EXTENSIONS OF FIRST ORDER LOGIC

Cambridge Tracts in Theoretical Computer Science

Titles in the series

1. G. Chaitin *Algorithmic Information Theory*
2. L.C. Paulson *Logic and Computation*
3. M. Spivey *Understanding Z*
4. G. Revesz *Lambda Calculus, Combinators and Functional Programming*
5. A. Ramsay *Formal Methods in Artificial Intelligence*
6. S. Vickers *Topology via Logic*
7. J-Y. Girard, Y. Lafont & P. Taylor *Proofs and Types*
8. J. Clifford *Formal Semantics & Pragmatics for Natural Language Processing*
9. M. Winslett *Updating Logical Databases*
10. K. McEvoy & J.V. Tucker (eds) *Theoretical Foundations of VLSI Design*
11. T.H. Tse *A Unifying Framework for Stuctured Analysis and Design Models*
12. G. Brewka *Nonmonotonic Reasoning*
14. S.G. Hoggar *Mathematics for Computer Graphics*
15. S. Dasgupta *Design Theory and Computer Science*
17. J.C.M. Baeten (ed) *Applications of Process Algebra*
18. J.C.M. Baeten & W. P. Weijland *Process Algebra*
19. M. Manzano *Extensions of First Order Logic*
21. D.A. Wolfram *The Clausal Theory of Types*
22. V. Stoltenberg-Hansen, I. Lindström & E. Griffor *Mathematical Theory of Domains*
23. E.-R. Olderog *Nets, Terms and Formulas*
26. P.D. Mosses *Action Semantics*
27. W.H. Hesselink *Programs, Recursion and Unbounded Choice*
29. P. Gärdenfors (ed) *Belief Revision*
30. M. Anthony & N. Biggs *Computational Learning Theory*
31. T.F. Melham *Higher Order Logic and Hardware Verification*
32. R.L. Carpenter *The Logic of Typed Feature Structures*
33. E.G. Manes *Predicate Transformer Semantics*
34. F. Nielson & H.R. Nielson *Two Level Functional Languages*
35. L. Feijs & H. Jonkers *Formal Specification and Design*
36. S. Mauw & G.J. Veltink (eds) *Algebraic Specification of Communication Protocols*
37. V. Stavridou *Formal Methods in Circuit Design*
38. N.Shankar *Metamathematics, Machines and Gödel's Proof*
39. J.B.Paris *The Uncertain Reasoner's Companion*
40. J.Desel & J.Esparza *Free Choice Petri Nets*
41. J.-J. Ch. Meyer & W. van der Hoek *Epistemic Logic for AI and Computer Science*

EXTENSIONS OF FIRST ORDER LOGIC

María Manzano
University of Barcelona

CAMBRIDGE
UNIVERSITY PRESS

CAMBRIDGE UNIVERSITY PRESS
Cambridge, New York, Melbourne, Madrid, Cape Town, Singapore, São Paulo

Cambridge University Press
The Edinburgh Building, Cambridge CB2 2RU, UK

Published in the United States of America by Cambridge University Press, New York

www.cambridge.org
Information on this title: www.cambridge.org/9780521354356

First published 1996
This digitally printed first paperback version 2005

A catalogue record for this publication is available from the British Library

ISBN-13 978-0-521-35435-6 hardback
ISBN-10 0-521-35435-8 hardback

ISBN-13 978-0-521-01902-6 paperback
ISBN-10 0-521-01902-8 paperback

Table of contents

Applying many-sorted logic to dynamic logic.

Preface.

This book considers various extensions of first order logic, giving detailed and elaborate treatment to many useful logical systems: second order logic (**SOL**), type theory (**RTT**, **ETT** and **FTT**), modal logic (**PML** and **FOML**), dynamic logic (**PDL**) and many-sorted logic (**MSL**). A substantial dose of logical perspective is also provided.

The second objective of this book is to pursue the thesis that most reasonable logical systems can be naturally translated into many-sorted first order logic. The thesis is maintained throughout the book, but only appears openly and explicitly in the last chapter. There, all the logic systems treated in the book are put in direct correspondence with many-sorted logic because this logic offers a unifying framework in which to place other logics. In itself, many-sorted logic is a natural logic for formalizing statements in a great variety of disciplines and it also has an efficient proof theory with a complete deductive calculus.

Currently, the proliferation of logics used in philosophy, computer science, artificial intelligence, mathematics and linguistics makes a working reduction of this variety an urgent issue. The aim is two-fold:

To be able to use only one deductive calculus and a unique theorem prover for all logics -*i.e.*, an **MSL** theorem prover;

To avoid the proofs of the metaproperties of the different existing logics by borrowing them from many-sorted logic.

The appeal of this approach is that it is so intuitive and easy that only common sense is needed to understand the construction. Besides, as the basic ingredients change, the recipe can be adapted and used to prepare different dishes. So with very little effort the results obtained are considerable. It is difficult to trace the development of this approach because almost every non-classical logic has found its standard counterpart at birth. Nevertheless, I like to credit most of the ideas involved in our current presentation to Henkin's paper "Completeness in the theory of types" (1950). However I do not want to be misleading; you are not going to find in this paper of 1950 anything like the translation of formulas into another formal language, or the open appearance of many-sorted logic. In connection with **SOL**, many-sorted logic appeared later, in Henkin's "Banishing the rule of substitution for functional variables" (1953), where a new second order calculus with the comprehension rule was presented. As noted in that paper, from this calculus it is possible to isolate the many-sorted calculus by leaving out the comprehension rule. Another remarkable discovery included in the 1953 paper is that we can weaken comprehension so that it applies only to a restricted class of formulas of our choice. This is of great help when treating the modal and dynamic logics where we restrict comprehension to the sets and relations defined by translations of formulas of **PML** or of **PDL**.

In Henkin 1950 paper the completeness of type theory is proved and the general models are presented. How did Henkin prove the completeness theorem for type theory? A very rapid answer to this question is: by changing the semantics and hence the logic. Roughly presented, the idea is very simple: The set of validities is so wide because our class of standard structures is too small. We have been very restrictive when requiring the relational universes of any model to contain all possible relations (where "possible" means in the background set theory used as metalanguage) and we have paid a high price for it. If we also allow nonstandard structures, and if we now interpret validity as being true in all general models, redefining all the semantic notions referring to this larger class of general structures, completeness (in both weak and strong senses), Löwenheim-Skolem, and all these theorems can be proven as in first order logic.

In addition to its usefulness, the general model's construction is far from being an ad hoc solution lacking naturalness and common sense. Throughout the pages of this book you will find good reasons for wondering whether the philosophy of standard structures is the only possible choice. The reasons are directly related to the following questions:

(1) Are we satisfied with the limitation on the class of models they require? Would it not be highly instructive to discover new and sensible models for a known existing theory?
(2) Don't we feel uneasy about crossing the border with set theory? Don't second order validities refer to the given set-theoretical environment instead of the logic in itself?
(3) Do we need all the expressive power they provide?
(4) Are we willing to pay the price that standard semantics demands?

Further motivation for using general models may be found in van Benthem's recent essay "The sources of complexity", where the author considers that with general semantics

> ...we achieve a moral rarity, being a combination of philosophical virtue with computational advantage,...

In fact, when considering the arguments used in the second chapter of this book, one can argue that the standard semantics is not logically adequate in the sense that it does not allow all logically possible interpretations of second order formulas as models because of the argument posed by Németi in the following form:

> We have to be placed in a set-theoretical universe, even assuming that there could be more than one such. Nevertheless, in the set theoretical universe you choose to be in, the GCH is either true or false. Assume it is true. Then, in every standard model for **SOL** the **SOL** formula φ expressing this hypothesis is true and so φ is valid. But since GCH is not derivable from ZFC, the result suggest that an interpretation $\mathcal{I}$ such that $\mathcal{I} \nvDash \varphi$ can not be excluded as "logically impossible". So, at least one $\mathcal{I}$ with $\mathcal{I} \vDash \neg\varphi$ is a logical possibility (by Paul Cohen's classical result). But such a model is not allowed in the standard semantics. So, we feel that the standard semantics does not include all logically possible worlds as models (we have to think about formulas, like GCH, which are both expressible in second order logic and independent from Zermelo-Fraenkel set theory). This argument is reinforced by the fact that there is an inexhaustible supply of independent formulas like GCH. In Henkin's general semantics many possibilities are restored as possible models; for instance, models with or without the GCH.

As you will see, the general model strategy is also used in modal logic and dynamic logic. Both logics are faithfully represented by many-sorted theories with a comprehension schema restricted to a definable subclass of many-sorted formulas.

A brief description of each chapter follows.

Chapter I. Standard Second Order Logic.
The first chapter is an introduction to standard second order logic with emphasis placed on the expressive power this logic provides. It consists of extending first order logic to second order logic by allowing quantification over sets and relations. Also mentioned are the model-theoretic counterparts of expressiveness, without overlooking the incompleteness result.

The definition of standard structure is given and the common relationships between standard structures are defined. Specifically, notions such as substructure, homomorphism, isomorphism and embedding are dealt with. A section is devoted to standard semantics where meaning is given to formulas of the formal language by introducing the related notions of satisfiability, validity and consequence. The question of what sets and relations are definable is then considered and a number of notions of definability are proposed. The chapter closes by proving a series of semantic theorems for standard second order logic, including the coincidence lemma, the substitution lemma and the isomorphism theorem.

Chapter II. Deductive Calculi.
A number of deductive calculus for second order logic are defined and soundness and incompleteness results are presented.

The chapter begins with an informal introduction defining what a calculus is, explaining the usual motivations for wanting a calculus, and stating the desired metaproperties of a calculus; ***i.e.***, that it would never drive us to erroneous reasoning and that it would also help us to derive all the consequences of a given set of hypotheses. Of the three calculi introduced, the first is a very simple extension of a first order calculus of sequents where the quantifiers' rules also cover the set and relation variables. It is defined for a second order language where equality among individuals is treated as in first order logic; that is, it is a primitive or logical symbol rather than a defined one. The calculus also contains the rules dealing with equality. Since we also have equality for predicates as primitive, we adjoin some equality rules for them and we will have the extensionality axiom as a rule without hypothesis. This calculus will not count as a second order calculus for many people. In fact, it is plain many-sorted, and in an imprecise way we can name it **MSL**. Adding comprehension or lambda rules we obtain proper second order calculus. Many deductions are done in full as exercises.

Another section is devoted to proving the soundness theorems for the three calculi. There is a very easy proof of incompleteness of **MSL** with standard semantics showing that $\exists xX\, Xx$ is valid in the standard semantics but is not derivable in **MSL**.

The chapter closes by proving the incompleteness result for second order logic with standard semantics, in both weak and strong senses, for any calculus.

Chapter III. Categoricity of Second Order Peano Arithmetic.
This chapter introduces Peano arithmetic in **SOL** and proves that with the standard semantics this theory is categorical; that is, any two second order models of Peano arithmetic are isomorphic. The question of non-standard models of first order Peano arithmetic is raised and put in direct correspondence with non-standard models of second order logic; quite different

meanings for the word "non-standard" which are, nevertheless, related.

Later it is proved that in Peano models it is possible to introduce recursive operations of any kind, but induction models where not all recursive operations can be introduced are also defined. The induction models which are not Peano models come in only two shapes: cycles and "spoons".

Chapter IV. Frames and General Structures.
This chapter consists of six sections. In the first, frames and general structures are informally introduced and the dichotomy between standard and non-standard views is discussed, arriving at the conclusion that it is intimately related with how the concept of subset is considered: that is, as a "logical" or undefined concept or as something to be defined in the logic.

In two other sections frames and general structures with the related semantics are introduced. The question of whether the general structures can be defined algebraically is dealt with in another section. The logics obtained by weakening comprehension, whose relevance is pointed out in this book, are also dealt with. The chapter closes by considering weak second order logic; that is, a logic where the concept of finiteness is taken from the metatheory and imposed as a "logical" concept.

Chapter V. Type Theory.
This chapter basically consists of the presentation of three different languages for type theory and a brief discussion of paradoxes and their solution in type theory. A deductive calculus for type theory is presented, which is a simple extension for all types of one for our second order calculus. The semantics of frames and general structures is also defined, and there is a very detailed proof of the equivalence of the usual definition of general structures with a proposed algebraic definition of general structures. The original functional presentation of Church is also treated, and the relationship with the previous relational presentation is given in full. Another section is devoted to equational type theory, a very illuminating logic where the only primitives are equality and abstraction and where the remaining logical concepts including connectors and quantifiers are definable. The chapter closes with our obtaining a calculus for this language. Limitations of time, space and knowledge have resulted in the omission of important subjects such as the beautiful definition of natural numbers in Church's paper, the connection of this presentation to the existing literature on models for typed lambda calculus, and perhaps also with Montague Grammar.

Chapter VI. Many-sorted Logic.

This chapter consists of eight sections devoted to many-sorted logic. There is a long introduction where reasons for using many-sorted logic are provided. The fact that in many branches of mathematics and computer science the natural structures are many-sorted is highlighted. The standard treatment of reduction to single-sorted structures and logic is raised and the weak points of this reduction are considered. It is seen that many-sorted logic has been used with success in computer science and also in a wide range of logics, as a unifier logic. Many-sorted language, semantics and deductive calculus are presented in detail and the completeness of this calculus is proved in full by extending the usual method. The chapter closes with the reduction of many-sorted logic to first order unsorted logic in the classical way; namely, unification of domains for the conversion of structures and relativization of quantifiers in the translation of formulas.

Chapter VII. Applying Many-Sorted Logic.

In the final chapter, in line with the philosophy presented throughout the book, all the logics thus far discussed, including modal and dynamic logic, are translated into many-sorted logic and their usual structures are converted into many-sorted structures thus giving us many-sorted theories. These theories are the standard counterparts of the original logics and are capable of representing them faithfully. In addition, some of the metaproperties of many-sorted semantics and calculus are transferred to these logics. In the first section of this chapter the general plan of the translation, its aims and usual steps are discussed. The second section is devoted to the translation of higher order logic into many-sorted logic. Using this translation technique we obtain completeness and soundness results for higher order logic. Modal logic is afterwards introduced, and a many-sorted theory, **MODO**, is proposed which proves the usual semantic theorems of compactness, enumerability and Löwenheim-Skolem and also tests the calculus indirectly by proving soundness and completeness. **MODO**(S4) does the same for the modal logic S4. For **PML** the many-sorted theory proposed is **SOLO**^{2}.

Readership.

This book is a monograph on extensions which can be used as an introductory texbook for Master's level students or senior undergraduates. It can also be used as a reference book since special attention has been given to the elaboration of conceptual distinctions and definitions. In fact, the book has been written like a novel, with a clear plot and an expected climax, and it is intended to be read as such, from cover to cover.

Since I wanted the book to be suitable for non-mathematicians too (including people not only in computer science, but also philosophers and linguists), it is not very demanding mathematically, the definitions are very detailed and the proofs are usually provided. Some choices were made in order to keep the book on a friendly level, but although the technical difficulty is rather low, a certain maturity of thinking is needed. Some of the frequent explanations attempt to achieve that in the form of a perspective of the logical landscape.

Prerequisites.

In order to read this book a modest knowledge of first order logic and set theory is needed, and it would be appropriate after introductory courses in both. For the benefit of potential readers short of the required background, some introductory books on first order logic and set theory are included in the bibliography.

Acknowledgments.

The book is also connected to my own intellectual and personal biography, not only in the obvious sense, in terms of the time it took me to write it, but because the subject has been around me (back and forth) for many years. The subject of my Master's thesis was completeness for second order logic and my PhD thesis was on second order logic as well. Both were presented in the Department of Logic in the University of Barcelona. It was decisive for this book that I spent the academic year 1977-1978 as a Fulbright Scholar in Berkeley, and that Leon Henkin guided me as my advisor. There I learnt many of the things that directly or indirectly, I hope, will show in these pages, including an intellectual appreciation of the beauty of teaching and the value of effort put into pedagogical issues. I have always thanked Leon Henkin for introducing me, with his enormous gifts for teaching, in a non-traumatic style, to his own wise overview of metamathematics and algebra. The subject presented was the usual one in graduate courses, but the presentation and insights were a challenge. The daily handwritten handouts in the unmistakable violet color of the Vietnamese copier... unforgettable!

When I first learnt about modal logic, the idea of translating it into first order many-sorted logic appeared immediately. Right from the start for me it was directly connected with what had been done in higher order logic. I have always had the feeling that this was just putting another piece of the puzzle in the right place. I soon discovered that this idea had already generated a whole industry and I became very happy afterwards when reading Johan van Benthem's survey and book. Wonderful, hats off! I applied the same treatment to dynamic logic and wrote a paper on this. I was in Leeds at that time, at the Centre for Theoretical Computer Science. Somehow this book grew from that paper and that visit.

In 1988 John Tucker and Karl Meinke organized an international workshop, held at the University of Leeds, where I met I Hajnal Andréka and Istvan Németi. Owing to what we like to call the Henkin connection, we shared the common ground that makes our understanding enjoyable. We talked about logic of programs, higher order logic, the general semantics of Henkin and the ontological, philosophical and practical consequences of the choice between standard or general semantics for it. I appreciate their help and encouragement during this period.

As this book begin to take shape and grow, several other people also helped me: Ildiko Sain, whose cleverness is only glimpsed in the incompleteness proof of Chapter II; Ramón Jansana, who suggested a shorter version of this incompleteness proof, which is included in the book. Several people, including Ramón and Johan van Benthem, questioned the advisability of including this incompleteness proof in such a book. I know they are right, and I apologize for my stubbornness, it has to do with the story of the proof and my emotional link with it until I obtained this readable, I feel, presentation. In addition, the computational importance of set-theoretic absoluteness can serve as a justification of my choice.

But, overall, I have to thank Antonia Huertas, whose support and help have been invaluable. Various places in the book show, I hope, some of her mathematical elegance. Of course, my students must be thanked, most especially Jordi López and Manuel Durán who suggested a few changes. I am also grateful to David Tranah for his patience and encouragement and to my Cambridge University Press referee for useful comments, on the whole.

In these pages of acknowledgments I also want to mention some of those whose indirect support helped me during this period; my sons and husband, my father, sister and brother, my female colleagues in the field of logic and philosophy of science and all my friends from Cervera del Maestre to San Diego.

CHAPTER I
STANDARD SECOND ORDER LOGIC.

1.- INTRODUCTION.

1.1. General idea.

Second order logic (**SOL**) is distinguished from first order logic in that it has relational as well as individual variables, and both types of variables can be quantified. Since it was Frege who pioneered the use of relational variables, second order logic is over one hundred years old; but the effective distinction between first and second order logic took the work of a few other people[1]. It was, in fact, implicit in Russell's work, but it was not made explicit until the work of Hilbert & Ackermann [1928]. First order logic was indeed only a fragment of the highly expressive language introduced by Frege [1879] and Russell [1908].

Thus, in second order logic we can say: "for all individuals, φ holds", as in first order logic, and formalize it as $\forall x\varphi$. We can also say: "for all properties, φ holds", unlike first order logic, and write it as $\forall X\varphi$. By $\forall X^2\varphi$ we express: "for all binary relations, φ holds". And so on....

Therefore, second order structures must contain different domains: the domain of individuals A, for variables of individual sort to range on; the unary relational domain A_1, as the range for the unary relational variables; the binary relational domain A_2, and so on. When we wish our second order logic to be standard, we want the formula $\forall X\varphi$ to mean: "for all possible subsets of A, φ holds". While we are doing that, we are taking the notion of subset from the background set theory we are using as metalanguage. That forces us to include in A_1 all subsets of A, even all those ghostly sets we could never describe or define. Consider the situation where A is an infinite set, say of cardinality α; $\mathcal{P}$A, the power set of A, which is the standard A_1, contains 2^α elements, whereas our formal language has just $\aleph_0$ formulas.

[1]See the historical notes in Church [1956], page 288.

We will see that adding to our universe of sets, $\mathbf{A}_1$, all the sets picked up by the so little descriptive quality of being a subset of **A**, which is the standard definition of structure, gives us a nonabsolute logic; *i.e.*, a logic whose concept of truth depends on the background set theory.

1.2. Expressive power[2].

Anyway, second order logic with standard semantics (based upon standard structures) has great expressive power (too much, we might say).
For instance:

(1) ***Arithmetical induction*** can be formulated and would retain all its expressive power as

$$\forall X(Xc \wedge \forall x(Xx \rightarrow X\sigma x) \rightarrow \forall x\, Xx)$$

This formula says: Any property which holds for zero and for the successor of any number having this property is a property of all numbers.

(2) The ***identity of individuals*** can be defined and not be, as in first order logic, a primitive relation. The most popular definition of identity is the Leibniz one, which in second order logic becomes:

$$\forall xy(x=y \leftrightarrow \forall X(Xx \leftrightarrow Xy))$$

This formula says: Two individuals are equal if and only if they share all their properties.

(3) The intuitive notion "most **R** are **S**" (*i.e.*, most things having property **R** also have property **S**), which is not expressible in a first order language with equality and with two unary relation symbols for **R** and **S**, can be expressed in **SOL** as

$$\neg\exists X^2(\forall x(\exists y\, X^2xy \leftrightarrow Rx \wedge Sx) \wedge \forall x(\exists y\, X^2yx \rightarrow Rx \wedge \neg Sx) \wedge \forall xyz(X^2xy \wedge X^2xz \rightarrow y=z)$$
$$\wedge\ \forall xyz(X^2xy \wedge X^2zy \rightarrow x=z))$$

This **SOL** formula expresses: there is no one-to-one function from **R∩S** into **R–S**. Everybody agrees that it captures the intuitive meaning of "most **R** are **S**", since it says that the set **R∩S** is "bigger" than the set **R–S**.

(4) Both ***finiteness*** and ***infinity***[3] can be formulated by a single formula. For instance,

---

[2]All the questions raised here are revisited in section 4.8.

[3]For more information about axioms of infinity, see Alonzo Church [1956], page 342. There you will find some

finiteness can be written as

$$\forall F(\forall xy(Fx{=}Fy \rightarrow x{=}y) \rightarrow \forall x\exists y\, x{=}Fy)$$

(every one-to-one function, f: **A** ⟶ **A**, on the whole universe of individuals, **A**, is also onto).

In fact, we are using functional variables in this formulation, but they can be easily removed in favor of relational ones by explicitly saying that our binary relation is a function with the whole universe as its domain. Can you write it with relation variables only?

(5) The axioms of ***well ordering***. When $\leq$ is an ordering, the formula

$$\forall X(\exists y\, Xy \rightarrow \exists u(Xu \wedge \forall z(Xz \rightarrow u{\leq}z)))$$

expresses that all non-empty subsets have a least element.

(6) The ***comprehension axioms***, stating that all definable relations exist.

$$\exists X^n \forall x_1..x_n(X^n x_1..x_n \leftrightarrow \varphi)$$

where X^n shall not be free in φ.

(7) The property of ***being countable*** can also be formulated within second order logic by just expressing: A set is countable iff there is a linear ordering relation on it such that every element has only finitely many predecessors.

(8) Even the ***continuum hypothesis***, CH, can be formulated in second order logic[4]. The formula φ_{CH} says: If the domain is of the same cardinality as $\mathbb{R}$, then every subset of the domain is either countable (finite or infinite) or else of the same cardinality as the whole domain. Thus, φ_{CH} is valid iff CH holds.

(9) Also the ***generalized continuum hypothesis***, GCH, can be expressed in second order logic; that is, the formula

$$\forall XY(\mathit{inf}(X) \wedge Y \sim \mathcal{P}X \rightarrow \forall Z(Z \subseteq Y \rightarrow Z \preceq X \vee Z \sim Y))$$

can be written completely in second order, as we shall see in section 4.8 below. This formula says: "Every subset Z of a set Y (Z ⊆ Y) that is equipollent to the power set of an infinite set **X** (**Y** ~ $\mathcal{P}$**X**) is either equipollent to that power set (**Z** ~ **Y**) or of equal or less power than the infinite set (**Z** ≼ **X**)."

Again, the formula φ_{GCH} is valid iff GCH holds. In fact, it has been known from early times that when using second order logic, the border with set theory has been

historical references.

[4]See section 4.8.

trespassed over. To set up the set of validities we need to specify which set theory will be used in the metalanguage in much more detail than in first order logic. Church, Henkin, Kreisel and Quine were aware of the situation long ago. Nowadays, one can find comments on it in almost any textbook[5].

We do not have to go into mathematics to find examples of thoughts needing second order logic to be expressed. Here are some colloquial examples:

(a) "Hay gente para todo" (there are all kinds of people). This can be formulated as:

$$\forall X \exists y\, Xy$$

(b) "There is at least one characteristic shared by all authoritarian regimes - either leftist or rightist." This can be formulated as:

$$\exists X \forall z(Az \wedge (Lz \vee Rz) \rightarrow Xz)$$

(c) "There are certain women who are able to love different men who don't share any quality." We can select the formalization:

$$\exists x(Wx \wedge \exists z \exists y(Mz \wedge My \wedge z \neq y \wedge Lxz \wedge Lxy \wedge \neg \exists X(Xz \wedge Xy)))$$

The problem is that most of them are trivially true or obviously false because the intended meaning is a bit more subtle.

(d) When we choose: "Mathematicians and philosophers share at least one quality", and we formalize it as

$$\exists Z \forall xy(Mx \wedge Py \rightarrow (Zx \wedge Zy))$$

we should not be satisfied either, since it is trivially true. (Think of the quality of being either a mathematician or a philosopher.)

1.3. Model-theoretic counterparts of expressiveness.

As a by-product of the expressive power of second order logic with standard semantics we obtain the following model-theoretic counterparts:

(1) The Peano axioms are categorical: any two second order models of the Peano axioms are isomorphic.

---

[5]Ebbinghaus, Flum & Thomas [1984], page 135 or van Benthem & Doets [1983], page 275.

(The proof of this was already in Dedekind. Chapter III will be devoted to this subject.)

(2) Second order logic is not a compact logic, that is: the compactness theorem fails.
(This result is a direct consequence of finiteness being expressable in the language. Think of the infinite set of formulas $\{\varphi_n / n\geq 2\}$, saying that there are at least n elements in the universe, and the formula expressing that the universe is finite. A detailed proof of the non-compactness is in 4.9.1 of this chapter.)

(3) The Löwenheim-Skolem theorem also fails.
(This result follows from the fact that being uncountable is expressible in the language: the formula expressing that the universe is uncountable has no countable model, as required for the Löwenheim-Skolem theorem.)

1.4. Incompleteness.

Therefore, in second order logic with standard semantics we will never find a strongly complete deductive calculus (*i.e.*, satisfying: if $\Gamma \models \varphi$, then $\Gamma \vdash \varphi$). The reason is that compactness, which could be proven from strong completeness, fails. We know even more: the set of validities is so unmanageable that we will never get a complete calculus, not even in the weak sense (*i.e.*, satisfying: if $\models \varphi$, then $\vdash \varphi$). This result follows from Gödel's incompleteness theorem together with item (1) above[6]. (In Chapter III we will sketch this incompleteness proof.)

As was pointed out by Németi and others, following ideas of Sain[7], we don't need the Gödel theorem to realize that a complete calculus can never be obtained. The observation was made with formulas such as CH in mind, formulas whose validity is based upon the background set theory we choose to have. (In Chapter II we will sketch this incompleteness proof.) Roughly posed, how can we define a calculus to generate as theorems the formulas in the unstable set of validities[8]?

---

[6]See van Heijenoort ed [1967], page 592 for the original proof. See Ebbinghaus, Flum & Thomas [1984], page 162 for a proof of the incompleteness of second order logic based on Trahtenbrot's theorem, which says that the set of sentences valid in all finite structures is not enumerable.

[7]Sain [1979] has important applications to computer science logics, philosophical logic and theory of semantics of natural languages. These applications also appear in Pasztor [1986], [1988] and Sain [1987]. See as well Barwise & Feferman eds [1985], page 600.

[8]In our Occidental tradition this has been maintained ever since the Heraclitean philosophers: "It is impossible to say anything true about things which change".

One might think that, perhaps, adding CH to the axioms of our background set theory will fix the situation. But, from Gödel's incompleteness, we know that this is not the case. It is not possible to give explicitly a complete axiom system for set theory; that is, a set of axioms such that every formula φ of the language of set theory or its negation $\neg\varphi$ is provable from the set of axioms. In fact, there is an inexhaustible supply of independent formulas like CH. However, even knowing that we can never achieve completeness, no one would stop us from defining a sound calculus. For instance, we can define a calculus just as an extension of the first order one, where the rules dealing with quantifiers also cover the relational quantification. Or we can extend the calculus a bit further by adding the comprehension schema to the calculus mentioned. The latter is the one commonly accepted as second order calculus. After that, we may or may not decide to add the axiom of choice or the axiom of extensionality or any other axiom we feel necessary. Any of these calculi is incomplete in the class of standard structures where the notion of subset is taken from the metalanguage (set theory). But if we leave open to interpretation in the structure what sets and relations are - *i.e.,* if we accept non-standard structures - the situation changes.

This is exactly what Henkin did when in 1949 he proved the completeness theorem for type theory. In Chapter IV we will introduce the general structures invented by Henkin and will experience the dramatic changes they operate in second order logic. The changes are of such a nature that for many people you are no longer in the premises of second order logic. In particular, second order logic with general semantics is quite a manageable logic - since it is compact, strongly complete and enjoys the Löwenheim-Skolem property -, but you pay for it with the loss of a great deal of the expressive power.

2.- SECOND ORDER GRAMMAR.

A specific second order language is defined by giving its alphabet and the rules for its calculus of formulas. The alphabet contains enough logical symbols, quantifiable variables of several types and a possibly empty set of operation constants. Between two second order languages the differences always lay in the alphabet and they may affect any of these sets, but while some of these differences can be considered just minor ones (for example, when they only affect the operation constants), others can have greater relevance (for instance, when they affect the quantifiable relation variables by restricting them to unary relation variables). The set of logical symbols of a second order language always contains enough connectives and quantifiers, but it might or might not include equality. As in first order logic, we say that the set of connectives is complete when all the truth functions can be defined in terms of connectives in the set and similarly for the quantifiers. The language is second order in so far as it contains quantifiable individual and relation variables.

Restricted SOL.

Some second order languages only have a finite number of kinds of relational variables, plus the individual variables which all of them have. For instance, monadic second order language[9] only contains individual and unary relation variables, both kinds being quantifiable. Binary second order language contains individuals, unary and binary relation variables. In general, n-ary second order language ($n \geq 1$) contains individual and i-ary relation variables for $1 \leq i \leq n$, where the number n represents the greatest degree of admissible quantification.

SOL.

Nevertheless, what is usually presented as second order language contains n-ary relation variables of any degree n (for $n \geq 1$, any positive integer). That is, it contains individual variables, unary relation variables, binary relation variables, etc. Unless otherwise explicitly stated, the second order languages used in this book, which belong to the class we are naming **SOL**, allow quantification for n-ary relation variables for any $n \geq 1$. These languages contain a first order basis, **FOL**, upon which we build the new second order features. **SOL** includes extended equality, for both individual and relation symbols. Equality is added as a logical symbol because, as we take it as primitive, it will have its genuine and fixed meaning; *i.e.*, independent of the standard/non-standard semantics issue. (In Chapter IV we discuss it extensively.) In general, second order language does not have equality for relations, but we will have it. There are several good reasons for this choice, to be discussed in section 4.8 of this chapter.

Extended SOL.

Sometimes, we also have function variables that can be quantified. As before, we might allow function quantification up to a certain n, or for any n. As long as we have relation variables, having function variables or not is only a matter of convenience. This variation is inessential because we can always rewrite the formula using only relation variables.

---

[9]Monadic second order logic has very special properties, as can be seen in Gurevich [1985].

λ-SOL.

On the other hand, some second order languages contain the abstractor λ[10]. λ-abstraction will allow us to built predicates from formulas. The use of the λ-abstractor, while very convenient, is not essential since it adds no expressive power to **SOL** as presented here. We have decided to include it because it will give a preliminary glimpse of a typed λ-calculus, to be presented later on. λ-abstraction could also be used to build functions from terms, but we are not using it in this sense.

Equality-free SOL.

In the literature of standard second order logic the equality sign for individuals is defined by Leibniz's indiscernibility principle. Therefore, there is no real need of having it as primitive and no difference between **SOL** and **Equality-free SOL**. (This is no longer true when we shift to non-standard semantics and so, to make things easier, we have decided to include primitive equality even in this standard chapter.)

The set of operation constants.

Besides variables and logical symbols, in each second order language there is a set of relation and/or function constants. We call them operation constants and they are in a set **OPER.CONS** of our choice. Every operation constant in **OPER.CONS** must be different from the rest of the symbols in the language and none is a string of other operation symbols. In the classical presentation of second order language the symbols in **OPER.CONS** are all of them first order; that is, they are symbols for functions and relations among individuals obtained from **FOL**. Following a quite standard procedure, individual constants are identified with zero-ary function constants and propositional symbols, if any, are zero-ary relation symbols. Nowadays it is also common to include symbols for functions and relations among relations or for functions or relations between individuals and relations, but the essential feature of **SOL** is the quantification of relations. In **SOL** the only proper second order relation symbols we are having are the logical symbols of equality for relations.

Pure SOL.

We can also have a second order language with no operation constants; *i.e.*, **OPER.CONS** $= \emptyset$. In this language we have individual and relation variables[11]. This language is the natural one to

---

[10]The lambda abstractor was first introduced by Alonzo Church, see Church [1940] and [1941].

[11]Denyer [1992] has proved that second order logic without individual quantification, which he terms "Pure second order logic", is decidable. Do not get confused, **Pure SOL** has individual variables that can be quantified.

express the properties of size of the domain.

2.1. Definitions (signature and alphabet).

To specify a particular second order language we will give its signature. From the signature we learn the kinds of quantifiable variables and we also learn the relation and function constants we are having and their types. The only thing we specify separately is whether we are having λ-abstraction or not.

A signature Σ is a pair $\langle$VAR, FUNC$\rangle$ where **VAR** is the set containing all the kinds of quantifiable variables (in higher order logic the kinds are types, in many-sorted logic they are sorts) and **FUNC** is a function whose domain is the set **OPER.CONS** of operation constants of the language and it gives types as values; ***i.e.***, finite sequences of members of **VAR**.

In 2.1.1 we will present the signature of a second order language in a very general case; ***i.e.***, it might have function variables as well as relation variables and all of them are quantified. Moreover, if we have functions of degree n, then we have functions of degree 1,...., n-1 as well; so we can continually go from unary variables to n-ary variables.

2.1.1. Signature of any second-order language.
By a second order signature Σ we mean an ordered pair $\Sigma = \langle$VAR, FUNC$\rangle$ where:

(i) **VAR** is a set such that: (1) $1 \in$ **VAR**, $\langle 0,1\rangle \in$ **VAR** and (2) whenever $\alpha \in$ **VAR** then $\alpha = \langle 0,1,\overset{n}{\ldots},1\rangle$ with n≥1 or $\alpha = \langle 1,\overset{n+1}{\ldots},1\rangle$.
Besides that, whenever $\alpha \in$ **VAR** and $\alpha = \langle 0,1,\overset{n}{\ldots},1\rangle$ with n>1 then also $\langle 0,1,\overset{n-1}{\ldots},1\rangle \in$ **VAR**. And whenever $\beta \in$ **VAR** and $\beta = \langle 1,\overset{n}{\ldots},1\rangle$ with n>1, then also $\langle 1,\overset{n-1}{\ldots},1\rangle \in$ **VAR**.

(ii) **FUNC** = **FUNC(Σ)** is a function whose values are of these forms: $\langle 0,1,\overset{n}{\ldots},1\rangle$ with n≥1 or $\langle 1,\overset{n+1}{\ldots},1\rangle$ with n≥0. We are using **OPER.CONS** as domain of **FUNC** and call its elements operation constants. ▮

Explanation.
The set **VAR** contains the kinds of quantifiable variables, while in **FUNC** we obtain the type of each operation constant. 1 is the type of individuals, $\langle 0,1,\overset{n}{\ldots},1\rangle$ is the type of n-ary

relations and $\langle 1,\overset{n+1}{\ldots},1\rangle$ is the type of n-ary functions. (So zero-ary functions are safely identified with individuals.) Since in second order logic our variables are for sets and relations, the kinds of variables are also types. In the classical presentation of second order logic the function and relation constants are always among individuals and so the types of relation constants are types of certain variables as well.

2.1.2. Signature of the classes of languages SOL and λ-SOL.

(i) VAR = $\{1, \langle 0,1\rangle, \langle 0,1,1\rangle, \langle 0,1,1,1\rangle,\ldots\}$

(ii) FUNC = FUNC(Σ) is a function defined as in 2.1.1 ▨

Remark.

The set VAR of any language in SOL is formed by two disjoint sets corresponding to individual and relation types. Since we want to keep the formulas easy to read, we are not using the types as superscripts, instead we will use the more conventional treatment of first order logic: we will use just a number indicating the arity of the variable or relation constant.

2.1.3. Alphabet of the λ-SOL language λ-L_2.

The alphabet of a second order language of signature Σ contains all the operation constants in **OPER.CONS**, logical symbols and an infinite number of variables for each type $\alpha \in$ VAR. Besides that, it may contain the symbol λ.

In particular, our λ-language (λ-L_2) will have:

(1) Connectives: $\neg, \vee, \wedge, \rightarrow, \leftrightarrow$.

(2) Quantifiers: $\forall, \exists$.

(3) Abstractor: λ.

(4) Parentheses:),(.

(5) Equality symbols: $E, E_1, E_2,\ldots$ (for individuals and relations).

They have types: $\langle 0,1,1\rangle$, $\langle 0,\langle 0,1\rangle,\langle 0,1\rangle\rangle$,...,$\langle 0,\langle 0,1,\overset{n}{\ldots},1\rangle,\langle 0,1,\overset{n}{\ldots},1\rangle\rangle$, etc.

(6) Falsity: $\perp$ (its type is 0).

(7) A set $\mathcal{V}$ of individual variables: $x, y, z, x_1, x_2, x_n,\ldots$ (their type is 1)
A set $\mathcal{V}_1$ of unary relation variables: $X^1, Y^1, Z^1, X^1_1, X^1_2, X^1_3,\ldots$ (their type is $\langle 0,1\rangle$.)
A set $\mathcal{V}_2$ of binary relation variables: $X^2, Y^2, Z^2, X^2_1, X^2_2, X^2_3,\ldots$ (their type is $\langle 0,1,1\rangle$)
and so on.
We will consider a countable infinite set, **OPER.CONS**, including:

(8) Zero-ary function constants: $a, b, c, c_1, c_2, c_3,\ldots$ (their type is 1, as the type of

individual variables)

Unary function constants: f^1, g^1, h^1, f_1^1, f_2^1, f_3^1,... (they have a type $\langle 1,1\rangle$, which is not a member of **VAR** because in there we just put the types of quantifiable variables)

Binary function constants: f^2, g^2, h^2, f_1^2, f_2^2, f_3^2,... (whose type is $\langle 1,1,1\rangle$)

and so on.

Unary relation constants: R^1, S^1, T^1, R_1^1, R_2^1, R_3^1,... (of type $\langle 0,1\rangle$)

Binary relation constants: R^2, S^2, T^2, R_1^2, R_2^2, R_3^2,... (of type $\langle 0,1,1\rangle$)

and so on. ▓

2.1.4. Alphabet of the SOL language L_2.

The alphabet L_2 is obtained from the alphabet of λ-L_2 by leaving out the λ-abstractor. ▓

2.2. Expressions: terms, predicates and formulas.

Now, from the set of finite strings of elements of the alphabet we are going to select the expressions of λ-L_2 and of L_2; that is, the predicates, formulas and terms of λ-L_2 and of L_2. The sets **TERM**(L_2), **TERM**(λ-L_2), **PRED**(L_2), **PRED**(λ-L_2), **FORM**(L_2) and **FORM**(λ-L_2) are defined in the expected way, giving rise to individual and relational quantification. They are the smallest sets obtained by the following inductive rules:

2.2.1. Terms.

(T1) Any individual variable x is a term.

(T2) Any individual constant b is a term.

(T3) If f is an n-ary function constant with arity n≥1 and $\tau_1,...,\tau_n$ are terms, then $f\tau_1...\tau_n$ is a term.

TERM(λ-L_2) is the smallest set obtained by these rules. ▓

TERM(L_2) = **TERM**(λ-L_2). ▓

2.2.2. Predicates.

(P1) Any n-ary relation X^n variable is a predicate of degree n.

(P2) Any n-ary relation P^n constant is a predicate of degree n.

(P3) Also, E, E_1, E_2,... are predicates of degree 2.

(P4) If ψ is any formula of λ-L_2 and $x_1,...,x_n$ are pairwise distinct individual variables, then $\lambda x_1...x_n\ \psi$ is an n-ary predicate (where the inductive definition of **FORM**(λ-L_2)

is presented below).

PRED(λ-L_2) is the smallest set obtained by these rules. ▓

PRED(L_2) is the smallest set obtained by rules (P1), (P2) and (P3). ▓

2.2.3. Formulas.

(F1) If Π is an n-ary predicate and $\tau_1,...,\tau_n$ are terms, then $\Pi\tau_1...\tau_n$ is a formula. In particular, $E\tau_1\tau_2$(written $\tau_1 = \tau_2$) is a formula when τ_1 and τ_2 are terms. $\perp$ is a formula.

(F2) If Π^n and Ψ^n are n-ary predicates, then $E_n\Pi^n\Psi^n$ (written $\Pi^n = \Psi^n$) is a formula.

(F3) If φ and ψ are formulas, then $\neg\varphi$, $(\varphi \vee \psi)$, $(\varphi \wedge \psi)$, $(\varphi \rightarrow \psi)$ and $(\varphi \leftrightarrow \psi)$ are formulas.

(F4) If φ is a formula and x is any individual variable, then $\forall x\varphi$ and $\exists x\varphi$ are both formulas.

(F5) If φ is a formula and X^n is any n-ary relation variable, then $\forall X^n\varphi$ and $\exists X^n\varphi$ are both formulas.

FORM(λ-L_2) is the smallest set obtained by these rules. ▓

FORM(L_2) is the smallest set obtained by these rules. ▓

2.2.4. Expressions.

The set union of the sets **TERM**(λ-L_2), **PRED**(λ-L_2) and **FORM**(λ-L_2) is the set of expressions of λ-L_2, denoted by **EXPR**(λ-L_2). ▓

The set union of the sets **TERM**(L_2), **PRED**(L_2) and **FORM**(L_2) is the set of expressions of L_2, denoted by **EXPR**(L_2). A member of any of them is an expression, denoted by ε. ▓

Remark.

Please recall that for a language without λ we suppress the rule (P4) of 2.2.2 and so the rules (F1) through (F5) of 2.2.3 are weakened since we then lack λ-predicates.

EXAMPLES

We have mentioned the comprehension schema. Here are some easy instances of it:

(1) $\exists Z\forall x(Zx \leftrightarrow \neg Rx)$. This says that there exists the complement of the set denoted by R.

(2) $\exists Z\forall x(Zx \leftrightarrow (Rx \wedge \neg Sx))$. This says that there exists the set difference of sets denoted by R and S.

(3) $\exists Z\forall x(Zx \leftrightarrow \exists y\, Rxy)$. The domain of the relation denoted by R exists.

(4) $\exists Z\forall x(Zx \leftrightarrow x=x)$. The universe exists. In the **Equality-free SOL** language the equality sign should be replaced by its definition, write $\forall X(Xx \leftrightarrow Xx)$ instead of $x=x$.

(5) $\exists Z^2\forall x\forall y(Z^2xy \leftrightarrow R^2yx)$. The reciprocal of a given relation exists.

(6) The restriction on the variable Z^n cannot be harmlessly dropped. Otherwise we would have monsters like this formula $\exists Z\forall x(Zx \leftrightarrow \neg Zx)$.

(7) In **λ-SOL** the comprehension axiom can be simply expressed as

$$\forall x_1...x_n(\lambda x_1...x_n\varphi\, x_1...x_n \leftrightarrow \varphi)$$

2.2.5. Cardinality of a language.

As usual, the cardinality of a language is the cardinality of the set of its formulas. Therefore, $\mathbf{CARD}(L_2) = \mathbf{CARD}(\lambda\text{-}L_2) = |\mathbf{FORM}(L_2)| = |\mathbf{FORM}(\lambda\text{-}L_2)| = \aleph_0$. ▮

2.3. Remarks on notation.

In (F3) we open the door to parentheses; since they can be annoying, we can suppress some of them by following the rules specified below:

(1) We can leave out external parentheses. Therefore, instead of

$$(((\varphi_1 \vee \neg\varphi_2) \vee \varphi_3) \vee (\neg\varphi_4 \vee \varphi_5)) \text{ we will write } ((\varphi_1 \vee \neg\varphi_2) \vee \varphi_3) \vee (\neg\varphi_4 \vee \varphi_5)$$

and instead of $(\varphi \rightarrow \psi)$ we will write $\varphi \rightarrow \psi$.

(2) In case of iterated disjunction or conjunction, the rule is association to the left. Therefore, instead of

$$((((\varphi_1 \vee \neg\varphi_2) \vee \varphi_3) \vee \varphi_4) \vee \varphi_5) \text{ we will write } \varphi_1 \vee \neg\varphi_2 \vee \varphi_3 \vee \varphi_4 \vee \varphi_5.$$

We might also write $\bigvee_{p\in\{1,...,5\}} \varphi_p$.

When we have a finite set of formulas Γ and we want to indicate its iterated disjunction, we will write $\bigvee_{\varphi\in\Gamma} \varphi$. If we wanted to indicate iterated conjunction of Γ, we would write $\bigwedge_{\varphi\in\Gamma} \varphi$.

(3) Disjunction and conjunction tie formulas more firmly than conditional and biconditional connectives. Therefore, we may suppress parentheses in the former. So, instead of the formula

$$((\varphi_1 \vee \neg\varphi_2) \rightarrow \varphi_3), \text{ we can write } \varphi_1 \vee \neg\varphi_2 \rightarrow \varphi_3$$

This conditional formula should not be mixed up with the disjunction formula

$\varphi_1 \vee (\neg\varphi_2 \rightarrow \varphi_3)$ which cannot be simplified.

Some other rules of simplification are as follows:

(4) An iterated quantification, $\forall x_1 \forall X_7^3 \forall X_4^2$ (or $\exists x_1 \exists X_7^3 \exists X_4^2$) can be simplified as $\forall x_1 X_7^3 X_4^2$ (or $\exists x_1 X_7^3 X_4^2$). Therefore, instead of

$$\forall x_1 \forall X_7^3 \forall X_4^2 \varphi \text{ (or } \exists x_1 \exists X_7^3 \exists X_4^2 \varphi) \text{ we will write } \forall x_1 X_7^3 X_4^2 \varphi \text{ (or } \exists x_1 X_7^3 X_4^2 \varphi).$$

(5) We use E as an individual binary predicate and E_n as a binary predicate of predicates of the same degree n. We shall be using for all of them the symbol =.

(6) To make the formulas more readable, very often we will use the initial of a name as an individual or relation constant. Similarly, to make the formulas more typable, we will suppress some superscripts.

(7) We will use $v, v_1, v_2, \ldots$ to refer indifferently to individual or relation variables.

(8) Beyond that, when tradition is too strong and our notation makes the formulas difficult to read, we will follow tradition. For instance, when talking about addition and multiplication we will use the symbols + and $\cdot$ as binary function constants and we will write the terms left and right of the symbols. In this case we will use parentheses to prevent ambiguity. Thus, we will write

$$(x+y) \text{ instead of } +xy$$

We are doing it already with equality; writing

$\tau = t$ (or $\Pi^n = \Psi^n$) instead of $E\tau t$ (or $E_n \Pi^n \Psi^n$)

Also, we will write

$\tau \neq t$ (or $\Pi^n \neq \Psi^n$) instead of $\neg\tau = t$ (or $\neg\Pi^n = \Psi^n$)

2.4. Induction.

Before concluding this brief introduction to the formal languages L_2 and λ-L_2, we want to make some remarks on induction. Each of the sets of formulas, predicates or terms is defined as the least set satisfying the definition. So, when you want to prove that they have a certain property, it is enough to verify the items specified in 2.4.1 below.

2.4.1. Proofs by induction on EXPR(λ-L_2).

If we want to show that all expressions of λ-L_2 have the property $\mathcal{P}$ we will have to prove:

(T1) All individual variables of λ-L_2 have the property $\mathcal{P}$.

(T2) All individual constants in **OPER.CONS** have the property $\mathcal{P}$.

(T3) If the terms $\tau_1,...,\tau_m \in$ TERM(λ-L_2) share the property $\mathcal{P}$, and f is an m-ary function constant of λ-L_2, then $f\tau_1...\tau_m$ has the property $\mathcal{P}$.

(P1) All relation variables of λ-L_2 have the property $\mathcal{P}$.

(P2) All relation constants in **OPER.CONS** have the property $\mathcal{P}$.

(P3) = has the property $\mathcal{P}$.

(P4) If $\varphi \in$ **FORM**(λ-L_2) has the property $\mathcal{P}$, then $\lambda x_1...x_n\ \varphi$ also has the property $\mathcal{P}$.

(F1) If the terms $\tau_1,...,\tau_m \in$ TERM(λ-L_2) share the property $\mathcal{P}$, and Π is an n-ary predicate of λ-L_2, then $\Pi\tau_1...\tau_m$ has the property $\mathcal{P}$. In particular, τ=t has the property $\mathcal{P}$, assuming that τ and t have the property $\mathcal{P}$. Also, $\perp$ has the property $\mathcal{P}$.

(F2) If the predicates Π^n and Ψ^n have the property $\mathcal{P}$, then $\Pi^n=\Psi^n$ has the property $\mathcal{P}$.

(F3) If the formulas φ and ψ share the property $\mathcal{P}$, then $\neg\varphi$, $(\varphi \wedge \psi)$, $(\varphi \vee \psi)$, $(\varphi \rightarrow \psi)$ and $(\varphi \leftrightarrow \psi)$ have the property $\mathcal{P}$.

(F4) If $\varphi \in$ **FORM**(λ-L_2) has the property $\mathcal{P}$ and x is an individual variable, then $\forall x\varphi$ and $\exists x\varphi$ also have the property $\mathcal{P}$.

(F5) If $\varphi \in$ **FORM**(λ-L_2) has the property $\mathcal{P}$ and X^n is an n-ary relation variable, then $\forall X^n\varphi$ and $\exists X^n\varphi$ also have the property $\mathcal{P}$. ▓

2.4.2. Proofs by induction on EXPR(L_2).
The precise definition is left to the reader. ▓

2.4.3. Definitions by recursion on EXPR(λ-L_2).
We use recursion to define new concepts. The general schema is the obvious one: we begin with the simplest expressions and while assuming that it is defined for arbitrary expressions, define it for the expressions built by rules given in 2.2. Since in the definition of a concept - for instance, a function H from the set of expressions into a set **B** - we want each expression to have a unique value, and our definition of H is based on the construction of expressions, we must be sure that every expression of λ-L_2 is built in just one way. We do not want an expression ε having two or more H-values. Therefore, the ***unique readability theorem*** must hold. This theorem, which I am not proving, can be stated as:

(1) Every term is either an individual variable, or an individual constant in **OPER.CONS**, or

it has the following form: (a) $f\,\tau_1...\tau_n$, where the n-ary function constant and the terms in (a) are uniquely determined.

(2) Every predicate other than equality is either a relation variable or a relation constant in **OPER.CONS** or it has the form $\lambda x_1...x_n\ \varphi$, where the individual variables and the formula are uniquely determined.

(3) Every formula has one of the following forms:
(a) $\Pi^n\tau_1...\tau_n$, (b) $\tau=t$, (c) $\perp$,
(d) $\Pi^n=\Psi^n$,
(e) $\neg\varphi$, (f) $(\varphi \wedge \psi)$, (g) $(\varphi \vee \psi)$, (h) $(\varphi \rightarrow \psi)$, (i) $(\varphi \leftrightarrow \psi)$,
(j) $\forall x\varphi$, (k) $\exists x\varphi$,
(l) $\forall X^n\varphi$, or (m) $\exists X^n\varphi$.
(where (a) through (m) are mutually exclusive and the expressions in all of them are uniquely determined).

When defining a concept C for each expression of $\lambda\text{-}L_2$ it is enough to do the following:

(T1) Define C for each individual variable of $\lambda\text{-}L_2$.

(T2) Define C for all the individual constants in **OPER.CONS**.

(T3) Assuming it is defined for all terms $\tau_1,...,\tau_n$ define C for $f\tau_1...\tau_n$ where f is an n-ary function constant.

(P1) Define C for each relation variable.

(P2) Define C for all the relation constants in **OPER.CONS**.

(P3) Define C also for $=$.

(P4) Define C for $\lambda x_1...x_n\ \varphi$, assuming it is defined for φ.

(F1) Assuming it is defined for all terms $\tau_1,...,\tau_n$ and for the n-ary predicate Π, define C for $\Pi\tau_1...\tau_n$. Define it also for $\tau=t$ and for $\perp$.

(F2) Assuming it is defined for Π^n and Ψ^n, define it also for $\Pi^n=\Psi^n$.

(F3) Define C for $\neg\varphi$, $(\varphi \wedge \psi)$, $(\varphi \vee \psi)$, $(\varphi \rightarrow \psi)$, and $(\varphi \leftrightarrow \psi)$, assuming it is defined for φ and ψ.

(F4) Define C for $\forall x\varphi$ and for $\exists x\varphi$, assuming it is defined for φ.

(F5) Define C for $\forall X^n\varphi$ and for $\exists X^n\varphi$, assuming it is defined for φ.

2.4.4. Definitions by recursion on EXPR(L_2).

Can you please do this? ▓

2.5. Free and bound variables.

Within a formula or a predicate a variable can be free or bound. The definition is an obvious extension to that of first order logic: a variable is free if it occurs in the expression and it is not within the scope of a quantifier or an abstractor and it is bound when it occurs in the expression but in the scope of a quantifier or an abstractor. In fact, a variable could never be bound in a term. Now we are going to define **FREE**(ε) for any expression ε. **FREE**(ε) will be defined to be the set of all the variables that freely occur in ε. The definition will, of course, be by induction.

2.5.1. Definition of FREE(ε) for $\varepsilon \in$EXPR(λ-L_2).

(T1) FREE(x) $= \{x\}$ for any individual variable of λ-L_2

(T2) FREE(f) $= \emptyset$ for any zero-ary function constant $f \in$OPER.CONS

(T3) FREE($f\tau_1 ... \tau_n$) $=$ FREE(τ_1) $\cup ... \cup$ FREE(τ_n)

(P1) FREE(X^n) $= \{X^n\}$ for any n-ary relation variable

(P2) FREE(R^n) $= \emptyset$ for any n-ary relation constant, $R^n \in$OPER.CONS

(P3) FREE($=$) $= \emptyset$

(P4) FREE($\lambda x_1 ... x_n\ \varphi$) $=$ FREE(φ)$-\{x_1, ..., x_n\}$

(F1) FREE($\Pi \tau_1 ... \tau_n$) $=$ FREE(Π) $\cup$ FREE(τ_1) $\cup ... \cup$ FREE(τ_n)
FREE($\tau = t$) $=$ FREE(τ) $\cup$ FREE(t)
FREE($\perp$) $= \emptyset$

(F2) FREE($\Pi^n = \Psi^n$) $=$ FREE(Π^n) $\cup$ FREE(Ψ^n)

(F3) FREE($\neg\varphi$) $=$ FREE(φ)
FREE($\varphi \nabla \psi$) $=$ FREE(φ) $\cup$ FREE(ψ), where ∇ is any binary connective

(F4) (F5) FREE($\exists v \varphi$) $=$ FREE($\forall v \varphi$) $=$ FREE(φ)$-\{v\}$, where v is a variable of any kind ▮

Let's define FREE(Γ) $= \bigcup_{\varphi \in \Gamma}$ FREE(φ). ▮

2.5.2. Definition of FREE(ε) for $\varepsilon \in$EXPR(L_2).

Suppress the rule (P4). ▮

2.5.3. Closed expressions.

A term τ is said to be *closed* when FREE(τ)$=\emptyset$. ▮

A formula φ is called a ***sentence*** when $\mathbf{FREE}(\varphi)=\emptyset$. ▓
$\mathbf{SENT}(\lambda\text{-}L_2)$ will denote the set of sentences of $\lambda\text{-}L_2$ and $\mathbf{SENT}(L_2)$ will denote the set of sentences of L_2. ▓

Remarks.
A closed predicate might contain variables bound by λ-abstraction. Since in a term a variable can never be bound, a closed term contains no variables.

2.5.4. Universal and existential closure.
The ***universal closure*** of a formula φ is the sentence obtained from it by placing in front of the formula universal quantifiers binding all the free variables in φ. In a similar way, we define the ***existential closure*** of a formula. We will write $\forall\varphi$ to denote the universal closure of φ and $\exists\varphi$ to denote its existential closure. ▓

Therefore, whenever $\mathbf{FREE}(\varphi) = \{v_1,...,v_n\}$, then $\forall\varphi \equiv \forall v_1...v_n\varphi$ and $\exists\varphi \equiv \exists v_1...v_n\varphi$. ▓

2.6. Substitution.

Quite often we need to substitute within a formula φ a term τ for an individual variable $x\in\mathbf{FREE}(\varphi)$ or a predicate Π^n for a relation variable $X^n\in\mathbf{FREE}(\varphi)$. In each case we obtain a formula ψ. We wish to define the substitution in such a way that φ expresses the same about x as ψ does about τ and equivalently for X^n and Π^n. We should carry out the substitution with care when bound variables are present in the expression. For instance, if we have the first order formula $\varphi \equiv \forall x\, Rxy$ and we replace the variable y by z, we will obtain the formula $\forall x\, Rxz$. But, if we replace y by x, we will get $\forall x\, Rxx$. The latter expresses that the relation denoted by R is reflexive, while the two previous ones are saying that a certain individual is in the relation with everything. What we are going to do in order to replace x by y is to change the quantified variable for a new one and then replace y by x. For instance, $\forall z\, Rzx$.

2.6.1. Substitution of a term for an individual variable in an expression of L_2.

(T1) $z\frac{\tau}{x} = \begin{cases} z\text{, if } x \not\equiv z \\ \tau\text{, if } x \equiv z \end{cases}$

(T2) $a\frac{\tau}{x} = a$

(T3) $[f^{n}\tau_1\ldots\tau_n]\frac{\tau}{x} = f^{n}\,\tau_1\frac{\tau}{x}\ldots\tau_n\frac{\tau}{x}$

(P1) $X^{n}\frac{\tau}{x} = X^{n}$

(P2) $R^{n}\frac{\tau}{x} = R^{n}$

(P3) $=\frac{\tau}{x} = \;=$

(F1) $[\Pi^{n}\tau_1\ldots\tau_n]\frac{\tau}{x} = \Pi^{n}\frac{\tau}{x}\,\tau_1\frac{\tau}{x}\ldots\tau_n\frac{\tau}{x}$

$[\tau_1=\tau_2]\frac{\tau}{x} = (\tau_1\frac{\tau}{x} = \tau_2\frac{\tau}{x})$

$\bot\frac{\tau}{x} = \bot$

(F2) $[\Pi^{n}=\Psi^{n}]\frac{\tau}{x} = (\Pi^{n}\frac{\tau}{x} = \Psi^{n}\frac{\tau}{x})$

(F3) $[\neg\varphi]\frac{\tau}{x} = \neg\,\varphi\frac{\tau}{x}$

$[\varphi \nabla \psi]\frac{\tau}{x} = \varphi\frac{\tau}{x} \nabla \psi\frac{\tau}{x}$ where ∇ is any binary connective

(F4) $$[\forall z\varphi]\frac{\tau}{x} = \begin{cases} \forall z\varphi \ (*) \\ \forall z\varphi\frac{\tau}{x} \ (**) \\ \forall y[\varphi\frac{y}{z}]\frac{\tau}{x} \ (***) \end{cases}$$

(*) if $x \notin$ **FREE**($\forall z\varphi$)

(**) if $x \in$ **FREE**($\forall z\varphi$) and $z \notin$ **FREE**(τ)

(***) if $x \in$ **FREE**($\forall z\varphi$) and $z \in$ **FREE**(τ). y is new and it is the variable with least index in a given ordering, so $y \notin$ **FREE**($\forall z\varphi$)$\cup$**FREE**(τ)

Similarly for $\exists z\varphi$.

(F5) $[\forall X^{n}\varphi]\frac{\tau}{x} = \forall X^{n}\varphi\frac{\tau}{x}$ ▩

2.6.2. Substitution of a term for an individual variable in an expression of λ-L_2.

For the language λ-L_2 we only have to add the following (P4)-rule:

(P4) $$[\lambda x_1\ldots x_n\,\varphi]\frac{\tau}{x} = \begin{cases} \lambda x_1\ldots x_n\varphi \ (*) \\ \lambda x_1\ldots x_n\varphi\frac{\tau}{x} \ (**) \\ \lambda x_1\ldots x_i y_{i+1}\ldots y_n[\varphi\frac{y_{i+1}\ldots y_n}{x_{i+1}\ldots x_n}]\frac{\tau}{x} \ (***) \end{cases}$$

(*) if $x \notin \mathbf{FREE}(\lambda x_1 ... x_n \varphi)$

(**) if $x \in \mathbf{FREE}(\lambda x_1 ... x_n \varphi)$ and $x_i \notin \mathbf{FREE}(\tau)$ for all $1 \leq i \leq n$

(***) if $x \in \mathbf{FREE}(\lambda x_1 ... x_n \varphi)$ and $\exists i 1 \leq i \leq n$ such that $x_j \in \mathbf{FREE}(\tau)$ $\forall j$ $i+1 \leq j \leq n$. The variables are distinct and new and are taken in a systematic way

(The pairwise distinct variables $y_{i+1},...,y_n$ satisfy

$y_{i+1},...,y_n \notin \mathbf{FREE}(\lambda x_1 ... x_n \varphi) \cup \mathbf{FREE}(\tau) \cup \{x_1,...,x_n\}$

Of course, the assumption that the problematic variables are at the end of the abstraction is inessential). ▒

Remark.

Please note that since the variables $x_1,...,x_n$ are pairwise distinct and the new variables $y_{i+1},...,y_n \notin \{x_1,...,x_n\}$, then

$$[...[\varphi \frac{y_{i+1}}{x_{i+1}}]...\frac{...y_n}{...x_n}]$$

can be unambiguously simplified as

$$[\varphi \frac{y_{i+1}...y_n}{x_{i+1}...x_n}]$$

The latter notation will be introduced below to denote the simultaneous substitution.

2.6.3. Substitution of a predicate for a relation variable in an expression of L_2.

(T1) $z \dfrac{\Pi^m}{X^m} = z$

(T2) $a \dfrac{\Pi^m}{X^m} = a$

(T3) $[f^n \tau_1 ... \tau_n] \dfrac{\Pi^m}{X^m} = f^n \tau_1 ... \tau_n$

(P1) $Z^n \dfrac{\Pi^m}{X^m} = \begin{cases} Z^n, \text{ if } X^m \not\equiv Z^n \\ \Pi^m, \text{ if } X^m \equiv Z^n \end{cases}$

(P2) $R^n \dfrac{\Pi^m}{X^m} = R^n$

(P3) $= \dfrac{\Pi^m}{X^m} = =$

(F1) $[\Pi^n \tau_1 ... \tau_n] \dfrac{\Pi^m}{X^m} = \Pi^n \dfrac{\Pi^m}{X^m} \tau_1 ... \tau_n$

$$[\tau_1=\tau_2]\frac{\Pi^m}{X^m} = \tau_1 = \tau_2$$

$$\bot\frac{\Pi^m}{X^m} = \bot$$

(F2) $$[\Pi^n=\Psi^n]\frac{\Pi^m}{X^m} = (\Pi^n\frac{\Pi^m}{X^m} = \Psi^n\frac{\Pi^m}{X^m})$$

(F3) $$[\neg\varphi]\frac{\Pi^m}{X^m} = \neg\,\varphi\frac{\Pi^m}{X^m}$$

$$[\varphi\ \nabla\ \psi]\frac{\Pi^m}{X^m} = \varphi\frac{\Pi^m}{X^m}\ \nabla\ \psi\frac{\Pi^m}{X^m}$$ where ∇ is a binary connective

(F4) $$[\forall z\varphi]\frac{\Pi^m}{X^m} = \forall z\varphi\frac{\Pi^m}{X^m}$$

Similarly for $\exists z\varphi$.

(F5) $$[\forall Z^n\varphi]\frac{\Pi^m}{X^m} = \begin{cases} \forall Z^n\varphi & (*) \\ \forall Z^n\varphi\frac{\Pi^m}{X^m} & (**) \\ \forall Y^n[\varphi\frac{Y^n}{Z^n}]\frac{\Pi^m}{X^m} & (***) \end{cases}$$

(*) if $X^m \notin \mathrm{FREE}(\forall Z^n\varphi)$

(**) if $X^m \in \mathrm{FREE}(\forall Z^n\varphi)$ and $Z^n \notin \mathrm{FREE}(\Pi^m)$

(***) if $X^m \in \mathrm{FREE}(\forall Z^n\varphi)$ and $Z^n \in \mathrm{FREE}(\Pi^m)$. Y^n is a new variable and it is the variable with least index in a given ordering, so

$Y^n \notin \mathrm{FREE}(\forall Z^n\varphi) \cup \mathrm{FREE}(\Pi^m)$

For existential quantification it is the same. ▓

2.6.4. Substitution of a predicate for a relation variable in an expression of λ-L_2.

For the language λ-L_2 we only have to add the following (P4)-rule:

(P4) $$[\lambda x_1..x_n\varphi]\frac{\Pi^m}{X^m} = \begin{cases} \lambda x_1..x_n\varphi & (*) \\ \lambda x_1..x_n\varphi\frac{\Pi^m}{X^m} & (**) \\ \lambda x_1..x_i y_{i+1}\cdots y_n[\varphi\frac{y_{i+1}..y_n}{x_{i+1}..x_n}]\frac{\Pi^m}{X^m} & (***) \end{cases}$$

(*) if $X^m \notin \mathrm{FREE}(\lambda x_1..x_n\varphi)$

(**) if $X^m \in$ **FREE**$(\lambda x_1 ... x_n \varphi)$ and $x_i \notin$ **FREE**(Π^m) for all $1 \leq i \leq n$

(***) if $X^m \in$ **FREE**$(\lambda x_1 ... x_n \varphi)$, $\exists i$ $1 \leq i \leq n$ such that $x_j \in$ **FREE**(Π^m) $\forall j$ $i+1 \leq j \leq n$. The variables are distinct, new and taken systematically from an ordering.

(The pairwise distinct variables $y_{i+1}, ..., y_n$ satisfy

$y_{i+1}, ..., y_n \notin$ (**FREE**$(\lambda x_1 ... x_n$ $\varphi)$ $\cup$ **FREE**(Π^m) $\cup$ $\{x_1, ..., x_n\})$

Besides that, we have to modify (F4).

$$\text{(F4)} \quad [\forall z\varphi]\frac{\Pi^m}{X^m} = \begin{cases} \forall z\varphi\frac{\Pi^m}{X^m} & (*) \\ \forall y[\varphi\frac{y}{z}]\frac{\Pi^m}{X^m} & (**) \end{cases}$$

(*) if $z \notin$ **FREE**(Π^m)

(**) if $z \in$ **FREE**(Π^m) and y is a new variable and it is the variable with least index in a given ordering, so $y \notin$ **FREE**(Π^m) $\cup$ **FREE**$(\forall z\varphi)$. ▒

2.6.5. Simultaneous substitution.

A good exercise for you is to define the simultaneous substitution of the expressions $\varepsilon_1, ..., \varepsilon_n$ for the pairwise distinct variables $v_1, ..., v_n$ (where each v_i is of the same type as ε_i) in **TERM**(L_2), **PRED**(L_2) and **FORM**(L_2). Define it as well for the language λ-L_2. ▒

3.- STANDARD STRUCTURES.

3.1. Definition of standard structures.

The second order languages we have introduced are both designed to talk about structures of signature $\Sigma = \langle$**VAR**, **FUNC**$\rangle$.

Standard structures of signature Σ are ordered tuples

$$\mathcal{A} = \langle \mathrm{A}, \langle \mathrm{A}_n \rangle_{n \geq 1}, \langle C^{\mathcal{A}} \rangle_{C \in \mathbf{OPER.CONS}} \rangle$$

such that:

(i) $\mathrm{A} \neq \emptyset$, the universe of individuals is a non-empty set.

(ii) For each $n \geq 1$, $A_n = \mathcal{P}A^n$; that is, the universe of n-ary relations is the power set of the n-ary cartesian product of **A**. Therefore, the n-ary relational universe contains all possible n-ary relations on **A**.

(iii) For each n-ary relation constant, $R \in$ **OPER.CONS** and **FUNC**$(R) = \langle 0,1,\overset{n}{\ldots},1 \rangle$, $R^{\mathcal{A}}$ is an n-ary relation on individuals. That is,

$$R^{\mathcal{A}} \subseteq A \times \overset{n}{\ldots} \times A$$

(Thus, $R^{\mathcal{A}}$ is a subset of the n-ary cartesian product of **A**, an element of $\mathcal{P}A^n$.)

(iv) For each n-ary function constant, $f \in$ **OPER.CONS** and **FUNC**$(f) = \langle 1,\overset{n+1}{\ldots},1 \rangle$, $f^{\mathcal{A}}$ is an n-ary function on individuals. That is,

$$f^{\mathcal{A}}: A \times \overset{n}{\ldots} \times A \longrightarrow A$$

For individual constants the condition reduces to belonging to **A**. ▮

Remarks.

It is clear that given a set **A** and a family of relations on **A** to put in $\langle C^{\mathcal{A}} \rangle_{C \in \mathbf{OPER.CONS}}$, there is just one standard structure

$$\mathcal{A} = \langle A, \langle \mathcal{P}A^n \rangle_{n \geq 1}, \langle C^{\mathcal{A}} \rangle_{C \in \mathbf{OPER.CONS}} \rangle$$

Since the relation universes are known once you have the individual universe, we can identify $\mathcal{A}$ with its first order basis,

$$\mathcal{A} = \langle A, \langle C^{\mathcal{A}} \rangle_{C \in \mathbf{OPER.CONS}} \rangle$$

Thus, the standard point of view according to which in **SOL** we want to talk about first order structures is justified.

3.2. Relations between standard structures established without the formal language.

Since our standard structures are basically first order, and we only change the formal language when shifting to **SOL**, it is not surprising that when we come to establish relations among structures and express them in the metalanguage, we repeat what we usually do in first order logic. We will use in the metalanguage variables (in **bold**), quantifiers and connectives; please see them as mere abbreviations of the corresponding English expressions.

The relations we will consider are always between structures of the same signature. In what follows $\mathcal{A}$ and $\mathcal{B}$ will be:

$$\mathcal{A} = \langle \mathbf{A}, \langle C^{\mathcal{A}} \rangle_{C \in \mathbf{OPER.CONS}} \rangle \text{ and } \mathcal{B} = \langle \mathbf{B}, \langle C^{\mathcal{B}} \rangle_{C \in \mathbf{OPER.CONS}} \rangle$$

3.2.1. Substructures.

Let $\mathcal{A}$ and $\mathcal{B}$ be two standard structures of the same signature. We say that $\mathcal{A}$ is a ***substructure*** of $\mathcal{B}$ iff

(i) $\mathbf{A} \subseteq \mathbf{B}$.

(ii) For every n-ary function constant $f \in$ **OPER.CONS**, then $f^{\mathcal{A}} = f^{\mathcal{B}} \upharpoonright \mathrm{A}^n$.
(As a special case, zero-ary functions are the same in both structures: $a^{\mathcal{A}} = b^{\mathcal{B}}$.)

(iii) For every n-ary relation constant $R \in$ **OPER.CONS**, then $R^{\mathcal{A}} = R^{\mathcal{B}} \cap \mathrm{A}^n$. ▒

$\mathcal{A} \sqsubseteq \mathcal{B}$ stands for "$\mathcal{A}$ is a substructure of $\mathcal{B}$". ▒
(The notation $f^{\mathcal{B}} \upharpoonright \mathrm{A}^n$ corresponds to the restriction of the function $f^{\mathcal{B}}$ to the n-ary cartesian product of A.)

3.2.2. Homomorphism.

Let $\mathcal{A}$ and $\mathcal{B}$ be two standard structures of the same signature. **h** is called a ***homomorphism*** from $\mathcal{A}$ into $\mathcal{B}$ iff

(i) **h**: $\mathbf{A} \longrightarrow \mathbf{B}$ (**h** is a function whose domain is **A** and whose values are in **B**).

(ii) For every n-ary function constant $f \in$ **OPER.CONS** and for every $\mathbf{x}_1,\ldots,\mathbf{x}_n \in \mathbf{A}$:

$$\mathbf{h}(f^{\mathcal{A}}(\mathbf{x}_1,\ldots,\mathbf{x}_n)) = f^{\mathcal{B}}(\mathbf{h}(\mathbf{x}_1),\ldots,\mathbf{h}(\mathbf{x}_n))$$

(as a special case, $\mathbf{h}(a^{\mathcal{A}}) = a^{\mathcal{B}}$).

(iii) For every n-ary relation constant $R \in$ **OPER.CONS** and for every $\mathbf{x}_1,\ldots,\mathbf{x}_n \in \mathbf{A}$:

$$\text{if } \langle \mathbf{x}_1,\ldots,\mathbf{x}_n \rangle \in R^{\mathcal{A}} \text{ then } \langle \mathbf{h}(\mathbf{x}_1),\ldots,\mathbf{h}(\mathbf{x}_n) \rangle \in R^{\mathcal{B}}. \text{ ▒}$$

$\mathcal{A} \xrightarrow{\mathbf{h}} \mathcal{B}$ stands for "**h** is a homomorphism from $\mathcal{A}$ into $\mathcal{B}$". ▒

$\mathcal{A} \longrightarrow \mathcal{B}$ stands for "there is h such that $\mathcal{A} \xrightarrow{\mathbf{h}} \mathcal{B}$". ▒

- When the function **h** satisfying all the previous conditions is ***onto***, we say that **h** is a homomorphism of $\mathcal{A}$ ***onto*** $\mathcal{B}$; *i.e.* surjective. ▒

•• When condition (iii) is changed so that the "if...then" condition is replaced by an "if and only if" condition, we say that the homomorphism is ***strong***. ▒

••• When $\mathcal{A} \xrightarrow{\mathbf{h}} \mathcal{B}$ and h is onto and the homomorphism is strong, we also say that $\mathcal{B}$ is a

homomorphic image of $\mathcal{A}$. ▒

3.2.3. Isomorphism.

Let $\mathcal{A}$ and $\mathcal{B}$ be two standard structures of the same signature. A function $\mathbf{h}: \mathbf{A} \longrightarrow \mathbf{B}$ is called an ***isomorphism*** from $\mathcal{A}$ onto $\mathcal{B}$ iff

(i) The function $\mathbf{h}$ is a bijection; that is, $\forall xy(\mathbf{h}(\mathbf{x}) = \mathbf{h}(\mathbf{y}) \rightarrow \mathbf{x} = \mathbf{y})$ and $\mathbf{h}[\mathbf{A}] = \mathbf{B}$, where $\mathbf{h}[\mathbf{A}]$ is the image of $\mathbf{A}$ under $\mathbf{h}$; *i.e.*, is surjective and injective.

(ii) This condition is the same as in homomorphisms.

(iii) For every n-ary relation constant $R \in \mathbf{OPER.CONS}$ and for every $\mathbf{x}_1,\ldots,\mathbf{x}_n \in \mathbf{A}$:

$$\langle \mathbf{x}_1,\ldots,\mathbf{x}_n\rangle \in R^{\mathcal{A}} \text{ iff } \langle \mathbf{h}(\mathbf{x}_1),\ldots,\mathbf{h}(\mathbf{x}_n)\rangle \in R^{\mathcal{B}}$$ ▒

$\mathcal{A} \overset{\mathbf{h}}{\cong} \mathcal{B}$ stands for "$\mathbf{h}$ is an isomorphism from $\mathcal{A}$ onto $\mathcal{B}$". ▒

$\mathcal{A} \cong \mathcal{B}$ stands for "there is an $\mathbf{h}$ such that $\mathcal{A} \overset{\mathbf{h}}{\cong} \mathcal{B}$". ▒

3.2.4. Embedding.

Let $\mathcal{A}$ and $\mathcal{B}$ be two standard structures of the same signature. A function $\mathbf{h}: \mathbf{A} \longrightarrow \mathbf{B}$ is called an ***embedding*** from $\mathcal{A}$ into $\mathcal{B}$ iff

(i) The function $\mathbf{h}$ is one-to-one; that is, $\forall xy(\mathbf{h}(\mathbf{x}) = \mathbf{h}(\mathbf{y}) \rightarrow \mathbf{x} = \mathbf{y})$.

Conditions (ii) and (iii) are the same as in isomorphisms. ▒

$\mathcal{A} \overset{\mathbf{h}}{\underset{\sim}{\sqsubseteq}} \mathcal{B}$ stands for "$\mathbf{h}$ is an embedding from $\mathcal{A}$ into $\mathcal{B}$".

$\mathcal{A} \underset{\sim}{\sqsubseteq} \mathcal{B}$ stands for "there is an h such that $\mathcal{A} \overset{\mathbf{h}}{\underset{\sim}{\sqsubseteq}} \mathcal{B}$". ▒

Proposition 1: Let $\mathbf{h}$ be a strong homomorphism from $\mathcal{A}$ into $\mathcal{B}$. $\mathbf{h}$ is an embedding if and only if $\mathbf{h}$ is an isomorphism from $\mathcal{A}$ into $\mathbf{h}[\mathcal{A}]$

(where $\mathbf{h}[\mathcal{A}] = \langle \mathbf{h}[\mathbf{A}], \langle \mathbf{h}[C^{\mathcal{A}}]\rangle_{C \in \mathbf{OPER.CONS}}\rangle$)

Proof

[$\Longrightarrow$] If $\mathbf{h}$ is an embedding from $\mathcal{A}$ into $\mathcal{B}$, it is clearly an isomorphism from $\mathcal{A}$ into $\mathbf{h}[\mathcal{A}]$ because on this range the function is onto.

[$\Longleftarrow$] If $\mathcal{A} \overset{\mathbf{h}}{\cong} \mathbf{h}[\mathcal{A}]$, then the strong homomorphism $\mathbf{h}: \mathcal{A} \longrightarrow \mathcal{B}$ is also an embedding since the function h is one-to-one. ∎

Proposition 2: Let $\mathbf{h}$ be a homomorphism from $\mathcal{A}$ into $\mathcal{B}$. Then $\mathbf{h}$ is an embedding if and only if $\mathbf{h}$ is an isomorphism from $\mathcal{A}$ into $\mathcal{B}\upharpoonright\mathbf{h}[A]$ (where $\mathcal{B}\upharpoonright\mathbf{h}[A]$ is a structure with domain $\mathbf{h}[A]$ having as n-ary functions the ones in $\mathcal{B}$ restricted to $\mathbf{h}[A]^n$ and as relations the intersection of the relations in $\mathcal{B}$ with $\mathbf{h}[A]^n$).

Proof

This is an easy corollary of proposition 1, since in this case $\mathbf{h}[\mathcal{A}] = \mathcal{B}\upharpoonright\mathbf{h}[A]$. ∎

Proposition 3: $\mathbf{h}$ is an embedding from $\mathcal{A}$ into $\mathcal{B}$ if and only if there is a structure $\mathcal{C}$ such that $\mathcal{C} \sqsubseteq \mathcal{B}$ and $\mathbf{h}$ is an isomorphism from $\mathcal{A}$ onto $\mathcal{C}$.

Proof

This proposition says: $\mathcal{A}$ is embedded into $\mathcal{B}$ if and only if there is a copy of $\mathcal{A}$ inside $\mathcal{B}$. Thus, we can draw this picture:

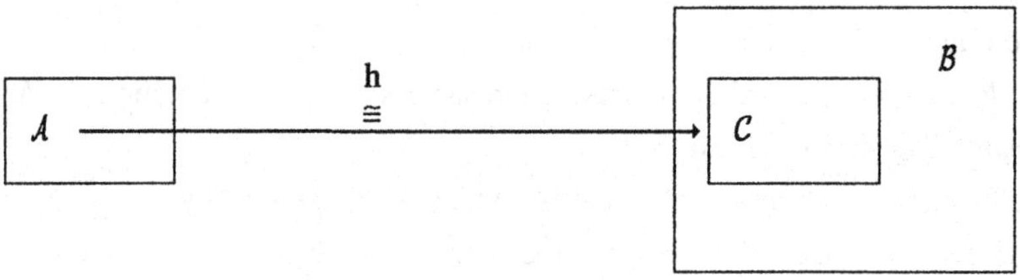

[⟹] By proposition 2, the structure $\mathcal{B}\upharpoonright\mathbf{h}[A]$ satisfies the required conditions.

[⟸] Can you please check that an isomorphism $\mathbf{h}$ from $\mathcal{A}$ into a substructure $\mathcal{C}$ of $\mathcal{B}$ is also an embedding from $\mathcal{A}$ into $\mathcal{B}$? ∎

Proposition 4: The concepts presented above are related among themselves as shown below:

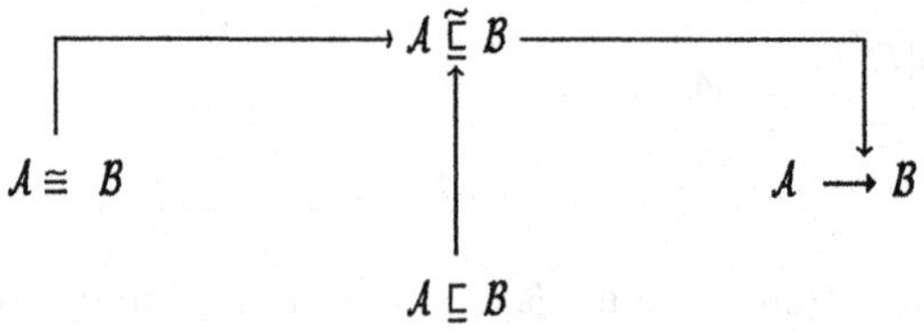

Proof

Most of the arrows follow from the definitions. To see that $\mathcal{A} \sqsubseteq \mathcal{B}$ implies $\mathcal{A} \mathrel{\tilde{\sqsubseteq}} \mathcal{B}$, use proposition 3. The copy of $\mathcal{A}$ inside $\mathcal{B}$ is $\mathcal{A}$ itself! ∎

3.2.5. Congruence relations and homomorphisms.

Given a structure $\mathcal{A}$ and a binary relation $\mathbf{R} \subseteq \mathbf{A} \times \mathbf{A}$, $\mathbf{R}$ is a congruence relation on $\mathcal{A}$ iff:

(i) $\mathbf{R}$ is an equivalence relation on $\mathbf{A}$; that is, it is reflexive, symmetric and transitive and its domain and range is $\mathbf{A}$.

(ii) For every n-ary function constant $f \in$ **OPER.CONS** and $x_1,...,x_n, y_1,...,y_n \in A$:

$$\text{if } \langle x_1,y_1\rangle \in R,...,\langle x_n,y_n\rangle \in R \text{ then } \langle f^{\mathcal{A}}(x_1,...,x_n), f^{\mathcal{A}}(y_1,...,y_n)\rangle \in R$$

(iii) For every n-ary relation constant $T \in$ **OPER.CONS** and $x_1,...,x_n, y_1,...,y_n \in A$:

$$\text{if } \langle x_1,y_1\rangle \in R,...,\langle x_n,y_n\rangle \in R, \text{ then } \langle x_1,...,x_n\rangle \in T^{\mathcal{A}} \text{ iff } \langle y_1,...,y_n\rangle \in T^{\mathcal{A}} \quad \blacksquare$$

Proposition 1: If **h** is a strong homomorphism from $\mathcal{A}$ into any other structure $\mathcal{B}$, then

$$\sim h = \{\langle x,y\rangle \in A \times A \,/\, h(x) = h(y)\}$$

is a congruence relation on $\mathcal{A}$.

Proof

Let **h** be a strong homomorphism. We want to prove that $\sim$**h** is a congruence relation.

(1) It is obvious that $\sim$**h** is an equivalence relation.

(2) For every n-ary function constant $f \in$ **OPER.CONS** and $x_1,...,x_n, y_1,...,y_n \in A$:

$$\text{if } \langle x_1,y_1\rangle \in \sim h,...,\langle x_n,y_n\rangle \in \sim h, \text{ then } h(x_1)=h(y_1),...,h(x_n)=h(y_n)$$

and so

$$\begin{aligned} h(f^{\mathcal{A}}(x_1...x_n)) &= f^{\mathcal{B}}(h(x_1)...h(x_n)) \\ &= f^{\mathcal{B}}(h(y_1)...h(y_n)) \\ &= h(f^{\mathcal{A}}(y_1...y_n)) \end{aligned}$$

Therefore, $\langle f^{\mathcal{A}}(x_1...x_n), f^{\mathcal{A}}(y_1...y_n)\rangle \in \sim h$

(3) For every n-ary relation constant $R \in$ **OPER.CONS** and $x_1,...,x_n, y_1,...,y_n \in A$:

$$\text{if } \langle x_1,y_1\rangle \in \sim h,...,\langle x_n,y_n\rangle \in \sim h, \text{ then } h(x_1)=h(y_1),...,h(x_n)=h(y_n)$$

and so

$$\begin{aligned} \langle x_1,...,x_n\rangle \in R^{\mathcal{A}} &\text{ iff } \langle h(x_1),...,h(x_n)\rangle \in R^{\mathcal{B}} \\ &\text{ iff } \langle h(y_1),...,h(y_n)\rangle \in R^{\mathcal{B}} \\ &\text{ iff } \langle y_1,...,y_n\rangle \in R^{\mathcal{A}} \quad \blacksquare \end{aligned}$$

Proposition 2: For every congruence relation $\approx$ on $\mathcal{A}$, there is a strong homomorphism **h** from $\mathcal{A}$ onto some other structure,

$$\mathcal{A}_\approx = \langle A_\approx, \langle C^{\mathcal{A}_\approx}\rangle_{C\in \mathbf{OPER.CONS}}\rangle$$

such that $\approx\, = \sim\mathbf{h}$.

Proof

Let a structure $\mathcal{A}_\approx$ be defined as follows:

(i) $A_\approx = \{[x]_\approx / x\in A\}$ is the set of equivalence classes induced by $\approx$.

(ii) For every n-ary function constant $f\in$ **OPER.CONS** and $x_1,\ldots,x_n\in A$

$$f^{\mathcal{A}_\approx}([x_1]_\approx,\ldots,[x_n]_\approx) = [f^{\mathcal{A}}(x_1,\ldots,x_n)]_\approx$$

(iii) For every n-ary relation constant $R\in$ **OPER.CONS** and $x_1,\ldots,x_n\in A$

$$\langle [x_1]_\approx,\ldots,[x_n]_\approx\rangle\in R^{\mathcal{A}_\approx} \text{ iff } \langle x_1,\ldots,x_n\rangle\in R^{\mathcal{A}}$$

Let **h** be the function which maps every element of **A** into its equivalence class; that is,

$$\begin{aligned}\mathbf{h}\colon A &\longrightarrow A_\approx\\ x &\longmapsto [x]_\approx\end{aligned}$$

1.- Clearly the function is onto.

2.- For every n-ary function constant $f\in$ **OPER.CONS** and $x_1,\ldots,x_n\in A$

$$\begin{aligned}\mathbf{h}(f^{\mathcal{A}}(x_1\ldots x_n)) &= [f^{\mathcal{A}}(x_1\ldots x_n)]_\approx\\ &= f^{\mathcal{A}_\approx}([x_1]_\approx,\ldots,[x_n]_\approx)\\ &= f^{\mathcal{A}_\approx}(\mathbf{h}(x_1),\ldots,\mathbf{h}(x_n))\end{aligned}$$

3.- For every n-ary relation constant $R\in$ **OPER.CONS** and $x_1,\ldots,x_n\in A$

$$\begin{aligned}\langle x_1,\ldots,x_n\rangle\in R^{\mathcal{A}} &\text{ iff } \langle [x_1]_\approx,\ldots,[x_n]_\approx\rangle\in R^{\mathcal{A}_\approx}\\ &\text{ iff } \langle \mathbf{h}(x_1),\ldots,\mathbf{h}(x_n)\rangle\in R^{\mathcal{A}_\approx}\end{aligned}$$

Besides that, it is easy to see that $\approx\, = \sim\mathbf{h}$, since

$$\begin{aligned}\langle x,y\rangle\in\,\approx &\text{ iff } [x]_\approx = [y]_\approx\\ &\text{ iff } \mathbf{h}(x) = \mathbf{h}(y)\\ &\text{ iff } \langle x,y\rangle\in\sim\mathbf{h}\end{aligned}$$ ∎

Proposition 3: If **h** is a strong homomorphisms from $\mathcal{A}$ onto $\mathcal{B}$, then $\mathcal{A}^{\sim\mathbf{h}} \cong \mathcal{B}$.

Proof

By propositions 1 and 2, there is a strong homomorphism from $\mathcal{A}$ onto $\mathcal{A}^{\sim h}$.

Furthermore, $\mathcal{A}^{\sim h} \cong \mathcal{B}$, since the function defined by

$$H: A^{\sim h} \longrightarrow B$$
$$[x]^{\sim h} \longmapsto h(x)$$

is an isomorphism; *i.e.*, it is:

(i) Well defined, one-to-one and onto.
Well defined, since $\langle x,y\rangle \in \sim h$ iff $[x]^{\sim h} = [y]^{\sim h}$ iff $h(x) = h(y)$.
One-to-one, since from $h(x) = h(y)$ it follows that $[x]^{\sim h} = [y]^{\sim h}$.
Onto, since h was onto.

(ii) For every n-ary function constant $f \in$ OPER.CONS and arbitrary elements of $A^{\sim h}$, $[x_1]^{\sim h},\ldots,[x_n]^{\sim h}$:

$$\begin{aligned} H(f^{\mathcal{A}^{\sim h}}([x_1]^{\sim h},\ldots,[x_n]^{\sim h})) &= H([f^{\mathcal{A}}(x_1,\ldots,x_n)]^{\sim h}) \\ &= h(f^{\mathcal{A}}(x_1,\ldots,x_n)) \\ &= f^{\mathcal{B}}(h(x_1),\ldots,h(x_n)) \\ &= f^{\mathcal{B}}(H([x_1]^{\sim h}),\ldots,H([x_n]^{\sim h})) \end{aligned}$$

(iii) For every n-ary relation constant $R \in$ OPER.CONS and arbitrary elements of $A^{\sim h}$, $[x_1]^{\sim h},\ldots,[x_n]^{\sim h}$:

$$\begin{aligned} \langle [x_1]^{\sim h},\ldots,[x_n]^{\sim h}\rangle \in R^{\mathcal{A}^{\sim h}} &\text{ iff } \langle x_1,\ldots,x_n\rangle \in R^{\mathcal{A}} \\ &\text{ iff } \langle h(x_1),\ldots,h(x_n)\rangle \in R^{\mathcal{B}} \\ &\text{ iff } \langle H([x_1]^{\sim h}),\ldots,H([x_n]^{\sim h})\rangle \in R^{\mathcal{B}}. \ ∎ \end{aligned}$$

Proposition 4: If h_1 and h_2 are two strong homomorphisms from $\mathcal{A}$ onto $\mathcal{B}_1$ and $\mathcal{B}_2$ respectively, and if $\sim h_1 = \sim h_2$, then $\mathcal{B}_1 \cong \mathcal{B}_2$.

Proof

It is an easy corollary of the previous proposition. ∎

4.- STANDARD SEMANTICS.

We have already introduced both the formal language of **SOL** (which is composed of symbols and strings of symbols) and the standard structures. Each standard structure is composed of a universe of individuals and universes for sets and relations defined on individuals; these universes have as members all possible sets and relations. Besides that, standing out in the structure, there are certain relations and functions between members of the universe of individuals. In semantics, we build a bridge between these different realities. The bridge is the notion of truth, or more generally, the concept of satisfaction of a formula under an interpretation.

The definition of interpretation simply extends its homologue for first order logic, which, in turn, extends propositional logic. Both logics are taken with their classical presentation and so the connectives are extensional and the individual quantification is performed over a unique universe of individuals. We say that a connective is extensional when its meaning can be completely described as a truth function over the set $\{T,F\}$ of standard truth values.
(Non-extensional connectives, also called intensional connectives, appear in modal logic.)

As the standard structures for second order logic are not the only ones to be considered in this book, non-standard semantics will also be handled (see Chapter IV). Thus, in second order logic, unlike first order logic, we have standard and non-standard interpretations. It is also true that in first order logic we also talk about non-standard structures, but they are in fact non-standard models of a particular theory (because they are not isomorphic to the intended model). What we don't have in **FOL** is a non-standard semantics. Therefore, the meaning of non-standard in **FOL** and in **SOL** is different. But different does not mean that they are not related, as we will explain in detail in section 2.2 of Chapter III.

4.1. Assignment.

4.1.1. In second order logic an ***assignment*** is a mapping from the set of variables into the universes

$$M: \mathcal{V} \cup (\bigcup_{n\geq 1} \mathcal{V}_n) \longrightarrow A \cup (\bigcup_{n\geq 1} A_n)$$

in such a way that $M[\mathcal{V}] \subseteq \mathbf{A}$ and $M[\mathcal{V}_n] \subseteq \mathbf{A}_n$ for each n; that is to say that n-ary relation variables always get their value in $\mathbf{A}_n$. ▒

4.1.2. If M is an assignment, x is an individual variable and $\mathbf{x}$ is any element of A, then $M_x^{\mathbf{x}}$ is an assignment which maps x to $\mathbf{x}$ and agrees with M on all variables distinct from x. Therefore,

$$M_x^{\mathbf{x}} = (M - \{\langle x, M(x)\rangle\}) \cup \{\langle x, \mathbf{x}\rangle\}$$ ▒

4.1.3. If M is an assignment, X^n is an n-ary relation variable and $\mathbf{X}^n$ is any element of $\mathbf{A}_n$, then $M_{X^n}^{\mathbf{X}^n}$ is an assignment which maps X^n to $\mathbf{X}^n$ and agrees with M on all other variables. Therefore,

$$M_{X^n}^{\mathbf{X}^n} = (M - \{\langle X^n, M(X^n)\rangle\}) \cup \{\langle X^n, \mathbf{X}^n\rangle\}$$ ▒

4.1.4. In a similar way we define $M_{v_1 \ldots v_n}^{\mathbf{v}_1 \ldots \mathbf{v}_n}$ for the pairwise distinct variables $v_1, \ldots, v_n$ of any type and the individuals and relations $\mathbf{v}_1, \ldots, \mathbf{v}_n$ of $\mathcal{A}$ of the same type as the variable of equal subscript.

$$M_{v_1 \ldots v_n}^{\mathbf{v}_1 \ldots \mathbf{v}_n} = (M - \{\langle v_1, M(v_1)\rangle, \ldots, \langle v_n, M(v_n)\rangle\}) \cup \{\langle v_1, \mathbf{v}_1\rangle, \ldots, \langle v_n, \mathbf{v}_n\rangle\}$$ ▒

4.2. Interpretation.

An interpretation $\mathcal{I}$ over a standard structure $\mathcal{A}$ is a pair $\langle \mathcal{A}, M\rangle$ where M is an assignment on $\mathcal{A}$. Once an interpretation is given, every term denotes an element in A and every formula is true or false under the interpretation. The satisfaction relation makes precise the notion of a formula being true under an interpretation. (We write $\mathcal{I}$ sat φ to indicate that $\mathcal{I}$ satisfies φ. We also say that φ holds in $\mathcal{I}$ or that $\mathcal{I}$ is a model of φ.) If τ is a term and $\mathbf{x} \in \mathbf{A}$, we write $\mathcal{I}(\tau) = \mathbf{x}$ to indicate that the term τ names the individual $\mathbf{x}$ in $\mathcal{I}$. Also, if Π^n is a predicate and $\mathbf{X}^n \in \mathbf{A}_n$, then we write $\mathcal{I}(\Pi^n) = \mathbf{X}^n$ to indicate that Π^n represents the relation $\mathbf{X}^n$ in $\mathcal{I}$.

If $\mathcal{I} = \langle \mathcal{A}, \mathrm{M} \rangle$ then we will write $\mathcal{I}^{\mathrm{v}_1..\mathrm{v}_n}_{v_1..v_n}$ instead of $\langle \mathcal{A}, \mathrm{M}^{\mathrm{v}_1...\mathrm{v}_n}_{v_1...v_n} \rangle$. ▮

4.2.1. Definition of denotation of terms and predicates and of satisfaction of formulas of λ-L_2.

Let $\mathcal{I} = \langle \mathcal{A}, \mathrm{M} \rangle$.

(T1) $\mathcal{I}(x) = \mathrm{M}(x)$

(T2) $\mathcal{I}(a) = a^{\mathcal{A}}$

(T3) $\mathcal{I}(f\tau_1...\tau_n) = f^{\mathcal{A}}(\mathcal{I}(\tau_1)...\mathcal{I}(\tau_n))$

(P1) $\mathcal{I}(X^n) = \mathrm{M}(X^n)$

(P2) $\mathcal{I}(R) = R^{\mathcal{A}}$

(P3) $\mathcal{I}(=) = \{\langle \mathrm{x,y} \rangle \in \mathrm{A}^2 / \mathrm{x} = \mathrm{y}\} \cup (\bigcup_{n \geq 1} \{\langle \mathrm{X}^n, \mathrm{Y}^n \rangle \in \mathrm{A}_n^2 / \mathrm{X}^n = \mathrm{Y}^n\})$

(equality is identity in every universe)

(P4) $\mathcal{I}(\lambda x_1...x_n\, \varphi) = \{\langle \mathrm{x}_1,...,\mathrm{x}_n \rangle \in \mathrm{A} \times \overset{(n}{\dots} \times \mathrm{A} \,/\, \mathcal{I}^{\mathrm{x}_1...\mathrm{x}_n}_{x_1...x_n} \text{ sat } \varphi\}$

(F1) $\mathcal{I}$ sat $\Pi\, \tau_1...\tau_n$ iff $\langle \mathcal{I}(\tau_1),...,\mathcal{I}(\tau_n) \rangle \in \mathcal{I}(\Pi)$

In particular, $\mathcal{I}$ sat $\tau_1 = \tau_2$ iff $\mathcal{I}(\tau_1) = \mathcal{I}(\tau_2)$.

Also, it is not true that $\mathcal{I}$ sat $\bot$

(F2) $\mathcal{I}$ sat $\Pi^n = \Psi^n$ iff $\mathcal{I}(\Pi^n) = \mathcal{I}(\Psi^n)$

(F3) $\mathcal{I}$ sat $\neg\varphi$ iff it is not true that $\mathcal{I}$ sat φ

$\mathcal{I}$ sat $\varphi \vee \psi$ iff $\mathcal{I}$ sat φ or $\mathcal{I}$ sat ψ

$\mathcal{I}$ sat $\varphi \wedge \psi$ iff $\mathcal{I}$ sat φ and $\mathcal{I}$ sat ψ

$\mathcal{I}$ sat $\varphi \rightarrow \psi$ iff if $\mathcal{I}$ sat φ then $\mathcal{I}$ sat ψ

$\mathcal{I}$ sat $\varphi \leftrightarrow \psi$ iff $\mathcal{I}$ sat φ if and only if $\mathcal{I}$ sat ψ

(F4) $\mathcal{I}$ sat $\forall x\varphi$ iff for all $\mathrm{x} \in \mathrm{A}$: $\mathcal{I}^{\mathrm{x}}_{x}$ sat φ

$\mathcal{I}$ sat $\exists x\varphi$ iff there is $\mathrm{x} \in \mathrm{A}$ such that: $\mathcal{I}^{\mathrm{x}}_{x}$ sat φ

(F5) $\mathcal{I}$ sat $\forall X^n\varphi$ iff for all $\mathrm{X}^n \in \mathrm{A}_n$: $\mathcal{I}^{\mathrm{X}^n}_{X^n}$ sat φ

$\mathcal{I}$ sat $\exists X^n\varphi$ iff there is $\mathrm{X}^n \in \mathrm{A}_n$ such that: $\mathcal{I}^{\mathrm{X}^n}_{X^n}$ sat φ ▮

4.2.2. Definition of denotation of terms and predicates and of satisfaction of formulas of L_2.
Suppress rule (P4) and realize that rules (F1) through (F5) vary their scope. ▮

4.2.3. Model of formulas.

(a) Given a formula φ, we say that $\mathcal{I}$ is ***a model of*** φ if and only if $\mathcal{I}$ sat φ. ▮

(b) Given a set of formulas Γ, $\mathcal{I}$ is ***a model of*** Γ if and only if $\mathcal{I}$ sat φ for every $\varphi \in \Gamma$. ▮

(c) The standard notation for these concepts is $\mathcal{I} \vDash \varphi$ and $\mathcal{I} \vDash \Gamma$. ▮

Remarks.

When φ is a sentence we do not need the assignment and sometimes we will say that the structure $\mathcal{A}$ is a model of φ or that φ is ***true in*** $\mathcal{A}$. So you can write $\mathcal{A} \vDash \varphi$.

As above, when Γ is a set of sentences we can say that $\mathcal{A}$ is a model of Γ, leaving out the assignment (you can write $\mathcal{A} \vDash \Gamma$). As we will see, the coincidence lemma in section 5.1 below justifies this procedure.

4.2.4. Satisfiability.

(a) A formula φ is ***satisfiable*** if and only if there is at least one interpretation $\mathcal{I}$ such that $\mathcal{I}$ is a model of φ. ▮

(b) A set of formulas Γ is ***satisfiable*** if and only if there is at least one interpretation $\mathcal{I}$ which simultaneously models each formula in Γ. ▮

(c) A formula φ is ***unsatisfiable*** if and only if it is not satisfiable. ▮

(d) A set of formulas Γ is ***unsatisfiable*** if and only if it is not satisfiable. ▮

4.3. Consequence and validity.

It is a popular prejudice to say that the relation of consequence is the basic notion of logic. In fact, in an abstract setting, a logic is nothing but a set of formulas defined from two things: the set of formulas of a formal language (**FORM**) and its consequence relation ($\vDash$). Thus, a logic could also be identified with $\langle$**FORM**, $\vDash\rangle$. For the classical binary relation of consequence the following definition has been accepted all through this century:

> A formula φ is a ***consequence*** of a set of formulas Γ when every model of Γ is also a model of φ.

What is the intuition we want to capture with this concept? From what other concepts should it be distinguished?

It is commonplace to say that in logic the main task is to analyze the pure logic concepts involved in correct reasoning, which has to be, up to a certain point, independent of the particular reasoning instances (since we accept that there are infinite correct reasonings following the same logic pattern). Consequence is the relation that holds between the hypothesis and the conclusion of a correct reasoning and all the correct reasonings following the same pattern. The idea is that if we translate into the formal language a correct reasoning expressed in a natural language obtaining Γ as hypothesis and φ as conclusion, no matter how we retranslate Γ and φ into English, we always obtain a correct reasoning again. Of course, we keep unchanged the meaning of the pure logical aspects (*i.e.*, connectors, quantifiers, identity). From our point of view, it is not the reasoning process that we want to model with this concept of consequence, but to attain a general description of the different situations, models or worlds where the hypothesis of a right reasoning, Γ, and its conclusion, φ, can take their truth values. The reasoning process itself is better modelled in a calculus. Thus, from this point of view, consequence is a semantic concept. We want to make it clear that in any valid or correct reasoning the particular truth values of the hypothesis and conclusion in a given model, situation or world are not decisive: an incorrect reasoning can have true hypothesis and conclusion, and there are correct reasonings with false conclusions. In fact, the key to the question is that a correct reasoning will never drive us from true hypothesis to false conclusion. So the intuition is that there is not a model, situation or world where both hypothesis and negation of conclusion are true. Technically, $\Gamma\cup\{\neg\varphi\}$ has no model. Thus, our semantic definition of consequence given some lines above seems adequate.

But, somehow, there also corresponds to our intuition of a correct reasoning the idea of contradiction between hypothesis and negation of the conclusion. Technically, $\Gamma\cup\{\neg\varphi\}$ is contradictory. The concept of a contradictory set of formulas is not semantic but proof-theoretical. As you will see in the next chapter, the reasoning process which takes place in our mind is better understood and modelled in proof theory in a logical calculus.

It is only natural that the concept of a contradictory set of formulas is close to the concept of an unsatisfiable set (without models), since the latter is the syntactical counterpart of the former in the same sense that $\models$ (consequence) and $\vdash$ (deducibility) correspond to one another.

We will also introduce validity as consequence from the empty set of formulas. (Thus, we define φ is valid iff φ is a consequence of $\emptyset$.) Since any interpretation models the empty set, that means that all interpretations are models of φ.

In the chapters which follow we will see that we can change the semantics of a formal language by changing the class of structures we want to talk about, but then we also change the consequence relation and, in a proper sense, we are then in the realm of a new logic. Therefore, the notation $\Gamma \models_{\mathcal{ST}} \varphi$ (φ is a consequence of Γ in the class of structures $\mathcal{ST}$ and $\Gamma \models_{\mathcal{T}} \varphi$ (φ is a consequence of Γ in the class of models of the theory $\mathcal{T}$) is telling you that a change of logic has been made which has to be treated with care.

4.3.1. Consequence.

(a) A formula φ is a ***consequence*** of a set of formulas Γ if and only if each interpretation $\mathcal{I}$ which happens to be a model of Γ is also a model of φ. ▓
Therefore, φ is a consequence of Γ, if and only if, for every structure $\mathcal{A}$ of signature Σ and every assignment M on its universes, if $\langle \mathcal{A}, M \rangle$ is a model of every $\psi \in \Gamma$, then $\langle \mathcal{A}, M \rangle$ is also a model of φ.

(b) We will write $\Gamma \models \varphi$ to indicate that φ is a consequence of Γ. ▓

(c) We will write $\Gamma \not\models \varphi$ to indicate that φ is not a consequence of Γ. In this case we also say that φ is ***independent*** of Γ. ▓

Remarks on notation.

Please note that in the above the same symbol, $\models$, is used for consequence and for models. Both notations are standard. To distinguish between uses you have to look at the left position.

Since we are considering standard structures and the semantic is based on them, sometimes to emphasize this fact, or to distinguish it from non-standard notions, we will write $\Gamma \models_{\mathcal{S.S}} \varphi$ instead of just $\Gamma \models \varphi$, where $\mathcal{S.S}$ represents the class of standard structures.

4.3.2. Validity.

(a) A formula φ is ***valid*** if and only if $\emptyset \models \varphi$. ▓

(b) We will write $\models \varphi$ for validities. ▓

(c) **VALID**($\models$) (or simply $\models$) represents the set of standard validities. ▓

Remarks on notation.

As before, sometimes we will write $\models_{\mathcal{S.S}} \varphi$ instead of just $\models \varphi$. In that case, $\models_{\mathcal{S.S}}$ would represent the set of standard validities.

4.3.3. Proposition. For all Γ and φ: $\Gamma \vDash \varphi$ iff $\Gamma\cup\{\neg\varphi\}$ is unsatisfiable.

Proof

[$\Rightarrow$] Let $\Gamma \vDash \varphi$. So, for all $\mathcal{I}$: If $\mathcal{I}$ is a model of Γ, then $\mathcal{I}$ is a model of φ. Therefore, there is no $\mathcal{I}$ such that $\mathcal{I}$ is a model of $\Gamma\cup\{\neg\varphi\}$. Thus, $\Gamma\cup\{\neg\varphi\}$ is unsatisfiable.

[$\Leftarrow$] Let $\Gamma\cup\{\neg\varphi\}$ be unsatisfiable. Then, there is no $\mathcal{I}$ such that $\mathcal{I}$ is a model of $\Gamma\cup\{\neg\varphi\}$. So, for all $\mathcal{I}$: If $\mathcal{I}$ is a model of Γ, then $\mathcal{I}$ is a model of φ. Thus, $\Gamma \vDash \varphi$. ▮

4.4. Logical equivalence.

The logical equivalence relation we are going to introduce below is a metaconcept and thus the symbol used for it does not belong to the alphabet of the object language, λ-L_2. Nevertheless, it is closely related to the connective $\leftrightarrow$, as you will be asked to prove below. The logical equivalence relation will be useful to customize your formal language by helping you to choose as primitive connectors a complete set of them.

4.4.1. Definition.

(a) Two formulas φ and ψ are ***logically equivalent*** if and only if $\varphi \vDash \psi$ and $\psi \vDash \varphi$. ▒

(b) We will write $\varphi \mathrel{\dashv\vDash} \psi$ to express this metaconcept. ▒

4.4.2. Proposition. For all φ and ψ: $\varphi \mathrel{\dashv\vDash} \psi$ iff $\vDash \varphi \leftrightarrow \psi$.
Can you please prove this? ▮

4.4.3. Proposition. For all φ and ψ:

(1) $\bot \mathrel{\dashv\vDash} \neg x{=}x$

(2) $\varphi \wedge \psi \mathrel{\dashv\vDash} \neg(\neg\varphi \vee \neg\psi)$

(3) $\varphi \rightarrow \psi \mathrel{\dashv\vDash} \neg\varphi \vee \psi$

(4) $\varphi \leftrightarrow \psi \mathrel{\dashv\vDash} \neg(\varphi \vee \psi) \vee \neg(\neg\varphi \vee \neg\psi)$

(5) $\forall v\varphi \mathrel{\dashv\vDash} \neg\exists v\neg\varphi$

Can you please prove this? ▮

4.4.4. Proposition. For all φ and ψ:

(1) $\neg\varphi \mathrel{\dashv\vDash} \varphi \rightarrow \bot$

(2) $\varphi \wedge \psi \mathrel{\dashv\vDash} (\varphi \rightarrow (\psi \rightarrow \bot)) \rightarrow \bot$

(3) $\varphi \vee \psi \mathrel{\dashv\vDash} (\varphi \rightarrow \bot) \rightarrow \psi$

(4) $\varphi \leftrightarrow \psi \models\mid ((\varphi \rightarrow \psi) \rightarrow ((\psi \rightarrow \varphi) \rightarrow \perp)) \rightarrow \perp$

(5) $\forall v\varphi \models\mid (\exists v(\varphi \rightarrow \perp)) \rightarrow \perp$

Can you please prove this? ∎

Remark.

Some other equivalences are typical of standard second order logic. For instance, the formula expressing identity of two individuals,

$\forall Z(Zx \leftrightarrow Zy)$, saying that they are in the same sets

is equivalent to the formula

$\forall Z^2(\forall z\, Z^2zz \rightarrow Z^2xy)$, saying that a pair of individuals belongs to all reflexive relations.

The reason for that equivalence is that identity is the least reflexive relation and that in standard structures all sets and relations are in the relation universes. In **Equality-free SOL** any of these formulas can be used to define equality for individuals.

4.5. Simplifying our language.

Right from the definition of satisfaction of formulas it is clear that we don't need all the connectives and quantifiers we have introduced so far. For some purposes - ***e.g.***, proofs by induction on the formation of formulas - we can assume that our language only has $\neg$ and $\vee$ as connectives and $\exists$ as quantifier. The formulas including the rest of the connectives $\perp$, $\wedge$, $\rightarrow$, $\leftrightarrow$ and the universal quantifier $\forall$ can be considered as abbreviations of the formulas with only $\neg$, $\vee$ and $\exists$. The well known equivalences we use to simplify our language are stated in proposition 4.4.3 above.

Some other sets of logical symbols seem preferable in other contexts, like the set $\{\perp, \rightarrow, \forall\}$ used in modal logic. In this latter case, proposition 4.4.4 resolves the problem.

To make the question more precise, you can obtain a language at least as expressive as our L_2, when you choose a proper subset of the basic connectives and quantifiers and then you prove that all the formulas of L_2 are defined by logically equivalent formulas using only the reduced set of connectives and quantifiers. For the language λ-L_2 the same reduction can be made. There is a reverse reduction from λ-L_2 to L_2, but you need the simultaneous substitution lemma in section 5.2.

4.5.1. Proposition. For all $\varphi \in$ **FORM**(L_2) there is a $\varphi^* \in$ **FORM**$(L_2 - \{\bot, \wedge, \rightarrow, \leftrightarrow, \forall\})$ such that $\varphi \mathrel{\models\!\dashv} \varphi^*$. (So the primitive formulas only contain $\neg, \vee$ and $\exists$.)

Proof

We firstly define by induction on formulas a map $*$ from the set **FORM**(L_2) into **FORM**$(L_2 - \{\bot, \wedge, \rightarrow, \leftrightarrow, \forall\})$.

(F1) $\bot^* = \neg x{=}x$

$\varphi^* = \varphi$ for the rest of the formulas obtained by this rule

(F2) $\varphi^* = \varphi$ for all the formulas obtained by this rule (if we were in language λ-L_2 you would need to define the obvious function on predicates changing the required λ-predicates)

(F3) $(\neg\varphi)^* = \neg\varphi^*$ $\qquad (\varphi \vee \psi)^* = \varphi^* \vee \psi^*$

$(\varphi \wedge \psi)^* = \neg(\neg\varphi^* \vee \neg\psi^*)$ $\qquad (\varphi \rightarrow \psi)^* = \neg\varphi^* \vee \psi^*$

$(\varphi \leftrightarrow \psi)^* = \neg(\varphi^* \vee \psi^*) \vee \neg(\neg\varphi^* \vee \neg\psi^*)$

(F4) $(\forall x\varphi)^* = \neg\exists x \neg\varphi^*$ $\qquad (\exists x\varphi)^* = \exists x\varphi^*$

(F5) $(\forall X^n\varphi)^* = \neg\exists X^n \neg\varphi^*$ $\qquad (\exists X^n\varphi)^* = \exists X^n\varphi^*$

Finally, using proposition 4.4.3 prove that $*$ has the desired properties. ∎

4.5.2. Proposition. For all $\varphi \in$ **FORM**(L_2) there is a $\varphi^{-} \in$ **FORM**$(L_2 - \{\neg, \wedge, \vee, \leftrightarrow, \exists\})$ such that $\varphi \mathrel{\models\!\dashv} \varphi^{-}$. (So the primitive formulas only contain $\bot$, $\rightarrow$ and $\forall$.)

Proof

We firstly define by induction on formulas a map $^{-}$ from the set **FORM**(L_2) into **FORM**$(L_2 - \{\neg, \wedge, \vee, \leftrightarrow, \exists\})$. This map is based on proposition 4.4.4 in the same sense as the previous map $*$ was based on proposition 4.4.3.

We secondly prove, using proposition 4.4.4, that $^{-}$ has the desired properties. ∎

4.5.3. Proposition. For all $\varphi \in$ **FORM**$(\lambda$-$L_2)$ there is a $\varphi^* \in$ **FORM**$(\lambda$-$L_2 - \{\bot, \wedge, \rightarrow, \leftrightarrow, \forall\}))$ such that $\varphi \mathrel{\models\!\dashv} \varphi^*$.

Proof

The proof proceeds as in 4.5.1. ∎

4.5.4. Proposition. For all $\varphi\in$FORM(λ-L_2) there is a $\varphi^{\blacksquare}\in$FORM($\lambda$-$L_2$–{¬,∧,∨,↔,∃}) such that $\varphi \models\!\mid \varphi^{\blacksquare}$. (So the primitive formulas only contain ⊥, → and ∀.)

Proof
The proof proceeds as in 4.5.2. ∎

4.6. Alternative presentation of standard semantics.

There is an alternative presentation of semantics which is basically a rewording of this, but where we add a universe of truth values and instead of relations we have characteristic functions. From a structure $\mathcal{A}$ defined according to definition 3.1 you easily pass to a structure $\mathcal{A}^{\#}$ obtained by an easy construction. You can work the transformation for yourself as follows:

(A) In the first place, from the signature Σ, we build a signature $\Sigma^{\#}$. We agree that the n-ary relations and n-ary characteristic functions share types: $\langle 0,1,\overset{n}{\ldots},1\rangle$ is the type for both. As a result, the set **VAR** remains unchanged. To the set **OPER.CONS** you can add the equality and the logical connectors with the expected values under **FUNC**.

(B) In the second place, take the structure $\mathcal{A}$ defined according to definition 3.1 above,

$$\mathcal{A}=\langle \mathrm{A},\langle \mathrm{A}_n\rangle_{n\geq 1},\langle C^{\mathcal{A}}\rangle_{C\in \mathbf{OPER.CONS}}\rangle$$

and build from it a structure $\mathcal{A}^{\#}$ of signature $\Sigma^{\#}$. Add a universe A_0 for truth values and in every universe A_n replace every relation by the corresponding characteristic function. Replace also each distinguished n-ary relation by its characteristic function; *i.e.*, instead of $\mathrm{R}\subseteq \mathrm{A}^n$, put the function

$$\chi_{\mathrm{R}}\colon \mathrm{A}^n \longrightarrow \{\mathrm{T},\mathrm{F}\}$$
$$\langle x_1,\ldots,x_n\rangle \longmapsto \mathrm{T} \quad \text{iff } \langle x_1,\ldots,x_n\rangle\in \mathrm{R}$$

Add to the structure $\mathcal{A}$ the truth functions for interpreting the connectives with their standard meaning. Add as well the characteristic functions for the prototypical relation of identity, for individuals and relations.

(C) Finally, for every assignment, M, the new assignment $\mathrm{M}^{\#}$ can also be easily adapted. Given a structure $\mathcal{A}^{\#}$ and an assignment $\mathrm{M}^{\#}$, form the interpretation $\mathcal{I}^{\#}=\langle \mathcal{A}^{\#},\mathrm{M}^{\#}\rangle$. Define recursively $\mathcal{I}^{\#}(\varepsilon)$ for each expression ε. Terms and predicates will denote elements of the universes, formulas will denote elements of A_0.

Of course, we want that for each formula φ and each interpretation $\mathcal{I}$,

$$\mathcal{I} \text{ sat } \varphi \text{ iff } \mathcal{I}^{\#}(\varphi) = \mathrm{T}$$

4.7. Definable sets and relations in a given structure.

Given a structure

$$\mathcal{A} = \langle \mathrm{A}, \langle \mathrm{A}_n \rangle_{n \geq 1}, \langle C^{\mathcal{A}} \rangle_{C \in \mathbf{OPER.CONS}} \rangle$$

and a second order language L_2 or λ-L_2, there are several kinds of relations which are related, in one way or another, with $\mathcal{A}$ and **FORM**(λ-L_2). Certainly we will distinguish: (1) first and second order relations ***on*** the universes of the structure, (2) relations ***into*** the universes of the structure, (3) ***definable*** relations of the structure using a given language and (4) ***parametrically definable*** relations of the structure using a given language. These sets of relations are not restricted to the category of relations among individuals; ***i.e.,*** not all of them are first order relations. Since in a second order structure of signature Σ the only relations displayed are the relations among individuals, in this approach we are viewing some hidden relations. Hidden in the structure, but definable with the second order language, are some relations which, even though they are not relations among individuals, are used to define first order relations.

Some of the distinctions introduced below are a bit artificial in the context of standard structures and semantics. In Chapter IV they will apply to a wide variety of structures and they will reach there their proper significance.

4.7.1. Definition of first order relations of the structure $\mathcal{A}$.

(a) If $\mathcal{A}$ is a second order structure, any subset of the n-ary cartesian product of the universe of individuals - *i.e.*, any $\mathrm{X} \subseteq \mathrm{A}^n$ - is an n-ary ***first order relation on $\mathcal{A}$.*** ▓

Let $\mathbf{REL}^{1st}(\mathcal{A})$ be the class of all first order relations on $\mathcal{A}$. ▓

(b) We say that an n-ary first order relation X is ***into*** $\mathcal{A}$ when $\mathrm{X} \in \mathrm{A}_n$ or $\mathrm{X} = R^{\mathcal{A}}$ for $R \in \mathbf{OPER.CONS}$. ▓

Let $\mathbf{REL}^{1st}(\in \mathcal{A})$ be the class of all first order relations into $\mathcal{A}$. ▓

Remarks.

All these relations are first order relations. In the universes of any second order structure $\mathcal{A}$

there are *only* relations among individuals; when the structure is standard, ***all*** the relations among individuals are in the universes of the structure. Thus, in standard structures all the n-ary first order relations ***on*** $\mathcal{A}$ are ***into*** $\mathcal{A}$.

Proposition: For standard structures:

(1) $\text{REL}^{1^{st}}(\mathcal{A}) = \bigcup_{n\geq 1} A_n$.

(2) $\text{REL}^{1^{st}}(\mathcal{A}) = \text{REL}^{1^{st}}(\in\mathcal{A})$.

Proof

Both follow easily from the definitions.

The reason for (1) is that in any structure $\mathcal{A}$,

$$\text{REL}^{1^{st}}(\mathcal{A}) = \bigcup_{n\geq 1} \mathcal{P}A^n$$

and in a standard structure, $A_n = \mathcal{P}A^n$ for all $n\geq 1$. ∎

4.7.2. Definition of second order relations of $\mathcal{A}$

(a) If $\mathcal{A}$ is a second order structure, $A_{i_1},\ldots,A_{i_n}$ are universes of $\mathcal{A}$ (either individual or relation universes; $A_{i_j} = A$ or $A_{i_j} = A_m$, with $m\geq 1$), any subset of the cartesian product of these universes - *i.e.*, any $X \subseteq A_{i_1}\times\ldots\times A_{i_n}$ - is an n-ary ***second order relation of*** $\mathcal{A}$ ▒

Let $\text{REL}(\mathcal{A})$ be the class of all second order relations of $\mathcal{A}$. ▒

(b) We say that an n-ary second order relation X is ***into*** $\mathcal{A}$ when $X\in A_n$ or $X = R^{\mathcal{A}}$ for $R\in$OPER.CONS. ▒

Let $\text{REL}(\in\mathcal{A})$ be the class of all second order relations into $\mathcal{A}$. ▒

(c) We can define the set of ***proper second order relations*** as

$$\text{REL}^{2^{nd}}(\mathcal{A}) = \text{REL}(\mathcal{A}) - \text{REL}^{1^{st}}(\mathcal{A}).$$ ▒

Remarks.

Of course, when all the $A_{i_j} = A$, then we have a one-sorted first order relation as defined in 4.7.1. In this way, the set of second order relations includes as a subset the first order relations.

On the other hand, due to our choice of signature, we do not have proper second order relations ***into*** the structure, but we could, with a different Σ.

For a structure $\mathcal{A}$ with a countably infinite universe of individuals, the set of first order relations of $\mathcal{A}$, $\mathbf{REL}^{1^{st}}(\mathcal{A})$, has $2^{\aleph_0}$ elements and the set of second order relations of $\mathcal{A}$, $\mathbf{REL}^{2^{nd}}(\mathcal{A})$, has $2^{2^{\aleph_0}}$

Proposition: It is clear from the definition that in our case:

(1) $\mathbf{REL}^{1^{st}}(\mathcal{A}) \subseteq \mathbf{REL}(\mathcal{A})$ but $\mathbf{REL}^{1^{st}}(\mathcal{A}) \neq \mathbf{REL}(\mathcal{A})$

(2) $\mathbf{REL}^{1^{st}}(\in\mathcal{A}) = \mathbf{REL}(\in\mathcal{A})$

Proof

Obvious. ▮

4.7.3. Definition of $\mathcal{A}$-definable first order relations using a given language.

(a) Let $\mathcal{A}$ be a second order structure and $\mathbf{X} \subseteq \mathrm{A}^n$ an n-ary relation on individuals. We say that $\mathbf{X}$ is an ***$\mathcal{A}$-definable first order relation using λ-L_2*** iff there exist a formula φ of λ-L_2, pairwise distinct individual variables $x_1,...,x_n$ such that $\mathbf{FREE}(\lambda x_1...x_n\ \varphi) = \emptyset$ and an interpretation $\mathcal{I}$ over $\mathcal{A}$ such that

$$\mathbf{X} = \mathcal{I}(\lambda x_1...x_n\ \varphi)$$ ▮

Let $\mathbf{DEF}^{1^{st}}(\mathcal{A},\lambda\text{-}L_2)$ be the smallest class containing all $\mathcal{A}$-definable first order relations using λ-L_2. ▮

(b) For the **SOL** language without λ-abstraction, L_2, we say that the formula φ along with the sequence of individual variables $\langle x_1,...,x_n\rangle$ ***defines*** X ***in the structure $\mathcal{A}$ using L_2*** when

$$\mathbf{X} = \{\langle \mathbf{x}_1,...,\mathbf{x}_n\rangle \ /\ \langle \mathcal{A}, \mathrm{M}^{\mathbf{x}_1...\mathbf{x}_n}_{x_1...x_n}\rangle \text{ sat } \varphi\}$$

where M is an assignment and $\mathbf{FREE}(\varphi) \subseteq \{x_1,...,x_n\}$. ▮

Let $\mathbf{DEF}^{1^{st}}(\mathcal{A},L_2)$ be the smallest class containing all $\mathcal{A}$-definable first order relations using L_2. ▮

Introducing a new notation: With the notation to be introduced in 5.1.2, we will simplify

$\langle \mathcal{A}, \mathrm{M}^{\mathbf{x}_1...\mathbf{x}_n}_{x_1...x_n}\rangle$ to $\mathcal{A}[^{\mathbf{x}_1...\mathbf{x}_n}_{x_1...x_n}]$ and also to $\mathcal{A}[\mathbf{x}_1...\mathbf{x}_n]$

in certain circumstances.

4.7.4. Definition of $\mathcal{A}$-definable second order relations using a given language.

X is an ***$\mathcal{A}$-definable second order relation using a language λ-L_2*** (or L_2) when **X** is a second order relation of $\mathcal{A}$ and there is a formula φ of λ-L_2 (or of L_2) such that

$$\mathbf{X} = \{\langle \mathbf{v}_1,...,\mathbf{v}_n\rangle \in \mathbf{A}_{i_1} \times ... \times \mathbf{A}_{i_n} \,/\, \mathcal{A}\,[{}^{\mathbf{v}_1 ... \mathbf{v}_n}_{v_1 ... v_n}]\ \text{sat}\ \varphi\}$$

where $\mathbf{FREE}(\varphi) \subseteq \{v_1,...,v_n\}$ and for each j, 1≤j≤n, the variable v_j is of type $i_j \in \mathbf{VAR}$.

Let $\mathbf{DEF}(\mathcal{A},L_2)$ and $\mathbf{DEF}(\mathcal{A},\lambda\text{-}L_2)$ be the corresponding sets.

Remark.

In the case (a) of 4.7.3, we say that the λ-predicate $\lambda x_1...x_n\ \varphi$ names **X** in $\mathcal{A}$. In both cases we can say that the formula φ along with the sequence of variables $\langle x_1,...,x_n\rangle$ defines **X** in the structure $\mathcal{A}$. Please notice that the order in the sequence is quite important because the same formula and variables define different relations with different orderings.

For instance, Rxy defines $R^{\mathcal{A}}$ and its converse:

$$R^{\mathcal{A}} = \mathcal{I}(\lambda xy\ Rxy) \ \text{ but } \ \mathcal{I}(\lambda yx\ Rxy) = (R^{\mathcal{A}})^{-1}$$

This remark also applies for the language L_2 ; *i.e.*, the same formula and variables define different relations with different orderings:

$$\{\langle \mathbf{x},\mathbf{y}\rangle / \mathcal{A}\,[{}^{\mathbf{xy}}_{xy}]\ \text{sat}\ Rxy\} = R^{\mathcal{A}} \ \text{ but } \ \{\langle \mathbf{y},\mathbf{x}\rangle / \mathcal{A}\,[{}^{\mathbf{xy}}_{xy}]\ \text{sat}\ Rxy\} = (R^{\mathcal{A}})^{-1}$$

Since our **SOL** languages are countable and so is the set of finite sequences of variables, the sets of definable relations are also countable - *i.e.*, of cardinality $\leq \aleph_0$.

Proposition: All the following conditions are true for standard structures.

(1) $\mathbf{DEF}(\mathcal{A},L_2) = \mathbf{DEF}(\mathcal{A},\lambda\text{-}L_2)$

(2) $\mathbf{DEF}^{1^{st}}(\mathcal{A},L_2) = \mathbf{DEF}^{1^{st}}(\mathcal{A},\lambda\text{-}L_2)$

(3) $\mathbf{DEF}^{1^{st}}(\mathcal{A},L_2) \subseteq \mathbf{DEF}(\mathcal{A},L_2)$ but $\mathbf{DEF}^{1^{st}}(\mathcal{A},L_2) \neq \mathbf{DEF}(\mathcal{A},L_2)$

Proof

Can you prove these? ▮

4.7.5. Definition of first and second order parametrically $\mathcal{A}$-definable relations using a given language.

(a) **X** is a ***parametrically $\mathcal{A}$-definable first order relation using*** λ-L_2 (or L_2) iff there are a formula φ, individual variables $x_1,...,x_n$ and variables $v_1,...,v_m$ of any types $i_1,...,i_m \in$ **VAR** such that

$$\mathbf{X} = \{\langle \mathbf{x}_1,...,\mathbf{x}_n\rangle \in \mathbf{A}^n \,/\, \mathcal{A}\left[{}^{\mathbf{x}_1...\mathbf{x}_n\ \mathbf{v}_1...\mathbf{v}_m}_{x_1...x_n\ v_1...v_m}\right] \text{ sat } \varphi\}$$

where $\mathbf{FREE}(\varphi) \subseteq \{x_1,...,x_n,v_1,...,v_m\}$ and the parameters $\mathbf{v}_1,...,\mathbf{v}_m$ are in $\mathbf{A}_{i_1},...,\mathbf{A}_{i_m}$ of types $i_1,...,i_m$. ▮

(b) **X** is a ***parametrically $\mathcal{A}$-definable second order relation using*** λ-L_2 (or L_2) iff there are a formula φ, variables $u_1,...,u_n$ and variables $v_1,...,v_m$ of any types $k_1,...,k_n,i_1,...,i_m \in$ **VAR** such that

$$\mathbf{X} = \{\langle \mathbf{u}_1,...,\mathbf{u}_n\rangle \in \mathbf{A}_{k_1}\times...\times\mathbf{A}_{k_n} \,/\, \mathcal{A}\left[{}^{\mathbf{u}_1...\mathbf{u}_n\ \mathbf{v}_1...\mathbf{v}_m}_{u_1...u_n\ v_1...v_m}\right] \text{ sat } \varphi\}$$

where $\mathbf{FREE}(\varphi) \subseteq \{u_1,...,u_n,v_1,...,v_m\}$ and the parameters $\mathbf{v}_1,...,\mathbf{v}_m$ are in $\mathbf{A}_{i_1},...,\mathbf{A}_{i_m}$ of types $i_1,...,i_m$. ▮

Let $\mathbf{PARAM.DEF}^{1^{st}}(\mathcal{A},L_2)$, $\mathbf{PARAM.DEF}^{1^{st}}(\mathcal{A},\lambda\text{-}L_2)$, $\mathbf{PARAM.DEF}(\mathcal{A},L_2)$ and $\mathbf{PARAM.DEF}(\mathcal{A},\lambda\text{-}L_2)$ be the corresponding sets. ▮

Remarks.

In a structure $\mathcal{A}$ of $\aleph_0$ individuals, since the set of finite sequences of parameters taking values in $\mathbf{A} \cup \{\mathbf{A}_n \,/\, n\geq 1\}$ has $2^{\aleph_0}$ members, the sets of parametrically definable relations have $\leq 2^{\aleph_0}$ members.

In any structure $\mathcal{A}$ it is easy to see that all n-ary first order relations in $\mathbf{A}_n$ are parametrically definable. To see this, just take the formula $X^n x_1...x_n$ and an interpretation where $\mathcal{I}(X^n)$ is the desired relation. Since all possible first order sets and relations are in the relational universes of a standard structure, all of them are parametrically definable; the notion of parametric definability is not useful in this context. As you will see in Chapter IV, it will be truly useful in the context of non-standard structures.

Proposition: Due to the choice of signature and also to the fact of being standard,

(1) $\text{REL}(\in\mathcal{A}) \subseteq \text{PARAM.DEF}^{1^{st}}(\mathcal{A},L_2)$.

(2) $\text{REL}^{1^{st}}(\mathcal{A}) = \text{PARAM.DEF}^{1^{st}}(\mathcal{A},L_2)$.

(3) $\text{DEF}^{1^{st}}(\mathcal{A},L_2) \subseteq \text{PARAM.DEF}^{1^{st}}(\mathcal{A},L_2)$.

Proof

Left to the reader. ▮

EXAMPLES.

All the classes of relations we have introduced so far can be represented in the following picture. Using the results obtained for standard structures in the previous propositions, we will stripe the empty areas.

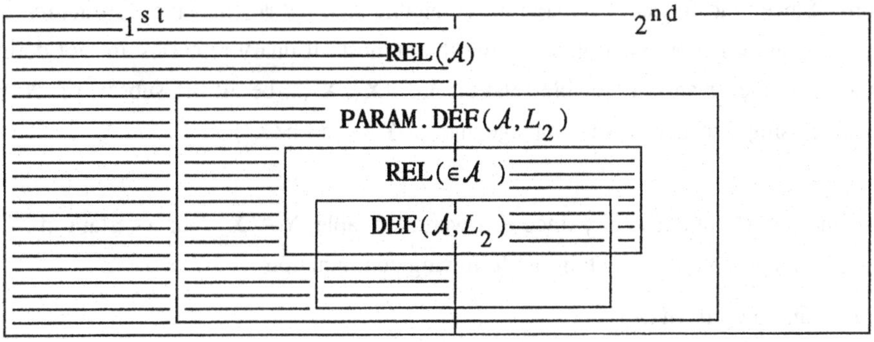

Boolean operations.

In a structure $\mathcal{A}$ having $R,T\in$OPER.CONS, we have that $R^{\mathcal{A}} \cup T^{\mathcal{A}}$, $R^{\mathcal{A}} \cap T^{\mathcal{A}}$ and all Boolean operations are definable by the very simple first order formulas: $Rx \vee Tx$, $Rx \wedge Tx$, etc. Also definable are the domain and the reciprocal of a given relation and the cartesian product of any two. In general, the class of definable relations is closed under all Boolean operations.

All the previous examples are of relations also definable in first order logic. The whole universe and the empty set are first order definable as well. To see the contrast, we can sketch the definition of a first order relation by second order means.

A typical first order SOL definable relation.

For instance, when we have a definable relation, let's say,

$$X^2 = \mathcal{I}(\lambda x_1 x_2\ \varphi)$$

we can define its reflexive and transitive closure; *i.e.*, its loop as

$$\mathcal{I}(\lambda y_1 y_2\ \forall X^2(\lambda x_1 x_2\ \varphi \subseteq X^2 \wedge \text{Refl.}X^2 \wedge \text{Trans.}X^2 \rightarrow X^2 y_1 y_2))$$

The formula

$$\forall X^2(\lambda x_1 x_2\ \varphi \subseteq X^2 \wedge \text{Refl.}X^2 \wedge \text{Trans.}X^2 \rightarrow X^2 y_1 y_2)$$

and the sequence of variables $\langle y_1, y_2\rangle$ define the smallest reflexive and transitive relation containing the original one. Of course, this formula can be written without abbreviations. (Can you do this?)

An example of a first order undefinable relation on the structure of natural numbers.

Let us consider the standard second order structure of natural numbers with the common operations. Since our formal language is countable and $\mathcal{P}\mathbb{N}$ has the cardinality of the continuum, by an easy computation we know that almost all unary relations are not definable. Here is an example of an undefinable relation. Let $X_0, X_1, \ldots$ be all the subsets of $\mathbb{N}$ which are definable using a second order language and let $Y = \{n \,/\, n \notin X_n\}$

It is clear that Y is not definable, since if it were definable, $Y = X_m$, for a certain m. This is impossible because from it we obtain the following contradiction

$$m \in Y \text{ if and only if } m \notin X_m$$

(Note, however, that this set Y, as any other subset of the universe of individuals - *i.e.*, as any other member of A_1 - is parametrically definable in the standard structure by the formula Xx.)

All the examples we have given so far are of first order relations. But with our second order language we can also define second order relations.

Membership.

Here is an example of a proper second order parametrically definable relation between individuals and sets:

$$\in_1 = \{\langle x,X\rangle \in A \times A_1 / x \in X\} = \{\langle x,X\rangle \in A \times A_1 / \mathcal{I}^{xX}_{xX} \text{ sat } Xx\}$$

Power set.

Let Z be any subset of A, *i.e.*, Z is an element of the universe of unary relations, $A_1 = \mathcal{P}A$. Using Z as parameter we will define the set of all its subsets by

$\{X \in A_1 \,/\, \mathcal{A}[XZ] \text{ sat } \forall z(Xz \rightarrow Zz)\}$

4.8. More about the expressive power of standard SOL.

Closely related to the concept of definability in a given structure is the more general one of being second order expressible. In this general case given a property stated in English what we want is to formalize it with the help of our **SOL**. But a property of what? And moreover, what do we mean by a property?

"The" mathematical universe.

So far we have been assuming that we are placed in a mathematical universe of sets and we have introduced our formal second order language to talk about structures in this mathematical universe. As you probably noticed, when we were describing the semantics of **SOL** we were talking about sets, pretending we knew what they were, implicitly assuming a working knowledge of our mathematical universe. This mathematical universe is our environment. We like to think that there are many possible mathematical environments and that we can move from one environment to another and talk about the changes, but only in our metalanguage which until now is English. There is no need to assume that there is a unique, platonic, environment, but we have to accept that we are in "a" universe and that while being in a given one things can be only one way; *i.e.*, true or false, independently of our knowledge. (These are the assumptions we necessarily make when choosing classical logic). Therefore, as a manner of speaking, we often say "the" mathematical universe. This only means that we are referring to an arbitrary but fixed mathematical universe. You can identify the mathematical universe with the so called Zermelo-Fraenkel hierarchy of sets. To help your intuition, you can imagine that all sets are placed in the cumulative hierarchy, $\langle \mathcal{V}, \in \rangle$, which we build by levels.

The Zermelo-Fraenkel hierarchy of sets.

Sets and membership are both primitive notions in set theory and so you will not find here a definition of what a set is, but rather an intuitive picture. The basic assumption we make is that sets are not given all at once from the start, but that we build them by levels, instead. At each level the way of forming a new set is to collect some of the available ones. To avoid possible problems in choosing sets to form new collections (for instance, we might need to assume that the universe of all sets is already a well defined collection) and being aware of the inconsistencies arriving from falling into a vicious circle[12], we can overcome this difficulty by introducing the unrestricted power set operation. Given a set x we put in $\mathcal{P}x$ all the subsets of x, without any further description of them: $\mathcal{P}x = \{y / y \subseteq x\}$. We will need the ordinal numbers, Ω, to arrange the levels, but this is not a problem because what we are doing now is giving a picture, not a definition in any technical sense.

By recursion on the ordinal numbers we form the chain of levels

$$\mathcal{V}(0) \subseteq \mathcal{V}(1) \subseteq \mathcal{V}(2) \subseteq \ldots$$

in the following way:

$\mathcal{V}(0) = \emptyset$ (in the first level we put the empty set)

$\mathcal{V}(1) = \mathcal{P}\,\mathcal{V}(0) = \{\emptyset\}$ (in the second level we put the set whose unique element is the empty set)

In fact, any time we have a level $\mathcal{V}(n)$ we build the level $\mathcal{V}(n+1) = \mathcal{P}\,\mathcal{V}(n)$ (in this level are all sets that can be constructed using the previous level)

To build the level $\mathcal{V}(\omega)$ we take the infinite union of the previous levels

$$\mathcal{V}(\omega) = \mathcal{V}(0) \cup \mathcal{V}(1) \cup \mathcal{V}(2)\ldots$$

and we continue,

$$\mathcal{V}(\omega+1) = \mathcal{P}\,\mathcal{V}(\omega)$$

In general, for every successor ordinal $\beta = \alpha+1$

$$\mathcal{V}(\beta) = \mathcal{P}\,\mathcal{V}(\alpha)$$

and for every limit ordinal λ

$$\mathcal{V}(\lambda) = \bigcup_{\alpha<\lambda} \mathcal{V}(\alpha)$$

Of course, this is a never ending chain, but we can add as a principle:

$$\mathcal{V} = \bigcup_{\beta\in\Omega} \mathcal{V}(\beta)$$

which says: sets are the members of the levels of the hierarchy, nothing else.

Thus, we build all our sets from the empty set; at successor levels we allow all possible

---

12For a discussion on paradoxes, see the introduction to Chapter V.

collections of previous sets to be new sets, while at limit levels we collect everything already present into one set. This is the common description of the Zermelo hierarchy of sets, which are usually represented by a never ending cone having in the axis all the ordinals. I prefer to represent it as a never ending staircase having as the surface all the ordinals.

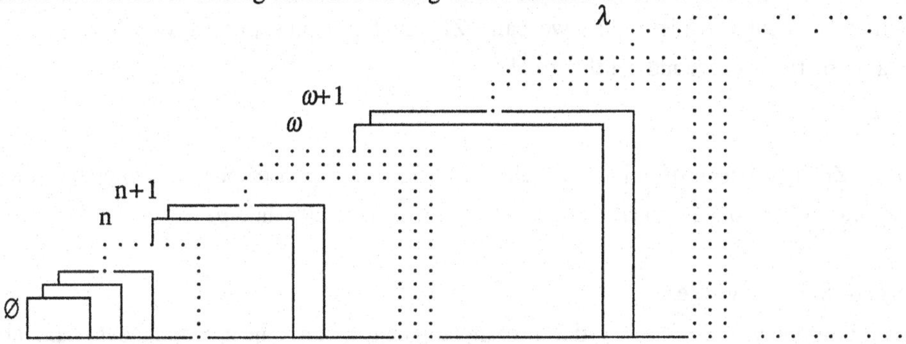

Since this is only a picture to help your intuition, you can entirely forget about it and rely on the axiomatic presentation.

Background set theory.

The Zermelo-Fraenkel axioms describe the simple principles of the cumulative hierarchy of "the" mathematical universe and they are usually written in FOL within a language, $L^{\in}$, having a binary relation constant, $\in$, as the only non-logical symbol. The notions of set and membership are primitives while the rest are defined by the well known definitions. So in the first order language $L^{\in}$ we formulate the famous axioms[13] and we thus obtain a first order theory, ZF.

What I want to say now is explained in Ebbinghaus, Flum & Thomas [1984], let me quote them:

> **Experience shows that all mathematical propositions can be formalized in L^{ε} (or variants of it), and that mathematical provable propositions have formalizations which are derivable from ZF. Thus it is in principle possible to imitate all mathematical reasoning in L^{ε} using the rules of the sequent calculus. In this sense, first order logic is sufficient for mathematics.** At the same time this experience shows that the properties of the universe which are

[13]The Zermelo-Fraenkel axioms for set theory can be found in Ebbinghaus, Flum & Thomas [1984], page 108.

> expressed in ZF are a sufficient basis for a set-theoretic development of mathematics. Thus ZF is a formalization of the set-theoretic assumptions about the universe upon which the mathematician ultimately relies. Since these set-theoretic assumptions can be viewed as the background for all mathematical considerations, we call ZF in this connection, a system of axioms for **background set theory.**[14]

Moreover, ZF is a bunch of axioms which can be seen as a part of our metalanguage (that is, as replacing some of our English) and as a formalized first order theory.

The formal SOL language.

We have introduced the second order formal language as an object language to talk about structures in our mathematical universe. That means that we have to respect certain rules: In the object language we can only talk about things in one environment at once (this assumption is the common one in classical logic.) Moreover, your object language cannot be used to talk about "the" mathematical universe as a whole.

The technical reason for the last restriction is that we always ask our structures to have sets as universes; thus, for example, a second order structure should never have a proper class as a universe. The reason for making such a technical restriction goes back to Tarski: when he settled the semantic concepts we are using today they were based on the careful distinction between object language and metalanguage. Allowing our SOL language to be interpreted in structures whose universes were the entire mathematical universe would require you to be able to define the truth of formulas of the object language in itself and this contradicts the well known Tarski theorem of undefinability of truth, since in that unlucky case we can reproduce the liar's paradox.

We introduce the formal language of SOL as peculiar strings of symbols and we give them a meaning by interpreting them in structures we take from the available mathematical universe. Where each structure has its own restricted universe of quantification we term this the domain of the structure.

---

[14]They use Φ_0 instead of ZF and L^S instead of L^{ε}.

Expressing properties in SOL.

If we look at the examples of formalizability in **SOL** we realize that there are certain differences between them. Sometimes, by formalizability in **SOL** we mean definability of a global relation in the domain of any structure, quite often we mean axiomatizability of a property of the domain, or axiomatizability of a class of structures with common properties. Sometimes, we mean categorical axiomatizability of a given structure with certain properties. On other occasions the property expressed is a property of "the" mathematical universe. I use the word property everywhere; this word is the key one. A property can be identified with a sentence of our metalanguage and, as was mentioned before, it is possible to introduce a language $L^{\in}$ for set theory as part of our metalanguage. The formal second order language is then expressing properties of the background set theory.

4.8.1. Axiomatizable property of the domain.

(a) A property $\mathcal{P}$ of the domain of individuals is ***axiomatizable*** if and only if there is a recursive set of sentences Γ of **Pure SOL** such that $\mathcal{A}$ is a model of Γ iff A has the property $\mathcal{P}$, for every standard structure $\mathcal{A}$. ▓

(b) A property $\mathcal{P}$ of the domain of individuals is ***finitely axiomatizable*** if and only if there is a sentence φ of **Pure SOL** such that $\mathcal{A}$ is a model of φ iff A has the property $\mathcal{P}$, for every standard structure $\mathcal{A}$. ▓

4.8.2. Global relation.

(a) A global n-ary relation R on "the" mathematical universe is ***first order and globally definable*** if and only if there is a **SOL** formula φ with $\mathrm{FREE}(\varphi)\subseteq\{x_1,...,x_n\}$ such that for every structure $\mathcal{A}$, $\{\langle \mathbf{x}_1,...,\mathbf{x}_n\rangle \,/\, \mathcal{A}[^{\mathbf{x}_1...\mathbf{x}_n}_{x_1...x_n}] \text{ sat } \varphi\} = \mathbf{R} \cap \mathbf{A}^n$. ▓

In λ-**SOL** we express the condition by saying: $\mathcal{A}(\lambda x_1...x_n\ \varphi) = \mathbf{R} \cap \mathbf{A}^n$. ▓

(b) A global n-ary relation **R** on "the" mathematical universe is ***second order and globally definable*** if and only if there is a **SOL** formula φ with $\mathrm{FREE}(\varphi)\subseteq\{v_1,...,v_n\}$ of types $i_1,...,i_n$ such that for every structure $\mathcal{A}$,

$$\{\langle \mathbf{v}_1,...,\mathbf{v}_n\rangle \in \mathbf{A}_{i_1}\times...\times\mathbf{A}_{i_n} \,/\, \mathcal{A}[^{\mathbf{v}_1...\mathbf{v}_n}_{v_1...v_n}] \text{ sat } \varphi\} = \mathbf{R} \cap (\mathbf{A}_{i_1}\times...\times\mathbf{A}_{i_n})$$ ▓

4.8.3. Axiomatizable class.

(a) A class of structures $\mathcal{K}$ is ***axiomatizable*** if and only if there is a recursive set of sentences Γ of **SOL** such that, for every structure $\mathcal{A}$: $\mathcal{A}\in\mathcal{K}$ iff $\mathcal{A}$ is a model of Γ. ▓

(b) A class of structures $\mathcal{K}$ is ***finitely axiomatizable*** if and only if there is a sentence φ of **SOL** such that, for every structure $\mathcal{A}$: $\mathcal{A}\in\mathcal{K}$ iff $\mathcal{A}$ is a model of φ. ▒

Remark.

Please bear in mind that 4.8.1 and 4.8.3 are similar but not identical.

4.8.4. Categorically axiomatizable structure.

(a) A given structure $\mathcal{B}$ is ***categorically axiomatizable*** if and only if there is a recursive set of sentences Γ such that $\mathcal{A}$ is a model of Γ iff $\mathcal{B}\cong\mathcal{A}$. ▒

(b) A given structure $\mathcal{B}$ is ***categorically finitely axiomatizable*** if and only if there is a sentence φ such that $\mathcal{A}$ is a model of φ iff $\mathcal{B}\cong\mathcal{A}$. ▒

4.8.5. Mathematical universe.

A property $\mathcal{P}$ of "the" mathematical universe is ***axiomatizable*** if and only if there is a sentence φ of **Pure SOL** such that, φ is valid iff $\mathcal{P}$ holds in "the" mathematical universe. ▒

EXAMPLES

(1) **Axioms of infinity.**

As we have already seen, finiteness of the domain and infinity (negation of finiteness) are second order axiomatizable. In fact, there are many second order formulas that can be used as axioms of infinity. Another easy formulation of infinity is the formula

$$\exists X(\forall xyz(Xxy \land Xyz \to Xxz) \land \forall x\, \neg Xxx \land \forall x\exists y\, Xxy)$$

saying that there is an irreflexive and transitive relation whose domain is the whole universe.

A word of caution is added here: there are several related concepts that should not be mixed up. There are certain axioms, even first order axioms, which require an infinite domain of individuals to be true in a structure, but they need the structure to be of a special signature and they fail in some infinite structures. For instance, the formula $\alpha_{\mathbf{DO}}$ obtained as the conjunction of the axioms for a dense ordering requires an infinite domain to be true in a structure, but not all the infinite structures are dense orderings. We do not call them axioms of infinity. For us, an infinity axiom is a formula φ of **Pure SOL** such that for every structure

$\mathcal{A}$, $\mathcal{A}$ is a model of φ if and only if the universe of individuals of $\mathcal{A}$ is infinite[15]. While the first order case - *e.g.* the axiom of dense order - is such that if $\mathcal{A}$ is a model of α_{DO}, then its universe is infinite, the reverse does not follow. For instance, the structure $\langle \mathbb{N}, \leq \rangle$ is infinite, but $\leq$ is not a dense ordering. For the set of axioms of arithmetic:

$\forall x\ \sigma x \neq c$ (zero is not the successor of any number)

$\forall xy(\sigma x = \sigma y \rightarrow x{=}y)$ (the successor function is one-to-one)

$\forall y(y \neq c \rightarrow \exists z\ \sigma z = y)$ (all non-zero numbers are successors)

nor is it an axiomatization of infinity.

It is obvious that we need an infinite structure to make these true, but they do not hold in many infinite structures; not all the functions in infinite structures have to obey these axioms. For example, they are false in the structure $\langle \mathbb{N}, 0, I \rangle$, where I is the identity function. What we need is to be able to say that in the domain of the structure such a function can be defined and we do that in **Pure SOL** using relation quantification.

We know that in first order logic neither finiteness of the domain nor infinity can be expressed by a single formula. The proof of this is that if they were, compactness would be lost.

When we say that finiteness is second order axiomatizable, we mean in standard second order logic. An infinite non-standard structure can be so poor that it fails to contain one-to-one but not onto relations. Since we can still write down the finiteness axiom in this form, it would hold in our infinite structure. Then the old ghost of Skolem's paradox shows up.

(2) **Identity.**

Although we have equality as primitive in **SOL** and in **λ-SOL**, we are going to study a bit the other possible option: when we are in **Equality-free SOL** and it is introduced as a definition of the identity relation.

What is identity?

Identity is a global relation on the mathematical universe. By the relation of identity we mean that binary relation which holds between any object and itself, and which fails to hold between any two distinct objects. (The sign to represent identity is the identity sign, or equality.) In any

[15]Notice that depending on our background set theory used in the metalanguage, some proposed axioms of infinity might not be acceptable: they might not be equivalent to our definition of infinity in the metalanguage. Problems show up when we are without the axiom of choice in the background set theory used in the metalanguage.

second order standard structure we can define a binary relation between individuals with this property. The way to do it is to use the Leibniz's indiscernibility principle saying that two things are identical when there is no property able to distinguish them. Namely, using the formula:

$\forall X(Xx \longleftrightarrow Xy)$

Identity for individuals in Equality-free SOL.

Therefore, our equality sign for individuals, =, is easily introduced in **Equality-free SOL** by the formal definition:

$\forall xy(x=y \longleftrightarrow \forall X(Xx \longleftrightarrow Xy))$

Thus, the expression $t=\tau$ (where t and τ are terms) should be understood in **Equality-free SOL** as replacing $\forall X(Xt \longleftrightarrow X\tau)$.

The relation defined by # is the true identity relation in any standard second order structure because we know that in the domain of unary relations all the possible relations are in and so all the singletons.

It could also be defined by the formula $\forall Z^2(\forall z\, Z^2zz \rightarrow Z^2xy)$ because the least reflexive relation is the identity, which we have in the domain of binary relations in any standard structure.

Identity in FOL.

Why do we have to take equality as primitive in first order logic? (That means, we do not define it, but instead we have to give a semantic rule to interpret the equality sign as the desired identity relation.)

The reason for this procedure is that there is no first order formula able to define it in every structure. We come close to accomplishing this when the first order language considered only has a finite number of relation constants. For instance, if the only relation constants we had were the unary relation constant R and the binary relation constant T, the formula

▬ $(Rx \longleftrightarrow Ry) \wedge \forall z(Txz \longleftrightarrow Tyz) \wedge \forall z(Tzx \longleftrightarrow Tzy)$

expresses that x and y cannot be distinguished in our formal language. This "definition" obeys the usual rules of reflexivity, symmetry and transitivity. But the definition is by no means perfect because we can give a first order model of ▬ where $\mathcal{I}(x)$ is not identical to

$\mathcal{I}(y)$. Here is a very simple one:

$\mathcal{I} = \langle \mathcal{A}, \mathrm{M} \rangle$, where $\mathcal{A} = \langle \{1,2,3\}, \mathrm{R}^{\mathcal{A}}, \mathrm{T}^{\mathcal{A}} \rangle$, $\mathrm{R}^{\mathcal{A}} = \{1,2,3\}$, $\mathrm{T}^{\mathcal{A}} = \emptyset$ and $\mathrm{M}(x) = 1$, $\mathrm{M}(y) = 2$

The formula ▪ is the best we can come up with in first order logic to formalize Lebniz's principle of indiscernibles. In contrast, one of the pleasant features of second order standard logic is that we can define the relation of identity and therefore we do not need to have the equality sign as a logical primitive sign. All I have said should serve to warn you that the possibility of defining identity is lost as long as there is no guarantee of having all possible sets as denotation, specifically, all the singletons. Or that our structure does not have the identity relation in the universe of binary relations. Then we are back to the situation encountered in first order logic.

Identity for relations in Equality-free SOL.

In general, identity for relations is neither introduced as a primitive logical symbol nor defined using the rest of the symbols. The main reason is that this identity relation between relations is not a first order but a proper second order relation. But is it possible to define identity? Can we use Leibniz's principle to introduce the identity for relations?

The answer to both questions is negative, since to follow Leibniz's patter we would need third order variables.

The extensionality principle could be used to introduce equality for relations; that is, the formula:

** $\forall X^n Y^n (X^n = Y^n \leftrightarrow \forall x_1 \ldots x_n (X^n x_1 \ldots x_n \leftrightarrow Y^n x_1 \ldots x_n))$

Thus, the formula $\Pi^n = \Psi^n$ (where Π^n and Ψ^n are n-ary predicates) should be understood as

* $\forall x_1 \ldots x_n (\Pi^n x_1 \ldots x_n \leftrightarrow \Psi^n x_1 \ldots x_n)$

The extensionality axiom taken as the definition of equality for relations gives us an equivalence relation. Being a definition, it does not work in this case as a way of avoiding non-extensional models, but from a non-extensional model we can always obtain an extensional one using the equivalence relation induced by *. However, the relation introduced by this definition is not always the prototypical identity relation for relations, but a rather weaker equivalence relation.

In fact, there is not a significant difference between having this definition and not. In the first place, because one usually works with extensional models; that is, we usually have extensionality in the metalanguage. In the second place, because whenever we have a second order non-extensional model, we can obtain from it an extensional model, using the equivalence relation induced by the definition of equality for relations formulated above, by passing to the quotient structure.

Extensionality in SOL.

In our **SOL** language we have equality as a primitive relation and the same in **λ-SOL.** Having it as primitive, the extensionality axiom, when added to your calculus, has the desired effect. For certain purposes - ***i.e.***, when we want to use **SOL** as a foundational system - it is good to have an extensionality axiom in the form **. The combined effect of this axiom and the comprehension axiom allows in **SOL** definition by abstraction. We can now state and prove that

$$\exists! X^n \forall x_1 \ldots x_n (X^n x_1 \ldots x_n \leftrightarrow \varphi), \text{ with } X^n \notin \mathrm{FREE}(\varphi)$$

(there is a unique relation defined by each formula and a certain sequence of variables)

Thus, **SOL** and **λ-SOL** are truly equivalent because the abstractor can be introduced in **SOL**. (In Chapter IV, subsection 3.4.5, the reverse problem is proposed; ***i.e.***, how to code **λ-SOL** into **SOL** by removing the abstractor).

Reasons to have equality as primitive.

Why do we insist on having the redundant **SOL** with primitive equality? The answer to this question is that the definitions given above do not work well in some cases:

(a) When you use non-standard structures, the formula # defines an equivalence relation but it could be different from identity. Therefore, if you want to have the prototypical identity, you should either have it as primitive, or define as well the concept of non-standard normal structure. We are choosing the first solution.

(b) In the second order calculi of **SOL** (C_2) and of **λ-SOL** (λ-C_2), the equality rules of reflexivity and equals substitution for individuals are derivable from the rest, using the definition of equality, but we will introduce a sub-calculus as well without comprehension (the calculus C_2^- of many-sorted logic, **MSL**), where this is no longer true. Therefore, when planning to have this calculus it is better to treat equality as in first order logic and to add the equality rules to the calculus.

(c) As I have said before, even in standard structures the equality for relations introduced by the extensionality axiom could be different from identity. When we have equality for relations as primitive, adding the extensionality axiom has the expected results.

(d) Having equality as primitive, the combined effect of the comprehension axiom and extensionality allows the definition by abstraction; making derivable the uniqueness of the relation defined by every formula and every string of variables.

(3) Countable and uncountable.

Based upon the formalization of finiteness, we can also formulate the property of being countable. To do it we need first to change the definition of finiteness a bit, to be able to say that a given set in the universe of unary relations is finite.

$$\varphi_{fin}(Z) \equiv \forall X^2(\forall x(Zx \longleftrightarrow \exists y\, X^2xy) \wedge \forall x(\exists y\, X^2yx \rightarrow Zx) \wedge \forall xyz(X^2xy \wedge X^2xz \rightarrow y{=}z) \wedge$$
$$\forall xyz(X^2xy \wedge X^2zy \rightarrow z{=}x) \rightarrow \forall x(Zx \rightarrow \exists y\, X^2yx))$$

is the desired formalization, since $\langle \mathcal{A},M \rangle$ sat $\varphi_{fin}(Z)$ iff $M(Z)$ is finite.

Now we express the idea that there is a strict linear ordering relation in the universe such that every element has only finitely many predecessors.

$$\varphi_{ctbl} \equiv \exists Y(\forall x\, \neg Yxx \wedge \forall xyz(Yxy \wedge Yyz \rightarrow Yxz) \wedge \forall xy(Yxy \vee Yyx \vee x{=}y) \wedge \forall x \exists X(\varphi_{fin}(X) \wedge$$
$$\forall y(Xy \longleftrightarrow Yyx))$$

is the formalization called for.

Of course, the property of being uncountable is the negation of this.

$$\varphi_{unc} \equiv \neg\varphi_{ctbl}$$

(4) Real numbers. (Categorically axiomatizable structure, 4.8.4.)

Another nice property of standard **SOL** is that real numbers can be characterized up to isomorphism. Just take the first order axioms for ordered fields and add to it the second order axiom

$$\forall ZY(\forall xy(Zx \wedge Yy \rightarrow x{\leq}y) \rightarrow \exists z \forall xy(Zx \wedge Yy \rightarrow x{\leq}z \wedge z{\leq}y))$$

which is a simplified version of Dedekind's cut axiom. (It says that whenever we cut the reals in two, there is an element on the boundary.) The formalization must work because we know that, up to isomorphism, the ordered field of real numbers is the only complete ordered field. Therefore, we have obtained a formula $\varphi_{\mathbb{R}}$ such that

$\mathcal{A}$ is a model of $\varphi_{\mathbb{R}}$ if and only if $\mathcal{A} \cong \langle \mathbb{R},0,1,+,\cdot,\leq \rangle$

(5) The continuum hypothesis. (Property of "the" mathematical universe, 4.8.5.)
In second order logic we can also express the continuum hypothesis. As you might know, this is the conjecture Cantor himself raised to answer the question posed by the problem of the real numbers (also called "the continuum"), which can be roughly represented by: are there cardinalities between $\aleph_0$ (the first infinite cardinal, the natural numbers) and the cardinality of the continuum, $|\mathbb{R}|$? Thus the continuum problem is the question: can a set of the same cardinality as $\mathbb{R}$ have as a subset an uncountable set whose cardinality is less than $|\mathbb{R}|$? This question originated when Cantor proved the uncountability of the reals; that is, $|\mathbb{R}|>\aleph_0$. The continuum hypothesis, CH, expresses the conjecture Cantor made for this problem; that is, there are no cardinalities between $\aleph_0$ and $|\mathbb{R}|$. We can express this with an **SOL** formula, φ_{CH}. Basically we want the formula φ_{CH} to say: a subset of a set of cardinality $|\mathbb{R}|$ can be either countable or else be of the same cardinality as the reals. The first thing we do is to change the definition of countability a bit, to be able to say that a set in the universe of unary relations is countable. We then obtain a formula such that

$$\langle \mathcal{A}, \mathrm{M}\rangle \text{ sat } \varphi_{ctbl}(X) \text{ iff } \mathrm{M}(X) \text{ is countable}$$

After that we need a formula to say that the universe of the structure has the same cardinality as $\mathbb{R}$. We can do this by removing the function and relation constants in the formula $\varphi_{\mathbb{R}}$, putting variables instead, and then getting the existential closure of it. (Since our language does not have function variables, we must use relation variables, do not forget to add the two conditions saying that they are functions and that their domain is the whole universe.) With the new formula, $\psi_{\mathbb{R}}$, we express the property of being of the same cardinality as $\mathbb{R}$:

$$\mathcal{A} \text{ is a model of } \psi_{\mathbb{R}} \text{ iff } \mathcal{A} \text{ is of the same cardinality as } \mathbb{R}$$

Our continuum hypothesis φ_{CH} would say: if the domain is of the same cardinality as $\mathbb{R}$, then every subset of the domain is either countable or else of the same cardinality as the whole domain. Can you finish it?

The continuum hypothesis can have this reading as well:

$$2^{\aleph_0} = \aleph_1 \text{ (since } |\mathbb{R}| = 2^{\aleph_0} = |\mathcal{P}\,\aleph_0|\text{, and we take } \aleph_1 \text{ as the first cardinal after } \aleph_0)$$

(6) The generalized continuum hypothesis. (Property of "the" mathematical universe, 4.8.5.)

The generalized continuum hypothesis, GCH, says: $2^{\aleph_\beta} = \aleph_\alpha$, for all α, $\alpha = \beta+1$. GCH can be easily expressed by saying: there are no cardinalities between the cardinality of an infinite set and the cardinality of its power set. As seen in the Introduction, the generalized continuum hypothesis can also be formulated in **SOL** by the formula φ_{GCH} expressing

$$\forall XY(\mathit{inf}(X) \land Y \sim \mathcal{P}X \rightarrow \forall Z(Z \subseteq Y \rightarrow Z \preceq X \lor Z \sim Y))$$

This formula says: "Every subset Z of a set Y ($Z \subseteq Y$) that is equipollent to the power set of an infinite set X ($Y \sim \mathcal{P}X$) is either equipollent to that power set ($Z \sim Y$) or of equal or less power than the infinite set ($Z \preceq X$)". The only not so obvious part is how to formulate $Y \sim \mathcal{P}X$ in second order logic. A definition due to Németi is to introduce a binary relation U between X and Y which, in a sense, contains a one-to-one function from $\mathcal{P}X$ onto Y: Every subset Z of X has a unique element of Y as the common image of all its members under the relation U. Besides that, the range of U is Y. All this is expressed by the formula

$$\exists U(U \subseteq X \times Y \land \forall Z(Z \subseteq X \rightarrow \exists! z(Yz \land \forall u(Zu \leftrightarrow Uuz) \land Y = Rec(U))))$$

This formula formalizes this idea:

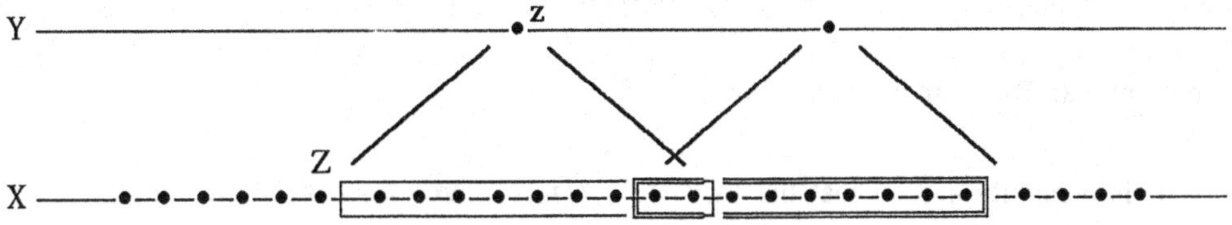

Since neither GCH nor its negation, ¬GCH, can be proved in Zermelo-Fraenkel set theory, the validity of the second order formula expressing GCH can be neither established nor refuted within the framework of Zermelo-Fraenkel set theory. That is why the expressive power of standard second order logic is too much.

A language which can express more than can be decided in Zermelo-Fraenkel set theory is non-stable. When that happens there is no hope of finding a complete deductive calculus. Based on this fact, we will sketch the proof of the incompleteness of **SOL** in the next chapter.

(7) Set theory[16].

The Zermelo-Fraenkel set theory, ZF, is a bunch of axioms which can be seen as a part of our metalanguage (that is, as replacing some of our English) or as a formalized first order theory. As a first order theory ZF might have models (assuming consistency), but the mathematical universe itself, $\mathcal{U} = \langle \mathcal{V}, \in \rangle$, is not one such because we do not accept as models anything having as its domain a class which is not a set. As a first order theory, Löwenheim-Skolem

[16] I strongly recommend you the introductory and motivating paper of Shoenfield [1977], pp. 317-344.

applies and therefore, if it had a model, it would have many "non-standard models" as well.

What happens when expressing Zermelo-Fraenkel axioms in **SOL**?

The separation and the replacement schemes now become single axioms,

$$\mathbf{SEP}^2 \equiv \forall X x \exists y \forall z (z \in y \longleftrightarrow z \in x \wedge Xx)$$

$$\mathbf{REP}^2 \equiv \forall F x \exists y \forall z (z \in y \longleftrightarrow \exists u (u \in x \wedge z = Fu))$$

whose strength makes second order Zermelo-Fraenkel theory ***almost*** categorical.
That is, $\mathcal{A} = \langle \mathrm{A}, \epsilon^{\mathcal{A}} \rangle$ is a model of ZF^2 if and only if for some strongly inaccessible κ: $\mathcal{A} \cong \langle \mathcal{V}(\kappa), \epsilon \rangle$ (where ZF^2 is the set of axioms obtained by replacing the separation and replacement schemes by their second order versions.)

As noted in van Benthem & Doets [1983]:

> It is generally agreed that the models $\langle \mathcal{V}(\kappa), \epsilon \rangle$ are "standard" to a high degree.
>
> If we add an axiom to ZF^2 saying that there are no inaccessibles, the system becomes categorical, defining $\langle \mathcal{V}(\kappa), \epsilon \rangle$ for the first inaccessible κ.

4.9. Negative results.

Due to the great expressive power of **SOL** it is easy to demonstrate that some very classical first order theorems do not hold in **SOL**. We are going to prove this here for compactness and Löwenheim-Skolem theorems. The weak and strong incompleteness theorems are proved in the next chapter.

4.9.1. The compactness theorem does not hold for SOL.

Proof
The compactness theorem says: For all Φ and ψ, if $\Phi \models \psi$ then $\Delta \models \psi$ for at least a finite subset of Φ, $\Delta \subseteq \Phi$.

Let Γ be the set of formulas

$$\varphi_n \equiv \exists x_1 \ldots x_n (\neg x_1 = x_2 \wedge \ldots \wedge \neg x_1 = x_n \wedge \ldots \wedge \neg x_{n-1} = x_n)$$

for $n \geq 2$, and take a formula expressing the infinity of the domain, φ_{inf}. It is easy to see that $\Gamma \vDash \varphi_{inf}$ but there is no finite subset of Γ, - *i.e.*, $\Delta \subseteq \Gamma$ with a finite number of elements - such that $\Delta \vDash \varphi_{inf}$

Let us take any finite subset $\Delta \subseteq \Gamma$. Since we only have a finite set of formulas from Γ, there is one with a maximum subscript. Let m be the maximum of the numbers n such that $\varphi_n \in \Delta$. As a model for Δ we can take a structure $\mathcal{A} = \langle\langle \mathbf{A} \rangle\rangle$ where $\mathbf{A}$ has $m+1$ elements. Clearly $\mathcal{A}$ is not a model of φ_{inf}. Therefore, $\Delta \nvDash \varphi_{inf}$. ▮

4.9.2. The strong completeness theorem does not hold for SOL with a sound calculus.
Since we have not introduced the calculus yet, the precise proof cannot be given, but it is easy to see how the argument should go.

The strong completeness theorem says: if $\Gamma \vDash \varphi$ then $\Gamma \vdash \varphi$, for all Γ and φ. But we know that compactness fails. Therefore, there are sets such that $\Gamma \vDash \varphi$ but for no finite Δ, $\Delta \subseteq \Gamma$, $\Delta \vDash \varphi$. In this situation, in a sound calculus accepting only finite rules of proof, we can never obtain a deduction of φ from Γ.

4.9.3. The Löwenheim-Skolem theorem does not hold for SOL.

Proof
For our countable language, the version of the Löwenheim-Skolem theorem we are refuting says: "If a countable set of sentences Γ has a model, then Γ has a model whose universe of individuals is countable". In fact, we will refute it for a set $\Gamma = \{\varphi\}$ formed by a single formula which is Löwenheim's original version (1915). Obviously, the failure of the stronger version is also proved.

We have already obtained the formula saying that the universe is uncountable, φ_{unc}. We know that for every structure $\mathcal{A}$, $\mathcal{A}$ is a model of φ_{unc} iff $\mathbf{A}$ is uncountable. This formula has an uncountable model but no model whose universe of individual is countable. ▮

4.9.4. The weak completeness theorem does not hold for SOL.
The classical proof is based on Gödel's incompleteness[17]. In the next chapter we are going to present a curious proof of the incompleteness of **SOL.**

5.- SEMANTIC THEOREMS.

5.1. Coincidence lemma.

This lemma shows that when dealing with closed expressions, assignments do not matter. Namely, the lemma says that when we have different assignments (on a structure $\mathcal{A}$) whose restriction to the set of free variables of a given expression is the very same function, then the interpretations obtained with any of these assignments agree on the given expression. We will state the lemma as follows:

5.1.1. Lemma. Let $\mathcal{A}$ be a second order structure, M_1 and M_2 two assignments on $\mathcal{A}$ and let $\mathcal{I}_1 = \langle \mathcal{A}, M_1 \rangle$ and $\mathcal{I}_2 = \langle \mathcal{A}, M_2 \rangle$ be the corresponding interpretations. Then:

(1) For any term τ such that $M_1 \upharpoonright \mathbf{FREE}(\tau) = M_2 \upharpoonright \mathbf{FREE}(\tau)$, we have $\mathcal{I}_1(\tau) = \mathcal{I}_2(\tau)$.

(2) For any predicate Π^n such that $M_1 \upharpoonright \mathbf{FREE}(\Pi^n) = M_2 \upharpoonright \mathbf{FREE}(\Pi^n)$, we have
$$\mathcal{I}_1(\Pi^n) = \mathcal{I}_2(\Pi^n)$$

(3) For any formula φ such that $M_1 \upharpoonright \mathbf{FREE}(\varphi) = M_2 \upharpoonright \mathbf{FREE}(\varphi)$, we have
$$\mathcal{I}_1 \text{ sat } \varphi \text{ iff } \mathcal{I}_2 \text{ sat } \varphi$$

Proof

(1) For the first statement, we use induction on terms. All three cases, (T1), (T2) and (T3) are straightforward.

(2) For the second statement we use induction on predicates. (P1), (P2) and (P3) are obvious, let us do case (P4).

(P4) Let $M_1 \upharpoonright \mathbf{FREE}(\lambda x_1 ... x_n\, \varphi) = M_2 \upharpoonright \mathbf{FREE}(\lambda x_1 ... x_n\, \varphi)$ and assume the theorem holds for formulas.

For any $x_1,...,x_n \in A$, we have $(M_1{}^{x_1...x_n}_{x_1...x_n}) \upharpoonright \mathbf{FREE}(\varphi) = (M_2{}^{x_1...x_n}_{x_1...x_n}) \upharpoonright \mathbf{FREE}(\varphi)$

[17]See Enderton [1972], page 272.

and since we assume that the theorem holds for formulas, it follows that

$$(\mathcal{I}_1{}^{x_1 \ldots x_n}_{x_1 \ldots x_n}) \text{ sat } \varphi \text{ iff } (\mathcal{I}_2{}^{x_1 \ldots x_n}_{x_1 \ldots x_n}) \text{ sat } \varphi$$

Therefore,

$$\mathcal{I}_1(\lambda x_1 .. x_n\ \varphi) = \{\langle x_1,\ldots,x_n\rangle \epsilon A \times \ldots \times A \,/ (\mathcal{I}_1{}^{x_1 \ldots x_n}_{x_1 \ldots x_n}) \text{ sat } \varphi\}$$

$$= \{\langle x_1,\ldots,x_n\rangle \epsilon A \times \ldots \times A \,/ (\mathcal{I}_2{}^{x_1 \ldots x_n}_{x_1 \ldots x_n}) \text{ sat } \varphi\}$$

$$= \mathcal{I}_2(\lambda x_1 \ldots x_n\ \varphi)$$

(3) For the third statement we will use induction on formulas. (F1), (F2) and (F3) are obvious. (F4) and (F5) are similar. Let us do case (F5).

(F5) Let $M_1 \restriction FREE(\exists Z^n \varphi) = M_2 \restriction FREE(\exists Z^n \varphi)$ and so, for every $Z^n \epsilon A_n$:

$$(M_1{}^{Z^n}_{Z^n}) \restriction FREE(\varphi) = (M_2{}^{Z^n}_{Z^n}) \restriction FREE(\varphi)$$

$$\mathcal{I}_1 \text{ sat } \exists Z^n\ \varphi \text{ iff there is } Z^n \epsilon A_n : \mathcal{I}_1{}^{Z^n}_{Z^n} \text{ sat } \varphi$$

$$\text{iff there is } Z^n \epsilon A_n : \mathcal{I}_2{}^{Z^n}_{Z^n} \text{ sat } \varphi$$

(by the induction hypothesis)

$$\text{iff } \mathcal{I}_2 \text{ sat } \exists Z^n \varphi \quad \blacksquare$$

5.1.2. Notation.

Thanks to the preceding lemma, we can simplify our notation, leaving out in some cases the reference to assignments.

(1) Let $\mathcal{A}$ be a structure and ε an expression of λ-L_2 such that $FREE(\varepsilon) \subseteq \{v_1,\ldots,v_n\}$, and let the variables be ordered by $\langle v_1,\ldots,v_n\rangle$ corresponding to the appearance in ε. Now let

$$\langle v_1,\ldots,v_n\rangle \text{ be a sequence of elements of } A \cup \bigcup_{n \geq 1} A_n$$

where the types of the members on it match with the types of variables, then instead of

$$\langle \mathcal{A}, M^{v_1 \ldots v_n}_{v_1 \ldots v_n}\rangle (\varepsilon) \text{ we will write } \mathcal{A}[{}^{v_1 \ldots v_n}_{v_1 \ldots v_n}] (\varepsilon) \text{ or } \mathcal{A}[v_1 \ldots v_n](\varepsilon)$$

for terms and predicates, and instead of

$$\langle \mathcal{A}, M^{v_1 \ldots v_n}_{v_1 \ldots v_n}\rangle \text{ sat } \varepsilon \text{ we will write } \mathcal{A}[{}^{v_1 \ldots v_n}_{v_1 \ldots v_n}] \text{ sat } \varepsilon \text{ or } \mathcal{A}[v_1 \ldots v_n] \text{ sat } \varepsilon$$

for formulas.

(2) For closed terms we can also suppress the reference to any assignment and write simply $\mathcal{A}(\tau)$ (instead of $\langle \mathcal{A},\mathrm{M}\rangle(\tau)$).

(3) For sentences we will say that $\mathcal{A}$ is a model of φ, or that $\mathcal{A}$ is a model of Γ.

5.2. Substitution lemma.

This lemma expresses the following fact: Between formal language and structure there is a kind of homomorphism, you can either substitute in the formula, or leave the formula unaltered and define a new assignment to make the changes. We will prove two lemmas, for individual variables and for relation variables. The precise statements of the lemmas are as follows.

5.2.1. Substitution lemma for individuals.

Let x be an individual variable and τ a term. Given a second order structure $\mathcal{A}$ and assignment M on $\mathcal{A}$,

(1) For every term t: $\langle \mathcal{A},\mathrm{M}_x^{\langle \mathcal{A},\mathrm{M}\rangle(\tau)}\rangle(t) = \langle \mathcal{A},\mathrm{M}\rangle(t\frac{\tau}{x})$

(2) For every n-ary predicate Π: $\langle \mathcal{A},\mathrm{M}_x^{\langle \mathcal{A},\mathrm{M}\rangle(\tau)}\rangle(\Pi) = \langle \mathcal{A},\mathrm{M}\rangle(\Pi\frac{\tau}{x})$

(3) For every formula φ: $\langle \mathcal{A},\mathrm{M}_x^{\langle \mathcal{A},\mathrm{M}\rangle(\tau)}\rangle$ sat φ iff $\langle \mathcal{A},\mathrm{M}\rangle$ sat $\varphi\frac{\tau}{x}$

Proof

Let $\langle \mathcal{A},\mathrm{M}\rangle = \mathcal{I}$ and write $\mathcal{I}_x^{\mathbf{x}}$ for $\langle \mathcal{A},\mathrm{M}_x^{\mathbf{x}}\rangle$.

The proof is quite straightforward. The only complex step is (P4).

(P4) To prove the lemma for $\lambda x_1...x_n\ \varphi$ we have to distinguish three cases:

First case: $x\notin$FREE$(\lambda x_1...x_n\ \varphi)$

$\mathcal{I}_x^{\mathcal{I}(\tau)}(\lambda x_1...x_n\ \varphi) = \mathcal{I}(\lambda x_1...x_n\ \varphi) = \mathcal{I}([\lambda x_1...x_n\ \varphi]\frac{\tau}{x})$

(by the coincidence lemma, since $\mathcal{I}\upharpoonright$FREE$(\lambda x_1...x_n\ \varphi) = \mathcal{I}_x^{\mathcal{I}(\tau)}\upharpoonright$FREE$(\lambda x_1...x_n\ \varphi)$)

Second case: $x\in$FREE$(\lambda x_1...x_n\ \varphi)$ and $x_i\notin$FREE(τ) for any $1\leq i\leq n$

$$\mathcal{I}_x^{\mathcal{I}(\tau)}(\lambda x_1...x_n\ \varphi) = \{\langle \mathbf{x}_1,...,\mathbf{x}_n\rangle \,/\, \mathcal{I}_{x\ x_1...x_n}^{\mathcal{I}(\tau)\mathbf{x}_1...\mathbf{x}_n} \text{ sat } \varphi\}$$

$$= \{\langle \mathbf{x}_1,...,\mathbf{x}_n\rangle \,/\, \mathcal{I}_{x_1...x_n x}^{\mathbf{x}_1...\mathbf{x}_n\mathcal{I}(\tau)} \text{ sat } \varphi\}$$

(since $x \not\equiv x_i$, $1 \leq i \leq n$)

$$= \{\langle \mathbf{x}_1,...,\mathbf{x}_n \rangle \,/\, \mathcal{I}^{\mathbf{x}_1...\mathbf{x}_n \mathcal{I}^{\mathbf{x}_1...\mathbf{x}_n}_{x_1...x_n}(\tau)}_{x_1...x_n x} \text{ sat } \varphi\}$$

(since $\mathcal{I}(\tau) = \mathcal{I}^{\mathbf{x}_1...\mathbf{x}_n}_{x_1...x_n}(\tau)$ because $x_i \notin \mathrm{FREE}(\tau)$ for any $1 \leq i \leq n$)

$$= \{\langle \mathbf{x}_1,...,\mathbf{x}_n \rangle \,/\, \mathcal{I}^{\mathbf{x}_1...\mathbf{x}_n}_{x_1...x_n} \text{ sat } \varphi\frac{\tau}{x}\}$$

(using the induction hypothesis on formulas, to be proven below)

$$= \mathcal{I}(\lambda x_1...x_n\ \varphi\frac{\tau}{x})$$

$$= \mathcal{I}([\lambda x_1...x_n\ \varphi]\frac{\tau}{x})$$

Third case: $x \in \mathrm{FREE}(\lambda x_1...x_n\ \varphi)$ and $x_{i+1},...,x_n \in \mathrm{FREE}(\tau)$ for an i, $1 \leq i \leq n$ and take $y_{i+1},...,y_n \notin \mathrm{FREE}(\lambda x_1...x_n\ \varphi) \cup \mathrm{FREE}(\tau) \cup \{x_1,...,x_n\}$

$$\mathcal{I}^{\mathcal{I}(\tau)}_{x}(\lambda x_1...x_n\ \varphi)$$

$$= \{\langle \mathbf{x}_1,...,\mathbf{x}_n \rangle \,/\, \mathcal{I}^{\mathcal{I}(\tau)\mathbf{x}_1...\mathbf{x}_n}_{x\ \ x_1...x_n} \text{ sat } \varphi\}$$

$$= \{\langle \mathbf{x}_1,...,\mathbf{x}_n \rangle \,/\, \mathcal{I}^{\mathcal{I}(\tau)\mathbf{x}_1...\mathbf{x}_i\mathbf{x}_{i+1}...\mathbf{x}_n\mathbf{x}_{i+1}...\mathbf{x}_n}_{x\ \ x_1...x_i y_{i+1}...y_n x_{i+1}...x_n} \text{ sat } \varphi\}$$

(by the coincidence lemma, since both interpretations agree on $\mathrm{FREE}(\varphi)$)

$$= \{\langle \mathbf{x}_1,...,\mathbf{x}_n \rangle \,/\, \mathcal{I}^{\mathcal{I}(\tau)\mathbf{x}_1...\mathbf{x}_i\mathbf{x}_{i+1}...\mathbf{x}_n}_{x\ \ x_1...x_i y_{i+1}...y_n} \text{ sat } \varphi\frac{y_{i+1}...y_n}{x_{i+1}...x_n}\}$$

(by the induction hypothesis, thanks to the fact that $\mathcal{I}^{\mathcal{I}(\tau)\mathbf{x}_1...\mathbf{x}_i\mathbf{x}_{i+1}...\mathbf{x}_n}_{x\ \ x_1...x_i y_{i+1}...y_n}(y_{i+1}) = \mathbf{x}_{i+1}$)

$$= \{\langle \mathbf{x}_1,...,\mathbf{x}_n \rangle \,/\, \mathcal{I}^{\mathbf{x}_1...\mathbf{x}_i\mathbf{x}_{i+1}...\mathbf{x}_n\mathcal{I}(\tau)}_{x_1...x_i y_{i+1}...y_n x} \text{ sat } \varphi\frac{y_{i+1}...y_n}{x_{i+1}...x_n}\}$$

(because all the variables are different)

$$= \{\langle \mathbf{x}_1,...,\mathbf{x}_n \rangle \,/\, \mathcal{I}^{\mathbf{x}_1...\mathbf{x}_i\mathbf{x}_{i+1}...\mathbf{x}_n}_{x_1...x_i y_{i+1}...y_n} \text{ sat } [\varphi\frac{y_{i+1}...y_n}{x_{i+1}...x_n}]\frac{\tau}{x}\}$$

(using the induction hypothesis and by coincidence lemma, for $\mathcal{I}(\tau) = \mathcal{I}^{\mathbf{x}_1...\mathbf{x}_i\mathbf{x}_{i+1}...\mathbf{x}_n}_{x_1...x_i y_{i+1}...y_n}(\tau)$)

$$= \mathcal{I}(\lambda x_1...x_i y_{i+1}...y_n\ [\varphi\frac{y_{i+1}...y_n}{x_{i+1}...x_n}]\frac{\tau}{x})$$

$$= \mathcal{I}([\lambda x_1...x_n\ \varphi]\frac{\tau}{x})\ \blacksquare$$

5.2.2. Substitution lemma for predicates.

Let X^m be a relation variable and Ψ^m a predicate. Given a second order structure $\mathcal{A}$ and assignment M on $\mathcal{A}$,

(1) For every term t: $\langle \mathcal{A}, M\frac{\langle \mathcal{A},M\rangle(\Psi^m)}{X^m}\rangle(t) = \langle \mathcal{A},M\rangle(t\frac{\Psi^m}{X^m})$

(2) For every predicate Π^n: $\langle \mathcal{A}, M\frac{\langle \mathcal{A},M\rangle(\Psi^m)}{X^m}\rangle(\Pi^n) = \langle \mathcal{A},M\rangle(\Pi^n\frac{\Psi^m}{X^m})$

(3) For every formula φ: $\langle \mathcal{A}, M\frac{\langle \mathcal{A},M\rangle(\Psi^m)}{X^m}\rangle$ sat φ iff $\langle \mathcal{A},M\rangle$ sat $(\varphi\frac{\Psi^m}{X^m})$

Proof

The proof is also easy, but long. Please do it. ∎

5.2.3. Simultaneous substitution lemma.

Following a similar procedure, you can state and prove a generalization of the above substitution lemmas. In the new one you will use the concept of simultaneous substitution. ∎

5.3. Isomorphism theorem.

The lesson to be learnt from this theorem is that isomorphic structures are so much alike that from a mathematical point of view they are considered as identical. From first order logic we learn that isomorphism there implies elementary equivalence; that is, there is no sentence of first order logic able to tell the difference between two isomorphic structures. In fact, something stronger is true: if $\mathcal{A}$ and $\mathcal{B}$ are isomorphic, whenever a formula is true in $\mathcal{A}$ for certain elements in A, the same formula is true in $\mathcal{B}$ for the corresponding (in the isomorphism) elements of **B**. But, **SOL** being a very strong and expressive language, we might have doubts about whether the isomorphism theorem generalizes for this logic. We will see below that isomorphic structures are secondary equivalent. Consequently, isomorphism is a finer classification of structures than secondary equivalence. In fact, something stronger is true, as you will see below.

5.3.1. Theorem.

Let $\mathcal{A} \overset{h}{\cong} \mathcal{B}$ and extend the function **h** so as to cover all the universes. (That is, define:

$$\bar{\mathbf{h}}: \mathbf{A} \cup (\bigcup_{n>0} \mathbf{A}_n) \longrightarrow \mathbf{B} \cup (\bigcup_{n>0} \mathbf{B}_n)$$
$$\mathbf{x} \longmapsto \mathbf{h}(\mathbf{x})$$
$$\mathbf{X}^n \longmapsto \{\langle \mathbf{h}(\mathbf{x}_1), \ldots, \mathbf{h}(\mathbf{x}_n)\rangle \,/\, \langle \mathbf{x}_1, \ldots, \mathbf{x}_n\rangle \in \mathbf{X}^n\})$$

Then

(1) For every term t: $\bar{\mathbf{h}}\,(\langle \mathcal{A},\mathrm{M}\rangle(t)) = \langle \mathcal{B},\bar{\mathbf{h}}\circ\mathrm{M}\rangle(t)$

(2) For every predicate Π^n: $\bar{\mathbf{h}}\,(\langle \mathcal{A},\mathrm{M}\rangle(\Pi^n)) = \langle \mathcal{B},\bar{\mathbf{h}}\circ\mathrm{M}\rangle(\Pi^n)$

(3) For every formula φ: $\langle \mathcal{A},\mathrm{M}\rangle$ sat φ iff $\langle \mathcal{B},\bar{\mathbf{h}}\circ\mathrm{M}\rangle$ sat (φ)

Proof

The proof is quite straightforward. In proving (P3); that is, that identity is respected, you have to use the fact that function $\bar{\mathbf{h}}$ is one-to-one. For (P4), (F4) and (F5) we use the fact that $\bar{\mathbf{h}}$ is a bijection. Let us see (P4) and (F4) in detail.

(P4) $\bar{\mathbf{h}}(\langle \mathcal{A},\mathrm{M}\rangle(\lambda x_1..x_n\varphi)) = \bar{\mathbf{h}}(\{\langle \mathbf{x}_1,\ldots,\mathbf{x}_n\rangle \in \mathbf{A}^n \,/\, \langle \mathcal{A},\mathrm{M}^{\mathbf{x}_1\ldots\mathbf{x}_n}_{x_1\ldots x_n}\rangle \text{ sat } \varphi\})$

$= \{\langle \bar{\mathbf{h}}(\mathbf{x}_1),\ldots,\bar{\mathbf{h}}(\mathbf{x}_n)\rangle \in \mathbf{B}^n \,/\, \langle \mathcal{A},\mathrm{M}^{\mathbf{x}_1\ldots\mathbf{x}_n}_{x_1\ldots x_n}\rangle \text{ sat } \varphi\}$

(by definition of $\bar{\mathbf{h}}$)

$= \{\langle \bar{\mathbf{h}}(\mathbf{x}_1),\ldots,\bar{\mathbf{h}}(\mathbf{x}_n)\rangle \in \mathbf{B}^n \,/\, \langle \mathcal{B},\bar{\mathbf{h}}\circ\mathrm{M}^{\mathbf{x}_1\ldots\mathbf{x}_n}_{x_1\ldots x_n}\rangle \text{ sat } \varphi\}$

(induction hypothesis for formulas)

$= \{\langle \bar{\mathbf{h}}(\mathbf{x}_1),\ldots,\bar{\mathbf{h}}(\mathbf{x}_n)\rangle \in \mathbf{B}^n/\langle \mathcal{B},(\bar{\mathbf{h}}\circ\mathrm{M})^{\bar{\mathbf{h}}(\mathbf{x}_1)\ldots\bar{\mathbf{h}}(\mathbf{x}_n)}_{x_1\ldots x_n}\rangle \text{ sat } \varphi\}$

(as you can see easily)

$= \{\langle \mathbf{y}_1,\ldots,\mathbf{y}_n\rangle \in \mathbf{B}^n/\langle \mathcal{B},(\bar{\mathbf{h}}\circ\mathrm{M})^{\mathbf{y}_1\ldots\mathbf{y}_n}_{x_1\ldots x_n}\rangle \text{ sat } \varphi\}$

(because the function $\bar{\mathbf{h}}$ is bijective)

(F4) $\langle \mathcal{A},\mathrm{M}\rangle$ sat $\exists x\,\varphi$ iff there is $\mathbf{x}\in\mathbf{A}$ such that $\langle \mathcal{A},\mathrm{M}^{\mathbf{x}}_{x}\rangle$ sat φ

iff there is $\mathbf{x}\in\mathbf{A}$ such that $\langle \mathcal{B},\bar{\mathbf{h}}\circ\mathrm{M}^{\mathbf{x}}_{x}\rangle$ sat φ

(induction hypothesis)

iff there is $\mathbf{y}\in\mathbf{B}$ such that $\langle \mathcal{B},(\bar{\mathbf{h}}\circ\mathrm{M})^{\mathbf{y}}_{x}\rangle$ sat φ

(because the function is a bijection)

iff $\langle \mathcal{B},\bar{\mathbf{h}}\circ\mathrm{M}\rangle$ sat $\exists x\,\varphi$ ∎

5.3.2. Corollary.

Let $\mathcal{A} \overset{\mathbf{h}}{\cong} \mathcal{B}$ and extend the function $\mathbf{h}$ as above.

(1) For every term t such that $\mathbf{FREE}(t) \subseteq \{v_1,\ldots,v_n\}$:

$$\bar{\mathbf{h}}\,(\mathcal{A}[{}^{\mathbf{v}_1\ldots\mathbf{v}_n}_{v_1\ldots v_n}](t)) = \mathcal{B}[{}^{\bar{\mathbf{h}}(\mathbf{v}_1)\ldots\bar{\mathbf{h}}(\mathbf{v}_n)}_{v_1\ldots v_n}](t)$$

(2) For every predicate Π^n such that $\mathbf{FREE}(\Pi^n) \subseteq \{v_1,\ldots,v_n\}$:

$$\bar{\mathbf{h}}\,(\mathcal{A}[{}^{\mathbf{v}_1\ldots\mathbf{v}_n}_{v_1\ldots v_n}](\Pi^n)) = \mathcal{B}[{}^{\bar{\mathbf{h}}(\mathbf{v}_1)\ldots\bar{\mathbf{h}}(\mathbf{v}_n)}_{v_1\ldots v_n}](\Pi^n)$$

(3) For every formula φ such that $\mathbf{FREE}(\varphi) \subseteq \{v_1,\ldots,v_n\}$:

$$\mathcal{A}[{}^{\mathbf{v}_1\ldots\mathbf{v}_n}_{v_1\ldots v_n}] \text{ sat } \varphi \quad \text{iff} \quad \mathcal{B}[{}^{\bar{\mathbf{h}}(\mathbf{v}_1)\ldots\bar{\mathbf{h}}(\mathbf{v}_n)}_{v_1\ldots v_n}] \text{ sat } \varphi \quad \blacksquare$$

CHAPTER II
DEDUCTIVE CALCULI.

1.- INTRODUCTION.

1.1. General idea.

In the preceding chapter we have introduced two second order languages, L_2 and λ-L_2 (both of them of signature Σ), and we have also introduced the standard structures. We have defined as well the semantic notions of consequency and validity. Everyone recognizes that among all formulas of any of these languages, validities are of a very special interest and that it is also very useful to establish whether or not a formula is a consequence of a set of formulas. Up to now, we can do it by resorting to direct verification of truth conditions; *i.e.*, using the semantic definitions of validity and consequence; the latter one is not very handy, since, in principle, it involves the checking of an infinite class of structures.

Two questions come immediately to mind: First of all, why are we so interested in validities? Secondly, can we generate them mechanically?

If you pay closer attention to first order validities you will find out that, due to the fact that they are always true in any structure, they do not describe any particular structure, situation or world. Their truth has nothing to do with the structure they are true in but with themselves and, in particular, their internal distribution of logical connectors and quantifiers. So, when you retranslate them back into English, they are very very cryptical. As opposed to this situation, standard second order validities are also able to talk about the enviroment; *i.e.*, "the" mathematical universe.

Are validities describing anything, are they sensibly talking about something? I like to think that first order validities are describing the logic in itself, they establish its laws, the laws of mathematical thought and reasoning. Therefore, whenever we are able to find rules to generate all the validities, we have the guarantee of having captured the essence of reasoning; *i.e.*, its logic perfume in the most radical and barbarous sense[18]. Within second order validities the logic is somewhat masked behind the underlying set theory and to distinguish between logical and set-theoretic properties remains an interesting task.

In propositional and first order logics, there is a mechanical way to establish the validity of a formula φ and to show that a formula ψ is a logical consequence of a set of formulas Γ: we can deduce ψ in a calculus using formulas in Γ as hypotheses by building up a deductive chain between hypothesis and conclusion; while when φ is a validity we do not use any hypothesis, φ is obtained using only the rules of the calculus.

A derivation in a calculus is an array of sequents obtained by following certain rules; namely, the calculus rules. The precise nature of the rules can vary, but they must be of a finite character and such that one can check by inspection whether or not their sequents have been obtained according to them. There is even an algorithm to check proofs. For propositional logic something stronger is true: there is also an algorithm to tell you whether or not a formula is a theorem of the calculus.

Can we have a calculus for second order logic? Why is it interesting to have one?

1.2. Motivations.

There are several reasons why we want to have a calculus. (1) Firstly, if we are thinking on the possibility of implementing the process of obtaining validities and consequences in a machine, a calculus with precise rules is easier to implement than the corresponding semantical definitions. (2) Secondly, if we want to model the reasoning and proof processes which take place in our minds, a calculus is a better candidate for being a model of this. The idea of a process of thinking is that from a certain hypothesis, let us say certain information or data obtained perhaps from observing the real world, we derive certain conclusions while sitting in a chair. We do not go out to check our conclusions in the real world, we just obtain them by a process of calculus in our minds. (3) Another motivation for wanting a calculus is that with its help we can prove things with limited mathematical resources; we do not have to go as deep into set theory as when using the semantical definition of consequence. In the latter case,

---

[18]As in **Das Parfum**, by Patrick Suskind.

sooner or later, we are going to need the full formalism of set theory. (4) Finally, I see certain psychological advantages in having a calculus; anybody can check the correctness of your proof and so the convincing part becomes easier[19]. (5) And, more than anything else, when the proof is done in a calculus, nobody is going to ask you to prove that your proof is indeed a proof (since, as mentioned above, there is even an algorithm to check the correctness of proofs).

1.3. Desired metaproperties of a calculus: soundness and completeness.

Of course, if a calculus is to be helpful it would never lead us to erroneous reasoning: it is not going to lead us from true hypothesis to false conclusions. It must be a ***sound calculus.***

Further, it is desirable that all the consequences of a set Γ should be derived from Γ; *i.e.*, we would like to have a ***complete calculus.***

When soundness is assumed, the completeness theorem establishes the equivalence between syntax and semantics of a certain language. Due to this equivalence, we can use the calculus to show that a formula is a consequence of a set of formulas, and we can use the semantics to show that a given formula is not derivable in the calculus.

There are two degrees of completeness; namely, strong and weak completeness.

(1) Each validity is a theorem. This is *weak completeness.*

(2) For every set of formulas Γ and formula φ, whenever $\Gamma \models \varphi$ then also φ can be derived from Γ using the calculus. This is ***strong completeness.***

Completeness in the weak sense can be viewed, from outside, in this way: the semantic definition of validity makes a selection from the set of all formulas by picking up all those formulas that accept as models any interpretation $\mathcal{I}$. The deductive calculus makes a parallel selection: choosing the formulas that are deducible on it using no hypothesis.

Let **THEO** be the subset of **FORM** whose elements are the logical theorems in the calculus. Let **VAL** be the set of validities.

---

[19]This path has been very common in the history of logic, ever since Leibniz.

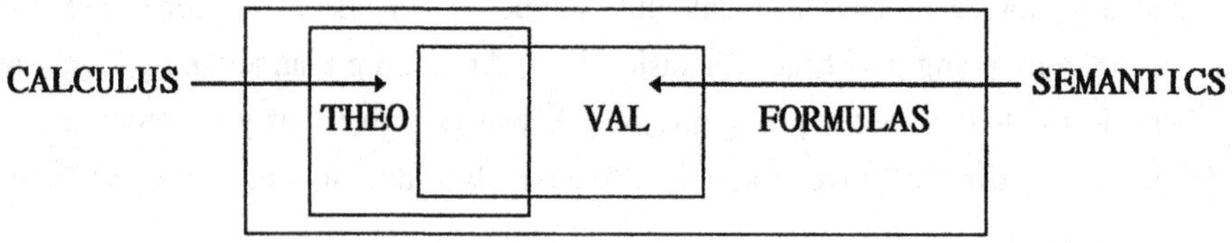

Do these sets coincide?

Proving that **THEO ⊆ VAL** is the objective of the soundness theorem, and proving **VAL ⊆ THEO** is that of the weak completeness theorem. If the calculus were sound and complete, the diagram should look like this:

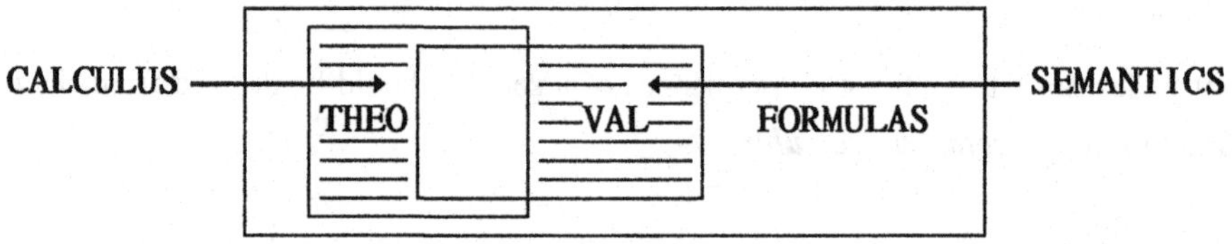

(the striped areas are empty)

Actually, when we construct a calculus we want to be able to use it to generate as logical theorems the set of valid formulas. Completeness and soundness assure us that the calculus is well constructed and useful to us: the method is dependable (soundness) and generally applicable (completeness).

Unfortunately, in standard second order logic the set of validities is not recursively enumerable. Therefore, no calculus can pick them up as theorems and any calculus we could define is incomplete. The set **VAL–THEO ≠ ∅** and so the diagram looks like this:

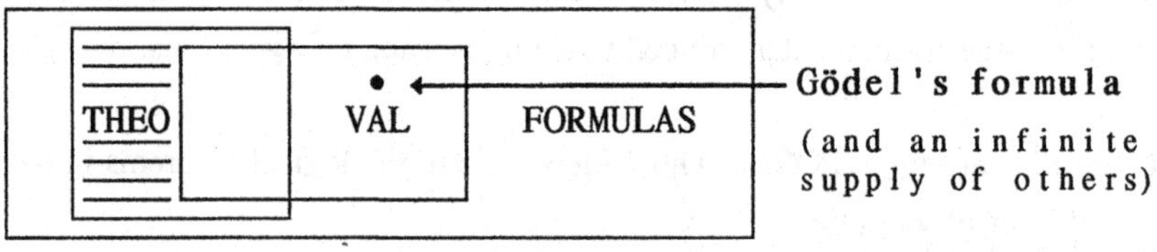

1.4. Our second order calculi.

As I have already explained in the preceding chapter, second order logic with standard semantics is not a compact logic and there is no hope of finding a complete calculus in the strong sense. It is impossible to find a weak complete calculus either. All we can do, as long as we insist on keeping the standard semantics, is to define a sound one. Which one?

In first order logic we have a very limited freedom when defining a calculus, since we know which formulas we want to obtain. Any finite set of rules is good as long as we can afterwards prove that with their help all and only the validities can be obtained. All first order complete calculi are equivalent.

In second order logic we have more freedom because we know from the beginning that not all the standard validities can be obtained. So almost any set of sound rules that allow us to get more than the first order validities will do. Somehow, you want your calculus to help you to isolate from the second order standard validities the set of what you feel are the "logical validities" (as opposed to the "set-theoretic" ones). It is strongly recommended that you are able to offer an alternative and natural semantics for the second order formulas and a completeness theorem for this semantics. Nevertheless there are certain sets of rules that have a pedigree: I will present below three of them.

The weakest of our calculi, C_2^-, is only an extension of the first order one which consists of allowing the rules dealing with quantifiers to take care of the relation quantification. It is defined for the language L_2 where equality among individuals is treated as in first order logic; that is, it is a primitive or logical symbol rather than a defined one. The interpretation of this symbol is the "true" identity relation. The calculus also contains the rules dealing with equality. Since we also have equality for predicates as primitive, we also adjoin some equality rules for them. We will have the extensionality axiom as a rule without hypothesis. This calculus will not count as a second order calculus for many people. In fact, this calculus is plain many-sorted and that is why, in a lousy way, I am also naming it **MSL**.

This many-sorted calculus was first isolated from the second order calculus by Henkin [1953] in a paper where he introduced the comprehension schema as a way of getting rid of the complex substitution rule of Church [1956].[20]

[20]Don't be surprised by the dates, Church [1956] is a revised version of a book which appeared in 1944.

He pointed out:

> In addition to the fact that F^{**} [similar to our calculus **SOL**] is formulated without reference to substitution for functional variables there is another advantage which we would claim for this system, namely, that it calls attention to the subsystem F^{*} [similar to our **MSL**]. The existence of this subsystem is generally obscured, in the ordinary formulation of second order functional calculus...
>
> Actually, the formal theorems of the system F^{*} form a very interesting class, as the following interpretation reveals.

And then he gives the definition of a frame; that is, of a many-sorted structure. The semantics based on frames makes **MSL** a complete calculus, as we will see later.

Besides this **MSL** calculus, we will have the C_2 calculus (also called **SOL**). The latter is obtained from the former by adding the comprehension schema as a rule without premises. It has been designed to be used with the language L_2 of **SOL** which does not contain the λ-abstractor.

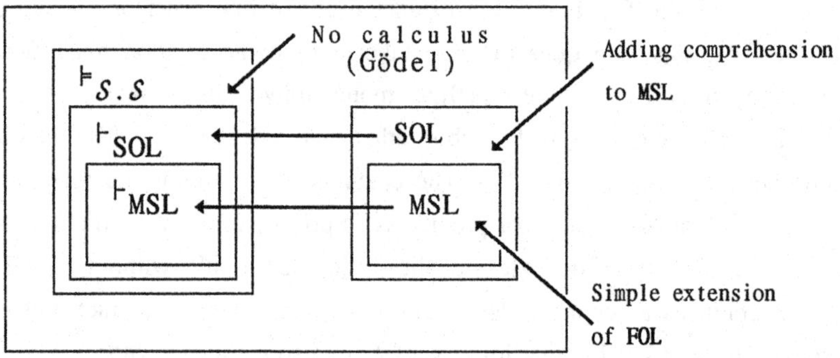

As you will see in chapter IV with both **MSL** and **SOL** calculi we can associate a specific and rather natural semantics; namely, the semantics based on frames and general structures.

In Henkin [1953] the possibility of defining a calculus between C_2^- - **MSL** - and C_2 - **SOL** - by restricting the comprehension axiom to certain kinds of formulas is also explored. I will use this idea in propositional modal logic and in dynamic logic.

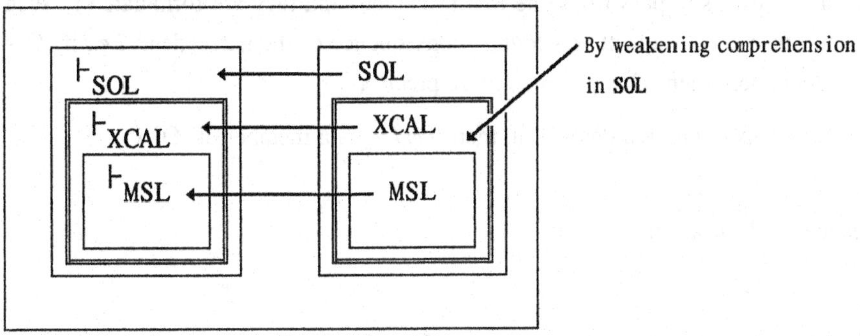

For the language **λ-SOL** we introduce a calculus which includes two λ-rules. We will show that the comprehension rule becomes a theorem of this calculus and, therefore, we do not need it as an axiom. We will call this calculus λ-C_2 (also, **λ-SOL**). This new calculus is equivalent to our previous calculus C_2, where we have equality for relations, comprehension and extensionality.

2.- SEQUENT CALCULI.

Very briefly I will present three sequent calculi for second order logic, two of them are equivalent in deductive power.

All three are based on the sequent calculus of Ebbinghaus, Flum & Thomas's ***Mathematical Logic*** [1984]; it has been enlarged with the extensionality axiom, with quantifier rules for the new quantification and with either λ-rules, or comprehension rule.

2.1. Deductions.

A deduction is a finite non-empty sequence of lines, each of which is a finite non-empty sequence of formulas $\varphi_1 ... \varphi_n \psi$ which is called a ***sequent*** whose ***antecedent*** is the sequence $\varphi_1 ... \varphi_n$ and whose ***consequent*** is ψ. In the following we will use the letters Ω and Θ for sequences of formulas (possible empty). We can also write sequences in the form $\Theta\ \varphi$. For a sequent we will use the notation $\Theta \hookrightarrow \psi$, where Θ is $\varphi_1 \ldots \varphi_n$. Θ is the antecedent and ψ the consequent.

Sequent rules allow us to pass from one line to another and they are formulated in such a way that in each line the consequent is a logical consequence of the antecedent; *i.e.*, if $\Theta \hookrightarrow \psi$ is a line in a deduction, then $\Theta \models \psi$. To be more precise,

if $\Theta \hookrightarrow \psi$ is a line in a deduction, then $\{\varphi / \varphi$ is a member of $\Theta\} \models \psi$

The rules are the following:

2.2. Sequent rules common to all calculi.

We introduce below the rules for calculus $\lambda\text{-}C_2$, C_2 and C_2^-. We will use the $\lambda\text{-}C_2$ calculus with the language $\lambda\text{-}L_2$, and the calculus C_2 and its subcalculus C_2^- with the λ-free language L_2.

2.2.1.- (HI) Hypothesis introduction.

$$\frac{}{\Omega \hookrightarrow \varphi}\text{, when } \varphi \in \Omega$$

2.2.2.- (M) Monotony.

$$\frac{\Omega \hookrightarrow \varphi}{\Theta \hookrightarrow \varphi}\text{, when all the formulas in } \Omega \text{ are also in } \Theta.$$

(*i.e.*, when $\Omega \subseteq \Theta$, if we identify a sequent, Ω or Θ, with the set of its members.)

2.2.3.- (PC) Proof by cases.

$$\frac{\begin{array}{lll}\Omega & \psi & \hookrightarrow \varphi \\ \Omega & \neg\psi & \hookrightarrow \varphi\end{array}}{\begin{array}{lll}\Omega & & \hookrightarrow \varphi\end{array}}$$

2.2.4.- (NC) Non contradiction.

$$\frac{\begin{array}{lll}\Omega & \neg\varphi & \hookrightarrow \psi \\ \Omega & \neg\varphi & \hookrightarrow \neg\psi\end{array}}{\begin{array}{lll}\Omega & & \hookrightarrow \varphi\end{array}}$$

2.2.5.- (IDA) Introducing disjunction in the antecedent.

$$\frac{\begin{array}{lll}\Omega & \varphi & \hookrightarrow \gamma \\ \Omega & \psi & \hookrightarrow \gamma\end{array}}{\Omega \quad \varphi \vee \psi \hookrightarrow \gamma}$$

2.2.6.- (IDC) Introducing disjunction in the consequent.

$$\frac{\Omega \hookrightarrow \varphi}{\Omega \hookrightarrow \varphi \vee \psi} \quad \text{and} \quad \frac{\Omega \hookrightarrow \varphi}{\Omega \hookrightarrow \psi \vee \varphi}$$

2.2.7.- (IPA) Introducing individual particularization in the antecedent.

$$\frac{\Omega \quad \varphi\frac{y}{x} \hookrightarrow \psi}{\Omega \quad \exists x\varphi \hookrightarrow \psi}, \; y \notin \text{FREE}(\Omega \cup \{\exists x\varphi, \psi\}), \; x \text{ and } y \text{ are individual variables}$$

2.2.8. (IPC) Introducing individual particularization in the consequent.

$$\frac{\Omega \hookrightarrow \varphi\frac{\tau}{x}}{\Omega \hookrightarrow \exists x\varphi} \quad \text{where } x \text{ and } \tau \text{ are a variable and a term}$$

2.2.9.- (RE) Reflexivity of equality for individuals.

$$\frac{}{\hookrightarrow \quad \tau = \tau}$$

2.2.10.- (ES) Equals substitution for individuals.

$$\frac{\Omega \quad \hookrightarrow \varphi\frac{\tau}{x}}{\Omega \; x = t \hookrightarrow \varphi\frac{t}{x}}$$

All the previous rules are also first order rules. Now we extend the calculus to cover relational quantification.

2.2.7^{n}.- (IPA)^{n} Introducing relation quantification in the antecedent.

$$\frac{\Omega \quad \varphi\frac{Y^n}{X^n} \hookrightarrow \psi}{\Omega \quad \exists X^n\varphi \hookrightarrow \psi}$$

(where X^n and Y^n are n-ary relation variables $Y^n \notin \text{FREE}(\Omega \cup \{\exists X^n\varphi, \psi\})$)

2.2.8^{n}.- (I.P.C)^{n} Introducing Relation Quantification in the Consequence.

$$\frac{\Omega \hookrightarrow \varphi\frac{\Pi^{n}}{X^{n}}}{\Omega \hookrightarrow \exists X^{n}\varphi}$$

(where Π^{n} is an n-ary predicate and X^{n} an n-ary relation variable)

2.2.11.- (Ext.) Extensionality.

$$\frac{}{\hookrightarrow \quad \forall X^{n}Y^{n}(X^{n} = Y^{n} \leftrightarrow \forall x_{1}...x_{n}(X^{n}x_{1}..x_{n} \leftrightarrow Y^{n}x_{1}...x_{n}))}$$

Let's call C_2^- the calculus having only these rules:
(HI), (M), (PC), (NC), (IDA), (IDC), (IPA), (IPC), (IPA)^n, (IPC)^n, (RE), (ES), (Ext.). ▮

Remarks.

(1) In **Equality-free SOL**, when introducing the equality by definition, you do not need the rules for equality because, due to your definition, they are derivable rules of the calculus. With a non-standard semantics it is better to have equality as primitive and to include the equality rules. Instead of having equality rules for relations, we have the more conventional axiom of extensionality.

(2) The calculus C_2^- can be seen as a simple extension of the first order calculus; it's being formulated in a second order language without the λ. Let us call $\vdash_{C_2^-}$ the set of logical theorems obtained on it. The elements of $\vdash_{C_2^-}$ are generalizations of theorems in a first order calculus (with minor transformations it is **MSL**), but there is nothing specific to **SOL** in this set. The set of theorems in this calculus is rather small and it is easy to prove that it is a subset of the set of standard validities:

$$\vdash_{C_2^-} \subseteq \models_{S.S}$$

Therefore, C_2^- can be proven to be a sound calculus in the standard sense. A new semantic could also be defined which makes this calculus complete and sound[21]. It is not the general semantics, though, but the semantics based on frames. I present it in Chapter IV.

[21]See Robbin [1969], page 139. The source is Henkin [1953].

2.3. Sequent rules for calculus C_2.

Nevertheless, one of the capabilities of second order logic we have mentioned many times is the definition of relations. We can do two things, we add either a comprehension schema or abstraction rules. The simpler one is to add to C_2^- the comprehension schema as a rule without hypothesis,

2.3.1.- (CS) Comprehension schema.

$$\frac{}{\hookrightarrow\ \exists X^n\ \forall x_1 \ldots x_n (X^n x_1 \ldots x_n \leftrightarrow \varphi)}\ , \text{ where } X^n \notin \mathrm{FREE}(\varphi)$$

and call the resulting calculus C_2. ∎

Now the set of theorems in C_2 includes all the occurrences of the comprehension schema. This calculus is complete and sound when its semantics is based upon the general structures which will be defined in Chapter IV.

2.4. Sequent rules for a calculus including lambda.

An equivalent formulation of C_2, but for a language with λ-abstraction, is the result of adding to the calculus C_2^- the rules for introducing the abstractor λ in the antecedent and in the consequent. As noted above, while using the language λ-L_2, the rules $(\mathrm{IPC})^n$ and $(\mathrm{IPA})^n$ for relation quantification are also more powerful, even though their formulation remains unchanged.

2.4.1.- (IAC) Introducing abstraction in the consequent.

$$\frac{\Omega\ \hookrightarrow\ \varphi\dfrac{\tau_1 \ldots \tau_n}{x_1 \ldots x_n}}{\Omega\ \hookrightarrow\ \lambda x_1 \ldots x_n\ \varphi\ \tau_1 \ldots \tau_n}\quad (x_1,\ldots,x_n \text{ are pairwise distinct individual variables})$$

2.4.2.- (IAA) Introducing abstraction in the antecedent.

$$\frac{\Omega\ \ \varphi\dfrac{\tau_1 \ldots \tau_n}{x_1 \ldots x_n}\ \hookrightarrow\ \psi}{\Omega\ \ \lambda x_1 \ldots x_n\ \varphi\ \tau_1 \ldots \tau_n\ \hookrightarrow\ \psi}\quad (x_1,\ldots,x_n \text{ are pairwise distinct individual variables})$$

Let us call this calculus λ-C_2. ▮

Remark.

Please note that the rules (IPA) and $(IPC)^n$ apply slightly differently in calculi C_2 and C_2^- than in λ-C_2. The reason is that in the two former we use the language of **SOL**, L_2, where we do not have λ-abstraction and so the predicates used in the substitution are always relation symbols, either variables or constants. In the λ-C_2 calculus we have the language of λ-**SOL**, λ-L_2, and we can have predicates with λ. Keep that in mind, it will be useful later.

2.5. Deductions.

(1) If, according to the C_2^- calculus rules, we obtain as a line the sequent $\Omega \hookrightarrow \varphi$ of formulas of L_2, we say that it ***is derivable in*** C_2^- and we write $\vdash_{C_2^-} \Omega\ \varphi$. ▮

(2) If, according to the C_2 calculus rules, we obtain as a line the sequent $\Omega \hookrightarrow \varphi$ of formulas of L_2, we say that it ***is derivable in*** C_2 and we write $\vdash_{C_2} \Omega\ \varphi$. ▮

(3) If, according to the λ-C_2 calculus rules, we obtain as a line the sequent $\Omega \hookrightarrow \varphi$ of formulas of λ-L_2, we say that it ***is derivable in*** λ-C_2 and we write $\vdash_{\lambda\text{-}C_2} \Omega\ \varphi$. ▮

(4) More generally, a formula φ ***is derivable from a set*** Δ of formulas in our C_2^- calculus (or in the C_2 or in the λ-C_2 calculus) if and only if there is a finite subset of Δ, $\{\varphi_1,\varphi_2,...,\varphi_n\}$, such that $\vdash_{C_2^-} \varphi_1\ \varphi_2...\varphi_n\ \varphi$ (or, such that $\vdash_{C_2} \varphi_1\ \varphi_2...\varphi_n\ \varphi$; or, such that $\vdash_{\lambda\text{-}C_2} \varphi_1\ \varphi_2...\varphi_n\ \varphi$). We will write $\Delta \vdash_{C_2^-} \varphi$. (Or, we will write $\Delta \vdash_{C_2} \varphi$; or, we will write $\Delta \vdash_{\lambda\text{-}C_2} \varphi$.) ▮

2.6. Derivable rules.

We have defined the calculi for the simplified language without $\land$, $\rightarrow$, $\leftrightarrow$, $\forall$ or $=$. To prove a theorem whose formulas are written with all the connectives, we can use the equivalences stated in Chapter I, 4.4.3. Nevertheless, any of these calculi can improve its performance by adding to it as many derivable rules as you like. A derivable rule is like a primitive one except for being unnecessary: the deductive power of the calculus is not going to enlarge. And so the significative difference between primitives and derivable rules is that the latter ones must be justified using the primitives rules to show that we can do without the derivable ones.

Here are some examples of derivable rules which can be added to any of the three calculi.

2.6.1. (SNC) Second non-contradiction rule.

$$\frac{\begin{array}{l}\Omega \hookrightarrow \psi \\ \Omega \hookrightarrow \neg\psi\end{array}}{\Omega \hookrightarrow \varphi}$$

Proof

1	Ω		$\hookrightarrow \psi$	premise
2	Ω		$\hookrightarrow \neg\psi$	premise
3	Ω	$\neg\varphi$	$\hookrightarrow \psi$	(M) in 1
4	Ω	$\neg\varphi$	$\hookrightarrow \neg\psi$	(M) in 2
5	Ω		$\hookrightarrow \varphi$	(NC) in 3,4

2.6.2. (T) Transitivity rule.

$$\frac{\begin{array}{lll}\Omega & & \hookrightarrow \varphi \\ \Omega & \varphi & \hookrightarrow \psi\end{array}}{\begin{array}{lll}\Omega & & \hookrightarrow \psi\end{array}}$$

Proof

1	Ω		$\hookrightarrow \varphi$	premise
2	Ω	φ	$\hookrightarrow \psi$	premise
3	Ω	$\neg\varphi$	$\hookrightarrow \varphi$	(M) in 1
4	Ω	$\neg\varphi$	$\hookrightarrow \neg\varphi$	(HI)
5	Ω	$\neg\varphi$	$\hookrightarrow \psi$	(SNC) in 3,4
6	Ω		$\hookrightarrow \psi$	(PC) in 2,5

2.6.3. (MP) Rule of "modus ponens".

$$\frac{\begin{array}{l}\Omega \hookrightarrow \varphi \rightarrow \psi \\ \Omega \hookrightarrow \varphi\end{array}}{\Omega \hookrightarrow \psi}\text{, that is, }\frac{\begin{array}{l}\Omega \hookrightarrow \neg\varphi \vee \psi \\ \Omega \hookrightarrow \varphi\end{array}}{\Omega \hookrightarrow \psi}$$

2.6.4.(MT) Rule of "modus tollens".

$$\frac{\begin{array}{l}\Omega \hookrightarrow \varphi \rightarrow \psi \\ \Omega \hookrightarrow \neg\psi\end{array}}{\Omega \hookrightarrow \neg\varphi}\text{, that is, }\frac{\begin{array}{l}\Omega \hookrightarrow \neg\varphi \vee \psi \\ \Omega \hookrightarrow \neg\psi\end{array}}{\Omega \hookrightarrow \neg\varphi}$$

Proof

1	Ω		$\hookrightarrow$	$\neg\varphi \vee \psi$	premise
2	Ω		$\hookrightarrow$	$\neg\psi$	premise
3	Ω	ψ	$\hookrightarrow$	$\neg\psi$	(M) in 2
4	Ω	ψ	$\hookrightarrow$	ψ	(HI)
5	Ω	ψ	$\hookrightarrow$	$\neg\varphi$	(SNC) in 3,4
6	Ω	$\neg\varphi$	$\hookrightarrow$	$\neg\varphi$	(HI)
7	Ω	$\neg\varphi\vee\psi$	$\hookrightarrow$	$\neg\varphi$	(IDA) in 5,6
8	Ω		$\hookrightarrow$	$\neg\varphi$	(T) in 1,7

2.6.5. (D) Deduction rule.

$$\frac{\Omega \quad \varphi \hookrightarrow \psi}{\Omega \quad \hookrightarrow \varphi \to \psi}\text{, that is, }\frac{\Omega \quad \varphi \hookrightarrow \psi}{\Omega \quad \hookrightarrow \neg\varphi \vee \psi}$$

Proof

1	Ω	φ	$\hookrightarrow$	ψ	premise
2	Ω	φ	$\hookrightarrow$	$\neg\varphi \vee \psi$	(IDC) in 1
3	Ω	$\neg\varphi$	$\hookrightarrow$	$\neg\varphi$	(HI)
4	Ω	$\neg\varphi$	$\hookrightarrow$	$\neg\varphi \vee \psi$	(IDC) in 3
5	Ω		$\hookrightarrow$	$\neg\varphi \vee \psi$	(PC) in 2,4

2.6.6. (DN) Double negation rule.

$$\frac{\Omega \hookrightarrow \neg\neg\varphi}{\Omega \hookrightarrow \varphi}\text{ and }\frac{\Omega \hookrightarrow \varphi}{\Omega \hookrightarrow \neg\neg\varphi}$$

Proof

1	Ω		$\hookrightarrow$	φ	premise
2	Ω	$\neg\varphi$	$\hookrightarrow$	φ	(M) in 1
3	Ω	$\neg\varphi$	$\hookrightarrow$	$\neg\varphi$	(HI)
4	Ω	$\neg\varphi$	$\hookrightarrow$	$\neg\neg\varphi$	(SNC) in 2,3
5	Ω	$\neg\neg\varphi$	$\hookrightarrow$	$\neg\neg\varphi$	(HI)
6	Ω		$\hookrightarrow$	$\neg\neg\varphi$	(PC) in 4,5

2.6.7. (IGC) Introducing individual generalization in the consequent.

$$\frac{\Omega \hookrightarrow \varphi\frac{y}{x}}{\Omega \hookrightarrow \forall x\varphi} \quad \text{where } y\notin \mathrm{FREE}(\Omega \cup \{\forall x\varphi\}) \text{, that is } \frac{\Omega \hookrightarrow \varphi\frac{y}{x}}{\Omega \hookrightarrow \neg\exists x\neg\varphi}$$

Proof

1	Ω		$\hookrightarrow \varphi\frac{y}{x}$	premise
2	Ω	$\neg\varphi\frac{y}{x}$	$\hookrightarrow \neg\varphi\frac{y}{x}$	(HI)
3	Ω	$\exists x\neg\varphi\frac{y}{x}$	$\hookrightarrow \neg\varphi\frac{y}{x}$	(IPA) in 2
4	Ω		$\hookrightarrow \exists x\neg\varphi\frac{y}{x} \rightarrow \neg\varphi\frac{y}{x}$	(D) in 3
5	Ω		$\hookrightarrow \neg\neg\varphi\frac{y}{x}$	(DN) in 1
6	Ω		$\hookrightarrow \neg\exists x\neg\varphi\frac{y}{x}$	(MT) in 5,4

2.6.7^{n}. (IGC)^{n} Introducing relation generalization in the consequent.

$$\frac{\Omega \hookrightarrow \varphi\frac{Y^{\mathrm{n}}}{X^{\mathrm{n}}}}{\Omega \hookrightarrow \forall X^{\mathrm{n}}\varphi} \quad \text{where } Y^{\mathrm{n}}\notin \mathrm{FREE}(\Omega \cup \{\forall X^{\mathrm{n}}\varphi\}) \text{, that is } \frac{\Omega \hookrightarrow \varphi\frac{Y^{\mathrm{n}}}{X^{\mathrm{n}}}}{\Omega \hookrightarrow \neg\exists X^{\mathrm{n}}\neg\varphi}$$

2.6.8. (EGC) Eliminating individual generalization in the consequent.

$$\frac{\Omega \hookrightarrow \forall x\varphi}{\Omega \hookrightarrow \varphi\frac{\tau}{x}} \text{, that is, } \frac{\Omega \hookrightarrow \neg\exists x\neg\varphi}{\Omega \hookrightarrow \varphi\frac{\tau}{x}}$$

Proof

1	Ω		$\hookrightarrow \neg\exists x\neg\varphi$	premise
2	Ω	$\neg\varphi\frac{\tau}{x}$	$\hookrightarrow \neg\exists x\neg\varphi$	(M) in 1
3	Ω	$\neg\varphi\frac{\tau}{x}$	$\hookrightarrow \neg\varphi\frac{\tau}{x}$	(HI)
4	Ω	$\neg\varphi\frac{\tau}{x}$	$\hookrightarrow \exists x\neg\varphi$	(IPC) in 3
5	Ω		$\hookrightarrow \varphi\frac{\tau}{x}$	(NC) in 2,4

2.6.8^{n}. (EGC)^{n} Eliminating relation generalization in the consequent.

$$\frac{\Omega \hookrightarrow \forall X^{\mathrm{n}}\varphi}{\Omega \hookrightarrow \varphi\frac{\tau}{X^{\mathrm{n}}}} \text{, that is, } \frac{\Omega \hookrightarrow \neg\exists X^{\mathrm{n}}\neg\varphi}{\Omega \hookrightarrow \varphi\frac{\tau}{X^{\mathrm{n}}}}$$

A similar proof can establish the rules for relational generalization, which you can add to our calculus. As above, calculus C_2^- is used only with a language without λ and these relational rules are weaker than in calculus λ-C_2 where we have a λ-language.

We can give as well a rule of introduction and another of elimination for every connective.

2.6.9. (ICC) Introducing conjunction in the consequent.

$$\frac{\Omega \hookrightarrow \varphi \qquad \Omega \hookrightarrow \psi}{\Omega \hookrightarrow \varphi \wedge \psi}$$

2.6.10. (ECC) Eliminating conjunction in the consequent.

$$\frac{\Omega \hookrightarrow \varphi \wedge \psi}{\Omega \hookrightarrow \varphi} \text{ and } \frac{\Omega \hookrightarrow \varphi \wedge \psi}{\Omega \hookrightarrow \psi}$$

2.6.11. (IBC) Introducing biconditional in the consequent.

$$\frac{\Omega \hookrightarrow \varphi \rightarrow \psi \qquad \Omega \hookrightarrow \psi \rightarrow \varphi}{\Omega \hookrightarrow \varphi \leftrightarrow \psi} \text{, that is, } \frac{\Omega \hookrightarrow \neg\varphi \vee \psi \qquad \Omega \hookrightarrow \neg\psi \vee \varphi}{\Omega \hookrightarrow \neg(\varphi \vee \psi) \vee \neg(\neg\varphi \vee \neg\psi)}$$

2.6.12. (EBC) Eliminating biconditional in the consequent.

$$\frac{\Omega \hookrightarrow \varphi \leftrightarrow \psi}{\Omega \hookrightarrow \varphi \rightarrow \psi} \text{ and } \frac{\Omega \hookrightarrow \varphi \leftrightarrow \psi}{\Omega \hookrightarrow \psi \rightarrow \varphi}$$

2.6.13. (I → C) Introducing conditional in the consequent.

$$\frac{\Omega \hookrightarrow \psi}{\Omega \hookrightarrow \varphi \rightarrow \psi} \text{ and } \frac{\Omega \hookrightarrow \neg\varphi}{\Omega \hookrightarrow \varphi \rightarrow \psi}$$

2.7. Equality and comprehension.

As I said before, in **Equality-free SOL**, where equality for individuals is introduced by

Leibniz's definition, the rules for equality need not be primitive since they can be proved as derivable rules using the remaining rules of λ-C_2.

2.7.1. (RE) Reflexivity of equality.

$$\frac{}{\tau = \tau}\ \text{, that is, }\ \frac{}{\forall X(X\tau \leftrightarrow X\tau)}$$

Proof

1	$X\tau$	$\hookrightarrow X\tau$	(HI)
2		$\hookrightarrow X\tau \rightarrow X\tau$	(D) in 1
3		$\hookrightarrow X\tau \leftrightarrow X\tau$	(IB) in 2,2
4		$\hookrightarrow \forall X(X\tau \leftrightarrow X\tau)$	(IGC)^1 in 3

2.7.2. (ES) Equals substitution.

$$\frac{\Omega \qquad \hookrightarrow \varphi\frac{\tau}{x}}{\Omega\ \ \tau = t \hookrightarrow \varphi\frac{t}{x}}\ \text{, that is, }\ \frac{\Omega \qquad\qquad \hookrightarrow \varphi\frac{\tau}{x}}{\Omega\ \ \forall X(X\tau \leftrightarrow Xt) \hookrightarrow \varphi\frac{t}{x}}$$

Proof

1	Ω			$\hookrightarrow \varphi\frac{\tau}{x}$	premise
2	Ω	$\forall X(X\tau \leftrightarrow Xt)$		$\hookrightarrow \forall X(X\tau \leftrightarrow Xt)$	(HI)
3	Ω	$\forall X(X\tau \leftrightarrow Xt)$		$\hookrightarrow \lambda x\varphi\, \tau \leftrightarrow \lambda x\varphi\, t$	(EGC)^1 in 2
4	Ω	$\forall X(X\tau \leftrightarrow Xt)$		$\hookrightarrow \varphi\frac{\tau}{x}$	(M) in 1
5	Ω	$\forall X(X\tau \leftrightarrow Xt)$		$\hookrightarrow \lambda x\varphi\, \tau$	(IAC) in 4
6	Ω	$\forall X(X\tau \leftrightarrow Xt)$		$\hookrightarrow \lambda x\varphi\, \tau \rightarrow \lambda x\varphi\, t$	(EBC) in 3
7	Ω	$\forall X(X\tau \leftrightarrow Xt)$		$\hookrightarrow \lambda x\varphi\, t$	(MP) in 6, 5
8	Ω	$\forall X(X\tau \leftrightarrow Xt)$	$\varphi\frac{t}{x}$	$\hookrightarrow \varphi\frac{t}{x}$	(HI)
9	Ω	$\forall X(X\tau \leftrightarrow Xt)$	$\lambda x\varphi\, t$	$\hookrightarrow \varphi\frac{t}{x}$	(IAA) in 8
10	Ω	$\forall X(X\tau \leftrightarrow Xt)$		$\hookrightarrow \varphi\frac{t}{x}$	(T) in 9, 7

As I have already mentioned, equality can also be introduced in **Equality-free SOL** using the property of reflexivity; *i.e.*, two individuals are equal when they belong to all reflexive relations. Here we prove the equivalence of the two definitions.

2.7.3. Theorem:

$\vdash_{\lambda\text{-}C_2} \forall xy(\forall Z(Zx \longmapsto Zy) \longmapsto \forall Y(\forall z Yzz \rightarrow Yxy))$

Proof

1	$\forall Z(Zx \longmapsto Zy)$ $\forall z\, Yzz$	$\hookrightarrow$	$\forall z\, Yzz$	(HI)
2	$\forall Z(Zx \longmapsto Zy)$ $\forall z\, Yzz$	$\hookrightarrow$	Yxx	(EGC) in 1
3	$\forall Z(Zx \longmapsto Zy)$ $\forall z\, Yzz$	$\hookrightarrow$	$\lambda y\, Yxy\, x$	(IAC) in 2
4	$\forall Z(Zx \longmapsto Zy)$ $\forall z\, Yzz$	$\hookrightarrow$	$\forall Z(Zx \longmapsto Zy)$	(HI)
5	$\forall Z(Zx \longmapsto Zy)$ $\forall z\, Yzz$	$\hookrightarrow$	$\lambda y\, Yxy\, x \rightarrow \lambda y\, Yxy\, y$	(EGC) in 4
6	$\forall Z(Zx \longmapsto Zy)$ $\forall z\, Yzz$	$\hookrightarrow$	$\lambda y\, Yxy\, y$	(MP) in 5, 3
7	$\forall Z(Zx \longmapsto Zy)$ $\forall z\, Yzz$ Yxy	$\hookrightarrow$	Yxy	(HI)
8	$\forall Z(Zx \longmapsto Zy)$ $\forall z\, Yzz$ $\lambda y\, Yxy\, y$	$\hookrightarrow$	Yxy	(IAA) in 7
9	$\forall Z(Zx \longmapsto Zy)$ $\forall z\, Yzz$	$\hookrightarrow$	Yxy	(T) in 6, 8
10	$\forall Z(Zx \longmapsto Zy)$	$\hookrightarrow$	$\forall z\, Yzz \rightarrow Yxy$	(D) in 9
11	$\forall Z(Zx \longmapsto Zy)$	$\hookrightarrow$	$\forall Y(\forall z\, Yzz \rightarrow Yxy)$	(IGC) in 10
12		$\hookrightarrow$	$\forall Z(Zx \longmapsto Zy) \rightarrow \forall Y(\forall z\, Yzz \rightarrow Yxy)$	(D) in 11
13	$\forall Y(\forall z\, Yzz \rightarrow Yxy)$	$\hookrightarrow$	$\forall Y(\forall z\, Yzz \rightarrow Yxy)$	(HI)
14	$\forall Y(\forall z\, Yzz \rightarrow Yxy)$	$\hookrightarrow$	$\forall z\, \lambda xy\, \forall Z(Zx \longmapsto Zy)zz \rightarrow \lambda xy\, \forall Z(Zx \longmapsto Zy)\, xy$	(EGC) in 13
15	$\forall Y(\forall z\, Yzz \longrightarrow Yxy)$ Zz	$\hookrightarrow$	Zz	(HI)
16	$\forall Y(\forall z\, Yzz \rightarrow Yxy)$	$\hookrightarrow$	$Zz \rightarrow Zz$	(D) in 15
17	$\forall Y(\forall z\, Yzz \rightarrow Yxy)$	$\hookrightarrow$	$Zz \longmapsto Zz$	(IB) in 16, 16
18	$\forall Y(\forall z\, Yzz \rightarrow Yxy)$	$\hookrightarrow$	$\forall Z(Zz \longmapsto Zz)$	(IGC) in 17
19	$\forall Y(\forall z\, Yzz \rightarrow Yxy)$	$\hookrightarrow$	$\lambda xy\, \forall Z(Zx \longmapsto Zy)\, zz$	(IAC) in 18
20	$\forall Y(\forall z\, Yzz \rightarrow Yxy)$	$\hookrightarrow$	$\forall z \lambda xy\, \forall Z(Zx \longmapsto Zy)\, zz$	(IGC) in 19
21	$\forall Y(\forall z\, Yzz \rightarrow Yxy)$	$\hookrightarrow$	$\lambda xy\, \forall Z(Zx \longmapsto Zy)\, xy$	(MP) in 14, 20
22	$\forall Y(\forall z\, Yzz \rightarrow Yxy)$ $\forall Z(Zx \longmapsto Zy)$	$\hookrightarrow$	$\forall Z(Zx \longmapsto Zy)$	(HI)
23	$\forall Y(\forall z\, Yzz \rightarrow Yxy)$ $\lambda xy \forall Z(Zx \longmapsto Zy)xy$	$\hookrightarrow$	$\forall Z(Zx \longmapsto Zy)$	(IAA) in 22
24	$\forall Y(\forall z\, Yzz \rightarrow Yxy)$	$\hookrightarrow$	$\forall Z(Zx \longmapsto Zy)$	(T) in 21, 23
25		$\hookrightarrow$	$\forall Y(\forall z\, Yzz \rightarrow Yxy) \rightarrow \forall Z(Zx \longmapsto Zy)$	(D) in 24
26			$\forall Z(Zx \longmapsto Zy) \longmapsto \forall Y(\forall z\, Yzz \rightarrow Yxy)$	(IBC) in 25, 12
27			$\forall xy(\forall Z\, (Zx \longmapsto Zy) \longmapsto \forall Y(\forall z\, Yzz \rightarrow Yxy))$	(IGC) in 26, twice

In calculus $\lambda\text{-}C_2$ we can prove comprehension as a theorem and, if you like, you can have it as a rule without premises. The proof involves rules of abstraction, but also the rule (IPC) is used for a λ-predicate.

2.7.4. Comprehension theorem.

$\vdash_{\lambda\text{-}C_2} \exists X^n \forall x_1 ... x_n (X^n x_1 ... x_n \leftrightarrow \varphi)$, where $X^n \notin \mathrm{FREE}(\varphi)$

Proof

1	$\varphi \hookrightarrow \varphi$		(HI)
2	$\varphi \hookrightarrow \lambda x_1 ... x_n \varphi\, x_1 ... x_n$		(IAC) in 1, (*)
3	$\hookrightarrow \varphi \rightarrow \lambda x_1 ... x_n \varphi\, x_1 ... x_n$		(D) in 2
4	$\lambda x_1 ... x_n \varphi\, x_1 ... x_n \hookrightarrow \varphi$		(IAA) in 1
5	$\hookrightarrow \lambda x_1 ... x_n \varphi\, x_1 ... x_n \rightarrow \varphi$		(D) in 4
6	$\hookrightarrow \lambda x_1 ... x_n \varphi\, x_1 ... x_n \leftrightarrow \varphi$		(IBC) in 5, 3
7	$\hookrightarrow \forall x_1 ... x_n (\lambda x_1 ... x_n \varphi\, x_1 ... x_n \leftrightarrow \varphi)$		(IGC) n times in 6
8	$\hookrightarrow \exists X^n \forall x_1 ... x_n (X^n x_1 ... x_n \leftrightarrow \varphi)$		$(\mathrm{IPC})^n$ in 7

(*) (because $\varphi \equiv \varphi \dfrac{x_1 ... x_n}{x_1 ... x_n}$)

I have mentioned that having comprehension and extensionality in the calculus C_2 the existence and uniqueness of the relation defined by every suitable formula is a theorem, that is, we can prove the following theorem.

2.7.5. Theorem.

$\vdash_{C_2} \exists ! X^n \forall x_1 ... x_n (X^n x_1 ... x_n \leftrightarrow \varphi)$

where $\exists !$ is understood as: there exists a unique.... In our case it is an abbreviation of the formula

$$\exists X^n \forall x_1 ... x_n (X^n x_1 ... x_n \leftrightarrow \varphi) \wedge \forall X^n Y^n (\forall x_1 ... x_n (X^n x_1 ... x_n \leftrightarrow \varphi) \wedge \forall x_1 ... x_n (Y^n x_1 ... x_n \leftrightarrow \varphi) \rightarrow X^n = Y^n)$$

General idea of the proof.

From the comprehension axiom we get the existence of a relation defined using the formula φ. From extensionality we obtain the uniqueness of such a relation.

Remarks.

What is the meaning of this theorem? As I see it, it merely says that whenever you have comprehension and extensionality you are able to give a name to the relation defined by a formula (using a given sequence of variables), since there is a unique one. That means, you can conservatively extend your language with an abstractor operator.

When written in terms of λ-notation, the comprehension axiom becomes

$$\forall x_1 ... x_n (\lambda x_1 ... x_n \varphi \, x_1 ... x_n \leftrightarrow \varphi)$$

It is not difficult to prove that in the calculus C_2 the rules dealing with abstraction are derivable ones. You have to use the comprehension axiom in the form given above. Can you please do this?

2.8. Deduction exercises.

2.8.1. Theorem.

$\vdash_{\lambda\text{-}C_2} \forall x\varphi \leftrightarrow \lambda x\varphi = \lambda x\, x{=}x$

This theorem gives you an idea to be used later: individual quantification can be defined in a second order language with abstraction enlarged with identity for relations.

Proof

1	$y{=}y$			(RE)
2	$\forall x\varphi$	$\hookrightarrow$	$y{=}y$	(M) in 1
3	$\forall x\varphi$	$\hookrightarrow$	$\lambda x\, x{=}x\, y$	(IAC) in 2
4	$\forall x\varphi$	$\hookrightarrow$	$\lambda x\varphi\, y \rightarrow \lambda x\, x{=}x\, y$	(I→C) in 3.
5	$\forall x\varphi$	$\hookrightarrow$	$\forall x\varphi$	(HI)
6	$\forall x\varphi$	$\hookrightarrow$	$\varphi\frac{y}{x}$	(EGC) in 5
7	$\forall x\varphi$	$\hookrightarrow$	$\lambda x\varphi\, y$	(IAC) in 6
8	$\forall x\varphi$	$\hookrightarrow$	$\lambda x\, x{=}x\, y \rightarrow \lambda x\varphi\, y$	(I→C) in 7.
9	$\forall x\varphi$	$\hookrightarrow$	$\lambda x\varphi\, y \leftrightarrow \lambda x\, x{=}x\, y$	(IBC) in 8, 4
10	$\forall x\varphi$	$\hookrightarrow$	$\forall x(\lambda x\varphi\, x \leftrightarrow \lambda x\, x{=}x\, x)$	(IGC) in 9
11		$\hookrightarrow$	$\forall XY(X{=}Y \leftrightarrow \forall x(Xx \leftrightarrow Yx))$	(Ext.)
12	$\forall x\varphi$	$\hookrightarrow$	$\forall XY(X{=}Y \leftrightarrow \forall x(Xx \leftrightarrow Yx))$	(M) in 11

13 $\forall x\varphi \quad \hookrightarrow \quad \lambda x\varphi = \lambda x\, x{=}x \leftrightarrow \forall x(\lambda x\varphi\, x \leftrightarrow \lambda x\, x{=}x\, x)$ (EGC) twice in 12

14 $\forall x\varphi \quad \hookrightarrow \quad \forall x(\lambda x\, \varphi\, x \leftrightarrow \lambda x\, x{=}x\, x) \to \lambda x\varphi = \lambda x\, x{=}x$ (EBC) in 13

15 $\forall x\varphi \quad \hookrightarrow \quad \lambda x\varphi = \lambda x\, x{=}x$ (MP) 14, 10

16 $\forall x\varphi \to \lambda x\varphi = \lambda x\, x{=}x$ (D) in 15

17 $\lambda x\varphi = \lambda x\, x{=}x \quad \hookrightarrow \quad \lambda x\varphi = \lambda x\, x{=}x$ (HI)

18 $\lambda x\varphi = \lambda x\, x{=}x \quad \hookrightarrow \quad \forall XY(X{=}Y \leftrightarrow \forall x(Xx \leftrightarrow Yx))$ (M) in 11

19 $\lambda x\varphi = \lambda x\, x{=}x \quad \hookrightarrow \quad \lambda x\varphi = \lambda x\, x{=}x \leftrightarrow \forall x(\lambda x\varphi\, x \leftrightarrow \lambda x\, x{=}x\, x)$ (EGC) in 18

20 $\lambda x\varphi = \lambda x\, x{=}x \quad \hookrightarrow \quad \lambda x\varphi = \lambda x\, x{=}x \to \forall x(\lambda x\varphi\, x \leftrightarrow \lambda x\, x{=}x\, x)$ (EBC) in 19

21 $\lambda x\varphi = \lambda x\, x{=}x \quad \hookrightarrow \quad \forall x(\lambda x\varphi\, x \leftrightarrow \lambda x\, x{=}x\, x)$ (MP) in 20, 17

22 $\lambda x\varphi = \lambda x\, x{=}x \quad \hookrightarrow \quad \lambda x\varphi\, y \leftrightarrow \lambda x\, x{=}x\, y$ (EGC) in 21

23 $\lambda x\varphi = \lambda x\, x{=}x \quad \hookrightarrow \quad \lambda x\, x{=}x\, y \to \lambda x\varphi\, y$ (EBC) in 22

24 $\hookrightarrow \quad y{=}y$ (RE)

25 $\lambda x\varphi = \lambda x\, x{=}x \quad \hookrightarrow \quad y{=}y$ (M) in 24

26 $\lambda x\varphi = \lambda x\, x{=}x \quad \hookrightarrow \quad \lambda x\, x{=}x\, y$ (IAC) in 25

27 $\lambda x\varphi = \lambda x\, x{=}x \quad \hookrightarrow \quad \lambda x\, \varphi\, y$ (MP) in 23,26

28 $\lambda x\varphi = \lambda x\, x{=}x \quad \varphi\frac{y}{x} \quad \hookrightarrow \quad \varphi\frac{y}{x}$ (HI)

29 $\lambda x\varphi = \lambda x\, x{=}x \quad \lambda x\, \varphi\, y \quad \hookrightarrow \quad \varphi\frac{y}{x}$ (IAA) in 28

30 $\lambda x\varphi = \lambda x\, x{=}x \quad \hookrightarrow \quad \varphi\frac{y}{x}$ (T) in 27,29

31 $\lambda x\varphi = \lambda x\, x{=}x \quad \hookrightarrow \quad \forall x\varphi$ (IGC) in 30

32 $\lambda x\varphi = \lambda x\, x{=}x \to \forall x\varphi$ (D) in 31

33 $\forall x\varphi \leftrightarrow \lambda x\varphi = \lambda x\, x{=}x$ (IBC) in 32, 16

2.8.2. Theorem.

Let $\Pi = \{\forall x\, \neg c = \sigma x,\ \forall xy\, (\sigma x = \sigma y \to x = y),\ \forall X(Xc \wedge \forall z(Xz \to X\sigma z) \to \forall x\, Xx)\}$. Then

$$\Pi \vdash_{\lambda\text{-}C_2} \forall x\, \neg x = \sigma x$$

(Here we prove that from second order Peano axioms it follows that no number is its own successor.)

Proof

1 $\Pi \quad \hookrightarrow \quad \forall x\, \neg c = \sigma x$ (HI)

2 $\Pi \quad \hookrightarrow \quad \neg c = \sigma c$ (EGC) in 1

3 $\Pi \quad \hookrightarrow \quad \lambda z\, \neg z = \sigma z\, c$ (IAC) in 2

4 $\Pi \quad \neg x = \sigma x \quad \hookrightarrow \quad \forall xy(\sigma x = \sigma y \to x = y)$ (HI)

5 $\Pi \quad \neg x = \sigma x \quad \hookrightarrow \quad \sigma x = \sigma\sigma x \to x = \sigma x$ (EGC) in 4, twice

6	Π	$\neg x = \sigma x \hookrightarrow \neg x = \sigma x$	(HI)
7	Π	$\neg x = \sigma x \hookrightarrow \neg\sigma x = \sigma\sigma x$	(MT) in 5, 6
8	Π	$\lambda z\, \neg z = \sigma z\ x \hookrightarrow \neg\sigma x = \sigma\sigma x$	(IAA) in 7
9	Π	$\lambda z\, \neg z = \sigma z\ x \hookrightarrow \lambda z\, \neg z = \sigma z\ \sigma x$	(IAC) in 8
10	Π	$\hookrightarrow \lambda z\, \neg z = \sigma z\ x \rightarrow \lambda z\, \neg z = \sigma z\ \sigma x$	(D) in 9
11	Π	$\hookrightarrow \forall x(\lambda z\, \neg z = \sigma z\ x \rightarrow \lambda z\, \neg z = \sigma z\ \sigma x)$	(IGC) in 10
12	Π	$\hookrightarrow \lambda z\, \neg z = \sigma z\ c \wedge \forall x(\lambda z\, \neg z = \sigma z\ x \rightarrow \lambda z\, \neg z = \sigma z\ \sigma x)$	(ICC) in 3, 11
13	Π	$\hookrightarrow \forall X(Xc \wedge \forall z(Xz \rightarrow X\sigma z) \rightarrow \forall x\, Xx)$	(HI)
14	Π	$\hookrightarrow \lambda z\, \neg z{=}\sigma z\ c \wedge \forall x(\lambda z \neg z{=}\sigma z\ x \rightarrow \lambda z\, \neg z{=}\sigma z\ \sigma x) \rightarrow \forall x\ \lambda z \neg z{=}\sigma z\ x$	(EGC) in 13
15	Π	$\hookrightarrow \forall x\ \lambda z\, \neg z = \sigma z\ x$	(MP) in 14, 12
16	Π	$\hookrightarrow \lambda z\, \neg z = \sigma z\ x$	(EGC) in 15
17	Π	$\lambda z\, \neg z = \sigma z\ x \hookrightarrow \neg x = \sigma x$	(IAA) in 6
18	Π	$\hookrightarrow \neg x = \sigma x$	(T) in 16, 17
19	Π	$\hookrightarrow \forall x \neg x = \sigma x$	(IGC) in 18

2.8.3. Theorem.

$\forall X(Xc \wedge \forall z(Xz \rightarrow X\sigma z) \rightarrow \forall x\, Xx) \vdash_{\lambda\text{-}C_2} \forall y(\forall x\, \neg y = \sigma x \rightarrow y = c)$

Proof

Can you prove this? ∎

2.8.4. Theorem.

$\vdash_{\lambda\text{-}C_2} \exists x X\ Xx$

Proof

Can you prove this? ∎

3.- SOUNDNESS THEOREM IN STANDARD SEMANTICS.

As has been already explained, the soundness theorem states that our calculus would never drive us to erroneous reasoning. Whenever we have derived a formula from a set of formulas using the calculus, we can be certain that an informal proof of it is also possible in standard structures. That is, the formula is a semantical consequence of the set of formulas in the standard sense.

Now we are going to state and prove the soundness theorems for the calculi introduced so far: λ-C_2, C_2 and C_2^-. The semantics used is the standard one and we write $\vDash_{\mathcal{S.S}}$ to remind ourselves of this fact. In addition, only λ-C_2 is used with a language including λ-abstraction.

We want to prove the following:

For every $\Gamma \subseteq$ **FORM** and every formula φ: If $\Gamma \vdash_{\mathbf{CAL}} \varphi$ then $\Gamma \vDash_{\mathcal{S.S}} \varphi$

(where **CAL** should be replaced by each of the three calculi considered and **FORM** should be understood as the set of formulas in the language used, with or without λ).

To prove this we should proceed as follows:

Let $\Gamma \vdash_{\mathbf{CAL}} \varphi$. By the definition 2.5 (finiteness of deduction) there is a finite sequence of formulas of Γ, $\Omega \subseteq \Gamma$, with elements $\varphi_1,...,\varphi_n$, such that $\vdash_{\mathbf{CAL}} \Omega\ \varphi$. That is, $\Omega \hookrightarrow \varphi$ is a sequent of our calculus **CAL**. The key is to prove that in this situation the sequent is correct, $\Omega \vDash_{\mathcal{S.S}} \varphi$ [properly, $\{\varphi_1,...,\varphi_n\} \vDash_{\mathcal{S.S}} \varphi$]. It is clear that from this we obtain that $\Gamma \vDash_{\mathcal{S.S}} \varphi$, because $\Omega \subseteq \Gamma$.

Therefore, we must show that all sequents in the calculus are correct. We have to show that the rules without premises are sound and the other rules preserve soundness.

3.1 The soundness of rules common to all three calculi in standard semantics.

I will prove the correctness for the language λ-L_2, since from it follows the correctness of the language without λ. I will use the shorter notation $\vDash$ (instead of $\vDash_{\mathcal{S.S}}$) for standard semantic notions. Besides that, to simplify the notation, we identify the sequence Ω with the set of its members, $\{\gamma / \gamma$ is in $\Omega\}$.

Proof

3.1.1 Soundness of (HI)

Trivially, if $\varphi \in \Omega$ then $\Omega \vDash \varphi$.

3.1.2. Soundness of (M)

If the sequent $\Omega \hookrightarrow \varphi$ is sound and $\Omega \subseteq \Theta$, since $\Omega \vDash \varphi$, $\Theta \vDash \varphi$ also.

3.1.3. Soundness of (PC)

Let $\Omega\ \varphi \hookrightarrow \psi$ and $\Omega\ \neg\varphi \hookrightarrow \psi$ be sound sequents. Therefore, $\Omega \cup \{\varphi\} \vDash \psi$ and $\Omega \cup \{\neg\varphi\} \vDash \psi$. To show that $\Omega \vDash \psi$ take any model $\mathcal{I}$ of Ω. Either $\mathcal{I}$ is a model of φ or $\mathcal{I}$ is a model of $\neg\varphi$. In any case, $\mathcal{I}$ is a model of ψ.

3.1.4. Soundness of (NC)

3.1.5. Soundness of (IDA)

3.1.6. Soundness of (IDC)

Let $\Omega \hookrightarrow \varphi$ be a sound sequent. Therefore, $\Omega \vDash \varphi$. Thus, $\Omega \vDash \varphi \vee \psi$, since any model of φ is also a model of $\varphi \vee \psi$.

3.1.7. Soundness of (IPA)

Let $\Omega\ \varphi\frac{y}{x} \hookrightarrow \psi$ be a sound sequent and $y \notin \mathbf{FREE}(\Omega \cup \{\exists x\varphi,\ \psi\})$. Therefore, $\Omega \cup \{\varphi\frac{y}{x}\} \vDash \psi$. We want to show that $\Omega \cup \{\exists x\varphi\} \vDash \psi$.

Let $\mathcal{I} = \langle \mathcal{A}, \mathrm{M}\rangle$ be a model of $\Omega \cup \{\exists x\varphi\}$. Then there must be an $\mathbf{x} \in \mathbf{A}$ such that $\mathcal{I}^{\mathbf{x}}_{x}$ sat φ, and also $\mathcal{I}^{\mathbf{xx}}_{yx}$ sat φ (because when $x \equiv y$ it is trivially true, and when $x \not\equiv y$, $y \notin \mathbf{FREE}(\varphi)$, and it follows by the coincidence lemma).

Since $\mathcal{I}^{\mathbf{x}}_{y}(y) = \mathrm{x}$, we have $\mathcal{I}^{\mathbf{x}\mathcal{I}^{\mathbf{x}}_{y}(y)}_{yx}$ sat φ.
Using the substitution lemma, $\mathcal{I}^{\mathbf{x}}_{y}$ sat $\varphi\frac{y}{x}$.
It is easy to see that $\mathcal{I}^{\mathbf{x}}_{y}$ sat ψ, because $y \notin \mathbf{FREE}(\Omega)$ and $\mathcal{I}$ was a model of Ω. Therefore, $\mathcal{I}^{\mathbf{x}}_{y}$ sat ψ. To see that $\mathcal{I}$ sat ψ remember that $y \notin \mathbf{FREE}(\psi)$ and apply the coincidence lemma.

3.1.8. Soundness of (IPC)

3.1.7^{n}. Soundness of (IPA)^{n}.

3.1.8^{n}. Soundness of (IPC)^{n}.

Let $\Omega \hookrightarrow \varphi\frac{\Pi^{\mathrm{n}}}{X^{\mathrm{n}}}$ be a sound sequent. Therefore, $\Omega \vDash \varphi\frac{\Pi^{\mathrm{n}}}{X^{\mathrm{n}}}$. We want to show that $\Omega \vDash \exists X^{\mathrm{n}}\varphi$.

Let $\mathcal{I}=\langle\mathcal{A},M\rangle$ be a model of Ω. Therefore, $\mathcal{I}$ is also a model of $\varphi\frac{\Pi^n}{X^n}$. By the substitution lemma we know that also $\mathcal{I}^{\mathcal{I}(\Pi^n)}_{X^n}$ is a model of φ.

In standard structures $A_n = \mathcal{P}A^n$ and so all n-ay relations are in this universe. Therefore, $\mathcal{I}(\Pi^n) \in A_n$. Then $\mathcal{I}$ sat $\exists X^n\varphi$.

3.1.9. Soundness of (RE)

Since this rule doesn't have premises, it must be shown that $\models \tau{=}\tau$.

Let $\mathcal{I}=\langle\mathcal{A},M\rangle$ be any model. Clearly, $\mathcal{I}$ is a model of $\tau{=}\tau$, because $\mathcal{I}$ is a function and the interpretation of $\tau{=}\tau$ is $\mathcal{I}(\tau)=\mathcal{I}(\tau)$.

3.1.10. Soundness of (ES)

3.1.11. Soundness of (Ext.)

This follows from the fact that our models are extensional.

Prove the remainder yourself. ▮

Once we have proved the soundness of all these rules, our calculus C_2^- is sound. But we have proved more, since we have not restricted ourselves to formulas of L_2 but of λ-L_2. Therefore, all these rules are sound in standard semantics, when applied for any second order language.

3.2. The soundness of lambda rules.

We have already proved the soundness of all rules common to C_2^- in the extended language λ-L_2. Therefore, the only thing that remains to be proven is the soundness of the two new rules dealing with λ-abstractor.

3.2.1. Soundness of (IAC)

Let the sequent $\Omega \hookrightarrow \varphi\frac{\tau_1...\tau_n}{x_1...x_n}$ be sound. That is, $\Omega \models \varphi\frac{\tau_1...\tau_n}{x_1...x_n}$.

Let $\mathcal{I}=\langle\mathcal{A},M\rangle$ be a model of Ω. We want to prove that $\mathcal{I}$ is a model of the formula

$\lambda x_1 ... x_n\ \varphi\ \tau_1 ... \tau_n$.

Since $\mathcal{I}$ is a model of Ω, then it is also a model of $\varphi \frac{\tau_1 ... \tau_n}{x_1 ... x_n}$.

Therefore, using the substitution lemma, $\mathcal{I}^{\mathcal{I}(\tau_1)...\mathcal{I}(\tau_n)}_{x_1...x_n}$ sat φ.

We know then that $\langle \mathcal{I}(\tau_1),...,\mathcal{I}(\tau_n)\rangle \in \mathcal{I}(\lambda x_1 ... x_n\ \varphi)$. Therefore,

$$\mathcal{I} \text{ sat } \lambda x_1 ... x_n\ \varphi\ \tau_1 ... \tau_n$$

3.2.2. Soundness of (IAA)

The proof uses the same definitions and lemmas as the preceding one. ∎

3.3. The soundness of comprehension.

We have to show that the comprehension rule is correct. Since it is a rule without premises, we must show

$$\models \exists X^n\ \forall x_1 ... x_n\ (X^n x_1 ... x_n \longleftrightarrow \varphi), \text{ for any } \varphi \text{ with } X^n \notin \text{FREE}(\varphi)$$

Since we are now using standard structures, all possible relations are in the universes and so, in particular, all the definable relations, as you can ensure yourself. ∎

Remark.

Please note that the condition that $X^n \notin \text{FREE}(\varphi)$ is very important, otherwise we would have as axioms formulas whose validity would be impossible to prove, for instance:

$$\exists X^n\ \forall x_1 ... x_n\ (X^n x_1 ... x_n \longleftrightarrow \neg X^n x_1 ... x_n)$$

4.- INCOMPLETENESS IN STANDARD STRUCTURES.

All second order calculi are incomplete while using standard semantics. The incompleteness is in both senses: weak and strong. We will prove here the incompleteness of C_2^- in the weak sense and also the incompleteness of any second order calculus in both senses.

4.1. Incompleteness of C_2^- in standard structures.

As expected, the calculus C_2^- is not complete when we consider standard semantics. Its incompleteness is a corollary of the incompleteness of C_2, but it can also be proved very easily from the two propositions stated below.

4.1.1. Theorem.

There is a formula γ of L_2 such that $\vDash_{S.S}\gamma$ but not $\vdash_{C_2^-}\gamma$.

Proof

To prove this, you will prove two propositions:

Proposition 1: The formula $\gamma \equiv \exists xX\, Xx$ is valid in the standard sense.

Proposition 2: The formula γ is not a theorem of C_2^-.

Proposition 1 is clear; $\exists xX\, Xx$ is valid since in any standard structure

$$\mathcal{A} = \langle A, \langle \mathcal{P}A^n \rangle_{n\geq 1}, \langle C^{\mathcal{A}} \rangle_{C\in \mathbf{OPER.CONS}} \rangle$$

not only $A \neq \emptyset$ but also $A \in A_1$.

You will prove Proposition 2 in two steps:

(A) To every formula $\varphi \in \mathbf{FORM}(L_2)$ we associate a truth value, φ^*, defined in this way:

(i) $\varphi^* = F$, for all atomic formulas except equalities. $\varphi^* = T$, when φ is an equality.

(ii) $(\neg\varphi)^* = \begin{cases} T, \text{ if } \varphi^* = F \\ F, \text{ if } \varphi^* = T \end{cases}$

(iii) $(\varphi \vee \psi)^* = \begin{cases} F, \text{ if } \varphi^* = F \text{ and } \psi^* = F \\ T, \text{ otherwise} \end{cases}$

(iv) $(\exists v\ \varphi)^* = \varphi^* = (\forall v\ \varphi)^*$, where v can be individual or predicative.

(B) Check that whenever $\vdash_{C_2^-}\varphi$ then $\varphi^* = T$. But $\gamma^* = F$. That proves that $\exists xX\, Xx$ is not a theorem in C_2^-. (For every rule of the general form

$$\frac{\begin{array}{lll}\Omega & \varphi \hookrightarrow & \psi \\ \Omega' & \varphi' \hookrightarrow & \psi'\end{array}}{\begin{array}{lll}\Theta & \hookrightarrow & \beta\end{array}}$$

you should check this: If $((\bigwedge_{\alpha\in\Omega} \alpha \wedge \varphi) \rightarrow \psi)^* = T$ and

$$((\bigwedge_{\alpha\in\Omega'} \alpha \wedge \varphi') \rightarrow \psi')^* = T \text{ then } (\bigwedge_{\alpha\in\Theta} \alpha \rightarrow \beta)^* = T.)$$

4.2. Incompleteness of second order logic in standard structures (strong sense).

To see that the strong completeness theorem does not hold in **SOL** we will see that there is a sentence which is a standard consequence of a set of sentences but it is not derivable from it in any of our calculi (in fact, in any sound calculus with finite rules of proof).

In I.4.9 we saw that strong completeness is impossible with standard semantics. Now we will prove this in more detail.

4.2.1. Theorem.

In L_2 there are a set of sentences Γ and a sentence γ such that $\Gamma \vDash_{S.S} \gamma$ but it is not the case that $\Gamma \vdash \gamma$ in any of our second order calculi.

Proof

Take the set of formulas $\Gamma = \{\varphi_n \,/\, n \geq 2\}$ saying that there are at least n elements and, as γ, an axiom of infinity. It is obvious that $\Gamma \vDash_{S.S} \gamma$.

To prove that $\Gamma \vdash_{CAL} \gamma$ is not the case, assume that $\Gamma \vdash_{CAL} \gamma$ in one of our calculi, C_2 or λ-C_2. Using the finiteness of deduction (definition 2.5), there is a finite sequence of elements of Γ, $\Omega \subseteq \Gamma$ such that $\Omega \hookrightarrow \gamma$ is a sequent in the calculus. But all our calculi are sound in the standard sense (sections 3.1, 3.2 and 3.3). Therefore, $\Omega \vDash_{S.S} \gamma$.

But the finite set Ω has finite models, since there is a φ_m in it with a maximum subscript, while the formula γ expresses infinity. Therefore, $\Omega \nvDash_{S.S} \gamma$ and we have a contradiction. Thus $\Gamma \vdash_{CAL} \gamma$ cannot hold. ∎

4.3. Incompleteness of second order logic in standard structures (weak sense).

Well known incompleteness proofs in the literature.

According to the weak incompleteness theorem of second order logic, there is no calculus for this logic able to select the set of standard validities. We have seen above that, due to the expressive power of standard second order logic, there is not a complete calculus in the strong sense. We also realize that Gödel's incompleteness theorem applies and, consequently, there is no complete calculus in the weak sense either. (A proof of incompleteness of **SOL** based on the incompleteness of arithmetic will appear in Chapter III.) There is an alternative proof of Gödel's weak incompleteness theorem: Using the expressive power of **SOL**, in particular the fact that finiteness is expressible in the language, we can obtain from Trahtenbrot's theorem the incompleteness of second order logic[22]. Here Trahtenbrot's theorem says that the set of **SOL**-sentences valid in all finite structures is not enumerable.

Fundamental basis of this proof.

In what follows I will sketch another incompleteness proof based on Sain [1979]. This proof also uses the expressive power of standard second order logic.

To follow the proof we have to be aware of the basic ontologic and semantic assumptions we make in classical logic. Apart from these, in the proof we are using well known results, tricks and techniques of set theory. Finally, we use the expressive power of **SOL** and a set-theoretic presentation of **SOL** specially designed for this proof. Thus, the proof is based four basic ideas:

(1) We should know what the ***assumptions we necessarily make when choosing classical logic*** are. Namely, that we are placed in "a" mathematical universe of sets which is our environment and that we introduce the formal (object) language to talk about structures in this mathematical universe. **SOL** is now our object language. As was mentioned already in I.4.8, it should be stressed that while there is no need to assume that there exists a unique mathematical universe, we have to accept that in our object language we can only talk about sets in one environment at once. Moreover, the object language cannot be used to talk about "the" mathematical universe as a whole. The reason for the last restriction is that we use Tarski's semantics; *i.e.*, we do want to carefully distinguish object language and metalanguage, since we do not want to contradict Tarski's theorem of undefinability of truth (which is a reproduction of the liar's paradox you will see described in Chapter V).

(2) We accept ZFC as our ***background set theory***. The axioms of ZFC are written in a language $L^{\in}$ of first order having a binary relation constant, $\in$, as the only non-logical symbol. This **FOL** is not our object language, but we consider it as part of our

[22]See Ebbinghaus, Flum & Thomas [1984], page 162.

metalanguage and its sentences can be seen as abbreviations of English sentences. Since they are just metalanguage, they are true or false, and when we quantify over all sets we do quantify over the whole class of all sets. But can we define truth and consequence of metalanguage in metalanguage? Are we not trapped in the very same black hole? Moreover, how can we express the change of mathematical universe?

(3) What we can do is to use some well known ***tricks, techniques and results of meta-set theory***. Specifically, the tricks used in relative consistency proofs and Gödel's and Cohen's results about the independence from ZFC of both the generalized continuum hypothesis and the negation of this hypothesis.

We think that our world now contains classes and $L^{\in}$ is a formal language for this new world. So we take Gödel-Bernays-Neumann (GBN) set theory as our underlying set theory in metalanguage using a first order language, $L^{\in}$, for our convenience. This is the usual move in consistency proofs[23] of set theory. To keep in a safe position we do as usual; we prove our formal theorems in a first order calculus, soundness is assumed, but we do not use completeness. Thus, we can use the fact that a set of sentences with a model is consistent, but not the reverse.

The difference of GBN from the better known Zermelo-Fraenkel set theory, ZF, is rather important for us: in GBN we can consider structures whose universes are proper classes instead of just sets. We may even consider $\mathcal{U} = \langle \mathcal{V}, \in^{\mathcal{U}} \rangle$, where $\mathcal{V}$ is the class of all sets, which we can consider fixed for the time being, otherwise unknown. $\mathcal{U}$ is not a structure in the usual sense - ***i.e.***, for no object language whatsoever -, since it has a proper class as a universe, but it can be considered in GBN.

There is an alternative trick, also common in consistency proofs, which is a relative interpretation of set theory into itself[24]. We can accept as classes "collections" of sets which are defined by formulas of $L^{\in}$, even when their existence is not ensured by any axiom of our metatheory. In this context, classes can be identified with the formulas defining them. For example, $x=x$ is the current mathematical universe. Moreover, the membership relation of a class need not be the global membership relation but could be any formula of $L^{\in}$ defining a binary relation. Thus, we can say that a class structure of set theory is a pair $\langle \mathbf{M}, \mathrm{E} \rangle$ where $\mathbf{M}$ and E are formulas; $\mathbf{M}$ defines the universe of the class structure and E its peculiar membership relation. To express the truth of a

[23]See Kunen [1980], page 110.

[24]Ibid. page 141. Both tricks are basically the same, but I prefer to use GBN in the main proof (theorem 4.3.6 below) and the relativization to formulas in the alternative proof (theorem 4.3.8).

formula φ in this class structure, we write derivability in background set theory of the formula obtained from φ by relativization to **M** and replacement of the membership sign by **E**. Thus,

"$\langle \mathbf{M},\mathbf{E}\rangle$ is a class model of φ" is now understood as "ZFC $\vdash \varphi^{\langle \mathbf{M},\mathbf{E}\rangle}$" (where $\varphi^{\langle \mathbf{M},\mathbf{E}\rangle}$ is relativized as defined below)

(4) We will use also the overwhelming *expressive power of* **SOL**, especially, its ability to express properties of our mathematical universe and, in particular, properties which are able to distinguish one mathematical universe from another; *i.e.*, formulas which are independent of ZFC. Please recall that we have a **SOL** formula, φ_{GCH}, such that

$$\models_{\mathcal{S.S}} \varphi_{\mathrm{GCH}} \text{ iff GCH holds in "the" mathematical universe}$$

General idea of the proof.

The original idea of this proof is that we can provide a set-theoretic development of second order logic; that is, in the mathematical universe of set theory we can find substitutes for the **SOL** formulas and so - since our formulas are treated as sets, we can talk about our formulas in the language of set theory, $L^{\in}$, exactly as we do with any other sets. In fact, we can use that the set of formulas of second order logic is definable in the math universe using the language of set theory. Also the concept of standard structure and the concept of validity can be defined set-theoretically. One can give a natural set-theoretical description of the notions of sequent and derivation, developing the whole syntax set-theoretically. We can easily agree that the mathematical resources needed for this task aren't very deep and the set-theoretical formulas used to define provability are of a very simple character, since they are what are usually termed persistent formulas. Finally, even the completeness theorem of second order logic can be formalized as a sentence of $L^{\in}$. If it were complete, the mathematical proof of completeness would have to be established with limited resources, *i.e.*, in the axiomatic basis of set theory (ZFC).

Then, using the known theorems of Cohen and Gödel, we can obtain the incompleteness of **SOL** from the fact that the generalized continuum hypothesis is expressible in **SOL**. That means that there is a formula φ_{GCH} such that this formula is valid in the standard semantics if and only if GCH holds in the mathematical universe we are assuming we are in when defining the semantic for **SOL**. Thus, when Cohen's model is considered as our enviroment, φ_{GCH} cannot be valid, but φ_{GCH} is valid when Gödel's model is taken as our enviroment. Of course, that the second order formula expressing the generalized continuum hypothesis is valid in one environment and not valid in another is not a contradiction, but nevertheless it is telling you already that something is getting wrong with the standard semantics.

It is important to see that the real contradiction we will obtain is that φ_{GCH} must be valid and must not be valid in the "same" mathematical enviroment. To obtain this contradiction the completeness of second order logic is assumed.

Let us term **CAL** the second order calculus of your choice; it could be C_2, λ-C_2 or any other of your preference.

The substance of the proof rest on the unbalanced relation between the set-theoretical formulas expressing $\vdash_{\mathbf{CAL}} \varphi_{\mathrm{GCH}}$ and $\models_{\mathcal{S}.\mathcal{S}} \varphi_{\mathrm{GCH}}$. While the first one is a persistent formula whose truth value does not change when we go up from a transitive class of sets to a wider one, the second one does change since the meaning of φ_{GCH} is involved.

Thus, the $L^{\in}$ formulas expressing provability and validity of this formula φ_{GCH} cannot be equivalent, as required by the completeness theorem.

Summarizing, $\vdash_{\mathbf{CAL}} \varphi_{\mathrm{GCH}}$ is persistent while $\models_{\mathcal{S}.\mathcal{S}} \varphi_{\mathrm{GCH}}$ is not, hence they can not coincide.

4.3.1. Preliminary definitions.

We introduce a first order language (**FOL**) to talk about sets. Our language only contains a binary relation symbol, $\in$, individual variables and logical symbols, including equality. Using formulas of this language we can syntactically extend the set of its operation constants by the common definitions for $\subseteq$, $\cap$, $\cup$, etc. To refer to this language we use the symbol $L^{\in}$.

The concepts and definitions to be introduced below for **FOL** correspond with the definitions introduced in section 4.7 of Chapter I for **SOL**. Given a set of sets, **B**, the structure implicitly considered is $\mathcal{B} = \langle \mathbf{B}, \in \rangle$, where $\in$ is the global relation of membership restricted to **B**. We use the same symbol for the membership relation in the structure and for the predicate of the language and rely on the context to distinguish them. We will also use first order structures $\mathcal{A} = \langle \mathrm{A}, \in^{\mathcal{A}} \rangle$, where $\in^{\mathcal{A}}$ is a binary relation on A (not necessarily the global one of membership).

Notation.

Given a set of sets **B**, a binary relation on **B**, $\in^{\mathcal{B}}$, a formula φ of **FORM**($L^{\in}$) and a sequence of variables $\langle x,y_1,...,y_n\rangle$, with $\mathbf{FREE}(\varphi) \subseteq \{x, y_1,...,y_n\}$ and sets $\mathbf{y}_1,...,\mathbf{y}_n \in \mathbf{B}$ you can introduce the notation

$$\langle \mathbf{B},\epsilon^{\mathcal{B}}\rangle \left[{}^{\mathbf{x}\,\mathbf{y}_1...\mathbf{y}_n}_{x\,y_1...y_n}\right] \text{ sat } \varphi$$

using for **FOL** an abbreviation corresponding to 5.1.2 of Chapter I. ▓

(Also the notation $\langle \mathbf{B},\epsilon^{\mathcal{B}}\rangle$ $[\mathbf{x}\,\mathbf{y}_1...\mathbf{y}_n]$ sat φ will be used.) ▓

Parametrically definable sets.

Given a set of sets, **B**, a binary relation on **B**, $\epsilon^{\mathcal{B}}$, a structure $\mathcal{B} = \langle \mathbf{B},\epsilon^{\mathcal{B}}\rangle$, and a set $\mathbf{X} \subseteq \mathbf{B}$, we say that the subset **X** ***is parametrically definable in*** $\mathcal{B}$ if and only if there exist a formula φ of L^{ϵ} and a sequence of variables $\langle x,y_1,...,y_n\rangle$, with $\mathbf{FREE}(\varphi) \subseteq \{x, y_1,...,y_n\}$ and sets $\mathbf{y}_1,...,\mathbf{y}_n \in \mathbf{B}$ such that

$$\mathbf{X} = \{\mathbf{x} \in \mathbf{B} \,/\, \langle \mathbf{B},\epsilon^{\mathcal{B}}\rangle \left[{}^{\mathbf{x}\,\mathbf{y}_1...\mathbf{y}_n}_{x\,y_1...y_n}\right] \text{ sat } \varphi\}$$ ▓

$\text{PARAM.DEF.}(\mathcal{B},L^{\epsilon}) = \{\mathbf{X} \subseteq \mathbf{B} \,/\, \mathbf{X} \text{ is parametrically definable in } \mathcal{B}\}$. ▓

Relative interpretation.

A ***relative interpretation*** of set theory into itself consists of two formulas, $\mathrm{M}(x,v)$ and $\mathrm{E}(x,y,v)$, with no other free variables than the ones shown and where v serves as a parameter. ▓

Class structure.

For a non-empty collection of sets, **C**, and a binary relation on it, $\epsilon^{\mathcal{C}}$, we introduce the class structure, $\mathcal{C} = \langle \mathbf{C},\epsilon^{\mathcal{C}}\rangle$ and we extend the usual semantic concepts of model of a formula, definability of a relation and other similar ones. ▓

Given a relative interpretation in terms of formulas **M** and **E**, we can certainly consider $\langle \mathbf{M},\mathbf{E}\rangle$ as a class structure. ▓

Substructure.

For class structures $\mathcal{A}$ and $\mathcal{B}$ we extend the notion of substructure writing $\mathcal{A} \sqsubseteq \mathcal{B}$ (similar definition as in I.3.2). ▓

4.3.2. More set theory.

Sets and classes in Gödel-Bernays-Neumann.

The only difference with the Zermelo hierarchy of sets is that GBN closes up because we add a top level where we allow as classes all collections of sets from $\mathcal{V}$; even the whole class of the ordinals, Ω, or the universal class of all sets, $\mathcal{V}$.

In GBN we have a comprehension principle for classes. Intuitively, the comprehension principle says that any definable subcollection of $\mathcal{V}$ constructed above is added to $\mathcal{V}$, and we obtain $\mathcal{V}^+$ this way. Thus,

$$\mathcal{V}^+ = \mathcal{V} \cup \{\{x \in \mathcal{V} / \varphi\} / \varphi \in \text{FORM}(L^{\in})\}$$

(the bound variables in the formula φ are for sets only).

The constructible universe.

Inside any Zermelo-Fraenkel model, $\mathcal{U} = \langle \mathcal{V}, \in^{\mathcal{U}} \rangle$, lies a usually smaller submodel; it is its constructible part. In a technical sense, the constructible part of a model of ZF is its smallest submodel containing the ordinal numbers and still being a model of ZF.

By analogy with the Zermelo hierarchy of sets $\mathcal{V}(\alpha)$, where α is an ordinal, we will give a picture of the constructible hierarchy of sets $\mathcal{L}(\alpha)$. We begin with the empty set as in $\mathcal{V}$, at limit ordinals we collect, as before, everything together. The only difference affects the crucial step α+1: while in $\mathcal{V}(\alpha+1)$ we were taking all the subsets of $\mathcal{V}(\alpha)$, in $\mathcal{L}(\alpha+1)$ we will take a selection of them. In forming $\mathcal{V}(\alpha+1)$ we defined $\mathcal{V}(\alpha+1) = \mathcal{P}\,\mathcal{V}(\alpha)$, including in $\mathcal{V}(\alpha+1)$ sets that could never be defined in our formal language $L^{\in}$, sets only chosen on the basis of the weak quality of being a subset. But this quality does not describe its members in a tight way, so we do not know what sets we are accepting. On the other hand, in forming $\mathcal{L}(\alpha+1)$ we will take only the definable subsets of $\mathcal{L}(\alpha)$. Thus, we form by recursion on the ordinal numbers the hierarchy of sets as follows:

For $\alpha = 0$, then $\mathcal{L}(\alpha) = \emptyset$.

If $\alpha = \beta+1$, then $\mathcal{L}(\alpha) = \text{PARAM.DEF}(\mathscr{L}(\beta), L^{\in})$ (where $\mathscr{L}(\beta) = \langle \mathcal{L}(\beta), \in^{\mathcal{U}} \cap \mathcal{L}(\beta)^2 \rangle$).

If α is a limit ordinal, then $\mathcal{L}(\alpha) = \bigcup_{\beta<\alpha} \mathcal{L}(\beta)$.

A set X is said to be ***constructible*** iff there is an α such that $X \in \mathcal{L}(\alpha)$. The class of constructible sets is called the ***constructible universe*** and is denoted by $\mathcal{L}$. Thus

$$\mathcal{L} = \bigcup_{\beta \in \Omega} \mathcal{L}(\beta).$$

Comparing $\mathcal{L}$ with the Zermelo hierarchy, it is clear that $\mathcal{L}(\alpha) \subseteq \mathcal{V}(\alpha)$ for all α. In fact, since finite sets can be easily defined, $\mathcal{L}(n) = \mathcal{V}(n)$ and so $\mathcal{L}(\omega) = \mathcal{V}(\omega)$. But, usually, $\mathcal{L}(\omega+1) \neq \mathcal{V}(\omega+1)$ because in $\mathcal{P}\omega$ there can be up to uncountably many sets and only a countable number of them are definable because we only have a countable number of formulas in $L^{\in}$. It is also easily seen that $\mathcal{L}(\alpha) \subseteq \mathcal{L}(\beta)$ when $\alpha \leq \beta$. But, if you compare the growth of this hierarchy with Zermelo's, the rate of the constructible one is quite slow.

The axiom of constructibility.

The axiom of constructibility is equivalent to the assertion that every set is constructible. That means that we only accept as sets the constructible ones. In an informal way we can state this axiom as $\mathcal{V} = \mathcal{L}$. Once you have the ordinals and the constructible sets, it can be expressed as $\forall x\, \Lambda(x)$, where $\forall x\, \Lambda(x)$ is the formula

$$\forall x \exists y\, (y \in \Omega \wedge x \in \mathcal{L}(y))$$

4.3.3. Characterizing some special classes of formulas[25].

As we mentioned above, when we take Gödel-Bernays–Neumann as the underlying set theory, we can consider models whose universes are classes rather than sets. We may even consider $\mathcal{U} = \langle \mathcal{V}, \in^{\mathcal{U}} \rangle$, where $\mathcal{V}$ is the class of all sets of our present mathematical universe, which we consider fixed, otherwise unknown. $\mathcal{U}$ is not a model in the usual sense (since its universe is not a set but a proper class), but it is a "model" in Gödel-Bernays-Neumann. We can extend some of the model-theoretic notation to models whose universe is a proper class but bearing in mind that we are in fact doing a trick and that our notions are introduced only in the metalanguage.

Definition 1: Truth in a class structure.

For proper class structures we have introduced the concept

$$\langle \mathcal{V}, \in^{\mathcal{U}} \rangle \left[{}^{a_1 \ldots a_n}_{x_1 \ldots x_n}\right] \textit{ is a model of } \varphi$$

(for a formula φ of the first order language $L^{\in}$, where FREE(φ) $\subseteq \{x_1,\ldots,x_n\}$, and sets $a_1,\ldots,a_n$). Based on it we also introduce:

$$\varphi \text{ is } \textit{true} \text{ for } a_1,\ldots,a_n \text{ iff } \langle \mathcal{V}, \in^{\mathcal{U}} \rangle \left[{}^{a_1 \ldots a_n}_{x_1 \ldots x_n}\right] \text{ is a model of } \varphi$$

(because we are taking $\mathcal{U} = \langle \mathcal{V}, \in^{\mathcal{U}} \rangle$ as "the" universe). ▮

[25]The definitions stated here come from Barwise [1975], Chapter I and Kunen [1980], Chapter IV.

Definition 2: Relativization.

If φ is a formula of $L^{\in}$ and $\langle \mathbf{M},\mathbf{E}\rangle$ is a relative interpretation, the ***relativization*** of φ to $\langle \mathbf{M},\mathbf{E}\rangle$, written $\varphi^{\langle \mathbf{M},\mathbf{E}\rangle}$, is the formula obtained from φ by replacing in φ every part of it of the form $x \in y$ by $\mathbf{M}(x) \wedge \mathbf{M}(y) \wedge \mathbf{E}(x,y)$, every existential quantifier $\exists x\, \psi$ by $\exists x\, (\mathbf{M}(x) \wedge \psi)$ and every part of it of the form $\forall x\, \psi$ by $\forall x\, (\mathbf{M}(x) \rightarrow \psi)$. ▒

(When $\mathbf{E}(x,y)$ is $x \in y$ we can omit the reference to $\mathbf{E}$ and simply write $\varphi^{\mathbf{M}}$.)

We call $\exists x\, (\mathbf{M}(x) \wedge \varphi)$ a ***bounded*** (or limited) quantifier. A formula where all quantifiers are bounded is a ***bounded formula.*** ▒

Remark.

In fact, definition 2 should have been made by recursion on the formation of formulas, defining precisely what to do at every step. Can you please do this?.

Definition 3.

For every class structure $\mathcal{M}$ based upon the relative interpretation $\langle \mathbf{M},\mathbf{E}\rangle$ (where $\mathcal{M}$ and $\langle \mathbf{M},\mathbf{E}\rangle$ can be identified):

$\mathcal{M}$ ***is a model of*** φ iff $\mathrm{ZFC} \vdash \varphi^{\langle \mathbf{M},\mathbf{E}\rangle}$ ▒

(when $\mathbf{FREE}(\varphi) \subseteq \{x_1,\ldots,x_n\}$ we can certainly extend the notation to deal with open formulas by giving a suitable interpretation of $x_1,\ldots,x_n$ as classes).

We can write $\varphi^{\langle \mathbf{M},\mathbf{E}\rangle}$ is ***true*** for the same thing. ▒

Definition 4.

Let φ be a formula of $L^{\in}$ such that $\mathbf{FREE}(\varphi) \subseteq \{x_1,\ldots,x_n\}$, $\mathcal{A} = \langle \mathbf{A}, \in^{\mathcal{A}}\rangle$ and $\mathcal{U} = \langle \mathcal{V}, \in^{\mathcal{U}}\rangle$. Let $\mathcal{A} \sqsubseteq \mathcal{U}$ and $\mathbf{A}$ be a transitive class.

(where a transitive class $\mathbf{X}$ satisfies: if $\mathbf{Y} \in^{\mathcal{U}} \mathbf{Z} \in^{\mathcal{U}} \mathbf{X}$, then $\mathbf{Y} \in^{\mathcal{U}} \mathbf{X}$).

φ is ***absolute*** for $\mathbf{A}$ iff for all $\mathbf{a}_1,\ldots,\mathbf{a}_n \in \mathbf{A}$:

$\mathcal{U}[\mathbf{a}_1,\ldots,\mathbf{a}_n]$ satisfies φ iff $\mathcal{A}[\mathbf{a}_1,\ldots,\mathbf{a}_n]$ satisfies φ ▒

The last condition can, in relative interpretations, be expressed as

$$\mathrm{ZFC} \vdash (\varphi \leftrightarrow \varphi^{\langle \mathbf{A}, \in^{\mathcal{A}}\rangle})(\mathbf{a}_1,\ldots,\mathbf{a}_n)$$

(where the reference to "the" current world is omitted, since we identify it with $x{=}x$). ▒

Also, a formula φ is ***absolute relative to a theory*** T for the transitive substructure $\mathcal{A} \sqsubseteq \mathcal{U}$ of a T-model $\mathcal{U}$ iff for all $a_1,...,a_n \in A$:

$\mathcal{U}[a_1,...,a_n]$ satisfies φ iff $\mathcal{A}[a_1,...,a_n]$ satisfies φ ▓

Definition 5.

Let φ be a formula of $L^{\in}$ such that $\text{FREE}(\varphi) \subseteq \{x_1,...,x_n\}$, $\mathcal{A} = \langle A, \in^{\mathcal{A}} \rangle$ and $\mathcal{U} = \langle V, \in^{\mathcal{U}} \rangle$. Let $\mathcal{A} \sqsubseteq \mathcal{U}$ and A be a transitive class.

φ is ***persistent*** for A iff for all $a_1,...,a_n \in A$:

$\mathcal{A}[a_1,...,a_n]$ satisfies φ implies $\mathcal{U}[a_1,...,a_n]$ satisfies φ ▓

On the other hand, the formula φ is ***persistent relative to a theory*** T for the transitive substructure $\mathcal{A} \sqsubseteq \mathcal{U}$ of a T-model $\mathcal{U}$ iff for all $a_1,...,a_n \in A$:

$\mathcal{A}[a_1,...,a_n]$ satisfies φ implies $\mathcal{U}[a_1,...,a_n]$ satisfies φ ▓

(The last condition can, in relative interpretations, be expressed as

$$\text{ZFC} \vdash (\varphi^{\langle A, \in^{\mathcal{A}} \rangle} \to \varphi)(a_1,...,a_n).)$$

Remark.

In the proof we will use a model $\mathcal{U}$ and its constructible part $\mathcal{L}$. The significance of these definitions is of great importance. Absolute formulas don't shift their meaning as we move from the model $\mathcal{L}$ to $\mathcal{U}$ and back again. Persistent formulas persist as we go up from $\mathcal{L}$ to $\mathcal{U}$; the truth of a persistent formula is not affected when we add new sets to our universe of set theory.

Definition 6.

Let Δ_0 be the class of $L^{\in}$ formulas which are ***bound*** formulas. We can define precisely what they are as follows:

The Δ_0 formulas are those built up inductively by the following rules:

(1) $x \in y$ and $x = y$ are Δ_0.

(2) If φ and ψ are Δ_0, so are $\neg\varphi$, $\varphi \wedge \psi$, $\varphi \vee \psi$, $\varphi \to \psi$ and $\varphi \leftrightarrow \psi$.

(3) If φ is Δ_0, so are $\exists x\,(x \in y \wedge \varphi)$ and $\forall x\,(x \in y \to \varphi)$. ▓

Σ_1 is the set of formulas of the form $\exists x_1 ... x_n\ \varphi$ with $\varphi \in \Delta_0$. ▓

4.3.4. The theorems of Gödel and Cohen.

In what follows we will state the well known theorems of Cohen and Gödel[26] as well as a preliminary result on absolute formulas.

Theorem 1.

(1) Every atomic formula is absolute for $\mathcal{L}$ as well as for every transitive class **B** (relative to any theory T).

(2) Every Δ_0 formula is absolute (relative to any theory T) for $\mathcal{L}$ and for every transitive class B, including the sets $\mathcal{L}(\alpha)$.

(3) Every Σ_1 formula is persistent for $\mathcal{L}$ (relative to any theory T).

Theorem 2. (Gödel)

Let ZFL denote ZF+axiom of constructibility.

If ZF is consistent and $\mathcal{U} = \langle \mathcal{V}, \in^{\mathcal{U}} \rangle$ is a model of ZF and $\mathscr{L} = \langle \mathcal{L}, \in^{\mathscr{L}} \rangle$ (where $\mathscr{L} \sqsubseteq \mathcal{U}$; *i.e.*, $\in^{\mathscr{L}} = \in^{\mathcal{U}} \cap (\mathcal{L} \times \mathcal{L})$) is the constructible part of it,

(1) $\mathscr{L}$ is a model of ZFL.

(2) $\mathscr{L}$ is a model of C (where C is the axiom of choice).

(3) $\mathscr{L}$ is a model of GCH.

The formal proof of the preceding theorem can be carried out in ZF and so:

Theorem 3.

(1) $\text{ZF} \vdash \text{ZFL}^{\Lambda(x)}$.

(2) $\text{ZFL} \vdash \text{C}$.

(3) $\text{ZFL} \vdash \text{GCH}$.

(4) $\text{ZFC} \vdash \text{GCH}^{\Lambda(x)}$.

Theorem 4. (Cohen)

If Zermelo-Fraenkel is consistent, then there is a model of ZFC+ ¬GCH. That is, a model of set theory with choice where the generalized continuum hypothesis is not true.

4.3.5. Set-theoretical presentation of SOL.

We will assume that our present mathematical universe is $\mathcal{U} = \langle \mathcal{V}, \in^{\mathcal{U}} \rangle$, that its constructible

[26] For a proof of them see Kunen [1983], Chapters VI and VII, pages 173 and 204.

part is $\mathscr{L} = \langle \mathcal{L}, \in^{\mathscr{L}} \rangle$ and that the second order language we are talking about is L_2 with the standard semantics of Chapter I. Finally, the language of set theory used is $L^{\in}$.

The propositions stated below follow from Sain [1979]

Proposition 1: One can provide a set-theoretical presentation of the formal language L_2. That is:

(1) $\mathbf{FORM}(L_2) \subseteq \mathcal{L}(\omega)$, where $\mathcal{L}(\omega) \subseteq \mathcal{V}$ is the set of hereditarily finite elements of $\mathcal{V}$. This is true since formulas are finite strings of symbols and we can match the symbols of L_2 with certain sets in $\mathcal{L}(\omega)$.

(2) $\mathbf{FORM}(L_2) = \{\varphi \in \mathcal{V} \mid \mathcal{U}\ [\varphi] \text{ sat } \xi\}$, where ξ is a set-theoretical formula, written in $L^{\in}$ (the language of set theory) with $\mathbf{FREE}(\xi) \subseteq \{x\}$. This formula defines in the mathematical universe, $\mathcal{U}$, the set $\mathbf{FORM}(L_2)$.

(3) For any $\varphi \in \mathbf{FORM}(L_2)$ there is a mathematical proof of this fact, expressed by

$$\text{ZFC} \vdash \text{"}[\varphi \in \mathbf{FORM}(L_2)]\text{"}, \text{ where "}[\varphi \in \mathbf{FORM}(L_2)]\text{" is a formula of } L^{\in}$$

(The formula "$[\varphi \in \mathbf{FORM}(L_2)]$" of $L^{\in}$ exists because both φ and $\mathbf{FORM}(L_2)$ are definable in $\mathcal{L}(\omega)$.)

For every $z \in \mathcal{L}(\omega)$, there is a name for it in the language of set theory whose denotation in $\mathcal{U}$ is precisely $\bar{z}$. In fact,

$$\text{"}[\varphi \in \mathbf{FORM}(L_2)]\text{" is the formula } \xi\frac{\bar{\varphi}}{x}.)$$

Proposition 2: The semantic concept of standard structure can be introduced set-theoretically. Structures are sets and can be defined by a formula η of $L^{\in}$. That is,

$$\mathcal{S.S} = \{\mathcal{A} \in \mathcal{V} \mid \mathcal{U}\ [\mathcal{A}] \text{ sat } \eta\}$$

(where η is a set-theoretical formula, written in the language $L^{\in}$, with $\mathbf{FREE}(\eta) \subseteq \{y\}$; this formula defines in the mathematical universe, $\mathcal{U}$, the class $\mathcal{S.S}$).

Proposition 3: The concepts of truth of a **SOL** formula in a standard second order structure and of validity can also be introduced set-theoretically.

(1) The binary relation of truth is

$$\mathbf{TRUTH}(\vDash_{\mathcal{S.S}}) = \{\langle \mathcal{A}, \varphi \rangle \in \mathcal{V} \times \mathcal{V} \mid \mathcal{U}\ [\mathcal{A}, \varphi] \text{ sat } \mathcal{K}\}$$

(where $\mathcal{K}$ is a set-theoretical formula, written in the language $L^{\in}$, with

FREE($\mathcal{K}$) $\subseteq \{z,v\}$; this formula defines in the mathematical universe, $\mathcal{U}$, the binary relation of truth of a formula in a structure).

(2) $\models_{\mathcal{S.S}} \psi$ iff $\mathcal{U}$ is a model of "$[\models_{\mathcal{S.S}} \psi]$", where "$[\models_{\mathcal{S.S}} \psi]$" is a formula of $L^{\in}$; namely the formula $\forall x\,(\eta\frac{x}{y} \rightarrow \mathcal{K}\frac{x\overline{\psi}}{zv})$.

(3) If PROP is a formula of $L^{\in}$ abbreviating a property $\mathcal{P}$ of the mathematical universe which can also be expressed in **SOL** by the formula φ_{PROP}, the following equivalences hold:

(3.a) $\mathcal{P}$ holds iff PROP holds
iff $\mathcal{U}$ is a model of PROP

(in accordance with our use of the language $L^{\in}$)

Also,

(3.b) $\models_{\mathcal{S.S}} \varphi_{\text{PROP}}$ iff PROP holds
iff $\mathcal{U}$ is a model of PROP

(because it is a property which can be expressed in L_2)

Furthermore,

(3.c) $\models_{\mathcal{S.S}} \varphi_{\text{PROP}}$ iff $\mathcal{U}$ is a model of "$[\models_{\mathcal{S.S}} \varphi_{\text{PROP}}]$"

(since validity of **SOL** formulas in $\mathcal{S.S}$ is a property of sets expressible in $L^{\in}$)

Finally, from mathematical experience and (3.b) & (3.c) above, we know that in most cases,

(3.d) $\models_{\mathcal{S.S}} \varphi_{\text{PROP}}$ iff PROP holds

is equivalent to

$$\text{ZFC} \vdash \text{"}[\models_{\mathcal{S.S}} \varphi_{\text{PROP}}]\text{"} \leftrightarrow \text{PROP}$$

Proposition 4. It is possible to give a natural set-theoretical description of the notions of sequent and derivation, developing the whole syntax set-theoretically. We can do this for our calculus C_2, or for any other. For this task the mathematical resources which are needed aren't very deep and the set-theoretical formula used to define the binary relation of ***being a proof of*** is absolute, while the formula defining the unary relation of ***is provable*** is persistent.

Let us assume that there is a calculus **CAL** for second order logic, we then express provability in **CAL** in set-theoretic terms; then, for any $\varphi \in$ **FORM**(L_2),

(1) $\vdash_{\text{CAL}} \varphi$ iff $\mathcal{U}$ is a model of "$[\vdash_{\text{CAL}} \varphi]$".

But "$[\vdash_{\text{CAL}} \varphi]$" is a persistent formula of $L^{\in}$ roughly saying $\exists x\,(x$ is a proof of $\overline{\varphi})$.

Thus:

(2) $\mathscr{L}$ is a model of "[$\vdash_{\mathbf{CAL}}\ \varphi$]" implies $\mathscr{U}$ is a model of "[$\vdash_{\mathbf{CAL}}\ \varphi$]"
(recall that $\mathscr{U}$ is our universe and $\mathscr{L}$ is its constructible part).
Using relative interpretation we express the above as:

(3) ZFC $\vdash$ "[$\vdash_{\mathbf{CAL}}\ \varphi$]"$^{\Lambda(x)}$ $\rightarrow$ "[$\vdash_{\mathbf{CAL}}\ \varphi$]".

Initial assumption 5. The completeness theorem can be formalized as an $L^{\in}$ sentence. A completeness proof for a complete logic has to be a mathematical proof and so it should be able to be carried out in the axiomatic basis of set theory. Therefore, if **CAL** were complete, its proof should be established in ZFC and so

ZFC$\vdash$ "[**CAL** is complete for ***S.S***]"

where "[CAL is complete for ***S.S***]" is again a sentence of the set-theoretical language $L^{\in}$. Basically, this formula says

$$\forall x\ (\xi(x) \rightarrow (\forall y\ (\eta\frac{y}{z} \rightarrow \kappa\frac{y\ x}{z\ v}) \rightarrow \exists w\ (w \text{ is a proof of } x)))$$

Initial assumption 6. The soundness theorem can be formalized as an $L^{\in}$ sentence. Its mathematical proof has to be carried out in the axiomatic basis of set theory. Therefore, if **CAL** were sound, its proof should be established in ZFC and so

ZFC$\vdash$ "[**CAL** is sound for ***S.S***]"

where "[**CAL** is sound for ***S.S***]" is a sentence of the set-theoretical language $L^{\in}$. Basically, this formula says

$$\forall x\ (\xi(x) \rightarrow (\exists w\ (w \text{ is a proof of } x) \rightarrow \forall y\ (\eta\frac{y}{z} \rightarrow \kappa\frac{y\ x}{z\ v})))$$

Initial assumption 7. Using the two previous assumptions:

ZFC$\vdash$ "[**CAL** is sound & complete for ***S.S***]"
(if **CAL** were sound and complete for ***S.S***)

4.3.6. Incompleteness theorem.
No sound calculus of **SOL** can be proved to be complete for the standard models of second order logic (assuming that ZFC is consistent).

Proof
Assume that ZFC is consistent and that we have a sound calculus **CAL** for **SOL**. Accept also the initial assumptions 5, 6 and 7 of 4.3.5. By our theorem 4 of 4.3.4 (Cohen), there is a model $\mathcal{U} = \langle \mathcal{W}, \in^{\mathcal{U}} \rangle$ of ZFC+ ¬GCH. That is, a model of set theory where the generalized continuum hypothesis does not hold.

Let $\mathcal{L} \subseteq \mathcal{W}$ be the constructible part of it. Then, by our theorem 2 of 4.3.4 (Gödel), $\mathscr{L} = \langle \mathcal{L}, \in^{\mathscr{L}} \rangle$ is a model of GCH (where $\mathscr{L} \sqsubseteq \mathcal{U}$; that is, $\in^{\mathscr{L}} = \in^{\mathcal{U}} \cap (\mathcal{L} \times \mathcal{L})$).

As noted in I.4.8, in **SOL** we can express GCH by the formula φ_{GCH}. So we have

$\models_{\mathcal{S.S}} \varphi_{GCH}$ iff GCH holds in "the" set-theoretical universe.

Therefore, while confining ourselves to $\mathscr{L}$ as set-theoretical universe,

$\models_{\mathcal{S.S}} \varphi_{GCH}$

Since by (2) of proposition 3 of 4.3.5 validity can be introduced set-theoretically by a formula of $L^{\in}$, we have that the set-theoretic formula expressing it is true in the constructible universe. Thus,

(*) $\mathscr{L}$ is a model of "$[\models_{\mathcal{S.S}} \varphi_{GCH}]$"

Now assume that we have a calculus **CAL** for **SOL** which is sound and complete. Not only can we express these properties in the language of set theory, but also the proof can be proved in set theory using only limited resources; that is, resources contained in ZF (the axiom of choice is needed only when you want completeness for an uncountable language). Then, by our initial assumption 5 of 4.3.5,

ZFC ⊢ "[**CAL** is complete for $\mathcal{S.S}$]"

where, again, "[**CAL** is complete for $\mathcal{S.S}$]" is a sentence of $L^{\in}$.
Therefore, eliminating the quantification we obtain

ZFC ⊢ "$[\models_{\mathcal{S.S}} \varphi_{GCH}]$" → "$[\vdash_{CAL} \varphi_{GCH}]$"

Since $\mathscr{L}$ is a model of ZFC (by the above theorem 2 of 4.3.4) and we are assuming soundness in the background set theory, also

$\mathscr{L}$ is a model of "$[\models_{\mathcal{S.S}} \varphi_{GCH}]$" → "$[\vdash_{CAL} \varphi_{GCH}]$"

Therefore, using (*)

$\mathscr{L}$ is a model of "[$\vdash_{CAL} \varphi_{GCH}$]"

Now we take the crucial step: As was noted in proposition 4 of 4.3.5, the formula expressing provability in the calculus is of a very easy and peculiar kind since it is a persistent formula whose truth value does not change when we go from the constructible universe $\mathscr{L}$ to the whole of $\mathcal{U}$ (recall that $\mathcal{L}$ is a transitive subclass of $\mathcal{W}$).

$\mathcal{U}$ is a model of "[$\vdash_{CAL} \varphi_{GCH}$]"

We will see also that the formula of $L^{\in}$ expressing the validity of φ_{GCH} is true in $\mathcal{U}$. To get it we will use several facts: (1) that the soundness theorem of second order logic is provable in set theory from the axiomatic basis of ZFC, (2) that $\mathcal{U}$ is a model of ZFC and (3) soundness in the background set theory.

By initial assumption 6 of 4.3.5, the soundness theorem of second order calculus can be expressed set-theoretically and its proof is provable in set theory.

ZFC $\vdash$ "[CAL is sound for $\mathcal{S.S}$]"

Therefore,

ZFC $\vdash$ "[$\vdash_{CAL} \varphi_{GCH}$]" $\rightarrow$ "[$\models_{\mathcal{S.S}} \varphi_{GCH}$]"

Since $\mathcal{U}$ is a model of ZFC and we are assuming soundness in the background set theory, then

$\mathcal{U}$ is a model of "[$\models_{\mathcal{S.S}} \varphi_{GCH}$]"

Therefore, using again proposition 3 of 4.3.5, we have that when our set-theoretic universe is $\mathcal{U}$,

$\models_{\mathcal{S.S}} \varphi_{GCH}$

But $\mathcal{U}$ is not a model of GCH, according to our starting point; namely, $\mathcal{U}$ is Cohen's class model. Therefore, taking $\mathcal{U}$ as "the" set-theoretical universe,

$\not\models_{\mathcal{S.S}} \varphi_{GCH}$ (by proposition 3 of 4.3.5)

This is a contradiction. ∎

Remarks.
This proof applies to any logic which is not absolute. In addition, we can reproduce the proof for any formula which is both expressible in **SOL** and independent of ZFC.

4.3.7. Conclusion.

What is the conclusion of all this?

There is a lesson to be learnt from this result and this lesson has several possible readings.

(1) There is one reading in the old-fashioned conservative style: You should not give your logics so much expressive power because then they refuse to have the machinery of calculus ready for you to be used. (It is clear that you cannot have both: expressive power plus good logical properties. In fact, there is the theorem of Lindström proved more than twenty years ago saying that first order logic is the strongest logic where all three theorems of completeness, compactness and Löwenheim-Skolem are true together.)

(2) There is a more liberal reading admitting that we have made several mistakes when defining the standard semantics of second order logic. We are taking standard structures where we take power sets as universes for sets and relations. While we are doing that, we are taking the notion of subset from the background set theory (we are treating it as a "logical" notion, let us say, as equality in **FOL**, and taking it from the metalanguage). The problem is that the category of being a subset is not tight and we end up in a no absolute logic. But the whole definition of standard semantic can be considered a kind of mistake.

After meditating some time over the above argument, we conclude that the strong incompleteness result comes not from the basic nature of second order reasoning, but instead from the way we build the mathematical "model" of second order reasoning when defining the standard semantics. Roughly speaking, without wanting to do so, when building the mathematical definitions for second order logic, we caused a "side effect" by tying to our metatheory (ZFC) the semantics of the object logic (**SOL**). These side effects, ***i.e.***, these ties, bring about theorems which are of the kind called artifacts in natural sciences. That means, these theorems are consequences of our way of modeling the phenomenon under investigation and therefore do not illuminate the basic nature of the phenomenon (higher order reasoning) itself. These considerations led to the recent proliferation of absolute versions of nonabsolute logics.

The pioneer absolute version of a nonabsolute logic is Henkin [1949], for type theory. In Chapter IV we will adapt it for second order logic. And here is where we obtain the inversion of our results and we arrive at the happy end of this story: We can make **SOL** a complete logic by changing the semantics.

4.3.8. An alternative proof of theorem 4.3.6.

(This follows another incompleteness proof, which is basically a rewording of the previous one.)

No sound calculus of **SOL** can be proved to be complete for the standard models of second order logic (assuming that ZFC is consistent).

Proof

Assume that ZFC is consistent and that we have a sound calculus for **SOL**.

In **SOL** we can express GCH by a formula φ_{GCH}. Thus,

$\models_{\mathcal{S.S}} \varphi_{\text{GCH}}$ iff GCH holds

By (2) of proposition 3 in 4.3.5, for every **SOL** formula there is a formula of $L^{\in}$ expressing its validity. Furthermore, as noted in (3.d) of that proposition, from the axiomatic basis of set theory it is generally easy to prove the equivalence of the $L^{\in}$ formula expressing validity of a given **SOL** formula which formulates a certain property of the mathematical enviroment and its direct set-theoretic formulation. In particular, that applies for the generalized continuum hypothesis. So

(1) $\text{ZFC} \vdash \text{"}[\models_{\mathcal{S.S}} \varphi_{\text{GCH}}]\text{"} \leftrightarrow \text{GCH}$

Using only **FOL**, from (1) we obtain:

(2) $\text{ZFC} \vdash \text{"}[\models_{\mathcal{S.S}} \varphi_{\text{GCH}}]\text{"}^{\Lambda(x)} \leftrightarrow \text{GCH}^{\Lambda(x)}$

But, by Gödel's result (theorem 3 in 4.3.4)

(3) $\text{ZFC} \vdash \text{GCH}^{\Lambda(x)}$

From results in lines (2) and (3), using only the calculus of **FOL**,

(4) $\text{ZFC} \vdash \text{"}[\models_{\mathcal{S.S}} \varphi_{\text{GCH}}]\text{"}^{\Lambda(x)}$

Now assume that we have a proof of the soundness and completeness of **CAL** with standard semantics. According to assumption 7 in 4.3.5,

$\text{ZFC} \vdash$ "[**CAL** is sound and complete for $\mathcal{S.S}$]"

Therefore,

(5) $ZFC \vdash "[\models_{S.S}\ \varphi_{GCH}]" \leftrightarrow "[\vdash_{CAL}\ \varphi_{GCH}]"$

From (5), using only the rules of first order calculus,

(6) $ZFC \vdash "[\models_{S.S}\ \varphi_{GCH}]"^{\Lambda(x)} \leftrightarrow "[\vdash_{CAL}\ \varphi_{GCH}]"^{\Lambda(x)}$

From this, using line (4) and the calculus of **FOL**,

(7) $ZFC \vdash "[\vdash_{CAL}\ \varphi_{GCH}]"^{\Lambda(x)}$

But, according to our proposition 4 of 4.3.5, derivability in the sequent calculus is a persistent notion and we express it as:

$$ZFC \vdash "[\vdash_{CAL}\ \varphi_{GCH}]"^{\Lambda(x)} \rightarrow "[\vdash_{CAL}\ \varphi_{GCH}]"$$

Of course, from this and line (7) we obtain:

$$ZFC \vdash "[\vdash_{CAL}\ \varphi_{GCH}]"$$

From this line and (5) we also obtain:

$$ZFC \vdash "[\models_{S.S}\ \varphi_{GCH}]"$$

Now, using line (1),

$$ZFC \vdash GCH.$$

But this contradicts Cohen's result (Theorem 4 of 4.3.4), since we are assuming the consistency of ZFC and soundness in the metatheory. ▮

CHAPTER III
CATEGORICITY OF SECOND ORDER PEANO ARITHMETIC.

1.- INTRODUCTION.

I would like to introduce the subject by quoting Henkin [1960].

> According to modern standards of logical rigor, each branch of pure mathematics must be founded in one of two ways: either its basic concepts must be **defined** in terms of the concepts of some prior branch of mathematics, in which case its theorems are deduced from those of the prior branch of mathematics with the aid of these definitions, or else its basic concepts are taken as **undefined** and its theorems are deduced from a set of axioms involving these undefined terms.
>
> The natural numbers, 0, 1, 2, 3,..., are among those mathematical entities about which we learn at the earliest age, and our knowledge of these numbers and their properties is largely of an intuitive character. Nevertheless, if we wish to establish a precise mathematical theory of these numbers, we cannot rely on unformulated intuition as the basis of the theory but must found the theory in one of the two ways mentioned above. Actually, both ways are possible. Starting with pure logic and the most elementary portions of the theory of sets as prior mathematical sciences, the German mathematician Frege showed how the basic notions of the theory of numbers can be defined in such a way as to permit a full development of this theory. On the other hand the Italian mathematician Peano, taking **natural number**, **zero** and **successor** as primitive undefined concepts, gave a system of axioms involving these terms which were equally adequate to allow a full development of the theory of natural numbers.

Of the two options mentioned, we are going to talk about Peano's. Peano's axioms appeared for the first time in his ***Aritmetices Principia*** in 1889 and again in his ***Formulaire de Mathematiques*** of 1896. Peano noticed that these axioms were already in Dedekind and that they were also partially anticipated by Peirce (who recursively defines addition and multiplication). The induction principle is much older, it seems to have been formulated and used by Pascal in 1654 and by Fermat in 1659.

As we have already explained, we need second order logic to properly express the induction axiom.

In this chapter we are going to study the second order Peano theory. We will compare the strength of the first order formulation of the induction schema with the second order axiom. We will show the categoricity of the Peano axioms in **SOL** and we will study the method of defining functions by recursion. For various reasons, we will define induction models and study their structures and the negative applicability of the method of defining functions by recursion in them. Almost the whole chapter is based on the above mentioned paper of Henkin quoted at the beginning, it is the best expository paper I have ever read.

2.- SECOND ORDER PEANO AXIOMS.

Note. Throughout this whole chapter our basic **SOL** language, L_2, will only contain c and σ as zero-ary and unary functions.

2.1. Definitions: Peano models and induction models.

Let Π be the most famous set of axioms in the world; namely,

$1P \equiv \forall x \neg c = \sigma x$

$2P \equiv \forall xy\ (\sigma x = \sigma y \rightarrow x = y)$

$3P \equiv \forall X\ (Xc \wedge \forall z(Xz \rightarrow X\sigma z) \rightarrow \forall x\, Xx)$

2.1.1. We will say that a model of these axioms is a ***Peano model*** (or a Peano structure). ▒

2.1.2. We will say that a model of 3P is an ***induction model.*** ▒

2.1.3. Let $PA^2 = CON(\Pi) = \{\varphi \in SENT(L_2) / \Pi \models \varphi\}$. ▒

EXAMPLES.

Please recall our convention for simplifying standard structures (Chapter I, section 3.1).

(1) The structure $\langle \mathbb{N}, 0, S \rangle$ of natural numbers, as we know them intuitively, with zero and

successor is a Peano model and also an induction model.

(2) The structure $\langle 2\mathbb{N},0,+2 \rangle$ of even numbers with zero and the function of adding 2 is also a Peano structure and an induction model.

(3) The structure $\langle \mathbb{N}^*,0^*,S^* \rangle$ where $\mathbb{N}^* = \{1,2,4,8,...\}$ is the set of powers of 2, and $S^*x = 2x$ for all $x \in \mathbb{N}^*$, is a Peano model and an induction model.

(4) The structure $\langle\{a\},a,f\rangle$, where f is the only possible function on $\{a\}$, is also an induction model, but it is not a Peano model. Notice, however, that this structure not only satisfies axiom 3P, but it also satisfies axiom 2P.

(5) The structure $\langle\{a,b\},a,g\rangle$, where $a \neq b$ and $g(x) = b$ for all x, is also an induction model, but it is not a Peano model. In this structure axiom 1P is also satisfied.

(6) The structure $\mathcal{A} = \langle A,c^{\mathcal{A}},\sigma^{\mathcal{A}} \rangle$ where $A = \{0,1,2,3,4,5\}$, $c^{\mathcal{A}} = 0$ and

$$\begin{aligned} \sigma^{\mathcal{A}}: A &\longrightarrow A \\ 0 &\longmapsto 1 \\ 1 &\longmapsto 2 \\ \vdots &\longmapsto \\ 5 &\longmapsto 0 \end{aligned}$$

is an induction model.

We can represent it as

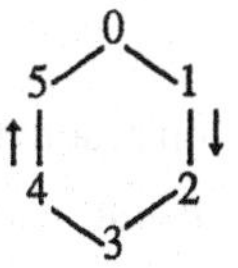

This structure is a model of 3P and also of 2P. However, it is not a model of 1P.

(7) The structure $\mathcal{B} = \langle B,c^{\mathcal{B}},\sigma^{\mathcal{B}} \rangle$ where $B = \{0,1,...,12\}$, $c^{\mathcal{B}} = 0$ and

$$\begin{aligned} \sigma^{\mathcal{B}}: B &\longrightarrow B \\ 0 &\longmapsto 1 \\ 1 &\longmapsto 2 \\ \vdots &\longmapsto \\ 11 &\longmapsto 12 \\ 12 &\longmapsto 7 \end{aligned}$$

is an induction model.

We can represent it as

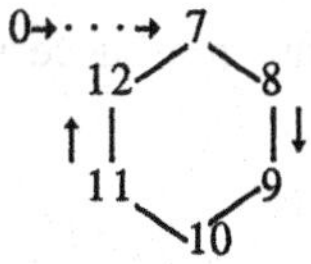

This structure is a model of 3P but also of 1P. However, it is not a model of 2P.

2.2. Comparison between the second order induction axiom and the first order induction schema.

The first thing to note is already in the heading: the second order induction axiom is not a schema but a single axiom. Besides that, its expressive power is stronger than the corresponding infinite set of first order induction axioms:

$$\varphi\frac{c}{x} \wedge \forall x(\varphi \rightarrow \varphi\frac{\sigma x}{x}) \rightarrow \forall x\, \varphi$$

(for any first order formula with **FREE**(φ) $= \{x\}$).

A first look shows you that in **FOL** we can only apply induction to a countable class of sets (since we only have a countable class of formulas), whereas in **SOL** with standard semantics induction applies to any subset of the universe of individuals and this set is uncountable. But here the important point is not the quantity of sets to which we can apply induction, but the quality of them. We would not have models non-isomorphic to the intended structure of natural numbers in **FOL**, if the string of standard numbers were definable in any model of first order Peano arithmetic, but it is not. Let me explain this point:

Every student of mathematical logic has constructed what is usually termed a non-standard model of the first order theory of the natural numbers; that is, a model non-isomorphic to the structure $\mathcal{N} = \langle \mathbb{N}, 0, S \rangle$. The construction can be carried out also for the enlarged model $\langle \mathbb{N}, 0, S, +, \cdot \rangle$; it is an easy corollary of compactness: we add to the sentences in the theory of natural numbers - that is, to **THEO**($\mathcal{N}$) $= \{\varphi \in$ **SENT**$(L_1) / \mathcal{N}$ is a model of $\varphi\}$ - an infinite list saying that a certain number is none of the successors of 0. While in the language we have the zero-ary constant c and the unary function constant σ, in an enlarged language with a new individual constant k, the sentences can be $k \neq c$, $k \neq \sigma c$, $k \neq \sigma\sigma c$,.... Since every finite subset of this new set of sentences has a model, then, by compactness, the whole set must have one, let us say $\mathcal{M}$. $\mathcal{M}$ is a model of the first order Peano Arithmetic, PA[1], and also a model of the new formulas $k \neq c$, $k \neq \sigma c$, $k \neq \sigma\sigma c$,.... Therefore, the universe of $\mathcal{M}$ contains non-standard numbers, *i.e.*, there are numbers which are not successors of zero. Call the set of standard numbers $\mathbb{N}(\mathcal{M})$, where

$$\mathbb{N}(\mathcal{M}) = \{\mathcal{M}(c), \mathcal{M}(\sigma c), \mathcal{M}(\sigma\sigma c), ...\}$$

It is easy to see that $\mathbb{N}(\mathcal{M})$ is not definable in **FOL** in the structure $\mathcal{M}$. Imagine that it were definable; that is,

$$\mathbb{N}(\mathcal{M}) = \{x / \mathcal{M}\ [x] \text{ sat } \beta\}$$

(for a first order formula with **FREE**(β) $= \{x\}$).

In that case we could apply induction for $\mathbb{N}(\mathcal{M})$, arriving at the contradiction that the universe of $\mathcal{M}$ contains no other elements but the ones in $\mathbb{N}(\mathcal{M})$. In fact, we can prove a broader statement establishing the link between standard models of PA^1 and definability of the set of its standard numbers.

Statement: Let $\mathcal{A}$ be a first order model of PA^1. Then $\mathcal{A}$ is standard if and only if the set of standard numbers, $\mathbb{N}(\mathcal{A})$, is definable in $\mathcal{A}$.

It is obvious that in standard models the formula $x{=}x$ defines the set of standard numbers. To prove the other direction of the statement you have to consider a model $\mathcal{A}$ of PA^1 where the set $\mathbb{N}(\mathcal{A})$ is definable by a formula β. In that case, the set of non-standard numbers would be defined by $\neg\beta$. We will see then that either $\mathcal{A}$ is standard - *i.e.*, in the Universe of $\mathcal{A}$ there are only standard numbers - or we arrive at the contradiction that the set of standard numbers is missing one element.

The formula

$$\exists x\, \neg\varphi \rightarrow (\neg\varphi\frac{c}{x} \vee \exists y(\neg\varphi\frac{\sigma y}{x} \wedge \varphi\frac{y}{x}))$$

is equivalent to the induction axiom and so it holds in $\mathcal{A}$, for any φ with $\mathbf{FREE}(\varphi) = \{x\}$. But look what happens when we consider the formula β. The interpretation in the model $\mathcal{A}$ is:

"If there exists $x\in A$ such that $x\notin\mathbb{N}(\mathcal{A})$, then either $\mathcal{A}(c)\notin\mathbb{N}(\mathcal{A})$ or there is a $y\in A$ such that $y\in\mathbb{N}(\mathcal{A})$ but not its successor, $\sigma^{\mathcal{A}}(y)\notin\mathbb{N}(\mathcal{A})$."

Therefore, if x is a non-standard number, we arrive at a contradiction: the set of standard numbers lacks an element.

Now it is easy to see the difference between the first and second order formulations of the induction axiom. With the former we cannot apply induction over standard numbers in a model having non-standard numbers. Therefore, the first order induction schema is unable to stop non-standard numbers. On the other hand, we will prove later that the second order induction axiom does stop non-standard numbers as Peano arithmetic is categorical in standard second order logic.

2.3. Non-standard models.

The existence of non-standard models of arithmetic was discovered by Skolem in the thirties, but for many years they received not much attention. In fact, they were used only as pathological counterexamples. Skolem himself used them to try, without succeeding, to divert the formalist stream of his epoch. It was not until 1949 that they received a very different treatment. Henkin proved the completeness of the theory of types at the time using non-standard structures. Although the meanings of non-standard in higher order logic and in arithmetic are not the same, they are very much related. At the end of his paper "Completeness in the theory of types" [1950], Henkin builds a non-standard model of arithmetic which is doubly non-standard. In fact, as you will see in this book, with Henkin's general semantics to be introduced in Chapter IV, we will prove in Chapter VII that **SOL** becomes strongly complete and thus compact. Therefore, we can make use of the same compactness argument we were employing before for **FOL**.

We cannot yet use compactness for **SOL** with Henkin's semantics, but you will see that a model of PA^2 having non-standard numbers in the universe of individuals must be non-standard in the second order sense.

Let's see this in detail:
In the preceding section we have briefly shown how to build a non-standard model of the first order theory of the natural numbers, a model non-isomorphic to the structure $\langle \mathbb{N},0,S,+,\cdot \rangle$. On the other hand, in **SOL** a non-standard structure $\mathcal{A}$ has a set **A** as universe of individuals and a family of sets $\langle A_n \rangle_{n\geq 1}$ such that each $A_n \subseteq \mathcal{P}A^n$, and $A_m \neq \mathcal{P}A^m$ for at least one $m\geq 1$. That is the condition of being non-standard in second order terms.

Take now our non-standard model of the first order theory of natural numbers, $\mathcal{M}$, and build a **SOL** structure out of it by choosing a family of sets $\langle M_n \rangle_{n\geq 1}$ such that each $M_n \subseteq \mathcal{P}M^n$ for all n. Let us term the resulting structure $\mathcal{M}^*$. Is $\mathcal{M}^*$ a model of second order Peano arithmetic? Since we have not described a precise way to build $\mathcal{M}^*$, the structure could not be a model of PA^2; but whatever the answer happened to be, we know from the start that if the structure $\mathcal{M}^*$ were a model of PA^2, then it must be non-standard in the second order sense. Specifically, $M_1 \neq \mathcal{P}M$. The reason is as follows: Consider the set of standard numbers in $\mathcal{M}$; that is, $\mathbb{N}(\mathcal{M})$. If the structure $\mathcal{M}^*$ were a model of PA^2, it would be in particular a model of the induction axiom. Imagine that the set of standard numbers, $\mathbb{N}(\mathcal{M})$, were in the universe of unary relations of $\mathcal{M}^*$. Since this set contains the zero and the successor of each of its members, $M = \mathbb{N}(\mathcal{N})$. But this is untrue because we know that in **M** there are non-standard numbers. What is the conclusion of all this? Very clearly, $\mathbb{N}(\mathcal{N}) \notin \mathbf{M}_1$ and so $\mathbf{M}_1 \neq \mathcal{P}\mathbf{M}$: The structure $\mathcal{N}^*$ is non-standard in the second order sense.

I hope I haven't driven you to a complete confusion when talking about non-standard second order models of Peano arithmetic. Haven't I said that second order Peano arithmetic is categorical? How could it have a model non-isomorphic to $\mathcal{N}$?

Well, as Skolem pointed out as early as 1929, second order Peano arithmetic is categorical only when "set" as it appears in the induction axiom is interpreted with its standard meaning; that is, when we take its meaning from metatheory by using standard semantics: $A_n = \mathcal{P}A^n$ for all n. But Henkin [1949] threw a positive light on the subject and made it possible to construct a non-standard model of PA^2 which is doubly so. Of course, we have to abandon the standard point of view and consider that the concept of set is attached to the model, accordingly changing the semantics.

Thus, when we open the door to non-standard interpretations, second order logic loses some of its expressive power and Peano arithmetic is no longer categorical. It is still stronger than first order Peano arithmetic since the consistency of PA^1 can be proved in PA^2. In fact, there is a **FOL** formula $\varphi_{CON(PA^1)}$ expressing the consistency of the first order version of Peano arithmetic such that

$$PA^1 \nvDash \varphi_{CON(PA^1)} \text{ (in FOL) but } PA^2 \vDash_{\mathcal{G}.\mathcal{S}} \varphi_{CON(PA^1)}$$

(in **SOL** with Henkin's semantics)

As we have already explained, the reason why first order Peano arithmetic is not categorical is that the set of standard numbers is not definable by a first order formula in a structure where we have non-standard numbers and then we lack induction for this set. The reason why second order Peano arithmetic with standard interpretation is categorical is that we have induction for all possible sets and a structure with non-standard numbers would never be a model of the second order induction axiom.

When we are in second order logic but we allow structures with nonfull relational universes, quantification only applies for the sets and relations that are present in the structure. Very likely the universe of unary relations would not have the set of standard numbers as one of its members. In the general structures of Henkin we put in the universes all sets and relations that are parametrically definable in the structure by second order formulas. Well, as in the first order case, the set of standard numbers is not definable either, by a second order formula in a structure having non-standard numbers.

3. CATEGORICITY OF PEANO AXIOMS.

To prove the categoricity of the Peano axioms we are going to follow the path which follows. We begin by proving two lemmas from which our theorem 1 is obtained.

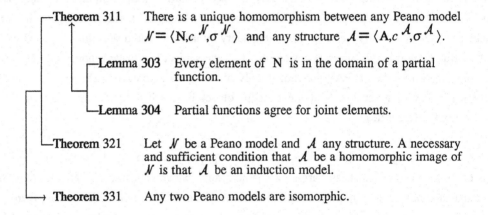

Theorem 311	There is a unique homomorphism between any Peano model $\mathcal{N}=\langle N, c^{\mathcal{N}}, \sigma^{\mathcal{N}}\rangle$ and any structure $\mathcal{A}=\langle A, c^{\mathcal{A}}, \sigma^{\mathcal{A}}\rangle$.
Lemma 303	Every element of N is in the domain of a partial function.
Lemma 304	Partial functions agree for joint elements.
Theorem 321	Let $\mathcal{N}$ be a Peano model and $\mathcal{A}$ any structure. A necessary and sufficient condition that $\mathcal{A}$ be a homomorphic image of $\mathcal{N}$ is that $\mathcal{A}$ be an induction model.
Theorem 331	Any two Peano models are isomorphic.

The first theorem we will prove is that of the existence of a unique homomorphism between any Peano model $\mathcal{N}=\langle N, c^{\mathcal{N}}, \sigma^{\mathcal{N}}\rangle$ and any structure $\mathcal{A}=\langle A, c^{\mathcal{A}}, \sigma^{\mathcal{A}}\rangle$. The homomorphism to be defined is the union of a chain of approximating functions. These functions are partial functions whose domains are segments of the natural numbers; *i.e.*, decreasing chains till zero. When we build a function as union of functions we have to be sure that the function covers all the domain aimed at and that the building functions do not conflict with each other; otherwise the union of functions could not be a function. Moreover, we want the final function to be a homomorphism and then some other requirements have to be met.

In the two lemmas which follow we will prove that the necessary conditions are satisfied to build the desired function. In theorem 1 we prove that there is a unique homomorphism between any Peano structure and any structure $\mathcal{A}$ of the same signature as $\mathcal{N}$.

The second theorem says that induction models are only homomorphic images of Peano structures. Using both theorems we easily prove that any two Peano models are isomorphic.

3.0. Partial functions.

Let $\mathcal{N} = \langle N, c^{\mathcal{N}}, \sigma^{\mathcal{N}} \rangle$ be a Peano model and $\mathcal{A} = \langle A, c^{\mathcal{A}}, \sigma^{\mathcal{A}} \rangle$ be any structure of the same signature.

3.0.1. Definition.
A subset $H \subseteq N$ is called a ***segment*** where it is a decreasing chain till $c^{\mathcal{N}}$. That is: $c^{\mathcal{N}} \in H$ and whenever $\sigma^{\mathcal{N}}(x) \in H$ then also $x \in H$, for all $x \in N$. ▓

Remark.

From this definition it is immediately clear that N and $\{c^{\mathcal{N}}\}$ are segments. In the second case we use axiom 1P.

3.0.2. Definition.
A ***partial function*** is a function f from a segment H into A satisfying the following two conditions:

(1) $f(c^{\mathcal{N}}) = c^{\mathcal{A}}$;

(2) $f(\sigma^{\mathcal{N}}(x)) = \sigma^{\mathcal{A}}(f(x))$

for all $x \in N$ such that $\sigma^{\mathcal{N}}(x) \in H$. ▓

3.0.3. Lemma: Every element of N is in the domain of a partial function.

Proof
We are going to define a subset of N using the condition of membership in the domain of a partial function. We will see that this subset contains $c^{\mathcal{N}}$ and that any time it contains an element, it also contains its successor. Therefore, using axiom 3P, this subset must be the whole of N. Let

$$G = \{x \in N \,/\, \exists f(f \text{ is a partial function } \& \text{ Dom } f \text{ is a segment } \& \; x \in \text{Dom } f)\}$$

Claim 1: $c^{\mathcal{N}} \in G$.

Because, by 1P, $\{c^{\mathcal{N}}\}$ is a segment and the function $f: \{c^{\mathcal{N}}\} \longrightarrow A$ defined by $f(c^{\mathcal{N}}) = c^{\mathcal{A}}$ is a partial function.

Claim 2: $\forall y(y \in G \Rightarrow \sigma^{\mathcal{N}}(y) \in G)$.

Let $y \in G$; that is, $y \in \text{Dom } f$ where f is a partial function and Dom f is a segment. If

$\sigma^{\mathcal{N}}(y) \in \text{Dom } f$, we finish. If $\sigma^{\mathcal{N}}(y) \notin \text{Dom } f$ then let $H = \text{Dom } f \cup \{\sigma^{\mathcal{N}}(y)\}$ and $f^* = f \cup \{\langle \sigma^{\mathcal{N}}(y), \sigma^{\mathcal{A}}(f(y)) \rangle\}$. We will see that H is a segment and f* is a partial function, and so $\sigma^{\mathcal{N}}(y) \in G$.

To see that H is a segment is immediate because Dom f was a segment and for the special case where $\sigma^{\mathcal{N}}(x) = \sigma^{\mathcal{N}}(y)$ then using 2P we obtain that $x = y$, and we know that $y \in \text{Dom } f$, so x is too. To see that f* is a partial function we need to prove that it satisfies:

(1) $f^*(c^{\mathcal{N}}) = c^{\mathcal{A}}$

(2) $f^*(\sigma^{\mathcal{N}}(x)) = \sigma^{\mathcal{A}}(f^*(x))$ for all $x \in N$ such that $\sigma^{\mathcal{N}}(x) \in H$.

For $c^{\mathcal{N}}$ this is clear; $f^*(c^{\mathcal{N}}) = f(c^{\mathcal{N}}) = c^{\mathcal{A}}$. When $\sigma^{\mathcal{N}}(x) \in \text{Dom } f$ it is also clear. For the special case where $\sigma^{\mathcal{N}}(x) = \sigma^{\mathcal{N}}(y)$, by 2P we obtain $x = y$. But $f^*(\sigma^{\mathcal{N}}(y)) = \sigma^{\mathcal{A}}(f(y)) = \sigma^{\mathcal{A}}(f^*(y))$, because we have defined f* that way. From claims 1, 2 and the induction axiom, the lemma follows. ▌

Remark.

Please notice that we have used all three axioms 1P, 2P and 3P.

3.0.4. Lemma: If f and g are partial functions and $x \in \text{Dom } f \cap \text{Dom } g$ then $f(x) = g(x)$.

Proof

As in the previous lemma, we are going to define a subset of **N** with the desired properties and will then prove, using 3P, that this set is all of **N**. Let

$$G = \{x \in N \,/\, \forall fg(f,g \text{ are partial functions } \& \ x \in \text{Dom } f \cap \text{Dom } g \Rightarrow f(x) = g(x))\}.$$

Claim 1: $c^{\mathcal{N}} \in G$.

Since $f(c^{\mathcal{N}}) = c^{\mathcal{A}}$ for any partial function f.

Claim 2: $\forall y(y \in G \Rightarrow \sigma^{\mathcal{N}}(y) \in G)$.

Let $y \in G$, f, g be two partial functions and assume that $\sigma^{\mathcal{N}}(y) \in \text{Dom } f \cap \text{Dom } g$. By condition (2) of partial functions: $f(\sigma^{\mathcal{N}}(y)) = \sigma^{\mathcal{A}}(f(y))$ and $g(\sigma^{\mathcal{N}}(y)) = \sigma^{\mathcal{A}}(g(y))$. Since $y \in G$: $f(y) = g(y)$, then $f(\sigma^{\mathcal{N}}(y)) = g(\sigma^{\mathcal{N}}(y))$. Thus, $\sigma^{\mathcal{N}}(y) \in G$. From claims 1,2 and the induction axiom, the lemma follows. ▌

3.1. Recursion theorem.

3.1.1. Theorem.
There exists a unique homomorphism between any Peano model $\mathcal{N} = \langle N, c^{\mathcal{N}}, \sigma^{\mathcal{N}} \rangle$ and any structure $\mathcal{A} = \langle A, c^{\mathcal{A}}, \sigma^{\mathcal{A}} \rangle$.

Proof
Combining the two preceding lemmas we obtain that for every $x \in N$ there is a unique $z \in A$ such that $z = f(x)$ for any partial function f. Define $h: N \longrightarrow A$ such that for every $x \in N$, $h(x)$ is that unique $z \in A$ described above. In other words, **h** is the union of all partial functions. It remains to be proven that this function is a homomorphism from $\mathcal{N}$ into $\mathcal{A}$ and that it is the only possible one. Clearly, $h(c^{\mathcal{N}}) = c^{\mathcal{A}}$, since $f(c^{\mathcal{N}}) = c^{\mathcal{A}}$ for all partial functions. Moreover, $h(\sigma^{\mathcal{N}}(y)) = f(\sigma^{\mathcal{N}}(y))$ for a partial function f, by lemma 3.0.3. Being a partial function, $f(\sigma^{\mathcal{N}}(y)) = \sigma^{\mathcal{A}}(f(y))$. By the definition of h, $h(y) = f(y)$. Thus, $h(\sigma^{\mathcal{N}}(y)) = \sigma^{\mathcal{A}}(h(y))$.

We have already proved that **h** is a homomorphism. It remains to be proven that our **h** is unique. We only have to think how h was defined using the partial functions. h itself is a partial function on the segment N. If we have another partial function f with domain N, by lemma 3.0.4 we obtain that $h = f$. ∎

3.2. Relationship between induction models and Peano models.

3.2.1. Theorem.
Let $\mathcal{N} = \langle N, c^{\mathcal{N}}, \sigma^{\mathcal{N}} \rangle$ be a Peano model and $\mathcal{A} = \langle A, c^{\mathcal{A}}, \sigma^{\mathcal{A}} \rangle$ any structure. A necessary and sufficient condition that $\mathcal{A}$ be a homomorphic image of $\mathcal{N}$ is that $\mathcal{A}$ be an induction model.

Proof
[⟹] Let $\mathcal{A}$ be a homomorphic image of $\mathcal{N}$ and h the homomorphism. We want to prove that $\mathcal{A}$ is a model of 3P. Consider a subset H of A such that $c^{\mathcal{A}} \in H$ and $\forall y(y \in H \Longrightarrow \sigma^{\mathcal{A}}(y) \in H)$. We want to show that $H = A$. Since we know that $\mathcal{A}$ is the homomorphic image of $\mathcal{N}$ and that $\mathcal{N}$ is a Peano model, we can use 3P for $\mathcal{N}$. Our strategy is:

We will define $G = \{x \in N \,/\, h(x) \in H\}$

We will prove that $c^{\mathcal{N}} \in G$ and that $\forall y(y \in G \Rightarrow \sigma^{\mathcal{N}}(y) \in G)$ and then we will use 3P for $\mathcal{N}$ obtaining $G = N$.

Conclusion:

Then, from $G = N$, we get that $\forall x(x \in N \Rightarrow h(x) \in H)$; that is, $H = \text{Rec } h$. But, by hypothesis, **h** is onto and so $\text{Rec } h = A$. Therefore, $H = A$, the desired result.

It is clear then that the only thing that remains to be proven is the following:

Claim 1: $c^{\mathcal{N}} \in G$.

That is obvious because we took $c^{\mathcal{A}} \in H$ and **h** was a homomorphism, so $h(c^{\mathcal{N}}) = c^{\mathcal{A}}$.

Claim 2: $\forall y(y \in G \Rightarrow \sigma^{\mathcal{N}}(y) \in G)$.

Take $y \in G$. $h(y) \in H$, by the definition of G. $\sigma^{\mathcal{A}}(h(y)) \in H$ because H contains all the successors of its members. But **h** is a homomorphism and then $\sigma^{\mathcal{A}}(h(y)) = h(\sigma^{\mathcal{N}}(y))$. Therefore, $\sigma^{\mathcal{N}}(y) \in G$. This direction of the proof is finished.

[$\Leftarrow$] Let $\mathcal{A}$ be an induction model and $\mathcal{N}$ a Peano model. From theorem 3.1.1 we infer the existence of a unique homomorphism, **h**, from $\mathcal{N}$ into $\mathcal{A}$. We have to prove that **h** is onto; *i.e.*, $\text{Rec } h = A$. We will define H to be Rec **h**; that is, $H = \{x \in A \,/\, \exists y(y \in N \;\&\; h(y) = x)\}$. We will prove that $c^{\mathcal{A}} \in H$ and that $\forall y(y \in H \Rightarrow \sigma^{\mathcal{A}}(y) \in H)$ and then use 3P for $\mathcal{A}$ obtaining $H = A$. It is then clear that we only need to prove the two claims stated below.

Claim 1: $c^{\mathcal{A}} \in H$.

Easy, $h(c^{\mathcal{N}}) = c^{\mathcal{A}}$ because **h** is a homomorphism.

Claim 2: $\forall y(y \in H \Rightarrow \sigma^{\mathcal{A}}(y) \in H)$.

Take any $y \in H$. From the definition of H, $h(x) = y$ for a $x \in N$. But **h** is a homomorphism and then $\sigma^{\mathcal{A}}(h(x)) = h(\sigma^{\mathcal{N}}(x))$ with $\sigma^{\mathcal{N}}(x) \in N$. Therefore, $\sigma^{\mathcal{A}}(y) \in H$. The proof of theorem 3.2.1 is complete. ▮

3.3. Isomorphism of Peano models.

3.3.1. Theorem.

Any two Peano models are isomorphic.

Proof

Let $\mathcal{N} = \langle N, c^{\mathcal{N}}, \sigma^{\mathcal{N}} \rangle$ and $\mathcal{N}^* = \langle N^*, c^{\mathcal{N}^*}, \sigma^{\mathcal{N}^*} \rangle$ be any two Peano models. By Theorem 3.2.1, there are a homomorphism h from $\mathcal{N}$ onto $\mathcal{N}^*$ and a homomorphism **h*** from $\mathcal{N}^*$ onto $\mathcal{N}$. It is easy to prove that the composition of the two, $h^* \circ h$, is a homomorphism from $\mathcal{N}$ into $\mathcal{N}$. Now, according to theorem 3.1.1 there is a unique homomorphism between $\mathcal{N}$ and $\mathcal{N}$. Obviously, the identity function from N onto N is also a homomorphism, therefore, **h*∘h** is the identity. From this it follows that **h** is one-to-one and, therefore, **h** is an isomorphism from $\mathcal{N}$ onto $\mathcal{N}^*$. ∎

Remark.
Since all Peano models are isomorphic, we can talk about "the" Peano model $\langle \mathbb{N}, 0, S \rangle$ as if there were a unique possible one. In what follows, when not otherwise specified, $\mathcal{N}$ is that model.

3.4. Peano arithmetic and the theory of natural numbers.

Let $\mathbf{THEO}(\mathcal{N}) = \{\varphi \in \mathbf{SENT}(L_2) / \mathcal{N}$ is a model of $\varphi\}$ be the theory of natural numbers in **SOL** and let $\mathrm{PA}^2 = \mathbf{CON}(\Pi) = \{\varphi \in \mathbf{SENT}(L_2) / \Pi \models \varphi\}$ be Peano arithmetic in **SOL**. Due to the expressive power of second order logic, these sets are the same, as we will prove now. As you know, the corresponding statement for first order logic is far from true.

3.4.1. Theorem.
For the standard model of natural numbers, $\mathcal{N}$, we have $\mathbf{THEO}(\mathcal{N}) = \mathrm{PA}^2$.

PROOF:
[⇒] Let $\varphi \in \mathbf{THEO}(\mathcal{N})$. We want to prove that φ is also a consequence of Π. So take any Peano model, say $\mathcal{N}^*$. Clearly, $\mathcal{N}^*$ is a model of φ, since $\mathcal{N}^* \cong \mathcal{N}$ (by Theorem 3.3.1 above) and because of the isomorphism theorem (Chapter I, section 5.3).
[⇐] Obvious. ∎

Remark.
Please notice that PA^2 contains the semantic consequences of Π and that this set is different from the theorems which can be proved from Π.

3.4.2. Corollary.
For every $\varphi \in \mathbf{SENT}(L_2)$, either $\Pi \models \varphi$ or $\Pi \models \neg\varphi$. ∎

Remark.
Corollary 3.4.2 says that the Peano axioms are semantically complete in second order logic.

3.5. Weak incompleteness of SOL with standard semantics.

We will enunciate the well known Gödel incompleteness theorem for Peano arithmetic. From it we will prove the incompleteness of **SOL**.

3.5.1. Gödel's incompleteness theorem for PA^2.

There is a sentence γ such that $\gamma \in THEO(\mathcal{N})$ but it is not the case that $PA^2 \vdash_{CAL} \gamma$ in any second order calculus[27].

Note.

The formula γ is the well known Gödel formula asserting of itself that it is not a theorem of Peano arithmetic; as it is in fact not a theorem of PA^2, it holds in the standard model of natural numbers, $\mathcal{N}$.

3.5.2. Incompleteness theorem of SOL.

There is a sentence φ such that $\models_{S.S} \varphi$ but it is not the case that $\vdash_{CAL} \varphi$.

Proof

We will see that there is a sentence $\varphi \in L_2$ such that $\models_{S.S} \varphi$, but it is not the case that $\vdash_{CAL} \varphi$. By Gödel's theorem stated in 3.5.1 above, $\gamma \in THEO(\mathcal{N})$. But, using 3.4.1 above, $\gamma \in PA^2$; equivalently, $\gamma \in CON(\Pi)$. Take $\varphi \equiv 1P \wedge 2P \wedge 3P \rightarrow \gamma$. Thus, $\models_{S.S} \varphi$ but not $\vdash_{CAL} \varphi$ (otherwise we will have $PA^2 \vdash_{CAL} \gamma$ contradicting 3.5.1). ∎

Remarks.

From the categoricity of second order Peano Arithmetic we have arrived to the conclusion that this set of sentences is complete in a certain sense; that is, every sentence of L_2 is either true in all models of Π or false. Therefore, for every sentence φ, either φ or $\neg\varphi$ is a "semantical theorem" of PA^2; ***i.e.***, $\Pi \models \varphi$ or $\Pi \models \neg\varphi$.

Please be aware that we are in **SOL** with standard semantics and this logic is incomplete, so we are not saying that PA^2 is a complete theory in the usual syntactic sense; ***i.e.***, $\Pi \vdash \varphi$ or

[27]You can find the proof in Robbin [1969], page 157.

$\Pi \vdash \neg\varphi$. On the contrary, if we compare this situation with the one encountered in **FOL**, we see that the syntactical incompleteness of PA^2 entails the incompleteness of **SOL** while in **FOL** the completeness of the calculus is not affected. Why is that? If you look back at the proof, we have used two facts which are lacking in PA^1; namely, PA^2 is categorical and the set of axioms, Π, is finite.

4.- PEANO MODELS AND PRIMITIVE RECURSION.

As we have shown already, Peano axiomatized natural numbers taking as primitive undefined notions those of ***natural number***, ***zero*** and ***successor*** and with only three axioms - namely, 1P, 2P and 3P - he was able to synthesize the main facts to such an extreme that any model of them is isomorphic to the intended model $\mathcal{N} = \langle \mathbb{N}, 0, S \rangle$.

Although these axioms are so important that all true statement about $\mathcal{N}$ expressible in the powerful L_2 are consequences of them (theorem 3.4), we get discouraged when we realize that the theorems that can be proved using only the primitive concepts have little mathematical content; for instance, our deduction exercises $\Pi \vdash_{\lambda\text{-}C_2} \forall x\, \neg x = \sigma x$ and $\forall X(Xc \wedge \forall z(Xz \rightarrow X\sigma z) \rightarrow \forall x\, Xx) \vdash_{\lambda\text{-}C_2} \forall y(\forall x\, \neg y = \sigma x \rightarrow y = c)$ (see 2.8.2 and 2.8.3 in Chapter II). To prove deeper results we need to introduce such concepts as new operations; for example, addition, multiplication, exponentiation, etc. Peano's idea was to define addition using the equations

$$\mathbf{x+0 = x}$$

$$\mathbf{x+Sy = S(x+y)}$$

for every **x, y** in $\mathbb{N}$.

In what sense do these equations define addition? Do they define addition only in the structure of natural numbers or in any Peano structure as well? We are going to see that our theorem 3.1.1 answers these questions and also, in a broader sense, it justifies the introduction of all primitive recursive functions.

In fact, the definition of addition is an example of definition using mathematical induction. When we have a Peano model $\mathcal{N}^* = \langle N^*, c^{\mathcal{N}^*}, \sigma^{\mathcal{N}^*} \rangle$ and a structure $\mathcal{A} = \langle A, c^{\mathcal{A}}, \sigma^{\mathcal{A}} \rangle$ we say that the equations

(A) $\mathbf{h}(c^{\mathcal{N}^*}) = c^{\mathcal{A}}$

$$h(\sigma^{\mathcal{N}^*}(y)) = \sigma^{\mathcal{A}}(h(y))$$

define **h** using mathematical induction.

So we can ask the same questions about this intended function **h** in the broader situation where any Peano structure is considered. That is, in what sense do these equations define **h**? Do they define **h** in any Peano model?

What is clear is that such a definition must be justified by showing that there is a unique function defined by these equations. In fact, we have done this already in theorem 3.1.1. We will see below how can we apply Theorem 3.1.1 to show that in Peano models there is a unique operation of addition, another of multiplication, exponentiation, etc. Nevertheless, a stronger result holds: In Peano models all recursive operations can be introduced using mathematical induction. From this stronger result we could have obtained as corollaries the existence of the above mentioned operations of addition, multiplication and exponentiation.

That is:

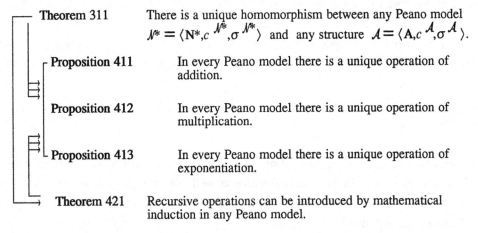

Theorem 311	There is a unique homomorphism between any Peano model $\mathcal{N}^* = \langle N^*, c^{\mathcal{N}^*}, \sigma^{\mathcal{N}^*} \rangle$ and any structure $\mathcal{A} = \langle A, c^{\mathcal{A}}, \sigma^{\mathcal{A}} \rangle$.
Proposition 411	In every Peano model there is a unique operation of addition.
Proposition 412	In every Peano model there is a unique operation of multiplication.
Proposition 413	In every Peano model there is a unique operation of exponentiation.
Theorem 421	Recursive operations can be introduced by mathematical induction in any Peano model.

We can also study the possibility of extending this method for defining functions to other kinds of structures such as induction models. In the following section we will see that it works for addition and multiplication, but does not work for exponentiation. Why is that? We will investigate the reasons for the failure of the introduction of recursive operations in general and arrive at the conclusion that a function needs to be what Henkin called universal to be definable using mathematical induction.

4.1. Addition, multiplication and exponentiation in Peano models.

4.1.1. **Proposition:** In every Peano model there is a unique operation of addition.

Proof

Let $\mathcal{N}^* = \langle N^*, c^{\mathcal{N}^*}, \sigma^{\mathcal{N}^*} \rangle$ be a Peano structure. We want to prove that there is a unique operation f satisfying:

(1.1) $f(x, c^{\mathcal{N}^*}) = x$

(1.2) $f(x, \sigma^{\mathcal{N}^*}(y)) = \sigma^{\mathcal{N}^*}(f(x,y))$

To prove this using theorem 3.1.1, we take the structure $\mathcal{N}^* = \langle N^*, c^{\mathcal{N}^*}, \sigma^{\mathcal{N}^*} \rangle$ and, for every $x \in N^*$, the structure $\mathcal{N}^*_x = \langle N^*, x, \sigma^{\mathcal{N}^*} \rangle$.

From the above mentioned theorem we infer that there is a unique homomorphism h_x between $\mathcal{N}^*$ and $\mathcal{N}^*_x$. The function h_x satisfies

(1) $h_x(c^{\mathcal{N}^*}) = x$

(2) $h_x(\sigma^{\mathcal{N}^*}(y)) = \sigma^{\mathcal{N}^*}(h_x(y))$, for every $y \in N^*$.

Defining f by the rule $f(x,y) = h_x(y)$ it is very easy to show that this function obeys (1.1) and (1.2). Therefore, the existence of the function f is established. To prove that such a function is also unique, we should consider another function g also satisfying the corresponding conditions (1.1) and (1.2). For every $x \in N^*$, we define g_x by the rule $g_x(y) = g(x,y)$, for every $y \in N^*$. This function satisfies the corresponding conditions (1) and (2). But, according to theorem 3.1.1 the function defined by equations (1) and (2) is unique. Therefore, for every $x \in N^*$, $h_x = g_x$. But then $h = g$. ▮

In theorem 4.1.1 we have shown, using theorem 3.1.1, that there is a unique operation defined by (1.1) and (1.2) for every $x, y \in N^*$. It is in this sense that theorem 3.1.1 justifies the definition of addition.

In Peano models we can introduce multiplication and exponentiation in a similar way, and justify them afterwards using theorem 3.1.1. We could prove, by similar arguments to the ones employed above, the following propositions:

4.1.2. Proposition: In every Peano model there is a unique operation of multiplication. ▮

4.1.3. Proposition: In every Peano model there is a unique operation of exponentiation. ▮

Remark.

We have to specify them as:

Multiplication. If $\mathcal{N}^* = \langle N^*, c^{\mathcal{N}^*}, \sigma^{\mathcal{N}^*} \rangle$ is a Peano structure, there is a unique operation **g** satisfying:

(2.1) $g(x, c^{\mathcal{N}^*}) = c^{\mathcal{N}^*}$

(2.2) $g(x, \sigma^{\mathcal{N}^*}(y)) = g(x,y) +^{\mathcal{N}^*} x$, for every $x, y \in N^*$.

Where $+^{\mathcal{N}^*}$ is the binary operation of addition.

Exponentiation. If $\mathcal{N}^* = \langle N^*, c^{\mathcal{N}^*}, \sigma^{\mathcal{N}^*} \rangle$ is a Peano structure, there is a unique operation **h** satisfying:

(3.1) $h(x, c^{\mathcal{N}^*}) = \sigma^{\mathcal{N}^*}(c^{\mathcal{N}^*})$

(3.2) $h(x, \sigma^{\mathcal{N}^*}(y)) = h(x,y) \cdot^{\mathcal{N}^*} x$, for every $x, y \in N^*$.

Where $\cdot^{\mathcal{N}^*}$ is the binary operation of multiplication.

In fact, as I have already explained, in Peano models all recursive operations can be introduced and justified by theorem 3.1.1. Therefore, instead of proving the two previous propositions, we are going to state and prove a broader statement from which both propositions follow as corollaries.

4.2. Theorem: recursive operations in Peano models.

4.2.1. Theorem: Recursive operations can be introduced by mathematical induction in any Peano model.

Proof

For the sake of simplicity, we are going to state and prove the theorem for the particular case where the function we want to introduce is a binary operation. That is:

Let $\mathcal{N}^* = \langle N^*, c^{\mathcal{N}^*}, \sigma^{\mathcal{N}^*} \rangle$ be a Peano model, **f** be a unary function on **N*** and **g** be a ternary function on **N***. There exists a binary operation **h** on **N*** such that:

(1.1) $h(x, c^{\mathcal{N}^*}) = f(x)$

(1.2) $h(x, \sigma^{\mathcal{N}^*}(y)) = g(x, y, h(x,y))$, holds for any $x, y \in N^*$.

In order to prove the theorem, we are going to prove the following lemma:

Lemma. If $\mathcal{N}^*= \langle N^*, c^{\mathcal{N}^*}, \sigma^{\mathcal{N}^*} \rangle$ is a Peano model, for every $x \in N^*$, there is a unique unary operation h_x on N^* such that:

(1) $h_x(c^{\mathcal{N}^*}) = f(x)$,

(2) $h_x(\sigma^{\mathcal{N}^*}(y)) = g(x,y,h_x(y))$ for every $y \in N^*$,

where f is a unary function and g is a ternary function on N^*.

Proof of lemma.

In the first place, we are going to prove existence. Let $N_1 = N^* \times N^*$, the cartesian product of N^*. For every $x \in N^*$, let $c_x^{\mathcal{N}^*} = \langle c^{\mathcal{N}^*}, f(x) \rangle$ and

$$\sigma_x^{\mathcal{N}^*}: N_1 \longrightarrow N_1$$

$$\langle y, z \rangle \longmapsto \langle \sigma^{\mathcal{N}^*}(y), g(x,y,z) \rangle \text{ for all } y,z \in N^*$$

Applying theorem 3.1.1 to the Peano model and the structure $\langle N_1, c_x^{\mathcal{N}^*}, \sigma_x^{\mathcal{N}^*} \rangle$, we see that for every $x \in N^*$ there exists a unique homomorphism m_x, such that:

(1) $m_x(c^{\mathcal{N}^*}) = c_x^{\mathcal{N}^*}$,

(2) $m_x(\sigma^{\mathcal{N}^*}(y)) = \sigma_x^{\mathcal{N}^*}(m_x(y))$ for every $y \in N^*$.

Take now the two projections Π_1 and Π_2 defined by:

$$\Pi_1: N_1 \longrightarrow N^* \qquad\qquad \Pi_2: N_1 \longrightarrow N^*$$

$$\langle x, y \rangle \longmapsto x \qquad\qquad \langle x, y \rangle \longmapsto y$$

for all $x,y \in N^*$

For every $x \in N^*$ we define:

$$h_x: N^* \longrightarrow N^* \qquad\qquad k_x: N^* \longrightarrow N^*$$

$$y \longmapsto \Pi_2(m_x(y)) \qquad\qquad y \longmapsto \Pi_1(m_x(y))$$

We will see that the function k_x is the identity on N^*.

Let $G = \{y \in N^* / k_x(y) = y\}$.

Claim 1: $c^{\mathcal{N}^*} \in G$.

Since $k_x(c^{\mathcal{N}^*}) = \Pi_1(m_x(c^{\mathcal{N}^*})) = \Pi_1(c_x^{\mathcal{N}^*}) = \Pi_1(\langle c^{\mathcal{N}^*}, f(x) \rangle) = c^{\mathcal{N}^*}$ as can be established using the definitions of k_x, $c_x^{\mathcal{N}^*}$ and Π_1 and the homomorphism condition for m_x.

Claim 2: $\forall y(y \in G \Rightarrow \sigma^{\mathcal{N}^*}(y) \in G)$.

Let $y \in G$; that is, $\mathbf{k}_x(y) = y$.

We have: $\mathbf{k}_x(\sigma^{\mathcal{N}^*}(y)) = \Pi_1(m_x(\sigma^{\mathcal{N}^*}(y))) = \Pi_1(\sigma_x^{\mathcal{N}^*}(m_x(y)))$.

But

$$\begin{aligned}\sigma_x^{\mathcal{N}^*}(m_x(y)) &= \sigma_x^{\mathcal{N}^*}(\langle \Pi_1(m_x(y)), \Pi_2(m_x(y))\rangle) \\ &= \langle\, \sigma^{\mathcal{N}^*}(\Pi_1(m_x(y))), g(x, \Pi_1(m_x(y)), \Pi_2(m_x(y)))\,\rangle \\ &= \langle\, \sigma^{\mathcal{N}^*}(k_x(y)), g(x, k_x(y), h_x(y))\,\rangle\end{aligned}$$

using the definitions of the functions involved.

Therefore, $k_x(\sigma^{\mathcal{N}^*}(y)) = \Pi_1(\sigma_x^{\mathcal{N}^*}(m_x(y))) = \sigma^{\mathcal{N}^*}(k_x(y)) = \sigma^{\mathcal{N}^*}(y)$

Using now axiom 3P, $\mathbf{G} = \mathbf{N}$. As expected, k_x is the identity.

We want to prove now that the function h_x satisfies conditions (1) and (2).

Claim 3: $h_x(c^{\mathcal{N}^*}) = f(x)$.

Since $h_x(c^{\mathcal{N}^*}) = \Pi_2(m_x(c^{\mathcal{N}^*})) = \Pi_2(c_x^{\mathcal{N}^*}) = \Pi_2(\langle c^{\mathcal{N}^*}, f(x)\rangle) = f(x)$.

Claim 4: $h_x(\sigma^{\mathcal{N}^*}(y)) = g(x, y, h_x(y))$.

Since

$$\begin{aligned}h_x(\sigma^{\mathcal{N}^*}(y)) &= \Pi_2(m_x(\sigma^{\mathcal{N}^*}(y))) = \Pi_2(\sigma_x^{\mathcal{N}^*}(m_x(y))) \\ &= \Pi_2(\langle\, \sigma^{\mathcal{N}^*}(k_x(y)), g(x, k_x(y), h_x(y))\,\rangle) \\ &= \Pi_2\langle\, \sigma^{\mathcal{N}^*}(y), g(x, y, h_x(y))\,\rangle = g(x, y, h_x(y))\end{aligned}$$

Having proved existence, to finish the proof of the lemma, it remains to show uniqueness. To do this, assume that there is another function $\mathbf{h}^*_x$ which also satisfies (1) and (2). Define $\mathbf{H} = \{y \in \mathbf{N} \,/\, \mathbf{h}_x(y) = \mathbf{h}^*_x(y)\}$ and use 3P to obtain that $\mathbf{H} = \mathbf{N}$.

From the lemma we obtain the theorem in a way similar to the one used in proving 4.1.1. The idea is that from the functions $\mathbf{h}_x$ we obtain the binary function $\mathbf{h}$ by the rule $\mathbf{h}(x,y) = \mathbf{h}_x(y)$. This function satisfies the two conditions (1.1) and (1.2) and is the only one with this property. ▮

Remark.

Using theorem 4.2.1. it is easy to obtain the propositions asserting the existence of a unique operation of addition, multiplication and exponentiation as corollaries.

Addition. Take f as the identity function on $\mathbf{N}^*$ and $g(x,y,z) = \sigma^{\mathcal{N}^*}(z)$. We get the desired result, $\mathbf{h}(\mathbf{x},c^{\mathcal{N}*}) = \mathbf{x}$ and $\mathbf{h}(\mathbf{x},\sigma^{\mathcal{N}*}(\mathbf{y})) = \sigma^{\mathcal{N}*}(\mathbf{h}(\mathbf{x},\mathbf{y}))$.

Multiplication. Take as f the constant function of value $c^{\mathcal{N}*}$ and $g(x,y,z) = z +^{\mathcal{N}*} x$. We then obtain: $h(x,c^{\mathcal{N}*}) = c^{\mathcal{N}*}$ and $\mathbf{h}(\mathbf{x},\sigma^{\mathcal{N}*}(\mathbf{y})) = \mathbf{h}(\mathbf{x},\mathbf{y}) +^{\mathcal{N}*} \mathbf{x}$.

Exponentiation. Take as f the constant function of value $\sigma^{\mathcal{N}*}(c^{\mathcal{N}*})$ and $g(x,y,z) = z \cdot^{\mathcal{N}*} x$. We get: $\mathbf{h}(\mathbf{x},c^{\mathcal{N}*}) = \sigma^{\mathcal{N}*}(c^{\mathcal{N}*})$ and $\mathbf{h}(\mathbf{x},\sigma^{\mathcal{N}*}(\mathbf{y})) = \mathbf{h}(\mathbf{x},\mathbf{y}) \cdot^{\mathcal{N}*} \mathbf{x}$.

5.- INDUCTION MODELS.

As I said before, induction models are second order structures where the axiom of induction is true. Of course, Peano models are a special kind of induction models but there are some other kinds of induction models as well. Induction models were introduced by Henkin in [1960]. According to Henkin's account, they have a pedagogical origin: he was trying to convince a fellow mathematician that a certain proof was deeply wrong. We will see now which one. We have seen already that our theorem 3.1.1 answers the questions raised to justify defining functions by mathematical induction.

When we have a Peano model $\mathcal{N}* = \langle N*, c^{\mathcal{N}*}, \sigma^{\mathcal{N}*} \rangle$ and a structure $\mathcal{A} = \langle A, c^{\mathcal{A}}, \sigma^{\mathcal{A}} \rangle$ we say that the equations

(A) $\mathbf{h}(c^{\mathcal{N}*}) = c^{\mathcal{A}}$
$\mathbf{h}(\sigma^{\mathcal{N}*}(\mathbf{y})) = \sigma^{\mathcal{A}}(\mathbf{h}(\mathbf{y}))$

define **h** using mathematical induction.

What is clear is that this definition must be justified by showing that there exists a unique function defined by these equations and we have done this already in theorem 3.1.1.

The wrong proof of the existence of such a function, say h, proceeds as follows:

> Let **G** be a subset of **N*** having as elements all $\mathbf{y} \in \mathbf{N}*$ such that h is defined for it using the equations (A); that is, we take **G** as Dom h. It is easy to show that $c^{\mathcal{N}*} \in \mathbf{G}$ and that whenever $\mathbf{y} \in \mathbf{G}$, $\sigma^{\mathcal{N}*}(\mathbf{y}) \in \mathbf{G}$ for any **y**. Therefore, using the induction axiom, $\mathbf{G} = \mathbf{N}*$.

As you will see later, the proof is completely wrong, but Henkin's colleague was convinced that the problem with it was not as deep as Henkin pretended, too many logical prejudices on Henkin's part!

What was Henkin's defense?
Besides arguing that in the proof when defining G we use the function **h** whose existence we want to prove, Henkin observed that we have only used the induction axiom and therefore, if the proof were correct, the recursion theorem would apply for any model of the induction axiom, not only for Peano models. Then Henkin defined induction models and showed that the mechanism of defining functions by mathematical induction does not always work in these models.

Once induction models are defined, we can study them. Although their creation was quite ***ad hoc***, they are very natural structures with a simple mathematical shape. They can be found in many different contexts, especially in a computing processes where we have an induction axiom governing the loop operator.

We are going to see that even though the induction axiom does not characterize its models up to isomorphism, it can be shown that they can be grouped in three wide categories: they are either Peano models, or cycles (residue class), or what Henkin named "spoons". The main reason why they can be grouped in this way is that axiom 3P never holds alone: it always entails either axiom 1P or 2P. Although the Peano axioms are semantically independent, there is a strong link between them.

5.1. Induction models and congruences.

5.1.1. **Proposition:** Take $\mathcal{N} = \langle \mathbb{N},0,S \rangle$. If $\mathcal{A}$ is an induction model, then $\mathcal{A} \cong \mathcal{N}/\!\sim$ for a certain congruence relation, ~.

Proof
Let $\mathcal{N} = \langle \mathbb{N},0,S \rangle$ be the natural numbers with zero and successor. Since $\mathcal{A}$ is an induction model, then by 3.2.1 $\mathcal{A}$ is a homomorphic image of $\mathcal{N}$. Now, using our proposition 4 of 3.2.5 in Chapter I, we obtain that $\mathcal{A} \cong \mathcal{N}/\!\sim$, for a certain congruence relation ~ on $\mathcal{N}$. ▮

5.2. Congruence relations on natural numbers.

We can extend the structure $\mathcal{N}$ by adjoining to it the operations of addition and multiplication and by considering also the natural ordering. That is, we take $\langle \mathbb{N},0,S,+,\cdot,< \rangle$. The extension is used only for convenience, since we have already seen that addition, multiplication and the ordering relation can be defined in $\mathcal{N}$. We will see that these operations allow us to give an explicit description of all congruence relations on the structure $\mathcal{N}$.

5.2.1. Definition.

Let m, n be any pair of natural numbers. We define the relation $R_{m,n}$ by the rule:

For any $x,y \in \mathbb{N}$, $\langle x,y \rangle \in R_{m,n}$ iff

(1) $x,y < n$ and $x = y$ or

(2) $x,y \geq n$ and $\exists z (z \in \mathbb{N} \,\&\, (x = y+(z \cdot m) \vee y = x+(z \cdot m))$ ▓

5.2.2. Theorem.

A binary relation R on $\mathbb{N}$ is a congruence relation on $\mathcal{N}$ if and only if it is the identity relation on $\mathbb{N}$ or there exist two natural numbers n, m such that $R = R_{m,n}$.

Proof

[$\Longrightarrow$] Let R be a congruence relation on $\mathcal{N}$ and assume that R is not the identity relation. Therefore, there exist $x,y \in \mathbb{N}$ such that $\langle x,y \rangle \in R$ and $x \neq y$. Let

$$n = \min\{x \in \mathbb{N} \,/\, \exists y(\langle x,y \rangle \in R \,\&\, y \neq x)\}$$

Since R is an equivalence relation different from identity, there exists $z \in \mathbb{N}$ such that $z \neq 0$ and $\langle n,n+z \rangle \in R$. Let

$$m = \min\{z \in \mathbb{N} \,/\, z \neq 0 \,\&\, \langle n,n+z \rangle \in R\}$$

Now that we have defined n and m, we can prove that $R = R_{m,n}$.

The elements of R which are not of the form $\langle x,x \rangle$ with $x<n$ are shown in the chart overleaf

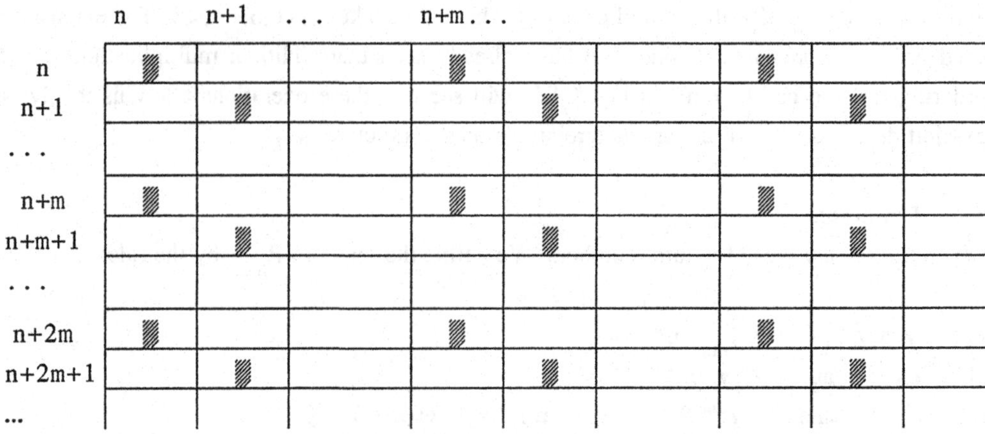

All these elements are in R, since it is a congruence relation and by definition of n and m. Is there any other element in R? The answer is no, since it can be shown that whenever **x,y≥n** and y≥x, we have **x** = n+w, **y** = n+w+v and

$\forall$**vw** (⟨n+w,n+w+v⟩∈R ⟹ ∃**z** v = m·z)

[⟸] For the other direction we need to prove that $\mathbf{R}_{m,n}$ is a congruence relation. The proof is quite straightforward and is left to the reader. ∎

Note.

The congruence relations $\mathbf{R}_{m,n}$ for n = 0 are the well known modular congruences, which have been extensively studied in number theory. If we look at the equivalence classes we see that there are m of them; namely,

[0]~ = {0,m,2m,...}

[1]~ = {1,m+1,2m+1,...}

⋮

[m-1]~ = {m-1,2m-1,3m-1,...}

The relations $\mathbf{R}_{m,n}$ with n≠0 have not received so much attention, but we have obtained already a clear intuitive picture of them. If we look at the equivalence classes we see that there are n+m of them, namely,

[0]~ = {0}

⋮

[m]~ = {m}

[n]~ = {n,n+m,n+2m,...}

$\vdots$

$[n+(m-1)]\sim = \{n+m-1, n+2m-1, \ldots\}$

5.3. Relative interdependence of Peano axioms.

5.3.1. Proposition: Every induction model is a model of either 1P or 2P.

Proof

Let $\mathcal{A}$ be an induction model. Then, using our Proposition 5.1.1, we know that $\mathcal{A}$ is isomorphic to $\mathcal{N}\sim$, for a certain congruence relation $\sim$ on $\mathcal{N}$. But now, using our Theorem 5.2.2, we know that there are just two possibilities:

(1) $\mathcal{A} \cong \mathcal{N}$, because when the congruence relation is identity, $\mathcal{N}\sim$ is just $\mathcal{N}$. In this situation $\mathcal{A}$ is a model of both 1P and 2P.

(2) $\mathcal{A} \cong \mathcal{N}\sim$ for one of the congruence relations $\mathbf{R}_{m,n}$. We have to distinguish here two possibilities: (a) for $n = 0$ and (b) for $n \neq 0$.

(a) For $n = 0$, $S\sim$ is a permutation,

$S\sim : \mathbb{N}\sim \longrightarrow \mathbb{N}\sim$

$[0]\sim \longmapsto [S0]\sim = [1]\sim$

$[1]\sim \longmapsto [S1]\sim = [2]\sim$

$\vdots$

$[m-1]\sim \longmapsto [S(m-1)]\sim = [m]\sim = [0]\sim$

Clearly, the structure $\mathcal{N}\sim$ is a cycle; namely, the system of residue classes module m. Axiom 2P is therefore satisfied. (See our examples 4 and 6 of section 2.1.)

(b) For $n \neq 0$, we have $[0]\sim = \{0\}$. Therefore,

$\forall x \in \mathbb{N}: x \neq 0 \Longrightarrow x \notin [0]\sim$

and so $\forall x \in \mathbb{N}: S(x) \notin [0]\sim$ because $\mathcal{N}$ is a Peano model satisfying 1P. We know that $[S(x)]\sim = S\sim([x]\sim)$ and so we have reached the conclusion:

$\forall [y]\sim \in \mathbb{N}\sim: S\sim([y]\sim) \neq [0]\sim$

The structure $\mathcal{N}\sim$ is a "spoon" and we have shown that it satisfies 1P. (See our examples 5 and 7 of section 2.1). Therefore, every induction model satisfies either 1P or 2P. ∎

6.- INDUCTION MODELS AND PRIMITIVE RECURSION IN INDUCTION MODELS.

We are going to see here that in induction models some operations such as addition and multiplication can be introduced by mathematical induction, but others such as exponentiation cannot. Besides this, we will see that both the addition and multiplication of any induction model $\mathcal{A}$ are the homomorphic images of the addition and multiplication on natural numbers, or, equivalently, they are the operations obtained by passing to the quotient. But in general (exponentiation is an example), if we have an operation f on natural numbers and a congruence relation ~ on $\mathbb{N}$ there is no guarantee of finding an operation g on $\mathcal{N}/\!\sim$ to be the operation obtained from passing to the quotient; that is, an operation being the homomorphic image of f under the homomorphism h corresponding to ~. We will show that the existence of such an operation g is attached by necessary and sufficient conditions to the compatibility of the operation f with the congruence relation ~.

Thus, addition and multiplication are what are usually termed universal operations, while exponentiation is not such an operation. Summarizing: Universal operations are compatible with congruence relations on natural numbers and, therefore, in passing from the structure of natural numbers to an induction model we are passing to a quotient structure where we obtain the homomorphic image of the universal operation.

6.1. Addition and multiplication in induction models.

6.1.1. Theorem: In every induction model there is a unique operation of addition.

Proof

In order to prove the theorem, we are going to state and prove two lemmas:

Lemma 1. If $\mathcal{A}=\langle A,c^{\mathcal{A}},\sigma^{\mathcal{A}}\rangle$ is an induction model, then for every $x\in A$ there is a unique unary operation h_x on A such that:

(1) $h_x(c^{\mathcal{A}})=x$

(2) $h_x(\sigma^{\mathcal{A}}(y))=\sigma^{\mathcal{A}}(h_x(y))$ for every $y\in A$

Lemma 2. If $\mathcal{A}=\langle A,c^{\mathcal{A}},\sigma^{\mathcal{A}}\rangle$ is an induction model, then there is a unique binary operation f on A such that:

(1.1) $f(x,c^{\mathcal{A}})=x$

(1.2) $f(x,\sigma^{\mathcal{A}}(y)) = \sigma^{\mathcal{A}}(f(x,y))$

Proof of lemma 1.

In the first place, we are going to prove uniqueness.

Let h_x and h^*_x be two unary operations satisfying (1) and (2) and define:

$$G = \{y \in A \,/\, h_x(y) = h^*_x(y)\}$$

Claim 1: $c^{\mathcal{A}} \in G$.

The reason is that both h_x and h^*_x satisfy (1)

Claim 2: $\forall y(y \in G \Rightarrow \sigma^{\mathcal{A}}(y) \in G)$.

Because if $y \in G$, then $h_x(y) = h^*_x(y)$. But both functions satisfy condition (2) and so

$$h_x(\sigma^{\mathcal{A}}(y)) = \sigma^{\mathcal{A}}(h_x(y)) = \sigma^{\mathcal{A}}(h^*_x(y)) = h^*_x(\sigma^{\mathcal{A}}(y))$$

Since $\mathcal{A}$ is an induction model, $\mathcal{A}$ is a model of 3P and so $G = A$ and then $h_x = h^*_x$.

We are going to prove now the existence of such a function. Let

$$H = \{x \in A \,/\, \exists h_x(h_x : A \longrightarrow A \;\&\; \text{satisfies (1) and (2)})\}$$

Claim 1: $c^{\mathcal{A}} \in H$.

Take as $h_{c^{\mathcal{A}}}$ the identity function on A. Clearly, it satisfies conditions (1) and (2).

Claim 2: $\forall y(y \in H \Rightarrow \sigma^{\mathcal{A}}(y) \in H)$.

If $y \in H$ then there is h_y satisfying the two conditions. Define $h_{\sigma^{\mathcal{A}}(y)}$ by the rule:

$$h_{\sigma^{\mathcal{A}}(y)}(x) = \sigma^{\mathcal{A}}(h_y(x)), \text{ for every } x \in A$$

This function satisfies (1), since $h_{\sigma^{\mathcal{A}}(y)}(c^{\mathcal{A}}) = \sigma^{\mathcal{A}}(h_y(c^{\mathcal{A}})) = \sigma^{\mathcal{A}}(y)$. It also satisfies (2), since

$$h_{\sigma^{\mathcal{A}}(y)}(\sigma^{\mathcal{A}}(x)) = \sigma^{\mathcal{A}}(h_y(\sigma^{\mathcal{A}}(x))) = \sigma^{\mathcal{A}}(\sigma^{\mathcal{A}}(h_y(x))) = \sigma^{\mathcal{A}}(h_{\sigma^{\mathcal{A}}(y)}(x))$$

Using now axiom 3P, $H = A$.

Proof of lemma 2.

In the first place we are going to prove the existence.

Let f be the binary function on A whose value, for every $x,y \in A$, is:

$$f(x,y) = h_x(y), \text{ where } h_x \text{ is the function of lemma 1}$$

It is easy to prove that f satisfies conditions (1.1) and (1.2)

To prove the uniqueness, let g be another function satisfying (1.1) and (1.2), we will show that $f = g$. For every $x \in A$ let g_x be the unary function on A such that $g_x(y) = g(x,y)$, for every $y \in A$. Therefore, using lemma 1, $g_x = h_x$, because it is easy to prove that g_x satisfies

(1) and (2).

To see it satisfies condition (1), recall that $g_x(c^{\mathcal{A}}) = g(x,c^{\mathcal{A}}) = x$. To see that it satisfies (2), look at the definition and use condition (1.2).

$$g_x(\sigma^{\mathcal{A}}(y)) = g(x,\sigma^{\mathcal{A}}(y)) = \sigma^{\mathcal{A}}(g(x,y)) = \sigma^{\mathcal{A}}(g_x(y))$$

Now, from the definition of f and g it follows that f = g. Theorem 6.1.1 is now finished, since the function satisfying (1.1) and (1.2) is addition. ▮

6.1.2. Theorem. Given the structure $\mathcal{N} = \langle \mathbb{N},0,S \rangle$ of natural numbers and the induction model $\mathcal{A} = \langle A,c^{\mathcal{A}},\sigma^{\mathcal{A}}\rangle$ the addition of $\mathcal{A}$, $+^{\mathcal{A}}$, is the homomorphic image of the addition, +, of $\mathcal{N}$.

Proof

Let **h** be the unique homomorphism of $\mathcal{N}$ onto $\mathcal{A}$ (Theorems 3.1.1 and 3.2.1). We will prove that the addition of $\mathcal{A}$ is the homomorphic image of the addition of $\mathcal{N}$. Clearly, we only need to show that for all $x,y\in\mathbb{N}$

$$h(x)+^{\mathcal{A}} h(y) = h(x+y)$$

Let $G = \{y\in\mathbb{N} \,/\, h(x)+^{\mathcal{A}} h(y) = h(x+y)\}$

Claim 1: $0\in G$.

We see that $h(x)+^{\mathcal{A}} h(0) = h(x)+^{\mathcal{A}} c^{\mathcal{A}} = h(x) = h(x+0)$

Claim 2: $\forall y(y\in G \Rightarrow S(y)\in G)$.

Let $y\in G$. Thus, $h(x+y) = h(x)+^{\mathcal{A}} h(y)$. Then, $h(x)+^{\mathcal{A}} h(S(y)) = h(x)+^{\mathcal{A}} \sigma^{\mathcal{A}}(h(y)) = \sigma^{\mathcal{A}}(h(x)+^{\mathcal{A}} h(y)) = \sigma^{\mathcal{A}}(h(x+y)) = h(S(x+y)) = h(x+S(y))$. Now, using 3P we get that $G = \mathbb{N}$. ▮

Remark.

Given an induction model $\mathcal{A} = \langle A,c^{\mathcal{A}},\sigma^{\mathcal{A}} \rangle$ we know from Proposition 5.1.1 that $\mathcal{A} \cong \mathcal{N}/\!\sim$ for the congruence relation ~ associated to that unique homomorphism **h** between $\mathcal{N}$ and $\mathcal{A}$ asserted in the recursion Theorem 3.1.1. It is easy to see that addition in $\mathcal{A}$, $+^{\mathcal{A}}$, is the operation obtained from + by passing to the quotient; *i.e.*, $x\!\sim +^{\mathcal{A}} y\!\sim = [x+y]\!\sim$.

6.1.3. Theorem. In every induction model there is a unique operation of multiplication.

Proof

In order to prove the theorem, we are going to state two lemmas which you are going to prove:

Lemma 1. If $\mathcal{A} = \langle A, c^{\mathcal{A}}, \sigma^{\mathcal{A}} \rangle$ is an induction model, then for every $x \in A$ there is a unique unary operation k_x on A such that

(1) $k_x(c^{\mathcal{A}}) = c^{\mathcal{A}}$,

(2) $k_x(\sigma^{\mathcal{A}}(y)) = (k_x(y)) +^{\mathcal{A}} x$ for every $y \in A$.

Lemma 2. If $\mathcal{A} = \langle A, c^{\mathcal{A}}, \sigma^{\mathcal{A}} \rangle$ is an induction model, then there is a unique binary operation h on A such that

(2.1) $h(x, c^{\mathcal{A}}) = c^{\mathcal{A}}$,

(2.2) $h(x, \sigma^{\mathcal{A}}(y)) = (h(x,y)) +^{\mathcal{A}} x$ for every $x, y \in A$. ▮

6.1.4. Theorem. Given the structure $\mathcal{N} = \langle \mathbb{N}, 0, S \rangle$ of natural numbers and the induction model $\mathcal{A} = \langle A, c^{\mathcal{A}}, \sigma^{\mathcal{A}} \rangle$, the multiplication of $\mathcal{A}$, $\cdot^{\mathcal{A}}$, is the homomorphic image of the multiplication, $\cdot$, of $\mathcal{N}$.

Proof

Can you please prove this? ▮

6.2. Exponential operation on induction models.

6.2.1. Theorem: Not every induction model has an exponential operation.

Proof

An exponential operation for an induction model $\mathcal{A} = \langle A, c^{\mathcal{A}}, \sigma^{\mathcal{A}} \rangle$ would be a binary function h on A such that

(3.1) $h(x, c^{\mathcal{A}}) = \sigma^{\mathcal{A}}(c^{\mathcal{A}})$,

(3.2) $h(x, \sigma^{\mathcal{A}}(y)) = h(x,y) \cdot^{\mathcal{A}} x$ for every $x, y \in A$.

We are going to define now an induction model where there is no function defined by (3.1) and (3.2).

Let $\mathcal{B} = \langle B, c^{\mathcal{B}}, \sigma^{\mathcal{B}} \rangle$ with $B = \{c^{\mathcal{B}}, p\}$ where $c^{\mathcal{B}} \neq p$ and $\sigma^{\mathcal{B}}(c^{\mathcal{B}}) = p$, while $\sigma^{\mathcal{B}}(p) = c^{\mathcal{B}}$. Clearly, $\mathcal{B}$ is an induction model. Nevertheless, equations (3.1) and (3.2) are unable to define a function, as can be shown by

$$h(c^{\mathcal{B}}, c^{\mathcal{B}}) = \sigma^{\mathcal{B}}(c^{\mathcal{B}}) = p$$

but also

$$\mathbf{h}(c^B, c^B) = \mathbf{h}(c^B, \sigma^B(\mathbf{p})) = (\mathbf{h}(c^B, \mathbf{p}))\cdot c^B = c^B \quad \blacksquare$$

6.3. Universal operations.

In the previous theorems we have seen that in induction models certain operations such as addition and multiplication can be defined by mathematical induction while others such as exponentiation cannot. Why is that? Is there any difference between addition and multiplication on the one hand and exponentiation on the other? Besides axiom 3P, what else do we need to define an operation by mathematical induction?

All these questions will get an answer in the following theorem where you will see that the condition of existence of the quotient operation is the compatibility of the congruence relation with the operation we want to define in the quotient.

6.3.1. Definition.
Let $\mathbf{f}$ be a binary operation on $\mathbb{N}$. Then $\mathbf{f}$ is a ***universal operation*** iff for all congruence relations $\sim$ on $\mathcal{N}$ it satisfies:

(*) $\forall \mathbf{x}\mathbf{y}\mathbf{x}_1\mathbf{y}_1 \in \mathbb{N}$: $\langle \mathbf{x},\mathbf{x}_1\rangle \in \sim \;\&\; \langle \mathbf{y},\mathbf{y}_1\rangle \in \sim \;\Rightarrow\; \langle \mathbf{f}(\mathbf{x},\mathbf{y}),\mathbf{f}(\mathbf{x}_1,\mathbf{y}_1)\rangle \in \sim$ $\blacksquare$

6.3.2. Theorem.
Let $\mathbf{f}$ be a binary operation on $\mathcal{N}$ and $\sim$ be a congruence relation on $\mathbb{N}$. Let $\mathbf{h}$ be the homomorphism corresponding to $\sim$. There exists a homomorphic image of $\mathbf{f}$ in $\mathcal{N}/\sim$ (a binary operation $\mathbf{g}$ on $\mathcal{N}/\sim$) if and only if $\mathbf{f}$ is universal.

Proof
Let $\mathbf{g} = \{\langle \mathbf{h}(\mathbf{x}),\mathbf{h}(\mathbf{y}),\mathbf{h}(\mathbf{z})\rangle \,/\, \mathbf{f}(\mathbf{x},\mathbf{y}) = \mathbf{z}\}$. It is enough to prove that $\mathbf{g}$ is a function if and only if condition (*) is respected.
[$\Rightarrow$] Let $\mathbf{g}$ be a function and imagine that $\langle \mathbf{x},\mathbf{x}_1\rangle \in \sim$ and $\langle \mathbf{y},\mathbf{y}_1\rangle \in \sim$. Therefore, $\mathbf{h}(\mathbf{x}) = \mathbf{h}(\mathbf{x}_1)$ and $\mathbf{h}(\mathbf{y}) = \mathbf{h}(\mathbf{y}_1)$. We want to prove that $\langle \mathbf{f}(\mathbf{x},\mathbf{y}),\mathbf{f}(\mathbf{x}_1,\mathbf{y}_1)\rangle \in \sim$. Since $\mathbf{g}$ is a function, from $\langle \mathbf{h}(\mathbf{x}),\mathbf{h}(\mathbf{y}),\mathbf{h}(\mathbf{z})\rangle \in \mathbf{g}$ and $\langle \mathbf{h}(\mathbf{x}_1),\mathbf{h}(\mathbf{y}_1),\mathbf{h}(\mathbf{v})\rangle \in \mathbf{g}$ we obtain

$$\mathbf{h}(\mathbf{f}(\mathbf{x},\mathbf{y})) = \mathbf{h}(\mathbf{z}) = \mathbf{h}(\mathbf{v}) = \mathbf{h}(\mathbf{f}(\mathbf{x}_1,\mathbf{y}_1))$$

[$\Leftarrow$] Let condition (*) be satisfied. To see that $\mathbf{g}$ is a function we need to show that whenever $\langle \mathbf{x},\mathbf{y},\mathbf{z}\rangle \in \mathbf{g}$ and $\langle \mathbf{x},\mathbf{y},\mathbf{v}\rangle \in \mathbf{g}$ then $\mathbf{z} = \mathbf{v}$. That is easy, using the definition of $\mathbf{g}$ and the condition (*). $\mathbf{g}$ is the operation obtained in the quotient. $\blacksquare$

6.3.3. Theorem.

Exponentiation is not a universal operation.

Proof

It is easy to see that exponentiation is not a universal operation. For instance, $\langle 2,2\rangle \in R_{3,0}$ and $\langle 0,3\rangle \in R_{3,0}$ but $\langle 2^0,2^3\rangle \notin R_{3,0}$. ∎

Let us assume that the operation j on $\mathbb{N}$ is obtained by primitive recursion from the operations f and g which are both universal. Is j also a universal operation? The example of the exponentiation shows that it is not always so. Nevertheless, you will see below that when j is commutative then it is also universal.

6.3.4. Theorem. Let j be a binary operation on natural numbers obtained by primitive recursion from the universal operations f and g. If j is commutative, then j is universal.

Proof

Let $jx0 = fx$ and $jxSy = gxy(jxy)$ for all $x,y \in \mathbb{N}$. Besides this, j is commutative and f, g are universal. Let $\sim$ be a congruence relation on $\mathcal{N}$. We want to prove that j is universal, but according to 6.3.2 this is equivalent to proving that there is a homomorphic image of j in $\mathcal{N}\sim$; *i.e.*, there is a unique $j\sim$ such that

$$j\sim([x]\sim,[y]\sim) = [jxy]\sim$$

To prove this we will prove first the following proposition:

Proposition: For every $x \in \mathbb{N}$, in $\langle \mathbb{N}\sim,[0]\sim,S\sim \rangle$ there is a unique $\tilde{j}_{[x]\sim}$ such that

(1) $\tilde{j}_{[x]\sim}[0]\sim = f\sim[x]\sim$,

(2) $\tilde{j}_{[x]\sim}S\sim[y]\sim = g\sim[x]\sim[y]\sim(\tilde{j}_{[x]\sim}[y]\sim)$

(where $f\sim$ and $g\sim$ are the homomorphic images of f and g whose existence is ensured by 6.3.2).

In the first place we will prove uniqueness.

Let $\tilde{j}_{[x]}$ and $\tilde{j}'_{[x]}$ be two operations satisfying (1) and (2). Define

$$G = \{[y]\sim \in \mathbb{N}\sim / \tilde{j}_{[x]}\sim[y]\sim = \tilde{j}'_{[x]\sim}[y]\sim\}$$

Claim 1: $[0]\sim \in G$.

Since $\tilde{j}_{[x]\sim}[0]\sim = f\sim[x]\sim = \tilde{j}'_{[x]\sim}[0]\sim$.

Claim 2: If $[y]\sim \in G$, then $S\sim[y]\sim \in G$.

Let $[y]\sim \in G$. Then, $\tilde{j}_{[x]\sim}[y]\sim = \tilde{j}'_{[x]\sim}[y]\sim$. But

$$\tilde{j}_{[x]\sim}S\sim[y]\sim = g\sim[x]\sim[y]\sim(\tilde{j}_{[x]\sim}[y]\sim) = g\sim[x]\sim[y]\sim(\tilde{j}'_{[x]\sim}[y]\sim) = \tilde{j}'_{[x]\sim}S\sim[y]\sim$$

Therefore, $S\sim[y]\sim \in G$. Now using P3 we get that $G = \mathbb{N}\sim$.

Now we will prove existence.

Let H be the set of all the elements of $\mathbb{N}\sim$ for which there exists a $j\sim_{[x]\sim}$. That is,

$$H = \{[x]\sim \in \mathbb{N}\sim / \exists \tilde{j}_{[x]\sim}(\tilde{j}_{[x]\sim} : \mathbb{N}\sim \longrightarrow \mathbb{N}\sim \text{ and it satisfies (1) and (2)}\}$$

Claim 1: $[0]\sim \in H$.

Define $\tilde{j}_{[0]\sim} = f\sim$; that is, $\tilde{j}_{[0]\sim}[x]\sim = f\sim[x]\sim = [fx]\sim$ for all $[x] \in \mathbb{N}\sim$. Now we have to see that it satisfies conditions (1) and (2). Obviously,

$$\tilde{j}_{[0]\sim}[0]\sim = f\sim[0]\sim.$$

Furthermore,

$$\tilde{j}_{[0]\sim}S\sim[y]\sim = f\sim S\sim[y]\sim = [fSy]\sim = [jSy0]\sim = [j0Sy]\sim = [g0y(j0y)]\sim = [g0y(jy0)]\sim$$
$$= [g0y(fy)]\sim = g\sim[0]\sim[y]\sim[fy]\sim = g\sim[0]\sim[y]\sim f\sim[y]\sim = g\sim[0]\sim[y]\sim(\tilde{j}_{[0]\sim}[y]\sim).$$

Claim 2: If $[y]\sim \in H$, then $S\sim[y]\sim \in H$.

Let $[y]\sim \in H$. Thus, there exists $\tilde{j}_{[y]\sim}$ satisfying $\tilde{j}_{[y]\sim}[0]\sim = f\sim[y]\sim$ and $\tilde{j}_{[y]\sim}S\sim[x]\sim = g\sim[y]\sim[x]\sim(\tilde{j}_{[y]\sim}[x]\sim)$. Define

$$\tilde{j}_{S\sim[y]\sim}[x]\sim = [jSyx]\sim$$

It is easy to see that this satisfies (1) and (2).

In the first place,

$$\tilde{j}_{S\sim[y]\sim}[0]\sim = [jSy0]\sim = [fSy]\sim = f\sim S\sim[y]\sim.$$

Furthermore,

$$\tilde{j}_{S\sim[y]\sim}S\sim[x]\sim = [jSySx]\sim = [gSyx(jSyx)]\sim = [gSyx(jxSy)]\sim = g\sim S\sim[y]\sim[x]\sim[jxSy]\sim =$$
$$g\sim S\sim[y]\sim[x]\sim(\tilde{j}_{S\sim[y]\sim}[x]\sim).$$

That proves the proposition. To finish the proof of the theorem you will prove that there exists a unique binary operation $j\sim$ on $\mathcal{N}\sim$. ▮

However, although all commutative operations are universal, not all universal operations have to be commutative, as you can see in the following theorem.

6.3.5. Theorem.

Not all universal operations are commutative.

Proof

For example, the operation j such that $jxy = x^2 \cdot y$ for all $x,y \in \mathbb{N}$ is a universal operation and it is obtained by primitive recursion from the universal functions f, g such that $fx = 0$ and $gxyz = z+x^2$ for all $x,y,z \in \mathbb{N}$; but j is not commutative. ∎

CHAPTER IV
FRAMES AND GENERAL STRUCTURES.

1.- INTRODUCTION.

1.1. Frames and general structures.

How did Henkin prove, in 1949, the completeness theorem for type theory?

A very quick answer to this question is: by changing the semantics and hence the logic. Roughly posed, the idea is very simple: the set of validities is so wide because our class of standard structures is too small. We are very restricted when asking the relational universes of any model to contain all possible relations (where possible means in the background set theory used as metalanguage). If we also allow non-standard structures (*i.e.*, structures where $A_n \subseteq \mathcal{P}A^n$, for all n, but for some m, $A_m \neq \mathcal{P}A^m$), then the set of validities in the very large class of structures which includes both classes is considerably reduced. In fact, it coincides with the set of sentences derivable in a calculus which is a simple extension of the first order one.

Apart from being a subset of the power set of the n-ary cartesian product of the universe of individuals, if we do not impose any other condition on the universes of a structure, it may well happen that it fails to contain certain relations that are definable in the structure using second order formulas. This means the comprehension schema does not necessarily hold. That is why we need structures where the relational universes obey certain closure conditions: Henkin's general models.

If we now interpret validity as being true in all general models, and redefine all the semantic notions referring to this larger class of general structures, completeness (in both weak and strong senses), Löwenheim-Skolem and all these theorems can be proved as in first order logic for both our C_2 and λ-C_2.

1.2. Standard / non-standard view.

So the standard and the non-standard semantics (where we also allow non-standard structures as models) make two completely different logics, since their consequence relations also differ. Both semantics are based on two completely different views of what kind of structures we want to talk about in second order logic.

What are those structures?

There are two ways of looking this question.

(1) **Standard point of view:** We want to talk about homogeneous structures. Our structures do not differ at all from the structures we studied in **FOL**.
This identification is understandable: when one chooses standard second order logic the reason could be the need of a stronger formal language where more can be expressed about the mathematical structures we want to study. These structures are the same as we were considering in first order logic. Our conceptualization of the world has not changed: our **OPER.CONS** is first order, and we still want to talk about a mathematical reality structured as a domain of individuals and certain fixed relations and functions on individuals[28]. The use of relation variables is only a device to try to fill the gap between what we can ***say*** in **FOL** about our structures and what we ***know*** about them.

(2) **Many-sorted point of view:** We want to talk about heterogeneous structures. It is obvious that we have several universes, even though they are related among themselves. It is true that the relations and functions we have given names to (those in **OPER.CONS**) are always relations among individuals of just one of our universes, but that is only one peculiarity of our signature, nothing essential. **SOL** is only a many-sorted theory.
Actually, recalling the arguments used in II.4.3, one can argue that the standard semantics is not logically adequate in the sense that it does not allow all logically possible interpretations of second order formulas as models. Consider the following.
We have to be placed in a set-theoretical universe, even assuming that there could be more than one such. Nevertheless, in the set-theoretical universe you choose to be in, the GCH is either true or false. Assume it is true. Then, in every standard model for **SOL** φ_{GCH} is true and φ_{GCH} is valid[29]. But since GCH is not derivable from ZFC, this

[28]This is the reason why in presenting second order logic in the classical and standard way we do not include second order relations in our signature Σ.

[29]To see the formula φ_{GCH} consult Chapter I, section 4.8.

suggests that an interpretation $\mathcal{I}$, such that $\mathcal{I} \nvDash \varphi_{GCH}$, cannot be excluded as "logically impossible". So at least one $\mathcal{I}$ with $\mathcal{I} \vDash \neg\varphi_{GCH}$ is a logical possibility (by Paul Cohen's classical result). But such a model is not allowed in the standard semantics. So it seems that the standard semantics does not include all logically possible worlds as models (we have to think about formulas, like GCH, which are both expressible in second order logic and independent of Zermelo-Fraenkel set theory). This argument is reinforced by the fact that there is an inexhaustible supply of independent formulas like GCH. In Henkin's general semantics many possibilities are restored as possible models; for instance, models with or without GCH. If the reader feels uneasy with having a too broad class with Henkin's general models, then we invite you to exclude them by adding axioms (like the axiom of choice, or the extensionality axiom mentioned above) to any desired calculus of second order logic. This way, by adding axioms, we can make the class of our general models as tight (as close to being standard) as we want without excluding some real logical possibilities, like an $\mathcal{I}$ such that $\mathcal{I} \nvDash \varphi_{GCH}$.

1.3. The concept of subset.

Imagine that we are pragmatic logicians with no pronounced opinion on the above and that we are searching for a natural semantics for the second order language we have already introduced. Since in **SOL** we have variables for each $\alpha \in$ **VAR**, it seems sensible to consider structures with different domains for every $\alpha \in$ **VAR**. But the set **VAR** is special; it tells us that a stratification has already taken place. Second order language seems to be designed to talk about very particular structures, having a non-empty set as universe of individuals and for every natural number n, a universe of n-ary relations on that set. So, to determine a structure, we have to fix the notion of subset. There are basically two ways, corresponding to the choice of standard/non-standard classes of structures.

(1) **Standard structures:** The notion of subset is taken from the background set theory and it is fixed. (So it is treated as a "logical" concept.)
When defining a structure, we say that a unary relation variable refers to any subset of the universe of individuals; that is, to any element of the power set of the universe of individuals. Similarly, a binary relation variable refers to any binary relation on the universe of individuals; that is, to any element of the power set of the cartesian product of the universe of individuals. In general, an n-ary relation variable refers to any n-ary relation on the universe of individuals; that is, to any element of the power set of the n-ary cartesian product of the universe of individuals. Structures of this kind are called

standard structures[30]. Choosing this semantics places ourselves with the people adopting the standard view, since the whole structure is known once we give the universe of individuals and the interpretation of the symbols in **OPER.CONS**. As we have already seen, we tie a particular set theory to the **SOL** semantics.

(2) **Non-standard structures:** The notion of subset is explicitly given within each model. (So it is treated as a concept "defined in the structure".)
We might think that the relations and functions we refer to when quantifying in second order logic do not always need to be all the possible ones. We often want to quantify over certain sets of sets and relations that are easier to control. That is, we want to have structures where the n-ary relation universe is a proper subset of the power set of the n-ary cartesian product of the universe of individuals. But we probably also want the class of structures taken as second order models to be natural and tight. We want certain similarities to exist between two second order structures. Henkin chooses to speak about structures at least containing all the sets and relations definable in the structure by **SOL** formulas, and so defining the celebrated general structures, which are some peculiar and natural non-standard structures. Their advantages and disadvantages will be considered later on. We shall see that in this case we are adopting the many-sorted view. There is also the possibility of adopting a semantic based on structures where the domains are closed but only under a restricted subset of the set of definable sets. In so far as this restricted class can be axiomatized, there is a calculus between C_2^- and C_2 to produce its theorems. Thus, the calculus obtained by weakening the comprehension schema also gets its natural semantics under the many-sorted point of view.

To help you to decide, you should remember that you are choosing between two different logics: in the first option the logic is unmanageable but the language is extremely powerful. In the second option the logic is OK but you pay a high price in expressive power. The second choice is also important in connection with other logics; it is most certainly a natural solution to the problem of incompleteness and can be used as a spring of inspiration in other logics.

Remarks.

(1) The meaning of non-standard.

Both in **FOL** and in **SOL** we talk about non-standard structures, but only in second order logic can non-standard semantics also be handled. Thus, in second order logic, unlike first order, we have standard and non-standard interpretations. In **FOL** the structures called

---

[30]They are also called principal interpretations and the logic based on them, full second order logic.

non-standard are in fact non-standard models of a particular theory and their characteristic is that they are not isomorphic to the intended model. Therefore, the meanings of non-standard in **FOL** and in **SOL** are different. But different does not mean that they are not related, as we have already explained in detail in section 2.2 of Chapter III.

(2) **Set theory.**

The two choices about the concept of subset are directly related to the Zermelo hierarchy and Gödel's constructible universe.

1.4. Summary.

Whenever we have a class of structures, we have the set of **SOL** sentences that are true in each structure in the class. And each time we have a set of sentences, we can ask whether there is a calculus to produce the sentences in the set as theorems.

We have $\mathcal{S.S}$, the class of standard structures, and accordingly, we find $\models_{\mathcal{S.S}}$, the set of validities in the class. We know that there is no complete calculus for $\models_{\mathcal{S.S}}$, since this set is not recursively enumerable.

But even knowing that there is no calculus in the standard sense, we have certain sequent rules which are sound and so we define a sequent calculus C_2. A weaker calculus is also defined, C_2^-. With these two calculi in hand, we produce the sets $\vdash_{C_2}$ and $\vdash_{C_2^-}$ of logical theorems in them, also termed $\vdash_{\mathbf{SOL}}$ and $\vdash_{\mathbf{MSL}}$.

Since $\vdash_{C_2}$ is a proper subset of $\models_{\mathcal{S.S}}$, in order to get the right semantics for it, we need to widen the class of structures to reduce the set of validities (the wider the class, the smaller the set, because to be valid in a wider class of structures a sentence needs to pass more, shall we say, "quality controls"). So we define structures in a wider sense (which we call frames) and general structures. They produce $\models_{\mathcal{F}}$ and $\models_{\mathcal{G.S}}$ and it happens (not by chance) that they are exactly the sets $\vdash_{\mathbf{MSL}}$ and $\vdash_{\mathbf{SOL}}$. That is, $\models_{\mathcal{F}} = \vdash_{\mathbf{MSL}}$ and $\models_{\mathcal{G.S}} = \vdash_{\mathbf{SOL}}$. It is easy to see that since $\mathcal{S.S} \subseteq \mathcal{G.S} \subseteq \mathcal{F}$ we have $\models_{\mathcal{F}} \subseteq \models_{\mathcal{G.S}} \subseteq \models_{\mathcal{S.S}}$.

Let me summarize this with a diagram:

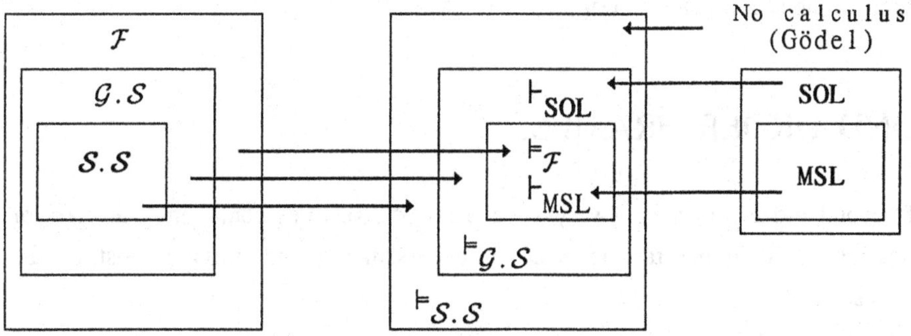

Therefore, when we interpret general validity as being true in all general models, and redefine all the semantic notions refering to this larger class of general structures, general completeness (in both weak and strong senses), Löwenheim-Skolem and all those theorems can be proven as in first order logic. A fortiori, the completeness result for this "natural" semantics gives you an extra reason for considering C_2 the "natural" second order calculus.

For the logics obtained by weakening comprehension, the picture looks like this:

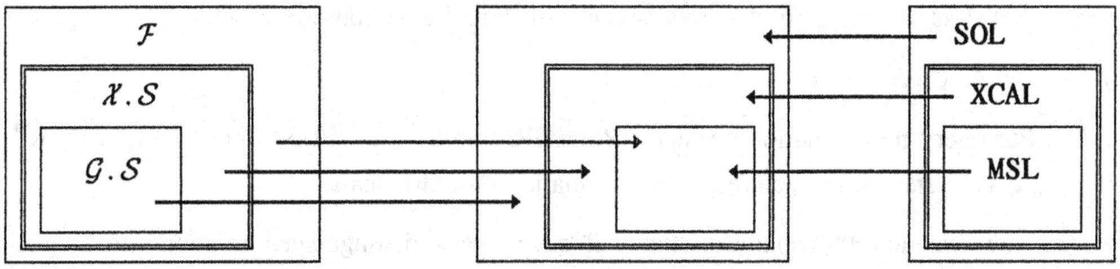

But second order logic loses a considerable amount of its expressive power. For example: when using general structures or just frames, the formula

$$\forall F(\forall xy(Fx=Fy \rightarrow x=y) \rightarrow \forall x\exists y\, x=Fy)$$

no longer means finiteness of the domain. This formula can be true in an infinite structure so poor that it fails to contain one-to-one not onto relations. Then the gap between what we know about our structures and what we can say in the formal language reopens and, as I said before, the old ghost of Skolem's paradox shows up.

Therefore, one has to choose expressive power or complete calculus. But even if you choose a complete calculus there is no reason why you have to abandon second order logic in favor of first order logic. We will show that complete second order logic is reducible to many-sorted logic, which turns out to be reducible to first order logic. But the first order version is not nearly so natural as the second order one[31].

2.- SECOND ORDER FRAMES.

The class of second order frames is a very wide class of structures containing the class of standard structures. This simple fact is basic to understanding and proving most of the theorems of this section.

2.1. Definition of frames.

2.1.1. Definition.

A ***second order frame*** $\mathcal{A}$ (some authors call them pre-structures) is defined by:

$$\mathcal{A} = \langle A, \langle A_n \rangle_{n\geq 1}, \langle C^{\mathcal{A}} \rangle_{C \in \mathbf{OPER.CONS}} \rangle$$

where

(i) $A \neq \emptyset$ is the universe of individuals which should be a non-empty set.

(ii) $\emptyset \neq A_n \subseteq \mathcal{P}A^n$, for each $n \geq 1$.

(iii) For every n-ary relation constant $R \in \mathbf{OPER.CONS}$ with $\mathbf{FUNC}(R) = \langle 0,1,\overset{n}{\ldots},1 \rangle$, $R^{\mathcal{A}}$ is, as in standard structures, an n-ary relation on individuals.

Now we add the condition that $R^{\mathcal{A}} \in A_n$; every distinguished relation must be a member of the corresponding universe.

(iv) For every n-ary function constant $f \in \mathbf{OPER.CONS}$ with $\mathbf{FUNC}(f) = \langle 1,1,\overset{n}{\ldots},1 \rangle$, $f^{\mathcal{A}}$ is an n-ary function on individuals. Furthermore, $f^{\mathcal{A}} \in A_{n+1}$.

Specifically, for individual constants we agree that the condition becomes $\{a^{\mathcal{A}}\} \in A_1$. ▮

Let's call the class of frames $\mathcal{F}$. ▮

Remarks.

Let us compare this definition with the previous one for standard structures in I.3.1. As you can see, we have changed the condition (ii) of standard structures. Now A_n can be any subset of the n-ary cartesian product of A. In (iii) and (iv) we have added the conditions to ensure

[31]For applications of many-sorted logic, see Meinke and Tucker eds, [1993].

that the relations and functions distinguished in the structure are included in the corresponding universes for quantification purposes.

2.1.2. Proposition: The class of standard structures is a proper subclass of the class of all frames.

Proof

From the definition, it is obvious that the class of standard structures is a proper subclass of the class of all frames. That is, $\mathcal{S.S} \subseteq \mathcal{F}$ and $\mathcal{S.S} \neq \mathcal{F}$. ▮

2.2. Semantics on frames.

The second order language L_2 remains unaltered when we shift to non-standard second order logic and the definitions of denotation of a term in a certain frame and of satisfaction of a formula in a frame closely parallel the standard definitions.

2.2.1. Denotation of terms and predicates and satisfaction of formulas in frames.

Given a frame $\mathcal{A}$ and an assignment M on it, we define the interpretation $\mathcal{I} = \langle \mathcal{A}, \mathrm{M} \rangle$, the denotation of terms and predicates and the satisfaction of formulas of L_2 exactly as with standard structures (see 4.2.1 of Chapter I). In particular, equality is also taken as primitive here and receives the same treatment. ▒

Caution.

However, when using frames there is no guarantee that the relation defined for a formula φ and the sequence of variables $x_1, x_2, \ldots, x_n$ would be in the universe of n-ary relations. That means, the corresponding $\mathcal{I}(\lambda x_1 \ldots x_n\, \varphi)$ would be a relation on individuals of $\mathcal{A}$ but not necessarily a member of A_n. That is the reason why we are using the semantics based on frames only for the λ-free language L_2.

2.2.2. Frame-model.

(a) Whenever we have an $\mathcal{A} \in \mathcal{F}$ and an assignment M such that $\langle \mathcal{A}, \mathrm{M} \rangle$ sat φ, we say that $\langle \mathcal{A}, \mathrm{M} \rangle$ is a *frame-model* of φ. ▒

(b) We also say that $\langle \mathcal{A}, \mathrm{M} \rangle$ is a *frame-model* of a set Γ of formulas when it is a frame-model of each $\gamma \in \Gamma$. ▒

Remark.

Since not all frames are standard structures, not all frame-models of a formula are also models (standard models) of the formula.

2.2.3. Consequence on frames.

We will write $\Gamma \models_{\mathcal{F}} \varphi$ to indicate that φ is a ***frame-consequence*** of Γ in the class of all frames, meaning that all frame-models of Γ are also frame-models of φ. ▒

Proposition: Frame-consequence implies consequence in standard structures.

Proof

Since $\mathcal{S.S} \subseteq \mathcal{F}$, it is easy to see that $\Gamma \models_{\mathcal{F}} \varphi$ implies $\Gamma \models_{\mathcal{S.S}} \varphi$, for all Γ and φ. ∎

2.2.4. Validity on frames.

We say that a formula φ is ***frame-valid*** if $\emptyset \models_{\mathcal{F}} \varphi$. We then write $\models_{\mathcal{F}} \varphi$. ▒

Proposition: Frame-validity implies validity in standard structures.

Proof

As before, for all φ: $\models_{\mathcal{F}} \varphi$ implies $\models_{\mathcal{S.S}} \varphi$, since $\mathcal{S.S} \subseteq \mathcal{F}$. ∎

2.2.5. Satisfiability on frames.

A formula φ is ***frame-satisfiable*** just when there is a frame-model of φ. ▒

Proposition: Frame-satisfiability does not imply satisfiability.

Proof

Of course, frame-satisfiability does not imply satisfiability (in standard structures), but the other way around. To see this, just think of the formula,

$$\exists xy(\forall X(Xx \longleftrightarrow Xy) \land \neg x{=}y)$$

which is frame-satisfiable but not satisfiable in $\mathcal{S.S}$. ∎

2.2.6. Equivalence in frames.

Two formulas φ and ψ are ***frame-equivalent*** (equivalent in the class of all frames) when we can prove that $\varphi \models_{\mathcal{F}} \psi$ and $\psi \models_{\mathcal{F}} \varphi$. ▒

EXERCISES.

It is obvious that frame-equivalence implies logical equivalence. But the relation of frame-equivalence is very strong and logical equivalence does not imply frame-equivalence. Nevertheless, you can verify yourself that for the logical symbols the equivalences given in propositions 4.4.2 through 4.4.4 of Chapter I are also frame-equivalences. The situation changes when we consider the two definitions of identity which could have been used in standard structures; namely,

$\forall Z(Zx \leftrightarrow Zy)$ and $\forall Z^2(\forall z\, Z^2zz \rightarrow Z^2xy)$

They are not frame-equivalent nor do they define identity in all frames. That means

$\{\langle x,y\rangle \in A^2 \,/\, \mathcal{I}^{xy}_{\mathbf{xy}} \text{ sat } \forall Z(Zx \leftrightarrow Zy)\}$

can be different from

$\{\langle x,y\rangle \in A^2 \,/\, \mathcal{I}^{xy}_{\mathbf{xy}} \text{ sat } \forall Z^2(\forall z\, Z^2zz \rightarrow Z^2xy)\}$

when $\mathcal{I}$ is an interpretation on a frame; they can be different as well from the identity relation.

Can you please state and prove as isolated propositions all the affirmations given above?

2.3. Soundness and completeness in frames.

Now we raise the natural question concerning the calculi C_2^- and C_2 and the new semantics based on frames.

C_2^- It can be proved that, as far as C_2^- is concerned, the semantics of frames is perfect. Using the language L_2, the rules of calculus C_2^- allow us to obtain all and only those formulas which are frame-valid. Thus, it can be shown

$$\vdash_{C_2^-} = \models_{\mathcal{F}}$$

That is, the calculus C_2^- is weak complete and sound in the class $\mathcal{F}$ of all frames. Besides this, for all Γ and φ of the language L_2: $\Gamma \models_{\mathcal{F}} \varphi$ iff $\Gamma \vdash_{C_2^-} \varphi$.

That is, the strong completeness and soundness of C_2^- in $\mathcal{F}$ are also theorems.

C_2 We will see that the semantics of frames is too flexible for the calculus C_2, since some of the logical theorems obtained in C_2 using comprehension are not valid in the class $\mathcal{F}$ of all frames. Therefore, the calculus C_2 with the semantics $\mathcal{F}$ is unsound.

2.3.1. Soundness of C_2^- in frames.

Lemma: $\Gamma \vdash_{C_2^-} \varphi$ implies $\Gamma \vDash_{\mathcal{F}} \varphi$, for all Γ and φ.

Proof

To prove this we would have to show that every theorem of Γ in calculus C_2^- is a consequence of it in the class of all frames. We can repeat what we did for standard structures. It is not, however, a corollary of the soundness of C_2^- in standard structures, since standard consequence does not imply frame-consequence. ∎

2.3.2. Unsoundness of C_2 in frames.

Lemma: There is a φ such that $\vdash_{C_2} \varphi$ but $\nvDash_{\mathcal{F}} \varphi$.

Proof

It is easy to see that there are theorems of the C_2 calculus which are not true in all frames. For example, the comprehension rule of C_2 allows us to deduce all the comprehension axioms as theorems. Nevertheless, the comprehension axiom has occurrences which are not valid in the class of all frames. To prove this, think of the formula $Rx \vee Tx$. The comprehension axiom corresponding to this formula says:

$$\exists X\, \forall x (Xx \longleftrightarrow Rx \vee Tx)$$

It is easy to see that this formula is not true in all frames. Take, for example, the frame

$$\mathcal{B} = \langle \{1,2,3\}, \langle \mathbf{B}_n \rangle_{n \geq 1}, \langle \{1\},\{2\} \rangle \rangle$$

where $\{1\} = R^{\mathcal{B}}$, $\{2\} = T^{\mathcal{B}}$ and $\mathbf{B}_1 = \{\{1\},\{2\}\}$. Since $\{1,2\} \notin \mathbf{B}_1$, the formula is false in $\mathcal{B}$. ∎

Remarks on the completeness of C_2^- and C_2 in frames.

The completeness of C_2^- in $\mathcal{F}$ is essentially nothing but the completeness of many-sorted logic. On the other hand, the completeness of the latter, **MSL**, can be done directly, following the common Henkin style procedures, or it can also be done using a well known technique of reduction to first order unsorted logic. In Chapter VI you will find both proofs. From the completeness result for **MSL** there follows the completeness of C_2^- in frames, and from that as a corollary, the completeness of C_2 in frames. But we know from the previous proposition of unsoundness that the semantics of frames is not suitable for the latter calculus.

In Chapter VII you will find a translation of second order formulas into many-sorted formulas and you will see that there is an easy way of using the completeness, compactness and Löwenheim-Skolem properties of many-sorted logic in the second order non-standard case.

2.4. Undefinability of identity in frames.

As we mention in Chapter I, section 4.8, in second order logic with standard semantics the equality symbol is not always treated as a primitive logic symbol, but introduced using the Leibniz indiscernibility criterion. What would have happened if, while being in **Equality-free SOL**, we had changed to the semantics based on frames but retained the definition of equality?

As we said there, we would have been back to the situation encountered in first order logic: where you can think of a frame $\mathcal{A}$ and an interpretation $\mathcal{I} = \langle \mathcal{A}, M \rangle$ such that $\mathcal{I}$ is a frame-model of $\forall X(Xx \leftrightarrow Xy)$ but where $\mathcal{I}(x) \neq \mathcal{I}(y)$. To see this, just take a frame $\mathcal{A}$ where $A = \{1,2,3\}$ and where $A_1 = \{\emptyset, A\}$.

What can be done to remedy this situation?

(A) **Abandoning Equality-free SOL.**

The easiest solution is the one we have already chosen. You take equality as a primitive logic symbol and proceed exactly as in **FOL**. More precisely,

(1) You add to the formal language the symbol $=$ as a primitive relation constant.

(2) You specify that its denotation will be the "true" identity relation which you place in a frame $\mathcal{A}$ as $=^{\mathcal{A}}$, or, instead of (2),

(3) You indicate that a formula $\tau = t$ is true in a frame-model $\mathcal{I}$ when and only when $\mathcal{I}(\tau) = \mathcal{I}(t)$.

Presumably, the calculus does not have (ES) or (RE) as primitive rules, since they can be obtained from the rest using Leibniz's definition. Now, with the loss of this definition, you have to:

(4) Add (ES) and (RE) as primitive rules of inference.

(B) **Discard the unwanted frames.**

Another solution to this problem is to introduce normal frames; ***i.e.***, where equality denotes identity. Since the case being analyzed is when equality is defined by Leibniz's definition, the easiest way to obtain your goal is to put in the frame all the singletons. Then your frame is certainly normal since it satisfies:

$$\forall xy \in A(\forall X \in A_1(x \in X \Leftrightarrow y \in X) \Longrightarrow x = y)$$

2.5. Frames and lambdas.

As we mentioned before, in the semantics of frames there is no guarantee that all λ-predicates have denotation in the frame. So, if you want to use the language λ-L_2, the first thing to decide is how to interpret simple formulas of the form

$$\lambda x_1...x_n\ \varphi\ \tau_1...\tau_n$$

in an interpretation $\mathcal{I} = \langle \mathcal{A}, \mathrm{M}\rangle$ where $\mathcal{I}(\lambda x_1...x_n\ \varphi) \notin \mathrm{A}_n$.

You should not give them the truth value true without careful thought because from the formula

$$\lambda x_1...x_n\ \varphi\ \tau_1...\tau_n \text{ of } \lambda\text{-}L_2, \text{ by the rule of (IPC).}$$

you obtain the formula of L_2,

$$\exists X^n\ X^n\tau_1...\tau_n$$

and this could be not true in $\mathcal{A}$ because $\mathcal{I}(\lambda x_1...x_n\ \varphi) \notin \mathrm{A}_n$.

What I am saying is that the corresponding sets of theorems of the calculus C_2^- in the language L_2 and in the language λ-L_2 are different, resulting in the unsoundness of C_2^- in frames for λ-L_2. And this is also true even for innocent looking formulas in **FORM**(L_2) like

$$\exists X^n\ X^n\tau_1...\tau_n$$

Please recall that we are free from this problem because we are using the language L_2. Therefore the rule (IPC) for relation variables is formulated for formulas without λ, and the predicates used in the substitution are always relation symbols, but the calculus C_2^- would not be sound for frames if we kept the current definitions but used language λ-L_2 instead of L_2.

Let us see precisely why:

Take as a definition of satisfaction of λ-formulas in frames the same as that in the standard case. You can check that $\lambda x\ \neg Rx\tau \vdash_{\mathrm{C}_2^-} \exists X\ X\tau$ (by the rule (IPC)).
But also $\lambda x\ \neg Rx\tau \not\models_{\mathcal{F}} \exists X\ X\tau$.
(To see that $\exists X\ X\tau$ is not a frame-consequence of $\lambda x\ \neg Rx\tau$ just take a frame $\mathcal{A}$ where

$$\mathrm{A} = \{0,1\} \text{ and } R^{\mathcal{A}} = \{0\} \text{ with } \mathrm{A}_1 = \{\{0\}\}$$

Use then an assignment M where $\langle \mathcal{A}, \mathrm{M}\rangle(\tau) = 1$.)

A further remark.

Of course, the calculus λ-C_2 is also unsound in frames, but this result is only natural, nothing dangerous or in need of a change. You have to think that the comprehension axioms are theorems of λ-C_2 but they are not frame-valid.

What can be done to remedy this situation?

(A) **Keeping the language λ-L_2 away from frames.**
The easiest solution is the one we have already chosen; we avoid the problem of dealing with λ-predicates with no denotation in the frame by the simple recipe of not mixing them together. So the semantics of frames will only be used with the lambda free language L_2.

(B) **Introducing a third truth value.**
You can certainly face the problem by introducing a semantics with three truth values, adding the unspecified truth value, U. The value U is primarily designed for simple formulas with λ-predicates defining relations which are out of the frame. If you depart from the alternative presentation of semantics introduced in 4.5 of Chapter I, the required transformation becomes easier. Basically, you add to the universe of truth values the unspecified truth value U, and the interpretation of connectors and quantifiers is changed to cover new cases.

2.6. Definable sets and relations in a given frame.

Given a frame

$$\mathcal{A} = \langle A, \langle A_n \rangle_{n\geq 1}, \langle C^{\mathcal{A}} \rangle_{C\in \mathbf{OPER.CONS}} \rangle$$

and a second order language L_2, there are several kinds of relations which are related, in one way or another, with $\mathcal{A}$ and **FORM**(L_2). In particular, we want to distinguish the same kinds of relations as in section 4.7 of Chapter I; namely: (1) first and second order relations *on* the universes of the frame, (2) relations ***into*** the universes of the frame, (3) ***definable*** relations of the frame using a given language and (4) ***parametrically definable*** relations of the frame using a given language.

Most of the distinctions introduced below are used afterwards to define general structures for second order logic.

2.6.1. Definition of first order relations of the frame $\mathcal{A}$

(a) Please recall the definition I.4.7.1 of an n-ary ***first order relation on*** $\mathcal{A}$ ▒

Let $\mathbf{REL}^{1st}(\mathcal{A})$ be the class of all first order relations of $\mathcal{A}$. ▒

(b) As in I.4.7.1, we say that an n-ary first order relation **X** is ***into*** $\mathcal{A}$ when $\mathbf{X}=R^{\mathcal{A}}$ for $R\in\mathbf{OPER.CONS}$ or $\mathbf{X}\in A_n$. ▒

Let $\mathbf{REL}^{1st}(\in\mathcal{A})$ be the class of all first order relations into $\mathcal{A}$. ▒

Remarks.

All these relations are first order. In the universes of any second order frame $\mathcal{A}$ there are ***only*** relations among individuals, but it is no longer true that all the n-ary first order relations ***on*** $\mathcal{A}$ are ***into*** $\mathcal{A}$.

Proposition.

For any frame $\mathcal{A}$:

(1) $\bigcup_{n\geq 1} A_n \subseteq \mathbf{REL}^{1st}(\mathcal{A})$.

(The reason is that $\mathbf{REL}^{1st}(\mathcal{A}) = \bigcup_{n\geq 1} \mathcal{P}(A^n)$ and in a frame, $A_n \subseteq \mathcal{P}A^n$ for all $n\geq 1$.)

(2) In any frame $\mathcal{A}$:

$$\mathbf{REL}^{1st}(\in\mathcal{A}) \subseteq \mathbf{REL}^{1st}(\mathcal{A})$$

(3) Due to our choice of signature, $\{C^{\mathcal{A}} / C\in\mathbf{OPER.CONS}\} \subseteq \mathbf{REL}^{1st}(\mathcal{A})$.

2.6.2. Definition of second order relations of $\mathcal{A}$

(a) Please recall the definition I.4.7.2 of an n-ary ***second order relation of*** $\mathcal{A}$ ▒

Let $\mathbf{REL}(\mathcal{A})$ be the class of all second order relations of $\mathcal{A}$. ▒

(b) We say that an n-ary second order relation **X** is ***into*** $\mathcal{A}$ as in I.4.7.2. ▒

Let $\mathbf{REL}(\in\mathcal{A})$ be the class of all second order relations into $\mathcal{A}$. ▒

Proposition.

(1) It is clear from the definition that

$$\mathbf{REL}^{1st}(\mathcal{A}) \subseteq \mathbf{REL}(\mathcal{A}) \text{ but } \mathbf{REL}^{1st}(\mathcal{A}) \neq \mathbf{REL}(\mathcal{A})$$

(2) Due to our choice of Σ,

$$\mathbf{REL}^{1st}(\in\mathcal{A}) = \mathbf{REL}(\in\mathcal{A})$$

(3) We can define the proper second order relations,

$$\text{REL}(\in\mathcal{A})^{2nd} = \text{REL}(\mathcal{A}) - \text{REL}^{1st}(\in\mathcal{A})$$

2.6.3. Definition of $\mathcal{A}$-definable first order relations using L_2.

As in section I.4.7.3, we say that the formula φ along with the sequence of individual variables $\langle x_1,\dots,x_n\rangle$ ***defines* X *in the structure* $\mathcal{A}$ *using* L_2** when

$$\mathbf{X} = \{\langle \mathbf{x}_1,\dots,\mathbf{x}_n\rangle \,/\, \mathcal{A}[{}^{\mathbf{x}_1\dots\mathbf{x}_n}_{x_1\dots x_n}] \text{ sat } \varphi\}$$

where $\text{FREE}(\varphi) \subseteq \{x_1,\dots,x_n\}$. ▒

Let $\text{DEF}^{1st}(\mathcal{A},L_2)$ be the smallest class containing all $\mathcal{A}$-definable first order relations using L_2. ▒

2.6.4. Definition of $\mathcal{A}$-definable second order relations using L_2.

Recall definition I.4.7.4 of a second order relation ***$\mathcal{A}$-definable using a language L_2***. ▒

Let $\text{DEF}(\mathcal{A},L_2)$ be the corresponding set. ▒

2.6.5. Definition of first and second order parametrically $\mathcal{A}$-definable relations using L_2.

(1) A first order relation **X** is parametrically $\mathcal{A}$-definable using L_2 iff there are a formula φ, individual variables $x_1,\dots,x_n$ and variables $v_1,\dots,v_m$ of any types $i_1,\dots,i_m \in \text{VAR}$ such that

$$\mathbf{X} = \{\langle \mathbf{x}_1,\dots,\mathbf{x}_n\rangle \in \mathbf{A}^n \,/\, \mathcal{A}[{}^{\mathbf{x}_1\dots\mathbf{x}_n\,\mathbf{v}_1\dots\mathbf{v}_m}_{x_1\;\;x_n\;v_1\;\;v_m}] \text{ sat } \varphi\}$$

where $\text{FREE}(\varphi) \subseteq \{x_1,\dots,x_n,v_1,\dots,v_m\}$ and the parameters $\mathbf{v}_1,\dots,\mathbf{v}_m$ are in $\mathbf{A}_{i_1},\dots,\mathbf{A}_{i_m}$ of types $i_1,\dots,i_m$. ▒

(2) A second order relation **X** is parametrically $\mathcal{A}$-definable using L_2 iff there are a formula φ, variables $u_1,\dots,u_n$ and variables $v_1,\dots,v_m$ of any types $k_1,\dots,k_n,i_1,\dots,i_m \in \text{VAR}$ such that

$$\mathbf{X} = \{\langle \mathbf{u}_1,\dots,\mathbf{u}_n\rangle \in \mathbf{A}_{k_1}\times\dots\times\mathbf{A}_{k_n} \,/\, \mathcal{A}[{}^{\mathbf{u}_1\dots\mathbf{u}_n\,\mathbf{v}_1\dots\mathbf{v}_m}_{u_1\;\;u_n\;v_1\;\;v_m}] \text{ sat } \varphi\}$$

where $\text{FREE}(\varphi) \subseteq \{u_1,\dots,u_n,v_1,\dots,v_m\}$ and the parameters $\mathbf{v}_1,\dots,\mathbf{v}_m$ are in $\mathbf{A}_{i_1},\dots,\mathbf{A}_{i_m}$ of types $i_1,\dots,i_m$. ▒

Let $\text{PARAM.DEF}^{1st}(\mathcal{A},L_2)$ and $\text{PARAM.DEF}(\mathcal{A},L_2)$ be the corresponding sets. ▒

Remarks.

In any structure

$$\mathcal{A} = \langle A, \langle A_n \rangle_{n\geq 1}, \langle C^{\mathcal{A}} \rangle_{C \in OPER.CONS} \rangle$$

it is easy to see that all n-ary first order relations in A_n are parametrically definable. What is no longer true is that all possible first order sets and relations are in the relational universes of a frame and so parametric definability serves us to define general structures for second order logic.

Proposition.

(1) $\mathrm{REL}(\in\mathcal{A}) \subseteq \mathrm{PARAM.DEF}^{1st}(\mathcal{A}, L_2)$, due to the choice of signature.

(2) $\mathrm{DEF}^{1st}(\mathcal{A}, L_2) \subseteq \mathrm{PARAM.DEF}^{1st}(\mathcal{A}, L_2)$.

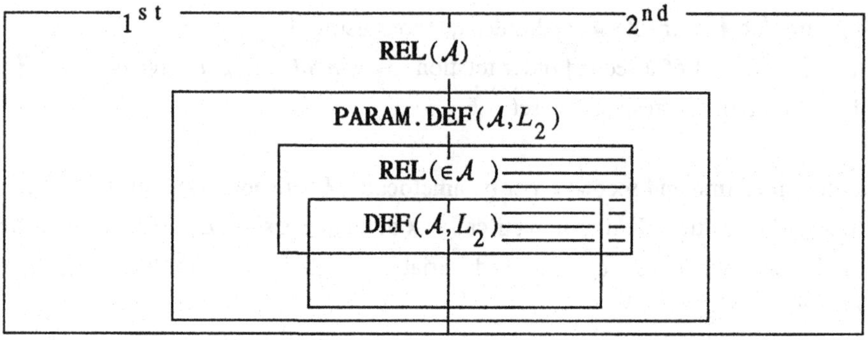

3.- GENERAL STRUCTURES.

We have seen that the C_2 calculus is unsound when using frames. Our aim has been to reduce the set of validities using non-standard semantics to be able to obtain all and only the second order theorems. The reduction operated by the non-standard semantics based on frames has been too dramatic and the comprehension axioms have been left out.

If we want the C_2 calculus to be sound, we need structures where the universes of sets and relations contain at least all the sets and relations that are definable using the formulas of SOL. What we need precisely are the general structures of Henkin.

There are at least three slightly different ways to define them:

(1) We can simply require that the calculus must be sound. In our case this is the same as requiring the structure to be a model of the set Γ containing all the comprehension

sentences[32]. Let us call this approach syntactical because we use the calculus. The condition required in this definition is a ***soundness condition.***

(2) We can require that all parametrically definable first order relations should be in the relational universes of the structure. When the calculus has the comprehension schema, the equivalence of this definition and the original is fairly obvious. Recall that a formula could define several relations depending on how we use the free variables in the formula and whether or not we accept parameters. Also, second order formulas are able to define first and second order relations; for instance, the formula Xx defines the membership relation which is not first order. In the relational universes of a second order structure we only put in the first order relations (*i.e.*, relations among individuals) but we also use the proper second order ones to build them. This second approach, semantical, is the most common one[33]. Let's denote by ***definable closure*** the condition required in this approach.

(3) We can give certain closure conditions on the relational universes to ensure that the definable relations are sitting in their proper place. The novelty of these conditions is that they are formulated independently of the formal language of **SOL**. This can be done in either a combinatorial, set-theoretical or algebraic approach[34]. In the third case the condition required would be the ***algebraic closure*** of the domains.

3.1. Definition of general structures.

3.1.1. Definition of general structures by soundness condition.

Let $\mathcal{A}$ be a frame. We say that $\mathcal{A}$ is a general structure if and only if it is a frame-model of the set Δ of all the comprehension sentences. ▮

3.1.2. Definition of general structures by definable closure.

Let $\mathcal{A}$ be a frame. We say that $\mathcal{A}$ is a general structure if and only if all parametrically $\mathcal{A}$-definable relations on individuals using the language L_2 are in the corresponding relation universes of the structure; *i.e.*, $A_n = \mathcal{P}A^n \cap \text{PARAM.DEF}(\mathcal{A},L_2)$. ▮

---

[32]They are the universal closure of occurrences of the comprehension schema.

[33]See Henkin [1950], see also Robbin [1969], page 140.

[34]This is advanced in a footnote in Henkin [1950] and developed differently in Andrews [1972.a] Boudreaux [1979] and Manzano [1982.b].

3.1.3. Proposition: The two definitions of general structures given so far are equivalent.

Proof

[$\Longrightarrow$] Let $\mathcal{A}$ be a general structure defined by the soundness condition. We want to see that all parametrically $\mathcal{A}$-definable relations on individuals using L_2 are in the relation universes. Let φ be a second order formula, $x_1,\ldots,x_n$ be pairwise distinct individual variables and $\langle v_1,\ldots,v_m\rangle$ the sequence, ordered by occurrence, of all the free variables of φ, apart from $x_1,\ldots,x_n$.

Take any n-ary relation variable X^n not free in φ. By hypothesis, $\mathcal{A}$ is a model of the sentence

$$\forall\ [\exists X^n \forall x_1\ldots x_n (X^n x_1\ldots x_n \leftrightarrow \varphi)];$$

here the symbol $\forall$ which is placed in front indicates the universal closure of the rest of the formula . Therefore, for all the $\mathbf{v}_1,\ldots,\mathbf{v}_m$ of the appropriate types,

$$\mathcal{A}\,[\mathbf{v}_1,\ldots,\mathbf{v}_m] \text{ is a model of } \exists X^n \forall x_1\ldots x_n (X^n x_1\ldots x_n \leftrightarrow \varphi)$$

Let $\mathcal{I} = \langle \mathcal{A}, \mathrm{M}\rangle$ where $\mathcal{I}(v_i) = \mathbf{v}_i$ for all i, $1 \leq i \leq m$. Obviously,

$$\mathcal{I} \text{ is a model of } \exists X^n \forall x_1\ldots x_n (X^n x_1\ldots x_n \leftrightarrow \varphi)$$

and so there is an $\mathbf{X}^n \in \mathbf{A}_n$ such that for all $\mathbf{x}_1,\ldots,\mathbf{x}_n \in \mathbf{A}$

$$\langle \mathbf{x}_1,\ldots,\mathbf{x}_n\rangle \in \mathbf{X}^n \text{ iff } \mathcal{I}^{\mathbf{x}_1\ldots\mathbf{x}_n}_{x_1\ldots x_n} \text{ sat } \varphi$$

$$\text{iff } \mathcal{A}\,[\mathbf{x}_1,\ldots,\mathbf{x}_n \mathbf{v}_1,\ldots,\mathbf{v}_m] \text{ sat } \varphi$$

This direction of the proof is now finished because this $\mathbf{X}^n \in \mathbf{A}_n$ is precisely the relation parametrically defined by the formula φ and the variables mentioned above.

[$\Longleftarrow$] Let $\mathcal{A}$ be a general structure defined by the definable closure condition. We want to see that all the comprehension sentences are true in $\mathcal{A}$. You can check this easily using the reverse of the steps we used for the other direction. ▌

Notation and remark.

From now on we can use freely any of these definitions, since we have checked that they are exactly the same, and so we can talk about "the" class of general structures.

The class of all general structures is named $\mathcal{G.S.}$ ▒

3.1.4. **Proposition:** The class of general structures is between the smaller class $\mathcal{S.S}$ and the bigger one $\mathcal{F}$. That is, $\mathcal{S.S} \subseteq \mathcal{G.S} \subseteq \mathcal{F}$.

Proof

The proof of this remark is simple; look at the definition of the concepts involved. ▮

3.2. Semantics based on general structures.

Since all general structures are frames, the semantic concepts defined in subsections 2.2.1 through 2.2.6 of this chapter for the second order language L_2 apply here. But we can also define a specific general semantics by the simple recipe of changing the word "frame" to "general" and the class $\mathcal{F}$ of frames to the class $\mathcal{G.S}$ of general structures. In particular, we write $\Gamma \models_{\mathcal{G.S}} \varphi$ to indicate that φ is a general consequence of Γ.

3.2.1. **Proposition:** General consequence is between frame-consequence and standard consequence.

Proof

Since $\mathcal{S.S} \subseteq \mathcal{G.S} \subseteq \mathcal{F}$, it is easy to see that

$\Gamma \models_{\mathcal{F}} \varphi$ implies $\Gamma \models_{\mathcal{G.S}} \varphi$ and that $\Gamma \models_{\mathcal{G.S}} \varphi$ implies $\Gamma \models_{\mathcal{S.S}} \varphi$, for all Γ and φ ▮

3.2.2. **Corollary:** General validity is between frame-validity and standard validity. That is, $\models_{\mathcal{F}} \varphi$ implies $\models_{\mathcal{G.S}} \varphi$ and $\models_{\mathcal{G.S}}$ implies $\models_{\mathcal{S.S}} \varphi$, for all φ. ▮

3.3. General structures and lambdas.

3.3.1. **Definition of denotation of terms and predicates and of satisfaction of formulas.**

It should be clear that general structures guarantee a denotation in the structure for all λ-predicates. Therefore, there is no need of keeping the language λ-L_2 away. Thus, all the definitions introduced in 4.2.1 of Chapter I apply here, in particular

$$\mathcal{I}(\lambda x_1..x_n\ \varphi) = \{\langle \mathrm{x}_1,...,\mathrm{x}_n\rangle \in \mathrm{A}^n \,/\, \mathcal{I}^{\mathrm{x}_1...\mathrm{x}_n}_{x_1...x_n} \text{ sat } \varphi\}$$

Can you please define them carefully? ▒

3.3.2. A proposed theorem.

If you were following the second option mentioned in section 2.5 of this Chapter, a nice definition for general structures is possible. This definition makes Kleene's three-valued semantics unnecessary; *i.e.*, the semantics collapses into the classical two-valued second order logic. Can you please formulate the suggested definition for general structure and prove its equivalence with the previous definition in two-valued logic? ▮

3.4. Soundness and completeness in general structures.

Before going further, let us check the new soundness result for the calculi C_2 and λ-C_2. We will see also that the completeness of both calculi follows easily from the completeness of C_2^- in frames. Moreover the calculus C_2^- is incomplete with the semantics on general structures.

3.4.1. Soundness of C_2 in general structures.

$\Gamma \vdash_{C_2} \varphi$ implies $\Gamma \vDash_{\mathcal{G.S}} \varphi$ for all Γ and φ, where $\Gamma \cup \{\varphi\} \subseteq$ **FORM**(L_2).

Proof

This follows easily from the fact that the calculus C_2^- is sound in frames (lemma 2.3.1 above) and the definition of general structures, since the only rule we have added to pass from C_2^- to C_2 is the comprehension schema, which is also what a frame needs to be a model of to become a general structure. That is, for all Γ and φ:

$$\Gamma \cup \Delta \vDash_{\mathcal{F}} \varphi \Leftrightarrow \Gamma \vDash_{\mathcal{G.S}} \varphi \text{ and } \Gamma \cup \Delta \vdash_{C_2^-} \varphi \Leftrightarrow \Gamma \vdash_{C_2} \varphi$$

where Δ is the set of all comprehension sentences.

Therefore,

$$\begin{array}{ccc} \Gamma \vdash_{C_2} \varphi & & \Gamma \vDash_{\mathcal{G.S}} \varphi \\ \Updownarrow & & \Updownarrow \\ \Gamma \cup \Delta \vdash_{C_2^-} \varphi & \Longrightarrow & \Gamma \cup \Delta \vDash_{\mathcal{F}} \varphi \end{array}$$ ▮

3.4.2. Soundness of λ-C_2 in general structures.

$\Gamma \vdash_{\lambda\text{-}C_2} \varphi$ implies $\Gamma \vDash_{\mathcal{G.S}} \varphi$ for all Γ and φ, where $\Gamma \cup \{\varphi\} \subseteq$ **FORM**(λ-L_2).

Proof

Can you please check that all the calculus rules are soundness preserving under the general semantics? All the proofs can be carried out as for standard structures (see II.3.1 and II.3.2), but this is not, however, a consequence of the soundness of λ-C_2 in the standard case. Notice that now the universes are full enough to contain all definable relations and, therefore, all the formulas with λ have a meaning in the structure; also recall that no universe is empty. The formula $\exists Xx\, Xx$ is not only true in all general structures, but also provable in λ-C_2. ∎

There is an alternative proof of the soundness of λ-C_2 using the result of C_2 (see 3.4.5 below).

3.4.3. Incompleteness of C_2^- in $\mathcal{G.S}$.

$\Gamma \models_{\mathcal{G.S}} \varphi$ does not imply $\Gamma \vdash_{C_2^-} \varphi$ for all Γ and φ, such that $\Gamma \cup \{\varphi\} \subseteq$ **FORM**(L_2).

Proof

The proof, very easy, follows from the observation that although $\exists Xx\, Xx$ is true in all general structures, it cannot be proved in C_2^-. (See II.4.1.) ∎

3.4.4. The completeness of C_2 in $\mathcal{G.S}$. follows from the completeness of C_2^- in $\mathcal{F}$.

If $\Sigma \models_{\mathcal{F}} \psi$ implies $\Sigma \vdash_{C_2^-} \psi$ for all Σ and ψ, then $\Gamma \models_{\mathcal{G.S}} \varphi$ implies $\Gamma \vdash_{C_2} \varphi$ for all Γ and φ (where $\Sigma \cup \Gamma \cup \{\psi, \varphi\} \subseteq$ **FORM**(L_2)).

Proof

Let us assume that we have the completeness of C_2^- in frames:

$$\Sigma \models_{\mathcal{F}} \psi \Rightarrow \Sigma \vdash_{C_2^-} \psi \text{ for all } \Sigma \text{ and } \psi, \text{ where } \Sigma \cup \{\psi\} \subseteq \textbf{FORM}(L_2)$$

Then, in particular, $\Gamma \cup \Delta \models_{\mathcal{F}} \varphi \;\Rightarrow\; \Gamma \cup \Delta \vdash_{C_2^-} \varphi$. The rest of the proof proceeds as in the proof of 3.4.1 but using completeness of C_2^- in frames instead of soundness. Thus,

$$\begin{array}{ccc} \Gamma \vdash_{C_2} \varphi & & \Gamma \models_{\mathcal{G.S}} \varphi \\ \Updownarrow & & \Updownarrow \\ \Gamma \cup \Delta \vdash_{C_2^-} \varphi & \Longleftarrow & \Gamma \cup \Delta \models_{\mathcal{F}} \varphi \end{array}$$

where Δ is the set of all comprehension sentences. ∎

We will prove the completeness of **MSL** in Chapter VI, which is basically the same as the completeness of C_2^- in frames. From it, the completeness of C_2 in general structures follows nicely, as you have seen above. In fact, in Chapter VII we will translate **SOL** into **MSL** to make the precise derivation.

3.4.5. The soundness and completeness of λ-C_2 in $\mathcal{G.S}$ follow from the soundness and completeness of C_2 in $\mathcal{G.S}$.

Of course, the completeness and soundness of λ-C_2 can be proved directly, but there is also a way of using the corresponding properties of C_2. What we have to do is to code the language λ-L_2 into L_2. You have to define the translation of each expression of λ-L_2 into an expression of L_2 and you want to use the following very general pattern:

$$\begin{array}{ccc} \Gamma \models_{\mathcal{G.S}} \varphi & & \Gamma \vdash_{\lambda\text{-}C_2} \varphi \\ \Updownarrow & & \Updownarrow \\ \Gamma^{\#} \models_{\mathcal{G.S}} \varphi^{\#} & \Longleftrightarrow & \Gamma^{\#} \vdash_{C_2} \varphi^{\#} \end{array}$$

Sketch of the proof.- To prove the theorem stated above you can take the following steps:

(A) Define $\psi^{\#}$ and prove $\psi \models_{\mathcal{G.S}} \psi^{\#}$ and $\psi^{\#} \models_{\mathcal{G.S}} \psi$, for every ψ of λ-L_2.

For every formula ψ of λ-L_2, find an equivalent lambda-free formula of L_2, $\psi^{\#}$. The definition has to be by induction on the formation of expressions; the only changes concern formulas with λ, where

$$(\lambda x_1 \dots x_n\ \varphi\ \tau_1 \dots \tau_n)^{\#} \equiv \varphi \frac{\tau_1 \dots \tau_n}{x_1 \dots x_n}$$

In the proof of the equivalence of both formulas you need to use the simultaneous substitution lemma for general semantics, where the substitution lemma for this semantics has an equivalent formulation and a similar proof to the ones given in section I.5.2 for standard semantics.

(B) Using the result of the previous step, prove:

$$\Gamma \models_{\mathcal{G.S}} \varphi \Longleftrightarrow \Gamma^{\#} \models_{\mathcal{G.S}} \varphi^{\#}$$

(C) Use the completeness and soundness of C_2 to obtain:

$$\Gamma^{\#} \models_{\mathcal{G.S}} \varphi^{\#} \Longleftrightarrow \Gamma^{\#} \vdash_{C_2} \varphi^{\#}$$

(D) Using the fact that the comprehension axiom is a theorem of the calculus λ-C_2 (II.2.7.4), prove the following:

$$\Gamma^{\#} \vdash_{C_2} \varphi^{\#} \iff \Gamma^{\#} \vdash_{\lambda\text{-}C_2} \varphi^{\#}$$

(E) Prove that $\psi \vdash_{\lambda\text{-}C_2} \psi^{\#}$ and $\psi^{\#} \vdash_{\lambda\text{-}C_2} \psi$, for every formula ψ of $\lambda\text{-}L_2$. (The inductive proof uses in the main step the rules (IAC) and (IAA) of section 2.4 in Chapter II.)

(F) Use the previous step to prove:

$$\Gamma^{\#} \vdash_{\lambda\text{-}C_2} \varphi^{\#} \iff \Gamma \vdash_{\lambda\text{-}C_2} \varphi \quad \blacksquare$$

4.- ALGEBRAIC DEFINITION OF GENERAL STRUCTURES.

We have given so far two equivalent definitions of general structures, but both of them depend on the formal language. Here, we are going to see another definition of the same concept using algebraic closure conditions on the domains.

In Chapter V, in the context of type theory, you will find the whole proof of the equivalence of the definition of general structures already introduced and the one presented in the algebraic approach. The equivalence of the corresponding second order definitions follows easily from this. Now we sketch a direct proof. As an exercise, you can complete the detailed proof (consult Chapter V for inspiration).

4.1. Fundamental relations of a structure.

Let **REL**($\mathcal{A}$) be the class of all relations on the universes of $\mathcal{A}$. This class includes all the relations of any finite arity n, n≥1. We are going to name certain relations in **REL**($\mathcal{A}$) and to define certain operations in it which will allow us to define by an algebraic procedure the class of all parametrically $\mathcal{A}$-definable first and second order relations. From this class we obtain the class of relations between individuals.

The fundamental relations and operations are the following:

(1) **Membership.** For every n≥1, let $\epsilon_n = \{\langle X, x_1, ..., x_n\rangle \epsilon A_n \times A^n / \langle x_1, ..., x_n\rangle \epsilon X\}$.

(2) **Difference.** For every $R, S \epsilon$ **REL**($\mathcal{A}$) of the same type - that is, both **R** and **S** are subsets of the same cartesian product of certain universes of $\mathcal{A}$ - then **R–S** will denote the usual set difference of sets.

(3) **Cartesian product.** For every $R \epsilon$ **REL**($\mathcal{A}$) we denote the cartesian product $A_n \times R$ in the

standard way, for every $n \geq 1$ and also, $A \times R$.

(4) **Permutation 1.** ("The last will be first...") Let $R \in \mathbf{REL}(\mathcal{A})$ and $R \subseteq A_{i_1} \times \ldots \times A_{i_n}$ with $n \geq 2$, where each A_{i_j} is either A or a certain A_k.

$$\mathrm{PER}_1(R) = \{\langle v_n, v_1, \ldots, v_{n-1}\rangle / \langle v_1, \ldots, v_n\rangle \in R\}$$

(5) **Permutation 2.** ("...and the first, second") Let $R \in \mathbf{REL}(\mathcal{A})$ as above,

$$\mathrm{PER}_2(R) = \{\langle v_2, v_1, v_3 \ldots, v_{n-1}\rangle / \langle v_1, \ldots, v_n\rangle \in R\}$$

(6) **Projection.** Let $R \in \mathbf{REL}(\mathcal{A})$ as above,

$$\mathrm{PROJ}(R) = \{\langle v_1, \ldots, v_{n-1}\rangle / \exists u \, \langle v_1, \ldots, v_{n-1}, u\rangle \in R\}$$

(7) **Singletons.** For every $R \in A$ or $R \in A_n$, $\{R\}$ is the singleton of R.

4.1.1. Closure under seven.

Let $\mathcal{A}$ be a second order frame and $\mathbf{REL}(\mathcal{A})$ the class of all relations on the universes of $\mathcal{A}$. For every $D \subseteq \mathbf{REL}(\mathcal{A})$, D is ***closed under seven*** if and only if all the fundamentals relations are in D and it is closed under all fundamental operations. ▓

4.1.2. Algebraically defined relations.

Given a second order frame $\mathcal{A}$, $\mathbf{ALG.DEF}(\mathcal{A})$ is defined as the least subset of $\mathbf{REL}(\mathcal{A})$ closed under seven. That is,

$$\mathbf{ALG.DEF}(\mathcal{A}) = \bigcap \{D / \mathbf{REL}(\in \mathcal{A}) \subseteq D \subseteq \mathbf{REL}(\mathcal{A}) \ \& \ D \text{ is closed under seven}\}$$ ▓

Remark.

Given a set $A \neq \emptyset$ and suitable interpretations for the symbols in **OPER.CONS**, there is not a unique frame $\mathcal{A}$ based on them. Therefore, for each A there are many $\mathbf{ALG.DEF}(\mathcal{A})$ also.

4.2. Algebraic definition of general structures.

4.2.1. Definition by algebraic closure.

A frame $\mathcal{A}$ is a general structure iff for every $n \geq 1$,

$$A_n = \mathcal{P}A^n \cap \mathbf{ALG.DEF}(\mathcal{A})$$ ▓

4.2.2. Proposition. This definition is equivalent to that given by definable closure.

Proof

You need to prove that

$$\text{ALG.DEF}(\mathcal{A}) = \text{PARAM.DEF}(\mathcal{A},L_2)$$

In the first place you prove by induction on formula formation that every parametrically defined relation is algebraically definable. Next you prove that the seven fundamental sets and relations can be parametrically defined. Can you please complete the details? ▮

5.- LOGICS OBTAINED BY WEAKENING THE SCHEMA OF COMPREHENSION.

In section 3.4 we have seen that the completeness and soundness in general structures of the calculus C_2 is an easy corollary of the completeness and soundness of C_2^- in frames. That technique is exportable. A variety of calculi can be obtained by weakening the comprehension schema; ***i.e.***, by restricting it to comprehension axioms in the form

$$\exists X^n \forall x_1...x_n (X^n x_1...x_n \leftrightarrow \varphi)$$

where the formula φ is taken not from the set of all second order formulas, but from a proper subset of this set. For instance, we can restrict comprehension to formulas without quantifiers, or to first order formulas[35]. We can, as well, restrict comprehension to formulas of other kinds, as will be done in Chapter VII, where we restrict it to the formulas of second order logic which are translations of modal formulas or of propositional dynamic formulas. I believe that any decidable set of formulas of the language will do.

Once a new calculus has been defined, how can we find the right semantics to prove the completeness and soundness of the new logic obtained?

You will see that we can base the whole construction on the completeness and soundness of many-sorted logic, since from it we prove these properties for C_2^- in frames. Then you proceed exactly as we did with the C_2 calculus when building the general structures.

Let us summarize the steps which have to be taken:

(A) Take the recursive set Δ^* of the comprehension sentences you want to consider and

[35]See Henkin [1953].

define a calculus, **CAL**, by adding to C_2^- the rule (CS), but restricted to the formulas you want to consider.

(B) Define the class $\mathcal{F}^*$ of all frames which are models of the set Δ^* of your comprehension sentences (that is, $\mathcal{F}^* = \text{MOD}(\Delta^*)$).

(C) Based on this class $\mathcal{F}^*$, you define the new semantics; namely, the main concepts of consequence and validity in $\mathcal{F}^*$.

(D) Having done all this, the soundness and completeness of **CAL** are obtained as a corollary of the soundness and completeness of C_2^- in $\mathcal{F}$. That is,

$$\Gamma \cup \Delta^* \vDash_{\mathcal{F}} \varphi \Leftrightarrow \Gamma \vDash_{\mathcal{F}^*} \varphi \text{ and } \Gamma \cup \Delta^* \vdash_{C_2^-} \varphi \Leftrightarrow \Gamma \vdash_{\text{CAL}} \varphi$$

Therefore,

$$\begin{array}{ccc} \Gamma \vdash_{\text{CAL}} \varphi & & \Gamma \vDash_{\mathcal{F}^*} \varphi \\ \Updownarrow & & \Updownarrow \\ \Gamma \cup \Delta^* \vdash_{C_2^-} \varphi & \Longleftrightarrow & \Gamma \cup \Delta^* \vDash_{\mathcal{F}} \varphi \end{array}$$

where Δ^* is the set of all comprehension sentences you are considering. ▮

6.- WEAK SECOND ORDER LOGIC.

6.1. General idea.

If you compare this logic with standard **SOL**, the language remains unaltered but the semantics changes. The only changes affect quantification, where the formula $\exists X\, \varphi$ means that there is a finite set such that φ. As you will see, quantification over finite sets and relations is enough for many purposes.

In weak-**SOL** we maintain what we named the standard point of view: you still want to talk about homogeneous first order structures and the quantification over sets and relations is only added to give the logic more expressive power. Also in common with the standard **SOL** is the fact that all the universes are known once the domain of individuals is given; for a first order structure, there is only one weak second order structure extending it. As in standard **SOL** you can identify the whole structure with the first order part of it.

Which structures are used for weak-**SOL**? To some extent the structures used to interpret weak second order formulas can be considered as second order frames whose relation universes contain all finite relations but only then. Accordingly, in a structure for weak second order logic the only assignment that will be used always assigns finite relations as values for the relation variables. The structures used to interpret weak-**SOL** are different from the second order frames in that we discard the condition requiring all the sets and relations distinguished in the structure to be in the corresponding universes for quantification purposes.

You can regard weak second order logic as the logic where the concept of finiteness is taken from the metatheory and imposed as a "logical" concept. It is not surprising that ***finiteness*** and ***infinity*** can be expressed; these two properties are weak second order finitely axiomatizable by the formula $\exists X\ \forall y\ Xy$ and its negation. Of course, in giving this axiom we are not getting any insight into the property of finiteness, we are just stating the fact that the universes of our weak second order structures only contain the finite sets and relations. And this fact is somewhat artificial, conventional.

Since singletons are finite and quantification over them is the only one needed to express ***identity***, this concept can be defined in weak second order logic by Leibniz's usual definition. Nevertheless, we will continue having equality as primitive.

It should be stressed that weak second order logic has an expressive power between first and second order standard logic, but it is not one of the logics obtained by weakening comprehension. In fact, comprehension fails as you can easily see: in a structure whose universe of individuals is infinite, the complement of a definable finite relation is not finite, thus it is not in the universe of relations.

6.2. Metaproperties of weak second order logic.

In Chapter I, section 4.9, we proved that standard **SOL** neither is compact nor satisfies the Löwenheim-Skolem metaproperties. In Chapter II, sections 4.2 and 4.3, the proofs of the incompleteness theorems for standard **SOL**, in both weak and strong senses, were also presented. In Chapter III, section 3.3 we saw that any second order Peano models are isomorphic. From this can be deduced (see section 3.6) the incompleteness of standard **SOL**.

In this chapter we have introduced the general semantics to obtain the inverse and positive results: compactness, completeness and Löwenheim-Skolem theorems will now be provable (Chapter VII, section 3). Of course, the other side of the coin is that you get non-standard models of natural numbers.

Our weak-**SOL** is easily seen to be ***non-compact*** and so the strong theorem of completeness will also fail for any sound calculus (apply the procedures of I.4.9). However, the ***downward Löwenheim-Skolem*** theorem can be proved for it. It has been noted already that comprehension schemas are not weak second order validities, even in the easier cases. Thus, our **SOL** calculus is not sound with this semantics. Since we can have in a weak structure infinite relations as distinguished elements but we cannot quantify over them, even the **MSL** calculus is unsound with this semantics. But is there any weak complete calculus for weak second order logic?

The answer is no, since weak-**SOL** is strong enough to characterize up to isomorphism the structure $\mathcal{N} = \langle \mathbb{N}, 0, S, +, \cdot \rangle$ of the natural numbers with zero, succesor, addition and multiplication.

Let us tabulate all this information:

	standard SOL	weak SOL	general SOL
Compactness	NO	NO	YES
Weak Completeness	NO	NO	YES
Downward Löwenheim-Skolem	NO	YES	YES
Characterization of natural numbers	YES	YES	NO

6.2.1. Downward Löwenheim-Skolem.

If $\Gamma \subseteq$ **SENT**(L_2) has a weak-model, then Γ has a weak-model with a countable universe of individuals.

Proof

Let $\mathcal{A}$ be a weak-model of a countable set of sentences Γ in our countable second order language L_2. We will build a countable structure taking the basic elements from $\mathcal{A}$. The universe of individuals is being built by levels, having in the first one the interpretation for all the individual constants. In each level we close the set so as to include the values for all the function constants and witnesses for all the formulas of the form $\exists v\ \varphi$ (where v is either individual or predicative).

Definition of a chain $\mathbf{B}(0) \subseteq \mathbf{B}(1) \subseteq \mathbf{B}(2) \subseteq \ldots$

We will define a sequence $\mathbf{B}(0) \subseteq \mathbf{B}(1) \subseteq \mathbf{B}(2) \subseteq \ldots$ of countable subsets of $\mathbf{A}$ with the following characteristics:

(1) The sets $\mathbf{B}(0), \mathbf{B}(1), \mathbf{B}(2), \ldots$ form a chain ordered by inclusion.

(2) For each $m \geq 1$ and $f \in$ **OPER.CONS** with $\mathrm{FUNC}(f) = \langle 1,1,\overset{n}{\ldots},1\rangle$, we have

$$\mathrm{Rec}(f^{\mathcal{A}} \restriction \mathbf{B}(m)^n) \subseteq \mathrm{B}(m+1)$$

(3) For every $\exists x\ \varphi$ and weak-assignment M having all the values in $\mathbf{B}(m)$ (and its finite sets and relations) such that $\langle \mathcal{A}, \mathrm{M}\rangle$ sat $\exists x\ \varphi$, we have

$$\text{there is an } \mathbf{x} \in \mathbf{B}(m+1) \text{ such that } \langle \mathcal{A}, \mathrm{M}^{\mathbf{x}}_{x}\rangle \text{ sat } \varphi$$

(4) For every $\exists X^n\ \varphi$ and weak-assignment M having all the values in $\mathbf{B}(m)$ (and its finite sets and relations) such that $\langle \mathcal{A}, \mathrm{M}\rangle$ sat $\exists X^n\ \varphi$, we have

$$\text{there is a finite } \mathbf{X}^n \subseteq \mathbf{B}(m+1) \text{ such that } \langle \mathcal{A}, \mathrm{M}^{\mathbf{X}^n}_{X^n}\rangle \text{ sat } \varphi.$$

We begin with $\mathbf{B}(0)$ by taking any countable subset of A which includes all the $f^{\mathcal{A}}$ for all the function symbols with $\mathrm{FUNC}(f) = \langle 1\rangle$.

Having defined $\mathbf{B}(m)$ we define $\mathrm{B}(m+1)$ by adding to it the values of $f^{\mathcal{A}}$ for all $\mathbf{x}_1,\ldots,\mathbf{x}_n \in \mathbf{B}(m)$ (for each $f \in$ **OPER.CONS** with $\mathrm{FUNC}(f) = \langle 1,1,\ldots,1\rangle$). Besides this, for every $\exists x\ \varphi$ such that $\langle \mathcal{A}, \mathrm{M}\rangle$ sat $\exists x\ \varphi$ in a weak assignment M having all the values in $\mathbf{B}(m)$ and its finite sets and relations, we take from

$$\{\mathbf{x} \in \mathbf{A} \,/\, \langle \mathcal{A}, \mathrm{M}^{\mathbf{x}}_{x}\rangle \text{ sat } \varphi\}$$

an element to put in $\mathbf{B}(m+1)$. The choice of this element can be done in various ways; if you want to be very specific, you can use an ordering of the set A and in each step take the witnesses with minimum index in this ordering.

Finally, for every $\exists X^n\ \varphi$ such that $\langle \mathcal{A}, \mathrm{M}\rangle$ sat $\exists X^n\ \varphi$ in a weak-assignment M having all the values in $\mathrm{B}(m)$ (and its finite sets and relations), we take from

$$\{\mathbf{X}^n \in \mathbf{A}_n \,/\, \langle \mathcal{A}, \mathrm{M}^{\mathbf{X}^n}_{X^n}\rangle \text{ sat } \varphi\}$$

one relation and put all its members in $\mathrm{B}(m+1)$. You can take the $\mathbf{X}^n$ with fewest new members and for the choice of new members you can use the ordering of the set A.

Definition of the structure $\mathcal{B}$.

Let $\mathcal{B} = \langle B, \langle B_n \rangle_{n\geq 1}, \langle C^{\mathcal{B}} \rangle_{C \in \text{OPER.CONS}} \rangle$ be defined as follows:

(i) $B = \bigcup_{m\geq 1} B(m)$.

(ii) For each $n\geq 1$, B_n includes all the finite n-ary relations on B.

(iii) For each n-ary relation constant, $R \in$ OPER.CONS and FUNC(R) $= \langle 0,1,\overset{n}{\ldots},1\rangle$,

$$R^{\mathcal{B}} = R^{\mathcal{A}} \cap B^n$$

(thus, $R^{\mathcal{B}}$ is a subset of the n-ary cartesian product of B, an element of $\mathcal{P}\, B^n$).

(iv) For each n-ary function constant, $f \in$ OPER.CONS and FUNC(f) $= \langle 1,\overset{n+1}{\ldots},1\rangle$,

$$f^{\mathcal{B}} = f^{\mathcal{A}}{\restriction} B^n$$

(it is not immediately obvious that $\text{Rec}(f^{\mathcal{A}}{\restriction} B^n) \subseteq B$, but it follows from our construction, as you can verify yourself).

Proposition 1: $\mathcal{B} \sqsubseteq \mathcal{A}$ (where $\mathcal{B}$ and $\mathcal{A}$ are here identified with its first order parts and $\sqsubseteq$ is the concept of substructure Chapter I, 3.2.1).

Proposition 2: For each $M: \mathcal{V} \cup (\bigcup_{n\geq 1} \mathcal{V}_n) \longrightarrow B \cup (\bigcup_{n\geq 1} B_n)$, $\mathcal{I} = \langle \mathcal{A}, M\rangle$ and $\mathcal{H} = \langle \mathcal{B}, M\rangle$,

$\mathcal{I}$ sat φ iff $\mathcal{H}$ sat φ, for all $\varphi \in$ SENT(L_2)

Proposition 3: The structure $\mathcal{B}$ has a countable universe of individuals.

Proposition 4: $\mathcal{B}$ is a weak model of Γ.

All four propositions can be easily proved. Can you please do this? ∎

6.2.2. Natural numbers and weak-SOL.

In weak-SOL the structure $\mathcal{N} = \langle \mathbb{N}, 0, S, +, \cdot \rangle$ can be characterized up to isomorphism.

Proof

As axioms take the finite set Δ of sentences including:

$\alpha_1 \equiv \forall x \neg \sigma x = c$

$\alpha_2 \equiv \forall xy (\sigma x = \sigma y \rightarrow x = y)$

$\alpha_3 \equiv \forall x (\neg x = c \rightarrow \exists y\, x = \sigma y)$

$\beta_1 \equiv \forall x\, x + c = x$

$\beta_2 \equiv \forall xy\, x + \sigma y = \sigma(x + y)$

$$\gamma_1 \equiv \forall x\; x \cdot c = c$$
$$\gamma_2 \equiv \forall xy\; x \cdot \sigma y = (x \cdot y) + x$$
$$\delta \equiv \forall x \exists Y \forall y\; (\exists z\; y + \sigma z = x \rightarrow Yy)$$

All the axioms but δ are first order formulas with the usual interpretation. The clue of the formalization rests in the axiom δ saying that for any natural number the set of its predecessors is finite. Due to this axiom, $\mathbb{Z}$-chains are excluded. Any model $\mathcal{A}$ of Δ is then reduced to a standard part

$$\mathbb{N}(\mathcal{A}) = \{c^{\mathcal{A}}, \sigma^{\mathcal{A}}(c^{\mathcal{A}}), \sigma^{\mathcal{A}}(\sigma^{\mathcal{A}}(c^{\mathcal{A}})), \ldots\}$$

Can you please verify all this? ▮

CHAPTER V
TYPE THEORY.

1.- INTRODUCTION.

1.1. General idea.

So far we are familiar with propositional logic (*i.e.*, zeroth order), first order logic and second order logic. In propositional logic no quantification is allowed; in first order logic we quantify over individuals; in second order logic we also quantify over sets and relations among individuals. Second order relations - as described in I.4.7 - only incidentally appear in this logic, since we have neither constants nor variables to refer to or to quantify over them. If we can refer to them using variables, we are in third order logic. When we quantify, as well, over second order relations, we are in fourth order logic. A logic which includes all logics of all finite orders (but only them) is known as finite type theory[36].

The structures we want to talk about in type theory must include different quantification domains corresponding to the different types of variables. The whole family of domains is known as the hierarchy of types. In the standard relational hierarchy of types we have, as in the standard second order structures, a universe of individuals, D, and for each $n \geq 1$, a universe of n-ary relations among individuals, $D_{\langle 0,1,\overset{n}{\ldots},1\rangle}$. In the standard case, $D_{\langle 0,1,\overset{n}{\ldots},1\rangle} = \mathcal{P} D^n$. Furthermore, in type theory we have universes for relations among relations; for instance, $D_{\langle 0,\langle 0,1,\overset{n}{\ldots},1\rangle\rangle}$ is the universe whose members are unary relations on n-ary relations on individuals, while $D_{\langle 0,\langle 0,1,\overset{n_1}{\ldots},1\rangle,\ldots,\langle 0,1,\overset{n_m}{\ldots},1\rangle\rangle}$ is the universe of m-ary relations among n_i-ary ($1 \leq i \leq n$) relations of individuals. In general, we will have a universe $D_{\langle 0,\alpha_1,\ldots,\alpha_n\rangle}$ for n-ary relations among relations of any finite type α_i; which in the standard case embodies the whole of $\mathcal{P}(D_{\alpha_1} \times \ldots \times D_{\alpha_n})$. Every finite type has a type symbol from the set TS, to be defined below. In the language we use for type theory we accordingly distinguish different levels or types of variables to quantify over. We cannot quantify over all properties, but only over all properties of a given type; for instance, we can say "for all unary properties of individuals", or,

[36]There is also transfinite type theory, but it is not treated in this book. See Andrews [1965].

"for all binary relations among individuals and unary properties of individuals", etc.

In the first of our presentations of type theory, **RTT**, sets and relations are defined by comprehension and we ask our theory to include all the definable ones. We want also to identify classes having the same objects, thus we also have extensionality. The calculus C_ω which we will use with **RTT** is a generalization to all types of the second order calculus C_2 presented in Chapter II. In particular, comprehension and extensionality for all types are expressed now in this form:

$$\exists X^\beta \forall X_1^{\alpha_1} \ldots X_n^{\alpha_n} (X^\beta (X_1^{\alpha_1} \ldots X_n^{\alpha_n}) \leftrightarrow \varphi)$$

where $\beta = \langle 0,\alpha_1,\ldots,\alpha_n \rangle$ and $X^\beta \notin \mathrm{FREE}(\varphi)$,

and

$$\forall X^\beta Y^\beta (X^\beta (X_1^{\alpha_1} \ldots X_n^{\alpha_n}) \leftrightarrow Y^\beta (X_1^{\alpha_1} \ldots X_n^{\alpha_n}) \rightarrow X^\beta = Y^\beta)$$

where $\beta = \langle 0,\alpha_1,\ldots,\alpha_n \rangle$

Type theory possesses not only a huge expressive power, but also a very simple and natural conception which is not appreciated enough because it is masked behind a complex language. In **RTT** the complexity has been kept to a minimum sacrificing some of the formal beauty. You find then a very powerful language, only paralleled by set theory, and a great degree of internal coherence. It is so much so, that the best known formal paradoxes cannot be formulated here. The reason is that, as you will see later and Russell pointed out at the beginning of the century[37], most of the formal paradoxes appeared because quantification is following a vicious circle schema. This schema is broken when you quantify in type theory, *i.e.*, where you restrict quantification to a given type.

Although it is usually recognized that part of the motivation for developing set theory was the discovery of paradoxes in naive set theory, type theory is far from being an *ad hoc* construction lacking naturalness and mathematical common sense. Let us quote Gandy[38]:

> The simple theory of types provides a straightforward, reasonably secure, foundation for the greater part of classical mathematics. That is why a number of authors (Carnap, Gödel, Tarski, Church, Turing) gave a precise

[37]Whitehead & Russell [1910-13]. See Russell [1908] for a brief exposition of type theory based on a discussion of paradoxes.

[38]See Gandy [1977].

> formulation of it, and used it as a basis for metamathematical investigations. The theory is straightforward because it embodies two principles which (at least before the advent of modern abstract concepts) were part of the mathematician's normal code of practice. Namely that a variable always has a precisely delimited range, and that a distinction must always be made between a function and its arguments. In this sense one might claim that all good mathematicians had anticipated simple type theory. [Indeed Turing made this claim for primitive man]. The claim goes too far, but it does draw attention to the fact that the justification for the theory is not to be found by considering it as a formal device to avoid Russell's paradox.

Type theory includes second order logic, whose success and miseries therefore extend to it. In particular, all we have said and proved for second order logic in the four previous chapters also applies here. Thus, it is a powerful expressive language with no complete calculus to generate the standard validities. We have also the possibility of introducing frames and general semantics to select the provable sentences of reasonable deductive calculi.

1.2. Paradoxes and their solution in type theory.

Around the turn of the century a growing number of paradoxes[39] appeared in mathematics; particularly in foundational theories such as set theory. At the beginning, contradictions seemed to affect only very big sets - such as the set of all sets or the ordinals - and it was thought that maybe the notion of infinite was the only cause for them. But when Russell discovered his paradox affecting the very basic notion of set definition, everybody was then convinced that the theory was in need of a substantial modification. Well known are the axiomatic solutions offered by Zermelo and his followers on one hand and by von Neumann and others, on the other. Another path was the one taken by Brouwer and the intuitionists. Finally, Russell made a great advance by proposing a new theory where paradoxes cannot be formulated because the language itself avoids the formulation of them. Although Russell's formulation of type theory is different from ours, the basic ideas are the same.

Known paradoxes abound; among them we will distinguish three. In 1926 Ramsey classified

[39]For a discussion of paradoxes focused in type theory and related topics, see Ramsey [1926], Beth [1965], Rogers [1971], Copi [1971], Quine [1976], Church [1976], Tarski [1956.b], Kripke [1975] and Sainsbury [1988].

paradoxes into two big groups:

- *Logical or mathematical paradoxes.*
- •• *Semantic or epistemological paradoxes.*

To formulate paradoxes in the first group only logical or mathematical notions are needed; for instance, the concept of class, or the notion of number. To express paradoxes in the second group you need to mix up language and metalanguage, using notions such as truth or the notion of designate.

Ramsey's classification is useful because it helps you to understand paradoxes, but especially, because it helps you to solve them, offering different solutions for paradoxes in different groups. Logical paradoxes are solved in simple type theory, but to solve semantical paradoxes you need either complex ramified type theory or the distinction between language and metalanguage proposed by Tarski[40]. Thus, you have to be aware that to express the truth of a sentence of the object language you should be using another language which serves as the metalanguage of the former.

Logical paradoxes.

Among these Russell's and Cantor's paradoxes are by far the best known. Russell's paradox questions the very basic concept of class definition, while Cantor's is based on the more elaborate - but equally central in mathematics - notion of cardinality.

Russell's paradox.

In naive set theory all properties are able to define sets, but if you take as defining property the property of not being a member of itself, we arrive at the following contradiction when analyzing the class $U = \{X/X \notin X\}$: Is U a member of U? If U were a member of U, it should satisfy the defining property; *i.e.*, it should not be a member of itself, $U \notin U$. On the other hand, if U were not a member of U it should not satisfy the defining property; *i.e.*, $U \in U$. Of course, the resulting statement, $U \in U \longleftrightarrow U \notin U$, is a contradiction.

This paradox does not appear in type theory because the string of symbols $X \notin X$ is not a formula of **RTT** and we cannot apply comprehension to it; our atomic formulas now have the form $X^{\alpha} \in Y^{\beta}$ (or $Y^{\beta}X^{\alpha}$) with $\beta = \langle 0, \alpha \rangle$, where the distinction of types is basic.

[40]See Church [1976] for a comparison between the two solutions.

Let me explain this in detail. It is usually admitted that type theory and set theory are two different alternatives for foundations, and some people tend to see the differences as merely notational. We will go in two steps from **RTT** to set theory, pointing out the weakness of the transition and where axiomatic set theory has to be mended.

(A) We agree that properties are able to define sets and we can identify properties with formulas defining them. Moreover, we can reduce relations to sets, since ordered pairs can be considered as sets and ordered tuples can be seen as nested pairs; therefore, relations are also sets. Of course, to say that X^{α} is in the set Y^{β} - where $\beta = \langle 0,\alpha \rangle$ - you can write either $Y^{\beta}X^{\alpha}$ or $X^{\alpha} \in Y^{\beta}$; it is certainly a superfluous change since both formulas have the same meaning and scope. At this point comprehension has the form:

$$\exists Y^{\beta}\, \forall X^{\alpha}(X^{\alpha} \in Y^{\beta} \longleftrightarrow \varphi)$$

with $\beta = \langle 0,\alpha \rangle$, where the distinction of types is not at all superfluous.

(B) If type distinction does not exist and we admit that our universe only contains sets, the axiom of definition of sets is expressed by the formula $\exists Y\, \forall X(X \in Y \longleftrightarrow \varphi)$. But without type distinction we can again take as defining formula φ, the formula $X \notin X$, obtaining $\exists Y\, \forall X(X \in Y \longleftrightarrow X \notin X)$. By the principle of extensionality, the set defined by this formula is unique, we call this set U. Thus, $\forall X(X \in U \longleftrightarrow X \notin X)$. The contradiction is reached when we try to determine whether or not this U is a member of itself; we then obtain $U \in U \longleftrightarrow U \notin U$. To avoid this problem, in axiomatic set theory either you distinguish between sets and classes, or you have separation instead of comprehension. The axiom of separation only allows you to define new sets from previously defined ones.

Cantor's paradox.

Consider the class U of all classes; namely, the universal class. It can be proven that the cardinality of the power set of it is bigger than the cardinality of the universal class and that it is less than or equal to it.

Let U be the set of all sets. Obviously, its cardinal $|U|$ surpasses any possible cardinal; *i.e.*, $|A| \preceq |U|$ for all A. Thus,

$$* \quad \exists X\, \forall Y(|Y| \preceq |X|)$$

But look what happens when we consider the class $\mathcal{P}U$. It is easy to see, and Cantor himself proved it, that the power set of a set has strictly greater cardinality than the set. The proof is based on these two facts:

(1) For any A, there is a one-to-one function mapping A into $\mathcal{P}A$; namely, the function

$$\begin{aligned} f: A &\longrightarrow \mathcal{P}A \\ x &\longmapsto \{x\} \end{aligned}$$

(2) But no function $\mathbf{h}$ from A to $\mathcal{P}A$ can be exhaustive. The reason is that for the class $X = \{x \in A / x \notin \mathbf{h}(x)\}$, which is certainly a member of $\mathcal{P}A$, there is no element z of A such that $\mathbf{h}(z) = X$. To prove this, assume that we have $\mathbf{h}(z) = X$ for a certain $z \in A$. Clearly, for any $x \in A$: $x \in X \longleftrightarrow x \notin \mathbf{h}(x)$. In particular, for this z: $z \in X \longleftrightarrow z \notin \mathbf{h}(z)$. Since $\mathbf{h}(z) = X$, we get the statement: $z \in \mathbf{h}(z) \longleftrightarrow z \notin \mathbf{h}(z)$. This is a contradiction.

We have then proved:

$\forall X\, \exists Y(|Y| \succ |X|)$

which is equivalent to $\neg \exists X\, \forall Y(|Y| \preceq |X|)$.

Therefore, we have obtained a contradiction to *.

The Cantor paradox cannot appear in type theory because a set and its power set are in different types. In axiomatic set theory the universal class is not a set and only the power set of a set is also a set.

Semantic paradoxes.

The oldest known contradiction of this kind is due to Epimenides, the Cretan. He said that all Cretans were liars, and all other statements made by Cretans were lies. The contradiction arose when questioning Epimenides' statement under its own light. Is it true?

An easy way to see it is as follows:

Let p be the statement: "I am lying". Of course, this is the same as saying: "It is not true that p" which can be formalized as $\neg Tp$. Thus,

* $p \equiv \neg Tp$

But the semantical property of truth has to be defined as $\forall x(Tx \longleftrightarrow x)$.

Now look what happens when we consider the formula p itself. In the first place,

** $Tp \longleftrightarrow p$

We can now use * and replace in the formula **, the formula p by its formalization, obtaining

- $Tp \leftrightarrow \neg Tp$

  Of course, this is a contradiction.

In simple type theory or in any other formalized theory where you distinguish language and metalanguage the formula $\forall x(Tx \leftrightarrow x)$ with its intended meaning cannot be a formula of the object language. So this formula does not belong to the theory.

Let us examine what is the link between paradoxes and their solution in Russell's view[41]:

> In all the above contradictions (which are merely selections from an indefinite number) there is a common characteristic, which we may describe as self-reference or reflexiveness. The remark of Epimenides must include itself in its own scope. If all classes, provided they are not members of themselves are members of U, this must also apply to U;...
>
> Thus all our contradictions have in common the assumption of a totality such that, if it were legitimate, it would at once be enlarged by new members defined in terms of itself.

1.3. Three presentations of type theory.

A relational theory of types.

In the first of our formulations of type theory, which we call **RTT**, the main concern is simplicity and understandability; so we are not having proposition or function variables, nor lambda abstraction; moreover, the set of operation constants is empty. It is well known that while function symbols are often convenient, they can be eliminated without real loss of expressive power. The calculus C_ω which we will use with **RTT** is a generalization to all types of the second order calculus C_2. Therefore, we have comprehension and extensionality for all types. We will also introduce **RTT** with lambda and, in this case, we will use the obvious extension of the calculus λ-C_2 (with lambda rules instead of comprehension). For **RTT** we will make a new algebraic definition of general structures and we will prove in full the equivalence with the common definition.

---

[41]See Russell [1908].

A functional theory of types.
Church's elegant formulation of functional type theory, **FTT**, is also presented in section 4. It is more complex than our previous **RTT** because:

(1) We abandon the relational presentation in favor of a functional presentation; relations are then converted into characteristic functions. Functions of any types are also allowed.
(2) The abstractor operator is used to introduce functions.
(3) Following a well known device originated by Schönfinkel, all the functions considered are unary and the usual n-ary functions and relations are converted into unary functions.
(4) We add propositional types and the ability to form new types from them.
(5) Our **OPER.CONS** is no longer empty, but it includes constants for equality, negation, disjunction, existential function and selector operator. It might contain as well some other constants whose meaning can vary with every structure.

In subsection 4.4 we show in detail how to transform **RTT** into **FTT**; *i.e.*, we convert the relational structures into unary functional structures and also we translate the formulas. We will prove the semantical equivalence of meaning of the original formulas in relational structures with their translated formulas in converted structures.

An equational theory of types.
In another section we will present **ETT**, a beautiful equational theory of types. This is a language for functional type theory where the only primitive notions are identity and abstraction. The basic ideas are taken from Henkin [1963] and [1975].

It is interesting to see how using only these two basic notions all the connectors and quantifiers are defined. A calculus for **ETT** is also defined and this calculus only contains two basic axioms for equality, including lambda conversion, and a replacement rule of inference.

2.- A RELATIONAL THEORY OF FINITE TYPES.

2.1. Definition (signature and alphabet).

2.1.1. Signature of the relational type theory.
By a signature Σ for the relational type theory **RTT** we mean an ordered pair $\Sigma = \langle$**TS,FUNC**$\rangle$ where:

(i) **TS** is the set of type symbols, which is obtained by observing the following formation rules:

(1) $1,0 \in$ **TS** (1 is the type symbol of individuals, while 0 is the type symbol of propositions).

(2) For any natural number n: If $\alpha_1,...,\alpha_n \in \mathbf{TS}-\{0\}$, then $\langle 0,\alpha_1,...,\alpha_n\rangle \in \mathbf{TS}$. (The new type $\langle 0,\alpha_1,...,\alpha_n\rangle$ is for n-ary relations among types $\alpha_1,...,\alpha_n$.)

(ii) **FUNC** = **FUNC**(Σ) is a function whose domain is **OPER.CONS**, the set of operation constants. This function tells you the type of your operation constants. In our present case, **FUNC** is empty because **OPER.CONS** is empty. ▒

2.1.2. Alphabet of the RTT language T_ω.

Let us call T_ω the **Pure RTT** language. The alphabet of this language includes[42]: Connectives, quantifiers, parentheses, equality for expressions of each nonzero type α (where equality itself has type $\langle 0,\alpha,\alpha\rangle$) and variables for each nonzero type. Namely,

For every $\alpha \in \mathbf{TS}-\{0\}$, an infinite countable set $\mathcal{V}_\alpha$ of variables of type α: X^α, Y^α, Z^α, U^α, V^α, W^α, X_1^α, X_2^α, X_3^α, etc. ▒

Remark and notation.

As you see, for the sake of simplicity, we are not considering proposition variables. Also, if you prefer it, you can leave out the superscript and indicate the type separately.

2.2. Expressions.

The expressions of T_ω are built from the following rules:

(E1) $\perp$ is an expression of T_ω whose type is 0.

(E2) If $\alpha \in \mathbf{TS}-\{0\}$, X^α is an expression of T_ω whose type is α.

(E3) For each $\alpha \in \mathbf{TS}-\{0\}$, $=^{\langle 0,\alpha,\alpha\rangle}$ is an expression whose type is the superscript.

(E4) If A is an expression of type $\langle 0,\alpha_1,...,\alpha_n\rangle$ and if $B_1,...,B_n$ are expressions of types $\alpha_1,...,\alpha_n$, then $A(B_1...B_n)$ is an expression of type 0.

(E5) If φ and ψ are expressions of type 0, then $\neg\varphi$, $(\varphi \vee \psi)$, $(\varphi \wedge \psi)$, $(\varphi \rightarrow \psi)$ and $(\varphi \longleftrightarrow \psi)$ are expressions of type 0.

---

[42]See Chapter I, 2.1.3, for details.

(E6) If φ is an expression of type 0 and X^{α} is a variable of any type α, then $\forall X^{\alpha}\varphi$ and $\exists X^{\alpha}\varphi$ are expressions of type 0.

EXPR(T_{ω}) is the smallest set obtained by these rules. ▒
FORM(T_{ω}) is the set of expressions of type 0. ▒

Remarks.
In our previous terminology for second order logic, expressions of type 1 are individual terms.

But what about the expression X^{α}, with $\alpha = \langle 0,\alpha_1,...,\alpha_n\rangle$?
It is both a term and a predicate. With an expression Y^{β} of type $\beta = \langle 0,\alpha\rangle$, it works as a term when forming the formula $Y^{\beta}X^{\alpha}$; but with the expressions $Z^{\alpha_1},...,Z^{\alpha_n}$, it works as a predicate when building the formula $X^{\alpha}(Z^{\alpha_1}...Z^{\alpha_n})$. That is why we are not using the terminology of terms and predicates.

2.3. Equality.

We have added the equality signs as primitive symbols, so we have no need of introducing them by definition, but it's certainly possible and in type theory with standard semantics this is the common approach. Let us see briefly how:
For each type α, $\alpha\in$ **TS**$-\{0\}$,

$$\forall X^{\alpha}\, Y^{\alpha}(=^{\langle 0,\alpha,\alpha\rangle}(X^{\alpha}\, Y^{\alpha}) \longleftrightarrow \forall Z^{\langle 0,\alpha\rangle}\,(Z^{\langle 0,\alpha\rangle}(X^{\alpha}) \longleftrightarrow Z^{\langle 0,\alpha\rangle}(Y^{\alpha})))$$

Thus, this definition just extends to all types the Leibnizian definition given in section 4.8 of Chapter I.

2.4. Free variables and substitution.

Can you please define **FREE**(ε) for all the expressions of T_{ω}? (The definition should agree basically with definition 2.5.1 of Chapter I.) ▒

Given a variable X^{α} and an expression ε^{α}, both of the same type α ($\alpha\in$ **TS**$-\{0\}$), you can define by induction on the formation of expressions the substitution for the expression ε^{α} by the variable X^{α} in any expression ε.

Can you please define substitution by following the pattern of definitions given in section 2.6 of Chapter I? ▒

2.5. Deductive calculus.

The calculus for **RTT**, named C_{ω}, is a simple generalization of the calculus C_2 in Chapter II.

Can you please extend that calculus by extending the rules dealing with quantifiers so as to cover the whole range of type theory quantification? Can you extend as well the extensionality rule (Ext.) and the comprehension rule (CS)? Finally, can you extend the equality rules (RE) and (ES) so as to cover all the expressions of type $\alpha \in TS-\{0\}$?. ▒

Remarks.
In equality-free type theory, where equality is introduced by definition, you do not need the equality rules because they are theorems which can be proved from the definition.

As an exercise, can you prove (RE) and (ES) for expressions of any type $\alpha \in TS-\{0\}$? In fact, if you identify equality of type 0 with the connective $\longleftrightarrow$ (meaning identity of truth values), the rules (RE) and (ES) also apply for type 0.

2.6. The relational standard structure and the relational standard hierarchy of types.

2.6.1. Definition.
The language T_{ω} of signature Σ introduced so far is primarily designed to talk about ***relational standard structures*** of the same signature,

$$\mathcal{D} = \langle \, D, \langle D_{\alpha} \rangle_{\alpha \in TS} \, \rangle$$

where:

(i) $D \neq \emptyset$ is a non-empty set.

(ii) $\langle D_{\alpha} \rangle_{\alpha \in TS}$ is the ***relational standard hierarchy of types***; *i.e.*

(a) $D_0 = \{T,F\}$ and $D_1 = D$,

(b) $D_{\langle 0,\alpha_1,...,\alpha_n \rangle} = \mathcal{P}(D_{\alpha_1} \times ... \times D_{\alpha_n})$. ▒

Remarks.

(1) Therefore, in $D_{\langle 0,\alpha_1,...,\alpha_n \rangle}$, we have put in all the relations **R** which hold for n-tuples $\langle X_1,...,X_n \rangle$ such that $X_i \in D_{\alpha_i}$ for each $i \in \{1,...,n\}$. Clearly, a standard structure is uniquely determined when you know its universe **D**.

(2) Also, it is a simple matter to pass from this hierarchy to another where, instead of ordinary relations, we put in the corresponding characteristic functions.

2.6.2. Assignments.

As in second order logic (see section 4.1 of Chapter I), assignments are functions giving to every variable in the language a value in the hierarchy of types. Thus,

For every X^α: $M(X^\alpha) \in D_\alpha$. ▒

Also, for all $X_1 \in D_{\alpha_1}$,..., $X_n \in D_{\alpha_n}$ and variables $X_1,...,X_n$ of types $\alpha_1,...,\alpha_n$, you will define $M^{X_1...X_n}_{X_1...X_n}$ in the expected way. ▒

2.6.3. Interpretations.

As in second order logic, an interpretation $\mathcal{I}$ over a relational standard structure $\mathcal{D}$ is a pair $\langle \mathcal{D}, M \rangle$, where M is an assignment. See the agreements in section 4.2 of Chapter I for simplification of notation. ▒

2.6.4. Denotation of expressions.

You can define the denotation of expressions in the expected way, adapting the definitions given in subsection 4.2.1 of Chapter I. ▒

Notation.

We are going to simplify our notation following the conventions introduced in Chapter I, subsection 5.1.2, so now you understand

(1) $\mathcal{D}[^{X_1...X_n}_{X_1...X_n}](\varepsilon^\alpha)$ as the denotation of an expression ε^α $(\alpha \in TS-\{0\})$ under certain conditions.

(2) $\mathcal{D}[^{X_1...X_n}_{X_1...X_n}]$ sat φ as asserting the satisfiability of the formula φ under certain

circumstances.

This notation is justified by the coincidence lemma, which can be proved for type theory exactly as we did for second order logic.

2.6.5. Standard satisfiability, validity and consequence.
Can you please define these concepts for type theory? (Try to adjust the definitions to the corresponding definitions for second order logic, sections 4.2 and 4.3 of Chapter I.) ▒

2.6.6. Logical equivalence.
Can you please define this concept for type theory? (Adjust the definition to the corresponding definition for second order logic, presented in sections 4.4 of Chapter I.) ▒

2.6.7. Simplifying your language.
Following the procedure introduced in section 4.5 of Chapter I, you can prove that **RTT** can have only $\neg$, $\vee$ and $\exists$ as basic symbols; *i.e.*, leaving out $\bot$, $\wedge$, $\rightarrow$, $\leftrightarrow$ and $\forall$. ▮

2.7. RTT with lambda.

2.7.1. The language λ-T_ω.
Our language λ-T_ω is the result of adding to T_ω the lambda's facilities with regard to defining new predicates. So, to the six rules given in 2.2 for the formation of expressions, you add

(E7) If $X_1,...,X_n$ are pairwise distinct variables of types $\alpha_1,...,\alpha_n$ and φ is an expression of type 0, then $\lambda(X_1...X_n)\ \varphi$ is an expression of type $\langle 0,\alpha_1,...,\alpha_n\rangle$. ▒

2.7.2. Denotation of expressions.
The denotation of expressions of λ-T_ω agrees basically with the definitions of 2.6.4 for T_ω. We only have to add that we want

$$\mathcal{I}(\lambda(X_1^{\alpha_1}...X_n^{\alpha_n})\ \varphi) = \{\langle \mathbf{X}_1...\mathbf{X}_n\rangle \in \mathbf{D}_{\alpha_1}\times...\times\mathbf{D}_{\alpha_n} / \ \mathcal{I}^{\mathbf{X}_1...\mathbf{X}_n}_{X_1^{\alpha_1}...X_n^{\alpha_n}} \text{ sat } \varphi\}$$ ▒

2.7.3. The calculus λ-$\mathbf{C}_\omega$.
This new calculus, to be used with language λ-T_ω, is the obvious extension of the calculus

λ-C_2. Thus, instead of the comprehension schema (CS) we will use the rules of (IAC) and (IAA) for introducing abstraction in the consequent and in the antecedent. Of course, we extend them to cover the new types.

Let $X_1,...,X_n$ be pairwise distinct variables of types $\alpha_1,...,\alpha_n$ and $\varepsilon_1,...,\varepsilon_n$ be expressions of types $\alpha_1,...,\alpha_n$ as well. We can state the rules as

(IAC) Introducing abstraction in the consequent.

$$\frac{\Omega \hookrightarrow \varphi\frac{\varepsilon_1 \ldots \varepsilon_n}{X_1 \ldots X_n}}{\Omega \hookrightarrow (\lambda(X_1 \ldots X_n)\varphi)(\varepsilon_1 \ldots \varepsilon_n)}$$

(IAA) Introducing abstraction in the antecedent.

$$\frac{\Omega\ \varphi\frac{\varepsilon_1 \ldots \varepsilon_n}{X_1 \ldots X_n} \hookrightarrow \psi}{\Omega\ (\lambda(X_1 \ldots X_n)\varphi)(\varepsilon_1 \ldots \varepsilon_n) \hookrightarrow \psi}$$ ▮

2.8. Incompleteness of standard type theory.

It is easy to prove that the calculus of section 2.5 of this chapter is sound, but it is not complete. As you know, there are two versions of the completeness theorem; namely, weak and strong. As you probably have suspected, the deductive calculus of type theory is incomplete in both weak and strong senses. The proofs of these points can be extracted from the corresponding ones for second order logic. In particular, for incompleteness in the strong sense, you can build the argument based on the formula expressing infinity (See Chapter I, section 4.9). In the weak sense, the argument based on the expressive power of type theory also applies (See Chapter II, section 4.3).

Can you please state and prove these theorems? ▮

2.9. Relational general structures and relational frames.

When one realizes that the calculus is incomplete and can never be made complete by adjoining new rules to it, we might wonder whether or not provable formulas in C_ω can be distinguished; whether or not they can be isolated from the valid but unprovable formulas. Let us quote Henkin[43]

> This broad, somehow, vague question, has several answers - among them (a), (b), (c) below -
>
> (a) It is known that there can be no decision procedure to determine automatically, in a finite number of steps, whether or not a given logically valid formula is provable.
>
> (b) We can describe certain sets of formulas of type 0 for which we can demonstrate that any formula of the set will be provable if, and only if, it is logically valid. Thus, we have completeness relative to each of these sets...*[He is referring to propositional type theory and to the first order portion of type theory]*
>
> (c) Returning to the totality of logically valid formulas of L, we can pick out from among them those which are provable by introducing certain non-classical notions of validity. These are defined by enlarging the notion of model, a possibility engendered by observing that the language L may be used to refer to other kinds of systems than those we have described so far. There are two different directions in which we can proceed, described below...*[He then describes the method of general models and the method of boolean models]*.

As was explained in detail in the introduction of the previous chapter, Henkin was able to prove the completeness of type theory by changing the semantics, introducing non-standard structures. In fact, Henkin's construction was carried out for the full formalism of type theory, but for a different calculus than ours. So now we are going to define frames and general structures, extending the corresponding concepts for second order logic and applying the same philosophy.

2.9.1. Relational frames.

A ***relational frame for type theory*** is defined as:

$$\mathcal{D} = \langle \mathrm{D}, \langle \mathrm{D}_\alpha \rangle_{\alpha \in \mathrm{TS}} \rangle$$

where:

(i) $\mathrm{D} \neq \emptyset$ is a non-empty set.

---

[43]See Henkin [1975].

(ii) $\langle D_\alpha \rangle_{\alpha \in TS}$ is *a relational hierarchy of types; i.e.*:

$D_0 = \{T,F\}$ and $D_1 = D$

$\emptyset \neq D_{\langle 0,\alpha_1,\ldots,\alpha_n \rangle} \subseteq \mathcal{P}(D_{\alpha_1} \times \ldots \times D_{\alpha_n})$ $\blacksquare$

(Thus, the universes of a frame are not necessarily full.)

2.9.2. Satisfiability, validity and consequence in relational frames.

The semantics on frames for type theory is an easy generalization of the semantics on frames for second order logic, so you should extend the concepts defined in section 2.2 of Chapter IV to the current language T_ω. $\blacksquare$

Remarks.

As in second order logic, the semantics of frames is unable to guarantee a denotation in the frame for all the definable predicates, so the comprehension schema is not necessarily true in all frame-models. On the other hand, in frames, it is not safe to introduce equality by definition, since, with non-full universes, it could be different from identity.

2.9.3. Soundness and completeness in relational frames.

In type theory you can prove essentially the same second order metatheorems concerning the deductive calculus and by the same methods. Please note that a subcalculus, C^-_ω, can also be defined and for it the semantics of frames is OK. This calculus is basically the calculus to be presented in Chapter VI for **MSL** and the completeness of the latter will be used in the last chapter for the former.

2.9.4. Definable sets and relations in a given relational frame.

(a) If $\mathcal{D}$ is a frame, $D_{\alpha_1},\ldots,D_{\alpha_n}$ are universes of $\mathcal{D}$ of any types $\alpha_i \in TS-\{0\}$ and $\alpha = \langle 0,\alpha_1,\ldots,\alpha_n \rangle$, then any subset of the cartesian product of these universes – *i.e.*, any $X \subseteq D_{\alpha_1} \times \ldots \times D_{\alpha_n}$ - is an n-ary ***relation of type** α **of** $\mathcal{D}$*. $\blacksquare$

Let $REL(\mathcal{D})$ be the class of all relations of $\mathcal{D}$. $\blacksquare$

Let $REL^\alpha(\mathcal{D})$ be the class of all relations of type α of $\mathcal{D}$. $\blacksquare$

(b) We say that a relation X is *into* $\mathcal{D}$ when $X \in D_\alpha$ for $\alpha \in ST-\{0\}$. $\blacksquare$

Let $REL(\in \mathcal{D})$ be the class of all relations into $\mathcal{D}$. $\blacksquare$

(c) An n-ary relation ($n \geq 1$) X of type α is ***$\mathcal{D}$-definable using a language** T_ω* when it is a relation of type α of $\mathcal{D}$ and there is a formula φ of T_ω such that:

$$X = \{\langle V_1,...,V_n\rangle \in D_{\alpha_1}\times...\times D_{\alpha_n} / \mathcal{D}[{}^{V_1...V_n}_{V_1...V_n}] \text{ sat } \varphi\}$$

where $FREE(\varphi) \subseteq \{V_1,...,V_n\}$ and each variable V_j (for $j\in\{1,...,n\}$) is of type $\alpha_j \in TS-\{0\}$. ▓

Let $DEF(\mathcal{D},T_\omega)$ and $DEF^\alpha(\mathcal{D},T_\omega)$ be the corresponding sets. ▓

(d) An n-ary relation ($n\geq 1$) X of type $\alpha = \langle 0,\alpha_1,...,\alpha_n\rangle$ is ***parametrically $\mathcal{D}$-definable using T_ω*** iff there are a formula φ, variables $U_1,...,U_n$ and variables $V_1,...,V_m$ of any types $\alpha_1,...,\alpha_n$, $\beta_1,...,\beta_m \in TS-\{0\}$ such that

$$X = \{\langle U_1,...,U_n\rangle \in D_{\alpha_1}\times...\times D_{\alpha_n} / \mathcal{D}[{}^{U_1...U_n\ V_1...V_m}_{U_1...U_n\ V_1...V_m}] \text{ sat } \varphi\}$$

where $FREE(\varphi) \subseteq \{U_1,...,U_n,V_1,...,V_m\}$ and the parameters $V_1,...,V_m$ are in $D_{\beta_1},...,D_{\beta_m}$ of types $\beta_1,...,\beta_m$. ▓

Let $PARAM.DEF(\mathcal{D},T_\omega)$ and $PARAM.DEF^\alpha(\mathcal{D},T_\omega)$ be the corresponding sets. ▓

2.9.5. Relational general structures.

Relational general structures for type theory are relational frames whose universes are closed under definability and where identity can be safely used. So we define,

$\mathcal{D}$ is a ***relational general structure*** iff $\mathcal{D} = \langle D, \langle D_\alpha\rangle_{\alpha\in TS}\rangle$ is a relational frame such that

(i) For every formula φ with $FREE(\varphi) \subseteq \{X_1,...,X_n,Y_1,...,Y_m\}$ (where $X_i \in \mathcal{V}_{\alpha_i}$ for all $1\leq i\leq n$ and $Y_j \in \mathcal{V}_{\alpha_j}$ for all $1\leq j\leq m$) and for every $X_1,...,X_n$ such that $X_i \in D_{\alpha_i}$ ($i\in\{1,...,n\}$), we have

$$\{\langle Y_1,...,Y_m\rangle \in D_{\beta_1}\times...\times D_{\beta_m} / \mathcal{D}[{}^{X_1...X_n\ Y_1...Y_m}_{X_1...X_n\ Y_1...Y_m}] \text{ sat } \varphi\} \in D_{\langle 0,\beta_1,...,\beta_m\rangle} \quad ▓$$

Note.

This condition can be expressed by saying that all parametrically $\mathcal{D}$-definable relations of all nonzero types have to be in the hierarchy of types of all relational general structures. This condition can be termed ***definable closure***.

For languages where equality is introduced by definition, a second condition should be added:

(ii) ***The structure must be normal.*** This condition can be made precise in various ways; for example, by saying that the formula

$$\forall X^{\langle 0,\alpha\rangle}(X^{\langle 0,\alpha\rangle}(X^{\alpha}) \longleftrightarrow X^{\langle 0,\alpha\rangle}(Y^{\alpha}))$$

must define the prototypical, genuine, authentic, identity relation. ▮

Remark.
In our case, condition (ii) follows from condition (i). The reason is that in any structure $\mathcal{D}$, all the singletons are parametrically definable using our language for type theory containing primitive equality. So, according to condition (i), all the singletons should be included in the universes of sets of all levels β ($\beta = \langle 0,\alpha\rangle$, where $\alpha \neq 0$). A structure $\mathcal{D}$ meeting this requirement must satisfy condition (ii) as well.

You can maintain both conditions in the definition of general structure because there is no harm in keeping condition (ii) and in this way the definition has a broader applicability.

3.- ALGEBRAIC DEFINITION OF RELATIONAL GENERAL STRUCTURE

In any relational general structure $\mathcal{D}$ there is a proper denotation for each parametrically definable relation and it can be proved that general relational structures provide a good semantics for type theory. The semantics fits so nicely that soundness and completeness theorems are facts.

The definition of relational general structures we are working with is linked to the formal language and is not constructive. In this section, a new definition is proposed[44] and the proof of the equivalence with the former definition is carried out in full. Since in general structures there is no difficulty about using the abstractor lambda and the proofs are neater with it, we are going to enlarge our language by giving it this facility. The new language will be named $\lambda\text{-}T_{\omega}$.

[44]This definition is taken from Manzano [1982 b].

3.1. Fundamental relations.

In what follows I will enunciate a number of fundamental relations. These relations are parametrically definable in themselves and, moreover, they are able to generate all parametrically definable relations. So we will require the relational general structures to contain, and be closed under, all the fundamental relations. As a theorem, we will prove first that all fundamental relations are parametrically definable, and then, a relational general structure according to the definable closure definition contains all of them. Conversely, we will prove another theorem saying that a relational general structure defined algebraically contains all parametrically definable relations.

The fundamental relations and operations of $\mathcal{D}$ are:

3.1.1. Membership.

For every $n\geq 1$, $\alpha_1,\ldots,\alpha_n \in TS-\{0\}$, we have a membership relation,

$$\in_{\langle 0,\langle 0,\alpha_1,\ldots,\alpha_n\rangle,\alpha_1,\ldots,\alpha_n\rangle} = \{\langle X,Y_1,\ldots,Y_n\rangle \in D_{\langle 0,\alpha_1,\ldots,\alpha_n\rangle} \times D_{\alpha_1} \times \ldots \times D_{\alpha_n} / \langle Y_1,\ldots,Y_n\rangle \in X\}.$$ ▓

3.1.2. Difference.

For every $X\in D_\beta$ and $Y\in D_\beta$ of the same type $\beta = \langle 0,\alpha_1,\ldots,\alpha_n\rangle$ with $n\geq 1$, $X-Y$ will denote the usual set difference. Thus,

$$X\text{-}Y = \{\langle Z_1,\ldots,Z_n\rangle \in D_{\alpha_1} \times \ldots \times D_{\alpha_n} / \langle Z_1,\ldots,Z_n\rangle \in X \wedge \langle Z_1,\ldots,Z_n\rangle \notin Y\}$$ ▓

3.1.3. Cartesian product.

For every $\beta\in TS-\{0\}$, $\langle 0,\alpha_1,\ldots,\alpha_n\rangle \in TS$ with $n\geq 1$, $X\in D_{\langle 0,\alpha_1,\ldots,\alpha_n\rangle}$, $D_\beta \times X$ will denote the cartesian product defined this way,

$$D_\beta \times X = \{\langle Z_1,\ldots,Z_{n+1}\rangle \in D_\beta \times D_{\alpha_1} \times \ldots \times D_{\alpha_n}\rangle / \langle Z_2,\ldots,Z_{n+1}\rangle \in X\}$$ ▓

3.1.4. Permutation 1. ("The last will be first...")

For every $n>1$, $\beta = \langle 0,\alpha_1,\ldots,\alpha_n\rangle \in TS$ and $X\in D_\beta$, let

$$PER_1(X) = \{\langle Z_n,Z_1,\ldots,Z_{n-1}\rangle / \langle Z_1,\ldots,Z_n\rangle \in X\}$$ ▓

3.1.5. Permutation 2. ("...and the first, second")

For every $n>1$, $\beta = \langle 0,\alpha_1,\ldots,\alpha_n\rangle \in TS$ and $X\in D_\beta$, let

$$PER_2(X) = \{\langle Z_2,Z_1,Z_3,\ldots,Z_n\rangle / \langle Z_1,\ldots,Z_n\rangle \in X\}$$ ▓

3.1.6. Projection.

For every $n>1$, $\beta = \langle 0,\alpha_1,...,\alpha_n \rangle \in TS$ and $X \in D_\beta$, let

$$PROJ(X) = \{ \langle Y_1,...,Y_{n-1} \rangle \,/\, \exists Z \, \langle Y_1,...,Y_{n-1},Z \rangle \in X \}$$ ▓

3.1.7. Singletons.

For every $\alpha \in TS-\{0\}$ and $X \in D_\alpha$, $\{X\}$ is the singleton of X. Thus,

$$\{X\} = \{Z \in D_\alpha \,/\, Z = X\}$$ ▓

3.2. Definition of relational general structure by algebraic closure of the domains.

3.2.1. Closure under seven.

Let $\mathcal{D} = \langle D, \langle D_\alpha \rangle_{\alpha \in TS} \rangle$ be a frame. $\mathcal{D}$ is ***closed under seven*** if and only if

(i) For every $\alpha_1,...,\alpha_n \in TS-\{0\}$, let $\beta = \langle 0, \langle 0,\alpha_1,...,\alpha_n \rangle, \alpha_1,...,\alpha_n \rangle$. The condition requires that $\in_\beta \in D_\beta$ for every β

(ii) Let $\alpha \in TS-\{0,1\}$. For all $X,Y \in D_\alpha$: $X-Y \in D_\alpha$.

(iii) Let $\beta, \alpha_1,...,\alpha_n \in TS-\{0\}$. For all $X \in D_{\langle 0,\alpha_1,...,\alpha_n \rangle}$: $D_\beta \times X \in D_{\langle 0,\beta,\alpha_1,...,\alpha_n \rangle}$.

(iv) Let $\alpha_1,...,\alpha_n \in TS-\{0\}$. For all $X \in D_{\langle 0,\alpha_1,...,\alpha_n \rangle}$: $PER_1(X) \in D_{\langle 0,\alpha_n,\alpha_1,...,\alpha_{n-1} \rangle}$.

(v) Let $\alpha_1,...,\alpha_n \in TS-\{0\}$. For all $X \in D_{\langle 0,\alpha_1,...,\alpha_n \rangle}$: $PER_2(X) \in D_{\langle 0,\alpha_2,\alpha_1,\alpha_3,...,\alpha_{n-1} \rangle}$.

(vi) Let $\alpha_1,...,\alpha_n \in TS-\{0\}$. For all $X \in D_{\langle 0,\alpha_1,...,\alpha_n \rangle}$: $PROJ(X) \in D_{\langle 0,\alpha_1,...,\alpha_n,\alpha_{n-1} \rangle}$.

(vii) Let $\alpha \in TS-\{0\}$. For all $X \in D_\alpha$: $\{X\} \in D_{\langle 0,\alpha \rangle}$. ▓

3.2.2. Algebraically defined relations.

Given a relational frame $\mathcal{D}$, let ALG.DEF($\mathcal{D}$) be the class of all relations of $\mathcal{D}$ - *i.e.*, all the members of REL($\in\mathcal{D}$) - closed under all the fundamental relations and operations and let ALG.DEF$^\alpha$($\mathcal{D}$) be the subclass whose members have type α. ▓

3.2.3. Definition of relational general structures.

Let $\mathcal{D}$ be a frame. $\mathcal{D}$ is a ***relational general structure*** iff $D_\alpha = \text{ALG.DEF}^\alpha(\mathcal{D})$ for every $\alpha \in TS-\{0\}$. ▓

3.3. Theorem.

Let $\mathcal{D}$ be a relational general structure for type theory defined by definable closure of the universes and respecting identity (*i.e.*, defined according to 2.9.5), then $\mathcal{D}$ also satisfies the algebraic conditions expressed in definition 3.2.3 (*i.e.*, $D_\alpha = \text{ALG.DEF}^\alpha(\mathcal{D})$ for every $\alpha \in TS-\{0\}$).

Proof

Let $\mathcal{D}$ be a relational general structure which all parametrically definable relations are in and where the equality sign denotes identity for each type. We will see that all fundamental relations are in the hierarchy of types of $\mathcal{D}$. In each of the seven cases we will prove that the fundamental relation is definable.

(1) **Membership.** Let $\beta = \langle 0, \langle 0, \alpha_1, \ldots, \alpha_n \rangle \rangle$ with $n \geq 1$. It is easy to see that

$$\in_\beta = \mathcal{D}\,(\lambda Z^{\langle 0,\alpha_1,\ldots,\alpha_n\rangle} X_1^{\alpha_1} \ldots X_n^{\alpha_n})\, Z^{\langle 0,\alpha_1,\ldots,\alpha_n\rangle}(X_1^{\alpha_1} \ldots X_n^{\alpha_n})$$

Thus, $\in_\beta$ is a definable relation and so $\in_\beta \in D_\beta$.

(2) **Difference.** Let $\beta \in TS-\{0\}$ and so $\beta = \langle 0, \alpha_1, \ldots, \alpha_n \rangle$ with $n \geq 1$. For the parameters X, $Y \in D_\beta$ it is easy to see that

$$X-Y = \mathcal{D}\,[X,Y](\lambda(X_1^{\alpha_1} \ldots X_n^{\alpha_n})\, (X^{\langle 0,\alpha_1,\ldots,\alpha_n\rangle}(X_1^{\alpha_1} \ldots X_n^{\alpha_n}) \wedge \neg Y^{\langle 0,\alpha_1,\ldots,\alpha_n\rangle}(X_1^{\alpha_1} \ldots X_n^{\alpha_n}))$$

Thus, $X-Y$ is parametrically definable and so, $X-Y \in D_\beta$.

(3) **Cartesian product.** Let $\beta \in TS-\{0\}$ and $\langle 0, \alpha_1, \ldots, \alpha_n \rangle \in TS$ with $n \geq 1$. For the parameter $X \in D_{\langle 0,\alpha_1,\ldots,\alpha_n\rangle}$

$$D_\beta \times X = \mathcal{D}\,[X]\,(\,\lambda(Z^\beta X_1^{\alpha_1} \ldots X_n^{\alpha_n})\, X^{\langle 0,\alpha_1,\ldots,\alpha_n\rangle}(X_1^{\alpha_1} \ldots X_n^{\alpha_n})\,)$$

Thus, $D_\beta \times X$ is parametrically definable and so, $D_\beta \times X \in D_{\langle 0,\beta,\alpha_1,\ldots,\alpha_n\rangle}$.

(4) **Permutation 1.** Let $\beta = \langle 0, \alpha_1, \ldots, \alpha_n \rangle \in TS$ with $n > 1$. For the parameter $X \in D_{\langle 0,\alpha_1,\ldots,\alpha_n\rangle}$

$$PER_1(X) = \mathcal{D}\,[X]\,(\lambda\,(X_n^{\;n} X_1^{\alpha_1} \ldots X_{n-1}^{\alpha_{n-1}})\, X^{\langle 0,\alpha_1,\ldots,\alpha_n\rangle}(X_1^{\alpha_1} \ldots X_n^{\alpha_n})\,)$$

Thus, $PER_1(X)$ is parametrically definable and so, $PER_1(X) \in D_{\langle 0,\alpha_n,\alpha_1,\ldots,\alpha_{n-1}\rangle}$.

(5) **Permutation 2.** Let $\beta = \langle 0, \alpha_1, \ldots, \alpha_n \rangle \in TS$ with $n > 1$. For the parameter $X \in D_{\langle 0,\alpha_1,\ldots,\alpha_n\rangle}$

$$PER_2(X) = \mathcal{D}\,[X]\,(\lambda\,(X_2^{\alpha_2} X_1^{\alpha_1} X_3^{\alpha_3} \ldots X_n^{\alpha_n})\, X^{\langle 0,\alpha_1,\ldots,\alpha_n\rangle}(X_1^{\alpha_1} \ldots X_n^{\alpha_n})\,)$$

Thus, $PER_2(X)$ is parametrically definable and so $PER_2(X) \in D_{\langle 0,\alpha_2,\alpha_1,\alpha_3,...,\alpha_{n-1}\rangle}$.

(6) **Projection.** Let $\beta = \langle 0,\alpha_1,...,\alpha_n\rangle \in TS$ with n>1. For the parameter $X \in D_{\langle 0,\alpha_1,...,\alpha_n\rangle}$

$$PROJ(X) = \mathcal{D}[X]\ (\lambda\ (X_1^{\alpha_1}...X_{n-1}^{\alpha_{n-1}})\ \exists Z^{n}\ X^{\langle 0,\alpha_1,...,\alpha_n\rangle}(X_1^{\alpha_1}...X_{n-1}^{\alpha_{n-1}},Z^{\alpha_n}))$$

Thus, $PROJ(X)$ is parametrically definable and so $PROJ(X) \in D_{\langle 0,\alpha_1,...,\alpha_{n-1}\rangle}$.

(7) **Singletons.** These are parametrically definable in structures where equality denotes identity. Thus, singletons belong to the corresponding universe. Let $\alpha \in TS-\{0\}$. For the parameter $X \in D_\alpha$

$$\{X\} = \mathcal{D}[X]\ (\lambda(Y^\alpha)\ Y^\alpha = X^\alpha)$$

Thus, $\{X\}$ is parametrically definable and so $\{X\} \in D_{\langle 0,\alpha\rangle}$. ▮

3.4. Some parametrically definable relations also included in the universes of relational general structures defined by algebraic closure.

Let $\mathcal{D}$ be a relational general structure defined by algebraic closure. In what follows I will enunciate a series of relations and operations between relations for which it is easy to give a neat definition in $\mathcal{D}$, either with or without parameters. It is also easy to show that they have to be in the universes of $\mathcal{D}$ because they are defined in set theory using the fundamental operations.

In each case two different proofs are required:

(1) The relation is parametrically defined in $\mathcal{D}$.

(2) The relation is set-theoretically defined in terms of the fundamental operations and relations and so it is in the corresponding universe of $\mathcal{D}$.

(All the proofs are left to the reader.)

3.4.1. **Intersection.** For each $X, Y \in D_\alpha$ with $\alpha \in TS-\{0\}$, then $X \cap Y$ is parametrically definable and also $X \cap Y \in D_\alpha$.

3.4.2. **Universes.** For each $\alpha \in TS-\{0\}$, D_α is definable. Moreover, $D_\alpha \in D_{\langle 0,\alpha\rangle}$.

3.4.3. Complement. For each $\alpha \in TS-\{0,1\}$ and $X \in D_\alpha$, $\sim X$ is definable. Moreover, $\sim X \in D_\alpha$.

3.4.4. Union. For each $X, Y \in D_\alpha$ with $\alpha \in TS-\{0\}$, $X \cup Y$ is parametrically definable and also $X \cup Y \in D_\alpha$.

3.4.5. Complement of the difference. For each $X, Y \in D_\alpha$ with $\alpha \in TS-\{0,1\}$, $X \rhd Y$ is parametrically definable and also $X \rhd Y \in D_\alpha$. Here $X \rhd Y = \sim(X-Y)$.

3.4.6. Complement of the symmetric difference. For each $X, Y \in D_\alpha$ with $\alpha \in TS-\{0,1\}$, $X \lhd\rhd Y$ is parametrically definable and also $X \lhd\rhd Y \in D_\alpha$. Here

$$X \lhd\rhd Y = \sim((X-Y) \cup (Y-X)).$$

3.4.7. Arbitrary permutations. For every $n>1$, every permutation σ over $\{1,\ldots,n\}$, $\alpha_1,\ldots,\alpha_n \in TS-\{0\}$ and $X \in D_{\langle 0,\alpha_1,\ldots,\alpha_n \rangle}$, $PER_{\langle \sigma(1),\ldots,\sigma(n) \rangle}$ is parametrically definable and also $PER_{\langle \sigma(1),\ldots,\sigma(n) \rangle} \in D_{\langle 0,\sigma(1),\ldots,\sigma(n) \rangle}$.

3.4.8. Arbitrary cartesian product. For each $X \in D_\alpha$, $Y \in D_\beta$ with $\alpha = \langle 0,\alpha_1,\ldots,\alpha_n \rangle \in TS$ and $\beta = \langle 0,\beta_1,\ldots,\beta_m \rangle \in TS$, $X \times Y$ is parametrically definable and also

$$X \times Y \in D_{\langle 0,\alpha_1,\ldots,\alpha_n,\beta_1,\ldots,\beta_m \rangle}$$

3.4.9. Complement of the projection of the complement. For each $X \in D_\alpha$, with $\alpha = \langle 0,\alpha_1,\ldots,\alpha_n \rangle \in TS$ $JORP(X)$ is parametrically definable and $JORP(X) \in D_{\langle 0,\alpha_1,\ldots,\alpha_{n-1} \rangle}$, where $JORP(X) = \sim PROJ(\sim X)$.

3.4.10. Identity relation. For each $\alpha \in TS-\{0\}$, ID_α is definable in all structures where all singletons belong to the corresponding universes. Also, $ID_\alpha \in D_{\langle 0,\alpha,\alpha \rangle}$, where $ID_\alpha = \{\langle X,Y \rangle / X = Y\}$.

3.4.11. Parameterization. For each $n>1$, $\beta = \langle 0,\alpha_1,\ldots,\alpha_n \rangle \in TS$, $X \in D_\beta$ and $Y \in D_{\alpha_n}$, let

$$PARAM_{\langle Y \rangle}(X) = \{\langle Z_1,\ldots,Z_{n-1} \rangle \in D_{\alpha_1} \times \ldots \times D_{\alpha_{n-1}} / \langle Z_1,\ldots,Z_{n-1},Y \rangle \in X\}.$$

(It is easy to see that this relation is parametrically definable and that it belongs to the corresponding universe in a general structure algebraically defined.)

3.4.12. Identification. For each $n>1$, $\beta = \langle 0,\alpha_1,\ldots,\alpha_n \rangle \in TS$ with $\alpha_{n-1} = \alpha_n$, $X \in D_\beta$, let

$$IDENT_{\langle n-1,n \rangle}(X) = \{\langle Z_1,\ldots,Z_{n-1} \rangle \in D_{\alpha_1} \times \ldots \times D_{\alpha_{n-1}} / \langle Z_1,\ldots,Z_{n-1},Z_{n-1} \rangle \in X\}$$

(It is easy to see that this relation is definable in $\mathcal{D}$ and that it belongs to the corresponding universe in a general structure algebraically defined.) ▮

3.5. Theorem.

Let $\mathcal{D}$ be a relational general structure algebraically defined (*i.e.*, according to definition 3.2.3), then all parametrically $\mathcal{D}$-definable relations are in the corresponding universes of $\mathcal{D}$.

Proof

Instead of proving the theorem directly, we will prove a simplified version of it, but, in order to justify the simplification, two lemmas will be proved first.

3.5.1. Lemma: conversion of variables into parameters.

If $\mathcal{D}$ is a relational general structure algebraically defined and $\mathcal{D}$ contains all parameter-free definable relations, then $\mathcal{D}$ also contains all parametrically definable relations.

3.5.2. Lemma: eliminating superfluous variables.

If $\mathcal{D}$ is a relational general structure algebraically defined and $\mathcal{D}$ contains all definable relations using neither parameters nor superfluous variables, then $\mathcal{D}$ also contains all parameter-free definable relations.

Proof of lemma 3.5.1: Let $\mathcal{D}$ be a relational general structure algebraically defined and let φ be a formula with $\mathbf{FREE}(\varphi) \subseteq \{X_1^{\alpha_1},...,X_n^{\alpha_n},Y_1^{\beta_1},...,Y_m^{\beta_m}\}$. It is easy to see that whenever

$$\mathcal{D}(\,\lambda(X_1^{\alpha_1}...X_n^{\alpha_n}\,Y_1^{\beta_1}...Y_m^{\beta_m})\;\varphi\,)\in \mathrm{D}_{\langle 0,\alpha_1,...,\alpha_n,\beta_1,...,\beta_m\rangle}$$

then, for every $\langle \mathrm{Y}_1,...,\mathrm{Y}_m\rangle \in \mathrm{D}_{\beta_1}\times...\times\mathrm{D}_{\beta_m}$,

$$\mathcal{D}[\mathrm{Y}_1,...,\mathrm{Y}_m]\,(\,\lambda(X_1^{\alpha_1}...X_n^{\alpha_n})\;\varphi\,)\in \mathrm{D}_{\langle 0,\alpha_1,...,\alpha_n\rangle}$$

because this relation is the result of applying the operation of parameterization m times and this operation is allowed in relational general structures defined algebraically (see 3.4.11).

Proof of lemma 3.5.2: Let $\mathcal{D}$ be a general structure algebraically defined and let φ be a formula with $\mathbf{FREE}(\varphi) = \{X_1^{\alpha_1},...,X_n^{\alpha_n}\}$. It is easy to see that whenever

$$\mathcal{D}(\,\lambda(X_1^{\alpha_1}...X_n^{\alpha_n})\;\varphi\,)\in \mathrm{D}_{\langle 0,\alpha_1,...,\alpha_n\rangle}$$

then, for every $Y_1^{\beta_1},\dots,Y_m^{\beta_m}$ not free in φ,

$$\mathcal{D}(\,\lambda(X_1^{\alpha_1}\dots X_n^{\alpha_n}\,Y_1^{\beta_1}\dots Y_m^{\beta_m})\;\varphi\,)\in \mathrm{D}_{\langle 0,\alpha_1,\dots,\alpha_n,\beta_1,\dots,\beta_m\rangle}$$

because the last relation can be obtained by applying the rule (iii) of definition 3.2.1.

Now, we return to the proof of theorem 3.5 in the simplified version. So let $\mathcal{D}$ be a relational general structure defined algebraically. We want to prove that for any formula φ with exactly n variables free, the n-ary relation defined by the formula is in the proper universe. That is, if **FREE**$(\varphi) = \{X_1^{\alpha_1},\dots,X_n^{\alpha_n}\}$, then

$$\mathcal{D}(\,\lambda(X_1^{\alpha_1}\dots X_n^{\alpha_n})\;\varphi\,)\in \mathrm{D}_{\langle 0,\alpha_1,\dots,\alpha_n\rangle}$$

This proof has to go by induction on the formation of formulas; *i.e.*, by formation of expressions using the rules (E1), (E4), (E5) and (E6).

(E1) Let $\varphi \equiv \bot$. It is easy to see that

$$\mathcal{D}(\,\lambda(X_1^{\alpha_1}\dots X_n^{\alpha_n})\;\varphi\,) = \emptyset \in \mathrm{D}_{\langle 0,\alpha_1,\dots,\alpha_n\rangle} \quad \text{(by 3.4.2 and 3.4.3)}$$

(E4) Let $\varphi \equiv Y^{\beta}\,(Y_1^{\beta_1}\dots Y_m^{\beta_m})$ with $\beta = \langle 0,\beta_1,\dots,\beta_m\rangle$ and **FREE**$(\varphi) = \{X_1^{\alpha_1},\dots,X_n^{\alpha_n}\}$, thus $n = m+1$ and **FREE**$(\varphi) = \{Y^{\beta},Y_1^{\beta_1},\dots,Y_m^{\beta_m}\}$.

In φ, variables can be repeated and the sequence $\langle X_1^{\alpha_1}\dots X_n^{\alpha_n}\rangle$ can be different from the order of appearance in the formula, but we do not have to consider the complex general case, since we can apply the results of 3.4.7 and 3.4.12. So take φ simply as $X_1^{\alpha_1}(X_2^{\alpha_2}\dots X_n^{\alpha_n})$ where $\alpha_1 = \langle 0,\alpha_2,\dots,\alpha_n\rangle$

Clearly

$$\mathcal{D}(\,\lambda(X_1^{\alpha_1}\dots X_n^{\alpha_n})\;\varphi\,) = \in_{\langle 0,\alpha_1,\dots,\alpha_n\rangle} \quad\text{and so, } \mathcal{D}(\,\lambda(X_1^{\alpha_1}\dots X_n^{\alpha_n})\;\varphi\,)\in \mathrm{D}_{\langle 0,\alpha_1,\dots,\alpha_n\rangle}$$

(E5) Let us assume that the theorem works for φ and ψ. Thus,

$$\mathcal{D}(\,\lambda(X_1^{\alpha_1}\dots X_n^{\alpha_n})\;\varphi\,)\in \mathrm{D}_{\langle 0,\alpha_1,\dots,\alpha_n\rangle} \quad\text{and}\quad \mathcal{D}(\,\lambda(Y_1^{\beta_1}\dots Y_m^{\beta_m})\;\varphi\,)\in \mathrm{D}_{\langle 0,\beta_1,\dots,\beta_m\rangle}$$

Take in a suitable ordering the variables $Z_1^{\gamma_1},\dots,Z_p^{\gamma_p}$ such that

$\{Z_1^{\gamma_1},\dots,Z_p^{\gamma_p}\} = \{X_1^{\alpha_1},\dots,X_n^{\alpha_n},Y_1^{\beta_1},\dots,Y_m^{\beta_m}\}$

Using condition (iii) of 3.2.1 and 3.4.7, it is easy to see that

$$\mathcal{D}(\,\lambda(Z_1^{\gamma_1}\dots Z_p^{\gamma_p})\,)\;\varphi\in \mathrm{D}_{\langle 0,\gamma_1,\dots,\gamma_p\rangle} \quad\text{and}\quad \mathcal{D}(\,\lambda(Z_1^{\gamma_1}\dots Z_p^{\gamma_p})\,)\psi\in \mathrm{D}_{\langle 0,\gamma_1,\dots,\gamma_p\rangle}$$

Let $\mathrm{X} = \mathcal{D}(\,\lambda(Z_1^{\gamma_1}\dots Z_p^{\gamma_p})\;\varphi\,)$ and $\mathrm{Y} = \mathcal{D}(\,\lambda(Z_1^{\gamma_1}\dots Z_p^{\gamma_p})\;\psi\,)$.

Clearly,

$\mathcal{D}(\lambda(X_1^{\alpha_1}...X_n^{\alpha_n})\neg\varphi) = \sim X \in D_{\langle 0,\alpha_1,...,\alpha_n\rangle}$ (by 3.4.3)

$\mathcal{D}(\lambda(Z_1^{\gamma_1}...Z_p^{\gamma_p})\varphi \wedge \psi) = X \cap Y \in D_{\langle 0,\gamma_1,...,\gamma_p\rangle}$ (by 3.4.3)

$\mathcal{D}(\lambda(Z_1^{\gamma_1}...Z_p^{\gamma_p})\varphi \vee \psi) = X \cup Y \in D_{\langle 0,\gamma_1,...,\gamma_p\rangle}$ (by 3.4.4)

$\mathcal{D}(\lambda(Z_1^{\gamma_1}...Z_p^{\gamma_p})\varphi \rightarrow \psi) = X \rhd Y \in D_{\langle 0,\gamma_1,...,\gamma_p\rangle}$ (by 3.4.5)

$\mathcal{D}(\lambda(Z_1^{\gamma_1}...Z_p^{\gamma_p})\varphi \leftrightarrow \psi) = X \lhd\!\rhd Y \in D_{\langle 0,\gamma_1,...,\gamma_p\rangle}$ (by 3.4.6)

(E6) Let us assume that the theorem works for φ. Thus,

$\mathcal{D}(\lambda(X_1^{\alpha_1}...X_n^{\alpha_n})\varphi) \in D_{\langle 0,\alpha_1,...,\alpha_n\rangle}$

We want to prove that the theorem works for $\exists Z^\beta\ \varphi$. There are two possibilities:

(1) $Z^\beta \not\equiv X_i^{\alpha_i}$ for all $i \in \{1,...,n\}$, $\alpha_i \in TS-\{0\}$. In this case

$\mathcal{D}(\lambda(X_1^{\alpha_1}...X_n^{\alpha_n})\varphi) = \mathcal{D}(\lambda(X_1^{\alpha_1}...X_n^{\alpha_n})\exists Z^\beta \varphi)$

(2) $Z^\beta \equiv X_i^{\alpha_i}$ for $i \in \{1,...,n\}$, $\alpha_i \in TS-\{0\}$. Assume that $i = n$. In this case,

$\mathcal{D}(\lambda(X_1^{\alpha_1}...X_n^{\alpha_n})\exists Z^\beta \varphi) = PROJ(\mathcal{D}(\lambda(X_1^{\alpha_1}...X_n^{\alpha_n})\varphi))$

In a similar way we prove it for $\forall Z^\beta\ \varphi$ (use 3.4.9). ∎

4. A FUNCTIONAL THEORY OF FINITE TYPES.

This is the rather elegant formulation of the simple type theory offered by Church as early as 1940. The main features of **FTT** are that juxtaposition will have the usual interpretation as denoting the application of function to argument, and the abstractor operator is used to define a new function.

4.1. Definition (signature and alphabet).

4.1.1. Signature.

Our signature Σ for the functional type theory **FTT** is an ordered pair $\Sigma = \langle TS, FUNC \rangle$ where:

(i) **TS** is built by observing the following formation rules

(1) $1,0 \in$ **TS**.

(2) If $\alpha,\beta \in$ **TS**, then $\langle\alpha\beta\rangle \in$ **TS**.

(ii) **FUNC** = **FUNC**(Σ) is a function whose domain is **OPER.CONS**; where

$$\{\neg^{\langle 00\rangle}, \vee^{\langle\langle 00\rangle 0\rangle}\} \cup \{\Sigma^{\langle 0\langle 0\alpha\rangle\rangle}, =^{\langle\langle 0\alpha\rangle\alpha\rangle} / \alpha \in \mathbf{TS}\} \subseteq \mathbf{OPER.CONS}$$

Among the members of **OPER.CONS** we very often have a selector operator, $\iota^{\langle\alpha\langle 0\alpha\rangle\rangle}$ for every $\alpha \in$ **TS**. The values of the function are specified in the superscripts. ▓

4.1.2. Alphabet of the FTT languages λ-F_ω and λ-cF_ω.

Let us call λ-F_ω our language for **FTT**; this language does not include the selector operator. When this operator is in the language, we term it λ-cF_ω. The alphabet of any of them includes:

(1) All the symbols in **OPER.CONS** and parentheses *),(* and lambda λ as improper symbols.

(2) Variables for all types; *i.e.*, including the propositional types. ▓

4.2. Expressions.

4.2.1. Definition.

The expressions of λ-F_ω (resp. of λ-cF_ω) are built from the following rules:

(E1) Any variable or constant alone is an expression whose type is indicated by the superscripts.

(E2) If A is an expression of type $\langle\alpha\beta\rangle$ and if B is an expression of type β, then (AB) is an expression of type α.

(E3) If A is an expression of type α and X^β is a variable of any type β, then $(\lambda X^\beta A)$ is an expression of type $\langle\alpha\beta\rangle$. ▓

EXPR(λ-F_ω) is the smallest set obtained by these rules. ▓

FORM(λ-F_ω) is the set of expressions of type 0. ▓

EXPR(λ-cF_ω) and **FORM**(λ-cF_ω) also include the choice function. ▓

4.2.2. Conventions of abbreviation.

Let φ and ψ be expressions of type 0 and A^α and B^α expressions of type α.

(1) $\neg\varphi$ stands for $(\neg^{\langle 00\rangle}\varphi)$.

(2) $(\varphi \vee \psi)$ stands for $((\vee^{\langle\langle 00\rangle 0\rangle}\varphi)\psi)$.

(3) $(\varphi \wedge \psi)$ stands for $\neg(\neg\varphi \vee \neg\psi)$.

(4) $(\varphi \rightarrow \psi)$ stands for $(\neg\varphi \vee \psi)$.

(5) $(\varphi \leftrightarrow \psi)$ stands for $((\varphi \rightarrow \psi) \wedge (\psi \rightarrow \varphi))$.

(6) $\exists X^{\alpha}\ \varphi$ stands for $(\Sigma^{\langle 0\langle 0\alpha\rangle\rangle}(\lambda X^{\alpha}\ \varphi))$.

(7) $\forall X^{\alpha}\ \varphi$ stands for $\neg\exists X^{\alpha}\ \neg\varphi$.

(8) $(A^{\alpha} = B^{\alpha})$ stands for $((=^{\langle\langle 0\alpha\rangle\alpha\rangle}A^{\alpha})\ B^{\alpha})$.

When $\alpha = 0$, we can write $(A^{\alpha} \leftrightarrow B^{\alpha})$ instead of $(A^{\alpha} = B^{\alpha})$.

(9) $A^{\alpha} \neq B^{\alpha}$ stands for $\neg(A^{\alpha} = B^{\alpha})$.

(10) $\iota X^{\alpha}\ \varphi$ stands for $\iota^{\langle\alpha\langle 0\alpha\rangle\rangle}(\lambda X^{\alpha}\ \varphi)$.

Besides these, we will follow the rules stated in section 2.3 of Chapter I for parenthesis elimination. Also, for simplifying the expressions obtained by using either the rule (E2) or (E3), we will follow association to the left.

4.3. Functional frames, functional general structures and functional standard structures.

The languages $\lambda\text{-}F_{\omega}$ and $\lambda\text{-}cF_{\omega}$ introduced above can receive standard and non-standard interpretation.

4.3.1. A ***functional frame*** $\mathcal{D}$ ***of type*** Σ is an ordered tuple

$$\mathcal{D} = \langle\, \mathrm{D}, \langle \mathrm{D}_{\alpha}\rangle_{\alpha\in \mathbf{TS}}, \langle C^{\mathcal{D}}\rangle_{C\in \mathbf{OPER.CONS}}\,\rangle$$

where:

(i) $\mathrm{D} \neq \emptyset$ is a set.

(ii) $\langle \mathrm{D}_{\alpha}\rangle_{\alpha\in\mathbf{TS}}$ is a functional hierarchy of types; *i.e.*,

(a) $\mathrm{D}_0 = \{\mathrm{T},\mathrm{F}\}$ and $\mathrm{D}_1 = \mathrm{D}$.

(b) $\mathrm{D}_{\langle\alpha\beta\rangle} \subseteq \{\mathrm{f} \,/\, \mathrm{f}\colon \mathrm{D}_{\beta} \longrightarrow \mathrm{D}_{\alpha}\}$. That is, $\mathrm{D}_{\langle\alpha\beta\rangle}$ is a set of functions from D_{β} into D_{α}.

(iii) For any $C\in$ **OPER.CONS** with **FUNC**$(C) = \langle\alpha\beta\rangle$, $C^{\mathcal{D}}\colon \mathrm{D}_{\beta} \longrightarrow \mathrm{D}_{\alpha}$. In particular,

$$(\neg^{\langle 00\rangle})^{\mathcal{D}}\colon \mathrm{D}_0 \longrightarrow \mathrm{D}_0$$
$$\mathrm{T} \longmapsto \mathrm{F}$$
$$\mathrm{F} \longmapsto \mathrm{T}$$

$$(\vee^{\langle\langle 00\rangle 0\rangle})^{\mathcal{D}}: \mathbf{D}_0 \longrightarrow \mathbf{D}_{\langle 00\rangle}$$

$$\mathrm{T} \longmapsto (\vee^{\langle\langle 00\rangle 0\rangle})^{\mathcal{D}}(\mathrm{T}) : \mathbf{D}_0 \longrightarrow \mathbf{D}_0$$
$$\mathbf{X} \longmapsto \mathrm{T}$$
$$\mathrm{F} \longmapsto (\vee^{\langle\langle 00\rangle 0\rangle})^{\mathcal{D}}(\mathrm{F}) : \mathbf{D}_0 \longrightarrow \mathbf{D}_0$$
$$\mathbf{X} \longmapsto \mathbf{X}$$

$$(\Sigma^{\langle 0\langle 0\alpha\rangle\rangle})^{\mathcal{D}}: \mathbf{D}_{\langle 0\alpha\rangle} \longrightarrow \mathbf{D}_0$$
$$\mathbf{f} \longmapsto \mathrm{T} \quad (*)$$
$$\mathbf{g} \longmapsto \mathrm{F} \quad \text{otherwise } (**)$$

(*)if the function $\mathbf{f}: \mathbf{D}_\alpha \rightarrow \mathbf{D}_0$
$\mathbf{X} \mapsto \mathrm{T}$

has a value T for at least one $\mathbf{X} \in \mathbf{D}_\alpha$.

(**) That is, when $\mathbf{g}: \mathbf{D}_\alpha \longrightarrow \mathbf{D}_0$
$\mathbf{X} \longmapsto \mathrm{F}$

is F for all $\mathbf{X} \in \mathbf{D}_\alpha$.

$$(=^{\langle\langle 0\alpha\rangle\alpha\rangle})^{\mathcal{D}}: \mathbf{D}_\alpha \longrightarrow \mathbf{D}_{\langle 0\alpha\rangle}$$

$$\mathbf{X} \longmapsto (=^{\langle\langle 0\alpha\rangle\alpha\rangle})^{\mathcal{D}}(\mathbf{X}): \mathbf{D}_\alpha \longrightarrow \mathbf{D}_0$$
$$\mathbf{X} \longmapsto \mathrm{T}$$
$$\mathbf{Y} \longmapsto \mathrm{F} \quad \text{otherwise } (*)$$

(*) that is, for all $\mathbf{Y} \neq \mathbf{X} \in \mathbf{D}_\alpha$.

For $\lambda\text{-}cF_\omega$ the interpretation of the selector operator is based on a choice function for every $\alpha \in \mathrm{TS}$.

$(\iota^{\langle\alpha\langle 0\alpha\rangle\rangle})^{\mathcal{D}}$ is an election function whose value for every singleton $\mathbf{f}: \mathbf{D}_\alpha \longrightarrow \mathbf{D}_0$ is the only element mapped into T by f. It is a fixed element of $\mathbf{D}_\alpha$ if f is always F for every $\mathbf{X} \in \mathbf{D}_\alpha$ or if there is more than one $\mathbf{X} \in \mathbf{D}_\alpha$ mapped into T by f. Now we fix one element of $\mathbf{D}_\alpha$ for every type α using a choice function, C, for type 1. This is done inductively by setting

$$\mathbf{a}^0 = \mathrm{F} = \mathrm{C}(\mathbf{D}_1)$$

and, for any α and β, taking $\mathbf{a}^{\langle\alpha\beta\rangle}$ to be the function of $\mathbf{D}_{\langle\alpha\beta\rangle}$ such that

$$\mathbf{a}^{\langle\alpha\beta\rangle}(\mathbf{X}) = \mathbf{a}^\alpha, \text{ for every } \mathbf{X} \in \mathbf{D}_\beta$$

(iv) All the members of $\{C^{\mathcal{D}}\}_{C \in \mathrm{OPER.CONS}}$ are in the corresponding universes for quantification needs. ▓

Remarks.

With this definition it is easy to see that:

(1) $(\neg^{\langle 00\rangle})^{\mathcal{D}}$ is the negation function, since $(\neg^{\langle 00\rangle})^{\mathcal{D}}(T) = F$ and $(\neg^{\langle 00\rangle})^{\mathcal{D}}(F) = T$.

(2) $(\vee^{\langle\langle 00\rangle 0\rangle})^{\mathcal{D}}$ is the disjunction function, since $(\vee^{\langle\langle 00\rangle 0\rangle})^{\mathcal{D}}(Y)(X) = F$ iff $Y = X = F$.

(3) $(\Sigma^{\langle 0\langle 0\alpha\rangle\rangle})^{\mathcal{D}}$ is the existential function. That is, $(\Sigma^{\langle 0\langle 0\alpha\rangle\rangle})^{\mathcal{D}}$ is a predicate of predicates saying that the last predicate is not empty, since $(\Sigma^{\langle 0\langle 0\alpha\rangle\rangle})^{\mathcal{D}}(X^{\langle 0\alpha\rangle}) = T$ iff $X^{\langle 0\alpha\rangle}(Y^{\alpha}) = T$ for at least one $Y^{\alpha} \in D_{\alpha}$.

Using this existential function we define the existential quantifier following the pattern given in 4.2.2. This function sends every function of type $\langle 0\alpha\rangle$ to the truth value true with the sole exception of the constant-false function of type $\langle 0\alpha\rangle$ which is sent to the truth value false.

(4) $(=^{\langle\langle 0\alpha\rangle\alpha\rangle})^{\mathcal{D}}$ is the identity function, since $(=^{\langle\langle 0\alpha\rangle\alpha\rangle})^{\mathcal{D}}(Y)(X) = T$ iff $Y = X$.

(5) $(\iota^{\langle\alpha\langle 0\alpha\rangle\rangle})^{\mathcal{D}}$ is the function sending every singleton in $D_{\langle 0\alpha\rangle}$ to its unique member supplemented with an election function defined for every type α. Since this function sends every singleton to its unique member, it acts as a reverse operation for equality.

Note.

As you see, we have primitive equality but with the standard semantics it is redundant, since the well known Leibnizian definition also applies.

4.3.2. A ***functional general structure*** is a functional frame where $D_{\langle\alpha\beta\rangle}$ includes all the $\mathcal{D}$-definable functions from D_{β} into D_{α}. ▓

4.3.3. A ***functional standard structure*** is a functional frame where $D_{\langle\alpha\beta\rangle}$ is the whole set of functions from D_{β} into D_{α}. ▓

4.3.4. Interpretations.

Let $\mathcal{D}$ be a functional frame and M an assignment on its universes; that is, a map from variables to universes respecting types. We will say that $\langle \mathcal{D}, M \rangle$ is an interpretation over the functional frame $\mathcal{D}$. As in the preceding chapters, we can also say that $\langle \mathcal{D}, M \rangle$ is a frame model. ▓

4.3.5. Denotation of expressions.

Given an interpretation $\mathcal{I} = \langle \mathcal{D}, M \rangle$, we define by induction on expression formation the value $\mathcal{I}(\varepsilon)$ for every $\varepsilon \in \mathbf{EXPR}(\lambda\text{-}F_\omega)$ (resp. $\varepsilon \in \mathbf{EXPR}(\lambda\text{-}cF_\omega)$)

(E1) $\mathcal{I}(X^\alpha) = M(X^\alpha)$ for any variable X^α of type α

$\mathcal{I}(C) = C^{\mathcal{A}}$ for any $C \in \mathbf{OPER.CONS}$.

(E2) $\mathcal{I}(AB) = \mathcal{I}(A)(\mathcal{I}(B))$ for any A of type $\langle\alpha\beta\rangle$ and B of type β.

(E3) $\mathcal{I}(\lambda X^\beta A)\colon \mathbf{D}_\beta \longrightarrow \mathbf{D}_\alpha$

$$\mathbf{X} \longmapsto \mathcal{I}^{\mathbf{X}}_{X^\beta}(A)$$

for any A of type α.

(where $\mathcal{I}^{\mathbf{X}}_{X^\beta}$ is defined as usual; see, for instance I.4.1). ▮

4.3.6. Satisfiability, validity, consequence and logical equivalence in functional frames.

Following the pattern introduced in section 2.2 of the previous chapter, you can easily build all these concepts for functional frames on the basis that

$\mathcal{I}$ sat φ iff $\mathcal{I}(\varphi) = T$ ▮

Remark.

Now it is easy to understand the conventions for abbreviation of 4.2.2.

4.4. From RTT to FTT.

Very briefly we will see how to go from a signature Σ for **RTT** to a signature Σ^* for **FTT** and how to convert relational frames of signature Σ to functional frames of signature Σ^*. For this process we will use the standard presentation of relations as characteristic functions and the conversion of n-ary functions into unary functions. The idea is very simple and has been used already in Chapter III, section 4.1, where instead of a binary function g, giving a value g(x,y) to any pair of numbers in the domain, we take a unary function $g_{\mathbf{x}}$ for every number in the domain. This function is defined as $g_{\mathbf{x}}(y) = g(x,y)$. Therefore, instead of the binary function of addition we have the function of adding x, (x+), for every number x. Furthermore, formulas of $\lambda\text{-}T_\omega$ will be translated into formulas of $\lambda\text{-}F_\omega$ in such a way that the semantical equivalence is guaranteed.

4.4.1. From the signature Σ to the signature Σ*.

Let $\Sigma = \langle$ TS,FUNC $\rangle$ be our starting signature for RTT where FUNC $= \emptyset$. We will define $\Sigma^* = \langle$ TS*,FUNC* $\rangle$ as follows:

(1) If $\alpha \in$ TS, then $\alpha = 0$, $\alpha = 1$ or $\alpha = \langle 0,\alpha_1,...,\alpha_n\rangle$ with $\alpha_i \in$ TS–{0} (1≤i≤n). In the first two cases, $\alpha^* = \alpha$. In the third, $\alpha^* = \langle 0\alpha_1^*\rangle$ for n = 1 and $\alpha^* = \langle\langle 0\alpha_n^*\rangle ... \rangle\alpha_1^*\rangle$, using the induction step where $\alpha_1,...,\alpha_n$ had obtained their values.

(2) FUNC $= \emptyset$ in our presentation, since **OPER.CONS** is empty too. But **FUNC*** is no longer empty since we treat connectives as operation constants, not as logical symbols.

$$
\begin{array}{lll}
\textbf{FUNC*: OPER.CONS} & \longrightarrow & \textbf{TS} \\
\neg^{\langle 00\rangle} & \longmapsto & \langle 00\rangle \\
\vee^{\langle\langle 00\rangle 0\rangle} & \longmapsto & \langle\langle 00\rangle 0\rangle \\
\Sigma^{\langle 0\langle 0\alpha\rangle\rangle} & \longmapsto & \langle 0\langle 0\alpha\rangle\rangle \\
=^{\langle\langle 0\alpha\rangle\alpha\rangle} & \longmapsto & \langle\langle 0\alpha\rangle\alpha\rangle
\end{array}
$$

4.4.2. From relational frames to funtional frames.

Let $\mathcal{D}$ be a relational frame of signature Σ. We will define a functional frame $\mathcal{T}$ of signature Σ*.

(1) Let $\mathcal{D} = \langle D,\langle D_\alpha\rangle_{\alpha\in TS}\rangle$ be a relational frame of signature Σ. By induction on types we will define a functional hierarchy $\mathcal{T} = \langle T,\langle T_{\alpha^*}\rangle_{\alpha^*\in TS^*}\rangle$, along with a series of bijections $\mathcal{X}_\alpha$ mapping elements of D_α into elements of T_{α^*}. Let us call the union $\mathcal{X}$.

$D_1 = T_{1^*}$ and $D_0 = T_{0^*}$.

$\mathcal{X}_0 : D_0 \longrightarrow T_{0^*}$ and $\mathcal{X}_1 : D_1 \longrightarrow T_{1^*}$ are both the identity functions.

If for $\alpha_1,...,\alpha_n$ we have defined the bijections $\mathcal{X}_{\alpha_1},...,\mathcal{X}_{\alpha_n}$ and the functional universes $T_{\alpha_1^*},...,T_{\alpha_n^*}$, for $\beta = \langle 0,\alpha_1,...,\alpha_n\rangle$ we define $\mathcal{X}_\beta$ and T_{β^*}. This definition will be by induction on n≥1.

Let n = 1; by hypothesis we have the bijection $\mathcal{X}_{\alpha_1}$ and the functional universe $T_{\alpha_1^*}$. Based on them we define

$$
\begin{array}{l}
\mathcal{X}_{\langle 0,\alpha_1\rangle} : D_{\langle 0,\alpha_1\rangle} \longrightarrow T_{\langle 0,\alpha_1^*\rangle} \\
\qquad X \longmapsto \mathcal{X}_{\langle 0,\alpha_1\rangle}(X) : T_{\alpha_1^*} \longrightarrow T_0 \\
\qquad\qquad\qquad Z \longmapsto (\mathcal{X}_{\langle 0,\alpha_1\rangle}(X))(Z)
\end{array}
$$

where $(\mathcal{X}_{\langle 0,\alpha_1\rangle}(X))(Z) = T$ iff $\mathcal{X}_{\alpha_1}^{-1}(Z) \in X$.

The universe $T_{\langle 0,\alpha_1^*\rangle} = \{\mathcal{X}_{\langle 0,\alpha_1\rangle}(X) \,/\, X \in D_{\langle 0,\alpha_1\rangle}\}$.

We assume that the definition has been done for n–1 and we do it for n.

$$\mathcal{H}_{\langle 0,\alpha_1,\dots,\alpha_n\rangle}: D_{\langle 0,\alpha_1,\dots,\alpha_n\rangle} \longrightarrow T_{\langle \dots \langle 0,\alpha_n^*\rangle \dots \alpha_1^*\rangle}$$

$$X \longmapsto \mathcal{H}_{\langle 0,\alpha_1,\dots,\alpha_n\rangle}(X): T_{\alpha_1^*} \longrightarrow T_{\langle \dots\langle 0,\alpha_n^*\rangle \dots \alpha_2^*\rangle}$$

$$Z_1 \longmapsto W$$

where $W = (\mathcal{H}_{\langle 0,\alpha_1,\dots,\alpha_n\rangle}(X))(Z_1)$ is defined as the nested function giving to any $Z_2 \in T_{\alpha_2^*}, \dots, Z_n \in T_{\alpha_n^*}$ the value T under $(\dots(W(Z_2))\dots)(Z_n)$ iff $\langle \mathcal{H}^{-1}_{\alpha_1}(Z_1), \mathcal{H}^{-1}_{\alpha_2}(Z_2), \dots$ $\dots, \mathcal{H}^{-1}_{\alpha_n}(Z_n)\rangle \in X$

The universe $T_{\langle \dots \langle 0,\alpha_n^*\rangle \dots,\alpha_1^*\rangle} = \{\mathcal{H}_{\langle 0,\alpha_1,\dots,\alpha_n\rangle}(X) \,/\, X \in D_{\langle 0,\alpha_1,\dots,\alpha_n\rangle}\}$.

(2) Let $\mathcal{T}$ be a functional frame having as a basis the functional hierarchy defined above and as interpretation for the new symbols in **OPER.CONS*** the standard ones, as described in 4.3.1 (iii). In fact, for any $\mathcal{D}$ of signature Σ there is a unique

$$\mathcal{T} = \langle T, \langle T_{\alpha^*}\rangle_{\alpha^* \in TS^*}, \langle C^{\mathcal{T}}\rangle_{C \in \text{OPER.CONS}^*}\rangle$$

along with a bijection $\mathcal{H}$ as described above. We will call the new structure $\mathcal{H}(\mathcal{D})$. ▮

4.4.3. Inductive definition of $\text{TRANS}_{\text{RTT} \mapsto \text{FTT}}$.

We will write TRANS as abbreviation of $\text{TRANS}_{\text{RTT} \mapsto \text{FTT}}$.

(E1) $\text{TRANS}(\bot) = \forall x^0\, x^0$

(E2) $\text{TRANS}(x^{\alpha}) = x^{\alpha^*}$

(E3) $\text{TRANS}(=^{\langle 0,\alpha,\alpha\rangle}) = =^{\langle\langle 0\alpha^*\rangle\alpha^*\rangle}$

(E4) $\text{TRANS}(A(B_1 \dots B_n)) = (\dots(\text{TRANS}(A)(\text{TRANS}(B_1)))\dots\text{TRANS}(B_n))$

(E5) $\text{TRANS}(\neg\varphi) = \neg^{\langle 00\rangle}\text{TRANS}(\varphi)$

$\text{TRANS}(\varphi \vee \psi) = (\vee^{\langle\langle 00\rangle 0\rangle}\text{TRANS}(\varphi))(\text{TRANS}(\psi)) = \text{TRANS}(\varphi) \vee \text{TRANS}(\psi)$

(E6) $\text{TRANS}(\exists x^{\alpha}\, \varphi) = \Sigma^{\langle 0\langle 0\alpha^*\rangle\rangle}(\lambda x^{\alpha^*}\, \varphi)$

(E7) $\text{TRANS}(\lambda(x_1^{\alpha_1} \dots x_n^{\alpha_n})\varphi) = \lambda x_1^{\alpha_1^*}(\dots(\lambda x_n^{\alpha_n^*}\, \text{TRANS}(\varphi))\dots)$

4.4.4. Theorem on semantic equivalence.

For every relational frame model $\langle \mathcal{D}, M\rangle$, there are a function $\mathcal{H}$ on the hierarchy of $\mathcal{D}$ and a functional frame-model $\langle \mathcal{H}(\mathcal{D}), M^*\rangle$ simultaneously defined, such that

(1) $\langle \mathcal{D}, M\rangle$ is a model of φ iff $\langle \mathcal{H}(\mathcal{D}), M^*\rangle(\text{TRANS}(\varphi)) = T$, for every $\varphi \in \text{FORM}(\lambda\text{-}T_\omega)$.

(2) For any expression $\varepsilon \in \text{EXPR}(\lambda\text{-}T_\omega) - \text{FORM}(\lambda\text{-}T_\omega)$

$\mathcal{H}(\langle D, M\rangle(\varepsilon)) = \langle \mathcal{H}(\mathcal{D}), M^*\rangle(\text{TRANS}(\varepsilon))$

Proof

Let $\langle \mathcal{D},\mathrm{M} \rangle$ be a relational frame-model and $\langle \mathcal{H}(\mathcal{D}),\mathrm{M}^* \rangle$ a functional frame-model where $\mathcal{H}$ is a bijection defined as in 4.4.2 and M^* is an assignment giving values in the structure $\mathcal{H}(\mathcal{D})$ to the variables of signature Σ^*, which is obtained by following the diagram:

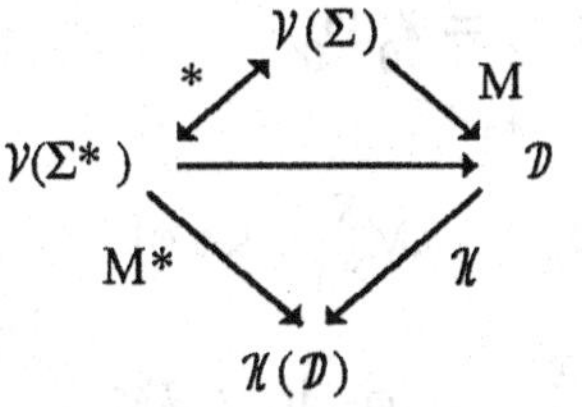

(E1) $\langle \mathcal{D},\mathrm{M} \rangle$ is a model of $\perp$ iff $\langle \mathcal{H}(\mathcal{D}),\mathrm{M}^* \rangle(\mathbf{TRANS}(\perp)) = \mathrm{T}$

(Since neither $\perp$ nor $\forall X^0 X^0$ has any model)

(E2) $\mathcal{H}(\langle \mathcal{D},\mathrm{M} \rangle(X^{\alpha})) = \mathcal{H}_{\alpha}(\mathrm{M}(X^{\alpha})) = \langle \mathcal{H}(\mathcal{D}),\mathrm{M}^* \rangle(\mathbf{TRANS}(X^{\alpha}))$

(E3) $\mathcal{H}(\langle \mathcal{D},\mathrm{M} \rangle(=^{\langle 0,\alpha,\alpha\rangle})) = \langle \mathcal{H}(\mathcal{D}),\mathrm{M}^* \rangle(=^{\langle\langle 0\alpha^*\rangle\alpha^*\rangle}) =$

$\langle \mathcal{H}(\mathcal{D}),\mathrm{M}^* \rangle\mathbf{TRANS}(=^{\langle 0,\alpha,\alpha\rangle})$. Because, by convention, equality is identity in all our structures.

(E4) For $\mathrm{n} = 1$, A of type $\langle 0,\alpha\rangle$ and B_1 of type α:

$\langle \mathcal{D},\mathrm{M} \rangle$ is a model of $A(B_1)$ iff $\langle \mathcal{D},\mathrm{M} \rangle(B_1) \in \langle \mathcal{D},\mathrm{M} \rangle(A)$

iff $\mathcal{H}_{\alpha}^{-1}(\mathcal{H}_{\alpha}\langle \mathcal{D},\mathrm{M} \rangle(B_1)) \in \langle \mathcal{D},\mathrm{M} \rangle(A)$

iff $\mathcal{H}_{\langle 0,\alpha\rangle}(\langle \mathcal{D},\mathrm{M} \rangle(A))(\mathcal{H}_{\alpha}\langle \mathcal{D},\mathrm{M} \rangle(B_1)) = \mathrm{T}$

iff $\langle \mathcal{H}(\mathcal{D}),\mathrm{M}^* \rangle(\mathbf{TRANS}(A))(\langle \mathcal{H}(\mathcal{D}),\mathrm{M}^* \rangle(\mathbf{TRANS}(B_1))) = \mathrm{T}$

iff $\langle \mathcal{H}(\mathcal{D}),\mathrm{M}^* \rangle(\mathbf{TRANS}(A(B_1))) = \mathrm{T}$

Let us assume that it has been proved for n–1 and prove it for n.

Let A be of type $\langle 0,\alpha_1,\ldots,\alpha_n\rangle$ and B_i of type α_i for every i, $1 \leq i \leq n$:

$\langle \mathcal{D},\mathrm{M} \rangle$ is a model of $A(B_1 \ldots B_n)$

iff $\langle\langle \mathcal{D},\mathrm{M} \rangle(B_1),\ldots,\langle \mathcal{D},\mathrm{M} \rangle(B_n)\rangle \in \langle \mathcal{D},\mathrm{M} \rangle(A)$

iff $\langle\mathcal{H}_{\alpha_1}^{-1}(\mathcal{H}_{\alpha_1}\langle \mathcal{D},\mathrm{M} \rangle(B_1)),\ldots,\mathcal{H}_{\alpha_n}^{-1}(\mathcal{H}_{\alpha_n}\langle \mathcal{D},\mathrm{M} \rangle(B_n))\rangle \in \langle \mathcal{D},\mathrm{M} \rangle(A)$

iff $(\ldots(\mathcal{H}_{\langle 0,\alpha_1,\ldots,\alpha_n\rangle}(\langle \mathcal{D},\mathrm{M} \rangle(A))(\mathcal{H}_{\alpha_1}\langle \mathcal{D},\mathrm{M} \rangle(B_1)))\ldots(\mathcal{H}_{\alpha_n}\langle \mathcal{D},\mathrm{M} \rangle(B_n))) = \mathrm{T}$

iff $(\ldots(\langle \mathcal{H}(\mathcal{D}),\mathrm{M}^* \rangle(\mathbf{TRANS}(A))(\langle \mathcal{H}(\mathcal{D}),\mathrm{M}^* \rangle(\mathbf{TRANS}(B_1)))\ldots$

$\ldots(\langle \mathcal{H}(\mathcal{D}),\mathrm{M}^* \rangle(\mathbf{TRANS}(B_n))) = \mathrm{T}$

iff $\langle \mathcal{I}(\mathcal{D}),M^* \rangle(\mathbf{TRANS}(A(B_1...B_n))) = T$

(E5) and (E6) are obvious.

(E7) For $n = 1$, X_1 of type α, formula φ.

$$\mathcal{I}(\langle \mathcal{D},M \rangle(\lambda(X_1)\varphi)) = \mathcal{I}(\{X\in\mathcal{D}_\alpha / \langle \mathcal{D},M^{\mathbf{X}}_{X_1} \rangle \text{ sat } \varphi\}) = Y\in\mathcal{I}_{\langle 0,\alpha\rangle}(D_{\langle 0,\alpha\rangle})$$

where $Y: \mathcal{I}_\alpha(D_\alpha) \longrightarrow \{T,F\} = \mathcal{I}_0(D_0)$

$$Z \longmapsto T \quad (*)$$

(*) iff $\mathcal{I}^{-1}_\alpha(Z)\in \{X\in D_\alpha / \langle \mathcal{D},M^{\mathbf{X}}_{X_1} \rangle \text{ sat } \varphi\}$

But $\mathcal{I}^{-1}_\alpha(Z)\in \{X\in D_\alpha / \langle \mathcal{D},M^{\mathbf{X}}_{X_1} \rangle \text{ sat } \varphi\}$ iff $\langle \mathcal{D},M^{\mathcal{I}^{-1}_\alpha(Z)}_{X_1} \rangle$ sat φ

iff $\langle \mathcal{I}(\mathcal{D}),M^{*\mathbf{Z}}_{X_1*} \rangle(\mathbf{TRANS}(\varphi)) = T$

iff $(\langle \mathcal{I}(\mathcal{D}),M^* \rangle(\lambda X_1{}^*\varphi))(Z) = T$

iff $(\langle \mathcal{I}(\mathcal{D}),M^* \rangle(\mathbf{TRANS}(\lambda(X_1)\varphi)))(Z) = T$

Therefore, $\mathcal{I}(\langle \mathcal{D},M \rangle(\lambda(X_1)\varphi)) = \langle \mathcal{I}(\mathcal{D}),M^* \rangle(\mathbf{TRANS}(\lambda(X_1)\varphi))$.

Let us assume that it is true for n-1 and so prove it for n.

Can you prove that $\mathcal{I}(\langle \mathcal{D},M \rangle(\lambda(X_1...X_n)\varphi)) = \langle \mathcal{I}(\mathcal{D}),M^* \rangle(\mathbf{TRANS}(\lambda(X_1...X_n)\varphi))$? ∎

5. EQUATIONAL PRESENTATION OF THE FUNCTIONAL THEORY OF FINITE TYPES.

5.1. Main features of ETT.

We have raised the question of equality all along. Mainly, we were concerned about the problem of defining it in terms of other logical symbols. We saw (Chapter I, section 4.8) that in **FOL** there is no way of defining the global relation of identity, while in standard **SOL** this definition is not only possible, but widely used.

In this section the reverse question is posed and affirmatively answered: Can we define with only equality and abstraction the remaining logical symbols?

The idea of reducing the other concepts to identity is an old one which was tackled with some success by Tarski [1923], who solved the case for connectors; Ramsey [1926], who raised the whole subject; and Quine [1937], who introduced quantifiers. It was finally answered in Henkin [1963] with an improvement in Andrews [1963]. Later, in 1975, Henkin wrote a whole paper on this subject in a volume[45] completely devoted to identity. This is an expository paper where you will find the ideas discussed but not developed in full, since no proof is included.

It is important to stress that the definitions of all these concepts are possible because, as in FTT, we have propositional variables of all finite orders; *i.e.*, **TS** includes 0 and all the types obtained from it. In fact, propositional type theory is an important subtheory of this presentation of type theory and can be studied separately. The calculus we will introduce for equational type theory, when working only in propositional types, generates all and only the validities of propositional types, as was shown in Henkin [1963]. The calculus is rather beautiful and natural and it seems to support Wittgenstein thesis on the foundation of mathematics, according to which mathematics consists not of tautologies, but of equations.

Equational type theory (**ETT**) is nothing but a presentation of functional type theory. Its signature is that presented in 4.1 for **FTT** but the set **OPER.CONS** needs only to contain equality. The alphabet of our formal language for **ETT**, which we term $\lambda\text{-}E_{\omega}$, only contains variables and equality as proper symbols, and parentheses and abstractor as improper ones. The rules for forming the expressions are (E1), (E2) and (E3) of 4.2. Thus,

$$\mathbf{FORM}(\lambda\text{-}E_{\omega}) = \mathbf{FORM}((\lambda\text{-}F_{\omega}) - (\{\neg^{\langle 00\rangle}, \vee^{\langle\langle 00\rangle 0\rangle}\} \cup \{\Sigma^{\langle 0\langle 0\alpha\rangle\rangle} \,/\, \alpha \in \mathbf{TS}\}))$$

Another language for **ETT** used here - termed $\lambda\text{-}cE_{\omega}$ - includes a selector operator, but restricted to certain types. We will use functional frames and functional standard structures and all the definitions introduced in 4.3 also apply here. Being but a presentation of functional type theory, we only need to prove that **FTT** can be reduced to **ETT**; namely, that the connectors and quantifiers can be expressed with equality and abstraction.

5.2. Connectors and quantifiers in ETT.

Since the only basic symbols of **ETT** are equality and abstraction and both of them are in **FTT**, we will show that they are sufficient by introducing the remaining basic symbols of **FTT** as abbreviations.

---

[45]**Philosophia** (Philosophical quarterly of Israel), vol. 5, nums. 1-2, January-April 1975.

5.2.1. Basic definitions.

For any formulas φ and ψ, $\varphi \longmapsto \psi$ can be used instead of $((=^{\langle\langle 00\rangle 0\rangle}\varphi)\psi)$.

(1) $\top^0$ stands for $((=^{\langle\langle 0\langle 00\rangle\rangle\langle 00\rangle\rangle}(\lambda X^0X^0))(\lambda X^0X^0))$

abbreviated as $\top \equiv_{\mathrm{Df}} \lambda X^0X^0 = \lambda X^0X^0$

(2) $\bot^0$ stands for $((=^{\langle\langle 0\langle 00\rangle\rangle\langle 00\rangle\rangle}(\lambda X^0X^0))(\lambda X^0\top^0))$

abbreviated as $\bot \equiv_{\mathrm{Df}} \lambda X^0X^0 = \lambda X^0\top$

(3) $\neg^{\langle 00\rangle}$ stands for $(\lambda X^0((=^{\langle\langle 00\rangle 0\rangle}\bot^0)X^0))$

abbreviated as $\neg \equiv_{\mathrm{Df}} \lambda X^0(\bot = X^0)$

(4) $\Sigma^{\langle 0\langle 0\alpha\rangle\rangle}$ stands for $(\lambda X^{\langle 0\alpha\rangle}(\neg^{\langle 00\rangle}((=^{\langle\langle 0\langle\alpha 0\rangle\rangle\langle\alpha 0\rangle\rangle}(\lambda X^\alpha(X^{\langle 0\alpha\rangle}X^\alpha)))(\lambda X^\alpha\bot^0))))$

abbreviated as $\Sigma \equiv_{\mathrm{Df}} \lambda X^{\langle 0\alpha\rangle}\lambda X^\alpha(X^{\langle 0\alpha\rangle}X^\alpha) \neq \lambda X^\alpha\bot$

(5) $\exists X^\alpha\varphi$ stands for $(\neg^{\langle 00\rangle}((=^{\langle\langle 0\langle\alpha 0\rangle\rangle\langle\alpha 0\rangle\rangle}(\lambda X^\alpha\varphi))(\lambda X^\alpha\bot^0)))$

abbreviated as $\exists X^\alpha\varphi \equiv_{\mathrm{Df}} \lambda X^\alpha\varphi \neq \lambda X^\alpha\bot$

(6) $\vee^{\langle 0\langle 00\rangle\rangle}$ stands for

$$(\lambda X^0(\lambda Y^0(\exists X^{\langle 00\rangle}(\neg^{\langle 00\rangle}((=^{\langle\langle 00\rangle 0\rangle}((=^{\langle\langle 00\rangle 0\rangle}(X^{\langle 00\rangle}(\neg^{\langle 00\rangle}X^0)))(X^{\langle 00\rangle}\top^0)))(\neg^{\langle 00\rangle}Y^0)))))))$$

abbreviated as $\vee \equiv_{\mathrm{Df}} \lambda X^0(\lambda Y^0\, \exists X^{\langle 00\rangle}((X^{\langle 00\rangle}\neg X^0 = X^{\langle 00\rangle}\top) \neq \neg Y^0))$ ▨

Explanation.

Let $\mathcal{I} = \langle \mathcal{D}, \mathrm{M} \rangle$ be a frame-model. It is easy to see that using the six definitions given above, $\mathcal{I}(\top) = \mathrm{T}$ while $\mathcal{I}(\bot) = \mathrm{F}$. Moreover, $\mathcal{I}(\neg)$ is a function of type $\langle 00\rangle$ whose value is T iff $\mathcal{I}(X^0) = \mathrm{F}$. Therefore, the symbol introduced in (1) is the name for truth, while in (2) we are defining falsehood. On the other hand, (3) is the negation function. Furthermore, $\mathcal{I}(\Sigma)$ is a function giving to sets of type $\langle 0\alpha\rangle$ the value T iff the set is not empty. Existential quantification can be reduced to this concept or be defined directly as in (5). Finally, even disjunction can be defined in terms of equality and lambda; as you see, the formula in (6) is a function which is F iff both $\mathcal{I}(X^0) = \mathrm{F}$ and $\mathcal{I}(Y^0) = \mathrm{F}$. Let us examine this in detail:

(a) When $\mathcal{I}(X^0) = \mathrm{T}$ and $\mathcal{I}(Y^0) = \mathrm{T}$, then $\mathcal{I}(\neg Y^0) = \mathrm{F}$ and inequality is T because, for the function $g\colon \mathrm{D}_0 \longrightarrow \mathrm{D}_0$ sending both T and F to T, the equation $X^{\langle 00\rangle}\neg X^0 = X^{\langle 00\rangle}\top$ is T.

(b) When $\mathcal{I}(X^0) = \mathrm{T}$ but $\mathcal{I}(Y^0) = \mathrm{F}$, then $\mathcal{I}(\neg Y^0) = \mathrm{T}$ and inequality is T because, for the identity function $\mathbf{i}\colon \mathrm{D}_0 \longrightarrow \mathrm{D}_0$, the equation $X^{\langle 00\rangle}\neg X^0 = X^{\langle 00\rangle}{}_\mathrm{T}$ is F.

(c) When $\mathcal{I}(X^0) = \mathrm{F}$ and $\mathcal{I}(Y^0) = \mathrm{T}$, then $\mathcal{I}(\neg Y^0) = \mathrm{F}$ and inequality is T because, for any function $\mathbf{f}\colon \mathrm{D}_0 \longrightarrow \mathrm{D}_0$, the equation $X^{\langle 00\rangle}\neg X^0 = X^{\langle 00\rangle}{}_\mathrm{T}$ is T.

(d) Finally, when $\mathcal{I}(X^0) = \mathrm{F}$ and $\mathcal{I}(Y^0) = \mathrm{F}$, then $\mathcal{I}(\neg Y^0) = \mathrm{T}$ and inequality can never be T because, for any function $\mathbf{h}\colon \mathrm{D}_0 \longrightarrow \mathrm{D}_0$, the equation $X^{\langle 00\rangle}\neg X^0 = X^{\langle 00\rangle}{}_\mathrm{T}$ is T.

5.2.2. Some other definitions of connectors.

Of course, with the basic definitions given above all the connectors and quantifiers can be introduced in our **ETT** by the usual definitions, but a direct definition is also possible as you will see below:

(1) $\wedge^{\langle 0\langle 00\rangle\rangle}$ stands for

$$(\lambda X^0(\lambda Y^0(\lambda X^{\langle 00\rangle}((=^{\langle\langle 00\rangle 0\rangle}(\lambda X^{\langle 00\rangle}(X^{\langle 00\rangle}((=X^0)Y^0)))(\lambda X^{\langle 00\rangle}(X^{\langle 00\rangle}{}_\mathrm{T}))))))$$

abbreviated as $\wedge \equiv_{\mathrm{Df}} \lambda X^0(\lambda Y^0(\lambda X^{\langle 00\rangle}(X^{\langle 00\rangle}X^0 = Y^0) = \lambda X^{\langle 00\rangle}(X^{\langle 00\rangle}{}_\mathrm{T})))$ ▮

(2) $\Pi^{\langle 0\langle 0\alpha\rangle\rangle}$ stands for $(\lambda X^{\langle 0\alpha\rangle}((=^{\langle\langle 0\langle\alpha 0\rangle\rangle\langle\alpha 0\rangle\rangle}(\lambda X^\alpha(X^{\langle 0\alpha\rangle}X^\alpha)))(\lambda X^\alpha{}_\mathrm{T}{}^0)))$

abbreviated as $\Sigma \equiv_{\mathrm{Df}} \lambda X^{\langle 0\alpha\rangle}\lambda X^\alpha(X^{\langle 0\alpha\rangle}X^\alpha) = \lambda X^\alpha{}_\mathrm{T}$

(3) $\forall X^\alpha\varphi$ stands for $((=^{\langle\langle 0\langle\alpha 0\rangle\rangle\langle\alpha 0\rangle\rangle}(\lambda X^\alpha\varphi))(\lambda X^\alpha{}_\mathrm{T}{}^0))$

abbreviated as $\forall X^\alpha\varphi \equiv_{\mathrm{Df}} \lambda X^\alpha\varphi = \lambda X^\alpha{}_\mathrm{T}$

(4) $\rightarrow^{\langle 0\langle 00\rangle\rangle}$ stands for $(\lambda X^0(\lambda Y^0((=^{\langle\langle 00\rangle 0\rangle}((\wedge^{\langle 0\langle 00\rangle\rangle}X^0)Y^0))X^0)))$

abbreviated as $\rightarrow \equiv_{\mathrm{Df}} \lambda X^0(\lambda Y^0((X^0 \wedge Y^0) = X^0))$ ▮

5.2.3. Theorem.

For all $\varphi \in$ **FORM**$(\lambda\text{-}F_\omega)$ there is a $\varphi^* \in$ **FORM**$(\lambda\text{-}E_\omega)$ such that $\varphi \mathrel{\models\!\!\!\dashv}_{\mathcal{G.S}} \varphi^*$. (The symbol $\models\!\!\!\dashv_{\mathcal{G.S}}$ stands for logical equivalence in functional general structures.)

Proof

This follows the usual pattern; that is,

(A) First define by induction on expressions a map $*$: **EXPR**$(\lambda\text{-}F_\omega) \longrightarrow$ **EXPR**$(\lambda\text{-}E_\omega)$ following the definitions given in 5.2.1.

(B) Then make explicit what is said in the above explanation and hence prove that the map $*$ has the desired properties. ▮

5.3. The selector operator in ETT.

Type theory with a selector operator also has a neat treatment in **ETT**. We introduce $\lambda\text{-}cE_{\omega}$ whose set of members includes a selector operator for type 1. Selector operators for any other type α, $\alpha \neq 1$, are introduced by definition. Let us see how this is done:

5.3.1. Definition.

(1) $\iota^{\langle 0\langle 00\rangle\rangle}$ stands for $(\lambda X^{\langle 00\rangle}((=^{\langle\langle 0\langle 00\rangle\rangle\langle 00\rangle\rangle}X^{\langle 00\rangle})(\lambda X^0 X^0)))$ ▓

5.4. A calculus for ETT.

The calculus we will present for **ETT** is an axiomatic one having four basic axioms and a rule of replacement. We will also present another calculus for a language with a selector operator which includes an axiom for descriptions.

5.4.1. Axioms.

(1) **(Ax.1). Only two truth values.**

$$(X^{\langle 00\rangle}\bot \wedge X^{\langle 00\rangle}\bot) = \forall X^0(X^{\langle 00\rangle}X^0)$$

(2) **(Ax.2). Equals substitution.**

$$(X^{\alpha} = Y^{\alpha}) \rightarrow (Z^{\langle 0\alpha\rangle}X^{\alpha} = Z^{\langle 0\alpha\rangle}Y^{\alpha})$$

(3) **(Ax.3). Extensionality.**

$$\forall X^{\beta}(X^{\langle\alpha\beta\rangle}X^{\beta} = Y^{\langle\alpha\beta\rangle}X^{\beta}) = (X^{\langle\alpha\beta\rangle} = Y^{\langle\alpha\beta\rangle})$$

(4) **(Ax.4). Lambda conversion.**

$$(\lambda X^{\beta}B^{\alpha})A^{\beta} = B^{\alpha}\frac{A^{\beta}}{X^{\beta}}$$

(5) **(Ax.5). Description.**

$$\iota^{\langle 1\langle 01\rangle\rangle}(\lambda X^1(X^1 = Y^1)) = Y^1$$ ▓

5.4.2. Rule of inference.

(R) **Replacement.**

To infer from φ and $A^{\alpha} = B^{\alpha}$ any formula ψ obtained from φ by replacing in φ a part of the form A^{α} by occurrences of B^{α}. ▓

Remarks on the calculus.

(1) Axiom (1) states that our logic only has two truth values.

(2) Axiom (2) expresses a basic substitutivity property of equality. It is possible to have instead of this axiom a particular version of it, namely,

$$(X^{\langle\alpha 0\rangle} = Y^{\langle\alpha 0\rangle}) \to (Z^{\langle 0\langle\alpha 0\rangle\rangle}X^{\langle\alpha 0\rangle} = Z^{\langle 0\langle\alpha 0\rangle\rangle}Y^{\langle\alpha 0\rangle})$$

from which our (Ax.2) follows as a theorem.

(3) Axiom (3) is the usual one for extensionality.

(4) Axiom (4) expresses the conversion property of the lambda abstractor. To avoid substitution and to simplify the proofs of certain metatheorems such as soundness, it is possible to have five simpler axioms instead of this one.

(Ax. 4.1) $((\lambda X^{\beta}X^{\beta})A^{\beta}) = A^{\beta}$

(Ax. 4.2) $((\lambda X^{\beta}Y^{\alpha})A^{\beta}) = Y^{\alpha}$ if $X^{\beta} \neq Y^{\alpha}$

(Ax. 4.3) $((\lambda X^{\beta}(B^{\langle\alpha\gamma\rangle}D^{\gamma}))A^{\beta}) = (((\lambda X^{\beta}B^{\langle\alpha\gamma\rangle})A^{\beta})((\lambda X^{\beta}D^{\gamma})A^{\beta}))$

(Ax. 4.4) $((\lambda X^{\beta}(\lambda X^{\beta}B^{\alpha}))A^{\beta}) = (\lambda X^{\beta}B^{\alpha})$

(Ax. 4.5) $((\lambda X^{\beta}(Y^{\gamma}B^{\alpha}))A^{\beta}) = (\lambda Y^{\gamma}((\lambda X^{\beta}B^{\alpha})A^{\beta}))$ if $Y^{\gamma} \neq X^{\alpha}$ and Y^{γ} does not occur free in A^{β}

Using these axioms our (Ax.4) follows as a theorem.

(5) Axiom (5) is an axiom of descriptions.

5.4.3. Deductions.

(1) A ***deduction of a formula*** φ ***in the calculus*** E is a finite sequence of formulas ending with φ, where each formula in the sequence either is an axiom or is inferred from previous formulas by the rule of inference. We will write $\vdash_{\mathrm{E}}$ to express that there is a deduction of φ in the calculus E. ▓

(2) A formula φ ***is derivable from a set*** Δ ***of formulas in*** E (and we write $\Delta \vdash_{\mathrm{E}} \varphi$) if and only if there are a finite subset of Δ, say Γ, and a finite sequence of formulas $\gamma_1,\dots,\gamma_n$ such that:

(a) $\gamma_n \equiv \varphi$

(b) Each γ_i is either a member of Γ, or a member of a deduction in E, or is obtained from γ_k and γ_j by the rule of replacement. ▓

CHAPTER VI
MANY-SORTED LOGIC

1.- INTRODUCTION.

1.1. Examples.

In many branches of mathematics and computer science we formalize statements concerning several types of objects. Thus the logical languages and the structures used to interpret them are conceived as ***many-sorted***; that is, the set of variables of the language will range over more than one universe or domain of objects.

There are plenty of examples of subjects where the semantics of formulas are many-sorted structures:

(1) In ***geometry***, to take a simple and ancient example, we use universes of points, lines, angles, triangles, rectangles, polygons, etc.

(2) In the ***theory of vector spaces*** we use a universe for vectors and a universe for the field of scalars. In addition, we may need to add universes for subspaces, metrics and linear maps.

(3) In the ***theory of groups*** we use structures where there are universes for the elements of a given group, for the subgroups, normal subgroups, homomorphisms, etc.

(4) In the ***theory of rings*** we use universes for individuals in the ring, along with subrings, ideals, homomorphisms, matrix rings, polynomial rings, etc.

(5) In ***second order logic*** our needs are: A universe for individuals, another for unary relations on individuals, one for binary relations on individuals, and so on.

(6) In ***simple type theory*** we use a universe of individuals, plus universes of sets of individuals, sets of sets of individuals, and so on.

(7) In ***making computations*** we invariably use structures that are many-sorted: typically they have universes of data, natural numbers and Booleans. In addition we may use universes for reals and strings of characters; and for finite or infinite arrays, or for finite or infinite streams, over any of the universes of data.

(8) In ***reasoning about computations*** we use a universe of states (where a state might be

considered as a set of memory registers used by the computer) and another universe for time. We may add universes for syntactic constructions such as programs and specifications.

What is the language and logic that best fits our needs in expressing and reasoning with statements in these subjects?

Having several universes of different sorts, we need a language which takes care of this fact; that is, a language with different sorts of quantifiable variables. Furthermore, we put in it the operation symbols to represent the operations in the structure. This language and its logic are many-sorted language and many-sorted logic.

1.2. Reduction to and comparison with first order logic.

First order logic is an established logic with many interesting properties: it has a complete and sound calculus; the logic is compact and it has the Löwenheim-Skolem property, to mention the most important ones.

First order logic as presented in most introductory texts (***e.g.***, van Dalen [1983]) is single-sorted or, more accurately, unsorted: the structures used in first order logic have only one universe or domain of objects and the formal language that refers to single-sorted structures only contains one kind of variable to refer to individual objects. Therefore, we might try, and have often done so, to fit or code our many-sorted structures and language into single-sorted structures and language. In fact, this is a standard approach to many-sorted logic.

This is possible and, indeed, is the approach taken in one of the pioneer papers, Hao Wang [1952]. Another pioneer paper in which the term many-sorted first appeared is Arnold Schmidt [1938].

So, it is well known that many-sorted logic reduces to one-sorted logic, and this approach is the one commonly used in textbooks[46]. The reduction is performed on two levels: a syntactical translation of many-sorted formulas into one-sorted formulas (known as ***relativization of quantifiers***) and a semantic conversion of many-sorted structures into one-sorted structures

[46]See: Herbert Enderton [1972], page 277 and Donald Monk [1976], page 483.

(called ***unification of domains***). What is not usually said in textbooks is that the reduction has a price.

In making the syntactical translation we take a first order language (with only one kind of variables) with the same operation symbols as used in the many-sorted language being translated, and we add to its alphabet a unary relation symbol representing each sort. Every quantified formula over a sort of the many-sorted language such as

$$\forall x^i \varphi(x^i)$$

will be replaced by a quantified conditional single-sorted formula whose antecedent expresses the fact of the quantified variable being of a certain sort. That is,

$$\forall x (Q^i x \rightarrow \varphi(x)')$$

The new single-sorted structure obtained by unification of domains will have only one universe: the union of all the universes in the many-sorted structure. The relations of the many-sorted structures become relations of the single-sorted structure, while the functions in the many-sorted structure are extended to obtain functions in the single-sorted structure whose domains are extended to the new unified universe.

I will describe the reduction in detail later, but let me first make a few remarks about the price of the coding of many-sorted logic in single-sorted logic.

(1) One of our aims in studying many-sorted logic is to find a logic that naturally fits the many-sorted structures we want to talk about. Therefore, the basic assumption of the single-sortedness of first order logic is inappropriate and we lose naturalness when shifting to first order logic.

(2) In 1967 Solomon Feferman, the first logician to develop many-sorted logic substantially[47], pointed out that as far as Craig's interpolation lemma[48] is concerned, the many-sorted language is better because an improved version of it can be formulated and proved on this premise of many-sortedness. The standard conversion of many-sorted into single-sorted gives us several theorems, such as Löwenheim-Skolem or compactness, but there is not a way to deduce the interpolation theorem for many-sorted logic directly

---

[47]It is extensively treated as well in: Kreisel & Krivine [1971], chapter 5, page 80 and in Zsuzsanna Markusz [1983]. It is briefly presented in Hao Wang [1964] chapter XII, and in the books already mentioned by: Herbert Enderton [1972], page 277 and Donald Monk [1976], page 483. It is also studied in Burmeister [1986].

[48]The one-sorted case is due to Craig [1957 b], the many-sorted one is proved in Feferman [1968]. The one-sorted version follows from the many-sorted one.

from Craig's interpolation theorem. As in unsorted logic, the interpolation lemma for many-sorted logic can be proved in model-theoretic style[49], or in proof-theoretic style, as in Feferman. Since it can be derived from the completeness of Gentzen's calculus without the cut rule, when interpolation fails for a certain logic it tells you that there is no great hope of finding a Gentzen style calculus. Therefore, interpolation serves as a test to know how good the proof theory of a given logic could be. From what I have said, it should be expected that the many-sorted calculus has a good proof theory, even better than the corresponding first order one.

In Ebbinghaus's opinion[50]:

> It is especially with interpolation that many-sortedness pays. As seen in Feferman [1974], the many-sorted version of the interpolation theorem together with its possible refinements is a powerful tool even for one-sorted model theory, offering for instance elegant proofs of various preservation theorems.

He also thinks:

> Interpolation properties seem to indicate some kind of balance between syntax and semantics. This can be seen, for instance, from the work of Zucker [1978] or from the fact that interpolation implies Beth's definability theorem, according to which implicit definitions can be made explicit. Hence we may expect that interpolation properties fail if syntax and semantics are not in an equilibrium.

(3) In a paper of Hook [1985] it is proved that a many-sorted theory could be interpretable in another many-sorted theory without their corresponding one-sorted translations being interpretable in one another. As he pointed out:

> A theory can be proved consistent by exhibiting an interpretation in a known consistent theory. A many-sorted theory, therefore, may be useful in a consistency proof for which the corresponding one-sorted theory would not suffice. (Even if another consistency proof is known, the proof using interpretations has the advantage of being finitary and purely syntactic.)

---

[49]See Kreisel & Krivine [1971], page 87, for a many-sorted language without equality. On page 91 you will find the proof for a many-sorted language with equality.

[50]See H.D Ebbinghaus [1985], page 68.

(4) Deductions in a many-sorted calculus are shorter than the corresponding deductions in the one-sorted calculus obtained in the reduction. They avoid useless conclusions such as the first order theorems of the one-sorted calculus which have no many-sorted counterparts because they are not translations of any many-sorted formula. The reason for this situation is that in the translation we add to the first order language a unary relation for each sort of the many-sorted language.
Therefore, from the point of view of automated theorem proving, whose major aim includes obtaining logical conclusions efficiently and quickly and avoiding useless results, the reduction to one-sorted logic is not acceptable[51].

It is clear that although many-sorted logic reduces to one-sorted logic, they have different properties. They differ in naturalness, in the strength of the interpolation property, and in the efficiency of the calculus, where the many-sorted logic is far better. Moreover, interpretation among many-sorted theories is not always preserved in the translation to one-sorted theories. It is also true (and obvious) that first order logic is contained in many-sorted logic.

However, both logics have a strongly complete calculus, and the compactness and Löwenheim-Skolem properties. (We will prove all these theorems later.)

As far as its model theory is concerned, notions such as submodel, homomorphic image, direct and reduced products, can be defined for the many-sorted case. Some well known theorems of first order logic, such as the Łos theorem and the Birkhoff theorem, can be generalized to many-sorted logic[52].

In addition, many-sorted elementary equivalence is preserved in passing to one-sorted language and structures[53]. That is, from any two many-sorted structures which are many-sortedly equivalent we obtain by unification of domains two single-sorted structures which are one-sortedly equivalent.

Is many-sorted logic a proper (or strict) extension of first order logic?

Lindström [1969] proves that first order logic is characterizable as the strongest logic to

---

[51]See Christoph Walther [1983] and A.E. Cohn [1983].

[52]See Zsuzsanna Markusz [1983], Meinke and Tucker [1990].

[53]See Daniel Dzierzgowski [1988].

simultaneously possess compactness and Löwenheim-Skolem metaproperties. It is also proved that first order logic is again the strongest logic with a finitary syntax to possess the Löwenheim-Skolem property and be complete. Therefore, many-sorted logic cannot be considered as a proper extension of first order logic.

Some terminological precision is in order here. There are various logics whose structures, as in many-sorted logic, have several universes: second order logic, third order logic, type theory; but their standard semantics is very specific and different from the many-sorted view. They are, in fact, extensions of first order logic in the strict sense and they are incomplete, non-compact and do not have the Löwenheim-Skolem property. On the other hand, certain expanded first order languages are also called extensions of first order logic. In so far as they are complete, compact and satisfy the Löwenheim-Skolem property, they cannot be considered proper extensions of first order language. Strictly speaking, many-sorted logic doesn't fit in this category because quantification is not extended, but changed. In first order logic we quantify over all the elements in a given universe, while in many-sorted logic we quantify over the universes obtained by a stratification of it.

1.3. Uses of many-sorted logic.

Many-sorted logic is not a proper extension of first order logic, but, attending to the other properties, it is often preferred to first order logic in computer science and linguistics[54]. As far as computer science is concerned, many-sorted logic is widely used. For example, in the following subjects:

(1) Abstract data types. Kamin [1979], ADJ [1979], Andréka & Németi [1979, 1980, 1981], Ehrig & Mahr [1985], Bergstra & Tucker [1984], Goguen & Meseguer [1985].

(2) Semantics and program verification. Andréka, Németi & Sain [1982], Németi [1981 a], Tucker & Zucker [1988], Makowsky & Sain [1990], Sain [1990], Pasztor [1988].

(3) Definition of program languages. Andréka, Németi & Sain [1982].

(4) Algebras for logic. Németi [1981 a, b], Meinke & Tucker [1990], Henkin, Monk & Tarski [1971] section II.8, Henkin, Monk & Tarski [1985] pages 148-150 and 255-260, Cirulis [1989] section 7(5).

(5) Data bases. Rónyai [1981], Knuth & Rónyai [1983]

(6) Dynamic logic. Pratt [1979 a, 1979 b, 1980 a, b], Németi [1981 a, 1982], Trnková &

[54]See Montague [1974] and Gallin [1975].

Reiterman [1987].

(7) Semantics of natural languages. Márkusz & Szöts [1981], Janssen [1983]

(8) Computer aided problem solving. Gergely & Szöts [1980].

(9) Knowledge representation of design. Márkusz [1981, 1982].

(10) Logic programming and automated deduction. Goguen & Meseguer [1984], Walther [1983], Cohn [1986], Schmidt & Schauß [1989].

Márkusz [1983] gave a detailed account of the use of many-sorted logic in computer science, especially the work of the Hungarian group. In fact, the preceding attempt at classification is based on Márkusz's.

Many-sorted logic has been used in pure mathematics as a way of finding new and non-standard models; for instance, Henkin's general models for higher order logic[55]. It turns out that this logic can be viewed from the perspective of many-sorted logic. As a result, in the light of the new semantics associated with it, higher order logic becomes complete.

Many-sorted logic can be useful for understanding dynamic logic in at least two different ways. Propositional dynamic logic can be translated into many-sorted logic and there is also the non-standard dynamic logic where the philosophy of Henkin's general models is successfully exploited. I will explain that in the next chapter.

1.4. Many-sorted logic as a unifier logic.

Nowadays, the proliferation of logics used in mathematics, computer science, philosophy and linguistics makes it an urgent issue to study the relationships between them and their possible conversions into one another.

Many-sorted logic is not only natural for reasoning about more than one type of objects with an efficient proof theory, but also a unifier for many other logics, even some non-classical ones such as modal or dynamic logic.

The following list includes some of the logics that, in principle, seem to be unifiable using many-sorted logic:

---

[55] See Leon Henkin [1950], [1975].

(1) ***Higher order logics*** (type theory and second order logic),
(2) ***Infinitary logic,***
(3) ***Non-classical logics*** (modal, temporal, multivalued),
(4) ***Logics of Programs*** (dynamic logic, Hoare-Floyd logics).

Therefore, the study of many-sorted logic and its model theory gives us a clue to the behavior of some other logics which can be translated into many-sorted logic and also allows us an easy way to compare different logics.

We will see in Chapter VII several examples of how many-sorted logic can act as a unifier:
(1) Higher order logic with the general semantics invented by Henkin.
(2) Modal logic with the semantics of Kripke models.
(3) Propositional dynamic logic.

2. STRUCTURES.

Our first aim is to classify mathematical structures by means of signatures in such a way that two structures have the same signature if and only if the same language can be used for each of them. Before going into the details of the formal definitions of signature and structure, let me explain informally what they are.

Structures are conceived as many-sorted; that is, they may have more than one universe (or domain) of objects (over each of which a special set of variables of the language will range). We use the index set **SORT**[56] for indexing the universes: for each $i \in$ **SORT**, A_i will be the universe of sort i. In particular, we specify that $0 \in$ **SORT** and that $A_0 = \{T,F\}$, A_0 being the truth value universe, the Boolean sort, where T(***truth***) and F(***falsity***) are distinct objects. We may instead have more than two truth value, but for our present purpose, classical logic is enough; we do not need many-valued logic. Three-valued logic can be obtained by taking $A_0 = \{T,F,U\}$, and adding the ***unspecified truth value.*** In Huertas [1994] the third value is used to define a partial many-sorted logic which is used as target logic when translating first order modal logic with the semantics of gaps.

[56]We don't have to impose any restriction on the cardinality of the index set. Nevertheless, since one is usually working with many-sorted logic and structures where the cardinality of **SORT** is less than or equal to $\aleph_0$, most of the proofs have been made for countable languages.

A structure has operations (*i.e.*, functions) over its universes of various kinds. For $i_0,\dots,i_n \in \mathbf{SORT}$, an n-place operation of type $\alpha = \langle i_0,\dots,i_n\rangle$ is a mapping from the cartesian product $\mathbf{A}_{i_1} \times \dots \times \mathbf{A}_{i_n}$ into $\mathbf{A}_{i_0}$. However, when $\mathbf{A}_{i_0}$ is the truth value universe, $\mathbf{A}_0$, we specify that it is an n-ary relation of type $\langle 0,i_1,\dots,i_n\rangle$. This case also covers the truth value operations: negation, disjunction, etc. We identify constants in the structure with functions from $\{\emptyset\}$ to $\mathbf{A}_i$; that is, of type $\langle i\rangle$.

We may also have n-ary untyped relations: functions from $(\bigcup_{i\in \mathbf{SORT}-\{0\}} \mathbf{A}_i)^n$ into $\mathbf{A}_0$. Untyped relations are of arity n, a positive integer. If we have untyped relations, we might have identity as a special one. (If we do not have untyped relations, we shall include an identity relation for each sort. Then, we have to add an equality sign for each sort.) In practice, one is usually working with typed relation symbols and the equality sign is only used between terms of the same type. A more general class of equations is needed in situations such as ramified type theory.

Let $S_\omega(\mathbf{SORT})$ be the set of all finite sequences of elements of **SORT**. Let **OPER.SYM** be an arbitrary set whose elements will be called operation symbols and let **FUNC** be a mapping from **OPER.SYM** into

$$[S_\omega(\mathbf{SORT})] \cup [\omega - \{0\}]$$

For any

$$\alpha \in [S_\omega(\mathbf{SORT})] \cup [\omega - \{0\}]$$

we let

$$[\mathbf{OPER.SYM}]_\alpha = \{ f \in \mathbf{OPER.SYM} \;/\; \mathbf{FUNC}(f) = \alpha\}$$

If $f \in [\mathbf{OPER.SYM}]_\alpha$, then f is an operation symbol which will be used to denote an operation of kind α in the interpreted language to be defined below (α is used to denote either a type or an arity). In particular, we want $\neg, \vee \in \mathbf{OPER.SYM}$.

We will also have a sign for the equality, E, whose interpretation in structure $\mathcal{A}$, $E^{\mathcal{A}}$, has to be a binary relation

$$\text{from } (\bigcup_{i\in \mathbf{SORT}-\{0\}} \mathbf{A}_i)^2 \text{ into } \mathbf{A}_0$$

In general, we want $E^{\mathcal{A}}$ to be normal; that is, the prototypical identity relation, the diagonal of

$$(\bigcup_{i\in \mathbf{SORT}-\{0\}} \mathbf{A}_i)^2$$

We do not require the universes in a structure to be pairwise disjoint. Therefore, we can have identical elements in different domains. This situation can only be expressed with untyped equality. On the other hand, we can restrict attention to normal structures because from a structure $\mathcal{A}$ we can construct a normal structure as long as it is established that $\mathcal{A}$ is a model of the axioms of equality. (The new normal structure will be the quotient structure induced by the equivalence relation $E^{\mathcal{A}}$.)

For $f \in [\mathbf{OPER.SYM}]_\alpha$, with $\alpha \in [S_\omega(\mathbf{SORT})]$ we say that f is an operation of type α, where $\alpha = \langle i_0, i_1, \ldots, i_n \rangle$. For $f \in [\mathbf{OPER.SYM}]_\alpha$, with $\alpha \in [\omega - \{0\}]$, we say that f is an untyped relation whose arity is α, where $\alpha = n$.

2.1. Definition (signature)

By a ***signature*** Σ we mean an ordered pair $\Sigma = \langle \mathbf{SORT}, \mathbf{FUNC} \rangle$ where:

(i) $\mathbf{SORT} = \mathbf{SORT}(\Sigma)$ is an index set with $0 \in \mathbf{SORT}$.

(ii) $\mathbf{FUNC} = \mathbf{FUNC}(\Sigma)$ is a function whose values are in $[S_\omega(\mathbf{SORT})] \cup [\omega - \{0\}]$. Elements of $S_\omega(\mathbf{SORT})$ are termed types while elements of $\omega - \{0\}$ are termed arities.
We use **OPER.SYM** as Dom(**FUNC**) and call its elements operation symbols. **OPER.SYM** is partitioned into disjoint subsets

$$[\mathbf{OPER.SYM}]_\alpha = \{ f \,/\, \mathbf{FUNC}(f) = \alpha \}$$

Every operation symbol in **OPER.SYM** is different from the rest and none is a string of other operation symbols.

(iii) $\neg, \vee, E \in \mathbf{OPER.SYM}$ and $\mathbf{FUNC}(\neg) = \langle 0,0 \rangle$, $\mathbf{FUNC}(\vee) = \langle 0,0,0 \rangle$, $\mathbf{FUNC}(E) = 2$.

(iv) In fact, $\neg$ and $\vee$ are the only f such that $\mathbf{FUNC}(f) = \langle i_0, i_1, \ldots, i_n \rangle$ with $0 \in \{i_1, \ldots, i_n\}$. ▮

2.2. Definition (structure).

By a ***structure*** $\mathcal{A}$ of signature $\Sigma = \langle \mathbf{SORT}, \mathbf{FUNC} \rangle$ we mean a pair

$$\mathcal{A} = \langle \langle A_i \rangle_{i \in \mathbf{SORT}}, \langle f^{\mathcal{A}} \rangle_{f \in \mathbf{OPER.SYM}} \rangle$$

as follows:

(i) $\langle A_i \rangle_{i\in \mathbf{SORT}}$ is a family of non-empty sets. For each $i \in \mathbf{SORT}$, A_i is the ith universe of $\mathcal{A}$. We have $A_0 = \{T,F\}$.

(ii) $\langle f^{\mathcal{A}} \rangle_{f\in \mathbf{OPER.SYM}}$ is a family of functions.

(iia) For each $f \in \mathbf{OPER.SYM}$ and $\mathbf{FUNC}\,(f) = \langle i_0,\dots,i_m \rangle$, we have

$$f^{\mathcal{A}}: A_{i_1} \times \dots \times A_{i_m} \longrightarrow A_{i_0}$$

In any structure $\mathcal{A}$ we will always have $\neg, \vee \in \mathbf{OPER.SYM}$ and we want all these symbols, in the two-valued logic, to be interpreted in the classical way, therefore:

$$\begin{array}{lll} \neg^{\mathcal{A}} : A_0 & \longrightarrow & A_0 \\ \quad T & \longmapsto & F \\ \quad F & \longmapsto & T \end{array} \qquad\qquad \begin{array}{lll} \vee^{\mathcal{A}} : A_0 \times A_0 & \longrightarrow & A_0 \\ \quad \langle T,T \rangle & \longmapsto & T \\ \quad \langle T,F \rangle & \longmapsto & T \\ \quad \langle F,T \rangle & \longmapsto & T \\ \quad \langle F,F \rangle & \longmapsto & F \end{array}$$

(iib) For $f \in \mathbf{OPER.SYM}$ and $\mathbf{FUNC}(f) = n$ we have an n-ary untyped relation:

$$f^{\mathcal{A}}: \left(\bigcup_{i\in \mathbf{SORT}-\{0\}} A_i\right)^n \longrightarrow A_0$$

In particular we have $E \in \mathbf{OPER.SYM}$, with $\mathbf{FUNC}(E) = 2$, whose intended meaning is identity. Therefore, $E^{\mathcal{A}}(x,y) = T$ iff $x = y$. The structures which interpret equality as identity are called normal structures; all our structures are going to be normal, without explicitly indicating so. ▒

Remarks.

(a) If $\mathbf{FUNC}(f) = \langle i_0,\dots,i_m \rangle$ and $\beta = \langle i_0,\dots,i_m \rangle$ is its type, $f^{\mathcal{A}}$ has type β; value type is i_0 while argument type is $\langle i_1,\dots,i_m \rangle$. Special cases are constants, proper functions, relations and connectives.

(a1) When $\mathbf{FUNC}(f) = \langle i \rangle$, f is an individual constant and $f^{\mathcal{A}} \in A_i$.

(a2) When f is a relation symbol with $\mathbf{FUNC}(f) = \langle 0,i_1,\dots,i_m \rangle$

$$f^{\mathcal{A}}: A_{i_1} \times \dots \times A_{i_m} \longrightarrow A_0$$

We can identify $f^{\mathcal{A}}$ with

$$\{\bar{x} \in A_{i_1} \times \dots \times A_{i_m} \,/\, f^{\mathcal{A}}(\bar{x}) = T\}$$

and will consequently say that

$f^{\mathcal{A}} \subseteq (A_{i_1} \times ... \times A_{i_m})$ is an m-ary typed relation (the type is $\beta = \langle 0, i_1, ..., i_m \rangle$)

(b) The cardinality of a many-sorted structure $\mathcal{A}$ is the sum of the cardinalities of the domains.

3.- FORMAL MANY-SORTED LANGUAGE.

To talk about a many-sorted structure $\mathcal{A}$ of signature Σ we need a many-sorted language L of the same signature.

3.1. Alphabet.

The alphabet of L includes all the operation symbols in **OPER.SYM**, the quantifiers and an infinite number of variables for each sort $i \in$ **SORT**$-\{0\}$. In particular, L contains:

(i) For each $i \in$ **SORT**$-\{0\}$: $v_0^i, v_1^i, v_2^i, ...$ (variables of sort i and whose type is i too). The set of variables, $\mathcal{V}$, is itself partitioned into disjoint subsets, $\{\mathcal{V}_i \, / \, i \in \textbf{SORT}-\{0\}\}$.
Thus, we let $\mathcal{V} = \bigcup \{\mathcal{V}_i \, / \, i \in \textbf{SORT}-\{0\}\}$.

(ii) All the operation symbols in **OPER.SYM**.

(iii) Quantifier: $\exists$. ▒

3.2. Expressions: formulas and terms.

Now, from the set of finite strings of elements of the alphabet we are going to select the expressions of L. We will use induction to define it.

(E1) Each variable of sort i is an expression of the same type (*i.e.*, the single type i).

(E2) If $f \in$ **OPER.SYM** and **FUNC**$(f) = \langle i_0, i_1, ..., i_m \rangle$, and $\varepsilon_1, ..., \varepsilon_m$ are expressions of single types $i_1, ..., i_m$, then $f \varepsilon_1 ... \varepsilon_m$ is an expression of type i_0.
If $R \in$ **OPER.SYM** and **FUNC**$(R) = n$, then for all the expressions of nonzero arbitrary single types $i_1, ..., i_n$ the string $R\varepsilon_1 ... \varepsilon_n$ is an expression of type 0.

(E3) If ε is an expression of type 0 and x^i is a variable of sort i, then $\exists x^i \varepsilon$ is an expression of type 0 as well.

Finally, no other string is an expression. ▮

We call **TERM** = **TERM**(*L*) the set of all expressions of single nonzero type i (*i.e.* i∈**SORT**–{0}) and use the Greek letter τ as a metavariable to refer to a term. When needed, we put a superscript, τ^{i}, to show the type of the term. ▮

We call **FORM** = **FORM**(*L*) the set of all expressions of type 0 and use the Greek letters φ and ψ as metavariables to refer to formulas. ▮

3.3. Remarks on notation.

(a) Case (E2) above covers:

(a1) when f is a proper function symbol.

(a2) when f is a connective (*i.e.* : $f \equiv \neg$ or $f \equiv \vee$) and the expressions concerned are of type 0. In this case, to make the formula more easily readable, we put the symbol $\vee$ between the terms (not preceding them) and we add parentheses on both sides. That is, instead of $\vee\varepsilon_1\varepsilon_2$ we write $(\varepsilon_1 \vee \varepsilon_2)$.

(a3) when f is a typed relation symbol, but not a connective. We use letters R, S, T in most cases, adding subscripts and/or superscripts to denote types when needed: $R^{\beta}_{0}, R^{\beta}_{1}, R^{\beta}_{2}, \ldots$

(a4) when f is an individual constant of sort i≠0, *i.e.*, **FUNC**(f) = ⟨i⟩. Then, by (2) in the definition of expressions, f followed by no terms, *i.e.*, f itself, is an expression of type i. We can, therefore, identify the type of the expression with the type of the constant symbol and with the corresponding sort. In this case we use the symbols $a, b, c, \ldots$, sometimes adding a superscript. .

(a5) when f is an untyped relation: $f \equiv R_n$ for $n \in \omega - \{0\}$. As a special binary untyped relation we have the equality sign: E. We will write $\tau_1 = \tau_2$ instead of $E\tau_1\tau_2$.

(b) In (a2) we open the door to parentheses; since they can be annoying, we can suppress some of them by following the rules specified in 2.3 of Chapter I. The rules are:

(b1) We can leave out external parentheses.

(b2) In case of iterated disjunction, the rule is association to the left.

(c) An iterated quantification over variables $x_1, \ldots, x_n$ of sorts $i_1, \ldots, i_n$, that is, $\exists x_1 \ldots \exists x_n$, can be simplified as $\exists x_1 \ldots x_n$.

(d) Beyond the above, when tradition is too strong and our notation makes the formulas difficult to read, we will follow tradition.

3.4. Abbreviations.

We will introduce new formulas as abbreviations:

(1) The formula $\varphi \wedge \psi$ abbreviates $\neg(\neg\varphi \vee \neg\psi)$.

(2) The formula $\varphi \to \psi$ abbreviates $\neg\varphi \vee \psi$.

(3) The formula $\varphi \leftrightarrow \psi$ abbreviates $\neg(\neg(\neg\varphi \vee \psi) \vee \neg(\neg\psi \vee \varphi))$.

(4) The formula $\forall x^i\varphi$ abbreviates $\neg\exists x^i\neg\varphi$.

3.5. Induction.

In **MSL** we also define new concepts for formulas or prove properties of all formulas using induction.

3.5.1. Proofs by induction on EXPR(L).

If we want to show that all expressions have the property $\mathcal{P}$ we will have to prove:

(E1) All variables in $\mathcal{V}$ have the property $\mathcal{P}$.

(E2) If the expressions $\varepsilon_1,...,\varepsilon_m$ of types $i_1,...,i_m$ share the property $\mathcal{P}$, and $f \in$ **OPER.SYM** and **FUNC**$(f) = \langle i_0, i_1,...,i_m\rangle$, then $f\varepsilon_1...\varepsilon_m$ has the property $\mathcal{P}$. This case covers all typed function and relation symbols.

If the expressions $\varepsilon_1,...,\varepsilon_m$ of arbitrary types $i_1,...,i_m$ share the property $\mathcal{P}$ and R is an untyped expression, then $R\varepsilon_1...\varepsilon_m$ has the property $\mathcal{P}$.

(E3) If $\varphi \in$ **FORM** has the property $\mathcal{P}$, then $\exists x^i\varphi$ also has the property $\mathcal{P}$. ▒

Remarks.

In fact, proofs by induction can be shaped in slightly different ways: formation of expressions, length of expressions, number of occurrences of logical symbols,.... According to the general schema chosen, the inductive step may vary to match it.

We use recursion to define new concepts. The general schema is the expected one: we begin with the simplest expressions and while assuming that the concept is defined for arbitrary expressions, define it for the expressions built by (E2) and (E3) of the definition of formulas and terms.

3.5.2. Definitions by recursion.

When defining a concept $\mathcal{C}$ for each expression it is enough to do the following:

(E1) Define $\mathcal{C}$ for each variable of sort i.

(E2) Assuming it is defined for all expressions $\varepsilon_1,\dots,\varepsilon_n$ of types $i_1,\dots,i_n$ define $\mathcal{C}$ for all possible $f\varepsilon_1\dots\varepsilon_n$.

(E3) Define $\mathcal{C}$ for $\exists x^i\varphi$, assuming it is defined for φ.

3.6. Free and bound variables.

Within a formula a variable can be free or bound. The definition is an obvious extension to that of first order logic: a variable is free if it occurs in the expression and it is not in the scope of a quantifier and it is bound when it occurs in the expression and also in the scope of a quantifier. In fact, a variable can only be bound in a formula and not in a term. Now we are going to define **FREE**(ε) for any expression ε. The definition will be designed to give the set of all the variables that occur freely in ε. It will, of course, be by recursion.

3.6.1. Definition.

(E1) $\mathbf{FREE}(x^i) = \{x^i\}$ for any variable of sort i

(E2) $\mathbf{FREE}(f\,\varepsilon_1\dots\varepsilon_n) = \mathbf{FREE}(\varepsilon_1) \cup\dots\cup \mathbf{FREE}(\varepsilon_n)$

(E3) $\mathbf{FREE}(\exists x^i\varepsilon) = \mathbf{FREE}(\varepsilon)-\{x^i\}$ ▓

3.6.2. Definition.

A term τ is said to be *closed* when $\mathbf{FREE}(\tau) = \emptyset$. ▓

A formula φ is called a *sentence* when $\mathbf{FREE}(\varphi) = \emptyset$. ▓

SENT = **SENT**(L) will denote the set of sentences of L. ▓

$\mathbf{FREE}(\Gamma) = \bigcup_{\varphi\in\Gamma} \mathbf{FREE}(\varphi)$. ▓

4.- SEMANTICS.

Given a language L and a structure $\mathcal{A}$, both of them sharing the same signature Σ, each closed term in L will denote an element in $\mathcal{A}$ and each sentence in L is true or false in $\mathcal{A}$. Nevertheless, we want to widen the scope of our definitions so that each term or formula gets an interpretation in $\mathcal{A}$. To do that we need to define assignments, where in many-sorted logic an assignment is a mapping

$$\mathrm{M}: \bigcup_{i \in \mathrm{SORT}-\{0\}} \mathcal{V}_i \longrightarrow \bigcup_{i \in \mathrm{SORT}-\{0\}} \mathrm{A}_i$$

in such a way that $\mathrm{M}[\mathcal{V}_i] \subseteq \mathrm{A}_i$; that is to say that variables of sort i always get their value in A_i.

An interpretation $\mathcal{I}$ over a structure $\mathcal{A}$ is a pair $\langle \mathcal{A}, \mathrm{M} \rangle$ where M is an assignment on $\mathcal{A}$.

4.1. Definitions.

4.1.1. Denotation.

Let $\mathcal{I} = \langle \mathcal{A}, \mathrm{M} \rangle$.

(E1) $\mathcal{I}(x^i) = \mathrm{M}(x^i)$

(E2) $\mathcal{I}(f\,\varepsilon_1 \ldots \varepsilon_n) = f^{\mathcal{A}}(\mathcal{I}(\varepsilon_1) \ldots \mathcal{I}(\varepsilon_n))$

As particular cases we have:

$\mathcal{I}(a_i) = a_i^{\mathcal{A}} \in \mathrm{A}_i$

$\mathcal{I}(f^{\beta}\tau_1 \ldots \tau_n) = (f^{\beta})^{\mathcal{A}}(\mathcal{I}(\tau_1), \ldots, \mathcal{I}(\tau_n))$

$\mathcal{I}(R^{\beta}\tau_1 \ldots \tau_n) = (R^{\beta})^{\mathcal{A}}(\mathcal{I}(\tau_1), \ldots, \mathcal{I}(\tau_n))$

(It is T or F according to the value of $\langle \mathcal{I}(\tau_1), \ldots, \mathcal{I}(\tau_n) \rangle$ in the characteristic function $(R^{\beta})^{\mathcal{A}}$.)

$\mathcal{I}(R_n\tau_1 \ldots \tau_n) = R_n^{\mathcal{A}}(\mathcal{I}(\tau_1), \ldots, \mathcal{I}(\tau_1))$

$\mathcal{I}(E\tau_1\tau_2) = E^{\mathcal{A}}(\mathcal{I}(\tau_1), \mathcal{I}(\tau_2))$

$\mathcal{I}(\neg\varphi) = \neg^{\mathcal{A}}\mathcal{I}(\varphi)$

$\mathcal{I}(\varphi \vee \psi) = \vee^{\mathcal{A}}(\mathcal{I}(\varphi), \mathcal{I}(\psi))$

(E3) $\mathcal{I}(\exists x^i\varphi) = \mathrm{T}$ iff $\{\mathrm{x}^i \in \mathrm{A}^i \,/\, \langle \mathcal{A}, \mathrm{M}_{x^i}^{\mathrm{x}^i} \rangle(\varphi) = \mathrm{T}\} \neq \emptyset$

(where $\mathrm{M}_{x^i}^{\mathrm{x}^i} = (\mathrm{M} - \{\langle x^i, \mathrm{M}(x^i) \rangle\}) \cup \{\langle x^i, \mathrm{x}^i \rangle\})$ ▒

Notation.

If $\langle \mathcal{A}, M\rangle = \mathcal{I}$, we will simplify $\langle \mathcal{A}, M_x^{x_i}\rangle$ as $\mathcal{I}_x^{x_i}$. ▓

4.1.2. Normal structures, models of formulas.

When $\mathcal{A}$ is a ***normal structure***, $\mathcal{I}(E\tau_1\tau_2) = \mathrm{T}$ iff $\mathcal{I}(\tau_1) = \mathcal{I}(\tau_2)$.

For a formula φ, we say that $\mathcal{I}$ ***is a model of*** φ if and only if $\mathcal{I}(\varphi) = \mathrm{T}$. In fact, when φ is a sentence we do not need the valuation and sometimes we will say that the structure $\mathcal{A}$ is a model of φ or that φ ***is true in*** $\mathcal{A}$. For a set Γ of formulas, $\mathcal{I}$ is a model of Γ if and only if $\mathcal{I}(\varphi) = \mathrm{T}$, for every $\varphi \in \Gamma$. As above, when Γ is a set of sentences we can say that $\mathcal{A}$ is a model of Γ, leaving out the valuation. ▓

(As you will see, the coincidence lemma justifies the above procedure.)

4.2. Satisfiability, validity, consequence and logical equivalence.

The definitions of these concepts are the obvious ones. To define them please see Chapter I, sections 4.3 and 4.4. ▓

Remark.

Recall that all our structures are normal and, therefore, when we say "all structures" we mean "all normal structures". If you decide to allow non-normal structures, then you should distinguish consequence and normal consequence, the latter restricted to normal structures. It is clear that consequence implies normal consequence.

5.- SUBSTITUTION OF A TERM FOR A VARIABLE.

Substitution is an operation where to each tuple of variable, term and expression there corresponds an expression. As you have seen already in other logics, usually the value-expression is the one obtained by erasing the variable and writing in the term in the original expression. But we do not want to substitute for bound variables, nor to change the meaning of the original formula, therefore the definition is a bit more complex than simple replacement.

(E1) $$z^{j}\frac{\tau}{x^{i}} = \begin{cases} \tau, \text{ if } x^{i} \equiv z^{j} \text{ (they are the same variable)} \\ z^{j}, \text{ otherwise} \end{cases}$$

(E2) We will distinguish:

(2a) If $f \in$ **OPER.SYM** and **FUNC**$(f) = \langle i_0, i_1, \ldots, i_m \rangle$ and $i_j \neq 0$ for all $j \in \{1, \ldots, n\}$, then

$$[f\tau_1 \ldots \tau_m]\frac{\tau}{x^{i}} = \begin{cases} f\tau_1 \ldots \tau_m & (*) \\ \text{but } f\ \tau_1\frac{\tau}{x^{i}} \ldots \tau_m\frac{\tau}{x^{i}} & (**) \end{cases}$$

(*) if x^{i} and τ have different types.

(**) otherwise.

(2b) If $R \in$ **OPER.SYM** and **FUNC**$(R) = \mathrm{m}$, then

$$[R\tau_1 \ldots \tau_m]\frac{\tau}{x^{i}} = R\ \tau_1\frac{\tau}{x^{i}} \ldots \tau_m\frac{\tau}{x^{i}}$$

(Notice that in that case we allow substitution between terms of different types.)

(2c) When the symbol is a negation or a disjunction, then

$$[\neg\varphi]\frac{\tau}{x^{i}} = \neg\varphi\frac{\tau}{x^{i}}$$

$$[\varphi \vee \psi]\frac{\tau}{x^{i}} = \varphi\frac{\tau}{x^{i}} \vee \psi\frac{\tau}{x^{i}}$$

(E3) $$[\exists z^{j}\varphi]\frac{\tau}{x^{i}} = \begin{cases} \exists z^{j}\varphi & (*) \\ \exists z^{j}\ \varphi\frac{\tau}{x^{i}} & (**) \\ \exists u^{j}[\varphi\frac{u^{j}}{z^{j}}]\frac{\tau}{x^{i}} & (***) \end{cases}$$

(*) if $x_{i} \notin$ **FREE**$(\exists z^{j}\varphi)$

(**) if $x^{i} \in$ **FREE**$(\exists z^{j}\varphi)$ and $z^{j} \notin$ **FREE**(τ)

(***) if $x^{i} \in$ **FREE**$(\exists z^{j}\varphi)$, $z^{j} \in$ **FREE**(τ) and u^{j} is a new variable

6. SEMANTIC THEOREMS.

6.1. Coincidence lemma.

6.1.1. Lemma.

Let $\mathcal{A}$ be a many-sorted structure, and M_1 and M_2 two assignments on $\mathcal{A}$. For any expression ε such that $M_1 \upharpoonright \mathbf{FREE}(\varepsilon) = M_2 \upharpoonright \mathbf{FREE}(\varepsilon)$, we have

$$\langle \mathcal{A}, M_1 \rangle(\varepsilon) = \langle \mathcal{A}, M_2 \rangle(\varepsilon)$$

Proof

The proof is a very easy induction exercise. ▮

6.1.2. Introducing a new notation.

Thanks to the coincidence lemma, we can avoid the use of assignments when dealing with formulas whose set of free variables is known.

(1) If $\mathbf{FREE}(\varepsilon) = \{x_1, x_2, \ldots, x_n\}$ respectively of types $i_1, \ldots, i_n$ and $\mathcal{A}$ is a many-sorted structure where the individuals $\mathbf{x}_1, \mathbf{x}_2, \ldots, \mathbf{x}_n$ are in the universes of sorts $i_1, \ldots, i_n$ and if M is any assignment, then instead of

$$\langle \mathcal{A}, M^{\mathbf{x}_1 \ldots \mathbf{x}_n}_{x_1 \ldots x_n} \rangle(\varepsilon) \text{ we will write } \mathcal{A}[^{\mathbf{x}_1 \ldots \mathbf{x}_n}_{x_1 \ldots x_n}](\varepsilon) \text{ or } \mathcal{A}[\mathbf{x}_1, \ldots, \mathbf{x}_n](\varepsilon)$$

when there is no ambiguity about the matching of variables and individuals.

(2) When we have closed expressions, *i.e.*, when $\mathbf{FREE}(\varepsilon) = \emptyset$, we can leave out any reference to assignments. Namely, instead of

$$\langle \mathcal{A}, M \rangle(\varepsilon) \text{ we will write } \mathcal{A}(\varepsilon)$$

6.2. Substitution lemma.

Given a many-sorted interpretation $\mathcal{I}$ (where $\mathcal{I} = \langle \mathcal{A}, M \rangle$), we have

$$\mathcal{I}^{\mathcal{I}(\tau)}_{x^i}(\varepsilon) = \mathcal{I}(\varepsilon \frac{\tau}{x^i})$$

for every expression ε of MSL and every term τ of type i.

Proof

This proof is also easy, but long. ▮

6.3. Equals substitution lemma.

Given a many-sorted interpretation $\mathcal{I}$,

$$\mathcal{I}(\varepsilon\frac{\tau}{x^i}) = \mathcal{I}(\varepsilon\frac{t}{x^i}) \text{ for every expression } \varepsilon$$

whenever $\mathcal{I}(\tau) = \mathcal{I}(t)$, and x^i has the same type as τ iff x^i has the same type as t.

Proof

The proof is an easy induction exercise. ▮

6.4. Isomorphism theorem.

6.4.1. Definition of isomorphism.

Let $\mathcal{A} = \langle\langle A_i\rangle_{i\in SORT}, \langle f^{\mathcal{A}}\rangle_{f\in OPER.SYM}\rangle$ and $\mathcal{B} = \langle\langle B_i\rangle_{i\in SORT}, \langle f^{\mathcal{B}}\rangle_{f\in OPER.SYM}\rangle$ be two many-sorted structures of the same signature and having disjoint universes.

A function $\mathbf{h} = \bigcup_{i\in SORT} \mathbf{h}_i$ is called an isomorphism from $\mathcal{A}$ onto $\mathcal{B}$ iff

(i) For every $i\in SORT$, $h_i: A_i \longrightarrow B_i$ is a bijection

(iia) For every $f\in OPER.SYM$ with $FUNC(f) = \langle i_0, i_1,\dots,i_m\rangle$ and $x_i,\dots,x_m$ in $A_{i_1},\dots,A_{i_m}$, we have

$$h(f^{\mathcal{A}}(x_i,\dots,x_m)) = f^{\mathcal{B}}(h(x_i),\dots,h(x_m))$$

Also, $h(\neg^{\mathcal{A}}(x,y)) = \neg^{\mathcal{B}}(h(x),h(y))$.

(iib) For every $f\in OPER.SYM$ with $FUNC(f) = n$ and $x_i,\dots,x_n$ in $\bigcup_{i\in SORT} A_i$, we have

$$h(f^{\mathcal{A}}(x_i,\dots,x_n)) = f^{\mathcal{B}}(h(x_i),\dots,h(x_n))$$ ▮

$\mathcal{A} \overset{\mathbf{h}}{\cong} \mathcal{B}$ stands for "**h** is an isomorphism from $\mathcal{A}$ onto $\mathcal{B}$". ▮

$\mathcal{A} \cong \mathcal{B}$ stands for "there is a **h** such that $\mathcal{A} \overset{\mathbf{h}}{\cong} \mathcal{B}$". ▮

6.4.2. Theorem.

Let $\mathcal{A}$ and $\mathcal{B}$ be two many-sorted structures with disjoint universes, $\mathcal{A} \overset{\mathbf{h}}{\cong} \mathcal{B}$ and let M be an assignment on $\mathcal{A}$. Then:

$$\mathbf{h}(\langle \mathcal{A},\mathrm{M}\rangle)(\varepsilon) = \langle \mathcal{B},\mathbf{h}\circ\mathrm{M}\rangle(\varepsilon)$$

for every expression ε.

Proof

Let $\mathcal{A}$, $\mathcal{B}$, h and M be as in the hypothesis of the theorem.

(E1) $\langle \mathcal{A},\mathrm{M}\rangle(x^{i}) = \mathrm{M}(x^{i})$

$\mathbf{h}(\langle \mathcal{A},\mathrm{M}\rangle(x^{i})) = \mathbf{h}(\mathrm{M}(x^{i})) = \mathbf{h}\circ\mathrm{M}(x^{i}) = \langle \mathcal{B},\mathbf{h}\circ\mathrm{M}\rangle(x^{i})$

(E2) Let $f \in$ **OPER.SYM** with **FUNC**$(f) = \langle \mathrm{i}_0, \mathrm{i}_1,...,\mathrm{i}_m\rangle$ and $\varepsilon_1,...,\varepsilon_m$ be expressions of types $\mathrm{i}_1,...,\mathrm{i}_m$

$\mathbf{h}(\langle \mathcal{A},\mathrm{M}\rangle(f\,\varepsilon_1...\varepsilon_m)) = \mathbf{h}(f^{\mathcal{A}}(\langle \mathcal{A},\mathrm{M}\rangle(\varepsilon_1),...,\langle \mathcal{A},\mathrm{M}\rangle(\varepsilon_m))) =$

$f^{\mathcal{B}}(\langle \mathcal{B},\mathbf{h}\circ\mathrm{M}\rangle(\varepsilon_1),...,\langle \mathcal{B},\mathbf{h}\circ\mathrm{M}\rangle(\varepsilon_m)) = \langle \mathcal{B},\mathbf{h}\circ\mathrm{M}\rangle(f\,\varepsilon_1...\varepsilon_m)$

(E3) $\mathbf{h}(\langle \mathcal{A},\mathrm{M}\rangle(\exists x^{i}\,\varphi)) = \mathrm{T}$ iff $\langle \mathcal{A},\mathrm{M}\rangle(\exists x^{i}\,\varphi) = \mathrm{T}$

iff $\{\mathrm{x}^{i}/\langle \mathcal{A},\mathrm{M}^{\mathrm{x}^{i}}_{x^{i}}\rangle(\varphi) = \mathrm{T}\} \neq \emptyset$

iff there is $\mathrm{x}^{i} \in \mathrm{A}_i$ such that $\langle \mathcal{A},\mathrm{M}^{\mathrm{x}^{i}}_{x^{i}}\rangle(\varphi) = \mathrm{T}$

iff there is $\mathbf{h}(\mathrm{x}^{i}) \in \mathrm{B}_i$ such that $\mathbf{h}(\langle \mathcal{A},\mathrm{M}^{\mathrm{x}^{i}}_{x^{i}}\rangle(\varphi)) = \mathrm{T}$

iff there is $\mathbf{h}(\mathrm{x}^{i}) \in \mathrm{B}_i$ such that $\langle \mathcal{B},\mathbf{h}\circ\mathrm{M}^{\mathrm{x}^{i}}_{x^{i}}\rangle(\varphi) = \mathrm{T}$

iff there is $\mathbf{h}(\mathrm{x}^{i}) \in \mathrm{B}_i$ such that $\langle \mathcal{B},(\mathbf{h}\circ\mathrm{M})^{\mathbf{h}(\mathrm{x}^{i})}_{x^{i}}\rangle(\varphi) = \mathrm{T}$

iff $\langle \mathcal{B},\mathbf{h}\circ\mathrm{M}\rangle(\exists x^{i}\,\varphi) = \mathrm{T}$ ∎

7.- THE COMPLETENESS OF MANY-SORTED LOGIC.

We have already introduced the formal language of many-sorted logic, many-sorted structures and the semantic concepts of consequency and validity. Now we will introduce a calculus to generate validities as logical theorems and to make it possible to mechanize the reasoning

reasoning proccess. Our calculus will be proved to be sound and strongly complete.

7.1. Deductive calculus.

Very briefly we will present a sequent calculus for many-sorted logic. As in second order logic, it is the sequent calculus of Ebbinghaus *et al* [1984]. Since this is the only calculus I will present for many-sorted logic, we will term it **MSL**.

7.1.1. Sequent rules.

As in second order logic, a deduction is a finite non-empty sequence of lines, each of which is a finite non-empty sequence of formulas: $\langle \varphi_1 \dots \varphi_n \psi \rangle$ is called a ***sequent*** with ***antecedent*** $\varphi_1, \dots, \varphi_n$ and ***consequent*** ψ.

The rules are the following:

(1) **(HI). Hypothesis introduction.**

(2) **(M). Monotony.**

(3) **(PC). Proof by cases.**

(4) **(NC). Non contradiction.**

(5) **(IDA). Introducing disjunction in the antecedent.**

(6) **(IDC). Introducing disjunction in the consequent.**

(7) **(IPA). Introducing particularization in the antecedent.**

$$\frac{\Omega \;\; \varphi\frac{y^i}{x^i} \;\hookrightarrow\; \psi}{\Omega \;\; \exists x^i \varphi \;\hookrightarrow\; \psi}, \; y^i \notin \mathrm{FREE}(\Omega \cup \{\exists x^i \varphi, \psi\})$$

(recall that y^i is of the same sort as x^i)

(8) **(IPC). Introducing particularization in the consequent.**

$$\frac{\Omega \;\hookrightarrow\; \varphi\frac{\tau}{x^i}}{\Omega \;\hookrightarrow\; \exists x^i \varphi}$$

(where x^i and τ are of the same type)

(9) **(RE). Reflexivity of equality.**

$$\frac{}{\tau = \tau}$$

(10) **(ES). Equals substitution.**

$$\frac{\Omega \hookrightarrow \varphi\frac{\tau}{x^{i}}}{\Omega\ \tau=t \hookrightarrow \varphi\frac{t}{x^{i}}}$$

(where x^{i} is of the same type as τ iff x^{i} is of the same type as t)

7.1.2. Deductions.

The concepts of derivable sequent in **MSL** and of derivable formula form a set of formulas as in second order logic, see Chapter I, section 2.5 for details. We will write the derivability sign $\vdash$ with a subscript when needed; namely, $\vdash_{\mathbf{MSL}}$. ▒

7.2. Syntactic notions.

In this section we will define some syntactic concepts, namely those of consistency, maximal consistency and the property of having witnesses. All three are properties of formulas and/or sets of formulas and in their definition we use derivability; ***i.e.***, the deductive calculus. We try to introduce consistency as a syntactic counterpart to satisfiability in the same sense as $\vdash$ and $\models$ would correspond to one another.

A set of formulas is contradictory (not consistent, or inconsistent) if and only if each formula in the language can be deduced from it. A set of formulas is maximally consistent when besides being consistent, each formula not in the set would make it inconsistent, if it were added to the set. A set of formulas contains witnesses if each existential formula comes with a witness. Let us define these concepts with care.

7.2.0. Preliminary definitions.

(1) $\Delta \subseteq$ **FORM** is ***contradictory*** iff for every $\varphi \in$ **FORM**, $\Delta \vdash \varphi$. ▒

(2) $\Delta \subseteq$ **FORM** is ***consistent*** iff it is not contradictory. ▒

(3) $\Delta \subseteq$ **FORM** is a ***maximally consistent*** set iff Δ is consistent and whenever $\varphi \in$ **FORM** and $\varphi \notin \Delta$, then $\Delta \cup \{\varphi\}$ is contradictory. ▒

(4) $\Delta \subseteq$ **FORM** ***contains witnesses*** iff for every existential formula, if $\exists x^{i}\varphi \in \Delta$, we have $\varphi\frac{\tau^{i}}{x^{i}} \in \Delta$, for some τ^{i} such that τ^{i} is a term of the same type as x^{i}. ▒

7.2.1. Theorems on consistency.

The following list includes some immediate corollaries of the definitions and the rules of the sequent calculus.

(1) If Δ is consistent and $\Gamma \subseteq \Delta$, then Γ is consistent.

(2) If Δ is contradictory and $\Delta \subseteq \Gamma$, then Γ is contradictory.

(3) If Δ is consistent, $\exists x^{i} \varphi \in \Delta$ and $z^{i} \notin \mathbf{FREE}(\Delta)$, then $\Delta \cup \{\varphi \frac{z^{i}}{x^{i}}\}$ is also consistent.

(4) $\Delta \subseteq \mathbf{FORM}$ is contradictory iff there is a $\varphi \in \mathbf{FORM}$ such that $\Delta \vdash \varphi$ and $\Delta \vdash \neg\varphi$.

Proof

The proof is left to the reader. ∎

7.2.2. Theorems on maximal consistency.

Let $\Delta \subseteq \mathbf{FORM}$ be a maximal consistent set and $\varphi, \psi \in \mathbf{FORM}$. Then all the following hold:

(1) If $\Delta \vdash \varphi$ then $\varphi \in \Delta$.

(2) If $\vdash \varphi$ then $\varphi \in \Delta$.

(3) $\neg\varphi \in \Delta$ iff $\varphi \notin \Delta$.

(4) $\varphi \vee \psi \in \Delta$ iff $\varphi \in \Delta$ or $\psi \in \Delta$.

(5) If $\Delta \cup \{\varphi\} \vdash \psi$ and $\Delta \cup \{\psi\} \vdash \varphi$ then: $\varphi \in \Delta$ iff $\psi \in \Delta$.

Proof

The proof is left to the reader. ∎

7.2.3. Theorem on witnesses.

Let $\Delta \subseteq \mathbf{FORM}$ be a maximal consistent set such that Δ contains witnesses. Then:

(1) $\exists x^{i} \varphi \in \Delta$ iff there is a term τ^{i} (of type i) such that $\varphi \frac{\tau^{i}}{x^{i}} \in \Delta$.

Proof

The proof is left to the reader. ∎

7.2.4. Lemma: finiteness of consistency.

A set Δ of formulas is consistent if and only if every finite subset of Δ is consistent.

Proof

[$\Rightarrow$] In this direction the proof is just theorem 7.2.1.(1) stated above.

[⟸] Let us suppose that every finite subset of Δ is consistent, but Δ itself is contradictory. Therefore, $\Delta \vdash \varphi$ and $\Delta \vdash \neg\varphi$ for a certain $\varphi \in$ **FORM**. But in a deduction from Δ only a finite number of formulas of this set are used: deductions are finite. Therefore, there are derivable sequents $\vdash \alpha_1 ... \alpha_n \varphi$ and $\vdash \beta_1 ... \beta_m \neg\varphi$. Of course, using repeatedly the monotony rule (M) of our calculus, we obtain the sequents

$$\vdash \alpha_1 ... \alpha_n \beta_1 ... \beta_m \varphi \text{ and } \vdash \alpha_1 ... \alpha_n \beta_1 ... \beta_m \neg\varphi$$

Therefore, $\{\alpha_1,...,\alpha_n,\beta_1,...,\beta_m\}$ is contradictory, by theorem 7.2.1.(4) on consistency. This contradicts our assumption of consistency of all finite subsets of Δ. ∎

7.3. Soundness.

As we have said before, a deductive calculus is sound when it can never lead us from true hypotheses to false conclusions. That is, if φ is deducible from Γ, then φ is also a semantic consequence of Γ.

7.3.1. Theorem

For each $\Gamma \subseteq$ **FORM** and $\varphi \in$ **FORM**, if $\Gamma \vdash \varphi$ then $\Gamma \vDash \varphi$.

Proof

This proof proceeds along the lines of the proof of the second order calculus. See Chapter I, section 3.1 for details. To prove the correctness of the rule (ES) for **MSL** you will need the lemma 6.3 stated above. ∎

7.3.2. Corollary.

If Δ has a model, then Δ is consistent.

Proof

Assume Δ has a model, but Δ is contradictory. Then, for a certain φ, $\Delta \vdash \varphi$ and $\Delta \vdash \neg\varphi$. But then, by soundness, $\Delta \vDash \varphi$ and $\Delta \vDash \neg\varphi$. This is impossible unless Δ has no model. ∎

7.4. Completeness theorem (countable language)[57].

We will prove the completeness theorem in its strong sense, $\Gamma \models \varphi$ implies $\Gamma \vdash \varphi$ (for any Γ, φ such that $\Gamma \cup \{\varphi\} \subseteq$ **FORM**(L)). To prove completeness and its corollaries we will follow the path:

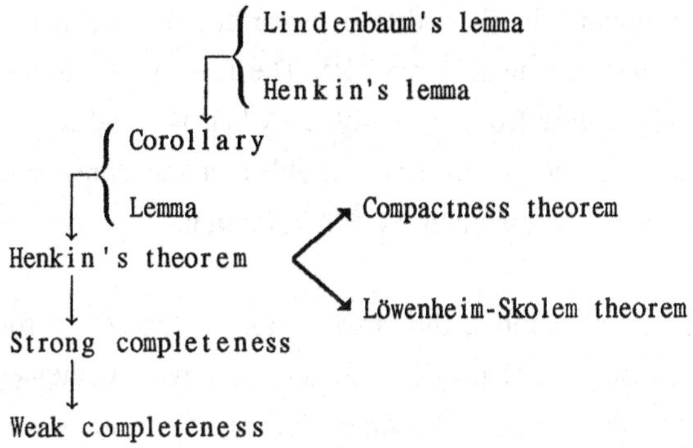

We will prove each of these theorems in the following form:

(1) **Lindenbaum lemma:** If $\Gamma \subseteq$ **FORM**(L) is consistent and **FREE**(Γ) finite, there exists Γ^* such that $\Gamma \subseteq \Gamma^* \subseteq$ **FORM**(L), Γ^* is maximally consistent and contains witnesses.

(2) **Henkin's lemma:** If Γ^* is maximally consistent and contains witnesses, then Γ^* has a countable model.

(3) **Corollary:** If $\Gamma \subseteq$ **FORM**(L) is consistent and **FREE**(Γ) is finite, then Γ has a countable model.

(4) **Lemma:** If $\Gamma \subseteq$ **FORM**(L) is consistent and $\Delta \subseteq$ **SENT**(L^*) is the class of sentences obtained from formulas in Γ by replacing every free variable by a new constant in L^* and if it happens that Δ has a countable model, then so has Γ.

(5) **Henkin's theorem:** If $\Gamma \subseteq$ **FORM**(L) is consistent, then Γ has a model whose domain is countable.

(6) **Strong completeness:** If $\Gamma \models \varphi$ then $\Gamma \vdash \varphi$

(7) **Weak completeness:** If $\models \varphi$ then $\vdash \varphi$.

[57]The cardinality of a many-sorted language is the cardinality of the set of its formulas and it is given by the cardinality of its symbols, including variables. Since we have variables for each sort, a language is not countable when the cardinality of **SORT** is greater than $\aleph_0$. The completeness proof for uncountable languages is similar, but we need the axiom of choice for ordering the formulas, and transfinite induction instead of finite induction.

(8) **Compactness theorem:** Γ has a model iff every finite subset of it has a model.

(9) **Löwenheim-Skolem:** If Γ has a model, then it has a countable model.

Before immersing ourselves in the proof, let us say a few remarks on strategy. First, we will prove that Henkin's theorem is a sufficient condition for completeness. Therefore, it is clear that the most important thing to do (in order to prove completeness) is to show that every consistent set of formulas has a countable model[58]. The rest of the strategy is easy to follow since Henkin's theorem will follow from the corollary when we find a way of leaving out the condition on the finiteness of the set of free variables in the consistent set. To prove the corollary we need Lindenbaum's lemma and the Henkin lemma.

In order to prove Lindenbaum's lemma, the enumeration of the set of formulas is a priority because we will use it to build a chain of consistent sets with witnesses whose union is a maximally consistent set with witnesses. To order the set of formulas we need the axiom of choice when we have an uncountable language, (which in fact we don't have!).

A maximally consistent set with witnesses is a very detailed description of a world. The idea is to construct a model following closely the instructions given by the formulas in the maximal consistent set. From a maximal consistent set with witnesses we obtain the tables of the operations of the model described. But which individuals are we going to choose to constitute the Universes of the model? We know (this is the philosophy of the isomorphism theorem) that what matters is not the individuals themselves but the relations that hold among them. Therefore, following Henkin, we will use the terms of the language as individuals in the universes of the model. Consequently, with a maximally consistent set of formulas Γ^* with witnesses, we can build a structure where we put in the operations described in Γ^*. As a first approach we build:

$$\mathcal{B} = \langle\langle\langle[\mathrm{TERM}(\mathcal{L})]_i\rangle_{i\in \mathbf{SORT}-\{0\}}, \{\mathrm{T},\mathrm{F}\}\rangle, \langle f^{\mathcal{B}}\rangle_{f\in \mathbf{OPER.SYM}}\rangle$$

where we define the function $f^{\mathcal{B}}$ over the universe of terms and the relation $R^{\mathcal{B}}$ gives truth values according to the oracle Γ^*. The value of the function for the terms $\tau_1,...,\tau_n$ is the term $f\tau_1...\tau_n$ while the relation gives the value T if and only if $R\tau_1...\tau_n\in\Gamma^*$. In particular,

$$E^{\mathcal{B}}(\tau_1, \tau_2) = \mathrm{T} \text{ iff } \tau_1 = \tau_2\in\Gamma^*$$

Besides that, we want the connectives to be standard; that is, $\neg^{\mathcal{B}}$ is the negation function and $\vee^{\mathcal{B}}$ is the disjunction function.

---

[58]Of course, the condition should be changed accordingly when the language is uncountable.

Since this structure is very likely not a normal one, we pass from it to the quotient structure induced by the identity in Γ^*; *i.e.*, the relation $E^{\mathcal{B}}$ defined using the equality formulas of Γ. It is not difficult to show that $E^{\mathcal{B}}$ is an equivalence relation and a congruence relation over all the functions in $\mathcal{B}$.

Now, we can prove in detail the lemmas and theorems in the chart above.

7.4.1.- Henkin's theorem implies strong completeness.

If every consistent set of formulas has a countable model, then

$$\text{If } \Gamma \models \varphi \text{ then } \Gamma \vdash \varphi$$

for every Γ and φ.

Proof

Assume Henkin's theorem. Suppose $\Gamma \models \varphi$. Therefore, $\Gamma \cup \{\neg\varphi\}$ is not satisfiable, it has no model. Using Henkin's theorem we conclude that $\Gamma \cup \{\neg\varphi\}$ is contradictory, hence $\Gamma \cup \{\neg\varphi\} \vdash \varphi$. But using our calculus rules (HI) and (PC) we obtain $\Gamma \vdash \varphi$. ▮

7.4.2. Lindenbaum lemma.

If $\Gamma \subseteq$ **FORM**(L) is consistent and **FREE**(Γ) is finite, then there exists a maximally consistent set Γ^* such that $\Gamma \subseteq \Gamma^*$ and Γ^* contains witnesses.

Proof

We want to extend Γ to a maximally consistent set with witnesses. We know that $\Gamma \subseteq$ **FORM**(L). Let $\varphi_1, \varphi_2, \varphi_3,...$ be an enumeration of **FORM**(L). Variables are also enumerated within their sorts:

$$y^i_1, y^i_2,...$$

By induction we will build a family $\langle \Gamma_n \rangle_{n \in \omega}$ of sets, each of them is a subset of **FORM**(L).[59]

$$\Gamma_0 = \Gamma$$

Assume that Γ_n has been built already and we want to build Γ_{n+1}.

[59]Here is where the changes should be made, for a non-denumerable language. We will need the well ordering theorem to order the formulas and instead of building $\aleph_0$ consistent sets, we will build as many as the cardinality of the language.

$$\Gamma_{n+1} = \begin{cases} \Gamma_n & (*) \\ \Gamma_n \cup \{\varphi_n\} & (**) \\ \Gamma_n \cup \{\varphi_n, \psi\frac{y^i_p}{x^i}\} & (***) \end{cases}$$

(*) if $\Gamma_n \cup \{\varphi_n\}$ is contradictory.

(**) if this set is consistent and φ_n is not an existential formula.

(***) if $\Gamma_n \cup \{\varphi_n\}$ is consistent, $\varphi_n \equiv \exists x^i \psi$, $y^i_p \notin$ **FREE**$(\Gamma_n \cup \{\varphi_n\})$, of the same sort as x^i and with the least p satisfying this condition.

Let $\Gamma^* = \bigcup_{n\in\omega} \Gamma_n$.

(1) **Proposition:** $\Gamma \subseteq \Gamma^*$.
Obvious.

(2) **Proposition:** For each positive integer n, Γ_n is consistent.
The proof is by induction.
$\Gamma_0 = \Gamma$ is consistent by hypothesis.
Assume Γ_n is consistent. Γ_{n+1} has to be of one of the following forms:
(1) $\Gamma_{n+1} = \Gamma_n$. In this case it is consistent by the induction hypothesis.
(2) $\Gamma_{n+1} = \Gamma_n \cup \{\varphi_n\}$. In this case it is consistent by construction.
(3) $\Gamma_{n+1} = \Gamma_n \cup \{\varphi_n, \psi\frac{y^i_p}{x^i}\}$, where $\varphi_n = \exists x^i \psi$ and $y^i_p \notin$ **FREE**$(\Gamma_n \cup \{\varphi_n\})$.
In this case it is not difficult to prove that Γ_{n+1} is consistent. We require that in Γ only a finite number of variables appear to ensure that we will always have new ones to use in the substitution.

(3) **Proposition:** Γ^* is consistent.
Let us suppose Γ^* is contradictory. By the lemma on finiteness of consistency, there must be a finite subset of Γ^*, say $\Delta = \{\delta_1,...,\delta_n\}$, such that Δ is contradictory.
Recall that all formulas in Δ are also in Γ^*. But being a member of Γ^* amounts at first to being a member of a certain Γ_n. We have defined the Γ_n's in such a way that they belong to an infinite chain $\Gamma_1 \subseteq \Gamma_2 \subseteq ... \subseteq \Gamma_n \subseteq \Gamma_{n+1} \subseteq ...$ ordered by inclusion.
Let Γ_p be the set of least index such that $\Delta \subseteq \Gamma_p$. By theorem 7.2.1.(2) on consistency, Γ_p is also contradictory. This conflicts with the above proposition (2).

(4) **Proposition:** Γ^* is maximally consistent.

Let $\varphi\in$ **FORM**(L)–Γ^*. We will show that $\Gamma^* \cup \{\varphi\}$ is contradictory.

Since **FORM**(L) has been ordered, φ must have a place in this ordering, let us say $\varphi \equiv \varphi_m$. We know that $\varphi_m \notin \Gamma_{m+1}$, its natural place. The only possible reason is that $\Gamma_m \cup \{\varphi_m\}$ is contradictory. Therefore, $\Gamma^* \cup \{\varphi_m\}$ is contradictory as well, because it contains as a subset a contradictory set.

(5) **Proposition:** Γ^* contains witnesses.

Let $\exists x^i \psi \in \Gamma^*$. As above, $\exists x^i \psi \equiv \varphi_n$ and it must be in Γ_{n+1}. Since Γ^* is consistent, $\Gamma_n \cup \{\exists x^i \psi\}$ is consistent too. According to our construction,

$$\Gamma_{n+1} = \Gamma_n \cup \{\exists x^i \psi, \psi \frac{y_p^i}{x^i}\} \quad \blacksquare$$

7.4.3. Henkin's lemma.

If Γ^* is maximally consistent and contains witnesses, then Γ^* has a countable model.

Proof

Let $\Gamma^* \subseteq$ **FORM**(L) be maximally consistent and containing witnesses. Since we have equality and we want our model to be normal, we need to construct a quotient structure. Therefore, we are going to construct the model described by the formulas in Γ^*, but we want the identity described in Γ^* to become the "true" identity relation. To do that we need to previously define an equivalence relation, the identity in our world Γ^*.

Definition: $\tau \approx t$ iff $\tau = t \in \Gamma^*$. $\blacksquare$

(1) **Proposition:** $\approx$ is an equivalence relation on $\bigcup_{i\in \mathbf{SORT}-\{0\}} [\mathbf{TERM}(L)]_i$.

Proof of proposition (1).

Reflexivity of $\approx$. For each $\tau \in$ **TERM**(L), $\vdash \tau = \tau$ by (RE). Since Γ^* is maximally consistent, $\tau = \tau \in \Gamma^*$.

Symmetry of $\approx$. We need to prove that for every $\tau, t \in$ **TERM**(L), whenever $\tau = t \in \Gamma^*$ then also $t = \tau \in \Gamma^*$.

Let $\tau = t \in \Gamma^*$:

$\Gamma^* \hookrightarrow \tau = t$			(HI)
$\hookrightarrow \tau = \tau$			(RE)
$\Gamma^*\ \tau = t$	$\hookrightarrow \tau = \tau$	$(\equiv [x = \tau]\frac{\tau}{x})$	(M)
$\Gamma^*\ \tau = t$	$\hookrightarrow t = \tau$	$(\equiv [x = \tau]\frac{t}{x})$	(ES)
$\Gamma^* \hookrightarrow t = \tau$			(M)

Therefore, $\Gamma^* \vdash t = \tau$. And so $t = \tau \in \Gamma^*$.

Transitivity of $\approx$. It has to be proven that whenever $\tau = \tau' \in \Gamma^*$ and $\tau' = t \in \Gamma^*$ we have $\tau = t \in \Gamma^*$. The proof is also very easy.

Notation. For a term τ, $[\tau]$ denotes the equivalence class of $\approx$ which τ is in.

We have proved that the relation is an equivalence. What we are going to do now is to define the structure $\mathcal{B}$ described in Γ^* and to use it to construct the quotient structure, $\mathcal{A}$. Before going into this construction, we prove that the relation $\approx$ is also a congruence on the structure $\mathcal{B}$; ***i. e.***, that all functions in $\mathcal{B}$ are respected by $\approx$.

(2) **Definition of $\mathcal{B}$.**

Let $\mathcal{B} = \langle\langle\langle[\mathbf{TERM}(L)]_i\rangle_{i\in \mathbf{SORT}-\{0\}}, \{T,F\}\rangle, \langle f^{\mathcal{B}}\rangle_{f\in \mathbf{OPER.SYM}}\rangle$ where:

(i) $B_i = [\mathbf{TERM}(L)]_i$ is the set of terms of type i, $i \neq 0$, $B_0 = \{T,F\}$.

(ii) For each $f \in \mathbf{OPER.SYM}$ such that $\mathbf{FUNC}(f) = \langle i_0, i_1, \ldots, i_n\rangle$ with $i_0 \neq 0$

$$f^{\mathcal{B}}(\tau_1, \ldots, \tau_n) = f\tau_1 \ldots \tau_n$$

for all sequences of terms $\langle \tau_1, \ldots, \tau_n\rangle$ where each τ_j $(1 \leq j \leq n)$ has type i_j.

(iii) For each $R \in \mathbf{OPER.SYM}$ such that $\mathbf{FUNC}(R) = \langle 0, i_1, \ldots, i_n\rangle$ with $i_1 \neq 0$

$$R^{\mathcal{B}}(\tau_1, \ldots, \tau_n) = T \text{ iff } R\tau_1 \ldots \tau_n \in \Gamma^*$$

for all sequences of terms $\langle \tau_1, \ldots, \tau_n\rangle$ where each τ_j $(1 \leq j \leq n)$ has type i_j.

Moreover the connectives are standard; that is, $\neg^{\mathcal{B}}$ is the negation function and $\vee^{\mathcal{B}}$ the disjunction function.

(iv) For each $R \in \mathbf{OPER.SYM}$ such that $\mathbf{FUNC}(R) = n$

$$R^{\mathcal{B}}(\tau_1, \ldots, \tau_n) = T \text{ iff } R\tau_1 \ldots \tau_n \in \Gamma^*$$

for all terms $\tau_1, \ldots, \tau_n$ of arbitrary nonzero types.

As a particular case we have:

$$E^{\mathcal{B}}(\tau_1, \tau_2) = T \text{ iff } \tau_1 = \tau_2 \in \Gamma^* \quad ▓$$

As you see, we take as the interpretation of equality in $\mathcal{B}$ the equivalence relation $\approx$. Of course, $E^{\mathcal{B}}$ while being an equivalence relation need not be the prototypic identity relation: the relation that holds between two individuals if and only if they are exactly the same one.

Therefore, although $\mathcal{B}$ is very likely not a normal model, we can obtain one from it. To do this we will pass from $\mathcal{B}$ to $\mathcal{B}/\approx$, the quotient structure. But first, as I said before, we will show that $\approx$ is a congruence relation on $\mathcal{B}$.

(3) **Proposition.** Let $f \in$ **OPER.SYM** with **FUNC**$(f) = \langle i_0, i_1,...,i_n\rangle$ and $i_0 \neq 0$:

$$\text{if } \tau_k \approx t_k (1 \leq k \leq n), \text{ then } f^{\mathcal{B}}(\tau_1,...,\tau_n) \approx f^{\mathcal{B}}(t_1,...,t_n)$$

for all terms of appropriate types; that is, τ_k and t_k both have type i_k $(1 \leq j \leq n)$.

Proof of proposition (3).

Assuming that $\tau_k = t_k \in \Gamma^*$ for all $k \in \{1,...,n\}$ and applying rule (ES) repeatedly it can be proved that

$$\Gamma^* \vdash f\tau_1...\tau_n = f t_1...t_k\tau_{k+1}...\tau_n \text{ for each } k\ (1 \leq k \leq n)$$

(induction is needed).

Therefore, $f\tau_1...\tau_n \approx f t_1...t_n$ and since all of these terms are the values of $f^{\mathcal{B}}$ for $\langle \tau_1,...,\tau_n\rangle$ and for $\langle t_1,...,t_n\rangle$, we get:

$$f^{\mathcal{B}}(\tau_1,...,\tau_n) \approx f^{\mathcal{B}}(t_1,...,t_n)$$

(4) **Proposition.** Let $R \in$ **OPER.SYM** with **FUNC**$(R) = \langle 0, i_1,...,i_n\rangle$ and $i_1 \neq 0$:

$$\text{if } \tau_k \approx t_k (1 \leq k \leq n), \text{ then } R^{\mathcal{B}}(\tau_1,...,\tau_n) \approx R^{\mathcal{B}}(t_1,...,t_n)$$

for all terms of appropriate types; that is, τ_k and t_k both have type i_k $(1 \leq j \leq n)$.

Proof of proposition (4).

Assuming that $\tau_k = t_k \in \Gamma^*$ for all $k \in \{1,...,n\}$ and applying rule (ES) repeatedly it can be proved that

$$\Gamma^* \cup \{R\tau_1...\tau_n\} \vdash R t_1...t_k\tau_{k+1}...\tau_n \text{ for each } k\ (1 \leq k \leq n)$$

and that

$$\Gamma^* \cup \{R t_1...t_n\} \vdash R\tau_1...\tau_k t_{k+1}...t_n \text{ for each } k\ (1 \leq k \leq n)$$

From this result we obtain:

$$\Gamma^* \cup \{R t_1...t_n\} \vdash R\tau_1...\tau_n \quad \Gamma^* \cup \{R\tau_1...\tau_n\} \vdash R t_1...t_n \text{ for each } k\ (1 \leq k \leq n)$$

Since Γ^* is a maximally consistent set, by 7.2.2.(5), we have:

$$R\tau_1...\tau_n \in \Gamma^* \text{ iff } R t_1...t_n \in \Gamma^*$$

Therefore, $R^{\mathcal{B}}(\tau_1,...,\tau_n) = R^{\mathcal{B}}(t_1,...,t_n)$

(5) **Proposition.** Let $R \in$ **OPER.SYM** with **FUNC**$(R) = n$:

$$\text{if } \tau_k \approx t_k \ (1 \le k \le n) \text{ then } R^{\mathcal{B}}(\tau_1,...,\tau_n) = R^{\mathcal{B}}(t_1,...,t_n)$$

for any terms of any nonzero types.

Proof of proposition (5).

Let $\tau_k \approx t_k$ (for each $k \in \{1,..,n\}$). Therefore, $\tau_k = t_k \in \Gamma^*$. By a similar procedure to that in the previous proposition (4), it can be proved that

$$\Gamma^* \cup \{R\tau_1...\tau_n\} \vdash Rt_1...t_n \text{ and } \Gamma^* \cup \{Rt_1...t_n\} \vdash R\tau_1...\tau_n$$

and therefore, $R_n\tau_1...\tau_n \in \Gamma^*$ iff $R_n t_1...t_n \in \Gamma^*$.

As before, $R^{\mathcal{B}}(\tau_1,...,\tau_n) = R^{\mathcal{B}}(t_1,...,t_n)$.

(6) **Definition of structure $\mathcal{A}$.**

Our structure $\mathcal{A}$ of signature $\Sigma = \langle \mathbf{SORT}, \mathbf{FUNC} \rangle$ will be a pair

$$\mathcal{A} = \langle \langle \mathrm{A_i} \rangle_{\mathrm{i} \in \mathbf{SORT}}, \langle f^{\mathcal{A}} \rangle_{f \in \mathbf{OPER.SYM}} \rangle$$

as follows:

(i) $\langle \mathrm{A_i} \rangle_{\mathrm{i} \in \mathbf{SORT}}$ is a family of sets, where for each $\mathrm{i} \in \mathbf{SORT}$, $\mathrm{A_i}$ is the ith universe of $\mathcal{A}$. Specifically,

(ia) For each $\mathrm{i} \in \mathbf{SORT}-\{0\}$, $\mathrm{A_i} = [\mathbf{TERM}(L)]_\mathrm{i}/_{\approx}$ is the set of equivalence classes of terms of type i under $\approx$. To name each class of terms of type i we choose a term of type i.

(ib) $\mathrm{A_0} = \{\mathrm{T,F}\}$.

(ii) $\langle f^{\mathcal{A}} \rangle_{f \in \mathbf{OPER.SYM}}$ is a family of functions.

For each $f \in \mathbf{OPER.SYM}$ such that $\mathbf{FUNC}(f) = \langle \mathrm{i_0,...i_m} \rangle$, we have $f^{\mathcal{A}} = f^{\mathcal{B}}/_{\approx}$. That is, it is a function $f^{\mathcal{A}}: \mathrm{A_{i_1}} \times ... \times \mathrm{A_{i_m}} \longrightarrow \mathrm{A_{i_0}}$ obtained from $f^{\mathcal{B}}$ by passing to the quotient. ▩

Remarks.

Because of the way we choose to name equivalence classes, although we can have two equal equivalence classes in two classes of terms of different types, they would receive different names. We will say that the class $[\tau^{\mathrm{i}}]$ has type i.

As you know, we say that $f^{\mathcal{A}}$ is an m-ary function of kind $\mathbf{FUNC}(f)$ and type $\langle \mathrm{i_0,i_1,...,i_m} \rangle$; value type is $\mathrm{i_0}$, argument type is $\langle \mathrm{i_1,...,i_m} \rangle$. You also know that as special cases we have: individual constants, relations, and connectives. Let us see the function in each case.

(iia) For each $f \in \mathbf{OPER.SYM}$ such that $\mathbf{FUNC}(f) = \langle \mathrm{i_0,...,i_m} \rangle$, $\mathrm{i_0} \neq 0$, and $\langle [\tau_1],...,[\tau_n] \rangle$ being a sequence of classes of terms where each $[\tau_k]$ has type $\mathrm{i_k}$ ($1 \le k \le n$), we have

$$f^{\mathcal{A}}([\tau_1],...,[\tau_n]) = f^{\mathcal{B}}/_{\approx}([\tau_1],...,[\tau_n]) = [f\tau_1...\tau_n]$$

Specifically, if a^i is an individual constant, then $(a^i)^{\mathcal{A}} = [a^i]$.

(iib) For each $R \in$ **OPER.SYM** such that **FUNC**$(R) = \langle 0,i_1,...,i_m\rangle$, and $\langle[\tau_1],...,[\tau_n]\rangle$ being a sequence of classes of terms where each $[\tau_k]$ has type i_k $(1 \le k \le n)$, we have

$$R^{\mathcal{A}}([\tau_1],...,[\tau_n]) = R^{\mathcal{B}}(\tau_1,...,\tau_n)$$

Therefore, it is T iff $R\tau_1...\tau_n \in \Gamma^*$.

(iic) For each $R \in$ **OPER.SYM** such that **FUNC**$(R) = n$, and $[\tau_1],...,[\tau_n]$ being classes of terms of nonzero sort, we have

$$R^{\mathcal{A}}([\tau_1],...,[\tau_n]) = R^{\mathcal{B}}(\tau_1,...,\tau_n)$$

Therefore, it is T iff $R\tau_1...\tau_n \in \Gamma^*$

(iid) $\neg^{\mathcal{A}}$ is negation and $\vee^{\mathcal{A}}$ is disjunction.

(7) **Definition of an interpretation $\mathcal{I}$.**

Let M be a map defined as:

$$\mathrm{M}: \bigcup_{i \in \mathrm{SORT}-\{0\}} \mathcal{V}_i \longrightarrow \bigcup_{i \in \mathrm{SORT}-\{0\}} \mathrm{A}_i$$
$$x^i \longmapsto [x^i]$$

and let $\mathcal{I} = \langle \mathcal{A}, \mathrm{M}\rangle$. ▓

(8) **Proposition:** $\mathcal{I}(\tau) = [\tau]$, for each term $\tau \in$ **TERM** and $\mathcal{I}(\varphi) = \mathrm{T}$ iff $\varphi \in \Gamma^*$, for each $\varphi \in$ **FORM**.

Proof of proposition (8).

(E1) $\mathcal{I}(x^i) = \mathrm{M}(x^i) = [x^i]$

(E2) We will show cases (2a) through (2f).

(2a) $\mathcal{I}(a^i) = (a^i)^{\mathcal{A}} = [a^i]$

(2b) $\mathcal{I}(f\tau_1...\tau_n) = f^{\mathcal{A}}(\mathcal{I}(\tau_1),...,\mathcal{I}(\tau_n)) = f^{\mathcal{A}}([\tau_1],...,[\tau_n]) = f^{\mathcal{B}}/_{\approx}([\tau_1],...,[\tau_n]) = [f\tau_1...\tau_n]$

(where f is a function symbol of type $\langle i_0,...,i_n\rangle$ with $i_0 \neq 0$).

The proof for terms is finished. In what follows we are going to prove the proposition for formulas. The induction used in the latter case is on the number of occurrences of $\neg, \vee$ and $\exists$.

(2c) $\mathcal{I}(R\tau_1...\tau_n) = R^{\mathcal{A}}(\mathcal{I}(\tau_1),...,\mathcal{I}(\tau_n)) = R^{\mathcal{A}}([\tau_1],...,[\tau_n]) = R^{\mathcal{B}}(\tau_1,...,\tau_n)$

Then it is T iff $R\tau_1...\tau_n \in \Gamma^*$ (where R is a relation symbol of type $\langle 0,i_1,...,i_n\rangle$).

(The proof uses the induction hypothesis on the terms τ_k $(1 \le k \le n)$ of type i_k.)

(2d) $\mathcal{I}(R\tau_1...\tau_n) = R^{\mathcal{A}}(\mathcal{I}(\tau_1),...,\mathcal{I}(\tau_n)) = R^{\mathcal{A}}([\tau_1],...,[\tau_n]) = R^{\mathcal{B}}(\tau_1,...,\tau_n)$

Then it is T iff $R\tau_1...\tau_n \in \Gamma^*$ (where R is a relation symbol of arity n).
(The proof uses the induction hypothesis on the terms τ_k ($1 \leq k \leq n$) of any types.)

(2e) $\mathcal{I}(\neg\varphi) = \neg^{\mathcal{A}}\mathcal{I}(\varphi) = \mathrm{T}$ iff $\mathcal{I}(\varphi) = \mathrm{F}$ iff $\varphi \notin \Gamma^*$ (induction hypothesis) iff $\neg\varphi \in \Gamma^*$ (maximal consistency)

(2f)

$$\mathcal{I}(\varphi \vee \psi) = \vee^{\mathcal{A}}(\mathcal{I}(\varphi), \mathcal{I}(\psi)) = \mathrm{F} \text{ iff } \mathcal{I}(\varphi) = \mathrm{F} \text{ and } \mathcal{I}(\psi) = \mathrm{F}$$
$$\text{iff } \varphi \notin \Gamma^* \text{ and } \psi \notin \Gamma^* \text{ (induction hypothesis)}$$
$$\text{iff } \varphi \vee \psi \notin \Gamma^* \text{ (maximal consistency)}$$

(E3) $\mathcal{I}(\exists x^i \varphi) = \mathrm{T}$ iff $\{[\tau^i] \in \mathrm{A}_i / \mathcal{I}_{x^i}^{[\tau^i]}(\varphi) = \mathrm{T}\} \neq \emptyset$

iff there is $[\tau^i] \in \mathrm{A}_i$ such that $\mathcal{I}_{x^i}^{[\tau^i]}(\varphi) = \mathrm{T}$

iff there is $\tau^i \in [\mathrm{TERM}]_i$ such that $\mathcal{I}_{x^i}^{\mathcal{I}(\tau^i)})(\varphi) = \mathrm{T}$

iff there is $\tau^i \in [\mathrm{TERM}]_i$ such that $\mathcal{I}(\varphi\frac{\tau^i}{x^i}) = \mathrm{T}$

(substitution lemma)

iff there is $\tau^i \in [\mathrm{TERM}]_i$ such that $\varphi\frac{\tau^i}{x^i} \in \Gamma^*$

(induction hypothesis)

iff $\exists x^i \varphi \in \Gamma^*$ (since Γ^* is maximally consistent)

(9) **Proposition:** $\mathcal{A}$ is countable.

Proof of proposition (9).

This is obvious, since $\mathrm{TERM}(L) = \bigcup_{i \in \mathrm{SORT}-\{0\}} [\mathrm{TERM}(L)]_i$ is countable. ∎

7.4.4. Corollary.

Whenever $\Gamma \subseteq \mathrm{FORM}(L)$ is consistent and $\mathrm{FREE}(\Gamma)$ is finite, Γ has a countable model. ∎

7.4.5. Lemma.

Let $\Gamma \subseteq \mathrm{FORM(L)}$ be consistent and $\Delta \subseteq \mathrm{SENT(L^*)}$ be the class of formulas obtained from those of Γ by replacing every free variable with a new individual constant of the same type.

If Δ has a countable model, then so does Γ.

Proof

Let Γ be consistent and Δ a set of sentences as explained in the hypothesis of the lemma. Let

$$\mathcal{B} = \langle \langle \mathrm{B}_i \rangle_{i \in \mathbf{SORT}\text{-}\{0\}}, \langle f^{\mathcal{B}} \rangle_{f \in \mathbf{OPER.SYM}^*} \rangle$$

be a model of Δ.

The reduction of $\mathcal{B}$ to **OPER.SYM** (that is $\mathcal{B} \restriction$**OPER.SYM**) along with the mapping M where each variable $v_m \in$**FREE**(Γ) of type i gets as value the constant c_m of the same type as that of that which is substituting for it in Δ, forms an interpretation $\mathcal{I}$ which is a model of Γ. ∎

7.4.6. Henkin's theorem.

Every consistent set of formulas has a countable model.

Proof

We have proven already this very same theorem assuming that the set of free variables in Γ is finite. Therefore, we only need to find a way of discarding the finiteness condition on **FREE**(Γ).

Let $\Gamma \subseteq$ **FORM**(L) and $L^* = L \cup (\bigcup_{i \in \mathbf{SORT}\text{-}\{0\}} \{c_1^i, c_2^i, \ldots\})$. Assume that the set of variables and the set of new constants are ordered within their sorts.

For every $\varphi \in \Gamma$ let $\bar{\varphi}$ be obtained from φ by substituting free variables for new constants of the same type. Let $\Delta = \{\bar{\varphi} \,/\, \varphi \in \Gamma\}$. We will prove that Δ is consistent. The reason why we want to prove the consistency of Δ is that from this fact it follows that Δ has a model, since **FREE**$(\Delta) = \emptyset$. Since we have proven already that models of Δ give models of Γ, our theorem will then be proved.

Proposition: Δ is consistent.

We will prove the consistency of Δ by proving that each finite subset of it has a model. Let $\Delta_0 \subseteq \Delta$ be a finite subset of Δ. In the corresponding Γ_0 only a finite number of variables can occur free, since Γ_0 itself is finite. We know that Γ_0, as a subset of Γ, must be consistent. Therefore, Γ_0 has a countable model (using 7.4.4).

Let that model be $\mathcal{I} = \langle \mathcal{A}, \mathrm{M} \rangle$.

Let $\bar{\mathcal{A}} = \langle \mathcal{A}, \langle \langle \mathrm{M}(x_n^i) \rangle_{n \in \omega} \rangle_{i \in \mathbf{SORT}\text{-}\{0\}} \rangle$ be an extension of $\mathcal{A}$ where we put as denotation of the new constants the interpretation in M of the variables of equal subscript; that is,

$$M(x^{i}_{n}) = \mathcal{I}(x^{i}_{n}) = \langle \mathcal{I},M\rangle(c^{i}_{n})$$

It is easy to see that $\langle \mathcal{I},M\rangle$ is a model of Δ_0. Since every finite subset of Δ has a model, each of them must be consistent. Therefore, Δ is consistent too. Now, from 7.4.2, 7.4.3 and 7.4.5 we conclude that Γ has a countable model. ▮

7.4.7. Strong completeness.
If $\Gamma \models \varphi$ then $\Gamma \vdash \varphi$.

Proof
This follows from 7.4.1 and 7.4.6. ▮

7.4.8. Weak completeness.
If $\models \varphi$ then $\vdash \varphi$.

Proof
This is a corollary of 7.4.7. ▮

7.5. Compactness theorem.

Γ has a model iff every finite subset of Γ has a model.

Proof
[$\Longrightarrow$] In this direction the proof is obvious.
[$\Longleftarrow$] Let us suppose that every finite subset of Γ has a model and imagine that Γ has, nevertheless, no model. By the Henkin lemma we conclude that Γ is an inconsistent set. Therefore, $\Gamma \vdash \varphi\wedge\neg\varphi$. But a deduction must be finite and so there is a finite set $\Delta \subseteq \Gamma$ such that $\Delta \vdash \varphi\wedge\neg\varphi$. But how can an inconsistent set have a model? The contradiction shows that Γ must have a model. ▮

7.6. Löwenheim-Skolem theorem.

Let Γ be a set of many-sorted sentences written in a countable language. If Γ has a model, then it has a countable model.

Proof

Let Γ be a set as explained in the hypothesis. Γ must be consistent. Then, by Henkin's theorem, it must have as well a countable model. ∎

8.- REDUCTION TO ONE-SORTED LOGIC.

As I said before, many-sorted logic easily reduces to one-sorted logic. To do this, we will define a syntactical translation (from many-sorted formulas and terms to one-sorted ones) and a semantic conversion of structures.

8.1. The syntactical translation (relativization of quantifiers).

Let L be a many-sorted language of signature Σ and **OPER.SYM** the set of its operation symbols. We will define a first order unsorted language, L^*, whose set of symbols includes all the symbols in L. Furthermore, L^* contains a unary relation symbol Q_i for each sort $i \in$ **SORT**$-\{0\}$. We shall treat the variables of L as variables of L^* also[60]. Let us say that the signature of the unsorted language is Σ^*.

In fact, the translation defined below is only the relativization of quantifiers to the new relation symbols in L^*. That it is, we will have structures with a unified domain and will consequently change the quantification over variables of sort i for a quantified conditional formula whose antecedent expresses the sort.

8.1.1. Definition.

$\mathbf{TRANS}_{\mathbf{MSL} \mapsto \mathbf{FOL}}$ is a function from the set of expressions in L to the set of expressions in L^*, it will be defined by induction.

In this section 8, we will abbreviate $\mathbf{TRANS}_{\mathbf{MSL} \mapsto \mathbf{FOL}}$ as **TRANS**.

(E1) $\mathbf{TRANS}(x_i) = x_i$ for each variable of every sort i

(E2) $\mathbf{TRANS}(f\, \tau_{i_1} ... \tau_{i_n}) = f\ \mathbf{TRANS}(\tau_{i_1}) ... \mathbf{TRANS}(\tau_{i_n})$

$\mathbf{TRANS}(R\tau_{i_1} ... \tau_{i_n}) = R\ \mathbf{TRANS}(\tau_{i_1}) ... \mathbf{TRANS}(\tau_{i_n})$

---

[60]This is impossible when the cardinality of **SORT** is greater than $\aleph_0$. (In this case, the precise definition of the translation is a bit more complex, but still possible.)

(E3) $\text{TRANS}(\exists x_i \varphi) = \exists x_i (Q_i x_i \wedge \text{TRANS}(\varphi))$, where the new symbol, $\wedge$, is a binary connective and we introduce $\alpha \wedge \beta$ as an abbreviation of the formula $\neg(\neg\alpha \vee \neg\beta)$

8.2. Conversion of structures.

8.2.1 From many-sorted structures to one sorted ones.

Let $\mathcal{A} = \langle \langle A_i \rangle_{i \in \text{SORT}-\{0\}}, \langle f^{\mathcal{A}} \rangle_{f \in \text{OPER.SYM}} \rangle$ be a many-sorted structure of signature Σ. We build a one sorted structure $\mathcal{A}^*$ by the method of unification of domains. We define:

$$\mathcal{A}^* = \langle \langle A_i \rangle_{i \in \text{SORT}-\{0\}}, \langle f^{\mathcal{A}^*} \rangle_{f \in \text{OPER.SYM}-\{\neg,\vee\}}, \langle Q_i^{\mathcal{A}^*} \rangle_{i \in \text{SORT}-\{0\}} \rangle$$

where

(i) The domain of $\mathcal{A}^*$ is the union of the domains of $\mathcal{A}$.

(iia) For each $f \in \text{OPER.SYM}$ with $\text{FUNC}(f) = \langle i_0, i_1, \ldots, i_n \rangle$ and $i_0 \neq 0$, then $f^{\mathcal{A}^*}$ is any extension of $f^{\mathcal{A}}$ such that

$$\text{Dom}(f^{\mathcal{A}^*}) = (\bigcup_{i \in \text{SORT}-\{0\}} A_i)^n \text{ and } f^{\mathcal{A}^*} \upharpoonright (A_{i_1} \times \ldots \times A_{i_n}) = f^{\mathcal{A}}$$

where all the new values are arbitrarily chosen. For instance, we can choose an element in the new unified domain and set it as the value of the new n-tuples. As you see, the only difference between $f^{\mathcal{A}}$ and $f^{\mathcal{A}^*}$ is that the domain of the latter is considerably bigger and so we need to specify values for the new tuples.

As a special case we have that for $f \in \text{OPER.SYM}$ such that $\text{FUNC}(f) = \langle i \rangle$, $f^{\mathcal{A}^*} = f^{\mathcal{A}}$. That is, constant elements in both structures are the same.

(iib) For each $R \in \text{OPER.SYM}$ such that either $\text{FUNC}(R) = \langle 0, i_1, \ldots, i_n \rangle$ or $\text{FUNC}(R) = n$, we have

$$R^{\mathcal{A}^*} = \{\langle x_1, \ldots, x_n \rangle \in A^{*n} / R^{\mathcal{A}}(x_1 \ldots x_n) = T\}$$

Specifically, $E^{\mathcal{A}^*} = E^{\mathcal{A}}$ and when our structure $\mathcal{A}$ is normal, $E^{\mathcal{A}^*}$ is the identity.

(iii) Each $Q_i^{\mathcal{A}^*} = A_i$. ▮

Remarks.

As you can see, in the structure $\mathcal{A}^*$ we want the interpretation of the new relation symbol Q_i to be the domain of sort i; that is, A_i. We say that $\mathcal{A}^*$ is obtained from $\mathcal{A}$ and has signature Σ^*. In fact, given a structure $\mathcal{A}$, there is more than one structure $\mathcal{A}^*$ obtained in this way, since there are many choices for the extensions of the functions in $\mathcal{A}$. The following theorems hold for any of these structures.

8.2.2. Theorem.

Given a normal structure $\mathcal{A}$ of signature Σ: $\mathcal{A}$ is a model of φ iff $\mathcal{A}^*$ is a model of **TRANS**(φ), for any sentence φ of L.

Proof

Let $\mathcal{A}$ be a normal structure of signature Σ and $\mathcal{A}^*$ a one-sorted structure obtained by unification of domains. We will make a broader statement, concerning any formula, from which the theorem follows:

Statement: For all many-sorted mappings M on $\mathcal{A}$ we have

$$\langle \mathcal{A},\mathrm{M}\rangle(\varepsilon) = \langle \mathcal{A}^*,\mathrm{M}\rangle(\mathbf{TRANS}(\varepsilon))$$

for any many-sorted term or formula ε.

Since we know from the coincidence lemma that when dealing with sentences, mappings don't matter, the only thing that has to be proved is the statement. To prove it, let M be a many-sorted mapping on $\mathcal{A}$. It is clear that M is also a one-sorted mapping on $\mathcal{A}^*$.

(E1) $\langle \mathcal{A},\mathrm{M}\rangle(x_i) = \mathrm{M}(x_i) = \langle \mathcal{A}^*,\mathrm{M}\rangle(x_i)$

(E2) $\langle \mathcal{A},\mathrm{M}\rangle(a_i) = a_i^{\mathcal{A}} = a_i^{\mathcal{A}^*} = \langle \mathcal{A}^*,\mathrm{M}\rangle(a_i)$

$\langle \mathcal{A},\mathrm{M}\rangle(f\,\varepsilon_1...\varepsilon_n) = f^{\mathcal{A}}(\langle \mathcal{A},\mathrm{M}\rangle(\varepsilon_1),...,\langle \mathcal{A},\mathrm{M}\rangle(\varepsilon_n)) = f^{\mathcal{A}^*}(\langle \mathcal{A}^*,\mathrm{M}\rangle(\varepsilon_1),...,\langle \mathcal{A}^*,\mathrm{M}\rangle(\varepsilon_n)) = \langle \mathcal{A}^*,\mathrm{M}\rangle(f\,\varepsilon_1...\varepsilon_n)$

(Using the induction hypothesis and the definition of $\mathcal{A}^*$. This proof applies for any $f \in$ **OPER.SYM.**)

(E3) $\langle \mathcal{A},\mathrm{M}\rangle(\exists x_i\varphi) = \mathrm{T}$ iff $\{\mathrm{x}_i \in \mathrm{A}_i \,/\, \langle \mathcal{A},\mathrm{M}_{x_i}^{\mathrm{x}_i}\rangle(\varphi) = \mathrm{T}\} \neq \emptyset$

But $\{\mathrm{x}_i \in \mathrm{A}_i \,/\, \langle \mathcal{A},\mathrm{M}_{x_i}^{\mathrm{x}_i}\rangle(\varphi) = \mathrm{T}\} = \{\mathrm{x}_i \in \mathrm{Q}_i^{\mathcal{A}^*} / \langle \mathcal{A}^*,\mathrm{M}_{x_i}^{\mathrm{x}_i}\rangle(\varphi) = \mathrm{T}\} =$

$\{\mathrm{x}_i \in \bigcup_{i \in \mathbf{SORT}-\{0\}} \mathrm{A}_i \,/\, \langle \mathrm{A}^*,\mathrm{M}_{x_i}^{\mathrm{x}_i}\rangle(Q_i x_i \wedge \mathbf{TRANS}(\varphi)) = \mathrm{T}\}$.

Therefore, $\langle \mathcal{A},\mathrm{M}\rangle(\exists x_i\varphi) = \mathrm{T}$ iff $\langle \mathcal{A}^*,\mathrm{M}\rangle(\mathbf{TRANS}(\exists x_i\varphi)) = \mathrm{T}$. ∎

8.2.3. From one-sorted structures to many-sorted ones.

A one-sorted structure $\mathcal{B}$ of signature Σ^* is not always convertible into a many-sorted structure. There are two problems that could stop the conversion:

(A) The relations Q_i^B corresponding to the new relation symbols Q_i that were not in the many-sorted **OPER.SYM** could be empty. In a many-sorted structure all the domains must be non-empty sets.

(B) For an $f \in$ **OPER.SYM**, f^B is just an operation on B and there is no reason why the values of $f^B \restriction (Q_{i_1}^B \times \ldots \times Q_{i_n}^B)$ should be in $Q_{i_0}^B$.

What we are going to do is to formulate in the first order language three conditions whose validity in a model makes it easily convertible into a many-sorted model. Let Π be the set of all sentences of the following forms:

(a) $\exists x\, Q_i x$, for each $i \in$ **SORT**$-\{0\}$

(b) $\forall x_1 \ldots x_n (Q_{i_1} x_1 \wedge \ldots \wedge Q_{i_n} x_n \rightarrow Q_{i_0} f x_1 \ldots x_n)$, where **FUNC**$(f) = \langle i_0, i_1, \ldots, i_n \rangle$, $f \in$ **OPER.SYM**

(c) $Q_i c$, for each $c \in$ **OPER.SYM** with **FUNC**$(c) = \langle i \rangle$

Now, a one-sorted model of Π, say B, can be transformed into a many-sorted structure $B^\diamond$.

8.2.4. Definition of the many-sorted structure $B^\diamond$.

Given a one-sorted model B of Π, we define

$$B^\diamond = \langle \langle \mathbf{B}_i^\diamond \rangle_{i \in \mathbf{SORT}}, \langle f^{B^\diamond} \rangle_{f \in \mathbf{OPER.SYM}} \rangle$$

where:

(i) For each $i \in$ **SORT**$-\{0\}$, $\mathbf{B}_i^\diamond = Q_i^B$ and $\mathbf{B}_0^\diamond = \{T, F\}$

(iia) For each $f \in$ **OPER.SYM** with **FUNC**$(f) = \langle i_0, i_1, \ldots, i_n \rangle$

$$f^{B^\diamond} = f^B \restriction (Q_{i_1}^B \times \ldots \times Q_{i_n}^B)$$

(iib) For each $f \in$ **OPER.SYM** with **FUNC**$(f) = \langle i \rangle$

$$f^{B^\diamond} = f^B$$

(iic) For each $R \in$ **OPER.SYM** such that **FUNC**$(R) = \langle 0, i_1, \ldots, i_m \rangle$, we have

$$R^{B^\diamond} : Q_{i_1}^B \times \ldots \times Q_{i_n}^B \longrightarrow \{T, F\}$$
$$\langle x_1, \ldots, x_n \rangle \longmapsto T \text{ iff } \langle x_1, \ldots, x_n \rangle \in R^B$$

For each $R \in$ **OPER.SYM** such that **FUNC**$(R) = n$, we have

$$R^{B^\diamond} : (\bigcup_{i \in \mathbf{SORT}-\{0\}} Q_i^B)^n \longrightarrow \{T, F\}$$
$$\langle x_1, \ldots, x_n \rangle \longmapsto T \text{ iff } \langle x_1, \ldots, x_n \rangle \in R^B$$

(iid) We add standard negation and standard disjunction for $\neg^{B^\Diamond}$ and $\vee^{B^\Diamond}$. ▮

Remarks.

Thanks to the sentences in Π, the original structure B has the properties that allow us to define $B^\Diamond$ the way we just did. It can be proven that $B^\Diamond$ is a normal many-sorted structure of signature Σ.

8.2.5. Theorem.

If B is a one-sorted structure which is a model of Π, then $B^\Diamond$ is a many-sorted structure. Furthermore, a many-sorted sentence φ is true in $B^\Diamond$ iff **TRANS**(φ) is true in B.

Proof

Let B be a model of Π. We want to prove that $B^\Diamond$ is a many-sorted structure. In fact,

(i) $\langle \mathbf{B}_i^\Diamond \rangle_{i \in \mathbf{SORT}}$ is a family of non-empty sets. This follows from the fact that $\exists x Q_i x \in \Pi$ and from the definition of the structure.

(ii) $\langle f^{B^\Diamond} \rangle_{f \in \mathbf{OPER.SYM}}$ is a family of functions. Let's see why:

(a) When **RANK**(f) = $\langle i_0,\dots,i_n \rangle$ with $i_0 \neq 0$, then, by definition of $B^\Diamond$, we restrict the function's domain to the new stratified domain. Since the structure B is a model of

$$\forall x_1 \dots x_n (Q_{i_1} x_1 \wedge \dots \wedge Q_{i_n} x_n \rightarrow Q_{i_0} f x_1 \dots x_n)$$

the values of function $f^{B^\Diamond}$ are in $Q^B_{i_0}$.

(b) When **FUNC**(f) = $\langle 0,i_1,\dots,i_n \rangle$ or when it is a constant or a connective, the definition of the structure along with axioms $Q_i c$ makes it obvious how to show that the structure fulfills the required type conditions.

(c) For untyped relations, there is nothing to show.

Now we have to prove that many-sorted truth in $B^\Diamond$ is equivalent to one-sorted truth in B of the translation. As in theorem 8.2.1, it is better to make a move to a more general statement concerning expressions, not necessarily closed.

Statement: For all many-sorted mappings M

$$\langle B^\Diamond, \mathrm{M} \rangle (\varepsilon) = \langle B, \mathrm{M} \rangle (\mathbf{TRANS}(\varepsilon))$$

for any many-sorted term or formula ε.

Can you prove this? ▮

8.2.6. Theorem.

Let $\Gamma \cup \{\varphi\} \subseteq$ **SENT**(L). In many-sorted logic

$$\Gamma \vDash \varphi \text{ iff } \Pi \cup \mathbf{TRANS}(\Gamma) \vDash \mathbf{TRANS}(\varphi)$$

in one-sorted logic (where $\mathbf{TRANS}(\Gamma) = \{\mathbf{TRANS}(\psi) \mathbin{/} \psi \in \Gamma\}$).

Proof

[$\Rightarrow$] Let $\mathcal{B}$ be a one-sorted model of $\Pi \cup \mathbf{TRANS}(\Gamma)$. Then $\mathcal{B}^{\lozenge}$ is a many-sorted model of Γ. Since our hypothesis is that $\Gamma \vDash \varphi$, $\mathcal{B}^{\lozenge}$ must be a model of φ too. Therefore, $\mathcal{B}$ is a model of φ.

[$\Leftarrow$] Let $\mathcal{A}$ be a many-sorted model of Γ. Then clearly $\mathcal{A}^*$ is a one-sorted model of Π and, by theorem 8.2.1, of **TRANS**(Γ). Since our hypothesis is that

$$\Pi \cup \mathbf{TRANS}(\Gamma) \vDash \mathbf{TRANS}(\varphi),$$

$\mathcal{A}^*$ is a model of **TRANS**(φ). Therefore, $\mathcal{A}$ is a model of φ. ▮

The previous theorem allows us to infer the following three theorems from the corresponding one-sorted results: compactness theorem, enumerability theorem and Löwenheim-Skolem theorem[61]. But we have proved them already directly. In Chapter VII translations are done in the reverse direction, from other logics into many-sorted logic, and you will see there how to transfer properties of the many-sorted calculus to the others.

---

[61]See Enderton [1972], p. 281.

CHAPTER VII
APPLYING MANY-SORTED LOGIC.

1.- GENERAL PLAN.

1.1. Aims.

As mentioned in the introduction to the previous chapter, many-sorted logic provides a unifying framework in which to place other logics. Currently, the proliferation of logics used in philosophy, computer science, artificial intelligence, mathematics and linguistics makes a working reduction of this variety an urgent issue. The aim is twofold:

(1) To be able to use only one deductive calculus and a unique theorem prover for all of them - *i.e.*, a **MSL** theorem prover - and

(2) To avoid proving the metaproperties of the different existing logics by borrowing them from many-sorted logic.

If a parallel practical effort were to be made in the direction of automating the translations of other logics into many-sorted logic, this would be a useful simplification. Moreover, you can compare different logics by comparing their different many-sorted theories.

The appeal of the approach is that it is so intuitive and easy that only common sense is needed to understand the construction. So with very little effort the results obtained are remarkably deep. It is difficult to trace the trend of this approach because almost every non-classical logic has found its standard shadow at birth, but I like to credit most of the ideas involved in our current presentation to Henkin [1950]. I do not want to be misleading, so you are not going to find in that paper anything like translation of formulas into another formal language, or the open appearance of many-sorted logic. In connection with **SOL**, many-sorted logic appeared later, in Henkin's [1953], where a new second order calculus with the comprehension rule was presented. As noted in that paper, from this calculus it is possible to isolate the many-sorted one by leaving out the comprehension rule.

Nowadays you will certainly find very similar ideas developed in great detail and it has been a flourishing research subject for almost twenty years. Van Benthem [1983, 1984], Fine [1975],

Gabbay [1976], Goldblatt & Thomason [1975] and Sahlqvist [1975] constitute a solid start. The most convenient reference is the survey written by van Benthem [1984]. The theory of correspondence is a whole subject in its own right. But, if I understand the ideas correctly, as far as modal logic is concerned, the lesson obtained is the reassurance of the needing of a new semantics for modal logic; namely, the alternative semantics of frames instead of structures. You can also see a very similar approach in the research groups of Gabbay and Németi.

In the present chapter we are going to develop, in a rather intuitive setting, the general plan of the unifying approach and to apply it to the logics studied in this book: second order logic and type theory. The examples of modal logic and dynamic logic are also presented, but with different results.

Before concluding this brief introduction, let me answer two possible criticisms:

(1) What is the price we pay for each of these reductions?

(2) Why do we choose many-sorted logic instead of second order logic, or unsorted first order logic?

The first question is just to reverse the criticisms we made of the reduction of **MSL** into **FOL**. In our case we only defend a ***working reduction*** into **MSL**; that is, we plan to use an automatic translator when possible, a theorem prover and a bunch of metatheorems already proved. You are free to formalize in the original logic and use it for other intuitive characterizations, if you feel it is more natural than its translation.

The second question has been answered in the introduction of Chapter VI except for, why no second order logic? In fact, we are using second order logic but with the Henkin semantics and this is many-sorted logic. We do not want standard second order logic because we would rather have a complete calculus.

1.2. Representation theorem.

The general plan, which has to be adapted to the particular cases, is as follows: The expressions of the logic to be studied - call it **XL** - are translated into a many-sorted language of a logic of a peculiar signature directly related to the signature of the original logic - call it $\Sigma\#$ and **MSL#** the logic, while the structures used to interpret the logic **XL** - call the class of them **ST(XL)** - are converted into structures for **MSL#** - call their class **ST(MSL#)**.

Thus, we need to define a recursive function **TRANS** to do the translation and a direct conversion of structures, **CONV**$_1$.

Thus, we have to add two preliminary provisos:

(A) The function

$$\mathbf{TRANS}: \mathbf{EXPR(XL)} \longrightarrow \mathbf{EXPR(MSL\#)}$$
$$\varepsilon \longmapsto \mathbf{TRANS}(\varepsilon)$$

must be defined by recursion on the formation of expressions of **XL**. We also want the translation to introduce at most a finite number of free variables in the closed expressions of **XL**.

On the other hand,

(B) The function

$$\mathbf{CONV_1}: \mathbf{ST(XL)} \longrightarrow \mathbf{ST(MSL\#)}$$
$$\mathcal{A} \longmapsto \mathbf{CONV_1}(\mathcal{A})$$

must be a conversion of structures for **XL** into many-sorted structures of a particular chosen signature. The aim is to be able to prove the direct semantic equivalence in the form of lemma 1 below.

Aside.

A possible approach is to add to the many-sorted structures new universes containing all the categories of mathematical objects you want to talk about (and you are able to talk to) in the logic **XL**. Thus, you can put into **CONV**$_1(\mathcal{A})$ universes containing the sets and relations defined in $\mathcal{A}$ by the constructs of **XL**. As a consequence, we seem to need shifting to **SOL** instead of **MSL**. But we know how to avoid using second order structures, taking first order many-sorted structures instead: We can use many-sorted universes and give the possible relations between different domains explicitly, by adding membership relation symbols to the language **MSL#** and membership relations (or something similar) to the many-sorted structures.

With the direct conversion of structures we want to obtain the equivalence of validity in the original structures for **XL** with validity of a certain class of **MSL#** formulas in **CONV**$_1$(**ST**(**MSL#**)). The efficiency and relevance of the results are based on the handyness of the class $\mathcal{S}^*$ (where $\mathcal{S}^* =$ **CONV**$_1$(**ST**(**MSL#**))). Thus, we ask: Can we "manage" the class $\mathcal{S}^*$? And, then, we concentrate on studying the class $\mathcal{S}^*$.

Of course, the first question to ask is whether or not $\mathcal{S}^*$ can be replaced by **MOD(Δ)**, where $\Delta \subseteq$ **FORM(MSL#)**. That is, we want a representation theorem for the validities of **XL**.

Let me summarize what we expect to achieve with the direct conversion.

Goal: lemma 1.

Lemma 1.- For every $\mathcal{A} \in$ **ST(XL)** there is a structure $\mathbf{CONV}_1(\mathcal{A}) \in$ **ST(MSL#)** such that

(a) $\mathcal{A}[\mathrm{v}_1...\mathrm{v}_n] \models \varphi$ in **XL** iff $\mathbf{CONV}_1(\mathcal{A})[^{\mathrm{v}_1...\mathrm{v}_n}_{v_1...v_n}](\mathbf{TRANS}(\varphi)[v_1...v_n]) = \mathrm{T}$ in **MSL#**.

(b) $\mathcal{A} \models \varphi$ in **XL** iff $\mathbf{CONV}_1(\mathcal{A})$ is a model of $\forall\mathbf{TRANS}(\varphi)$ in **MSL#**

for every sentence φ of **XL**.

(Here $v_1,...,v_n$ are the free variables appearing in the translation, if any, and $\mathrm{v}_1,...,\mathrm{v}_n$ are suitable elements in both the original and the converted structure. $\forall\mathbf{TRANS}(\varphi)$ is the universal closure of the translation of φ. Finally, $\mathcal{A}[\mathrm{v}_1...\mathrm{v}_n] \models \varphi$ stands for the truth of the formula φ with the parameters $\mathrm{v}_1...\mathrm{v}_n$, which is a concept of the logic **XL**. When the translation does not produce free variables, only the item (b) is applicable; in some other occasions (b) follows from (a)).

From this lemma 1, or a slightly modified version of it, you can easily obtain as a corollary theorem 1.

Theorem 1.- Let $\mathcal{S}^* = \mathbf{CONV}_1(\mathbf{ST(XL)})$

$\models \varphi$ in **XL** iff $\models_{\mathcal{S}^*} \forall\mathbf{TRANS}(\varphi)$ in **MSL#**

for all sentences φ of the logic **XL**.

1.2.1. Theorem.

Lemma 1 implies Theorem 1.

Proof

Theorem 1 says that the validity in **XL** of a sentence φ corresponds to the validity of $\forall\mathbf{TRANS}(\varphi)$ in the class $\mathcal{S}^*$ of many-sorted structures obtained by direct conversion. The proof is obvious in so as we are not proving validity of the formula $\forall\mathbf{TRANS}(\varphi)$ in the whole class **ST(MSL#)**, but something far more modest: the validity of this formula in the restricted class $\mathcal{S}^*$, which is the range of the conversion function; *i.e.*, $\mathbf{CONV}_1(\mathbf{ST(XL)})$. When the translation introduces no free variables, only item (b) of lemma 1 is used. ▌

Thus, the key to both definitions - ***i.e.***, **TRANS** and $\mathbf{CONV_1}$ - is to simplify the proof of the semantic equivalence and in this respect the relevance of the result obtained strongly depends on the "closeness" - in a sense open to various interpretations - of the class $\mathcal{S}^*$ to the class of all many-sorted models of the universal closure of the class of translations of **VAL(XL)**, the validities of **XL** in its own semantics. Thus we want

$\mathcal{S}^*$ to be "close" to **MOD(∀TRANS(VAL(XL)))**

We may also require that every expression ε of **XL** defines in its own structures, $\mathcal{A} \in$ **ST(XL)** "almost the same" object as **TRANS**(ε) defines in $\mathbf{CONV_1}(\mathcal{A})$. Thus,

$\mathcal{A}(\varepsilon) \approx \mathbf{CONV_1}(\mathcal{A})(\mathbf{TRANS}(\varepsilon))$

One of the first objectives is to be able to prove a representation theorem for the logic **XL**. That is, our aim is to prove the following theorem.

Goal: representation theorem.

Representation theorem.- There is a recursive set of sentences Δ, $\Delta \subseteq$ **SENT(MSL#)**, with $\mathbf{CONV_1}$**(ST(XL))** $\subseteq$ **MOD**(Δ) such that

$\models \varphi$ in the logic **XL** iff $\Delta \models \forall$**TRANS**(φ) in **MSL#**

for every sentence φ of **XL**.

From this theorem the enumerability of **XL** follows as a corollary.

Enumerability of **XL**.- The set **VAL(XL)** is recursively enumerable.

1.2.2. Theorem.

Representation theorem implies enumerability theorem for the logic **XL**.

Proof

By the representation theorem we have: There is a recursive set Δ of sentences, $\Delta \subseteq$ **SENT(MSL#)**, such that $\mathbf{CONV_1}$**(ST(XL))** $\subseteq$ **MOD**(Δ) and $\models \varphi$ in **XL** iff $\Delta \models \forall$**TRANS**(φ) in **MSL#**, for all $\varphi \in$ **SENT(XL)**. The set Δ is recursive and then **CON**(Δ) = {$\varphi \in$ **SENT(XL)**/ $\Delta \models \varphi$} is recursively enumerable. **TRANS** and its inverse are also recursive. ▮

What has been achieved?

We mentioned that we wanted to use a unique theorem prover for all of our logics and to avoid the proofs of the meta-propierties of these logics. With the representation theorem we have already achieved a great deal. First, we know that the logic **XL** is enumerable and thus a calculus for it is a natural demand, but we also know that in **MSL#** we can emulate such a calculus.

Can we proceed further?
When the original logic **XL** has a defined concept of consequence we can try to prove a theorem stating the relationship between consequence in **XL** and consequence in **MSL#**. In fact, from the theorems proved already we can prove the following theorem.

Theorem 2.- There is a recursive set of many-sorted sentences, $\Delta \subseteq$ **SENT(MSL#)**, with $\mathbf{CONV_1(ST(XL))} \subseteq \mathbf{MOD}(\Delta)$ such that:

If $\mathbf{TRANS}(\Pi) \cup \Delta \models \mathbf{TRANS}(\varphi)$ in **MSL#**, then $\Pi \models \varphi$ in **XL**,

for all $\Pi \cup \{\varphi\} \subseteq$ **SENT(XL)**. (Assuming that at most n variables appear in the translation.)

1.2.3. Theorem.
Lemma 1 and representation theorem imply theorem 2.

Proof
Let us assume lemma 1 and the representation theorem and let $\Pi \cup \{\varphi\} \subseteq$ **SENT(XL)**. Let us assume $\mathbf{TRANS}(\Pi) \cup \Delta \models \mathbf{TRANS}(\varphi)$ in **MSL#** and take $\mathcal{A} \in \mathbf{ST(XL)}$ such that $\mathcal{A}[\mathrm{v}_1 \ldots \mathrm{v}_n] \models \pi$ for all $\pi \in \Pi$. By lemma 1, there is $\mathbf{CONV_1}(\mathcal{A}) \in \mathbf{ST(MSL\#)}$ such that $\mathbf{CONV_1}(\mathcal{A})[{}^{\mathrm{v}_1 \ldots \mathrm{v}_n}_{v_1 \ldots v_n}] \models \mathbf{TRANS}(\pi)$ for every $\pi \in \Pi$. (Here $v_1, \ldots, v_n$ are the free variables appearing in the translation, if any, and $\mathrm{v}_1, \ldots, \mathrm{v}_n$ are suitable elements in both the original and the converted structure.) By the representation theorem, $\mathbf{CONV_1}(\mathcal{A}) \in \mathbf{MOD}(\Delta)$. Therefore, $\mathbf{CONV_1}(\mathcal{A})[{}^{\mathrm{v}_1 \ldots \mathrm{v}_n}_{v_1 \ldots v_n}] \models \mathbf{TRANS}(\varphi)$. By lemma 1, again, $\mathcal{A}[\mathrm{v}_1 \ldots \mathrm{v}_n] \models \varphi$. ∎

Remark.
In the proof we have not used the full strength of the representation theorem, but only the fact that $\mathbf{CONV_1}(\mathcal{A}) \in \mathbf{MOD}(\Delta)$. So we can state a lemma with this minimum requisite.
Lemma 2 (weak version).-There is a recursive set Δ of many-sorted sentences, $\Delta \subseteq$ **SENT(MSL#)**, such that $\mathbf{CONV_1(ST(XL))} \subseteq \mathbf{MOD}(\Delta)$.

In particular, with lemma 1 and the lemma stated above we can prove theorem 2, as you can do by yourself.

What else can be done?

Very often we can do better than in theorem 2 because we can prove the equivalence of consequence in **XL** with consequence in a theory of **MSL#**. From this result, which we term the main theorem, we obtain compactness and Löwenheim-Skolem for **XL** using the metaproperties of **MSL#**. (We put **MSL#** instead of just **MSL** to remind you that a particular signature is being used; but, of course, this is not needed. Do not be confused, we have proved the metaproperties of **MSL** in the general case; *i.e.*, for any many-sorted signature Σ.)

1.3. Main theorem.

In order to prove the main theorem a reverse conversion of structures will be defined. Two possible situations are going to be considered here: (1) when $\mathcal{S}^*$ is axiomatizable and (2) when it is axiomatizable only up to isomorphism or many-sorted equivalence. In either case, we have found a recursive Δ coding $\mathcal{S}^*$ and we can define a reverse conversion of structures. In fact, a weaker requirement can be accepted because we only need that the models of Δ cannot be distinguished by translation of formulas of **XL**.

(1) Let $\mathbf{CONV_1(ST(XL))} = \mathbf{MOD}(\Delta)$ for a recursive Δ. Thus, we have gotten an affirmative answer to the question of axiomatizability - *i.e.*, our $\mathcal{S}^* = \mathbf{MOD}(\Delta)$ - and we define a reverse conversion of structures

$$\mathbf{CONV_2}: \mathbf{ST(MSL\#)} \supseteq \mathbf{MOD}(\Delta) \longrightarrow \mathbf{ST(XL)}$$
$$\mathcal{C} \in \mathbf{MOD}(\Delta) \longmapsto \mathbf{CONV_2}(\mathcal{C})$$

from the relation $\mathbf{CONV_1^{-1}}$; where, with this definition, you want to be able to prove the reverse semantic equivalence in the form given below.

(2) Let $\mathbf{CONV_1(ST(XL))} \subseteq \mathbf{MOD}(\Delta)$ for a recursive Δ and let $\mathbf{MOD}(\Delta)$ be so close to $\mathcal{S}^*$ that all the elements of this class are either isomorphic or equivalent to converted structures. In this case we can get rid of structures in $\mathbf{MOD}(\Delta)$-$\mathcal{S}^*$ because we can define a function $\mathbf{H}: \mathbf{MOD}(\Delta) \longrightarrow \mathcal{S}^*$ such that for each $\mathcal{C} \in \mathbf{MOD}(\Delta)$, $\mathcal{C} \cong \mathbf{H}(\mathcal{C})$ or $\mathcal{C} \equiv \mathbf{H}(\mathcal{C})$ and $\mathbf{H}(\mathcal{C}) \in \mathcal{S}^*$. For each $\mathbf{H}(\mathcal{C})$ obtained in this way, we try first to define a reverse structure in **ST(XL)**. Our function $\mathbf{CONV_2}$ is probably obtained by composition.

$$\begin{array}{ccc} ST(MSL\#) \supseteq MOD(\Delta) & \longrightarrow & CONV_1(ST(XL)) \subseteq ST(MSL\#) \\ & {}_{CONV_2}\searrow & \downarrow \\ & & ST(XL) \end{array}$$

In any case we want the strong version of lemma 2 to be easily proved.

Goal: strong version of lemma 2.

Strong version of lemma 2.- There is a recursive set Δ of many-sorted sentences, $\Delta \subseteq$ **SENT(MSL#)**, with **CONV**$_1$**(ST(XL))** $\subseteq$ **MOD**(Δ) satisfying: for every many-sorted structure $\mathcal{C} \in$ **MOD**(Δ) there is an **XL**-structure **CONV**$_2(\mathcal{C}) \in$ **ST(XL)** such that

(a) **CONV**$_2(\mathcal{C}),[\mathrm{v}_1 \ldots \mathrm{v}_n] \models \varphi$ in **XL** iff $\mathcal{C}[{}^{\mathrm{v}_1 \ldots \mathrm{v}_n}_{v_1 \ldots v_n}]$(**TRANS**$(\varphi)[v_1 \ldots v_n]) = \mathrm{T}$ in **MSL#**

(b) **CONV**$_2(\mathcal{C}) \models \varphi$ in **XL** iff $\mathcal{C}$ is a model of $\forall$**TRANS**(φ) in **MSL#**

for all sentences of **XL**. (Here $v_1,\ldots,v_n$ are the free variables appearing in the translation, if any, and $\mathrm{v}_1,\ldots,\mathrm{v}_n$ are suitable elements in both the original and the converted structure. $\forall$**TRANS**(φ) is the universal closure of the translation of φ. $\mathcal{A},[\mathrm{v}_1 \ldots \mathrm{v}_n] \models \varphi$ stands for the truth of the formula φ with the parameters $\mathrm{v}_1 \ldots \mathrm{v}_n$, which is a concept of the logic **XL**. When the translation does not produce free variables, only the item (b) is applicable; in some other occasions (b) follows from (a)).

Now we will see how to use lemma 1 and the strong version of lemma 2 to obtain the main theorem.

Main Theorem.- There is a recursive $\Delta \subseteq$ **SENT(MSL#)** with **CONV**$_1$**(ST(XL))** $\subseteq$ **MOD**(Δ) such that:

$\Pi \models \varphi$ in the logic **XL** iff **TRANS**$(\Pi) \cup \Delta \models$ **TRANS**$((\varphi)$ in **MSL#**,

for all $\Pi \cup \{\varphi\} \subseteq$ **SENT(XL)**. (Assuming that at most n variables appear in the translation.)

1.3.1. Theorem.

Lemma 1 and the strong version of lemma 2 imply the main theorem (with the additional assumption that at most n variables - namely, $v_1,\ldots,v_n$ - are used in **TRANS**, the translation function).

Proof

Let $\Pi \cup \{\varphi\} \subseteq$ **SENT(XL)** and let us assume lemma 1 and the strong version of lemma 2. Let Δ be the set of sentences obtained in the strong version of lemma 2.

[$\Longrightarrow$] Let $\Pi \models \varphi$ in **XL** and $\mathcal{B}[{}^{\mathbf{v}_1 \ldots \mathbf{v}_n}_{v_1 \ldots v_n}]$ be a model of **TRANS**$(\Pi) \cup \Delta$. Since Δ only contains sentences, $\mathcal{B} \in$ **MOD**(Δ); by the strong version of lemma 2 there is a structure **CONV**$_2(\mathcal{B}) \in$ **ST(XL)** such that **CONV**$_2(\mathcal{B}),[\mathbf{v}_1 \ldots \mathbf{v}_n] \models \pi$, for all $\pi \in \Pi$.

Thus, **CONV**$_2(\mathcal{B}),[\mathbf{v}_1 \ldots \mathbf{v}_n] \models \varphi$. Using again the strong version of lemma 2, $\mathcal{B}[{}^{\mathbf{v}_1 \ldots \mathbf{v}_n}_{v_1 \ldots v_n}]$ is a model of **TRANS**(φ).

[$\Longleftarrow$] Let us assume **TRANS**$(\Pi) \cup \Delta \models$ **TRANS**(φ) in **MSL#** and take $\mathcal{A} \in$ **ST(XL)** such that $\mathcal{A},[\mathbf{v}_1 \ldots \mathbf{v}_n] \models \pi$, all $\pi \in \Pi$. By lemma 1, there is **CONV**$_1(\mathcal{A}) \in$ **ST(MSL#)** such that **CONV**$_1(\mathcal{A})[{}^{\mathbf{v}_1 \ldots \mathbf{v}_n}_{v_1 \ldots v_n}] \models$ **TRANS**(π) for every $\pi \in \Pi$. Besides, **CONV**$_1(\mathcal{A}) \in$ **MOD**(Δ). Therefore, **CONV**$_1(\mathcal{A})[{}^{\mathbf{v}_1 \ldots \mathbf{v}_n}_{v_1 \ldots v_n}] \models$ **TRANS**(φ). By lemma 1, again, $\mathcal{A},[\mathbf{v}_1 \ldots \mathbf{v}_n] \models \varphi$. ▮

Remark.

When the logics treated have a global notion of consequence or when the function **TRANS** produces no free variables, the global version of this theorem is enough.

Global Main Theorem.- There is a recursive set of many-sorted sentences, $\Delta \subseteq$ **SENT(MSL#)**, with **CONV**$_1$(**ST(XL)**) $\subseteq$ **MOD**(Δ) such that:

$$\Pi \models \varphi \text{ in } \mathbf{XL} \text{ iff } \forall\mathbf{TRANS}(\Pi) \cup \Delta \models \forall\mathbf{TRANS}((\varphi) \text{ in } \mathbf{MSL\#},$$

for all $\Pi \cup \{\varphi\} \subseteq$ **SENT(XL)**.

This global version has an easy proof, since no free variables have to be dealt with and only the items (b) in both lemma 1 and the strong version of lemma 2 are used.

Now we will see how to obtain compactness and Löwenheim-Skolem for **XL** using the main theorem.

Compactness of **XL**.- If $\Pi \models \varphi$ in **XL**, then there is a finite subset of it, $\Gamma \subseteq \Pi$, such that $\Gamma \models \varphi$.

1.3.2. Theorem.

The main theorem implies compactness of **XL**.

Proof

Let us assume the main theorem. We want to prove compactness of **XL** using the compactness of may-sorted logic. Let $\Pi \models \varphi$ in **XL**. Using the main theorem, there is

$\Delta \subseteq$ **SENT(MSL#)** with $\mathbf{CONV}_1(\mathbf{ST(XL)}) \subseteq \mathbf{MOD}(\Delta)$ such that

$$\mathbf{TRANS}(\Pi) \cup \Delta \models \mathbf{TRANS}(\varphi)$$

By compactness of **MSL#**, there is a finite subset of $\mathbf{TRANS}(\Pi) \cup \Delta$, say Σ (where $\Sigma = \{\mathbf{TRANS}(\pi_1),...,\mathbf{TRANS}(\pi_n)\} \cup \{\delta_1,...,\delta_n\}$) such that $\Sigma \models \mathbf{TRANS}(\varphi)$. Obviously, $\Sigma \cup \Delta \models \mathbf{TRANS}(\varphi)$. Using the main theorem again, $\{\pi_1,...,\pi_n\} \models \varphi$ in **XL**. ▌

Löwenheim-Skolem for **XL**.- If $\Pi \subseteq$ **SENT(XL)** has a model, then it has a countable model.

1.3.3. Theorem.

The main theorem implies Löwenheim-Skolem for **XL**. (With the additional assumptions that the language **XL** is countable and the reverse conversion, $\mathbf{CONV}_2$, converts countable models into countable models.)

Proof

Let $\Pi \subseteq$ **SENT(XL)** be a set of sentences of a countable language and assume that Π has a model, say $\mathcal{A}$. By lemma 1, $\forall\mathbf{TRANS}(\Pi)$ also has a model, $\mathbf{CONV}_1(\mathcal{A})$. Since $\mathbf{CONV}_1(\mathcal{A}) \in \mathbf{CONV}_1(\mathbf{ST(XL)}) \subseteq \mathbf{MOD}(\Delta)$, $\mathbf{CONV}_1(\mathcal{A}) \in \mathbf{MOD}(\forall\mathbf{TRANS}(\Pi) \cup \Delta)$. Since in **MSL#** Löwenheim-Skolem holds, $\forall\mathbf{TRANS}(\Pi) \cup \Delta$ has a countable model, $\mathcal{D}$. By the strong version of lemma 2 and the assumption on the cardinality, Π also has a countable model, $\mathbf{CONV}_2(\mathcal{D})$. ▌

1.3.4. Theorem.

The main theorem implies enumerability for **XL**.

Proof

Obvious, take Π as $\emptyset$ in the main theorem and proceed as in 1.2.2. ▌

1.4. Testing a given calculus for XL.

Up to now, we have defined a translation, **TRANS**, of formulas of **XL** into **MSL#** and at least a direct conversion of structures, $\mathbf{CONV}_1$, such that lemma 1 and its corollary theorem 1 are satisfied. We have also produced a recursive set of many-sorted axioms, Δ, such that at least we know the truth of the lemma establishing that $\mathbf{CONV}_1(\mathbf{ST(XL)}) \subseteq \mathbf{MOD}(\Delta)$. In what follows, we will also assume that the function **TRANS** respects the connectors.

When we have a calculus in **XL**, which we term **CAL(XL)**, we can also try to borrow soundness and completeness of **MSL#** by applying the results in **XL**. Therefore, we have to check whether or not the **MSL#** theory Δ is enough to produce as theorems the logical theorems of the logic **XL**. In what follows we will assume (1) **CAL(XL)** is finitary - *i.e.*, deductions are finite, hypotheses of the rules are also finite - (2) **CAL(XL)** contains the classical propositional calculus and (3) the deduction theorem holds in **CAL(XL)**.

There are several questions we would like to ask, the basic one being as follows: Are the axioms and/or rules of the calculus of **XL** easily converted by translation into theorems of Δ or derived rules of **MSL#**?

Therefore, we try to prove our lemma 3.

Goal: lemma 3.

Lemma 3.- If $\vdash \varphi$ in **CAL(XL)**, then $\Delta \vdash \forall$**TRANS**(φ) in **MSL#** (where Δ is the set of sentences obtained in any version of lemma 2).

From this lemma 3, theorem 3 follows easily.

Theorem 3.- $\Pi \vdash \varphi$ in **CAL(XL)** implies **TRANS**$(\Pi) \cup \Delta \vdash$ **TRANS**(φ) in **MSL#**, for all $\Pi \cup \{\varphi\} \subseteq$ **SENT(XL)** (where Δ is the set of sentences obtained in any version of lemma 2).

1.4.1. Theorem 3.

Lemma 3 implies theorem 3 (assuming the properties of the calculus and the behavior of the function **TRANS** stated above).

Proof

Let $\Pi \vdash \varphi$ in **CAL(XL)**. Then, there is a finite set $\{\pi_1,...,\pi_n\} \subseteq \Pi$ such that $\{\pi_1,...,\pi_n\} \vdash \varphi$. By the deduction theorem and certain propositional rules, $\vdash \pi_1 \wedge ... \wedge \pi_n \rightarrow \varphi$. By lemma 3, $\Delta \vdash \forall$**TRANS**$(\pi_1 \wedge ... \wedge \pi_n \rightarrow \varphi)$ in **MSL#**. Since the function **TRANS** respects connectives, and certain rules of quantifiers which apply also in the many-sorted calculus, $\Delta \vdash$ **TRANS**$(\pi_1) \wedge ... \wedge$ **TRANS**$(\pi_n) \rightarrow$ **TRANS**(φ). Therefore,

TRANS$(\Pi) \cup \Delta \vdash$ **TRANS**(φ) ▮

From this theorem 3 and theorem 2 in the preceding section, we obtain soundness for **CAL(XL)**.

Soundness of **CAL(XL)**.- If $\Pi \vdash \varphi$ in **CAL(XL)**, then $\Pi \models \varphi$ in **ST(XL)**.

1.4.2. Theorem.

Theorem 2 and theorem 3 imply soundness of **CAL(XL)**.

Proof

Let $\Pi \vdash \varphi$ in **CAL(XL)**. By theorem 3 above, **TRANS**(Π) $\cup\, \Delta \vdash$ **TRANS**(φ) (where Δ is the set of sentences obtained in any version of lemma 2). By soundness of **MSL#**, **TRANS**(Π) $\cup\, \Delta \vDash$ **TRANS**(φ). By theorem 2, $\Pi \vDash \varphi$. ∎

Remark.

When the logic **XL** has a global relation of consequence, or when the translation produces no free variables, theorem 3 can be modified to its global version.

Global theorem 3.- $\Pi \vdash \varphi$ in **CAL(XL)** implies $\forall$**TRANS**(Π) $\cup\, \Delta \vdash \forall$**TRANS**($\varphi$) in **MSL#**, for all $\Pi \cup \{\varphi\} \subseteq$ **SENT(XL)** (where Δ is the set of sentences obtained in any version of lemma 2).

We have proved already the soundness of the calculus and we want to use the metaproperties of **MSL#** to prove completeness of **CAL(XL)** as well. When the calculus being tested is very similar to the many-sorted calculus, we can try to prove directly the lemma on calculus equivalence. Thus, we try to prove lemma 4.

Goal: lemma 4.

Lemma 4.- $\vdash \varphi$ in **CAL(XL)** if and only if $\Delta \vdash \forall$**TRANS**(φ) in **MSL#**, all $\varphi \in$ **SENT(XL)** (where Δ comes from lemma 2, in any of its versions).

From lemma 4 and certain assumptions about the behavior of the calculus, theorem 4 follows easily.

Theorem 4.- $\Pi \vdash \varphi$ in **CAL(XL)** if and only if **TRANS**(Π) $\cup\, \Delta \vdash$ **TRANS**(φ) in **MSL#**, all $\Pi \cup \{\varphi\} \subseteq$ **SENT(XL)** (where Δ is the set of sentences obtained in any version of lemma 2).

1.4.3. Theorem.

Lemma 4 implies theorem 4 (assuming the same as in 1.4.1).

Proof

Obvious. ∎

Remark.

When the logic **XL** has a global relation of consequence, or when the translation produces no free variables, theorem 4 can be modified to its global version.

Global theorem 4.- $\Pi \vdash \varphi$ in **CAL(XL)** if and only if $\forall$**TRANS**(Π) $\cup \Delta \vdash \forall$**TRANS**($\varphi$) in **MSL#**, all $\Pi \cup \{\varphi\} \subseteq$ **SENT(XL)** (where Δ is the set of sentences obtained in any version of lemma 2).

We will see below that completeness of the calculus for **XL** follows immediately from theorem 4 and the main theorem.

Completeness of **CAL(XL)**.- If $\Pi \vDash \varphi$ in **ST(XL)**, then $\Pi \vdash \varphi$ in **CAL(XL)**.

1.4.4. Theorem.

Theorem 4 and the main theorem imply soundness and completeness of **CAL(XL)**.

Proof

Assume theorem 4 and the main theorem and use completeness and soundness of **MSL#**.

$$\begin{array}{ccc}
\Pi \vDash \varphi & \overset{(*)}{\Longleftrightarrow} & \mathbf{TRANS}(\Pi) \cup \Delta \vDash \mathbf{TRANS}(\varphi) \\
 & & \Updownarrow (**) \\
\Pi \vdash_{\mathbf{CAL(XL)}} \varphi & \underset{(***)}{\Longleftrightarrow} & \mathbf{TRANS}(\Pi) \cup \Delta \vdash_{\mathbf{MSL\#}} \mathbf{TRANS}(\varphi)
\end{array}$$

If you look at the schema, (*) is the main theorem, (**) is completeness and soundness of MSL, (***) is theorem 4. Therefore, following the arrow in the clockwise direction you obtain completeness,

$$\Pi \vDash \varphi \Longrightarrow \Pi \vdash_{\mathbf{CAL(XL)}} \varphi$$

and in the reverse sense, soundness,

$$\Pi \vdash_{\mathbf{CAL(XL)}} \varphi \Longrightarrow \Pi \vDash \varphi \quad \blacksquare$$

It is not necessary to prove lemma 4 directly to obtain completeness; we can just as well use lemma 3 and use the canonical model construction of the logic **XL** to prove the other direction. The canonical model construction may vary from one logic to another but in the general case is based on the existence and properties of the maximally consistent sets of formulas and allows us to reduce derivability in the logic to truth in the canonical model. What we propose is to prove the above mentioned reduction directly for the translation.

Goal: lemma 5.

Let $\mathcal{A}_{\mathbf{CAN}}$ be the canonical model of **XL**. If $\mathbf{CONV}_1(\mathcal{A}_{\mathbf{CAN}}) \models \forall\mathbf{TRANS}(\varphi)$, then $\vdash_{\mathbf{CAL(XL)}}$.

From lemma 5 and lemma 3 we prove lemma 4.

1.4.5. Theorem.

Lemma 5 and lemma 3 imply lemma 4.

Proof

Let Δ be the set of sentences obtained in any version of lemma 2 and assume that $\Delta \vdash \forall\mathbf{TRANS}(\varphi)$. By soundness, $\Delta \models \forall\mathbf{TRANS}(\varphi)$. Since $\mathbf{CONV}_1(\mathcal{A}_{\mathbf{CAN}}) \in \mathbf{MOD}(\Delta)$, by lemma 2, $\mathbf{CONV}_1(\mathcal{A}_{\mathbf{CAN}}) \models \forall\mathbf{TRANS}(\varphi)$. By lemma 5, $\vdash_{\mathbf{CAL(XL)}}\varphi$. If we use now lemma 3 we obtain

$$\vdash_{\mathbf{CAL(XL)}} \text{ iff } \Delta \vdash \forall\mathbf{TRANS}(\varphi). \quad \blacksquare$$

2.- HIGHER ORDER LOGIC AS MANY-SORTED LOGIC.

2.0. Preliminaries.

We are going to introduce a many-sorted language with a higher order appearance which will be used as a target language of our higher order formulas. In the first place, the logic we want to translate into **MSL** is **SOL** supplemented with the general semantics of Henkin (in Chapter IV). The calculus whose properties are going to be tested is C_2. For the relational type theory **RTT** with the calculus C_ω you can define the transformation yourself as a straightforward generalization of what has been done for second order logic.

According with the general plan traced in the previous section, formulas of **SOL** (or of **RTT**) will be translated into formulas of **MSL** and we will also convert general structures of **SOL** (or of **RTT**) into structures of **MSL** and viceversa. Recall that the goal in the direct conversion of structures is to prove lemma 1; ***i.e.***, that the truth of a **SOL** sentence in a **SOL** structure $\mathcal{A}$ is equivalent to the truth of its translation on its direct converted structure, $\mathbf{CONV}_1(\mathcal{A})$. Similarly for **RTT**. So we have to define both the translation and the conversion of structures. The very first thing we have to do is to look at the similarities and differences of **SOL** and **RTT** with **MSL**.

Let us begin with the structures.

(1) **MSL structures.**

A many-sorted structure has, of course, universes for each sort, but the different universes do not maintain any predetermined relationship fixed from the metatheory. (We only demand from them that they be non-empty sets.) This does not mean that they cannot be related among themselves, but, if they were, we have to make explicit throughout the relations of the structure; ***i.e.***, we have to choose specific relations and add them to

$$\langle f^{\mathcal{A}}\rangle_{f \in \mathbf{OPER.SYM}}$$

(2) **SOL structures and RTT structures.**

On the other hand, it is clear that second order structures and relational structures for type theory are a special kind of many-sorted structures: They are like many-sorted structures because they have different domains, but the domains are not as freely chosen as in **MSL.**

In second order structures we have the domain of individuals (which is a non-empty set), but the rest of the domains in the structure are not completely new sets since they are sets and relations between individuals. Thus, we build the rest of the domains in the structure out of elements in the domain of individuals. In second order structures, unlike many-sorted ones, we require the domain of n-ary relations to be a subset of the power set of the n-fold cartesian product of the domain of individuals

that is, if $\mathcal{A}$ is a second order structure, then $A_1 \subseteq \mathcal{P}A$, $A_2 \subseteq \mathcal{P}A^2$, etc.

We have been using several kinds of second order structures: namely, standard second order structures (Chapter I) and general structures and frames (Chapter IV).

(a) In standard second order structures, since

$$A_n = \mathcal{P}A^n$$

as long as we know the universe of individuals, A, we rely completely on the metatheory to decide what is going to be added as n-ary relations; the characteristic of being an n-ary relation is taken from set theory and there is no relation in the structure telling us.

(b) In frames and general structures we still want $A_n \subseteq \mathcal{P}A^n$ but the decision of what is going to be put in A_n, which possible relations are going to be actual in structure $\mathcal{A}$, is, to some extent, peculiar for every structure $\mathcal{A}$. Besides that, in general structures the universes are extensional and closed under definability.

In relational structures the situation is similar, since the universes in the relational hierarchy of types, $\langle \mathcal{D}_\alpha \rangle_{\alpha \in \mathbf{TS}}$, are built from $\mathcal{D}_0$ and $\mathcal{D}_1$ as explained in Chapter V, and we also accept standard and non-standard structures.

(3) **The offspring of SOL and MSL (also, of RTT and MSL).**

Now we work with general structures and so we want our many-sorted structures to be similar to them. In this case we have to put membership explicitly inside the structure; that is the reason why we add to the operation constants in **SOL** (or in **RTT**) all the membership relation symbols, whose intended meaning is membership. But what does it mean to say that their intended meaning is genuine membership? Moreover, how can we force the many-sorted universes to be extensional and closed under definability?

To answer these questions, keep on reading. The solution is to require the structure to be a model of the set Δ including the axioms of extensionality, comprehension and the disjoint universes requirement. In this case we can prove theorem 2.3.5 saying that given a many-sorted structure $\mathcal{A} \in \mathbf{MOD}(\Delta)$ in which the membership relation symbols are arbitrarily interpreted, we can find an isomorphic many-sorted structure $\mathcal{B} = \mathbf{H}(\mathcal{A})$

where the interpretation of membership is the genuine membership relation. For **RTT** the solution is basically the same.

On the other hand, what are the similarities and differences between the formal languages of **SOL** and **MSL**? and between **RTT** and **MSL**?

(1) **SOL language.**

For reasons of simplicity, the second order language we will consider only has relation constants in **OPER.CONS**, it will have equality for individuals and relations and the rest of the logic symbols are reduced to $\neg$ and $\vee$, while the quantifier is $\exists$. As you know, this is not a reduction in the scope of the theorem, since this language is equivalent to our L_2 of Chapter I (See proposition 4.5.1 in that chapter).

Linked to the characteristics of second order structures expounded above, in second order logic we accept as a formula the string of variables

$$X^n x_1 .. x_n$$

since the interpretation of X^n is an n-ary relation on elements of **A** and it makes sense to interpret

$$X^n x_1 .. x_n \quad \text{as} \quad \langle \mathbf{x}_1, ..., \mathbf{x}_n \rangle \in \mathbf{X}^n$$

(2) **RTT language.**

Just as we did in **SOL**, we can consider a simplified language for **RTT** with the same logic symbols; namely, $\neg$, $\vee$ and $\exists$. In **RTT** the formula

$$X^{\alpha}(Y^{\alpha_1} ... Y^{\alpha_n}) \quad \text{where} \quad \alpha = \langle 0, \alpha_1, ..., \alpha_n \rangle$$

is interpreted along the same lines.

(3) **MSL language.**

On the other hand, a string of variables such as $X^n x_1 ... x_n$ (or $X^{\alpha}(Y^{\alpha_1} ... Y^{\alpha_n})$) is not a formula in many-sorted logic since the interpretations of these variables are only elements of different domains, not necessarily related to each other.

(4) **The offspring of SOL and MSL (and of RTT with MSL).**

All these little differences have an easy solution: We add to the many-sorted language membership relation symbols and to the many-sorted structures membership relations as relation constants. In this way we can explicitly show in many-sorted structures what is implicitly given in second order or in type theory.

Idea of the translation.

Let us see how we do this:

From the second order signature Σ we pass to a many-sorted signature $\Sigma^{\square}$ (or to $\Sigma^{\bullet}$, if we depart from a type theory signature) with a higher order look. In both cases the main difference is the addition of membership relation constants, but there are also little details of make-up:

(A) The variables now have sorts instead of stratified types (we can keep the same variables, but strictly speaking their subscript are only for sorts).

(B) The set **OPER.CONS** of second order language, which is basically first order, is now enlarged to include new symbols for the membership relations. We do the same for type theory.

(C) We include, as well, the sort 0 and the connectives as operation symbols.

(D) In second order logic we have the formula

$$X^{n}x_{1}..x_{n}$$

which in many-sorted logic is meaningless, but in many-sorted logic we have

$$\varepsilon_{n}x_{1}..x_{n}X^{n}$$

which was not in **SOL** and the latter will have in **MSL** basically the same meaning as the first has in **SOL**. In the same way, in type theory we have

$$X^{\alpha}(Y^{\alpha_1}...Y^{\alpha_n}) \text{ with } \alpha = \langle 0,\alpha_1,...,\alpha_n\rangle$$

whereas, in the corresponding $\mathbf{MSL}^{\bullet}$ we have

$$\epsilon_{\beta}Y^{\alpha_1}...Y^{\alpha_n}X^{\alpha}, \text{ where } \beta = \langle 0,\alpha_1,...,\alpha_n,\alpha\rangle$$

Therefore, in the translation we will make each of them to be the translation of the other.

Idea of the conversion of structures.

What will we do with the structures?

(A) A second order or a type theory structure is basically a peculiar many-sorted structure since it has several domains. We want the many-sorted structure to have higher order appearance and, in particular, what we do in the direct conversion of structures is to add the membership relations explicitly to the second order or type theory structure (we just copy them from $\mathcal{A}$).

(B) In the reverse conversion we have to think what is needed to obtain from a many-sorted structure a second order one and, in particular, a general structure.

- The first thing is that even though in a many-sorted structure of signature $\Sigma^\square$ we have relations whose intended meaning is membership, we have to ask them to *behave* as membership relations (asking them to respect extensionality rules and, in certain cases, also comprehension) and, furthermore, to *be* genuine membership.

•• The second thing is that even in the improbable case of having the genuine membership relation among domains, when comprehension is not demanded in the previous step, they do not have to be closed under definability.

For relational general structures we follow the same path.

What will be done to solve both problems is to require the structures to be models of extensionality and comprehension and then to define a new structure where membership is authentic. The idea is as simple as that:

If we have a structure A where

$$A = \{0,1,3\}, \ A_1 = \{5,9,2\} \ \text{ and } \ \varepsilon_1^A = \{\langle 0,5\rangle,\langle 0,9\rangle,\langle 1,5\rangle,\langle 3,2\rangle,\langle 1,2\rangle\}$$

we pass to a structure B where

$$B = \{0,1,3\}, \ B_1 = \{\{0,1\},\{0\},\{3,1\}\} \ \text{ and }$$
$$\varepsilon_1^B = \{\langle 0,\{0,1\}\rangle,\langle 0,\{0\}\rangle,\langle 1,\{0,1\}\rangle,\langle 3,\{3,1\}\rangle,\langle 1,\{3,1\}\rangle\}$$

(Strictly speaking, we do not take these, but their corresponding characteristic functions.) For relational general structures we follow the same path.

Remark.
In this section we will develop the **SOL** case carefully; you are asked to do the same for **RTT**.

2.1 The formal many-sorted language $MSL^\square$.

2.1.1. The many-sorted signature $\Sigma^\square$.
Let **SORT** be the smallest set with the following properties:
(i) $0,1 \in$ **SORT**. (0 is the Boolean and 1 is the individuals sort.)
(ii)   For each natural number $n \geq 1$, we have $\langle 0,1,\overset{n}{...},1\rangle \in$ **SORT**. ($\langle 0,1,\overset{n}{...},1\rangle$ is the sort of

domains of n-ary relations on individuals. To help your intuition, we take it to be the type of n-ary relations on individuals as well.)

The signature $\Sigma^{\square} = \langle \mathbf{SORT}, \mathbf{FUNC} \rangle$ is such that:

(1) $\mathbf{SORT} = \mathbf{SORT}(\Sigma^{\square})$ is the set defined above.

(2) $\mathbf{FUNC} = \mathbf{FUNC}(\Sigma^{\square})$ is a function which takes as arguments the elements of **OPER.CONS** of second order logic (that means, only relation symbols on individuals, including equality for every sort; that is an equality of type $\langle 0,1,1 \rangle$, another of type $\langle 0, \langle 0,1 \rangle, \langle 0,1 \rangle \rangle$, etc.) enlarged with the new membership relation symbols (we also put in $\neg$ and $\vee$ as we did in many-sorted logic). Call the resulting set of symbols $\mathbf{OPER.SYM}^{\square}$.

Now we define

$$\mathbf{FUNC}: \mathbf{OPER.SYM}^{\square} \longrightarrow [S_{\omega}(\mathbf{SORT})]$$

where:

- Almost all the values of **FUNC** are of the following kind: $\langle 0,1,\overset{n}{\ldots},1 \rangle$. That is, they are relations among individuals whose interpretation will be a characteristic function. We have also values $\langle 0,0 \rangle$ and $\langle 0,0,0 \rangle$ for $\neg$ and $\vee$.

•• For the new membership relations ε_n,

$$\mathbf{FUNC}(\varepsilon_n) = \langle 0,1,\overset{n}{\ldots},1,\langle 0,1,\overset{n}{\ldots},1 \rangle \rangle$$ ▮

2.1.2. Alphabet of $\mathbf{MSL}^{\square}$.

The alphabet of many-sorted logic suited for **SOL** must contain all the symbols in $\mathbf{OPER.SYM}^{\square}$ (that includes the membership relation symbols ε_n) and a countable set of variables for each $i \in \mathbf{SORT} - \{0\}$. To simplify things, let us use the same variables as in **SOL**: $x_1, x_2, \ldots$ for variables of sort 1; $X^1_1, X^1_2, X^1_3, \ldots$ for variables of sort $\langle 0,1 \rangle$; $X^2_1, X^2_2, X^2_3, \ldots$ for variables of sort $\langle 0,1,1 \rangle$;...;$X^n_1, X^n_2, X^n_3, \ldots$ for variables of sort $\langle 0,1,\overset{n}{\ldots},1 \rangle$; etc.

Besides all that, we have the existential quantifier: $\exists$. ▮

2.1.3. Expressions.

The set of expressions of this many-sorted language, $\mathbf{MSL}^{\square}$, is defined in the same way as that of any other many-sorted language and therefore is different from the second order language only in the following:

(1) $X^n x_1 \ldots x_n$ is no longer a formula in $\mathbf{MSL}^{\square}$ (since it is only a string of variables).

(2) $\varepsilon_n x_1 \ldots x_n X^n$, unlike second order logic, is indeed a formula (of course, $x_1, \ldots, x_n$ should be

variables of individual sort). ▓

2.2. The syntactical translation.

The syntactical translation from **SOL** to this $\mathbf{MSL}^{\square}$ leaves every formula the same except the atomic formulas of the kind mentioned above; *i.e.*:

$$\mathbf{TRANS}^{\square}(X^{n}x_1...x_n) = \varepsilon_n x_1...x_n X^{n}$$

2.2.1. Definition by recursion.

Could you please define $\mathbf{TRANS}^{\square}$ properly? ▓

2.2.2. Notation and remark:

$\mathbf{TRANS}^{\square}(\Gamma) = \{\mathbf{TRANS}^{\square}(\gamma) \,/\, \gamma\in\Gamma\}$.

Please be aware that the translation does not introduce free variables in the formulas being translated; *i.e.*, the translation of a sentence is a sentence. Therefore, only item (b) is needed in both lemmas 1 and 2 to prove the main theorem.

2.3 Structures.

As mentioned already, a many-sorted structure $\mathcal{A}$ of this signature $\Sigma^{\square}$ has, of course, universes for each sort and membership-like relations. But this is not enough to guarantee a genuine membership and second order relation between universes. On the other hand, the second order logic we are studying is Henkin's; *i.e.*, with the general semantics. That means our **SOL** structures have disjoint universes, they are extensional and also they are closed under definability. So we want to define direct and reverse conversion of structures but demanding these properties both in **SOL** and in **MSL**.

2.3.1. Direct conversion of structures.

Let us define

$$\mathbf{CONV}_1\colon \mathbf{ST(SOL)} \longrightarrow \mathbf{ST}(\mathbf{MSL}^{\square})$$
$$\mathcal{A} \longmapsto \mathcal{A}^*$$

where, when $\mathcal{A} = \langle \mathrm{A}, \langle \mathrm{A}_n\rangle_{n\geq 1}, \langle C^{\mathcal{A}}\rangle_{C\in\mathbf{OPER.CONS}}\rangle$ we take

$$\mathcal{A}^* = \langle A, \langle A_n \rangle_{n\geq 0}, \langle f^{\mathcal{A}} \rangle_{f\in \mathbf{OPER.SYM}^{\square}} \rangle$$

with $A_0 = \{T,F\}$ and:

(i) when $C \in \mathbf{OPER.CONS} \cap \mathbf{OPER.SYM}^{\square}$ we put in $\mathcal{A}^*$ the characteristic function of $C^{\mathcal{A}}$, $C^{\mathcal{A}^*} = \{\langle x_1,...,x_n,X\rangle \in A^n \times A_0 \,/\, X = T \text{ iff } \langle x_1,...,x_n\rangle \in C^{\mathcal{A}}\}$.

(ii) when $C \in \mathbf{OPER.SYM}^{\square} - \mathbf{OPER.CONS}$, C is either a connective or membership. Thus,

$$\varepsilon_n^{\mathcal{A}^*} = \{\langle x_1,...,x_n,X^n,Y\rangle \in A^n \times A_n \times A_0 \,/\, Y = T \text{ iff } \langle x_1,...,x_n\rangle \in X^n\}$$

Besides this, all the connectives are standard. ▓

Remark and notation.

(1) Basically, $\mathcal{A}^*$ is a copy of $\mathcal{A}$ where membership is explicit and all the distinguished relations are replaced by their characteristic functions. Clearly, $\mathbf{CONV}_1$ is a one-to-one function.

(2) Let us refer to $\mathbf{CONV}_1(\mathbf{ST(SOL)})$ as $\mathcal{S}^*$.

2.3.2. Lemma 1 (b).

For every second order general structure, $\mathcal{A} \in \mathbf{ST(SOL)}$, there is a many-sorted structure, $\mathbf{CONV}_1(\mathcal{A}) \in \mathbf{CONV}_1(\mathbf{ST(SOL)})$, such that

$\mathcal{A}$ is a model of φ iff $\mathbf{CONV}_1(\mathcal{A})$ is a model of $\mathbf{TRANS}^{\square}(\varphi)$

for every sentence φ of **SOL**.

Proof

We will make a broader statement concerning all formulas from which the lemma easily follows. The statement says:

For every general structure $\mathcal{A} \in \mathbf{ST(SOL)}$ and assignment M on $\mathcal{A}$, there is a many-sorted structure $\mathcal{A}^* = \mathbf{CONV}_1(\mathcal{A})$ such that

$\langle \mathcal{A}, M\rangle$ is a model of φ iff $\langle \mathcal{A}^*, M\rangle$ is a model of $\mathbf{TRANS}^{\square}(\varphi)$

for any formula φ of **SOL**.

Could you please prove the statement by induction on the formation of formulas? ▮

2.3.3. Theorem 1.

For every sentence φ of **SOL**: $\models_{\mathcal{G.S}} \varphi$ in **SOL** iff $\models_{\mathcal{S}^*} \mathbf{TRANS}(\varphi)$ in $\mathbf{MSL}^{\square}$.

Proof

Use 1.2.1 and 2.3.2 to get this. ▮

2.3.4. Reverse conversion of structures.

We will make the reverse conversion of structures in four steps.

(A) The structures we want to work with are $\mathbf{MSL}^{¤}$ models of extensionality and comprehension with disjoint universes. So first we express these properties in $\mathbf{MSL}^{¤}$.

$$\Delta = \{Ext^{(n)} \,/\, n\geq 1\} \cup \{\forall Comph^{(n)}_{\varphi} \,/\, n\geq 1 \ \&\ \varphi\in \mathbf{FORM(MSL)}\} \cup \{Disj_{n,m} \,/\, n\neq m \ \&\ n,m\geq 1\}$$

where:

$$Ext^{(n)} = \forall X^n Y^n (\forall x_1 \ldots x_n (\varepsilon_n x_1 \ldots x_n X^n \leftrightarrow \varepsilon_n x_1 \ldots x_n Y^n) \rightarrow X^n = Y^n)$$

$$\forall Comph^{(n)}_{\varphi} = \forall \exists X^n \forall x_1 \ldots x_n (\varepsilon_n x_1 \ldots x_n X^n \leftrightarrow \varphi), \text{ where } X^n \notin \mathbf{FREE}(\varphi)$$

$$Disj_{n,m} = \neg \exists X^n Y^m \; X^n = Y^m \text{ (for } n\neq m)$$

(B) From a many-sorted structure $\mathcal{A}$ of signature $\Sigma^{¤}$ which is a model of Δ, we pass to another many-sorted structure $\mathcal{B}$ of the same signature but where membership is the typical second order relation. Thus, we define a function

$$\mathbf{H{:}MOD}(\Delta) \longrightarrow \mathbf{CONV_1(ST(SOL))}$$

If $\mathcal{A}$ is a model of Δ, $\mathcal{B} = \mathbf{H}(\mathcal{A})$ is basically a general second order structure with the genuine membership relation.

(C) We define an isomorphism f from $\mathcal{A}$ onto $\mathcal{B}$ which is also the identity on universes of sort 0 and 1.

(D) From a **MS**-structure $\mathcal{B}\in\mathbf{CONV_1(ST(SOL))}$ of the kind mentioned in step two, we define a **SOL** structure by an easy make-up transformation; namely, erasing the membership relation and adapting the signature to a second order one. Also characteristic functions turn back to relations. This is just to reverse the transformation done in $\mathbf{CONV_1}$.

2.3.5. Theorem.

There is a function $\mathbf{H{:}\ MOD}(\Delta) \longrightarrow \mathbf{CONV_1(ST(SOL))}$ sending every many-sorted model of Δ, $\mathcal{A}\in\mathbf{MOD}(\Delta)$, to another many-sorted structure of the same signature such that $\mathcal{A} \cong \mathbf{H}(\mathcal{A})$.

Proof

Definition of H.

Let $\mathcal{A} = \langle\langle A_i\rangle_{i\in SORT}, \langle R^{\mathcal{A}}\rangle_{R\in OPER.SYM^{\square}}\rangle$ be a given normal many-sorted structure of signature $\Sigma^{\square}$ which is a model of Δ. We define $\mathcal{B} = H(\mathcal{A})$ as follows:

$$\mathcal{B} = \langle\langle B_i\rangle_{i\in SORT}, \langle R^{\mathcal{B}}\rangle_{R\in OPER.SYM^{\square}}\rangle$$

where:

(i) $B_0 = A_0 = \{T,F\}$

(ii) $B_1 = A_1$

(iii) $B_{\langle 0,1,\dots,1\rangle} = \{\{\langle x_1,\dots,x_n\rangle\in(B_1)^n \,/\, \varepsilon_n^{\mathcal{A}}\langle x_1,\dots,x_n,Y^n\rangle = T\} \,/\, Y^n\in A_{\langle 0,1,\dots,1\rangle}\}$
for each $n\geq 1$.

(iv) We define $\varepsilon_n^{\mathcal{B}}$ to be the genuine membership relation, which means:
$\varepsilon_n^{\mathcal{B}}\langle x_1,\dots,x_n, X^n\rangle = T$ iff $\langle x_1,\dots,x_n\rangle\in X^n$, for each $x_1,\dots,x_n\in B_1$ and $X^n\in B_{\langle 0,1,\dots,1\rangle}$
(this can be done now, because of the selection of domains).

(v) The structure $\mathcal{B}$ is normal; *i.e.*, identity is treated as a logical symbol, being the authentic relation on all sorts.

(vi) All the other relations in $\mathcal{B}$ are the ones in $\mathcal{A}$. That is,

$$R^{\mathcal{A}} = R^{\mathcal{B}} \text{ for each } R\in OPER.SYM^{\square}-\{\varepsilon_n \,/\, n\geq 1\}$$

(this is possible because all the relations we are concerned with now, are either relations on individuals or truth functions). ▮

Explanation of the definition of $\mathcal{B}$ (doing "genetic architecture"): In $\mathcal{A}$ we have different domains for each sort. The domains were chosen arbitrarily, but there are certain links among them. In particular, the "pretended" membership relations of the structure $\mathcal{A}$, $\varepsilon_n^{\mathcal{A}}$. On the other hand, we want the structure $H(\mathcal{A})$ to be an offspring of **SOL** and of **MSL**.

Therefore, in building $B_{\langle 0,1,\dots,1\rangle}$ we want to choose a subset of $\mathcal{P}(B_1{}^n)$. That's the **SOL** heritage. But we want the selected relations and sets to keep in touch with the membership relations in $\mathcal{A}$: We follow instructions coded in the "membership" relations of $\mathcal{A}$ very closely.

Now we will define an isomorphism f of $\mathcal{A}$ onto $\mathcal{B}$ which is the identity on sorts 0 and 1.

Definition of f.

Let f be a function from the universes of $\mathcal{A}$ onto those in $\mathcal{B}$

$$f: \bigcup_{i \in SORT} A_i \longrightarrow \bigcup_{i \in SORT} B_i$$

defined by:

(i) $f \restriction A_0$ is the identity.

(ii) $f \restriction A_1$ is also the identity.

(iii) For each $Y^n \in A_{\langle 0,1,\ldots,1 \rangle}$:

$$f(Y^n) = \{ \langle x_1,\ldots,x_n \rangle \in (B_1)^n \,/\, \varepsilon_n^{\mathcal{A}} \langle x_1,\ldots,x_n,Y^n \rangle = T \}$$ ▨

Claim: f is a bijection.

(a) This function is onto because on the individual sort it is the identity and all the elements in $B_{\langle 0,1,\ldots,1 \rangle}$ are of the form $f(Y^n)$, since we defined it that way.

(b) Is this function one-to-one? We can easily see that the answer is yes. Let $f(Y^n) = f(X^n)$. That implies

$$\varepsilon_n^{\mathcal{A}} \langle x_1,\ldots,x_n,Y^n \rangle = T \text{ iff } \varepsilon_n^{\mathcal{A}} \langle x_1,\ldots,x_n,X^n \rangle = T$$

from which it necessarily follows that $Y^n = X^n$, since $\mathcal{A}$ is a model of extensionality:

$$Ext^{(n)} = \forall X^n Y^n (\forall x_1 \ldots x_n (\varepsilon_n x_1 \ldots x_n X^n \leftrightarrow \varepsilon_n x_1 \ldots x_n Y^n) \to X^n = Y^n)$$

Claim: f is also an isomorphism.

We have to prove:

(1) $\neg^{\mathcal{A}} \langle x,y \rangle = \neg^{\mathcal{B}} \langle f(x),f(y) \rangle$, for $x,y \in A_0$ and $\vee^{\mathcal{A}} \langle x,y,z \rangle = \vee^{\mathcal{B}} \langle f(x),f(y),f(z) \rangle$, for each $x,y,z \in A_0$.

(2) For each $R^{\mathcal{A}}$ in $\mathcal{A}$, $x_1,\ldots,x_n \in A_1$ (where $R \in \mathbf{OPER.SYM}^{\Omega} - (\{\neg,\vee\} \cup \{\varepsilon_n \,/\, n \geq 1\})$

$$R^{\mathcal{A}} \langle x_1,\ldots,x_n \rangle = T \text{ iff } R^{\mathcal{B}} \langle f(x_1),\ldots,f(x_n) \rangle = T$$

(3) For the membership relations and $x_1,\ldots,x_n \in A_1$, $X^n \in A_{\langle 0,1,\ldots,1 \rangle}$:

$$\varepsilon_n^{\mathcal{A}} \langle x_1,\ldots,x_n,X^n \rangle = T \text{ iff } \varepsilon^{\mathcal{B}} \langle f(x_1),\ldots,f(x_n),f(X^n) \rangle = T$$

(1) is obvious, since $\neg^{\mathcal{A}} = \neg^{\mathcal{B}}$, $\vee^{\mathcal{A}} = \vee^{\mathcal{B}}$ and f on A_0 is the identity.

(2) is also obvious, since all those relations are on elements of individual sort and f is the identity on them while $R^{\mathcal{A}} = R^{\mathcal{B}}$. Also, identical elements of $\mathcal{A}$ have identical images in $\mathcal{B}$ and vice-versa; just look at the definition of the biyection f and the properties of $\mathcal{A}$ and $\mathcal{B}$.

(3) follows easily, because $f(x_1) = x_1,\ldots,f(x_n) = x_n$ and

$$f(X^n) = \{ \langle x_1,\ldots,x_n \rangle \in B_1^n \,/\, \varepsilon_n^{\mathcal{A}} \langle x_1,\ldots,x_n,X^n \rangle = T \}$$

Furthermore, $\varepsilon^{\mathcal{B}}$ is genuine membership. ▮

2.3.6. **Definition of $CONV_2$.**

Let us define $CONV_2$ as $CONV_1^{-1} \circ H$, where **H** is the function defined in 2.3.5. ▮

2.3.7. **Strong version of lemma 2 (item (b)).**

There is a recursive $\Delta \subseteq SENT(MSL)$ with $CONV_1(ST(SOL)) \subseteq MOD(\Delta)$ such that, for every many-sorted structure $\mathcal{C} \in MOD(\Delta)$ there is a SOL-structure $CONV_2(\mathcal{C}) \in ST(SOL)$ such that

$$CONV_2(\mathcal{C}) \text{ is a model of } \varphi \text{ iff } \mathcal{C} \text{ is a model of } TRANS^{\square}(\varphi)$$

for all sentences of **SOL**.

Proof

Let Δ be the set of axioms defined in 2.3.4 above and $CONV_1$ the function defined in 2.3.1. Clearly $CONV_1(ST(SOL)) \subseteq MOD(\Delta)$ because our structures are general structures. Let **H** be as defined in 2.3.5 and $CONV_2$ as defined in 2.3.6. Let $\mathcal{C} \in MOD(\Delta)$. Thus $CONV_2(\mathcal{C}) \in ST(SOL)$. Let φ be a sentence of SOL and $TRANS^{\square}(\varphi)$ its translation.

[$\Longrightarrow$] If $CONV_2(\mathcal{C})$ is a model of φ, then $H(\mathcal{C})$ is a model of $TRANS^{\square}(\varphi)$, by 2.3.2 (lemma 1). Since $\mathcal{C} \cong H(\mathcal{C})$, by the isomorphism theorem (6.4.2. in Chapter VI), $\mathcal{C}$ is a model of $TRANS^{\square}(\varphi)$.

[$\Longleftarrow$] If $\mathcal{C}$ is a model of $TRANS^{\square}(\varphi)$, then $H(\mathcal{C}) \in CONV_1(ST(SOL))$ and it is a model of $\Delta \cup \{TRANS^{\square}(\varphi)\}$, by the isomorphism theorem 6.4.2. of Chapter VI. By lemma 1 (2.3.2), $CONV_1^{-1}(H(\mathcal{C}))$ is a model of $TRANS^{\square}(\varphi)$. ▮

2.4. The equivalence SOL-$MSL^{\square}$.

2.4.1. **Main theorem.**

$\Pi \models_{\mathcal{G.S}} \varphi$ in second order logic iff $TRANS^{\square}(\Pi) \cup \Delta \models TRANS^{\square}(\varphi)$ in many-sorted logic.

Proof

Use 1.3.1, lemma 1 for **SOL** (2.3.2 above) and the strong version of lemma 2 for **SOL** (2.3.7). ▮

2.4.2. Compactness of SOL with general semantics.

If $\Pi \models_{\mathcal{G.S}} \varphi$ in second order logic, there is a finite Γ, $\Gamma \subseteq \Pi$, such that $\Gamma \models_{\mathcal{G.S}} \varphi$.

Proof

Use 2.4.1 and 1.3.2. ▮

2.4.3. Enumerability of SOL with general semantics.

The set $\mathbf{VAL}_{\mathcal{G.S}}(\mathbf{SOL})$ of valid formulas in general semantics is recursively enumerable.

Proof

Use 2.4.1 and 1.3.4. ▮

2.4.4. Löwenheim-Skolem of SOL with general semantics.

If a set of sentences of **SOL** has a general model, then it has a countable general model.

Proof

Use 2.4.1 and 1.3.3 and the fact that reverse conversion respects cardinality. ▮

The enumerability and compactness theorems taken together tell us that a strongly complete calculus exists. But we want to know more, we want to test for completeness an actual one: our calculus C_2.

2.4.5. Theorem 4.

$\Pi \vdash \varphi$ in second order calculus C_2 iff $\mathbf{TRANS}^{\square}(\Pi) \cup \Delta \vdash \mathbf{TRANS}^{\square}(\varphi)$ in many-sorted calculus, **MSL**.

Proof

Every proof of **SOL** with assumptions in Π leads to a proof in **MSL** from assumptions in $\mathbf{TRANS}^{\square}(\Pi) \cup \Delta$ and vice versa. Only remember that all our many-sorted rules are the same as in second order logic and the translation only changes simple formulas. When in second order logic we use extensionality or the comprehension rule, in many-sorted we take the corresponding sentence by the rule of (HI). ▮

Using these theorems and the completeness and soundness of many-sorted logic, we can do without a direct proof of the completeness of **SOL**.

The equivalence between these two theories, **SOL** and Δ-**MSL**$^{\square}$, is shown in the figure:

$$\begin{array}{ccc}
\Pi \models_{\mathcal{G.S}} \varphi & \Longleftrightarrow & \mathrm{TRANS}^{\square}(\Pi) \cup \Delta \models \mathrm{TRANS}^{\square}(\varphi) \\
\Updownarrow & & \Updownarrow \\
\Pi \vdash_{C_2} \varphi & \Longleftrightarrow & \mathrm{TRANS}^{\square}(\Pi) \cup \Delta \vdash \mathrm{TRANS}^{\square}(\varphi)
\end{array}$$

Let's prove them.

2.4.6. Soundness and completeness of SOL.
$\Pi \models_{\mathcal{G.S}} \varphi$ iff $\Pi \vdash_{C_2} \varphi$ for al $\Pi \cup \{\varphi\} \subseteq \mathrm{SENT}(L_2)$.

Proof
Now, using the arrows of theorems 2.4.1 (main theorem) and 2.4.5 and completeness and soundness of the many-sorted logic, we have given an alternative proof of the completeness and soundness of the **SOL** calculus C_2. ∎

3.- MODAL LOGIC.

3.1. Some history.

The history of modal logic[62] begins in the classical epoch, including work of Aristotle (died in 322 BC), the Megarians[63] and the Stoics[64], and is followed by the work done by certain medieval logicians. The subject was almost entirely forgotten until Lewis reconsidered it at the beginning of this century.

Modal logicians needed to create a formalism able to capture dynamic situations, where truth could be relativized. Right from the start, the connections between modal and temporal notions were clear, being debated by the Megarians and the Stoics. The systematic approach began early in this century with Lewis [1912], Łukasiewicz [1953] and Carnap [1947]. After that the golden era comes with Kanger [1957a, b], Hintikka [1961, 1969], Prior [1957, 1967] and Kripke [1959, 1975]. The novelty in this approach is the discovery that modal logic can receive a well structured Tarskian semantics. A further step was taken by Lemmon [1957, 1966], Lemmon & Scott [1977] and Segerberg [1971, 1977] where the completeness theory for modal logic is fully developed. There was a change of perspective taken by van Benthem[65], Thomason, Goldblatt and others, known as correspondence theory. This step is performed when the intuitively obvious questions concerning the relationship with classical logic are taken in depth and a new semantics is given to modal logic.

In Aristotle the main subject rests on the differences between ***necessity*** and ***possibility***. Whenever we have a proposition φ, let $\Box\varphi$ mean that φ is necessary, while $\Diamond\varphi$ means that φ is possible. It seems that for Aristotle the contradiction between the pairs $\Box\varphi$ and $\neg\Box\varphi$ is clear and also the contradiction between $\Diamond\varphi$ and $\neg\Diamond\varphi$. He also thinks that neither of the pairs $\Box\varphi$ and $\Box\neg\varphi$ or $\Diamond\varphi$ and $\Diamond\neg\varphi$ is contradictory. He accepts the formula $\alpha \equiv \Box\varphi \rightarrow \Diamond\varphi$ as

[62]For details of the history see Kneale & Kneale [1962], Lemmon & Scott [1977], pp. 1-39 and Bull & Segerberg [1984], pp. 1-81. In fact, most of this section is based on them.

[63]The founder of the Megarian school was Euclides, a disciple of Socrates and elder contemporary of Plato. One of its prominent members was Diodorus Cronus, who was active as a teacher at the end of the fourth century BC.

[64]The founder of the Stoic school, which originates from the teaching of the Megarians, was Zeno of Citium (died in 264 BC). The best known head of the Stoic school was Chrysippus (280-207 BC).

[65]See van Benthem [1984, 1983]; the first is a survey paper in this particular trend, the second is a book devoted to the same subject.

expressing a true proposition - *i.e.*, necessity implies possibility - but he has doubts about the formula $\beta \equiv \Diamond\varphi \rightarrow \Diamond\neg\varphi$. He sees the problem in accepting both α and β. In fact α and β are using a different meaning for the word "possibility". In the first sense it is proper possibility, in the second it is contingency. Necessity and possibility can receive different interpretations: for instance, logical necessity, physical necessity, moral or temporal. In the general case we want $\Box\varphi$ to mean "always φ", but this "always" is shaped differently according to the laws of logic, physics, civil law or religion, time and our chosen conceptual systems about them.

In logic, necessity, possibility and contingency of propositions were in principle philosophical concepts, but they can also be seen in a technical way as validity, satisfiability and contingency; *i.e.*, by using the records of their truth tables propositions can be classified as satisfiabilities and contradictions, where satisfiabilities can also be classified as tautologies and contingencies.

satisfiabilities (at least one T) $\Diamond\varphi$	tautologies or validities (always T) $\Box\varphi$
	contingencies (both T and F values) $\Diamond\varphi\wedge\Diamond\neg\varphi$
	contradictions (always F) $\Box\neg\varphi$

In fact, modal logic can be seen as a metalanguage for talking semantics and for precisely that reason it has been accused of misunderstanding the difference between ***use*** and ***mention***[66].

I am not going to enter into the details of the history; nevertheless, I would like to emphasize two aspects of the ancient treatment of modality:

(1) The connections between modal and temporal notions were debated by the Megarians and Stoics. According to Boethius, Diodorus Cronus sees the connection in this way[67]:

> Diodorus defines the possible as that which either is or will be; the impossible as that which, being false, will not be true; the necessary as that

[66]See Quine [1943, 1947].

[67]Kneale & Kneale [1962], page 117.

which, being true, will not be false; and the non-necessary as that which either is already or will be false.

(2) The so called material implication paradoxes, which are considered as the starting point of modal research in this century, were anticipated by the medieval logicians[68].

Bull & Segerberg [1984] describe the twentieth century development of modal logic along the lines of three different traditions: syntactical, algebraic and model-theoretic.

Syntactical tradition.

Lewis [1912] is officially the first modal paper in this century. The original analysis of Lewis concerns disjunction. He sees the difference between these two sentences:

$\alpha \equiv$ Either Socrates died, or Socrates is a stone.

$\beta \equiv$ Either Frank does not love me or he does.

While α is true just because of the empirical fact that Socrates died and will be false when replacing Socrates by a living person, β is always true independently of me and Frank. The crucial question is, "Should we express in our object language the difference between the disjunction in α and β?"

Lewis thinks we should, and so he defines his well known modal systems. His method can be roughly described in this way: You define first a formal language in a purely syntactical way, including symbols to deal with the observed features you want to treat. Therefore, in the beginning, the formulas have no meaning at all. From the set of all the formulas you want to be able to select the subset including all the formulas you think must be taken as valid formulas, bearing in mind that you would like to have a recursive axiomatization of the set of validities. Nevertheless, if your semantics is only intuitive, how can you prove the completeness of your axiomatization?, how can you arrive at a unique axiomatization? The answer is that there is nothing like "the calculus" of **PML**; there are plenty. In this syntactical tradition many axiomatizations were born: Lewis himself gave us five of them; namely, the so called systems S1 through S5.

Algebraic tradition.

The interpretation of connectives as truth functions is certainly very useful and handy. Therefore, the first question in the algebraic tradition was, "can we do something similar with

[68]Ibid., page 281.

the new unary modal operators ($\Box$ and $\Diamond$) we have introduced?" Since there are only four unary truth functions and none of them gives us a satisfactory interpretation of the new modal operators, we have to add new truth values and take our modal operator to be a unary truth function over the enhanced set of truth values. This is the approach taken by Łukasiewicz. He took three truth values and defined:

ψ	$\Diamond\psi$
1	1
1/2	1
0	0

ψ	$\Box\psi$
1	1
1/2	0
0	0

Also in the origins of this algebraic tradition are the works done by Tarski & Jónsson in 1949, introducing what they called ***relation atom structures***[69]. They used them as representations of "abstract" Boolean algebras with operators. Later on, basically the same structures were introduced by Kripke in the modelist tradition and ever since we call them Kripke models. With Kripke semantics modal logic reached the standard of rigor and preciseness common to other branches of mathematical logic; the metaproperties of the calculus can then be successfully tackled. Rasiowa [1974] gave us also an algebraic logic treatment of modal logic, besides her algebraic treatment of classical logic.

Model-theoretic tradition.

Not counting the algebraic approach, which is frequently described as syntax in disguise, Carnap was the first to give a semantics for modal logic. It is generally understood that in Carnap three intellectual sources join: Frege, Leibniz and Wittgenstein. From Frege he took his ideas and interest in semantics, including the distinction between intension and extension. (Carnap was one of the few students Frege ever had.) From Leibniz, Carnap took the idea of interpreting necessity as truth in all possible worlds, consequently giving us a specific semantic for S5. From Wittgenstein he took the very general ideas about descriptions of states and the conception of a world of atoms.

Carnap takes a universe of "descriptions of states" containing sets of atomic propositions. Later on, his descriptions of states become in the literature "worlds". Given a collection $\mathcal{U}$ of state descriptions and a particular description of states, s, the atomic proposition P is true at s of $\mathcal{U}$ if and only if P is a member of s, while the formula $\Box\varphi$ is valid in the collection $\mathcal{U}$ if

[69]See Jónsson & Tarski [1951], also see Henkin, Monk & Tarski [1971], section 2.7.

and only if, for all t in $\mathcal{U}$, φ is valid in t. We state it formally as

$\mathcal{U},s \models P$ iff $P \in s$ and $\mathcal{U},s \models \Box\varphi$ iff for all $t \in \mathcal{U}$: $\mathcal{U},t \models \varphi$

Carnap's models can be defined as

$\langle \mathcal{U}, v \rangle$, where $\mathcal{U}$ is the universe, taken as a collection of state descriptions or possible worlds, and v is a valuation giving a truth value to each proposition constant and each world.

When you introduce a semantics for a formal language, the related notion of validity helps you to select a subset of the set of all formulas; namely, the set where all the validities are included. It was then proved that the set of formulas selected in this way is precisely the set of theorems in Lewis's logic S5. Therefore, Lewis's axiomatic logic S5 is complete in Carnap's semantics. In what follows we will use the semantic of Kripke, but you will see how Carnap's ideas can also be nicely exploited in the canonical models.

Modal logic has split into many different branches. To quote Bull & Segerberg[70]:

> In addition to more traditional pursuits we are now seeing phenomena as diverse as the application of modal predicate logic to philosophical problems at a new level of sophistication (Fine [1977a, 1977b, 1980, 1981]), the analysis of conditionals started by Stalnaker (Stalnaker [1968], D. Lewis [1973]), the generalization of model theory with modal notions (Mortimer [1974], Bowen [1978]), in-depth studies of the so-called provability interpretation (Boolos [1979]; see also Chapter II.9 of this Handbook), the advent of dynamic logic (Pratt [1980b] and Chapter II.10 of the Handbook) and Montague grammar (see Montague [1974]).

3.2. A formal language for PML.

3.2.1. Alphabet:

The alphabet of **PML** contains:

(1) A set **ATOM.PROP** of atomic formulas with $\bot \in$ **ATOM.PROP**, $\bot$ is ***falsity***. We will use the letter P for elements of **ATOM.PROP**; when needed, we will add subscripts:

[70]See Bull & Segerberg [1984], page 3.

P_0, P_1, P_2, etc.

(2) The connectives: $\neg$, $\vee$, $\wedge$, $\rightarrow$ and $\leftrightarrow$.

(3) Modal operators: $\Diamond$ and $\Box$.

(4) Parentheses:) and (. These are improper symbols. ▮

3.2.2. Formulas:

Formulas of **PML** are finite strings of symbols and they are inductively defined from the symbols in the alphabet by using the rules of the calculus of formulas given below. The set **FORM(PML)** of formulas of **PML** is the smallest set satisfying:

(F1) **ATOM.PROP** $\subseteq$ **FORM(PML)** (Thus, $\bot \in$ **FORM(PML)**).

(F2) If $\varphi \in$ **FORM(PML)** and $\psi \in$ **FORM(PML)**, then $\neg\varphi$, $(\varphi \vee \psi)$, $(\varphi \wedge \psi)$, $(\varphi \rightarrow \psi)$ and $(\varphi \leftrightarrow \psi)$ are in **FORM(PML)**.

(F3) If $\varphi \in$ **FORM(PML)**, then $\Diamond\varphi$ and $\Box\varphi$ are in **FORM(PML)**. ▮

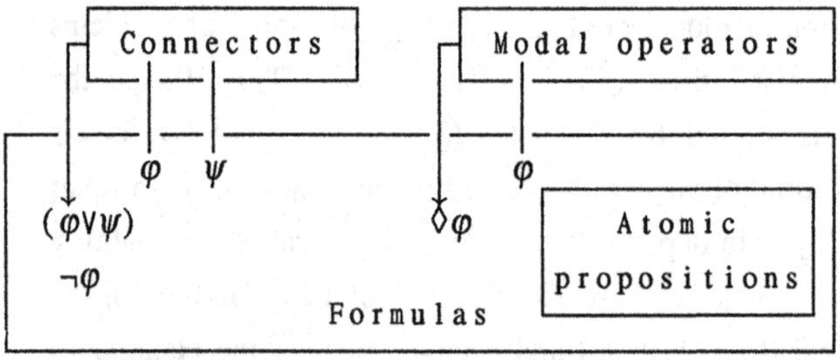

3.2.3. Schemes.

A ***schema*** in modal logic (as in any other logic) is a collection of formulas with the same syntactic form. For instance, the schema $\Box\varphi \rightarrow \Diamond\varphi$ represents the whole set of formulas

$\{\Box\psi \rightarrow \Diamond\psi \,/\, \psi \in$ **FORM(PML)**$\}$ ▮

3.2.4. A simplified language.

Of course, some other selections of primitives are also possible. In modal logic the common choice is: $\bot$, $\rightarrow$ and $\Box$ as basic symbols. See section 4.5 of Chapter I for details. $\Diamond\varphi$ can be defined as an abbreviation for $\neg\Box\neg\varphi$.

3.3.- Modal propositional logics.

Two different but related concepts are going to be discussed now: ways of defining precise modal logics and what a modal logic is. In both cases our point of departure is quite conventional, that means we accept either explicitly or implicitly the propositional logic.

From a broad but classical, model-theoretic point of view, whenever you have a class of mathematical structures, a formal language and a satisfaction relation between them both, you have a logic. With these basic components we obtain the set of valid formulas or semantic theorems in this logic which can be seen as an exhaustive description of what is common to all the structures in the class, including a description of the pure logical aspects - *i.e.* the meaning of the logic symbols used in the language. Since there is no unique way of describing a class of mathematical structures and this is so partially because there is not a unique language, we can agree that we are in the scope of modal logic at least when our language is modal and the satisfaction relation tells us how to interpret the modal formulas, while giving to the connectors their standard meaning.

From a syntactic and somewhat restrictive point of view, we have a logic when we have a formal language and a set of axioms and/or deduction rules, including the propositional ones, allowing us to select from the set of all formulas the set of theorems of our logic. As in the preceding case, we agree that we are in the realm of modal logic when at least our language is modal and our deduction rules describe the behavior of the modal operators and include the propositional calculus. Since we accept both the semantic and the syntactic approaches to a modal logic as sensible, we have to say that, in a rough sense, a modal logic is a set of modal formulas containing the pure propositional theorems of propositional modal logic.

When the logic is semantically presented, a further question we can ask is whether this set of formulas can be obtained independently of the semantics by means of a recursive syntactic procedure; that is, whether the set of formulas can be characterized by axioms and/or rules of inference. The answer could be positive, giving a recursive axiomatization of the logic, or negative, proving that your set of formulas is not recursively enumerable. When the logic is presented in pure syntactic terms, you have to investigate what semantics can be given to the formulas.

Whenever a modal logic **XM** is introduced, we have among its theorems the set of all pure propositional theorems of propositional modal logic. For propositional logic many equivalent deductive calculi are known. There are axiomatic calculi, natural deduction calculi, sequent calculi, etc. Any calculus in any of these classes, when running over the set **FORM(PL)**, produces the set of validities of propositional logic. So there is only one propositional logic and we can talk about ***the calculus*** of propositional logic as if there were only one, since we always get as logical theorems the set of validities of propositional logic; ***i.e.***, $\vdash_{PC}$(PL) = VAL(PL), for the calculus is sound and complete. Let us call the propositional calculus PC.

When we take the calculus of propositional logic, but we allow it to run over the set of formulas of propositional modal logic, we obtain the set $\vdash_{PC}$(PML) of propositional theorems of propositional modal logic. There is nothing modal in this set but the language; when applying PC rules, the formulas of the form $\Diamond\varphi$ and $\Box\varphi$ count as atomic.

In **PML** there are many possible choices of logics and in that case, even if they can be axiomatized, there is nothing like ***the calculus*** of **PML**, but a wide range of non-equivalent calculi from which you are free to choose for a particular task the one that best fulfills your needs. The reason is that the intended meaning of your modal operators can vary from a Leibnizian sense of necessity to a temporal interpretation of these operators and therefore the formulas in your logic, whose goal is to describe the meaning and/or the behavior of these operators, have to be adapted.

3.3.1. Definition:

A ***modal logic*** is any B such that $\vdash_{PC}$**(PML)** $\subseteq$ B $\subseteq$ **FORM(PML)** and B is closed under the rule of ***modus ponens*** (MP); ***i.e.***, if $\varphi \in$ B and $\varphi \rightarrow \psi \in$ B, then $\psi \in$ B. ▓

3.3.2. Definition:

Any member of the modal logic B is a ***theorem*** of B and conversely. In symbols, $\varphi \in$ B iff $\vdash_B \varphi$. ▓

3.3.3. Definition:

A formula φ is ***deducible*** in the logic B from the set Γ (written as $\Gamma \vdash_B \varphi$) iff there is a finite subset of Γ, say $\{\gamma_1,...,\gamma_n\}$, such that $\gamma_1 \wedge ... \wedge \gamma_n \rightarrow \varphi \in$ B. (When n = 0 we agree that $\gamma_1 \wedge ... \wedge \gamma_n \rightarrow \varphi \equiv \varphi$. Thus, we again get: $\vdash_B \varphi$ iff $\varphi \in$ B.) ▓

Remarks.

(1) In model theory, B will rather be called a ***theory***, in computer science the common

name is *logic* , in modal logic it has been called *system* . At present, the practice in the field of modal logic is quite flexible and there is no harm in having all three names as synonymous in this context. In fact, the usual modal systems differ from a plain theory because they are closed under a rule of substitution, since the axioms are scheme axioms.

(2) Please note how the theoremhood symbol $\vdash_B$ has been introduced, there is no presupposition of existence of a calculus; B might be non-axiomatizable. Also, to be deducible in a logic B does not imply the use of a calculus; in the definition we have only used the previously introduced notion of theoremhood. Of course, when you have a calculus you also have a logic, but not the other way around. If you have both, you can give the logic and the calculus the same initial.

(3) The definition of a modal logic is too broad, since we accept as modal logic the set $\vdash_{PC}$(PML), where there are no modal features but the language. Also, we accept as a modal logic the contradictory set of all modal formulas. Moreover, we are not requiring that the formulas of a modal logic should be obtained by means of a calculus, not even we ask the set B to be closed under formation of schemas (or equivalently, a rule of substitution).

None of the three items above constitutes a problem in itself, but we have to be aware of them.

3.3.4. Proposition.

Some basic properties of the operator $\vdash_B$ are:

(1) ***Monotony on hypotheses*** : If $\Gamma \subseteq \Pi$ and $\Gamma \vdash_B \varphi$, then $\Pi \vdash_B \varphi$.

(2) ***Monotony on logics*** : If $B \subseteq A$ and $\Gamma \vdash_B \varphi$, then $\Gamma \vdash_A \varphi$.

(3) ***Generalized*** (MP): If $\Gamma \vdash_B \varphi$ and $\Gamma \vdash_B \varphi \rightarrow \psi$, then $\Gamma \vdash_B \psi$.

(4) ***Deduction theorem*** : $\Gamma \cup \{\varphi\} \vdash_B \psi$ iff $\Gamma \vdash_B \varphi \rightarrow \psi$.

Proof

The proof is left to the reader. ▮

3.3.5. Definition:

Given a decidable set of formulas Γ and a finite set of rules H, a ***proof of*** φ ***in the calculus*** Γ_H is a finite sequence of formulas each of which either is in $\vdash_{PC}$(PML) $\cup\ \Gamma$ or has been obtained from previous formulas in the sequence by any of the rules of (H) or (MP). When there is a proof of φ in Γ_H we write $\vdash_{\Gamma_H} \varphi$. ▮

Remark.

Please notice that the calculus Γ_H includes PC, although the notation does not mention it explicitly.

3.3.6. Definition:

A logic B is ***axiomatizable*** iff there is a calculus Γ_H such that $B = \{\varphi / \vdash_{\Gamma_H} \varphi\}$. ▌

A logic B is ***finitely axiomatizable*** iff B is axiomatizable by a calculus Γ_H and there is a finite set of schema axioms producing Γ as particular instances. ▌

3.3.7. Definition:

A logic B is ***consistent*** iff no $\vdash_B \bot$.

3.3.8. Consistency and maximal consistency.

Let B be a modal logic and $\Pi \subseteq$ FORM(PML).

(1) Π is B-***consistent*** iff no $\Pi \vdash_B \bot$.

(2) Π is B-***contradictory*** iff $\Pi \vdash_B \bot$.

(3) Π is ***maximally B-consistent*** iff Π is B-consistent and for all $\psi \in$ FORM(PML):

If $\psi \notin \Pi$ then $\Pi \cup \{\psi\}$ is B-contradictory ▌

3.3.9. Theorems on consistency.

(1) If Π is B-consistent and $\Gamma \subseteq \Pi$ then Γ is B-consistent.

(2) If Π is B-contradictory and $\Pi \subseteq \Gamma$ then Γ is B-contradictory.

(3) Π is B-consistent iff every finite subset of Π is B-consistent.

Proof

The proof is left to the reader. ▌

3.3.10. Theorems on maximal consistency.

Let $\Delta \subseteq$ FORM(PML) be a maximal B-consistent set, then the items (1) through (5) stated in theorem 7.2.2 of Chapter VI are also true for PML. Namely,

(1) If $\Delta \vdash_B \varphi$ then $\varphi \in \Delta$.

(2) If $\vdash_B \varphi$ then $\varphi \in \Delta$

(3) $\neg\varphi \in \Delta$ iff $\varphi \notin \Delta$.

(4) $\varphi \vee \psi \in \Delta$ iff $\varphi \in \Delta$ or $\psi \in \Delta$.

(5) If $\Delta \cup \{\varphi\} \vdash_B \psi$ and $\Delta \cup \{\psi\} \vdash_B \varphi$, then $\varphi \in \Delta$ iff $\psi \in \Delta$.

Proof

The proof is left to the reader. ∎

3.3.11. Lindenbaum lemma.

If Γ is B-consistent, then there is a maximally B-consistent set Δ such that $\Gamma \subseteq \Delta$.

Proof

The proof is a simplified version of one explained for **MSL**, see 7.4.2 of Chapter VI for details. ∎

3.3.12. More theorems on maximal consistency.

Let $\Delta \subseteq$ FORM(PML) be a maximal B-consistent set.

(1) $B = \bigcap \{\Gamma / \Gamma$ is maximally B-consistent$\}$.

(2) If $\Delta \subseteq \Gamma$ and Γ is maximally B-consistent, then $\Gamma = \Delta$.

(3) Let $\Sigma \subseteq$ FORM(PML). If for every maximally B-consistent set Γ such that $\Sigma \subseteq \Gamma$, $\varphi \in \Gamma$ holds, then $\Sigma \vdash_B \varphi$.

Proof

The proof is left to the reader. ∎

3.4. Normal modal logics.

Normal modal logics form a class of modal logics whose distinguishing characteristic is to contain all the occurrences of the axiom schema K and Df◊ and to be closed as well under the modal rule of necessitation. The smallest normal modal logic is the logic ***K***, which we will define later.

3.4.1. Definition.

The ***calculus*** $\{K, Df\Diamond\}_{(N)}$ is obtained by adding to your favorite PC the schema axioms K, Df◊ and the rule (N).

The new axioms and rules are:

K **Distribution of □ with respect to →.** $\Box(\varphi \rightarrow \psi) \rightarrow (\Box\varphi \rightarrow \Box\psi)$.

Df$\Diamond$ **Definition of the diamond.** $\Diamond\varphi \leftrightarrow \neg\Box\neg\varphi$.

(N) **Necessitation:** If $\vdash \varphi$, then $\vdash \Box\varphi$. ▓

3.4.2. Definition:

The ***logic K*** is the smallest modal logic containing the schema axioms Df$\Diamond$ and K and being closed under the rule (N); *i.e.*, if $\varphi \in K$, then $\Box\varphi \in K$. So $K = \{\varphi / \vdash_{\{K, Df\Diamond\}_{(N)}} \varphi\}$. ▓

Remark.

An equivalent formulation for *K* is as follows: *K* is the smallest modal logic containing Df$\Diamond$ and being closed under the rule (KN): If $\vdash \gamma_1 \wedge \ldots \wedge \gamma_n \rightarrow \varphi$, then $\vdash \Box\gamma_1 \wedge \ldots \wedge \Box\gamma_n \rightarrow \Box\varphi$,

i.e., if $\gamma_1 \wedge \ldots \wedge \gamma_n \rightarrow \varphi \in K$ then $\Box\gamma_1 \wedge \ldots \wedge \Box\gamma_n \rightarrow \Box\varphi \in K$

(when n=0 we have: $\vdash \varphi$ implies $\vdash \Box\varphi$).

3.4.3. Definition:

A ***normal modal logic*** is any modal logic containing the logic *K* which is closed under the rules of the calculus $\{K, Df\Diamond\}_{(N)}$. ▓

There are many normal logics, but the best known and studied are the axiomatizable normal modal logics obtained when adding to the logic *K* any combination of the schema axioms

D $\Box\varphi \rightarrow \Diamond\varphi$

T $\Box\varphi \rightarrow \varphi$

B $\varphi \rightarrow \Box\Diamond\varphi$

4 $\Box\varphi \rightarrow \Box\Box\varphi$

5 $\Diamond\varphi \rightarrow \Box\Diamond\varphi$

and closing the extended set over the rules of the calculus $\{K, Df\Diamond\}_{(N)}$.

Including the logic *K*, there are only fifteen distinct normal systems obtained in this way[71]. To name a particular logic in this set we follow the standard notation which consist of adding to *K* the list of new schema axioms; for example, *KT* is the normal modal logic obtained by adding the axiom schema T to the logic *K* and closing the set under the rules of the calculus $\{K, Df\Diamond\}_{(N)}$. The Lewis systems S4 and S5 become here *KT*4 and *KT*5. From what has been said, the notation $KX_1 \ldots X_n$ is not only a name, but it also tells you that the logic is axiomatizable and what the axioms are. So when we write that the formula φ is a theorem of

[71]The proof that the 32 logics so obtained are in fact only 15 can be found in Chellas [1980], page 163.

the normal modal logic $KX_1...X_n$, we will write $\vdash_{KX_1...X_n} \varphi$ denoting not only membership of φ of $KX_1...X_n$, but also deducibility in the calculus

$$\{K, Df\Diamond, X_1...X_n\}_{(N)}$$

3.4.4. Theorem.
All normal modal logics obtained from D, T, B, 4 and 5 are contained in S5.

Proof
Can you prove this? ▮

3.5. Consistency of all normal modal logics contained in S5.

To prove that a formula is not a theorem of a given logic **XL** it is often possible and certainly useful to have a lemma reducing provability in **XL** to validity in **PL**; simply because using that lemma our problem reduces to proving that a certain formula is not a valid propositional formula. To prove this lemma we need to define a function converting our modal formulas into propositional formulas. The function we are defining leaves the modal formula $\perp$ unchanged, making it then easy to prove the consistency of the modal logic **XL**; *i.e.*, that $\perp$ is not a theorem of **XL**. We will prove the lemma for the logic S5, since this logic includes all the normal modal logics we are interested in.

3.5.1. Definition of the erasure function.

$$\begin{aligned} \text{ERAS: FORM(PML)} &\longrightarrow \text{FORM(PL)} \\ \perp &\longmapsto \perp \\ P &\longmapsto P \\ \neg\varphi &\longmapsto \neg(\text{ERAS}(\varphi)) \\ \varphi\vee\psi &\longmapsto \text{ERAS}(\varphi)\vee\text{ERAS}(\psi) \\ \Diamond\varphi &\longmapsto \text{ERAS}(\varphi) \end{aligned}$$

For the rest of the formulas the function does exactly the same; that is, it leaves everything unchanged except the modal operators which are erased. ▮

3.5.2. Lemma.
For all $\varphi \in$ **FORM(PML)**: If $\vdash_{S5} \varphi$, then $\models$ **ERAS**(φ) in **PL**.

Proof

We will prove that the erasure transformations of the axioms of S5 are all valid and that the rules of inference hold under erasure.

$\mathbf{ERAS(K)} = \mathbf{ERAS}(\Box(\varphi \to \psi) \to (\Box\varphi \to \Box\psi)) = (\mathbf{ERAS}(\varphi) \to \mathbf{ERAS}(\psi)) \to (\mathbf{ERAS}(\varphi) \to \mathbf{ERAS}(\psi))$

$\mathbf{ERAS(T)} = \mathbf{ERAS}(\Box\varphi \to \varphi) = \mathbf{ERAS}(\varphi) \to \mathbf{ERAS}(\varphi)$

$\mathbf{ERAS(5)} = \mathbf{ERAS}(\Diamond\varphi \to \Box\Diamond\varphi) = \mathbf{ERAS}(\varphi) \to \mathbf{ERAS}(\varphi)$

It is obvious that **ERAS(K), ERAS(T)** and **ERAS(5)** are all valid propositional formulas. An inference rule holds under erasure when we can prove that it converts tautologies into tautologies. Therefore, our rule of necessitation, (N), holds under erasure, since $\mathbf{ERAS}(\varphi) = \mathbf{ERAS}(\Box\varphi)$. Of course, the rules belonging to the propositional calculus hold under erasure, since the propositional calculus is correct in propositional logic. ∎

3.5.3. Theorem.

The logic S5 is consistent.

Proof

Using the lemma, every theorem of S5 is transformed into a valid formula of propositional logic. But $\bot$ is not a valid formula of propositional logic and $\mathbf{ERAS}(\bot) = \bot$, so $\bot$ is not a theorem of S5. ∎

3.5.4. Corollary:

All modal logics contained in S5 are consistent.

Proof

Use the theorem saying that any subset of a consistent set is also consistent (see 3.3.9. (1)) and 3.5.3 above. ∎

3.5.5. Corollary:

S4 is consistent.

Proof

Use $S4 \subseteq S5$. ∎

3.6. Kripke models.

In **PML** the notion of truth is not an absolute one, but relative to certain states or worlds; given a modal structure, a formula of **PML** is not simply true or false, but true or false in a certain world of the modal structure. Therefore, in modal logic a formula has not a truth value as interpretation, but a set of worlds; namely, the set of all worlds where the formula is true. Generally, worlds are not isolated, but related among themselves by the so-called accessibility relation. From a certain world **w** we see a formula $\Diamond\varphi$ as true when there is at least one world reachable from **w** where the formula φ is true, while the formula $\Box\varphi$ is true when φ is true in all the worlds reachable from w. **PM**-standard structures (or Kripke models) are composed of a domain of worlds (or states), a specially chosen binary relation on states and certain unary relations on states. With the sole exception of the logic K which accepts as models any Kripke structure, each modal logic presented so far accepts as models the members of a restricted class of Kripke models characterized by some peculiarity of the accessibility relation. In fact, you can see the modal axioms of a given modal logic as trying to describe their own accessibility relation. However, you will see later that this view places you in a *cul de sac.*

3.6.1. Definition of Kripke's models.

$\mathcal{M} = \langle \mathbf{W}, \mathbf{R}, \langle P^{\mathcal{M}} \rangle_{P \in \mathbf{ATOM.PROP}} \rangle$ is a **PM**-structure or a Kripke model iff

(1) $\mathbf{W} \neq \emptyset$ is a non-empty set whose elements are called worlds or states.

(2) **R** is a binary relation on worlds; that is, $\mathbf{R} \subseteq \mathbf{W} \times \mathbf{W}$.

(3) For each $P \in$ **ATOM.PROP**, $P^{\mathcal{M}}$ is a set of states; that is, $P^{\mathcal{M}} \subseteq \mathbf{W}$. (The idea behind this is that in $P^{\mathcal{M}}$ are all the worlds where P is true.) ▮

3.6.2. Interpretation.

When a **PM**-structure $\mathcal{M}$ is given, each formula φ gets an interpretation, $\mathcal{M}(\varphi)$, easily seen as a truth value for every world in $\mathcal{M}$. The interpretation of φ, $\mathcal{M}(\varphi)$, is the set of worlds or states where φ is true. Clearly the structure $\mathcal{M}$ provides us with such an interpretation for the atomic formulas in **ATOM.PROP**. Recursively, we are going to extend the definition to cover any formula.

$\mathcal{M}(P) = P^{\mathcal{M}}$ $\qquad\qquad$ $\mathcal{M}(\bot) = \emptyset$

$\mathcal{M}(\neg\varphi) = \mathbf{W} - \mathcal{M}(\varphi)$ $\qquad\qquad$ $\mathcal{M}(\varphi \vee \psi) = \mathcal{M}(\varphi) \cup \mathcal{M}(\psi)$

$\mathcal{M}(\varphi \wedge \psi) = \mathcal{M}(\varphi) \cap \mathcal{M}(\psi)$ $\qquad\qquad$ $\mathcal{M}(\varphi \rightarrow \psi) = \mathcal{M}(\neg\varphi) \cup \mathcal{M}(\psi)$

$\mathcal{M}(\varphi \leftrightarrow \psi) = (\mathcal{M}(\varphi) \cap \mathcal{M}(\psi)) \cup (\mathbf{W}-(\mathcal{M}(\varphi) \cup \mathcal{M}(\psi)))$
$\mathcal{M}(\Diamond\varphi) = \{s \in \mathbf{W} / \exists t \in \mathbf{W} (\langle s,t\rangle \in \mathbf{R} \ \& \ t \in \mathcal{M}(\varphi))\}$
$\mathcal{M}(\Box\varphi) = \{s \in \mathbf{W} / \forall t \in \mathbf{W}(\langle s,t\rangle \in \mathbf{R} \Rightarrow t \in \mathcal{M}(\varphi))\}$ ▓

3.6.3. Satisfiability, validity and consequence in Kripke models.

Given a Kripke model $\mathcal{M}$, a state s and formula φ we define several semantic concepts:

(1) $\mathcal{M}, s \models \varphi$ (φ is ***true at state*** s in $\mathcal{M}$) iff $s \in \mathcal{M}(\varphi)$. ▓

(2) $\mathcal{M} \models \varphi$ (φ is ***valid in*** $\mathcal{M}$) iff $\mathcal{M}, s \models \varphi$ for all s in W of $\mathcal{M}$; *i.e.*, $\mathcal{M}(\varphi) = \mathbf{W}$. ▓

Let $\mathcal{C}$ be a class of Kripke models.

(3) $\models_{\mathcal{C}} \varphi$ (φ is ***valid*** in the class $\mathcal{C}$) iff $\mathcal{M} \models \varphi$, for all $\mathcal{M} \in \mathcal{C}$. ▓

(4) $\models \varphi$ (φ is ***valid***) iff $\mathcal{M} \models \varphi$, for all Kripke models $\mathcal{M}$. ▓

Let Γ be a set of modal formulas and φ a formula.

(5) $\mathcal{M}, s \models \Gamma$ (Γ is ***satisfiable at state*** s of $\mathcal{M}$) iff $\mathcal{M}, s \models \varphi$, for all $\varphi \in \Gamma$. ▓

(6) $\mathcal{M} \models \Gamma$ (Γ is ***valid in*** $\mathcal{M}$) iff for every state s in $\mathcal{M}$: $\mathcal{M}, s \models \Gamma$. ▓

(7) $\Gamma \models_{\mathcal{C}} \varphi$ (φ is a ***consequence*** of Γ in the class $\mathcal{C}$) iff for every $\mathcal{M} \in \mathcal{C}$ and state s in $\mathcal{M}$: whenever $s \in \bigcap \{\mathcal{M}(\psi) / \psi \in \Gamma\}$ we have $s \in \mathcal{M}(\varphi)$. ▓

(8) $\Gamma \models \varphi$ (φ is a ***consequence*** of Γ) iff for every Kripke model $\mathcal{M}$ and state s in $\mathcal{M}$: whenever $s \in \bigcap \{\mathcal{M}(\psi) / \psi \in \Gamma\}$ we have $s \in \mathcal{M}(\varphi)$. ▓

Remark.

In **PML** two kinds of consequence relations are sometimes defined: local and global. (Local consequence implies global.) Our consequence relation is the strongest; *i.e.*, we are taking local consequence.

3.6.4. Definition of the canonical model of B.

Let B be a consistent normal modal logic. We define the ***canonical model of* B** as the PM-structure

$$\mathcal{A}_{B} = \langle \mathbf{W}_{B}, \mathbf{R}_{B}, \langle P^{\mathcal{A}_{B}}\rangle_{P \in \mathbf{ATOM.PROP}}\rangle$$

where:

(1) $\mathbf{W}_{B} = \{s \subseteq \mathbf{FORM(PML)} / s \text{ is maximally B-consistent}\}$

(2) $\mathbf{R}_{B} \subseteq \mathbf{W}_{B} \times \mathbf{W}_{B}$ is defined by: $\langle s,t\rangle \in \mathbf{R}_{B}$ iff $\{\varphi / \Box\varphi \in s\} \subseteq t$

(3) $P^{\mathcal{A}_{B}} = \{s \in \mathbf{W}_{B} / P \in s\}$ for all $P \in \mathbf{ATOM.PROP}$ ▓

Remarks.

The canonical model is quite a sensible one. We have adapted Carnap's idea when taking a universe of state descriptions. What better and more detailed description of a state than a maximal consistent set of formulas? The accessibility relation also has an intuitive interpretation as it establishes that the world t is an alternative to s when all the necessary truths of s are realized.

3.6.5. Proposition.

Let B be a consistent normal modal logic and $\mathcal{A}_B$ its canonical model. For every $\varphi \in$FORM(PML) and $s \in W_B$:

$\Box\varphi \in s$ iff for every $t \in W_B$, if $\langle s,t\rangle \in R_B$ then $\varphi \in t$

Proof

Let B be a consistent normal logic and $\mathcal{A}_B$ its canonical model. Let $\varphi \in$FORM(PML).

[$\Longrightarrow$] Let $\Box\varphi \in s$. Assume that $t \in W_B$ and $\langle s,t\rangle \in R_B$. By definition of R_B:

$\{\psi / \Box\psi \in s\} \subseteq t$

Therefore, $\varphi \in t$.

[$\Longleftarrow$] Assume that for every $t \in W_B$, if $\langle s,t\rangle \in R_B$ then, $\varphi \in t$. That is, for every maximally B-consistent set t, if $\{\psi / \Box\psi \in s\} \subseteq t$, then $\varphi \in t$. By the item (3) in 3.3.12, $\{\psi / \Box\psi \in s\} \vdash_B \varphi$. By definition of $\vdash_B$, it follows that $\gamma_1 \wedge ... \wedge \gamma_n \rightarrow \varphi \in B$ for certain $\gamma_1,...,\gamma_n$ such that $\Box\gamma_i \in s$ $(1 \leq i \leq n)$. Then, $\Box\gamma_1 \wedge ... \wedge \Box\gamma_n \rightarrow \Box\varphi \in B$, since B is a normal logic. Therefore, $s \vdash_B \Box\varphi$. By 3.3.10, $\Box\varphi \in s$. ∎

3.6.6. Definitions.

(1) A normal modal logic B is: ***sound with respect to a given class of structures*** $\mathcal{C}$ iff:

$$\text{If } \Gamma \vdash_B \varphi \text{ implies } \Gamma \models_{\mathcal{C}} \varphi \quad ∎$$

(2) A normal modal logic B is: ***strongly complete with respect to a given class of structures*** $\mathcal{C}$ iff:

$$\text{If } \Gamma \models_{\mathcal{C}} \varphi \text{ implies } \Gamma \vdash_B \varphi \quad ∎$$

(3) A normal modal logic B is: ***weakly complete with respect to a given class of structures*** $\mathcal{C}$ iff:

$$\text{If } \models_{\mathcal{C}} \varphi \text{ implies } \vdash_B \varphi \quad ∎$$

(4) A normal modal logic B is: ***determined by a given class of structures*** $\mathcal{C}$ iff: B is sound and weakly complete with respect to $\mathcal{C}$. ▮

3.6.7. Properties of the accessibility relation.

It is easy to see that the schema axioms K and Df◊ are valid in the whole class of the Kripke models defined in 3.6.1. above. Thus, they do not describe any property of the accessibility relation R. On the other hand, the axioms D, T, B, 4 and 5 are not valid in all the Kripke models. As it happens, each of them is true in Kripke models where the relation R has a definite property; in particular,

(1) K and Df◊ are valid in the whole class of Kripke models. Furthermore, the rule (N) preserves consequence.

(2) D is valid in the class of models where R is ***serial*** ; *i.e.*, for every $s \in \mathbf{W}$, there is $t \in \mathbf{W}$ such that $\langle s,t \rangle \in \mathbf{R}$.

(3) T is valid in the class of models where R is ***reflexive.***

(4) B is valid when R is ***symmetric.***

(5) 4 is valid for ***transitive*** R.

(6) 5 is valid for ***euclidean*** R; *i.e.*, for every $s,t,z \in \mathbf{W}$, if $\langle s,t \rangle \in \mathbf{R}$ and $\langle s,z \rangle \in \mathbf{R}$, then $\langle t,z \rangle \in \mathbf{R}$.

Proof

Can you prove the assertions made in (1)-(6) above? ▮

3.6.8. Corollary: soundness of the normal logics obtained from the axioms D, T, B, 4 and 5.

(1) The logic ***K*** is sound in the whole class of Kripke models.

(2) The logic ***KD*** is sound in the class of models where R is ***serial.***

(3) The logic ***KT*** is sound in the class of models where R is ***reflexive.***

(4) The logic ***KB*** is sound in the class of models where R is ***symmetric.***

(5) The logic ***K4*** is sound in the class of models where R is ***transitive.***

(6) The logic ***K5*** is sound in the class of models where R is ***euclidean.*** ▮

Remark.

3.6.7 and its corollary 3.6.8 are not saying that the only models of the usual axioms for normal logics are models where the accessibility relation has the associated property, although, fortunately, the canonical model for each of the logics obtained with these axioms has the required properties. In fact, with the usual semantics for modal logic (*i.e.*, the one we have presented), there is not a converse for 3.6.7. However, the completeness theorem for modal logic is formulated in such a way that the accessibility relation with its intended properties is imposed from outside; *i.e.*, the class of models with respect to which we prove completeness is not being fully and exclusively characterized by the modal logic axioms. This can be seen as a kind of failure and some people feel the need of an absolute sense of completeness and, accordingly, they change the semantics (frames $\langle \mathbf{W}, \mathbf{R} \rangle$ instead of models). When making such a change you are in what can be described as ***pure modal logic***; *i.e.*, where the actual models are disregarded and you are mentally placed in standard second order logic.

We will leave the semantic of modal logic unchanged because we feel that pure modal logic is too abstract and standard second order logic in this context is a kind of mistake which is offering too much expressive power while the desired properties of a calculus are missing. What will be done, in section 4 below, is to introduce a many-sorted theory representing modal logic. The properties of the accessibility relation can now be given axiomatically in the many-sorted theory. The novelty of the approach, if any, is that we do not have to take such a strong logic - such as full second order logic - which is lacking the logical properties of the calculus. Moreover, the logic we are introducing is not too weak as far as its expressive power is concerned, since the properties of the accessibility relation can be successfully characterized: We are taking one of the logics mentioned in section 5 of Chapter IV; that is, a logic between **MSL** and **SOL** obtained by weakening comprehension.

3.7. A formal language for FOML.

In this section we introduce a first order modal language and will be modeling Leibniz's possible worlds using very simple structures. Thus, we are modeling the intuitive notions of possibility and necessity based on Leibniz's idea of possibility as truth in at least one possible world, and necessity as truth in every possible world. The models we are introducing serve the purpose of fixing Leibniz's ideas in the way Carnap and the modelists understood them. It will provide us with a very specific semantics (in fact, a semantics for S5 only), but with the appeal of its intuitive charm. We will approach modal logic from a semantic point of view; thus, to begin with, we have neither axioms or rules. Nevertheless, we will call these models simple S5-models for obvious reasons.

3.7.1. Alphabet.

In **FOML** we have the following list of symbols:

(1) Individual variables: $x, y, z, x_1, x_2, \ldots$

(2) The connectives: $\perp, \neg, \rightarrow, \wedge, \vee$ and $\leftrightarrow$.

(3) Quantifiers: $\forall$ and $\exists$.

(4) Equality symbol: =.

(5) Modal operator symbols: $\Box$ and $\Diamond$.

(6) Relation constants: $R \in$ **REL.CONS**. These are arranged by the mapping

$$\mathbf{FUNC}: \mathbf{REL.CONS} \longrightarrow \mathbb{N}-\{0\}$$

which assigns the arity.

(7) Parentheses:) and (. ▮

3.7.2. Formulas.

The rules for forming formulas are the expected ones for **FOL** and the modal rule saying that from a formula φ we can form $\Box\varphi$ and $\Diamond\varphi$. ▮

Let us denote the smallest set of formulas obtained by these rules **FORM(FOML)**. ▮

3.8. Semantics.

When dealing with the system S5, very simple structures[72] can be used; namely, structures with a single domain of individuals for all possible worlds. Other than that, the accessibility relation between possible worlds is not needed[73].

3.8.1. Definition of structures, assignments and models.

$\mathcal{A} = \langle \mathrm{W}, \mathrm{A}, \langle P^{\mathcal{A}} \rangle_{P \in \mathbf{REL.CONS}} \rangle$ is a structure for our **FOML** (S5) iff:

(1) $\mathrm{W} \neq \emptyset$ is a universe of possible worlds or states.

(2) $\mathrm{A} \neq \emptyset$ is the universe of individuals.

(3) For every $P \in$ **REL.CONS** with $\mathbf{FUNC}(P) = \mathrm{n}$, $P^{\mathcal{A}} \subseteq \mathrm{A}^{\mathrm{n}} \times \mathrm{W}$. ▮

To be able to define the interpretation for all the formulas, we also need ***assignments*** of variables; that is, functions $\mathrm{M}: \mathcal{V} \longrightarrow \mathrm{A}$ from the set $\mathcal{V}$ of the individual variables into the universe of individuals. ▮

---

[72]See Bowen [1979], for a full introduction to the semantics of **FOML**.

[73]See Hughes & Cresswell [1984], page 123. Also, see Goldblatt [1992]. The reason is that from the canonical model of S5 whose accessibility relation is an equivalence, we obtain a submodel whose accessibility relation is universal. This model also characterizes S5 and the accessibility relation , being universal, is dispensable.

Given $\mathcal{A}$ and M as above, an interpretation (or model) is the pair $\langle \mathcal{A}, \mathrm{M}\rangle$; $\mathcal{I} = \langle \mathcal{A}, \mathrm{M}\rangle$. ▮
Given M as above, given an individual variable x and a certain $\mathrm{x} \in \mathrm{A}$, we define $\mathrm{M}_x^{\mathrm{x}}$ as $(\mathrm{M}-\{\langle x,\mathrm{M}(x)\rangle\} \cup \{\langle x,\mathrm{x}\rangle\}$ while $\mathcal{I}_x^{\mathrm{x}} = \langle \mathcal{A}, \mathrm{M}_x^{\mathrm{x}}\rangle$. ▮

3.8.2. Interpretation of a formula in a state or world.
Let $\mathcal{I} = \langle \mathcal{A},\mathrm{M}\rangle$, where $\mathcal{A}$ is a modal structure and M an assignment, and let $\mathrm{s} \in \mathbf{W}$ be a world in $\mathcal{A}$.

$\mathcal{I},\mathrm{s} \models Px_1..x_n$ iff $\langle \mathrm{M}(x_1),...,\mathrm{M}(x_n),\mathrm{s}\rangle \in P^{\mathcal{A}}$

$\mathcal{I},\mathrm{s} \models \forall x\varphi$ iff for all $\mathrm{x} \in \mathrm{A}$: $\langle \mathcal{A}, \mathrm{M}_x^{\mathrm{x}}\rangle,\mathrm{s} \models \varphi$

$\mathcal{I},\mathrm{s} \models \Box\varphi$ iff for all $\mathrm{t} \in \mathrm{W}$: $\mathcal{I},\mathrm{t} \models \varphi$

(For the rest of the formulas the definitions are the expected ones.) ▮

3.8.3. Truth and validity in a model.
Let $\mathcal{I} = \langle \mathcal{A},\mathrm{M}\rangle$ for a given $\mathcal{A}$ and M. Let s be a world of $\mathcal{A}$ and $\alpha \in$ FORM(FOML):

(1) α is ***true at state*** s in $\mathcal{I}$ iff $\mathcal{I},\mathrm{s} \models \alpha$.

(2) $\mathcal{I}$ is a ***model of*** α iff for every world $\mathrm{s} \in \mathrm{W}$: $\mathcal{I},\mathrm{s} \models \alpha$.

(3) $\Gamma \models \varphi$ iff for all $\mathrm{s} \in \mathbf{W}$ and $\mathcal{I}$: $\mathcal{I},\mathrm{s} \models \gamma$ for all $\gamma \in \Gamma$ implies $\mathcal{I},\mathrm{s} \models \varphi$. ▮

Notation remark.
Of course, the function M is of relevance only when giving truth values to open formulas, since in FOML we can also prove the coincidence lemma. Accordingly, we write $\mathcal{A},\mathrm{s} \models \alpha$ when α is a sentence or when α is true at s for every M.

3.9. A Deductive calculus for FOML(S5).

The deductive calculus for S5 consists of:

(1) A calculus for first order predicate logic. (You can take the calculus of MSL presented in section 7.1 of Chapter VI without the sorts.)

(2) The modal axioms Df◊, K, T and 5.

(3) The modal rule of necessitation.

(See section 3.4 for details on the modal calculus.) ▮

4.- PROPOSITIONAL MODAL LOGIC AS MANY-SORTED LOGIC.

4.1. The formal many-sorted logic.

4.1.1. The signature Σ^*.

Let SORT = {0,1,⟨0,1⟩}.

The signature Σ^*=⟨SORT,FUNC⟩ is such that:

(1) SORT is the set defined above.

(2) $FUNC^*$ is a function which takes as arguments the elements of $OPER.SYM^*$ consisting of: ATOM.PROP of PML, the equalities among individuals and among sets, E_1 and E_2, a binary relation S among individuals, the connectives and the membership relation ε_1.

$$\text{FUNC: OPER.SYM}^* \longrightarrow [S_{\omega}(\text{SORT})]$$

where:

(i) $FUNC^*(\perp) = \langle 0 \rangle$

(ii) $FUNC^*(\neg) = \langle 0,0 \rangle$

(iii) $FUNC^*(\rightarrow) = \langle 0,0,0 \rangle$ and the same for the rest of the binary connectors

(iv) $FUNC^*(S) = \langle 0,1,1 \rangle$

(v) $FUNC^*(P) = \langle 0,1 \rangle$, for each $P \in$ ATOM.PROP

(vi) $FUNC^*(\varepsilon_1) = \langle 0,1,\langle 0,1 \rangle \rangle$

(vii) $FUNC^*(E_1) = \langle 0,1,1 \rangle$

(viii) $FUNC^*(E_2) = \langle 0,\langle 0,1 \rangle,\langle 0,1 \rangle \rangle$ ▮

4.1.2. Alphabet of MSL^*.

The alphabet of a many-sorted language suited for PML must contain all operation symbols in $OPER.SYM^*$ and a countable set of variables for each $i \in$ SORT–{0}.

We will use lower-case for individual variables ($u,v,w,\ldots, u_1, u_2, u_3,\ldots$) and upper-case for set variables ($X,Y,Z,\ldots, X_1, X_2, X_3,\ldots$for unary relation variables of sort ⟨0,1⟩).

As well as all that, we have the universal and existential quantifiers: $\forall$ and $\exists$. ▮

4.1.3. Expressions.

The set of expressions of this language is defined in the many-sorted fashion. As usual, formulas are the expressions of type 0. Recall that now $P \in$ **ATOM.PROP** is no longer an atomic formula but a unary relation symbol of type $\langle 0,1 \rangle$. Therefore we need a term (a variable) to form an atomic formula. ▮

4.2. Translating function.

From **PML** we pass to a many-sorted language of signature Σ^{*}.

4.2.1. Definition.

With every φ of **PML** and individual variable u we associate as its translation a formula **TRANS**$^{*}(\varphi)[u]$ in the many-sorted language, defined by:

(F1) **TRANS**$^{*}(\bot)[u] \equiv u \neq u$

TRANS$^{*}(P)[u] \equiv Pu$ for each $P \in$ **ATOM.PROP**

(F2) **TRANS**$^{*}(\neg\varphi)[u] \equiv \neg$**TRANS**$^{*}(\varphi)[u]$

TRANS$^{*}(\varphi \rightarrow \psi)[u] \equiv$ **TRANS**$^{*}(\varphi)[u] \rightarrow$ **TRANS**$^{*}(\psi)[u]$ (similarly for the rest of the connectors)

(F3) **TRANS**$^{*}(\Box\varphi)[u] \equiv \forall w(Suw \rightarrow$**TRANS**$^{*}(\varphi)[w])$ where w must be a new variable; the first one in a chosen ordering

TRANS$^{*}(\Diamond\varphi)[u] \equiv \exists w(Suw \wedge$**TRANS**$^{*}(\varphi)[w])$ where w must be a new variable ▮

Remark.

As is evident, the operation **TRANS*** respects the connectives and gives you only restricted quantification. Moreover, only a variable occurs free.

4.2.2. Translation of the axioms for normal logics.

K $\Box(\varphi \rightarrow \psi) \rightarrow (\Box\varphi \rightarrow \Box\psi)$

TRANS*(K)$[u] \equiv$

$\forall v(Suv \rightarrow ($**TRANS**$^{*}(\varphi)[v] \rightarrow$ **TRANS**$^{*}(\psi)[v])) \rightarrow$

$(\forall v(Suv \rightarrow$ **TRANS**$^{*}(\varphi)[v]) \rightarrow \forall v(Suv \rightarrow$ **TRANS**$^{*}(\psi)[v]))$

Df$\Diamond$ $\Diamond\varphi \longleftrightarrow \neg\Box\neg\varphi$

TRANS*(Df$\Diamond$) $\equiv \exists v(Suv \wedge$ **TRANS**$^{*}(\varphi)[v]) \longleftrightarrow \neg\forall v(Suv \rightarrow \neg$**TRANS**$^{*}(\varphi)[v])$

D $\Box\varphi \rightarrow \Diamond\varphi$

TRANS*(D)$[u] \equiv \forall v(Suv \rightarrow$ **TRANS**$^{*}(\varphi)[v]) \rightarrow \exists v(Suv \wedge$ **TRANS**$^{*}(\varphi)[v])$

T $\Box\varphi \rightarrow \varphi$

TRANS*(T)$[u] \equiv \forall v(Suv \rightarrow$ **TRANS**$^{*}(\varphi)[v]) \rightarrow$ **TRANS**$^{*}(\varphi)[u]$

B $\varphi \rightarrow \Box\Diamond\varphi$

$\mathbf{TRANS}^{*}(\mathrm{B})[u] \equiv \mathbf{TRANS}^{*}(\varphi)[u] \rightarrow \forall v(Suv \rightarrow \exists w(Svw \wedge \mathbf{TRANS}^{*}(\varphi)[w]))$

4 $\Box\varphi \rightarrow \Box\Box\varphi$

$\mathbf{TRANS}^{*}(4)[u] \equiv \forall v(Suv \rightarrow \mathbf{TRANS}^{*}(\varphi)[v]) \rightarrow \forall v(Suv \rightarrow \forall w(Svw \rightarrow \mathbf{TRANS}^{*}(\varphi)[w]))$

5 $\Diamond\varphi \rightarrow \Box\Diamond\varphi$

$\mathbf{TRANS}^{*}(5)[u] \equiv \exists v(Suv \wedge \mathbf{TRANS}^{*}(\varphi)[v]) \rightarrow \forall v(Suv \rightarrow \exists w(Svw \wedge \mathbf{TRANS}^{*}(\varphi)[w]))$

4.2.3. Theorem.

(a) $\vdash_{\mathbf{MSL}} \forall u\, \mathbf{TRANS}^{*}(\mathrm{K})[u]$

(b) $\vdash_{\mathbf{MSL}} \forall u \mathbf{TRANS}^{*}(\mathrm{Df}\Diamond)[u]$

(c) If $\vdash_{\mathbf{MSL}} \forall u \mathbf{TRANS}^{*}(\varphi)[u]$, then $\vdash_{\mathbf{MSL}} \forall u \mathbf{TRANS}^{*}(\Box\varphi)[u]$ (condition related to the modal rule of necessitation)

(d) If $\vdash_{\mathbf{MSL}} \forall u(\mathbf{TRANS}^{*}(\gamma_1)[u] \wedge ... \wedge \mathbf{TRANS}^{*}(\gamma_n)[u] \rightarrow \mathbf{TRANS}^{*}(\varphi)[u])$ then $\vdash_{\mathbf{MSL}} \forall u(\mathbf{TRANS}^{*}(\Box\gamma_1)[u] \wedge ... \wedge \mathbf{TRANS}^{*}(\Box\gamma_n)[u] \rightarrow \mathbf{TRANS}^{*}(\Box\varphi)[u])$. (This is the condition related to the modal derived rule (KN))

Proof

Can you prove all these in the **MSL** calculus? ▮

4.3. General structures and frames built on PM-structures.

Recall that from a many-sorted structure of signature $\Sigma^{\Box}$ we can always pass to a second order structure (frame); therefore we can restrict attention to structures where the domain of sort $\langle 0,1 \rangle$ is a subset of the power set of the universe of individuals (see 2.3.4 through 2.3.7). In fact, Σ^{*} is a special case of $\Sigma^{\Box}$ and the above remark also applies. In all those structures where universes are shaped as in second order logic, we can discard the membership relations since they are redundant. If we also discard the Boolean sort and identify characteristic functions with the corresponding n-ary relations, we are in classical second order. All that reduction makes our task easier and we will do it. We also will use the lambda notation. Our second order structures will be models of comprehension sentences for a wide class of formulas including all the translations of propositional modal formulas. Thus, we are using one of the logics mentioned in section 5 of Chapter IV; that is, a logic obtained by weakening comprehension. In a lousy way, I will term them general structures.

4.3.1. Frames built on PM-structures.

Given a PM-structure $\mathcal{A}$,

$$\mathcal{A} = \langle \mathbf{W}, \mathbf{R}, \langle P^{\mathcal{A}} \rangle_{P \in \mathrm{ATOM.PROP}} \rangle$$

we say that $\mathcal{AF}$ is a frame built on $\mathcal{A}$ iff

$$\mathcal{AF} = \langle \mathbf{W}, \mathbf{W}', \mathbf{R}, \langle P^{\mathcal{A}} \rangle_{P \in \mathrm{ATOM.PROP}} \rangle$$

where:

(i) $\mathbf{W}' \subseteq \mathcal{P}\mathbf{W}$

(ii) $P^{\mathcal{A}} \in \mathbf{W}'$, for all $P \in$ ATOM.PROP ▒

4.3.2. General structures built on PM-strucutres.

Given a PM-structure $\mathcal{A}$ we say that $\mathcal{AG}$ is a general structure built on $\mathcal{A}$ iff

$$\mathcal{AG} = \langle \mathbf{W}, \mathbf{W}', \mathbf{R}, \langle P^{\mathcal{A}} \rangle_{P \in \mathrm{ATOM.PROP}} \rangle$$

satisfies:

The set **W'** includes **DEF**($\mathcal{A}$,**PML**). If we abbreviate this set as **DEF**, the conditions are:

(1) $\emptyset \in \mathbf{DEF}$ and $\mathbf{W} \in \mathbf{DEF}$

(2) $\{P^{\mathcal{A}} / P \in \mathrm{ATOM.PROP}\} \subseteq \mathbf{DEF}$

(3) $\forall TS(T, S \in \mathbf{DEF} \Longrightarrow T \cup S, \mathbf{W} - T \in \mathbf{DEF})$

(4) $\forall T(T \in \mathbf{DEF} \Longrightarrow \mathrm{Dom}(\mathbf{R} \cap (\mathbf{W} \times T)) \in \mathbf{DEF})$

In addition,

(5) $\forall w(w \in \mathbf{W} \Longrightarrow \{w\} \in \mathbf{W}')$

(6) $\forall w(w \in \mathbf{W} \Longrightarrow \mathrm{Rec}(\mathbf{R} \cap (\{w\} \times \mathbf{W})) \in \mathbf{W}')$ ▒

Let $\mathbf{CONV}_1$ be a function giving to each modal structure $\mathcal{A}$ the least general structure $\mathcal{AG}$ defined as above; *i.e.*, the intersection of general structures. ▒

Let $\mathcal{F}$ be the class of all frames built on modal structures and $\mathcal{G}$ the class of all general structures defined as above. ▒

Remark.

The idea behind this construction is to have in the universes of the structure all sets that can be defined in $\mathcal{A}$ by **PML** formulas. As you will see later, we have a bit more than that.

4.3.3. Lemma.

Let $\mathcal{G}$ be the whole class of general structures built on modal structures, then

$\mathcal{G} \subseteq \{\mathcal{B} / \exists \mathcal{A}$ ($\mathcal{A}$ is a **PM**-structure & $\mathcal{B} \in \mathcal{F}$ is built on $\mathcal{A}$ & $\{\mathcal{A}(\varphi) / \varphi \in$ **FORM(PML)**$\} \subseteq$ **W'**$)\}$

Proof

We want to show that given a **PM**-structure $\mathcal{A}$ and a general structure $\mathcal{AG}$ built on $\mathcal{A}$

$$\mathcal{AG} = \langle \mathbf{W}, \mathbf{W'}, \mathbf{R}, \langle P^{\mathcal{A}} \rangle_{P \in \mathbf{ATOM.PROP}} \rangle$$

then any set definable in $\mathcal{A}$ by a modal formula is in the corresponding domain of $\mathcal{AG}$.

The proof will be by induction over the construction of formulas.

$\mathcal{A}(\bot) = \emptyset$ and $\mathcal{A}(P) = P^{\mathcal{A}}$ are all in **W'** (conditions (1) & (2)). Whenever $\mathcal{A}(\varphi) \in \mathbf{W'}$ and $\mathcal{A}(\psi) \in \mathbf{W'}$ then $\mathcal{A}(\neg\varphi) = \mathbf{W} - \mathcal{A}(\varphi)$, $\mathcal{A}(\varphi \vee \psi) = \mathcal{A}(\varphi) \cup \mathcal{A}(\psi)$ and all the other Boolean combinations are all in **W'** (condition (3)). If $\mathcal{A}(\varphi) \in \mathbf{W'}$ then $\mathcal{A}(\Diamond\varphi) = \mathrm{Dom}(\mathbf{R} \cap (\mathbf{W} \times \mathcal{A}(\varphi)))$ is also in **W'** (condition (4)). Also, $\mathcal{A}(\Box\varphi) \in \mathbf{W'}$. ∎

4.3.4. Lemma.

Given a **PM**-structure $\mathcal{A}$ and a general structure $\mathcal{AG}$ built on it,

$$\mathcal{AG}(\lambda u \mathbf{TRANS}^{*}(\varphi)[u]) = \mathcal{A}(\varphi), \text{ for all } \varphi \in \mathbf{FORM(PML)}$$

Proof

(F1) $\mathcal{A}(\bot) = \emptyset = \mathcal{AG}(\lambda u\, u \neq u) = \mathcal{AG}(\lambda u\, \mathbf{TRANS}^{*}(\bot)[u])$

$\mathcal{A}(P) = P^{\mathcal{A}} = \mathcal{AG}(\lambda u\, Pu) = \mathcal{AG}(\lambda u\, \mathbf{TRANS}^{*}(P)[u])$

(F2) $\mathcal{A}(\neg\varphi) = \mathbf{W} - \mathcal{A}(\varphi) = \mathbf{W} - \mathcal{AG}(\lambda u\, \mathbf{TRANS}^{*}(\varphi)[u]) = \mathcal{AG}(\lambda u\, \mathbf{TRANS}^{*}(\neg\varphi)[u])$

(by induction hypothesis, $\mathcal{AG}(\lambda u\, \mathbf{TRANS}^{*}(\varphi)[u]) = \mathcal{A}(\varphi)$)

$\mathcal{A}(\varphi \rightarrow \psi) = (\mathbf{W} - \mathcal{A}(\varphi)) \cup \mathcal{A}(\psi) = \mathcal{AG}(\lambda u\, \mathbf{TRANS}^{*}(\neg\varphi)[u]) \cup \mathcal{AG}(\lambda u\, \mathbf{TRANS}^{*}(\psi)[u]) =$ $\mathcal{AG}(\lambda u\, \mathbf{TRANS}^{*}(\varphi \rightarrow \psi)[u])$, using the induction hypothesis needed; similarly for the rest of the formulas obtained by this rule (F2).

(F3) $\mathcal{A}(\Diamond\varphi) = \mathrm{Dom}(\mathbf{R} \cap (\mathbf{W} \times \mathcal{A}(\varphi)) = \mathcal{AG}(\lambda u\, \exists w(Suw \wedge \mathbf{TRANS}^{*}(\varphi)[w])) =$ $\mathcal{AG}(\lambda u\, \mathbf{TRANS}^{*}(\Diamond\varphi)[u])$; for $\mathcal{A}(\Box\varphi)$ it is similar ∎

4.3.5. Corollary.

For any general structure $\mathcal{AG}$ built on a **PM**-structure $\mathcal{A}$

$\mathcal{A}, s \models \varphi$ in **PML** iff $\mathcal{AG}[s](\mathbf{TRANS}^{*}(\varphi)[u]) = \mathrm{T}$ in $\mathbf{MSL}^{*}$ ∎

(where $\mathcal{AG}[s](\mathbf{TRANS}^{*}(\varphi)[u])$ is an abbreviation of $\langle \mathcal{AG}, \mathrm{M}_u^s \rangle(\mathbf{TRANS}^{*}(\varphi)[u])$).

4.3.6. Corollary (Lemma 1 (a)).

From the above corollary, it easily follows that for any **PM**-structure $\mathcal{A}$

(a) $\mathcal{A}, s \models \varphi$ in **PML** iff $\mathbf{CONV}_1(\mathcal{A})[s](\mathbf{TRANS}^*(\varphi)[u]) = \mathrm{T}$ in $\mathbf{MSL}^*$ ▮

4.3.7. Corollary (Lemma 1 (b)).

(b) $\mathcal{A} \models \varphi$ in **PML** iff $\mathbf{CONV}_1(\mathcal{A})$ is a model of $\forall u(\mathbf{TRANS}^*(\varphi)[u])$ in $\mathbf{MSL}^*$. ▮

4.3.8. Theorem 1.

$\models \varphi$ in **PML** iff $\models_{\mathcal{G}} \forall u(\mathbf{TRANS}^*(\varphi)[u])$ in $\mathbf{MSL}^*$.

Proof

Use 4.3.5 and 1.2.1. ▮

4.4. The MODO theory.

I will define a theory, **MODO**, which will be proven to be syntactically and semantically equivalent to the modal logic *K*.

4.4.1. Definition: MODO.

The set Δ of axioms of this theory are:

(1) Comprehension sentences for a restricted class of formulas including the translations of **PML** formulas; that is, all of the form

$$\forall \exists X \forall u(\varepsilon_1 uX \leftrightarrow \varphi), \text{ for each } \varphi \in \mathbf{TRANS}^*(\mathbf{PML})[u] \cup I \cup \Sigma$$

where $I = \{u{=}v / v$ is any individual variable such that $u \not\equiv v\}$, $\Sigma = \{Suv / v$ is any individual variable such that $u \not\equiv v\}$.

(2) Extensionality. ▮

4.4.2. Definition: MODO(S4).

To the set Δ of axioms in **MODO** we add the second order abstract conditions for the axioms T and 4,

MS(T) $\forall uY(\forall v(Suv \rightarrow \varepsilon_1 vY) \rightarrow \varepsilon_1 uY)$

MS(4) $\forall uY(\forall v(Suv \rightarrow \varepsilon_1 vY) \rightarrow \forall v(Suv \rightarrow \forall w(Svw \rightarrow \varepsilon_1 wY)))$

and call the resulting set **MODO(S4)**. ▮

4.4.3. Theorem.

The class $\mathcal{G}$ of general structures built on PM-structures is axiomatized by Δ; ***i.e.***, $\mathbf{MOD}(\Delta) = \mathcal{G}$.

Proof

Our models are extensional. We have to prove that all the rules given in definition 4.3.2 for general structures give new sets which are definable by formulas of $\mathbf{TRANS}^{*}(\mathbf{PML})$ or in $I \cup \Sigma$; and conversely. Recall that we are now taking many-sorted structures of signature Σ^{*} and we are considering them as second order structures because we are taking a universe of individuals and another of sets. If you do not want to make such an identification, you can convert every $\mathcal{A} \in \mathbf{MOD}(\Delta)$ into a SOL-structure, $\mathbf{H}(\mathcal{A})$, and then prove $\mathcal{G} = \mathbf{H}(\mathbf{MOD}(\Delta))$ instead. (Use the function **H** defined in 2.3.5.)

[$\Longrightarrow$] Let $\mathcal{A} \in \mathbf{MOD}(\Delta)$, we want to prove that $\mathcal{A} \in \mathcal{G}$. The proof is similar to theorem 3.3 of Chapter V.

(1) $\emptyset$ is definable by $\perp$ and **W** by its negation. (We use the fact that difference and complement of definable sets are also definable.)

(2) $P^{\mathcal{A}}$ is definable by Pu, and $Pu \equiv \mathbf{TRANS}^{*}(P)[u]$.

(3) Boolean operations over definable sets are also definable.

(4) $\mathrm{Dom}(\mathbf{R} \cap (\mathbf{W} \times \mathbf{T}))$ is also definable by $\mathbf{TRANS}^{*}(\Diamond\varphi)[u]$, when **T** is definable by $\mathbf{TRANS}^{*}(\varphi)[u]$.

(5) Unitary classes are definable with individual parameters in **W**. Of course, the definition uses formulas in I.

(6) $\mathrm{Rec}(\mathbf{R} \cap (\{\mathbf{w}\} \times \mathbf{W}))$ is also definable by Suv, using u as a parameter.

[$\Longleftarrow$] Let $\mathcal{A} \in \mathcal{G}$. We want to prove that $\mathcal{A} \in \mathbf{MOD}(\Delta)$; ***i.e.***, we want to prove that comprehension sentences in our chosen Δ are all satisfied.

(1) For formulas in I, $u = v$ defines a singleton. Singletons are in $\mathcal{A}$ by condition (5).

(2) For formulas in Σ, when we take u as a parameter, Suv defines the set of all points reached by **R** from a given $\mathbf{w} \in \mathbf{W}$. This set is in **W'** by condition (6).

(3) For all the formulas in $\mathbf{TRANS}^{*}(\mathbf{PML})$, the proof has to be by induction on $\varphi \in \mathbf{FORM}(\mathbf{PML})$.

   (F1) $\varphi \equiv \perp$. $\mathbf{TRANS}^{*}(\varphi)$ defines $\emptyset$, which is in **W'** by condition (1).
   $\varphi \equiv P$. $\mathbf{TRANS}^{*}(\varphi)$ defines $P^{\mathcal{A}}$, which belongs to **W'** by condition (2).

   (F2) Assume that the theorem holds for α and β. **X** is defined by $\mathbf{TRANS}^{*}(\alpha)$ and **Y** is defined by $\mathbf{TRANS}^{*}(\beta)$. Since the function $\mathbf{TRANS}^{*}$ respects connectives, the negation, disjunction, etc. of α and β are translated as negation, disjunction, etc. of their translations and these formulas define the complement, union, etc. of **X** and **Y**. Since condition (3) of definition 4.3.2 is satisfied, these sets are in **W'**.

(F3) $\varphi \equiv \Diamond\alpha$. Assume that the theorem holds for α and that $\mathbf{TRANS}^*(\alpha)[u]$ defines **X** in $\mathcal{A}$. Then $\Diamond\alpha$ is translated as $\exists v(Suv \wedge \mathbf{TRANS}^*(\alpha)[v])$ and the latter defines Dom(**R** ∩ (**W**×**X**)) in $\mathcal{A}$. By condition (5), this set is in **W'**. For $\varphi \equiv \Box\varphi$ the result follows from conditions (4) and (3). ▮

4.4.4. Representation theorem for *K*.

$\models \varphi$ in the whole class of Kripke structures (*i.e.*, in the class of structures for the logic *K*) iff **MODO** $\models \forall u(\mathbf{TRANS}^*(\varphi)[u])$ in **MSL**.

Proof

Use theorems 4.4.3 and 4.3.8. ▮

4.4.5. The powerful theory MODO.

The theory **MODO**, **MODO** $= \Delta$, will enable us to prove the equivalence of the first order conditions for the axioms D, T, B, 4 and 5 with the second order abstract conditions for the translations of these axioms. In each case we will make a replacement in the abstract condition for the relevant axiom using sets defined by comprehension. We can make such a substitution because we have comprehension and quantifier rules for set variables.

(1) $\Delta \vdash \mathrm{MS(D)} \leftrightarrow \alpha_{\mathrm{D}}$

$\mathrm{MS(D)} \equiv \forall uY(\forall v(Suv \rightarrow Yv) \rightarrow \exists v(Suv \wedge Yv))$

$\alpha_{\mathrm{D}} \equiv \forall u\exists vSuv$

The proof is easy, replace Y by $\lambda v\, v = v$ in the elimination of the quantifier in MS(D). That is, take this comprehension axiom:

$$\exists Y\forall v(\varepsilon_1 vY \leftrightarrow \mathbf{TRANS}^*(\neg\bot)[v])$$

Since $\vdash \forall u(\mathbf{TRANS}^*(\Diamond\neg\bot)[u]) \leftrightarrow \alpha_{\mathrm{D}}$, we also get

$$\Delta \vdash \forall u(\mathbf{TRANS}^*(\Diamond\neg\bot)[u]) \leftrightarrow \mathrm{MS(D)}$$

(2) $\Delta \vdash \mathrm{MS(T)} \leftrightarrow \alpha_{\mathrm{T}}$

$\mathrm{MS(T)} \equiv \forall uY(\forall v(Suv \rightarrow Yv) \rightarrow Yu)$

$\alpha_{\mathrm{T}} \equiv \forall uSuu$

Replace Y by $\lambda vSuv$ in the elimination of the quantifier in MS(T). That is, take this comprehension axiom:

$$\exists Y \forall v(\varepsilon_1 vY \longleftrightarrow Suv)$$

(3) $\Delta \vdash MS(B) \longleftrightarrow \alpha_B$

$MS(B) \equiv \forall uY(Yu \to \forall v(Suv \to \exists w(Svw \wedge Yw)))$

$\alpha_B \equiv \forall uv(Suv \to Svu)$

Replace Y by $\lambda v\, u = v$ in the elimination of the quantifier in MS(B). That is, take this comprehension axiom:

$$\exists Y \forall v(\varepsilon_1 vY \longleftrightarrow u=v)$$

(4) $\Delta \vdash MS(4) \longleftrightarrow \alpha_4$

$MS(4) \equiv \forall uY(\forall v(Suv \to Yv) \to \forall v(Suv \to \forall w(Svw \to Yw)))$

$\alpha_4 \equiv \forall uvw(Suv \wedge Svw \to Suw)$

Replace Y by $\lambda v Suv$ in the elimination of the quantifier in MS(4). That is, take this comprehension axiom:

$$\exists Y \forall v(\varepsilon_1 vY \longleftrightarrow Suv)$$

(5) $\Delta \vdash MS(5) \longleftrightarrow \alpha_5$

$MS(5) \equiv \forall uY(\exists v(Suv \wedge Yv) \to \forall v(Suv \to \exists w(Svw \wedge Yw)))$

$\alpha_5 \equiv \forall uv(Suv \wedge Suw \to Svw)$

Replace Y by $\lambda v\, v = w$ in the elimination of the quantifier in MS(5).

4.5. Reverse conversion.

4.5.1. Definition.

From a model $\mathcal{B}$ of Δ, which we are viewing as a SOL-structure, we obtain a modal structure by the simple procedure of deleting the universe of sets, W'. So we can define

$$\mathbf{CONV_2} = \mathbf{CONV_1^{-1}}$$

as a function from **MOD(Δ)** ⊆ **ST(SOL)** into **ST(PML)**. ▮

4.5.2. Strong version of lemma 2.

There is a recursive **Δ ⊆ SENT(MSL*)** such that **CONV$_1$(ST(PML)) ⊆ MOD(Δ)** and for every $\mathcal{B}$∈**MOD(Δ)** in **ST(SOL)** there is **CONV$_2$($\mathcal{B}$)∈ST(PML)**. For every φ∈**FORM(PML)**,

(a) $\text{CONV}_2(\mathcal{B}),s \models \varphi$ in PML iff $\mathcal{B}[s]$ is a model of $\text{TRANS}^{*}(\varphi)[u]$ in MSL^{*}.

(b) $\text{CONV}_2(\mathcal{B}) \models \varphi$ in PML iff $\mathcal{B}$ is a model of $\forall u(\text{TRANS}^{*}(\varphi)[u])$ in MSL^{*}.

Proof

Take $\Delta = \text{MODO}$. Let $\mathcal{B} \in \text{MOD}(\Delta) \subseteq \text{ST(SOL)}$, φ a formula of PML, $\text{TRANS}^{*}(\varphi)[u]$ its translation and $\forall u(\text{TRANS}^{*}(\varphi)[u])$ its quantified closed translation. Since it is a model of Δ, we have $\text{CONV}_2(\mathcal{B})$ in ST(PML). By corollaries 4.3.6 and 4.3.7,

(a) $\text{CONV}_2(\mathcal{B}),s \models \varphi$ in PML iff $\mathcal{B}[s]$ is a model of $\text{TRANS}^{*}(\varphi)[u]$ in MSL^{*}.

(b) $\text{CONV}_2(\mathcal{B}) \models \varphi$ in PML iff $\mathcal{B}$ is a model of $\forall u(\text{TRANS}^{*}(\varphi)[u])$ in MSL^{*}. ▮

4.5.3. Main theorem for *K*.

There is a recursive $\Delta \subseteq \text{SENT}(\text{MSL}^{*})$ with $\text{CONV}_1(\text{ST(PML)}) \subseteq \text{MOD}(\Delta)$ such that $\Pi \models \varphi$ (in the whole class of Kripke structures) iff $\text{TRANS}^{*}(\Pi)[u] \cup \Delta \models \text{TRANS}^{*}(\varphi)[u]$ in MSL.

Proof

Take $\Delta = \text{MODO}$. Similar to 1.3.1, use 4.3.6, 4.3.7, 4.4.3 and 4.5.2. ▮

4.5.4. Compactness of *K*.

If $\Pi \models \varphi$ (in the whole class of Kripke structures), then there is a finite $\Gamma \subseteq \Pi$ such that $\Gamma \models \varphi$, for any $\Pi \cup \{\varphi\} \subseteq \text{FORM(PML)}$.

Proof

Use 1.3.2 and 4.5.3. ▮

4.5.5. Enumerability of *K*.

The set of all valid formulas in Kripke structures is recursively enumerable.

Proof

Use 1.2.2, 4.4.3 and 4.4.4. The definition of $\mathcal{G}$ is recursive. ▮

4.5.6. Löwenheim-Skolem for *K*.

Let $\Pi \subseteq \text{FORM(PML)}$. If Π has a Kripke model, then it has a countable model with a countable domain.

Proof
Use 1.3.4, 4.3.7, 4.4.3, 4.5.2 and the fact that countable models are converted into countable models. ▮

4.5.7. Representation theorem for S4.
Let $\mathcal{C}$ be the class of reflexive and transitive Kripke structures.

$$\models_{\mathcal{C}} \varphi \text{ iff } \mathbf{MODO(S4)} \models \forall u(\mathbf{TRANS}^{*}(\varphi)[u])$$

for every formula φ of PML.

Proof
[⟹] Let $\models_{\mathcal{C}} \varphi$ where $\mathcal{C}$ is the class of reflexive and transitive structures. Let $\mathcal{B}$ be a model of **MODO**(S4). Thus, $\mathcal{B}$ is a model of Δ. By 4.4.5 and soundness of **SOL**, $\mathcal{B}$ is reflexive and transitive. $\mathbf{CONV}_2(\mathcal{B})$ is reflexive and transitive, then $\mathbf{CONV}_2(\mathcal{B}) \models \varphi$.

$\mathcal{B}$ is a model of $\forall u(\mathbf{TRANS}^{*}(\varphi)[u])$ (by 4.5.2)

[⟸] Let $\mathbf{MODO(S4)} \models \forall u(\mathbf{TRANS}^{*}(\varphi)[u])$. Let $\mathcal{A}$ be any reflexive and transitive structure. $\mathbf{CONV}_1(\mathcal{A}) \in \mathcal{G}$ is a model of Δ (4.4.3) and of α_T and α_4. By 4.4.5 and soundness of SOL, it is also a model of MS(T) and of MS(4). Therefore, $\mathbf{CONV}_1(\mathcal{A})$ is a model of

$\forall u(\mathbf{TRANS}^{*}(\varphi)[u])$

By 4.3.7, $\mathcal{A}$ is a model of φ. ▮

4.5.8. Main theorem for S4.
Let $\mathcal{C}$ be the class of reflexive and transitive Kripke structures.

$$\Pi \models_{\mathcal{C}} \varphi \text{ iff } \mathbf{TRANS}^{*}(\Pi)[u] \cup \mathbf{MODO(S4)} \models \mathbf{TRANS}^{*}(\varphi)[u]$$

for any $\Pi \cup \{\varphi\} \subseteq$ **FORM(PML)**.

Proof
Use 4.4.5, 4.3.6 and 4.5.2. ▮

4.5.9. Compactness of S4.
Let $\mathcal{C}$ be the class of reflexive and transitive Kripke structures.

If $\Pi \models_{\mathcal{C}} \varphi$ then there is a finite $\Gamma \subseteq \Pi$ such that $\Gamma \models_{\mathcal{C}} \varphi$

Proof

Use 1.3.2 and 4.5.8. ∎

4.5.10. Enumerability of S4.

The set of all valid formulas in reflexive Kripke structures is recursively enumerable.

Proof

Use 1.2.2 and 4.5.7. ∎

4.5.11. Löwenheim-Skolem for S4.

Let $\Pi \subseteq$ **FORM(PML)**. If Π has a reflexive and transitive Kripke model, then it has a countable one.

Proof

Use 1.3.3 and 4.5.8. ∎

4.6. Testing the calculus.

4.6.1. Lemma 3 for the logic *K*.

Let $\varphi \in$ FORM(PML). If $\vdash_K \varphi$, then MODO $\vdash_{\text{MSL}} \forall u(\mathbf{TRANS}^{\bullet}(\varphi)[u])$.

Proof

Use 4.2.3. ∎

4.6.2. Theorem 3 for the logic *K*.

For all $\Pi \cup \{\varphi\} \subseteq$ **FORM(PML)**:

If $\Pi \vdash_K \varphi$, then $\mathbf{TRANS}^{\bullet}(\Pi)[u] \cup \mathbf{MODO} \vdash_{\text{MSL}} \mathbf{TRANS}^{\bullet}(\varphi)[u]$

Proof

The result easily follows from 4.6.1. We can use 1.4.1 because the calculus of K is finitary, the deduction theorem holds and the function **TRANS**$^{\bullet}$ respects connectives. ∎

4.6.3. Lemma 3 for the logic S4.

If $\vdash_{S4} \varphi$, then MODO(S4) $\vdash_{\text{MSL}} \forall u(\mathbf{TRANS}^{\bullet}(\varphi)[u])$.

Proof

Use 4.6.1. Moreover, when in the proof of φ we use T or 4, in **MSL** we take MS(T) or MS(4). From them and the rule of comprehension you easily obtain the particular instance of **TRANS***(T) and **TRANS***(4) you want. ▮

4.6.4. Theorem 3 for the logic S4.

For all $\Pi \cup \{\varphi\} \subseteq$ **FORM(PML)**,

$$\text{If } \Pi \vdash_{S4} \varphi, \text{ then } \mathbf{TRANS}^*(\Pi)[u] \cup \mathbf{MODO}(S4) \vdash_{MSL} \mathbf{TRANS}^*(\varphi)[u]$$

Proof

Exactly as above; use 4.6.3 and 1.4.1. ▮

4.6.5. Definition of the canonical general structure.

Given a consistent normal logic B and its canonical model

$$\mathcal{A}_B = \langle W_B, R_B, \langle P^{\mathcal{A}_B} \rangle_{P \in ATOM.PROP} \rangle$$

we define the canonical general structure, $\mathcal{A}_B\mathcal{G}$, as $\mathrm{CONV}_1(\mathcal{A}_B)$. ▮

4.6.6. Proposition.

For every $\varphi \in$ **FORM(PML)** and $t \in W_B$: $\mathcal{A}_B\mathcal{G}[t] \vDash \mathbf{TRANS}^*(\varphi)[u]$ iff $\varphi \in t$.

Proof

The proof will be on induction on the formation of formulas.

(F1) $\mathcal{A}_B\mathcal{G}[t] \nvDash \mathbf{TRANS}^*(\bot)[u]$ iff $\bot \notin t$ (since t is maximally B-consistent)

$$\begin{aligned} \mathcal{A}_B\mathcal{G}[s] \vDash \mathbf{TRANS}^*(P)[u] &\text{ iff } \mathcal{A}_B\mathcal{G}[s] \vDash Pu \\ &\text{ iff } s \in P^{\mathcal{A}_B} \\ &\text{ iff } P \in s \end{aligned}$$

(F2) Assume that the proposition holds for φ and ψ.

$$\begin{aligned} \mathcal{A}_B\mathcal{G}[s] \vDash \mathbf{TRANS}^*(\neg\varphi)[u] &\text{ iff } \mathcal{A}_B\mathcal{G}[s] \vDash \neg\mathbf{TRANS}^*(\varphi)[u] \\ &\text{ iff } \mathcal{A}_B\mathcal{G}[s] \nvDash \mathbf{TRANS}^*(\varphi)[u] \\ &\text{ iff } \varphi \notin s \end{aligned}$$

$$\text{iff } \neg\varphi \in s$$

$$\mathcal{A}_B\mathcal{G}[s] \models \text{TRANS}^*(\varphi \wedge \psi)[u] \text{ iff}$$

$$\mathcal{A}_B\mathcal{G}[s] \models \text{TRANS}^*(\varphi)[u] \text{ and } \mathcal{A}_B\mathcal{G}[s] \models \text{TRANS}^*(\psi)[u]$$

$$\text{iff } \varphi \in s \text{ and } \psi \in s$$

$$\text{iff } (\varphi \wedge \psi) \in s$$

(F3) Assume that the proposition holds for φ.

$$\mathcal{A}_B\mathcal{G}[s] \models \text{TRANS}^*(\Box\varphi)[u] \text{ iff } \mathcal{A}_B\mathcal{G}[s] \models \forall v(Suv \rightarrow \text{TRANS}^*(\varphi)[u])$$

$$\text{iff for every } t \in W_B\text{: } \langle s,t\rangle \in R_B \text{ implies } \mathcal{A}_B\mathcal{G}[t] \models \text{TRANS}^*(\varphi)[v])$$

$$\text{iff for every } t \in W_B\text{: if } \langle s,t\rangle \in R_B\text{, then } \varphi \in t$$

$$\text{iff } \Box\varphi \in s \text{ (by 3.6.5)} \blacksquare$$

4.6.7. Proposition.

For the consistent normal logic $\boldsymbol{K}$, $\mathcal{A}_{\boldsymbol{K}}\mathcal{G}$ is a model of MODO.

Proof

Clearly $\mathcal{A}_{\boldsymbol{K}}\mathcal{G}$ is a model of all comprehension axioms in MODO (see 4.4.3). Furthermore, it satisfies extensionality. ∎

4.6.8. Lemma 5.

For all $\varphi \in$ FORM(PML), if $\mathcal{A}_{\boldsymbol{K}}\mathcal{G} \models \forall u(\text{TRANS}^*(\varphi)[u])$ then $\vdash_{\boldsymbol{K}} \varphi$.

Proof

Let $\varphi \in$ FORM(PML). Assume that $\mathcal{A}_{\boldsymbol{K}}\mathcal{G} \models \forall u(\text{TRANS}^*(\varphi)[u])$. Therefore, for all maximally $\boldsymbol{K}$-consistent sets s, $\mathcal{A}_{\boldsymbol{K}}\mathcal{G}[s] \models \text{TRANS}^*(\varphi)[u]$. By 4.6.6, for every maximally $\boldsymbol{K}$-consistent set s, $\varphi \in s$. By 3.3.10 (3), $\vdash_{\boldsymbol{K}} \varphi$. ∎

4.6.9. Lemma 4 for the logic *K*.

For all $\varphi \in$ FORM(PML), MODO $\vdash_{\text{MSL}} \forall u(\text{TRANS}^*(\varphi)[u])$ iff $\vdash_{\boldsymbol{K}} \varphi$.

Proof

Use 1.4.5, 4.6.8 and 4.6.1. To prove that MODO $\vdash_{\text{MSL}} \forall u(\text{TRANS}^*(\varphi)[u])$ implies $\vdash_{\boldsymbol{K}} \varphi$, assume that MODO $\vdash_{\text{MSL}} \forall u(\text{TRANS}^*(\varphi)[u])$. By soundness of MSL

$\mathbf{MODO} \vDash \forall u(\mathbf{TRANS}^*(\varphi)[u])$

We finish because, by 4.6.7, $\mathcal{A}_K\mathcal{G}$ is a model of **MODO.** ∎

4.6.10. Theorem 4 for the logic *K*.

For all $\Pi \cup \{\varphi\} \subseteq$ **FORM(PML)**, $\mathbf{TRANS}^*(\Pi)[u] \cup \mathbf{MODO} \vdash_{\mathrm{MSL}} \mathbf{TRANS}^*(\varphi)[u]$ iff $\Pi \vdash_K \varphi$.

Proof

Use 4.6.9 and 1.4.3 (since the calculus *K* is finitary, it has the deduction theorem, the function **TRANS*** respects the connectives and the usual quantification rules). ∎

4.6.11. Completeness and soundness of the calculus *K*.

For all $\Pi \cup \{\varphi\} \subseteq$ **FORM(PML)**, $\Pi \vdash_K \varphi$ iff $\Pi \vDash \varphi$.

Proof

Use 4.6.10 and 4.5.3. ∎

4.6.12. Proposition.

For the consistent normal logic S4, $\mathcal{A}_{S4}\mathcal{G}$ is a model of MODO(S4).

Proof

By 4.6.7 this model satisfies comprehension and extensionality. We will prove that $\mathcal{A}_{S4}\mathcal{G}$ has a reflexive and transitive accessibility relation. Hence, using 4.4.5 it follows that it is a model of MS(4) and MS(T). For reflexiveness: Let s be any maximally S4-consistent set. We want to prove that

$$\{\varphi \,/\, \Box\varphi \in s\} \subseteq s$$

Let $\Box\varphi \in s$. Since $\Box\varphi \to \varphi \in S4$ and $S4 \subseteq s$, and it is closed under (MP), $\varphi \in s$. For transitivity: Let s, t and w be maximally S4-consistent sets of formulas, and assume that $\{\varphi \,/\, \Box\varphi \in s\} \subseteq t$ and that $\{\varphi \,/\, \Box\varphi \in t\} \subseteq w$. We want to prove that

$$\{\varphi \,/\, \Box\varphi \in s\} \subseteq w$$

Let $\Box\varphi \in s$. Since $\Box\varphi \to \Box\Box\varphi \in S4$, $S4 \subseteq s$ and it is closed under M.P., $\Box\Box\varphi \in s$. Therefore, $\Box\varphi \in t$ and so $\varphi \in w$. ∎

4.6.13. Lemma 5..

For all $\varphi \in$ FORM(PML): If $\mathcal{A}_{S4}\mathcal{G} \vDash \forall u(\text{TRANS}^{*}(\varphi)[u])$ then $\vdash_{S4} \varphi$.

Proof

This is similar to the proof of 4.6.8. Use 4.6.12 instead of 4.6.7. ▮

4.6.14. Lemma 4 for the logic S4.

For all $\varphi \in$ FORM(PML): MODO(S4) $\vdash_{MSL} \forall u(\text{TRANS}^{*}(\varphi)[u])$ iff $\vdash_{S4} \varphi$.

Proof

Use 4.6.13 and 4.6.3. ▮

4.6.15. Theorem 4 for the logic S4.

For all $\Pi \cup \{\varphi\} \subseteq$ FORM(PML): $\text{TRANS}^{*}(\Pi)[u] \cup$ MODO(S4) $\vdash_{MSL} \text{TRANS}^{*}(\varphi)[u]$ iff $\Pi \vdash_{S4} \varphi$.

Proof

Use 4.6.14 and 1.4.3. ▮

4.6.16. Completeness and soundness of the calculus S4.

For all $\Pi \cup \{\varphi\} \subseteq$ FORM(PML), $\Pi \vdash_{S4} \varphi$ iff $\Pi \vDash_{\mathcal{C}} \varphi$ in the class $\mathcal{C}$ of reflexive and transitive Kripke structures.

Proof

Use 4.6.15 and 4.5.8. ▮

5.- FIRST ORDER MODAL LOGIC AS MANY-SORTED LOGIC.

This section is devoted to translating the first order modal system S5, FOML(S5) into MSL. We define a syntactical translation from FOML into MSL and prove the semantical interconnection between the original and the new. The translation is very useful because it enables us to prove compactness, enumerability, Löwenheim-Skolem, soundness and completeness theorems for the modal logic S5.

5.1. The formal many-sorted language MSL$^\blacklozenge$.

Now we shall present the many-sorted language we will consider, bearing in mind that we want to translate into this logic the **FOML**.

5.1.1. The signature $\Sigma^\blacklozenge$.

Let **SORT** = {0,1,2}.

The signature $\Sigma^\blacklozenge = \langle$SORT,FUNC$^\blacklozenge\rangle$ is such that:

(1) **SORT** is the set defined above.

(2) **FUNC**$^\blacklozenge$ is a function which takes as arguments the elements of **OPER.SYM**$^\blacklozenge$ consisting of: **REL.CONS** of **FOML**, the equalities among individuals of sorts 1 and 2, *i.e.*, E_1, E_2, and the connectives. All the values of this function are as in 4.1.1 but

$$\text{FUNC}^\blacklozenge(P) = \langle 0,2,\overset{n}{\ldots},2,1\rangle$$ ▓

5.1.2. Alphabet of MSL$^\blacklozenge$.

Two-sorted first order languages have two sorts of variables, ranging over the two universes. We will use lower-case variables u, v, w, u_1, u_2 for sort 1 (worlds), and the lower-case variables x, y, z, x_1, x_2,... for sort 2 (individuals).

We also have the symbols in **OPER.SYM**$^\blacklozenge$ and the quantifiers. ▓

5.1.3. Expressions.

The set of expressions of this language is defined in the many-sorted fashion. ▓

5.2. Translating function.

5.2.1. Definition.

The translating function, **TRANS**$^\blacklozenge$, respects connectors and basically extends the definition 4.2.1. Let v be a variable of sort 1. We list the novelties below:

$$\text{TRANS}^\blacklozenge(Px_1 \ldots x_n)[v] \equiv Px_1 \ldots x_n v$$

$$\text{TRANS}^\blacklozenge(\forall x\alpha)[v] \equiv \forall x \text{TRANS}^\blacklozenge(\alpha)[v]$$

$$\mathbf{TRANS}^{\blacklozenge}(\Box\alpha)[v] \equiv \forall v \mathbf{TRANS}^{\blacklozenge}(\alpha)[v]$$ ▮

Remarks.

(1) Note that the "same" variables of sort 2 (individuals) that appear in $\mathbf{TRANS}^{\blacklozenge}(\alpha)[v]$ appear as variables of α, and that there is only one variable of sort 1 (worlds), free or bound.

(2) As you see, the translation of necessitations differs from the one obtained by the function $\mathbf{TRANS}^{\bullet}$.

5.3. Theorems on semantic equivalence FOML-MSL.

In the following theorems we shall use basically the same structures for modal models and many-sorted ones, and for that we can introduce a simplified notation for certain assignments of many-sorted variables. (The only difference being that in our chosen presentation of MSL a truth-value universe is included; thus, strictly speaking $\mathbf{CONV}_1$ is not the identity, but the result of adding the universe A_0 and the standard presentation of the connectors. In the same way, $\mathbf{CONV}_2$ is not the identity but the result of erasing the universe A_0 and the standard presentation of the connectors.)

5.3.1. Conversion of structures.

If $\mathcal{A} = \langle W, A, \langle P^{\mathcal{A}}\rangle_{P\in \mathbf{REL.CONS}}\rangle$ is an S5-modal structure, $\mathbf{CONV}_1(\mathcal{A}) = \mathcal{A}^*$ is defined as

$$\mathcal{A}^* = \langle A_0, A_1, A_2, \langle P^{\mathcal{A}^*}\rangle_{P\in \mathbf{OPER.SYM}^{\blacklozenge}}\rangle$$

where $A_0 = \{T,F\}$, $A_1 = W$, $A_2 = A$ and $P^{\mathcal{A}^*} = P^{\mathcal{A}}$ for $P\in\mathbf{REL.CONS}$ or it is a standard connective or equality. ▮

The reverse conversion, $\mathbf{CONV}_2$, does the opposite. ▮

On notation: To simplify our notation, we will identify $\mathcal{A}$ with $\mathbf{CONV}_1(\mathcal{A})$ and $\mathcal{B}$ with $\mathbf{CONV}_2(\mathcal{B})$. Thus we are taking both functions as identity.

5.3.2. Assignments.

We only need a special kind of assignments to appear; namely, those that get a single value $s\in A_1$ over all the variables of sort 1. We shall write G_s - where $G_s(\mathcal{V}_2) \subseteq A_2$ and $G_s(\mathcal{V}_1) = \{s\}$ with $s\in A_1$. ▮

If M is an assignment of **FOML**, we shall call M* any assignment of $\mathbf{MSL}^{\blacklozenge}$ such that $M^*(x) = M(x)$ for every $x \in \mathcal{V}_2$. And we shall write M^*_s if also $M^*(u) = s$ for every $u \in \mathcal{V}_1$ with $s \in A_1$. ▓

5.3.3. Theorem.

Let α be a formula of **FOML**, $\mathcal{A} = \langle W, A, \langle P^{\mathcal{A}} \rangle_{P \in \mathrm{REL.CONS}} \rangle$ a structure for S5, $s \in W$ and M an assignment of variables in **FOML**:

$$\langle \mathcal{A}, M \rangle, s \models \alpha \text{ in } \mathbf{FOML} \text{ iff } \langle \mathcal{A}, M^* \rangle[s] \models \mathbf{TRANS}^{\blacklozenge}(\alpha)[v] \text{ in } \mathbf{MSL}^{\blacklozenge}.$$

(where we identify $\mathcal{A}$ with $\mathbf{CONV}_1(\mathcal{A})$ and $\langle \mathcal{A}, M^* \rangle[s]$ is $\langle \mathcal{A}, M^*_s \rangle$ because in the translation there is only a free variable of sort 1; namely, v).

Proof

We are going to do this by induction over the construction of α.

(F1) If α is an atomic formula, that is $\alpha \equiv Px_1 \dots x_n$ or $\alpha \equiv \bot$:

$$\begin{aligned} \langle \mathcal{A}, M \rangle, s \models Px_1 \dots x_n \ &\text{iff } \langle M(x_1), \dots, M(x_n), s \rangle \in P^{\mathcal{A}} \\ &\text{iff } \langle M^*_s(x_1), \dots, M^*_s(x_n), M^*_s(v) \rangle \in P^{\mathcal{A}} \end{aligned}$$

(since $P^{\mathcal{A}} = P^{\mathcal{A}^*}$)

$$\begin{aligned} &\text{iff } \langle \mathcal{A}^*, M^*_s \rangle \models Px_1 \dots x_n v \\ &\text{iff } \langle \mathcal{A}, M^*_s \rangle \models \mathbf{TRANS}^{\blacklozenge}(\alpha)[v] \\ &\text{iff } \langle \mathcal{A}, M^* \rangle[s] \models \mathbf{TRANS}^{\blacklozenge}(\alpha)[v] \end{aligned}$$

$$\begin{aligned} \langle \mathcal{A}, M \rangle, s \models \bot \ &\text{iff } \langle \mathcal{A}^*, M^*_s \rangle \models v \neq v \\ &\text{iff } \langle \mathcal{A}, M^*_s \rangle \models \mathbf{TRANS}^{\blacklozenge}(\bot)[v] \\ &\text{iff } \langle \mathcal{A}, M^* \rangle[s] \models \mathbf{TRANS}^{\blacklozenge}(\bot)[v] \end{aligned}$$

(F2) If $\alpha \equiv \neg\beta$ (respectively, $\alpha \equiv \beta \to \gamma$, or $\alpha \equiv \beta \wedge \gamma$, or $\alpha \equiv \beta \vee \gamma$, or $\alpha \equiv \beta \leftrightarrow \gamma$) and the theorem holds for β (respectively for β and γ) then it holds for α. The proof is trivial.

(F3) If $\alpha \equiv \forall x\beta$ and the theorem is true for β, then:

$$\begin{aligned} \langle \mathcal{A}, M \rangle, s \models \forall x\beta \ &\text{iff for all } \mathrm{x} \in A \ \langle \mathcal{A}, M^{\mathrm{x}}_{x} \rangle, s \models \beta \\ &\text{iff for all } \mathrm{x} \in A \ \langle \mathcal{A}, (M^{\mathrm{x}}_{x})^*_s \rangle \models \mathbf{TRANS}^{\blacklozenge}(\beta)[v] \end{aligned}$$

iff for all $x \in A$ $\langle \mathcal{A}, (M^*_s)^x_x \rangle \models TRANS^\blacklozenge(\beta)[v]$

(since $(M^x_x)^*_s = (M^*_s)^x_x$)

iff $\langle \mathcal{A}, M^*_s \rangle \models \forall x\, TRANS^\blacklozenge(\beta)[v]$

iff $\langle \mathcal{A}, M^*_s \rangle \models TRANS^\blacklozenge(\forall x\beta)[v]$

iff $\langle \mathcal{A}, M^* \rangle[s] \models TRANS^\blacklozenge(\forall x\beta)[v]$

(similarly for $\exists x\beta$)

(F4) If $\alpha \equiv \Box\beta$ and the theorem holds for β, then:

$\langle \mathcal{A}, M \rangle, s \models \Box\beta$ iff for all $t \in W$ $\langle \mathcal{A}, M \rangle, t \models \beta$

iff for all $t \in W$ $\langle \mathcal{A}, M^*_t \rangle \models TRANS^\blacklozenge(\beta)[v]$

iff for all $t \in W$ $\langle \mathcal{A}, (M^*_s)^t_v \rangle \models TRANS^\blacklozenge(\beta)[v]$

iff $\langle \mathcal{A}, M^*_s \rangle \models \forall v TRANS^\blacklozenge(\beta)[v]$

iff $\langle \mathcal{A}, M^*_s \rangle \models TRANS^\blacklozenge(\Box\beta)[v]$ ▮

iff $\langle \mathcal{A}, M^* \rangle[s] \models TRANS^\blacklozenge(\Box\beta)[v]$

(similarly for $\Diamond\beta$) ▮

5.3.4. Corollaries (lemma 1).

(1) Let α be a formula of **FOML**, $\mathcal{A} = \langle W, A, \langle P^{\mathcal{A}} \rangle_{P \in REL.CONS} \rangle$ a modal structure for S5 and M an assignment:

$\langle \mathcal{A}, M \rangle \models \alpha$ in **FOML** iff $\langle \mathcal{A}, M^* \rangle \models \forall u TRANS^\blacklozenge(\alpha)[u]$ in **MSL**$^\blacklozenge$

(where $\mathcal{A}$ is identified with **CONV**$_1(\mathcal{A})$ and M^* is defined in 5.3.2).

(2) Let α be a sentence of **FOML**, $\mathcal{A}$ a structure for S5 and $s \in W$ a world of $\mathcal{A}$:

(a) $\mathcal{A}, s \models \alpha$ in **FOML** iff $\mathcal{A}[s] \models TRANS^\blacklozenge(\alpha)[v]$ in **MSL**$^\blacklozenge$

(b) $\mathcal{A} \models \alpha$ in **FOML** iff $\mathcal{A}$ is a model of the sentence of **MSL**$^\blacklozenge$ $\forall u TRANS^\blacklozenge(\alpha)[u]$

Proof

(1) follows easily from 5.3.3 and its definitions. For (2) we see that: (a) follows from 5.3.3 and the coincidence theorem which can be proved easily for the logic **FOML**. (b) is then obvious. ▮

5.3.5. Representation theorem.

For all sentences α of **FOML**,

$\models \alpha$ in **FOML** iff $\models \forall v(TRANS^\blacklozenge(\alpha)[v])$ in **MSL**$^\blacklozenge$

Proof

[$\Longrightarrow$] Let $\models \alpha$. For all $\mathcal{A}$ and $s \in \mathbf{W}$ we have $\mathcal{A}, s \models \alpha$. By 5.3.4, $\mathcal{A}[s] \models$ **TRANS**$^{\blacklozenge}(\alpha)[v]$ for all $s \in \mathbf{W}$. (We identify $\mathcal{A}$ with **CONV**$_1(\mathcal{A})$). Therefore, $\mathcal{A} \models \forall v($**TRANS**$^{\blacklozenge}(\alpha)[v])$. So $\models \forall v($**TRANS**$^{\blacklozenge}(\alpha)[v])$.

[$\Longleftarrow$] Let $\models \forall v($**TRANS**$^{\blacklozenge}(\alpha)[v])$. For all $\mathcal{B} \in$ ST(MSL$^{\blacklozenge}$) and $s \in \mathbf{B}_1$, $\mathcal{B}[s] \models$ **TRANS**$^{\blacklozenge}(\alpha)[v]$. Therefore, for all $s \in \mathbf{B}_1$, $\mathcal{B}, s \models \alpha$. (We identify $\mathcal{B}$ with **CONV**$_2(\mathcal{B})$). So $\models \alpha$.

5.3.6. Enumerability theorem.

The set of S5-valid formulas is recursively enumerable.

Proof

Use 1.2.2 and 5.3.5. ▮

5.3.7. Strong version of lemma 2.

For every many-sorted structure $\mathcal{B}$ of signature $\Sigma^{\blacklozenge}$ there is a structure **CONV**$_2(\mathcal{B})$, **CONV**$_2(\mathcal{B}) \in$ **ST(FOML)** satisfying:

(a) **CONV**$_2(\mathcal{B}), s \models \varphi$ in **FOML** iff $\mathcal{B}[s] \models$ **TRANS**$^{\blacklozenge}(\alpha)[v]$ in **MSL**$^{\blacklozenge}$

(b) **CONV**$_2(\mathcal{B}) \models \varphi$ in **FOML** iff $\mathcal{B} \models \forall v($**TRANS**$^{\blacklozenge}(\alpha)[v])$ in **MSL**$^{\blacklozenge}$

Proof

The proof is straightforward using 5.3.3. You identify $\mathcal{B}$ and **CONV**$_2$. ▮

5.3.8. Main theorem.

Let Π be a set of sentences of **FOML** and φ a sentence of **FOML**:

$\Pi \models \varphi$ in modal logic iff **TRANS**$^{\blacklozenge}(\Pi)[v] \models$ **TRANS**$^{\blacklozenge}(\varphi)[v]$ in **MSL**$^{\blacklozenge}$

Proof

Use 5.3.4, 5.3.7 and 1.3.1. ▮

5.4. Metaproperties of FOML-S5: compactness and Löwenheim Skolem.

We have now proved that the $\mathbf{MSL}^{\blacklozenge}$ formulas which result from the translation of the modal theory S5 are semantically interconnected with the primitive ones; that is, the $\mathbf{MSL}^{\blacklozenge}$ theory which is the translation of S5 is semantically a faithful reproduction of this one. From this representation theorem we have derived enumerability for **FOML**. We have also proved the main theorem from where we can prove compactness and Löwenheim-Skolem for **FOML**-S5.

5.5. Soundness and completeness of S5.

As in the preceding section, we shall prove the soundness and completeness of S5 using the corresponding results of **MSL**; namely, the theorems 7.3. and 7.4. of Chapter VI. To be able to apply these, we shall prove lemmas 3 and 4 (recall section 1.4 in this chapter).

5.5.1. Lemma 3.

If $\vdash_{S5}\alpha$ then $\vdash_{\mathbf{MSL}} \forall v(\mathbf{TRANS}^{\blacklozenge}\alpha[u])$, for every sentence α of **FOML**.

Proof

Since the first-order part of S5 is the same than in many-sorted logic, we only have to check that the axioms of S5 are translated into theorems of $\mathbf{MSL}^{\blacklozenge}$ and that the translation of the rule of necessitation is a derived rule of $\mathbf{MSL}^{\blacklozenge}$.

Df◊ $\exists v\mathbf{TRANS}^{\blacklozenge}(\alpha)[v] \leftrightarrow \neg\forall v\mathbf{TRANS}^{\blacklozenge}(\neg\alpha)[u]$

K $\forall v(\mathbf{TRANS}^{\blacklozenge}(\alpha)[v] \rightarrow \mathbf{TRANS}^{\blacklozenge}(\beta)[v]) \rightarrow (\forall v\mathbf{TRANS}^{\blacklozenge}(\alpha)[v] \rightarrow \forall v\mathbf{TRANS}^{\blacklozenge}(\beta)[v])$

5 $\exists v\mathbf{TRANS}^{\blacklozenge}(\alpha)[v] \rightarrow \forall v(\exists v\mathbf{TRANS}^{\blacklozenge}(\alpha)[v])$

All these translations are theorems of our calculus $\mathbf{MSL}^{\blacklozenge}$ with very easy proofs. The rule of necessitation, (N), is translated into

If $\vdash_{\mathbf{MSL}}\mathbf{TRANS}^{\blacklozenge}(\alpha)[v]$, then $\vdash_{\mathbf{MSL}}\forall v\mathbf{TRANS}^{\blacklozenge}(\alpha)[v]$

which is a derived rule of the many-sorted calculus. ▮

5.5.2. Theorem 3.

If $\Gamma\vdash_{S5}\alpha$ then $\forall v\mathbf{TRANS}^{\blacklozenge}(\Gamma)[v] \vdash_{\mathbf{MSL}} \forall v\mathbf{TRANS}^{\blacklozenge}\alpha[v]$, where $\Gamma\cup\{\alpha\}\subseteq \mathbf{SENT}(\mathbf{FOML})$.

Proof

Due to the properties of the calculus, you can use 1.4.1. Also apply 5.5.1. ▮

5.5.3. Lemma 4 for the logic S5.

For all $\alpha \in$ SENT(FOML), $\vdash_{MSL} \forall v$TRANS$^{\blacklozenge}(\alpha)[v]$ iff $\vdash_{S5}\alpha$.

Proof

The proof is left to the reader. ▮

5.5.4. Soundness and completeness of S5.

$\Gamma \vdash_{S5}\alpha$ iff $\Gamma \models \alpha$, for every $\Gamma \cup \{\alpha\} \subseteq$ SENT(FOML).

Proof

Use 1.4.4, 5.5.3 and 5.3.8. ▮

6.- DYNAMIC LOGIC.

6.1. General idea.

Propositional dynamic logic[74] (**PDL**) is a powerful program logic used as a metalanguage for talking about computer programs. A program - *i.e.*, an algorithm - is basically a mechanical procedure allowing us to obtain certain values from certain data. During the execution of a program the memory registers of the computer change; thus, a program can be seen as a dynamic object - that is, as an object able to make the computer pass from one state to another. A state can be seen as the content of the memory registers used by the program. Due to the change of state, the truth values of the formulas describing it also change. The objective of the logic of programs is to create a logical-mathematical basis to be able to express our reasoning about computer programs. Which properties of programs would we like to express in the logic of programs? In the first place, it is very useful to be able to express and prove that a certain program is correct; that is, its adequacy to the aim for which it was designed. It is also interesting to express the property of halting or ending; that is, that the program is not inducing a never-ending computation. Another important property is equivalence between programs. It is also interesting to formalize the very general features of the most common programs; for instance, ***WHILE*** programs or ***IF THEN*** programs. It would also be very nice to have a deductive calculus in which to verify our reasoning about computer programs. **PDL** provides all that: it is a program logic in which most of the interesting properties of computer programs can be expressed; in particular, all the properties just mentioned. **PDL** possesses a weakly complete calculus but it is not a compact logic.

In classical logic - and, in particular, in model theory - our point of departure is a well known mathematical reality and we introduce the formal language to talk about it, the bridge between these two mathematical realities being the notion of truth, and based on it, the notion of consequence. The deductive calculus, with its deduction rules, is a mechanical replica of the notion of consequence which we obtain later.

In contrast with this situation, in the case of the programming languages, what we have first, our immediate reality, is the formalism and its rules and we search for a semantics for it. It is obvious that the real model of what is happening is the *CPU*, its memory registers, but this

[74]A survey of dynamic logic is in Harel [1984].

model is too complex and beyond the limits of a nice concise and rigorous mathematical analysis. For the philosophers the situation is not new, due to the similarities with modal logic, where the definition of the modal systems came before the definition of the semantics. It is quite curious that - certainly for different reasons - modal logic was the font of inspiration for the logic of programs.

Why are we not taking classical logic whose languages, calculus and structures are so well known and studied?
In principle, classical logic is static, there is no need to consider a change of truth values due to anything like a change of state. In modal logic we do express these changes and this is the reason why **PDL** uses modal logic as its basis. Modal models, in particular, Kripke models, suit **PDL** perfectly. **W** is now a universe of states. With each program we associate an accessibility relation in such a way that a pair of states, $\langle s,t \rangle$, is in that relation if and only if there is a computation of the program transforming the state **s** into the state t. Thus, a program is conceived as a binary relation between initial and final states.

Associating an accessibility relation to every basic program, we have to deal with several of them simultaneously; dynamic logic is multi-modal. As you will see, what we do to express this is to put a program letter into the square or diamond. Besides this extension of considering several accessibility relations simultaneously, we combine them by program operators. In fact, this is the most important feature of **PDL** and you will see how the axioms of this logic are not describing, as are the axioms in modal logic, the accessibility relation in itself, but the operation our program operators perform in them.

The connections between modal logic and propositional dynamic logic have been investigated in several places[75], mainly on the basis of Tarskian algebraic logic[76].

6.2. A formal language for PDL.

6.2.1. Alphabet.

The alphabet of **PDL** contains:

(1) Two disjoint sets **ATOM.PROP** and **ATOM.PROG**, of atomic formulas and programs

[75]See Orlowska [1989] and Venema [1989].

[76]Henkin, Monk & Tarski [1971, 1985], Tarski & Givant [1987].

with $\bot \in$ **ATOM.PROP**. We will use the letter P for elements of **ATOM.PROP** other than $\bot$, and Q for those in **ATOM.PROG**. When needed, we will add subscripts: P_0, P_1, P_2,... and the same for atomic programs.

(2) The connectives: $\neg$, $\wedge$, $\vee$, $\rightarrow$ and $\leftrightarrow$.

(3) Program operators: $\cup$, ; and *.

(4) Test operator: ?

(5) Modal operators: $\langle\rangle$ and $[]$.

(6) Parentheses:) and (. ▮

6.2.2. Definition of formulas and programs.

Formulas and programs of **PDL** are inductively defined from the symbols in the alphabet.

FORM(PDL) and **PROG(PDL)** (respectively, formulas of **PDL** and programs of **PDL**) are the smallest sets satisfying:

(F1) and (F2) as in definition 3.2.2 for modal logic.

(F3) If $\varphi \in$ **FORM(PDL)** and $a \in$ **PROG(PDL)**, then $\langle a\rangle\varphi$ and $[a]\varphi$ are in **FORM(PDL)**.

(G1) **ATOM.PROG** $\subseteq$ **PROG(PDL)**.

(G2) If $a \in$ **PROG(PDL)** and $b \in$ **PROG(PDL)** then $(a;b)$, $(a \cup b)$ and a^* are all in **PROG(PDL)**.

(G3) Whenever $\varphi \in$ **FORM(PDL)** then $(\varphi?) \in$ **PROG(PDL)**. ▮

Remark.

As you see, for each $\varphi \in$ **FORM(PDL)** we have a whole class of necessitations,

$\{[a]\varphi / a \in$ **PROG(PDL)**$\}$

6.2.3. Intuitive meaning of formulas and programs.

$(a;b)$	means	"do a followed by b".
$(a \cup b)$	means	"do a or b".
a^*	means	"do a any (but finite) number of times"
$\langle a\rangle\varphi$	means	"a is totally sound with respect to output condition φ"
$[a]\varphi$	means	"a is partially sound with respect to output condition φ"

6.3. Semantics.

In **PDL**, as in **ML**, the notion of truth is not an absolute one, but relative to certain states. PD structures are composed from a domain of states (or worlds), certain unary relations on states and certain binary relations on states.

6.3.1. Definition of Kripke structures.

$\mathcal{A} = \langle W, \langle P^{\mathcal{A}} \rangle_{P \in \mathrm{ATOM.PROP}}, \langle Q^{\mathcal{A}} \rangle_{Q \in \mathrm{ATOM.PROG}} \rangle$ is a **PDL** structure iff

(1) $W \neq \emptyset$ is a non-empty set whose elements are called states.

(2) For each $P \in$ ATOM.PROP, $P^{\mathcal{A}}$ is a set of states; that is, $P^{\mathcal{A}} \subseteq W$.

(3) For every $Q \in$ ATOM.PROG, $Q^{\mathcal{A}}$ is a binary relation on states; that is, $Q^{\mathcal{A}} \subseteq W \times W$.

(Each program gets as interpretation a set of pairs of states: initial and final states.) ▮

Notation remark.

We will say that $\mathcal{A}$ is of signature σ, where:

$$\begin{aligned} \sigma: \quad \mathrm{ATOM.PROP} \cup \mathrm{ATOM.PROG} &\longrightarrow \{\langle 0,1\rangle, \langle 0,1,1\rangle\} \\ P \in \mathrm{ATOM.PROP} &\longmapsto \langle 0,1\rangle \\ Q \in \mathrm{ATOM.PROG} &\longmapsto \langle 0,1,1\rangle \end{aligned}$$

6.3.2. Definition of interpretation.

When a **PD**-structure $\mathcal{A}$ is given, each formula $\varphi \in$ **FORM(PDL)** gets a value $\mathcal{A}(\varphi)$ and every program a of **PROG(PDL)** also gets a value $\mathcal{A}(a)$. The interpretation of φ, $\mathcal{A}(\varphi)$, is the set of states where φ is true and the interpretation of a, $\mathcal{A}(a)$, is a relation of pairs of initial and final states between which program a can lead us. So we extend for all the formulas and programs the values given in the structure for the atomic ones.

Assume that we have a structure $\mathcal{A}$ of signature σ. Let us define $\mathcal{A}(\varphi)$ and $\mathcal{A}(a)$ by induction on the formation of formulas and programs. The interpretation of formulas is as in modal logic (definition 3.6.1. in this chapter). So we will only present it here for programs.

(G1) $\mathcal{A}(Q) = Q^{\mathcal{A}}$

(G2) $\mathcal{A}(a \cup b) = \mathcal{A}(a) \cup \mathcal{A}(b)$

$\mathcal{A}(a;b) = \mathcal{A}(a) \circ \mathcal{A}(b)$

$\mathcal{A}(a^*) = (\mathcal{A}(a))^*$

(where $(\mathcal{A}(a))^* = \{\langle s,t\rangle \in W^2 \,/\, \exists k \exists s_0,\ldots,s_k (s_0 = s \;\&\; s_k = t \;\&\; \forall i (i \in \{1,\ldots,k\} \Rightarrow \langle s_{i-1}, s_i\rangle \in \mathcal{A}(a)))\}$.

(G3) $\mathcal{A}(\varphi?) = \{\langle s,s\rangle / s \in \mathcal{A}(\varphi)\}$ ▮

Remark.

As you see, $\mathcal{A}(a^*)$ is the reflexive and transitive closure of $\mathcal{A}(a)$. For instance, if your relation $\mathcal{A}(a)$ is the successor function, $\mathcal{A}(a) = \{\langle n,m\rangle \in \mathbb{N}^2 / m = n+1\}$, then $\mathcal{A}(a^*)$ is the ordering relation; $\mathcal{A}(a^*) = \{\langle n,m\rangle \in \mathbb{N}^2 / n \leq m\}$.

6.3.3. Truth, satisfiability, validity and consequence.

Given a PD-structure $\mathcal{A}$, state s and formula $\varphi \in$ FORM(PDL):

(1) $\mathcal{A}, s \models \varphi$ (φ is ***true at state*** s in $\mathcal{A}$) iff $s \in \mathcal{A}(\varphi)$. ▮

(2) $\mathcal{A} \models \varphi$ (φ is ***valid in*** $\mathcal{A}$) iff $\mathcal{A}, s \models \varphi$ for all s in W of $\mathcal{A}$. ▮

(3) $\models \varphi$ (φ is ***valid***) iff $\mathcal{A} \models \varphi$ for all PD-structures $\mathcal{A}$ with signature σ. ▮

Let $\Gamma \cup \{\varphi\} \subseteq$ FORM(PDL).

(4) $\mathcal{A}, s \models \Gamma$ (Γ is ***satisfiable at state*** s of $\mathcal{A}$) iff $\mathcal{A}, s \models \varphi$, all $\varphi \in \Gamma$. ▮

(5) $\mathcal{A} \models_{\exists} \Gamma$ (Γ is ***satisfiable at*** $\mathcal{A}$) iff there is a state s such that $\mathcal{A}, s \models \Gamma$. ▮

(6) $\mathcal{A} \models_{\forall} \Gamma$ (Γ is ***valid in*** $\mathcal{A}$) iff for every state s in $\mathcal{A}$: $\mathcal{A}, s \models \Gamma$. ▮

(7) $\Gamma \models_{L} \varphi$ (φ is a ***local consequence*** of Γ) iff for every PD-structure $\mathcal{A}$ and state s in $\mathcal{A}$: whenever $s \in \bigcap\{\mathcal{A}(\psi) / \psi \in \Gamma\}$ then $s \in \mathcal{A}(\varphi)$ ▮

(8) $\Gamma \models_{G} \varphi$ (φ is a ***global consequence*** of Γ) iff for every PD-structure $\mathcal{A}$:

whenever $\bigcap\{\mathcal{A}(\psi) / \psi \in \Gamma\} = W$ then $\mathcal{A}(\varphi) = W$. ▮

Remark.

In PDL we use two kinds of consequence relations: local and global. Local consequence implies global.

6.3.4. Definability in dynamic structures.

Given a structure $\mathcal{A}$ of signature σ, we say that the set $R \subseteq W$ is ***dynamic definable*** in $\mathcal{A}$ just if $R = \mathcal{A}(\varphi)$ for a certain $\varphi \in$ FORM(PDL). And we say that the relation $R \subseteq W \times W$ is ***dynamic definable*** in $\mathcal{A}$ when $R = \mathcal{A}(a)$ for a certain $a \in$ PROG(PDL). ▮

6.3.5. Expressing properties of programs in PDL.

Here are some examples of formalizations in PDL.

(1) *IF* φ *THEN a ELSE b* $\qquad$ $((\varphi?;a) \cup (\neg\varphi?;b))$

(2) *WHILE* φ *DO* a $((\varphi?;a)^*;\neg\varphi?)$

(3) *STOP* $\bot?$

(4) *REPEAT* a *UNTIL* φ $(a;(\neg\varphi?;a)^*)$

(5) $\langle a\rangle\varphi$ means that a is totally sound with respect to φ, but only in the weak sense. From certain states a takes us to states where φ is true, but for non-deterministic programs, a can just as well take us to states where φ is no longer true.

(6) $[a]\varphi$ means that a is partially sound with respect to φ in the strong sense. The problem is that for a never-ending a the formula $[a]\varphi$ is valid, independently of φ.

(7) We put $[a]\varphi \wedge \langle a\rangle\varphi$ to express total soundness in the strong sense.

(8) $[a]\bot$ expresses that the program has no end.

(9) $\langle a\rangle\varphi \leftrightarrow \langle b\rangle\varphi$ expresses that, as far as condition φ is concerned, the programs a and b are equivalent.

(10) If we want a deterministic program, we can impose this condition: $\langle a\rangle\varphi \rightarrow [a]\varphi$.

6.4. The logic PDL.

PDL shall be described as a normal modal logic in the language of **PDL**; that is, a logic containing ***K*** and closed under the rules of the calculus $\{K,Df\Diamond\}_{(N)}$. (For details, see section 3.4 of this chapter.) In particular, **PDL** is the smallest normal logic containing the schema axioms listed in 6.4.1 below.

6.4.1. Axioms.

A1. $\langle a;b\rangle\varphi \leftrightarrow \langle a\rangle\langle b\rangle\varphi$

A2. $\langle a\cup b\rangle\varphi \leftrightarrow (\langle a\rangle\varphi \vee \langle b\rangle\varphi)$

A3. $\langle a^*\rangle\varphi \leftrightarrow (\varphi \vee \langle a\rangle\langle a^*\rangle\varphi)$

A4. $\langle\varphi?\rangle\psi \leftrightarrow \varphi \wedge \psi$

A5. $[a]\varphi \leftrightarrow \neg\langle a\rangle\neg\varphi$

A6. $[a^*](\varphi \rightarrow [a]\varphi) \rightarrow (\varphi \rightarrow [a^*]\varphi)$

6.4.2. Deductive calculus.

PDL has the axioms for PC, the schema axiom K,

(K) $[a](\varphi \rightarrow \psi) \rightarrow ([a]\varphi \rightarrow [a]\psi)$

the axioms listed in 6.4.1 and it is closed under modus ponens (MP) and necessitation in this general form:

(N) If $\vdash \varphi$, then $\vdash [a]\varphi$ ▮

6.4.3. Known metaproperties of PDL.

A very well known result about **PDL** is that this calculus is sound and complete in the weak sense. That means: $\models \varphi$ iff $\vdash \varphi$, for any formula φ[77].

6.4.4. Non-compactness of PDL.

PDL is not compact.

Proof

We will see that there is a set Γ of sentences such that $\Gamma \models \varphi$ but for no finite subset Σ of Γ, $\Sigma \models \varphi$. The non-compactness of **PDL** is in both senses: local and global.

(1) The non-compactness of **PDL** with local consequence can be proved easily using the set Γ given by $\Gamma = \{P, [Q]P, [Q;Q]P, \ldots, [Q^n]P, \ldots\}$, where Q^n is the repeated composition of Q n times, and the formula $\varphi \equiv [Q^*]P$.
Clearly $\Gamma \models_L \varphi$, but for no finite $\Gamma_0 \subseteq \Gamma$ do we have $\Gamma_0 \models_L \varphi$. To see this, take a finite subset of Γ. Let n be the highest exponent of formulas occurring in this subset. We will give a structure $\mathcal{A}$ where for a state s in $\mathcal{A}$,

$$s \in \bigcap \{\mathcal{A}(\gamma) / \gamma \in \Gamma_0\} \text{ but } s \notin \mathcal{A}(\varphi)$$

Take $\mathcal{A} = \langle \mathbb{N}, P^{\mathcal{A}}, Q^{\mathcal{A}} \rangle$ where $P^{\mathcal{A}} = \{0, \ldots, n\}$ and $Q^{\mathcal{A}}$ is the successor function.
Take s as 0.

(2) The non-compactness of **PDL** with global consequence is shown easily by using the set Γ given by

$$\Gamma = \{P_1 \rightarrow P_2, P_1 \rightarrow [Q]P_2, P_1 \rightarrow [Q;Q]P_2, \ldots, P_1 \rightarrow [Q^n]P_2, \ldots\}$$

and the formula $\varphi \equiv P_1 \rightarrow [Q^*]P_2$.
Clearly $\Gamma \models_G \varphi$, but for no finite $\Gamma_0 \subseteq \Gamma$ do we have $\Gamma_0 \models_G \varphi$. To see this, take a finite subset of Γ.

Let $P_1 \rightarrow [Q^n]P_2$ be a formula not in Γ_0.

Take $\mathcal{A} = \langle \mathbb{N}, P_1^{\mathcal{A}}, P_2^{\mathcal{A}}, Q^{\mathcal{A}} \rangle$ where $P_1^{\mathcal{A}} = \{0\}$, $P_2^{\mathcal{A}} = \mathbb{N} - \{n\}$ and $Q^{\mathcal{A}}$ is the successor function.

Since $\mathcal{A}(P_1) = \{0\}$, in any state other than 0, every formula of Γ is true.

In the state 0, the formulas $P_1 \rightarrow [Q^m]P_2$ are true for $m \neq n$; the only exception being

[77]The completeness proof of this calculus is in Harel [1984], also in Goldblatt [1992].

for $m = n$. Since this formula is not in Γ_0,

$$\bigcap\{\mathcal{A}(\gamma)/\ \gamma\in\Gamma_0\} = \mathbb{N} \text{ but } \mathcal{A}(\varphi) \neq \mathbb{N} \quad \blacksquare$$

Remark.
It is clear, then, that the calculus cannot be complete in the strong sense.

7.- PROPOSITIONAL DYNAMIC LOGIC AS MANY-SORTED LOGIC.

What I want to do now is to present a many-sorted theory, **SOLO^2**, which is equivalent to **PDL**, both syntactically and semantically. As we did before in the cases dealing with **SOL**, or when we translated modal logic into **MSL**, we are going to define a syntactical translation from **PDL** into **MSL** and a semantical conversion of structures. Furthermore, I will define a theory whose axioms are: comprehension sentences for translations of **PDL** formulas and program; and abstract conditions for certain axioms in **PDL**. As you will see, the treatment I will apply to **PDL** is similar to the one used for **PML**.

Based upon **PD**-structures, we build many-sorted structures. Of special use are the extended dynamic frames. The idea behind this construction is to build structures with universes for: (1) states, (2) sets defined on the set of states and (3) relations defined on the sets of states. In extended dynamic frames we want to have in the universes for sets and relations all the dynamically definable ones.

On the other hand, when we translate formulas and programs of **PDL** we want the new **MSL** formula to define in a many-sorted structure the same set or relation that the original formula was defining in a **PD** structure, both structures having a common basis. Since we will be using several kinds of many-sorted structures (*i.e.*, extended dynamic frames, general structures and standard second order structures), the conclusion changes according to the kind being used.

7.1. Formal many-sorted language MSL$^{♪}$.

7.1.1. The signature $\Sigma^{♪}$.
Let **SORT** $= \{0,1,\langle 0,1\rangle,\langle 0,1,1\rangle\}$.

The signature $\Sigma^{♪} = \langle \mathbf{SORT}, \mathbf{FUNC} \rangle$ is such that:

(1) **SORT** is the set defined above.

(2) $\mathbf{FUNC}^{♪}$ is a function which takes as arguments the elements of $\mathbf{OPER.SYM}^{♪}$ consisting of: **ATOM.PROP** and **ATOM.PROG** of **PDL**, the equalities among individuals, sets and relations, E_1, E_2, E_3, the connective functions and the membership relations ε_1 and ε_2.

$$\mathbf{FUNC}^{♪}: \mathbf{OPER.SYM}^{♪} \longrightarrow [\mathrm{S}_{\omega}(\mathbf{SORT})]$$

where: all the values are the expected ones; see the values given in 4.1.1 by the "sister" function $\mathbf{FUNC}^{\bullet}$. Of course, we add:

$\mathbf{FUNC}^{♪}(Q) = \langle 0,1,1 \rangle$, for $Q \in \mathbf{ATOM.PROG}$

$\mathbf{FUNC}^{♪}(E_3) = \langle 0, \langle 0,1,1 \rangle, \langle 0,1,1 \rangle \rangle$

$\mathbf{FUNC}^{♪}(\varepsilon_2) = \langle 0,1,1,\langle 0,1,1 \rangle \rangle$ ▓

7.1.2. Alphabet.

The alphabet of a many-sorted language suited for **PDL** must contain all operation symbols in $\mathbf{OPER.SYM}^{♪}$ and a countable set of variables for each $i \in \mathbf{SORT} - \{0\}$.

We will use lower-case for individual variables of sort 1, ($u, v, z, \ldots, u_1, u_2, u_3, \ldots$) and upper-case for relational variables ($X, Y, Z, \ldots, X_1, X_2, X_3, \ldots$ for unary relation variables of sort $\langle 0,1 \rangle$ and $X^2, Y^2, Z^2, \ldots, X^2_1, X^2_2, X^2_3, \ldots$ for binary relation variables of sort $\langle 0,1,1 \rangle$).

As well as all that, we have the quantifiers: $\exists$ and $\forall$. ▓

7.1.3. Expressions.

The set of expressions of this language is defined in the many-sorted fashion. As usual, formulas are the expressions of type 0. Recall that now $P \in \mathbf{ATOM.PROP}$ is no longer an atomic formula but a unary relation symbol of type $\langle 0,1 \rangle$, while $Q \in \mathbf{ATOM.PROG}$ is a binary relation symbol of type $\langle 0,1,1 \rangle$. ▓

7.2. Translating function.

From **PDL** with $\mathbf{ATOM.PROP} \cup \mathbf{ATOM.PROG}$ as propositional and program constants, we pass to a many-sorted language of signature $\Sigma^{\flat}$ having

$$\langle\langle P\rangle_{P\in \mathbf{ATOM.PROP}}, \langle Q\rangle_{Q\in \mathbf{ATOM.PROG}}\rangle$$

as unary and binary relation symbols.

7.2.1. Definition.

With every $\varphi\in$ **FORM(PDL)** and individual variable u we associate as its translation a formula $\mathbf{TRANS}^{\flat}(\varphi)[u]$ in the many-sorted language. With every program $a\in$ **PROG(PDL)** and all variables u, v, we associate a formula $\mathbf{TRANS}^{\flat}(a)[u,v]$:

TRANS$^{\flat}$ coincides with **TRANS*** of definition 4.2.1 for the formulas obtained by the rules (F1) and (F2).

(F3) $\mathbf{TRANS}^{\flat}(\langle a\rangle\varphi)[u] \equiv \exists v(\mathbf{TRANS}^{\flat}(a)[u,v] \wedge \mathbf{TRANS}^{\flat}(\varphi)[v])$ where v must be a new variable (the first one in a given ordering) and $\mathbf{TRANS}^{\flat}(a)[u,v]$ is defined below. Similarly for $[a]\varphi$.

(G1) $\mathbf{TRANS}^{\flat}(Q)[u,v] \equiv Quv$ for each $Q\in$ **ATOM.PROG**

(G2) $\mathbf{TRANS}^{\flat}(a;b)[u,v] \equiv \exists w(\mathbf{TRANS}^{\flat}(a)[u,w] \wedge \mathbf{TRANS}^{\flat}(b)[w,v])$

$\mathbf{TRANS}^{\flat}(a \cup b)[u,v] \equiv \mathbf{TRANS}^{\flat}(a)[u,v] \vee \mathbf{TRANS}^{\flat}(b)[u,v]$

$\mathbf{TRANS}^{\flat}(a^*)[u,v] \equiv \forall X^2(\mathbf{TRANS}^{\flat}(a) \subseteq X^2 \wedge \mathrm{Refl}\, X^2 \wedge \mathrm{Trans}\, X^2 \rightarrow \varepsilon_2 uvX^2)$

which is an abbreviation for

$$\forall X^2(\forall uv(\mathbf{TRANS}^{\flat}(a)[u,v] \rightarrow \varepsilon_2 uvX^2) \wedge \forall u\, \varepsilon_2 uuX^2 \wedge \forall wuv(\varepsilon_2 wuX^2 \wedge \varepsilon_2 uvX^2 \rightarrow \varepsilon_2 wvX^2) \rightarrow \varepsilon_2 uvX^2)$$

(G3) $\mathbf{TRANS}^{\flat}(\varphi?)[u,v] \equiv \mathbf{TRANS}^{\flat}(\varphi)[u] \wedge u = v$ ∎

Remarks.

(1) Then $\mathbf{TRANS}^{\flat}(a^*)$ represents the smallest reflexive and transitive relation containing the original $\mathbf{TRANS}^{\flat}(a)$.

(2) As you see, each loop-free formula or program of **PDL** is translated into a formula of **MSL** where in fact only individual quantification is needed. We need quantification over sort $\langle 0,1,1\rangle$ for translating the loop.

7.3. Structures and frames built on PD-structures.

Please read the comment at the beginning of section 4.3; $\Sigma^{\flat}$ is a special case of $\Sigma^{\square}$ too.

7.3.1. Frames built on PD-structures of signature σ.

Given a PD-structure $\mathcal{A}$, of signature σ,

$$\mathcal{A} = \langle \mathbf{W}, \langle P^{\mathcal{A}} \rangle_{P \in \mathrm{ATOM.PROP}}, \langle Q^{\mathcal{A}} \rangle_{Q \in \mathrm{ATOM.PROG}} \rangle$$

we say that $\mathcal{AF}$ is a ***frame built on*** $\mathcal{A}$ iff

$$\mathcal{AF} = \langle \mathbf{W}, \mathbf{W}', \mathbf{W}'', \langle P^{\mathcal{A}} \rangle_{P \in \mathrm{ATOM.PROP}}, \langle Q^{\mathcal{A}} \rangle_{Q \in \mathrm{ATOM.PROG}} \rangle$$

where:

(i) $\mathbf{W}' \subseteq \mathcal{P}\mathbf{W}$ and $P^{\mathcal{A}} \in \mathbf{W}'$, for all $P \in$ ATOM.PROP,

(ii) $\mathbf{W}'' \subseteq \mathcal{P}(\mathbf{W} \times \mathbf{W})$ and $Q^{\mathcal{A}} \in \mathbf{W}''$, for all $Q \in$ ATOM.PROG. ▮

The class of frames built on structures of signature σ will be denoted by $\mathcal{F}$. ▮

Remarks on notation.

In what follows we will be using frames, second order standard structures, general structures and what I baptized as extended dynamic frames; all of them are built on PD-structures of signature σ.

7.3.2. Extended dynamic frames.

Given a PD-structure $\mathcal{A}$ we say that $\mathcal{AE}$ is an extended dynamic frame built on $\mathcal{A}$ iff

$$\mathcal{AE} = \langle \mathbf{W}, \mathbf{W}', \mathbf{W}'', \langle P^{\mathcal{A}} \rangle_{P \in \mathrm{PROP.CONS}}, \langle Q^{\mathcal{A}} \rangle_{Q \in \mathrm{PROG.CONS}} \rangle$$

satisfies:

(1) $\emptyset \in \mathbf{W}'$ and $\mathbf{W} \in \mathbf{W}'$

(2) $\{P^{\mathcal{A}} / P \in \mathrm{ATOM.PROP}\} \subseteq \mathbf{W}'$ and $\{Q^{\mathcal{A}} / Q \in \mathrm{ATOM.PROG}\} \subseteq \mathbf{W}''$

(3) $\forall RS(R,S \in \mathbf{W}' \Longrightarrow R \cup S, \mathbf{W}-R \in \mathbf{W}')$

(4) $\forall RS(R,S \in \mathbf{W}'' \Longrightarrow R \cup S, R \circ S, R^* \in \mathbf{W}'')$

(5) $\forall R(R \in \mathbf{W}' \Longrightarrow I_R \in \mathbf{W}'')$ (where I_R is the identity on R)

(6) $\forall RS(R \in \mathbf{W}'' \;\&\; S \in \mathbf{W}' \Longrightarrow \mathrm{Dom}(R \cap (\mathbf{W} \times S)) \in \mathbf{W}')$ ▮

The class of extended dynamic frames built on structures of signature σ will be denoted by $\mathcal{E}$. ▮

Let CONV_1 be a function giving to each $\mathcal{A} \in \mathrm{ST(PDL)}$ as value a unique extended dynamic frame built on $\mathcal{A}$; namely, the least extended dynamic frame built on $\mathcal{A}$. ▮

Remark.

The idea behind this construction (of the extended dynamic frames) is to have in the universes of the structure all sets and relations that can be defined in $\mathcal{A}$ by **PDL** formulas and programs. Lemma 7.3.3 shows that the aim has been achieved.

7.3.3. Lemma.

$\mathcal{E} \subseteq \{\mathcal{B} / \exists\mathcal{A}\,(\mathcal{A}$ of signature σ & $\mathcal{B} \in \mathcal{F}$ is built on $\mathcal{A}$ & $\{\mathcal{A}(\varphi)/\varphi \in \mathbf{FORM(PDL)}\} \subseteq \mathbf{W'}$ & $\{\mathcal{A}(a)/a \in \mathbf{PROG(PDL)}\} \subseteq \mathbf{W''})\}$

Proof

We want to show that given a **PD**-structure $\mathcal{A}$ of signature σ and an extended dynamic frame $\mathcal{AE}$ built on $\mathcal{A}$

$$\mathcal{AE} = \langle \mathbf{W}, \mathbf{W'}, \mathbf{W''}, \langle P^{\mathcal{A}}\rangle_{P \in \mathbf{ATOM.PROP}}, \langle Q^{\mathcal{A}}\rangle_{Q \in \mathbf{ATOM.PROG}}\rangle$$

then any set or relation dynamic definable in $\mathcal{A}$ is in the corresponding domain of $\mathcal{AE}$. The proof is rather obvious, since conditions on extended dynamic frames are quite ***ad hoc*** (see the similar proof of lemma 4.3.3). ▮

7.3.4. Lemma.

Given a structure $\mathcal{A}$ of signature σ and an extended dynamic frame $\mathcal{AE}$ built on it,

$$\mathcal{AE}(\lambda u \mathbf{TRANS}^{♪}(\varphi)[u]) = \mathcal{A}(\varphi), \text{ for all } \varphi \in \mathbf{FORM(PDL)}$$
$$\mathcal{AE}(\lambda uv \mathbf{TRANS}^{♪}(a)[u,v]) = \mathcal{A}(a), \text{ for all } a \in \mathbf{PROG(PDL)}$$

Proof

The proof, by induction on the construction of formulas and programs, is rather straightforward, see the similar proof of the lemma 4.3.4. Now, we prove that

$$\mathcal{A}(a^*) = \mathcal{AE}(\lambda uv \mathbf{TRANS}^{♪}(a^*)[u,v]).$$

First $\mathcal{A}(a^*) = (\mathcal{A}(a))^* \in \mathbf{W''}$ since $\mathcal{AE}$ is an extended dynamic frame and condition (4) holds. Moreover, $\mathcal{A}(a)) \subseteq \mathcal{A}(a^*)$ and $\mathcal{A}(a^*)$ is reflexive and transitive and it is the least relation with this condition. Therefore,

$$\mathcal{AE}(\lambda uv\ \forall X^2(\mathbf{TRANS}^{♪}(a) \subseteq X^2 \wedge \mathrm{Refl}\, X^2 \wedge \mathrm{Trans}\, X^2 \rightarrow \varepsilon_2 uvX^2)) = \mathcal{A}(a^*) \quad ▮$$

7.3.5. Corollary.

For every extended dynamic frame $\mathcal{AE}$ built on a **PD**-structure $\mathcal{A}$ of signature σ

$$\mathcal{A}, s \models \varphi \text{ in } \mathbf{PDL} \text{ iff } \mathcal{AE}[s](\mathbf{TRANS}^{♪}(\varphi)[u]) = \mathrm{T} \text{ in } \mathrm{MSL} \quad ▮$$

7.3.6. Corollary: lemma 1 (b) for PDL.

$\mathcal{A} \models \varphi$ in PDL iff CONV$_1$(TRANS$^{♪}$(φ)[u]) in MSL. ▮

7.3.7. Corollary: theorem 1.

$\models \varphi$ in PDL iff $\models_{\mathcal{E}} \forall u$TRANS$^{♪}$($\varphi$)[$u$] in MSL.

Proof

Use 7.3.5 and 1.2.1. ▮

7.4. The SOLO^2 theory.

7.4.1. Definition.

We will define a theory which will be proven to be syntactically and semantically equivalent to PDL. The axioms of this theory are:

(1) Comprehension sentences for translations of PDL formulas and programs; that is, all of the form

$$\exists X^2 \forall uv(\varepsilon_2 uvX^2 \leftrightarrow \text{TRANS}^{♪}(a)[u,v]), \text{ for each } a \in \text{PROG(PDL)}$$

$$\exists X \forall u(\varepsilon_1 uX \leftrightarrow \text{TRANS}^{♪}(\varphi)[u]), \text{ for each } \varphi \in \text{FORM(PDL)}$$

(2) Extensionality; for both, sets and relations.

(3) The $\Sigma^{♪}$ many-sorted abstract conditions for PDL axioms A4 and A6.

$$\text{MS(A4)} \equiv \forall X^2 Yu(\exists w(\varepsilon_2 uwX^{2*} \wedge \varepsilon_1 wY) \leftrightarrow (\varepsilon_1 uY \vee \exists v(\varepsilon_2 uvX^2 \wedge \exists w(\varepsilon_2 vwX^{2*} \wedge \varepsilon_1 wY))))$$

$$\text{MS(A6)} \equiv \forall X^2 Yu(\forall w(\varepsilon_2 uwX^{2*} \rightarrow (\varepsilon_1 wY \rightarrow \forall v(\varepsilon_2 wvX^2 \rightarrow \varepsilon_1 vY))) \rightarrow (\varepsilon_1 uY \rightarrow \forall w(\varepsilon_2 uwX^{2*} \rightarrow \varepsilon_1 wY)))$$

(where $\varepsilon_2 uwX^{2*}$ is short for $\forall Z^2(X^2 \subseteq Z^2 \wedge \text{Refl } Z^2 \wedge \text{Trans } Z^2 \rightarrow \varepsilon_2 uwZ^2)$). ▮

7.4.2. Lemma.

For each extended dynamic frame, $\mathcal{AE} \in \mathcal{E}$, $\mathcal{AE}$ is a model of SOLO^2.

Proof

It is easy to see that the comprehension sentences for translations are all satisfied, since by lemma 7.3.4,

$$\mathcal{A}(\varphi) = \mathcal{AE}(\lambda u \mathbf{TRANS}^{\flat}(\varphi)[u]) \text{ and } \mathcal{A}(a) = \mathcal{AE}(\lambda uv \mathbf{TRANS}^{\flat}(a)[u,v])$$

and by lemma 7.3.3 they are in **W'** and **W''**.

What happens with **MS(A4)** and **MS(A6)**?

Claim 1.- $\mathcal{AE}(\mathbf{MS(A4)}) = \mathrm{T}$

Remember that

$$\mathbf{MS(A4)} \equiv \forall X^2 Yu(\exists w(\varepsilon_2 uwX^{2*} \wedge \varepsilon_1 wY) \leftrightarrow (\varepsilon_1 uY \vee \exists v(\varepsilon_2 uvX^2 \wedge \exists w(\varepsilon_2 vwX^{2*} \wedge \varepsilon_1 wY))))$$

Let $\mathrm{S}^2 \in \mathbf{W''}$, $\mathrm{R} \in \mathbf{W'}$ and $\mathrm{s} \in \mathbf{W}$ be any members of these universes. Recall that

$$\mathrm{S}^{2*} = \{\langle \mathrm{s,t} \rangle \in \mathbf{W}^2 \,/\, \exists \mathrm{k} \exists \mathrm{s}_0,\ldots,\mathrm{s}_\mathrm{k} \,(\mathrm{s}_0 = \mathrm{s} \wedge \mathrm{s}_\mathrm{k} = \mathrm{t} \wedge \forall \mathrm{i}(\mathrm{i} \in \{1,\ldots,\mathrm{k}\} \rightarrow \langle \mathrm{s}_{\mathrm{i-1}}, \mathrm{s}_\mathrm{i} \rangle \in \mathrm{S}^2))\}$$

is the smallest reflexive and transitive relation containing S^2. Besides all that, $\mathrm{S}^{2*} \in \mathbf{W''}$ by condition (4). Therefore,

$$\mathrm{S}^{2*} = \mathcal{AE}[\mathrm{S}^2](\lambda uv\, \varepsilon_2 uvX^{2*})$$

(since $\varepsilon_2 uvX^{2*}$ is short for $\forall \mathrm{Z}^2 (X^2 \subseteq \mathrm{Z}^2 \wedge \mathrm{Refl}\ \mathrm{Z}^2 \wedge \mathrm{Trans}\ \mathrm{Z}^2 \rightarrow \varepsilon_2 uv\mathrm{Z}^2)$).

We want to prove that

$$\mathcal{AE}[\mathrm{S}^2,\mathrm{R},\mathrm{s}](\exists w(\varepsilon_2 uwX^{2*} \wedge \varepsilon_1 wY)) = \mathrm{T}$$

$$\text{iff } \mathcal{AE}[\mathrm{S}^2,\mathrm{R},\mathrm{s}](\varepsilon_1 uY \vee \exists v(\varepsilon_2 uvX^2 \wedge \exists w(\varepsilon_2 vwX^{2*} \wedge \varepsilon_1 wY))) = \mathrm{T}$$

[$\Longrightarrow$] Assume that $\mathcal{AE}[\mathrm{S}^2,\mathrm{R},\mathrm{s}](\exists w(\varepsilon_2 uwX^{2*} \wedge \varepsilon_1 wY)) = \mathrm{T}$

Therefore, there is **t** such that $\mathrm{t} \in \mathbf{R}$ and $\langle \mathrm{s,t} \rangle \in \mathrm{S}^{2*}$. If $\mathrm{t} = \mathrm{s}$ we have finished, since then $\mathrm{s} \in \mathbf{R}$ and therefore,

$$\mathcal{AE}[\mathrm{S}^2,\mathrm{R},\mathrm{s}](\varepsilon_1 uY \vee \exists v(\varepsilon_2 uvX^2 \wedge \exists w(\varepsilon_2 vwX^{2*} \wedge \varepsilon_1 wY))) = \mathrm{T}$$

If $\mathrm{t} \neq \mathrm{s}$ there must be $\mathrm{s}_0,\ldots,\mathrm{s}_\mathrm{k}$ such that $\mathrm{s}_0 = \mathrm{s}$, $\mathrm{s}_\mathrm{k} = \mathrm{t}$ and $\langle \mathrm{s}_{\mathrm{i-1}}, \mathrm{s}_\mathrm{i} \rangle \in \mathrm{S}^2$ for $1 \leq \mathrm{i} \leq \mathrm{k}$. Therefore, $\langle \mathrm{s,s}_1 \rangle \in \mathrm{S}^2$, $\langle \mathrm{s}_1,\mathrm{t} \rangle \in \mathrm{S}^{2*}$ and $\mathrm{t} \in \mathbf{R}$. Therefore,

$$\mathcal{AE}[\mathrm{S}^2,\mathrm{R},\mathrm{s}](\varepsilon_1 uY \vee \exists v(\varepsilon_2 uvX^2 \wedge \exists w(\varepsilon_2 vwX^{2*} \wedge \varepsilon_1 wY))) = \mathrm{T}$$

[$\Longleftarrow$] This is quite obvious; use reflexivity of the loop in one case and transitive closure of the loop in the other.

Claim 2.- $\mathcal{AE}(\mathbf{MS(A6)}) = \mathrm{T}$

Remember that

$$MS(A6) \equiv \forall X^2 Yu(\forall w(\varepsilon_2 uwX^{2*} \rightarrow (\varepsilon_1 wY \rightarrow \forall v(\varepsilon_2 wvX^2 \rightarrow \varepsilon_1 vY)) \rightarrow (\varepsilon_1 uY \rightarrow \forall w(\varepsilon_2 uwX^{2*} \rightarrow \varepsilon_1 wY))))$$

Let $S^2 \in \mathbf{W}''$, $R \in \mathbf{W}'$ and $s \in \mathbf{W}$. Assume that

$$\mathcal{AE}[S^2,R,s]\forall w(\varepsilon_2 uwX^{2*} \rightarrow (\varepsilon_1 wY \rightarrow \forall v(\varepsilon_2 wvX^2 \rightarrow \varepsilon_1 vY))) = T$$

and let $s \in R$. We want to show that

$$\mathcal{AE}[S^2,R,s]\forall w(\varepsilon_2 uwX^{2*} \rightarrow \varepsilon_1 wY) = T$$

So let $\langle s,t\rangle \in S^{2*}$ and prove that $t \in R$. Since $\langle s,t\rangle \in S^{2*}$ there must be $\langle s,s_1\rangle \in S^2,\ldots,\langle s_k,t\rangle \in S^2$. We know that $\langle s,s\rangle \in S^{2*}$ and since $s \in R$, then we have that for all r, whenever $\langle s,r\rangle \in S^2$, we also have $r \in R$. Therefore, $t \in R$. ▮

7.4.3. Corollary: Weak version of lemma 2.
$CONV_1(ST(PDL)) \subseteq MOD(SOLO^2)$. ▮

7.4.4. Lemma 3.
For each $\varphi \in \mathbf{FORM(PDL)}$:

whenever $\vdash \varphi$ in **PDL** then we have $\mathbf{SOLO}^2 \vdash \forall u\mathbf{TRANS}^{♪}(\varphi)[u]$ in **MSL**.

Proof
We have to prove (1) and (2) below:

(1) If φ is an axiom of **PDL** then $\forall u\mathbf{TRANS}^{♪}(\varphi)[u]$ is a theorem of $\mathbf{SOLO}^2$.
(2) Inference rules are respected.

Claim 1.- If φ is a tautology then $\vdash \forall u\mathbf{TRANS}^{♪}(\varphi)[u]$.
Let φ be a tautology. That means $\varphi \equiv \varphi_1 \square_1 \ldots \square_n \varphi_{n+1}$ with $\square_i$ an arbitrary connector and each φ_j is either an atomic formula, a negation, or a formula of logical form $[a]\psi$ or $\langle a\rangle\psi$.
In this case

$$\mathbf{TRANS}^{♪}(\varphi)[u] \equiv \mathbf{TRANS}^{♪}(\varphi_1)[u] \;\square_1 \ldots \square_n\; \mathbf{TRANS}^{♪}(\varphi_{n+1})[u]$$

and it is also a tautology of **MSL**. Tautologies are derivables in **MSL** calculus. Therefore,

$\vdash \mathbf{TRANS}^{♪}(\varphi)[u]$ in **MSL**.

Using this derived rule of generalization, $\vdash \forall u\, \mathbf{TRANS}^{♪}(\varphi)[u]$ in **MSL**.

Claim 2.- The formulas

$$\forall u \mathbf{TRANS}^{♪}(\mathrm{A1})[u],\ \forall u \mathbf{TRANS}^{♪}(\mathrm{A2})[u],\ \forall u \mathbf{TRANS}^{♪}(\mathrm{A3})[u],\ \forall u \mathbf{TRANS}^{♪}(\mathrm{A5})[u] \ \text{ and } \ \mathrm{K}$$

are all theorems of the **MSL** calculus. The proof is long, but without interest.

Claim 3.- $\forall u \mathbf{TRANS}^{♪}(\mathrm{A4})[u]$ and $\forall u \mathbf{TRANS}^{♪}(\mathrm{A6})[u]$ are theorems of $\mathbf{SOLO}^2$.

Since in $\mathbf{SOLO}^2$ we have the **MSL** abstract conditions for A4 and A6, along with the comprehension sentences for translations of **PDL** formulas and programs, the proof is very easy.

Claim 4.- The rules of inference are also respected.

It is obvious that: whenever $\varphi \in \mathbf{PDL}$ and $\varphi \rightarrow \psi \in \mathbf{PDL}$ implies $\psi \in \mathbf{PDL}$, we also have

$$\forall u \mathbf{TRANS}^{♪}(\varphi)[u],\ \forall u(\mathbf{TRANS}^{♪}(\varphi)[u] \rightarrow \mathbf{TRANS}^{♪}(\psi)[u]) \vdash \forall u \mathbf{TRANS}^{♪}(\psi)[u] \ \text{ in } \mathbf{MSL}$$

It is also clear that: whenever $\varphi \in \mathbf{PDL}$ implies $[a]\varphi \in \mathbf{PDL}$ also

$$\forall u \mathbf{TRANS}^{♪}(\varphi)[u] \vdash \forall uw(\mathbf{TRANS}^{♪}(a)[u,w] \rightarrow \mathbf{TRANS}^{♪}(\varphi)[w]) \ \text{ in } \mathbf{MSL} \ \blacksquare$$

Conclusion.

$$\begin{array}{ccccc}
\models \varphi & \overset{(1)}{\Longleftrightarrow} & \models_{\mathcal{E}} \forall u \mathbf{TRANS}^{♪}(\varphi)[u] & \overset{(2)}{\Longleftarrow} & \mathbf{SOLO}^2 \models_{\mathcal{F}} \forall u \mathbf{TRANS}^{♪}(\varphi)[u] \\
(5)\Updownarrow & & & & (3)\Updownarrow \\
\vdash \varphi & & \underset{(4)}{\Longrightarrow} & & \mathbf{SOLO}^2 \vdash_{\mathbf{MSL}} \forall u \mathbf{TRANS}^{♪}(\varphi)[u]
\end{array}$$

The double arrow in (1) is lemma 1 (7.3.6 above)

The single left arrow in (2) follows from the fact that $\mathcal{E} \subseteq \mathcal{F}$ and lemma 7.4.2.

The double arrow in (3) is the soundness and completeness of **MSL**.

The single right arrow in (4) is lemma 3 (7.4.4 above)

The double arrow in (5) is completeness and soundness of **PDL**.

Therefore, we have proven that

$$\models \varphi \Longleftrightarrow \mathrm{SOLO}^2 \models_{\mathcal{F}} \forall u \mathrm{TRANS}^{♪}(\varphi)[u]$$

and that

$$\vdash \varphi \Longleftrightarrow \mathrm{SOLO}^2 \vdash_{\mathrm{MSL}} \forall u \mathrm{TRANS}^{♪}(\varphi)[u]$$

BIBLIOGRAPHY.

Abramsky, S., Gabbay, D. & Maibaum, T. eds [1991]. **Handbook of Logic in Computer Science**, vols. I-III. Oxford: Oxford University Press.

Addisson, Henkin and Tarski eds. [1965]. **The Theory of Models (Proceedings of the 1963 International Symposium at Berkeley)**. Amsterdam: North-Holland.

ADJ (Wagner E. G., Wright J. B. & Thatcher J. W.) [1979]. "Many-sorted and ordered algebraic theories". **Reseach report RC 7595, IBM** T. J. Watson Research Center, NY. Yorktown Heights.

Andréka, H., Monk, J & Németi, I. eds. [1991]. **Algebraic Logic (Proc. Conf. Budapest 1988), Colloq. Math. Soc. J. Bolyai**, vol. 54, Amsterdam: North-Holland.

Andréka, H. & Németi, I. [1979, 1980, 1981, 1985]. "Applications of universal algebra, Model theory and categories in computer science (survey and bibliography).I, II-IV". Part I.: **CL&CL** vol. 13. pp. 252-282. Part II.: **CL&CL** vol. 14. pp. 7-20. Part III.: **Third Hungarian Comp. Sci. Conference (Budapest, Jan. 1981)**, Invited papers, pp. 75-93. Part IV.: Preprint Math. Inst. Hungar. Ac. Sc., 1985.

Andréka, H., Németi, I. & Sain, I. [1982]. "A complete logic for reasoning about programs via nonstandard model theory I-II". **Theoretical Computer Science**, vol. 17. Part I: num. 2, pp. 193-212. Part II: num. 3, pp. 259-278.

Andrews, P. B. [1963]. "A reduction of the axioms for the theory of propositional types". **The Journal of Symbolic** Logic, vol. 52, pp. 345-350.

- [1965] **A Transfinite Type Theory with Type Variables.** Amsterdam: North Holland.

- [1972a]. "General models, descriptions, and choice in type theory". **The Journal of Symbolic Logic**, vol. 37, num. 2, pp. 385-394.

- [1972b]. "General models and extensionality". **The Journal of Symbolic Logic.** vol. 37, num. 2, pp. 394-397.

- [1986]. **An Introduction to Mathematical Logic and Type Theory: To Truth through Proof.** Orlando, Fla: Academic Press.

Barcan, R. C. [1946]. "A Functional calculus of first order based on strict implication". **The Journal of Symbolic** Logic, vol. 11, pp. 1-16.

Barwise, J. [1975]. **Admissible Sets and Structures: An Approach to Definability Theory.** Berlin: Springer-Verlag.

- [1977]: "An introduction to first order logic". In Barwise ed. [1977]

- ed. [1977]. **Handbook of Mathematical Logic**. Amsterdam: North-Holland.

- [1985]. "Model-theoretic logics: background and aims". In Barwise, J. & Feferman, S. eds. [1985].

Barwise, J. & Feferman, S. eds. [1985]. **Model-Theoretic Logics.** Berlin: Springer-Verlag.

Bell, J. L. [1969]. **Models and Ultraproducts.** Amsterdam: North-Holland.

van Benthem, J. [1975]. "A note on modal formulae and relational properties". **The Journal of Symbolic Logic**, vol. 40, num.1, pp.55-58.

_ [1983]. **Modal Logic and Classical Logic.** Naples: Bibliopolis.

- [1984]. "Correspondence theory", In Gabbay, D. & Guenthner, F. eds. [1984]. vol. II, pp. 167-247.

[1995]. "The sources of complexity: Content versus wrapping", In Marx, M. & Polós, L. eds. [1995].

van Benthem, J. & Doets, K. [1983]. "Higher-order logic". In Gabbay, D & Guenthner, F. eds. [1983, 1984], vol. I, pp. 275-329.

Bergstra, J., Tiuryn, J. & Tucker, J. [1982]. "Floyd's principle, correctness theories and program equivalence". **Theoretical Computer Science,** vol. 17, pp. 113-149.

Bergstra, J. & Tucker, J. [1982]. "Expressiveness and the completeness of Hoare's logic". **Journal of Computer and System Sciences,** vol. 25, pp. 267-284.

- [1984]. "Hoare's logic for programming languages with two data types". **Theoretical Computer Science,** vol. 28, pp. 213-221.

Beth, E. [1965]. **The Foundations of Mathematics.** Amsterdam: North-Holland.

Boolos, G. [1979]. **The Unprovability of Consistency: An Essay in Modal Logic.** Cambridge: Cambridge University Press.

Boudreaux, J. C. [1979]. "Defining general structures". **Notre Dame Journal of Formal Logic,** vol. XX, num. 3, pp. 465-488.

Bowen, K. A. [1979]. **Model Theory for Modal Logic.** Dordrecht: Reidel.

Bull, R. & Segerberg, K. [1984]. "Basic modal logic". In Gabbay, D. & Guenthner, F. eds. [1984], vol. II, pp. 1-81.

Burmeister, P. [1986]. **A Model Theoretic Oriented Approach to Partial Algebras**, Berlin: Akademie-Verlag.

Bustos, E. et al. [1994]. **Perspectivas Actuales de Lógica y Filosofía de la Ciencia,** Madrid: Siglo XXI de España Editores, S. A.

Carnap, R. [1947]. **Meaning and Necessity: A Study in Semantics and Modal Logic.** Chicago: The Chicago University Press.

Chagrova,L.A. [1991]: "Undecidable problems in correspondence theory". **The Journal of Symbolic Logic**, vol. 56, pp. 1261-1272.

Chang, C. C. & Keisler, H. J. [1973]. **Model Theory.** Amsterdam: North-Holland.

Chellas, B. F. [1980]. **Modal Logic: An Introduction.** Cambridge: Cambridge University Press.

Church, A. [1940]. "A formulation of the simple theory of types". **The Journal of Symbolic Logic**, vol. 5, pp. 56-68.

- [1941]. **The Calculi of Lambda-Conversion.** (Annals of Mathematical Studies. num. 6.) Princeton: Princeton University Press.

- [1956]. **Introduction to Mathematical Logic.** Princeton, NY: Princeton University Press.

- [1976]. "Comparison of Russell's resolution of the semantical antinomies with that of Tarski. **The Journal of Symbolic Logic**, vol. 41, pp. 747-760.

Cirulis, J. [1989]. "An algebraization of first-order logic with terms", In Andréka, H., Monk, J. & Németi, I., eds. [1991]

Cohn, A. E. [1983]. "Improving the expressiveness of many-sorted logic". AAAI-83, Washington, pp. 84-87.

- [1986]. "Many-sorted logic = unsorted logic + control?", In Bramer M. ed. **Expert systems 86**, Cambridge: Cambridge University Press, pp. 184-194.

Copi, I. [1971]. **The Theory of Logical Types.** London: Routledge & Kegan Paul.

Craig, W. [1957a]. "Linear reasoning. A new form of the Herbrand-Gentzen theorem". **The Journal of Symbolic Logic**, vol. 22, pp. 250-268.

- [1957b]. "Three uses of the Herbrand-Gentzen theorem in relating model theory and proof theory". **The Journal of Symbolic Logic**, vol. 22, pp. 269-285.

Crossley, J. N. ed. [1975]. **Algebra and Logic.** Lecture Notes in Mathematics 450. Berlin: Springer-Verlag.

van Dalen, D. [1983]. **Logic and Structure.** Berlin: Springer-Verlag.

Denyer, N. [1992]. "Pure second-order logic". **Notre Dame Journal of Formal Logic**, vol. 33, num. 2, pp. 220.

Dziergowski, D. [1988]. "Many-sorted elementary equivalence". **Notre Dame Journal of Formal Logic**, vol. 29, num. 4, pp. 530-542.

Ebbinghaus, H. D. [1985]. "Extended logics: The general framework". In Barwise, J. and Feferman, S. eds. [1985].

Ebbinghaus, H. D., Flum, J. & Thomas, W. [1984]. **Mathematical Logic.** Berlin: Springer-Verlag.

Ehrig, H. & Mahr, B. [1985]. "Fundamentals of algebraic specification 1", **EATCS** 6, Berlin: Springer-Verlag.

Enderton, H. B. [1972]. **A Mathematical Introduction to Logic.** New York: Academic Press.

Feferman, S. [1968]. "Lectures on proof theory", **Proceedings of the Summer School in Logic (Leeds, 1967)**. Lecture Notes in Mathematics, vol. 70, pp. 1-107. Berlin: Springer-Verlag.

- [1974]. "Applications of many-sorted interpolation theorems". In Henkin, L. et al. eds. [1974].

Fine, K. [1975]. "Some connections between elementary and modal logic". In Kanger, S. ed. [1975].

- [1977a]. "Prior on the construction of possible worlds and instants". In Prior, A. & Fine, K. eds. [1977]

- [1977b]. "Properties, propositions and sets". **Journal of Philosophical Logic**, vol. 6, pp. 135-191.

- [1980, 1981, 1982]. "First order modal theories", Parts I, II, III. Part I, Sets: **Nous**, vol. 15, pp. 177-205. Part II, Propositions: **Studia Logica**, vol. 34, pp. 159-202. Part III, Facts: **Synthèse**, vol. 53, pp. 43-122.

Fischer, M & Ladner, R. [1979]. "Propositional modal logic of programs". **Proc. 9th ACM Symp. Theory of Comput**, vol. 18, pp. 194-211.

Frege, G. [1879]. **Begriffsschrift, eine der Arithmetischen Nachgebildete Formlesprache des Reinen Denkens**. English translation in van Heijenoort, J. ed. [1967], pp. 5-82.

Gabbay, D. [1976]. **Investigations in Modal and Tense Logics with Applications to Problems in Philosophy and Linguistics**. Dordrecht, Netherlands: Reidel.

Gabbay, D. & Guenthner, F. eds. [1983, 1984]. **Handbook of Philosophical Logic**, vols. I-IV. Dordrecht, Netherlands: Reidel.

Gallin, D. [1975]. **Intentional and Higher-Order Modal** Logic. Amsterdam: North-Holland.

Galton, A. ed. [1987]. **Temporal Logics and their Applications**. London: Academic Press.

Gandy, R. O. [1956]. "On the axiom of extensionality". **The Journal of Symbolic Logic**, vol. 21, pp. 36-48.

- [1977]. "The simple theory of types". In Gandy, R. O. & Hyland, M. eds. [1977].

Gandy, R.O. and Hyland, M. eds. [1977]. **Logic Colloquium** 76. Amsterdam: North-Holland.

Garson, J. [1984]. "Quantification in modal logic". In Gabbay, D. and Guenthner, F. eds. [1984].

Gergely, T. & Szöts, M. [1980]. "Logical foundations of problem solving". **Proceeding II. IMAI, Leningrad**. Repino, USSR.

Gödel, K. [1933]. "Eine Interpretation des intuitionistischen Aussagenkalküls". **Ergebnisse eines mathematischen Kolloquiums**, vol. 4, pp. 34-40.

Goguen, J. A. & Meseguer, J. [1984]. "Equality, types, modules and (why not?) generics for logic programming". **Journal of Logic Programming**, vol. 1, num. 2, pp. 179-210.

- [1985]. "Completeness of many-sorted equational logic". **Houston Journal of Mathematics**, vol. 11, num. 3

Goldblatt, R. [1975]. "First-order definability in modal logic". **The Journal of Symbolic Logic**, vol. 40, n.1, pp. 35-40.

- [1976]. "Metamathematics of modal logic". Parts I-II. **Reports on Mathematical Logic**. Part I: vol. 6, pp. 41-78. Part II: vol. 7, pp. 21-52.

- [1989]. "On closure under canonical embedding algebras". In Andréka, H., Monk, J & Németi, I. eds. [1991].

- [1992]. **Logics of Time and Computation**. CSLI. Lecture Notes, No. 7.

Goldblatt, R. & Thomason, S. K. [1975]. "Axiomatic classes in propositional modal logic". In Crossley, J. N. ed. [1975], pp. 163-173.

Gurevich, Y. [1985]. "Monadic second-order theories". In Barwise, J. & Feferman, S. eds. [1985], pp 479-501.

Harel, D. [1984]. "Dynamic logic". In Gabbay, D. & Guenthner, F. eds. [1984], vol. II. pp. 497-607.

Harrington, L. et al. eds. [1985]. **Harvey Friedman's Research Foundations of Mathematics**. Amsterdam: North-Holland.

van Heijenoort, J. [1967]. **From Frege to Gödel: A Source Book in Mathematical Logic, 1879-1931**. Cambridge, Mas: Harvard University Press.

Henkin, L. [1949]. "The completeness of the first order functional calculus". **The Journal of Symbolic Logic**, vol. 14, pp. 159-166.

- [1950]. "Completeness in the theory of types".**The Journal of Symbolic Logic**, vol. 15, pp. 81-91.

- [1953]. "Banishing the rule of substitution for functional variables". **The Journal of Symbolic Logic**, vol. 18, num. 3. pp. 201-208.

- [1960]. "On mathematical induction". **The American Mathematical Monthly**, vol. 67, num. 4.

- [1963]. "A theory of propositional types". **Fundamenta Mathematicae**, vol. 52, pp. 323-344.

- [1975]. "Identity as a logical primitive". **Philosophia**, vol. 5, pp. 31-45.

Henkin, L. et al. eds. [1974]. **Proceedings of the Tarski Symposium (Berkeley, 1971)**. (Proceedings of Symposia in Pure Mathematics, vol. XXV). Providence, RI.: American Mathematical Society.

Henkin, L., Monk, J. & Tarski, A. [1971]. **Cylindric Algebras, Part I**. Amsterdam: North-Holland.

[1985]. **Cylindric Algebras Part II**. Amsterdam: North-Holland.

Henkin, L., Monk, J., Tarski, A., Andréka, H. & Németi, I. [1981]. **Cylindric Set Algebras.** Lecture Notes in Mathematics. Berlin: Springer-Verlag.

Hilbert, D. and Ackermann, W. [1928]. **Grundzege der theoretischen Logik.** English translation in Hilbert, D. & Ackermann, N. [1938].

- [1938]. **Principles of Mathematical Logic.** New York: Chelsea.

Hintikka, J. [1961]. "Modality and quantification". **Theoria,**,vol. 27, pp. 119-128.

- [1969]. **Models for Modalities: Selected Essays.** Dordrecht, Netherlands: Reidel.

Hook, J. L. [1985]. "A note on interpretations of many-sorted theories". **The Journal of Symbolic Logic**, vol. 50, num. 2, pp. 372-374.

Huertas, A. [1994]. **Modal Logic (of Predicates) and (Partial and Heterogeneous) Non-Classical Logic.** Doctoral dissertation. Department of Logic. University of Barcelona.

Huertas, A. & Manzano, M. [1991a]. "Conversión de S5 en lógica bivariada". In Vide, M.ed. [1991].

- [1991b]. "Many-sorted Logic as a unifying framework". In Abstracts of the 9th International Congress of Logic, Methodology and Philosophy of Science. Uppsala University. **The Journal of Symbolic Logic**, vol. 58, num. 2. pag. 755.

Hughes, G. E & Cresswell, M. J. [1968]. **An Introduction to Modal Logic.** London: Methuen.

- [1984]. **A Companion to Modal Logic.** London: Methuen.

Janssen, T. [1983]. **Foundation and Applications of Montague Grammar.** Amsterdam: Mathematisch Centrum.

Jónsson, B. & Tarski, A. [1951, 1952]. "Boolean algebras with operators", Parts I-II. **American Journal of Mathematics**, Part I: vol. 73, pp. 891-939. Part II: vol. 74. pp. 127-162.

Kamin, S. [1979] "Rationalizing many-sorted algebraic theories". Reseach report RC 7595, IBM T. J. Watson Research Center, Yorktown Heights, NY.

Kanger, S. [1957a]. "The morning star paradox". **Theoria**, vol, 23. pp. 1-11.

- "A note on quantification and modality". **Theoria**, vol. 23, pp. 131-134.

Kanger, S. ed. [1975]. **Proceedings of the Third Scandinavian Logic Symposium.** Amsterdam: North-Holland.

Kneale, W. & Kneale, M. [1962]. **The Development of Logic.** Oxford: Oxford University Press.

Knuth, E. & Rónyai, L. [1983]. "Closed convex reference schemes. (A junction between computer science, cylindric and partial algebras.)", In **Proc. IFIP Conf**, Hungary.

Kozen, D. ed [1982]. **Logics of Programs** (Workshop, Yorktown Heights, NY, May 1981). Lecture Notes in Computer Science. 131. Berlin: Springer-Verlag.

Kozen, D. & Parikh, R. [1981]. "An elementary proof of the completeness of PDL". **Theoretical Computer Science**, vol. 14, pp. 113-118.

Kreisel, G. & Krivine, J.L. [1971]. **Elements of Mathematical Logic.** Amsterdam: North-Holland.

Kripke, S. [1959]. "A completeness theorem in modal logic". **The Journal of Symbolic Logic**, vol. 24, pp. 1-14.

- [1963a]. "Semantical analysis of modal logic I: Normal modal propositional calculi". **Zeitschrift für mathematische Logik und Grundlagen der Mathematik**, num. 9, pp. 113-116.

- [1963b]. "Semantical considerations on modal logics". **Acta Philosophica Fennica**, num. 16, pp. 83-94.

- [1965]. "Semantical analysis of modal logic II. In Leblanc, H. ed. [1973]

- [1975]. "Outline of a theory of truth". **The Journal of Philosophy**, vol. 72, pp. 690-716.

Kunen, K. [1980]. **Set Theory. An Introduction to Independence Proofs.** Studies in Logic and the Foundations of Mathematics. Amsterdam: North-Holland.

Kurucz, A., Manzano, M & Sain, I. [1994]. "How to increase applicability of a mathematical concept to real higher order phenomena". In Marx, M. & Polós, L. eds. [1995].

Leblanc, H. ed. [1973]. **Truth, Syntax and Modality.** Amsterdam: North-Holland.

Lemmon, E. [1957]. "New foundations for Lewis modal systems". **The Journal of Symbolic Logic**, vol. 22, pp. 176-186.

- [1966]. "Algebraic semantics for modal logics". **The Journal of Symbolic** Logic, vol. 31, pp. 191-218.

Lemmon, E. & Scott, D. [1977]. An **Introduction to Modal** Logic. Oxford: Blackwell.

Lewis, D. [1912]. "Implication and the algebra of logic". **Mind**, vol. 21, pp. 522-531.

- [1968]."Counterpart theory and quantified modal logic". **The Journal of Symbolic Logic, vol.** 13, pp. 126.

- **[1973]. Counterfactuals.** Cambridge, MA: Harvard University Press.

Lindström, P. [1969]. "On extensions of elementary logic". **Theoria**, vol. 35, pp. 1-11.

Łukasiewicz, J. [1953]. "A system of modal logic". **Journal of Computing Systems**, vol. 1. pp. 111-149

- [1970]. **Selected Works.** Amsterdam: North-Holland.

Maddux, R.,D., [1988]. Review of Henkin, L., Monk, J, & Tarski, A. [1985], **The Journal of Symbolic Logic**, pp. 239-241.

Makowsky, J. A. & Sain, I. [1990] "Weak second order characterizations of various program verification systems". **Theoretical Computer Science**, to appear.

Manzano, M. [1978]. **Sistemas Intermedios.** Fundación Juan March. Serie Universitaria. num. 62. Madrid.

- [1980]. **Teoría de Tipos.** Barcelona: Ediciones de la Universidad de Barcelona.
- [1982a]. "Los sistemas inductivos". In **Lógica, Epistemología y Teoría de la Ciencia.** Estudios de Educación. Madrid, MEC. pp. 19-34.
- [1982b]. "Los sistemas generales". In **Estudios de Lógica** y **Filosofía de la Ciencia.** Serie: Manuales Universitarios. Salamanca: Ediciones Universidad de Salamanca.
- [1985]. "Formalización en Teoría de tipos del Predicado de Existencia Conceptual de Mario Bunge." **Theoría**, vol. 2, pp. 513-534.
- [1986a]. "El nuevo traje del Emperador: de cómo la sofisticada lógica modal no lucía más que modelos clásicos, de primer orden" [for modal propositional logic]. In Proc. I Simposio Hispano-Mexicano de Filosofía (1984). Salamanca: Ediciones Universidad de Salamanca.
- [1986b]. "Nuevos hechos, viejos lenguajes". **V Congrés Catalá de Lógica.** Barcelona: PPU. pp. 17-22.
- [1987]. "Emperor's new clothes". In **Logic Colloquium'85.** Abstract in **The Journal of Symbolic Logic**, vol. 52.
- [1989a]. "SOLO: A second order theory equivalent to propositional dynamic logic". In **Logic Colloquium**'87. Abstract in **The Journal of Symbolic Logic**, vol. 54.
- [1989b]. **Teoría de Modelos.** AUT/126. Madrid: Alianza Editorial. English translation, Oxford: Oxford University Press (to appear).
- [1990]. "Lógica dinámica". **Agora**, vol. 9, pp. 31-43.
- [1991]. "La Bella y la Bestia. (perdón, Lógica e Informática)". **Arbor**, num. 54,. March 1991, Madrid, pp. 17-42.
- [1993a]. "Introduction to many-sorted logic". In Meinke, K. & Tucker, J. eds. [1993].
- [1993b]. "La gallina de los huevos de oro. (Capacidad expresiva, metateoría de conjuntos e incompletud)". **Actas del I Congreso de la Sociedad de Lógica, Metodología y Filosofía de la Ciencia.** Madrid: Departamento de Reprografía de la UNED.
- [1994]. "Lógica multivariada: matadora de lógicas." In Bustos, E. et al. eds [1994].

Márkusz, Z. [1981]. "Knowledge representation of design in many-sorted logic". **Proc. Seventh. Inter. Joint Conf. on Artif. Intell. IJCAI-81 (Vancouver)**, pp. 264-269.

- [1982]. "Design in logic". **Computer-Aided Design**, vol. 14, num. 6, pp. 335-343.
- [1983]. **On First Order Many Sorted Logic.** Parts I, II. Computer and Automation Institute. Hungarian Academy of Sciences. Budapest: Tamulmányok 151/1983.

Márkusz, Z. & Szöts, M [1981 b]. "On semantics of programming languages defined by universal algebraic tools". In **Mathematical Logic in Computer Science. Proc. Coll. Salgótarján, 1978. Colloq. Math.** Soc. J. **Bólyai,** vol. 26, pp. 491-507. Amsterdam: North-Holland.

Marx, M. & Polós, L. eds. [1995]. **Logic @ Work.** Oxford: Oxford University Press.

Meinke, K. [1991]. "A Recursive second order initial algebra specification of primitive recursion". Report DCS 91.14. Department of Computer Science, University College of Swansea.

Meinke, K. & Tucker, J. [1990]. "Universal algebra". In Abramsky, S., Gabbay, D. & Maibaum, T. eds [1991].

Meinke, K. & Tucker, J. eds. [1993]. **Many-Sorted Logic and its Applications.** Chichester: John Wiley & sons.

Meseguer, J. [1989]. "General logics". In Ebbinghaus, H. D. et al. eds. **Proc. Logic. Colloquium'87.** Amsterdam: North-Holland.

Monk, J. D. [1976]. **Mathematical Logic.** Berlin: Springer-Verlag.

Montague, R. [1974]. **Formal Philosophy: Selected Papers of R. Montague.** Thomson, E. H. ed., New Haven, Conn., and London: Yale University Press.

Mortimer, M. [1974]. "Some results in modal model theory". **The Journal of Symbolic Logic,** vol. 39, pp. 496-508.

Németi, I. [1981a]. "Connections between algebraic logic and initial algebra semantics of CF languages". In **Mathematical Logic in Computer Science (Proc. Coll. Salgótarján 1978). Colloq. Math. Soc. J. Bolyai,** vol. 26, pp. 561-605. Amsterdam: North-Holland.

\- [1981b]. "Dynamic algebras of programs". **Fundamentals of Computing theory'81.** Lecture Notes in Computer Science, vol. 117, pp. 281-290. Springer-Verlag.

\- [1981c]. "Nonstandard dynamic logic". In Kozen, D. ed [1982]

\- [1982]. "Every free algebra in the variety generated by the representable dynamic algebras is separable and representable". **Theoretical Computer Science,** vol. 17, pp. 343-347.

\- [1989]. "Algebraizations of quantifier logics, an introductory overview". **Studia Logica,** to appear.

Orlowska, E. [1989]. "Relational interpretation of modal logics". In Andréka, H., Monk, J & Németi, I. eds. [1991].

Parikh, R. [1981]. "Propositional dynamic logics of programs: A survey". In Engeler, E. ed. **Logic of Programs.** Lecture Notes in Computer Science. num. 125. Springer-Verlag.

Pasztor, A. [1986]. "Non-standard algorithmic and dynamic logic". **Journal Symbolic Computation,** vol. 2, pp. 59-81.

- [1988]. "Recursive programs and denotational semantics in absolute logics of programs". **Technical Report** #FIU-SCS-87-1. Florida International University, School of Computer Science.

Pratt, V. R. [1979a]. "Models of program logic". **20th IEEE Conference on Foundation of Computer Science** (San Juan, PR, 1979).

- [1979b]. "Dynamic algebras: examples, constructions, applications", MIT/LCS/TM-138, MIT Laboratory for Computer Science, May, 1980.

- [1980a]. "Dynamic algebras and the nature of induction", In **Proc. 12th ACM Symp. on Theory of Computing**, pp. 22-28. Los Angeles, Calif., May, 1980.

- [1980b]. " Application of modal logic to programming". **Studia Logica**, vol. 34, pp. 257-274.

Prior, A. [1957]. **Time and Modality.** Oxford: Clarendon Press.

- [1967]. **Past, Present and Future.** Oxford: Clarendon Press.

Prior,A. & Fine, K. eds. [1977]. **Worlds, Times and Selves.** London: Duckworth.

Quine, W. [1937]. "Logic based on inclusion and abstraction". **The Journal of Symbolic Logic**, vol. 2, pp. 145-152.

- [1943]. "Notes on existence and neccessity". **Journal of Philosophy**, vol. 40, pp. 113-127.

- [1947]. "The problem of interpreting modal logic". **The Journal of Symbolic Logic**, vol. 12, pp. 43-48.

- [1976]. **The ways of paradoxes and other essays.** Cambridge, Mass.: Harvard University Press.

Ramsey, F. [1926]. **The Foundations of Mathematics.** Proc. London Math. Soc. Ser 2. 338-384.

Rasiowa, H. [1974]. **An Algebraic Study of Non-Classical Logics.** Amsterdam: North-Holland.

Rescher, N. ed. [1968]. **Studies in Logical Theory.** Oxford: Blackwell.

Rijke, M. ed. [1993]. **Diamonds and Defaults.** Dordrecht, Netherlands: Kluwer Academic Publishers.

Robbin, J. W. [1969]. **Mathematical Logic: a First Course.** New York: W. A. Benjamin.

Rogers, H. [1967]. **Theory of Recursive Functions and Effective Computability. Series in Higher Mathematics.** New York: McGraw-Hill.

Rogers, R. [1971]. **Mathematical logic and formalized theories.** Amsterdam: North-Holland.

Rónyai, L. [1981]. "On basic concepts of query language SDLA/SET". (in Hungarian).

Russell, B. [1908]. "Mathematical logic as based in the theory of types". In van Heijenoort, J. ed. [1967]

Sahlqvist, H. [1975]. "Completeness and correspondence in the first and second order semantics for modal logic". In Kanger, S. ed. [1975], pp. 110-143.

Sain, I. [1979]. "There are general rules for specifying semantics: Observations on Abstract Model Theory." **CL & CL**, vol. XIII, pp. 195-250.

- [1984]. "Structured nonstandard dynamic logic", **Zeitschrift für Math. Logic u. Grundlagen der Math. Heft 3**, vol. 30, pp. 481-497.

- [1987]. "Total correctness in nonstandard logics of programs". **Theoretical Computer Science**, vol. 35, pp. 285-321.

- [1988]. "Comparing and characterizing the powers of established program verification methods", In Meinke, K. & Tucker, J. eds. [1993].

- [1990]. "Temporal Logics need their clocks". **Theoretical Computer Science**, to appear.

Sainsbury, R. [1988]. **Paradoxes.** Cambridge: Cambridge University Press.

Schmidt, A. [1938]. "Uber deduktive Theorien mit mehreren Sorten von Grunddingen". **Mathematische Annalen**, vol. 115, pp. 485-506.

Schmidt, M. & Schauß [1989]. **Computational Aspects of an Order-Sorted Logic with Term Declarations.** Lecture Notes in Artificial Intelligence 395. Berlin: Springer-Verlag.

Segerberg, K. [1971]. "An essay in classical modal logic". **Filosofiska Studier**, vol. 13. University of Uppsala.

Shoenfield, J. [1967]. **Mathematical Logic.** Reading, Mass.: Addison-Wesley.

- [1977]. "Axioms of set theory". In Barwise, J. ed. [1977].

Stalnaker, R. [1968]. "A theory of conditionals". In Rescher, N. ed. [1968], pp. 98-112.

Tarski, A. [1923] "Sur le terme primitif de la logistique". **Fundamenta Mathematicae**, vol. IV, p. 196.

- [1956a]. "The concept of truth in formalized languages". In Tarski, A. [1956b].

- [1956b]. **Logic, semantics, metamathematics.** Papers from 1923 to 1938. Oxford: Clarendon Press.

Tarski, A. & Givant, S. [1987]. "A formalization of set theory without variables". **AMS Colloquium Publications**, vol. 41. Providence, RI.

Thomason, S. K. [1972]. "Semantic analysis of tense logics". **The Journal of Symbolic Logic**, vol. 37, pp. 150-158.

- [1974]. "An incompleteness theorem in modal logic". **Theoria.** vol. 40, pp. 30-34

- [1975]. "Reduction of second-order logic to modal logic". **Zeitschrift für Math. Logic u. Grundlagen der Math.** vol. 21, pp. 107-114.

Trnková, V. & Reiterman, J., [1987] "Dynamic algebras with test". **J. Computer System Sciences**, vol. 35, 2, pp. 229-242

Tucker, J. V. & Zucker, J. I. [1988] **Program Correcteness Over Abstract Data Types with Error-State Semantics.** Amsterdam: North-Holland.

Väänänen, J. [1985]. "Set-theoretic definability of logics". In Barwise, J. & Feferman, S. eds. [1985].

Venema, Y. [1989]. "Two-dimensional modal logics for relational algebras and temporal logic of intervals", University of Amsterdam.

Vide, M. ed. [1991]. **Lenguajes Naturales y Lenguajes Formales.** Barcelona: PPU.

Walther, C. [1983]. **A Many-Sorted Calculus Based on Resolution and Paramodulation.** London: Pitman.

Wang, H. [1952]. "Logic of many-sorted theories". **The Journal of Symbolic Logic**, vol. 17, num. 2, pp. 105-116.

\- [1964]. **A Survey of Mathematical Logic.** Pekin: Science Press and Amsterdam: North-Holland.

Whitehead, A. N & Russell, B. [1910, 1912, 1913]. **Principia Mathematica.** New York: Cambridge University Press.

Zeman, J. J. [1973]. **Modal Logic: The Lewis-Modal Systems.** Oxford: Clarendon Press.

Zucker, J. I. [1978]. "The adequacy problem for classical logic". **Journal of Philosophical Logic**, vol. 7, pp. 517-535.

List of notation.

Index.

G

H

M

N

T

W

Z

Index of authors.

W

Z

Index of authors.

T

V

Z

W